The Literary Structure
of the Old Testament

The Literary Structure of the Old Testament

A Commentary on Genesis–Malachi

David A. Dorsey

Baker Academic

Grand Rapids, Michigan

© 1999 by David A. Dorsey

Published by Baker Academic
a division of Baker Publishing Group
P.O. Box 6287, Grand Rapids, MI 49516-6287
www.bakeracademic.com

Paperback edition published in 2004
ISBN 0-8010-2793-4

Printed in the United States of America

The Library of Congress has cataloged the hardcover edition as follows:
Dorsey, David A., 1949–
    The literary structure of the Old Testament : a commentary on Genesis–Malachi / David A. Dorsey.
       p. cm.
    Includes bibliographical references and index.
    ISBN 0-8010-2187-1
    1. Bible. O.T. Commentaries. 2. Bible as literature. I. Title.
BS1151.2.D67   1999
221.6′6—dc21   99-40433

In Memory of
Opal Pearl Dorsey
1920–1997

Contents

Unit 6: Minor Prophets

Unit 7: Conclusion

Preface

I began writing this book some ten years ago, although my interest in Hebrew literary structure goes back a decade before that. My fascination with the subject was kindled when I began teaching Old Testament courses in seminary. At that time I was struck by the apparent lack of order within many of the biblical books. Jeremiah seemed hopelessly confused in its organization; so did Isaiah and Hosea and most of the prophets. Song of Songs and Ecclesiastes appeared to be in almost complete disarray, and even the more orderly historical books, such as Joshua and Kings, showed signs of strangely careless organization. Why did the biblical authors write like this? I would never write a book, an article, or even a private letter with such carelessness of arrangement.

I was intrigued by the possibility that the Hebrew authors might have organized their compositions according to literary conventions that were different from ours. I began to discover, over a period of years, that several structuring patterns rarely used by us were remarkably common in the books of the Hebrew Bible, particularly chiasmus (symmetry), parallelism, and sevenfold patterns. I was increasingly struck by how often these patterns had been utilized to arrange biblical books. The task of analyzing the structures of the books of the Old Testament was a long and arduous one. I experienced many frustrations, and I am still not sure of a few analyses. But I am hopeful that I have made some important gains.

In the course of my research, the work of certain scholars was invaluable, including that of James Muilenburg, D. W. Gooding, James Limburg, H. Van Dyke Parunak, S. Bar-Efrat, Robert E. Longacre, Umberto Cassuto, William L. Holladay, William H. Shea, Robert Alter, Adele Berlin, and J. Cheryl Exum. I was also helped by the work of the Summer Institute of Linguistics, particularly the studies of Wilbur Pickering, John Beekman, John Callow, and Michael Kopesec.

At first I planned to include analyses of all the books of the Old Testament. Then reason set in, and I selected a small sampling of biblical books on which to focus. In the end, however, Kenneth Miller, my colleague at Evangelical School of Theology, convinced me to reverse this decision and return to my original (foolhardy) plan. I am keenly aware that what I have gained in breadth by greater coverage I have lost in depth. But I am satisfied with the decision, and I hope that the resulting product will be more useful to readers.

A number of individuals have been of invaluable assistance to me during the writing of this book. Encouragement and help have come from friends and colleagues alike: Susan Mittan, Ted and Diane Clem, Bill and Susan Mahan, Janet Hensel, David Dubble, Barbara Key (Kepler), Jane and Larry Baudoin, Michael True, and Janet Stauffer, as well as professors H. Douglas Buckwalter, Richard E. Averbeck, Barbara Snyder, Eugene H. Merrill, Alice Via, and Anson F. Rainey. Dr. Alan W. Pense, chairman of the seminary's board, and Dr. Kirby N. Keller, the seminary's president and dean, have been wonderfully supportive and gracious throughout the entire process. Many other members of the seminary community, including both staff and students, have contributed to the project in various practical ways.

Doug Buckwalter's assistance in the editing process was a labor of love. He graciously read and edited the entire manuscript, offering hundreds of excellent suggestions. The final product is far better because of his keen eye and fine recommendations.

I owe more than I could express to my wife Jan. She has been a source of continuous encouragement, inspiration, and practical assistance throughout the years. She has tirelessly and courageously helped me through the difficulties caused by the chronic, sometimes debilitating illness with which I have had to struggle during these past twenty years. Her prayers and support are probably the main reason (humanly

9

speaking) that I have been able to complete the present work. In addition, her many valuable suggestions have enriched the book throughout.

During the years that I worked on this book, both of my parents died. My father, Alden Jake Dorsey, passed away in 1991; and my mother, Opal Pearl Dorsey, died in 1997. I regret that neither of them lived to see the book's publication.

It was my mother who gave me a love for literature. She read to my brother Stephen and me regularly, from as early as I can remember. I still have many fond memories of those wondrous bedtime stories, whose structures—like those of the Bible—were designed for the ear, not the eye. It is to her memory that I gratefully dedicate this book.

Abbreviations

General

BHS   Biblia Hebraica Stuttgartensia

Old Testament Books

Gen.	Genesis	Eccles.	Ecclesiastes
Exod.	Exodus	Song	Song of Songs
Lev.	Leviticus	Isa.	Isaiah
Num.	Numbers	Jer.	Jeremiah
Deut.	Deuteronomy	Lam.	Lamentations
Josh.	Joshua	Ezek.	Ezekiel
Judg.	Judges	Dan.	Daniel
Ruth	Ruth	Hos.	Hosea
1 Sam.	1 Samuel	Joel	Joel
2 Sam.	2 Samuel	Amos	Amos
1 Kings	1 Kings	Obad.	Obadiah
2 Kings	2 Kings	Jon.	Jonah
1 Chron.	1 Chronicles	Mic.	Micah
2 Chron.	2 Chronicles	Nah.	Nahum
Ezra	Ezra	Hab.	Habakkuk
Neh.	Nehemiah	Zeph.	Zephaniah
Esth.	Esther	Hag.	Haggai
Job	Job	Zech.	Zechariah
Ps.	Psalms	Mal.	Malachi
Prov.	Proverbs		

Note: where Hebrew and English verse enumerations diverge, English verse numbers will be given first, followed by Hebrew verse numbers in square brackets; for example: Psalm 3:1–2 [3:2–3] indicates that the English numeration is 3:1–2, and the Hebrew is 3:2–3.

Unit 1
Introduction

1

Introduction

All literary compositions have structure. A book, a personal letter, a sermon, even a recipe, has an internal arrangement, sometimes referred to as "surface structure."[1] A typical sermon, for example, may be organized into three parts: introduction, body of three points, and conclusion. A sermon would not be appreciated or understandable if it simply consisted of hundreds of unrelated statements, one after another without any discernible order. The practice of structuring communication, whether written or oral, is universal among humans, as shown by studies among numerous languages and dialects throughout the world.[2] Humans need and appreciate communication that is arranged and organized.

This was true in ancient Israel. The pages of the Old Testament reflect a keen interest in literary structure. Hebrew authors and editors generally took great pains to arrange their compositions in ways that would help convey their messages.

The purpose of the present work is twofold: (1) to study the internal structures of each of the books in the Old Testament and (2) to consider the relationship between each book's structure and its meaning and message.

The Difficulty of Studying Literary Structure

Analyzing the structures of Old Testament books is difficult for two reasons. First, the Hebrew authors used no visual, graphic structure markers to help readers follow their organization. The original manuscripts of their compositions, like most written works from ancient times, probably contained few if any graphic indicators of their organization. The chapter and verse divisions in the Old Testament were added centuries after the Old Testament books were written. In contrast to modern Bibles, the text of ancient Hebrew manuscripts generally ran on and on without break, filling column after column from top to bottom and from side to side, without set-off titles, subtitles, indentations, or any other visual structure indicators.[3]

Modern readers are unaccustomed to such lack of visual helps. In modern texts an array of graphic techniques make an author's organizational intentions clear. As H. Van Dyke Parunak observes:

> Graphical signals bombard the reader of a book in modern western culture. Italics or underlining highlight words and phrases of special importance, while parentheses, footnotes, and appendices remove peripheral material from the direct course of the writer's argument. Chapter headings, section titles, and paragraph indentations divide the text into segments whose limits coincide with units of the writer's thought. Tables of contents outline the entire book, and sometimes even chapters or articles within the book.[4]

---

1. According to S. Bar-Efrat, "Some Observations on the Analysis of Structure in Biblical Narrative," *Vetus Testamentum* 30 (1980) 155, "structure can be defined as the network of relations among the parts of an object or a unit." Modern structuralists like Claude Lévi-Strauss, Ferdinand de Saussure, and Noam Chomsky distinguish a composition's "surface structure" from its "deep structure." For application of this more subjective study of thematic structure to biblical literature, see Robert M. Polzin, *Biblical Structuralism: Method and Subjectivity in the Study of Ancient Texts* (Semeia Supplements; Missoula, Mont.: Scholars Press, 1977); see also Jean Piaget, *Structuralism*, trans. Chaninah Maschler (New York: Harper & Row, 1970); Robert C. Culley, "Structural Analysis: Is It Done with Mirrors?" *Interpretation* 28 (1974) 165–81; Anthony C. Thiselton, "Keeping up with Recent Studies II: Structuralism and Biblical Studies: Method or Ideology?" *Expository Times* 89 (1978) 329–35; R. E. Longacre, *An Anatomy of Speech Notions* (Lisse: de Ridder, 1976), 98–196.

2. Longacre, *Anatomy of Speech Notions*; idem, "The Paragraph as a Grammatical Unit," *Syntax and Semantics* 12 (1979) 116–17; Joseph E. Grimes, *The Thread of Discourse* (The Hague: Mouton, 1975), 91–96, 101–11.

3. To be sure, some extant ancient texts contain a few graphic structural indicators (e.g., the slash marks sometimes used to indicate new paragraphs in the Akkadian el-Amarna correspondence); but in general the modern reader is struck by the visual blandness and uniformity that characterize the columns of ancient texts.

4. H. Van Dyke Parunak, "Oral Typesetting: Some Uses of Biblical Structure," *Biblica* 62 (1981) 153.

The absence of such visual structure markers does not mean that ancient authors were un-mindful of the structure of their compositions or that their compositions had less rigorous structural patterns than our modern books. On the contrary, numerous linguistic studies of var-ious unwritten tribal languages suggest that au-rally oriented compositions generally feature sophisticated structural patterns, indeed often more sophisticated than our modern Western counterparts.[5] The blandness of an ancient text's appearance reflects rather the cultural reality that ancient texts were written primarily to be heard, not seen.[6] Texts were normally intended to be read aloud, whether one was reading alone or to an audience.[7] Accordingly, an ancient writer was compelled to use structural signals that would be perceptible to the listening audi-ence. Signals were geared for the ear, not the eye, since visual markers would be of little value to a listening audience.[8]

To study structure in the Hebrew Bible, then, requires paying serious attention to verbal structure indicators—as we do, for example, when we listen to a sermon and try to grasp its general outline and main points. The Hebrew Bible is full of such verbal structure cues (e.g., Amos's repeating line "for three transgressions of x, even for four, I will not turn back my wrath"

or the periodic "these are the generations of x" in Genesis). To follow a biblical author's organi-zation, one must learn to watch (or listen!) for aural structure markers.

The second difficulty in studying structure in the Hebrew Bible is that ancient Hebrew struc-turing patterns and techniques were different from ours.[9] For example, symmetry, parallelism, and structured repetition (terms I will define shortly) appear throughout Old Testament liter-ature; these and related patterns are so foreign to modern readers that it is easy to miss—or misunderstand—them. To investigate structure in the Hebrew Bible, the reader must lay aside Western expectations and watch for these less familiar structuring conventions that were in-digenous to ancient Israel—much as modern linguists must do when working with unwritten tribal languages.[10]

Steps in Studying Literary Structure

To study a composition's structure is simply to identify and explain the composition's internal organization (i.e., its layout or arrangement). This involves three steps: (1) identifying the com-position's constituent parts ("units"), (2) analyz-ing the arrangement of those parts, and (3) con-sidering the relationship of the composition's structure to its meaning (i.e., identifying the structure's role in conveying the composition's message).

Identify the Constituent Units of a Composition

The first step in analyzing the structure of a composition is to identify its constituent units. Any piece of literature, written or oral, is made up of a number of parts, or units, that constitute the basic building blocks of the composition. For example, a sermon might have five major parts: introduction, three main points, and con-clusion. The phenomenon of organizing compo-sitions into parts, sometimes called "packag-ing,"[11] appears to stem from a basic limitation of the human mind:

The human mind cannot handle large quantities of information unless it applies the "packaging" prin-ciple. . . . It would seem that there are certain gen-

5. See, for example, the statements, examples, and bibli-ography in Parunak, "Oral Typesetting," 154 n. 2; Longacre, "Paragraph as a Grammatical Unit," 117–34; Wilbur Picker-ing, *A Framework for Discourse Analysis* (Arlington: Summer Institute of Linguistics/University of Texas at Arlington Press, 1980).

6. According to Parunak, "Oral Typesetting," 153, another reason ancient writers generally eschewed such space-taking graphic signals might have been the expense of writing mate-rial, which was so precious that previous documents were often erased to reuse the underlying papyrus or parchment.

7. H. Van Dyke Parunak, "Some Axioms for Literary Ar-chitecture" (paper read at the Midwest Regional Meeting of the American Oriental Society and the Society of Biblical Lit-erature at Ann Arbor, Mich., 23 Feb. 1981); Josef Balog, "Voces Paginarum," *Philologus* 82/36 (1926–27) 35–109, 202–40; G. L. Hendrickson, "Ancient Reading," *Classical Journal* 25 (1929–30) 182–96; Yehoshua Gitay, "Deutero-Isaiah: Oral or Written?" *Journal of Biblical Literature* 99 (1980) 190–94. Augustine (*Confessions* 6.3) expresses his astonishment at seeing Ambrose read a book without moving his lips.

8. Texts written in an aural society would naturally tend to use aurally oriented rather than visually oriented division markers. Parunak, "Some Axioms for Literary Architecture," 4, notes: "The printed page can display information in two di-mensions. But spoken language is one dimensional, in the sense that one word follows another in strictly linear order. We are used to taking full advantage of the two dimensional resources of the written medium. But in an aural society, ac-customed only to one dimensional, spoken language, even written materials are likely to retain the characteristics of one dimensionality." See also John Beekman, John Callow, and Michael Kopesec, *The Semantic Structure of Written Commu-nication* (Dallas: Summer Institute of Linguistics, 1981), 33.

9. The difference between Hebrew literary conventions and ours is best known in the area of Hebrew poetry. Some of the patterns and techniques used in Hebrew poetry are rather foreign to us—such as the use of parallelism, chiasmus, and the disregard for rhyme and strict meter.

10. For an example, see Longacre, "Paragraph as a Gram-matical Unit," 120.

11. This phenomenon is discussed in Beekman, Callow, and Kopesec, *Semantic Structure of Written Communication*, 14–15.

eral characteristics of the mind which are shared by all people and which determine when a quantity of information has reached a point at which it should be organized into separate packages rather than continue on.[12]

From their studies of written and oral compositions of various language groups, John Beekman, John Callow, and Michael Kopesec observe that seven seems to be the universally mean number in literary packaging, with groupings of anywhere from three to nine being relatively common.[13]

A composition is normally made up of a hierarchy of units; that is, the composition's major units are themselves composed of smaller units, which in turn are made up of even smaller units, and so on. A typical story is composed of several major parts; each part has a series of episodes; each episode comprises several paragraphs; and each paragraph is composed of several sentences. The Book of Judges, for example, is composed of three larger units: prologue (1:1–3:6), main body (3:7–16:31), and epilogue (17:1–21:25). The main body, in turn, comprises seven stories about the seven major judges. Each of these stories is composed of a series of episodes; each episode is made up of paragraphs; and each paragraph is made up of sentences. Beekman, Callow, and Kopesec describe this hierarchical process as follows:

> A corollary principle to the observation made by [George] Miller brings hierarchy into consideration. As information accumulates, smaller units, ranging in number from three to nine, will be combined to form a larger unit. When the number of these larger units reaches a number between three and nine, they in turn must be combined, and so the hierarchical process becomes essential to an understanding of language and an analysis of the structure of communication.[14]

An analysis of the literary structure of an Old Testament book should begin with the identifi-

cation of its constituent units, including its primary-level, secondary-level, and, if necessary, tertiary-level units. The task of identifying units will be discussed in more detail in chapter 2.

Analyze the Arrangement of the Units

The second step in studying the structure of a composition is to analyze the arrangement of its units. The composition's constituent units are of necessity arranged in one fashion or another. In this book, for instance, I arranged the major literary units (i.e., chapters) in a linear (a-b-c) pattern, beginning with a general introduction (this chapter), followed by several chapters dealing with more specific introductory matters, followed in turn by a series of chapters on the successive books of the Old Testament. The Book of Jonah, on the other hand, has (in addition to its chronologically linear scheme) a distinctly parallel arrangement scheme:

```
a  Jonah's commissioning (1:1–3)
  b  Jonah and the pagan sailors (1:4–16)
    c  Jonah's pious, grateful prayer (1:17–2:10 [2:1–11])
a' Jonah's recommissioning (3:1–3a)
  b' Jonah and the pagan Ninevites (3:3b–10)
    c' Jonah's angry, resentful prayer (4:1–4)
      d  God's lesson for Jonah (4:5–11)
```

Nonlinear schemes, particularly symmetric (a-b-c-b'-a')[15] and parallel (a-b-c-a'-b'-c') patterns, are quite popular in the Old Testament. The task of analyzing the arrangement of units will be discussed in greater detail in chapter 3.

Consider the Relationship of Structure to Meaning

The third step in analyzing the structure of a composition is to consider the relationship of the composition's structure to its meaning and message. The organization of a literary work contributes to and is an integral part of the work's meaning.[16] To put it differently, a composition's layout generally reflects the author's main focus, points of emphasis, agenda, etc., and accordingly represents an important avenue to better understand the author's meaning.

For example, in a symmetric (chiastic) arrangement the central unit generally functions

12. Ibid., 15.
13. Ibid., 15. Pickering, *Framework for Discourse Analysis*, 10, agrees. The idea of seven as the mean number for packaging was first proposed by psychologist George Miller, "The Magical Number Seven, Plus or Minus Two: Some Limits on Our Capacity for Information Processing," *Psychological Review* 63 (1956) 81–97. Miller concludes that the pattern reflects an inherent characteristic of the human mind.
14. Beekman, Callow, and Kopesec, *Semantic Structure of Written Communication*, 14–15; cf. Pickering, *Framework for Discourse Analysis*, 10, 18; Bar-Efrat, "Analysis of Structure in Biblical Narrative," 156. This principle is sometimes referred to as "recursion"; see, e.g., Beekman, Callow, and Kopesec, *Semantic Structure of Written Communication*, 18, 131; H. Van Dyke Parunak, *Structural Studies in Ezekiel* (Ph.D. diss., Harvard University, 1978), 9 n. 12.

15. The use of a prime sign after a letter indicates that the unit so marked in some way matches an earlier unit marked with the same letter. For example, a stanza marked b' is understood to echo or match a previous stanza labeled b.
16. This is pointed out by various scholars. For example, Muilenburg, "Form Criticism and Beyond," *Journal of Biblical Literature* 88 (1969) 9, suggests: "The correct analysis of the structure of a passage is of considerable consequence . . . for a grasp of the writer's intent and meaning"; see also Bar-Efrat, "Analysis of Structure in Biblical Narrative," 172.

as the turning point or climax or highlight of the piece (e.g., a-b-c-d-c'-b'-a'). Thus in the symmetrically arranged Book of Amos the central unit (Amos 5:1–17) features Amos's call to repentance; in the Song of Songs the center (Song 3:6–5:1) serves as the book's climax, celebrating the lovers' wedding; and in Ruth the center (chap. 2) represents the story's turning point— the meeting of Ruth and Boaz. Therefore, if a composition is found to have a symmetric configuration, the central unit's key role in the book should be considered. On the other hand, in a linear scheme or parallel pattern, the final unit often carries the climax or highlight (as it does in Jonah). This subject will be discussed at greater length in chapter 4.

Previous Research on Literary Structure

Interest in literary structure in the Hebrew Bible has blossomed during the past few years; but the subject is by no means new to biblical scholarship.

Early Efforts

One of the earliest known efforts to identify literary units in the books of the Old Testament is evidenced by the isolated Hebrew letters *sāmek* (ס, standing for *sĕtumâ*, "closed") and *pēh* (פ, standing for *pĕtuaḥ*, "open") found throughout the Hebrew Bible. These letters occur periodically in every book of the Hebrew Bible and generally, though not always, mark natural breaks in the text.[17] *Pēh* marks the beginning of a longer ("open") section; *sāmek* marks a shorter ("closed") section. In the Pentateuch there are 290 open sections and 379 closed sections.[18] In Genesis 22–25, for example, *pēh* appears before 22:1, 20; 25:1, 19, and *sāmek* before 23:1; 24:1; 25:12. Each of these coincides nicely with the beginning of a new episode or natural break within a story. These unit markers predate the Mishnah (third century A.D.) and therefore represent an early effort to determine the internal structure of the various books of the Hebrew Bible.[19]

Another early attempt to mark the internal structure of the books of the Old Testament was the division of the books into chapters. The chapter divisions of the Bible were first developed by Stephen Langton, Archbishop of Canterbury, in the thirteenth century and were in-

corporated into Hebrew manuscripts by A.D. 1330.[20] The chapter divisions, like the *sĕtumâ* and *pĕtuaḥ* divisions, generally, but not always, correspond to natural units within the books.[21] They represent a genuine attempt to identify internal structure within the biblical books.

The British School

Modern interest in organizational patterns in the Hebrew Bible began in England with the 1753 study of Bishop Robert Lowth.[22] Studying the Hebrew practice of arranging poetic verses in what he called parallelism, Lowth noticed that Hebrew poetry was generally organized into verses, with each verse usually composed of two matching lines. Lowth identified three common types of matching between the two lines: synonymous, antithetic, and synthetic parallelism. In synonymous parallelism, the second line repeats the basic idea of the first line:

> The heavens declare the glory of God
> the skies show forth his handiwork.
> —Psalm 19:1 [19:2]

In antithetic parallelism, the second line contrasts the basic idea of the first line:

> The Lord knows the way of the righteous
> but the way of the wicked will perish.
> —Psalm 1:6

Synthetic parallelism is a kind of catchall third category, in which the second line in one way or another furthers the thought of the first line:

> The Lord is my Shepherd
> I shall not want.
> —Psalm 23:1

Lowth's work inspired others to search for similar or additional patterns on larger and even book-length levels. His most influential student, John Jebb, took the next step.[23] Jebb observed that the patterns Lowth had discovered within

17. Robert H. Pfeiffer, *Introduction to the Old Testament* (New York: Harper, 1948), 81, notes three poorly placed divisions following Exod. 6:28; Isa. 56:9; Hag. 1:14.
18. Ibid., 81.
19. Emanuel Tov, *Textual Criticism of the Hebrew Bible* (Minneapolis: Fortress, 1992), 50–51.

20. Pfeiffer, *Introduction to the Old Testament*, 81; Tov, *Textual Criticism of the Hebrew Bible*, 52. Verse divisions in the Hebrew Bible, on the other hand, predate the Mishnah (ca. A.D. 200), although they were not finally standardized until the ben Asher text (tenth century); the enumeration of the verses of both Old and New Testaments was established by Robert Stephanus in 1551 (Pfeiffer, *Introduction to the Old Testament*, 80).
21. Tov, *Textual Criticism of the Hebrew Bible*, 52, mentions a few ill-chosen chapter breaks: Gen. 2:1; Exod. 17:1; 22:1; Deut. 12:1; Ps. 43:1; Isa. 10:1.
22. Robert Lowth, *Lectures on the Sacred Poetry of the Hebrews* (1753; repr. London: Tegg, 1835).
23. John Jebb, *Sacred Literature* (London: Cadell & Davies, 1820).

Hebrew verses also occurred on the paragraph or stanza level. An entire stanza, for example, might be arranged according to synonymous parallelism (e.g., a-b-c ‖ a'-b'-c'). Jebb also made another exceedingly important contribution to the study of Hebrew literary structure: he identified a fourth type of Hebrew parallelism, the chiasmus or introverted pattern, in which the elements in the second line match those in the first line in reverse order (a-b-c ‖ c'-b'-a'). Combining his two contributions, he wrote: "There are stanzas so constructed, that, whatever be the number of lines, the first shall be parallel with the last; the second with the next-to-last; and so throughout, in an order that looks inward, or, to borrow a military phrase, from flanks to centre. This may be called introverted parallelism."[24]

In 1824, Thomas Boys proposed that if the biblical writers utilized these structural patterns on verse and paragraph/stanza levels, they would undoubtedly have used the same patterns in even larger, book-length segments.[25] To demonstrate this, Boys carried out what seems to have been the first modern structural analyses of entire biblical books, studying the internal organization of 1 Thessalonians, 2 Thessalonians, Philemon, 2 Peter, and some of the Psalms.[26] While Boys's analyses may have been forced, his basic assumption was intriguing, and it inspired others to search for chiastic and other patterns to explain the layouts of various books of the Bible.

The most thoroughgoing of these efforts was that of E. W. Bullinger, who, following Boys's example, published structural analyses of virtually every book of the Bible in the second half of the nineteenth century.[27] In the twentieth century

two scholars continued to build on the foundations of the British school: Nils W. Lund, who offered structural analyses of biblical books in both Testaments (including Philemon, Revelation, and Habakkuk), and Yehuda Radday, who published a series of five studies in which he sought to demonstrate the chiastic arrangements of several books in the Hebrew Bible.[28] Even though these efforts were largely unconvincing, they succeeded in repeatedly calling attention to the issue of literary structure within the Hebrew Bible.[29]

The Continental School

Independent of the British school, and a few years behind it, several Continental scholars pursued similar lines regarding structure in the Old Testament. In 1896, D. H. Müller published his study of some of the structuring patterns used by the Hebrew prophets.[30] Focusing primarily on the paragraph or strophic level, Müller identified the same patterns already discovered by Lowth and Jebb (Müller's "responsion" is Lowth's "synonymous" and "antithetic" parallelism; and his "inclusion" is the same as Jebb's "chiasmus"). In addition, Müller also discovered another Hebrew structuring technique, which he called "concatenatio"; in this technique (sometimes called "pearling"), the same feature occurs at the end of one unit and at the beginning of the next.

During the next fifty years or so, A. Condamin, Umberto Cassuto, and Enrico Galbiati applied Müller's principles on larger and even book-length levels, offering structural studies of Jeremiah, Isaiah, Lamentations, and Exodus.[31]

---

24. Ibid., 57. Another helpful contribution made by Jebb was his suggestion that Lowth's "synonymous parallelism" was never strictly synonymous. Jebb prefers to call it, instead, "cognate parallelism" to allow for the variety of correspondences attested.

25. Thomas Boys, *Tactica Sacra* (London: Hamilton, 1824). Boys's methodology is instructive: he begins by determining the book's constituent paragraphs, utilizing the microstructural patterns that Lowth and Jebb had discovered; and he then examines how the paragraphs had been organized to form the entire book, assuming that they followed those same patterns used on smaller levels (i.e., the four types of parallelism identified by Lowth and Jebb).

26. Thomas Boys, *Key to the Book of Psalms* (London: Seeley, 1825). Using Boys's own marginal notes on the psalms not treated in the first edition, E. Bullinger revised and reissued this work in 1890 (London).

27. E. W. Bullinger, *The Companion Bible* (London: Oxford University Press, n.d.). Another British scholar of the nineteenth century, John Forbes, pursued structural features in various smaller units and also attempted structural analysis of the entire Book of Romans; see his *The Symmetrical Structure of Scripture* (Edinburgh: Clark, 1854) and *Analytical Commentary on the Epistle to the Romans* (Edinburgh: Clark, 1868).

28. Nils W. Lund, *Chiasmus in the New Testament* (Chapel Hill: University of North Carolina Press, 1942); idem, "The Literary Structure of the Book of Habakkuk," *Journal of Biblical Literature* 53 (1934) 355–70; Yehuda Radday, "On Chiasm in Biblical Narrative," *Beth Miqra* 20–21 (1964) 48–72 [in Hebrew]; idem, "Chiasm in Samuel," *Linguistica Biblica* 9–10 (1971) 21–31; idem, "Chiasm in Torah," *Linguistica Biblica* 19 (1972) 12–23; idem, "Chiasm in Joshua, Judges, and Others," *Linguistica Biblica* 27–28 (1973) 6–13; idem, "Chiasm in Kings," *Linguistica Biblica* 31 (1974) 52–67.

29. For a brief history of structural studies by the British and Continental schools, see Parunak, *Structural Studies in Ezekiel*, 2–24. A dated but still useful survey of trends in literary approaches to the Bible is found in Richard Coggins, "Keeping up with Recent Studies X: The Literary Approach to the Bible," *Expository Times* 92 (1984) 9–14.

30. D. H. Müller, *Die Propheten in ihrer ursprünglichen Form* (Vienna: Hölder, 1896).

31. A. Condamin, *Le Livre de Jérémie* (Études Bibliques; Paris: Lecoffre, 1902); idem, *Le Livre d'Isaïe* (Études Bibliques; Paris: Lecoffre, 1905); idem, "Symmetrical Repetitions in Lamentations Chapters i and ii," *Journal of Theological Studies* 7 (1905) 137–40; Umberto Cassuto, "The Prophecies of Jeremiah concerning the Gentiles," in *Biblical and Oriental Studies*, trans. Israel Abrahams (Jerusalem: Magnes, 1973), 1.178–226; Enrico Galbiati, *La Struttura Letteraria dell' Esodo* (Scrinium Theologicum 3; Rome: Paoline, 1956).

Recent Studies

The last several decades have seen a dramatic increase in the investigation of literary structure in the Old Testament. One major impetus for the renewed flurry of structural studies was the famous 1968 Society of Biblical Literature presidential address by James Muilenburg, in which he called for a new focus on the literary characteristics of biblical texts.[32] Since then, literary studies of the Hebrew Bible have appeared at an ever-increasing rate, and many of these have contributed, at least indirectly, to the understanding of literary structure in the Old Testament.[33]

At the same time, some far more convincing structural analyses of whole books have begun to appear. D. W. Gooding's work on the Book of Judges, for example, is particularly noteworthy,

as is Parunak's on Ezekiel, J. Cheryl Exum's on the Song of Songs, and William Shea's on Lamentations.[34] These and other contributions will be discussed in more detail in the following chapters.

Scope of the Present Study

Despite all the renewed activity in recent decades, there is still no comprehensive study of literary structure in the Hebrew Bible and few adequate analyses of the structures of individual Old Testament books. The field of research is still in its infancy,[35] and a comprehensive investigation is one of the greatest needs in biblical studies today. The goal of the present work is to help meet that need.

The first part of this book (chaps. 1–5) explores introductory issues, particularly procedure and methodology. The second part (chaps. 6–38) comprises a series of structural studies of each book of the Hebrew Bible. Each of these studies has two main objectives: (1) to analyze the internal organization of the biblical book and (2) to consider how an understanding of the book's structure sheds light on the book's meaning and message.[36] A concluding chapter (39) summarizes the work and offers suggestions for further study.

---

32. Muilenburg's address was subsequently published as "Form Criticism and Beyond," *Journal of Biblical Literature* 88 (1969) 1–18. See also his important article, "A Study in Hebrew Rhetoric: Repetition and Style," in *Congress Volume: Copenhagen 1953* (Vetus Testamentum Supplement 1; Leiden: Brill, 1953), 97–111. Muilenburg himself ("Form Criticism and Beyond," 12–18) made an important contribution to the study of Hebrew structuring practices by identifying some of the techniques used by the biblical writers to introduce and conclude literary units.

33. Mention should be made of the valuable work of a number of scholars: William L. Holladay, "Recovery of Poetic Passages in Jeremiah," *Journal of Biblical Literature* 85 (1966) 401–35, esp. pp. 406–12; idem, *The Architecture of Jeremiah 1–20* (London: Associated Universities Press, 1976); S. Bar-Efrat, *Narrative Art in the Bible* (Sheffield: Almond, 1989); idem, "Analysis of Structure in Biblical Narrative"; Jacob Licht, *Storytelling in the Bible* (Jerusalem: Magnes, 1978); Michael Fishbane, *Text and Texture: Close Readings of Selected Biblical Texts* (New York: Schocken, 1979); idem, "Recent Work on Biblical Narrative," *Prooftexts* 1 (1981) 99–104; Parunak, "Oral Typesetting"; idem, "Some Axioms for Literary Architecture"; William H. Shea, "The Chiastic Structure of the Song of Songs," *Zeitschrift für die alttestamentliche Wissenschaft* 92 (1980) 379–96; Robert Alter, *The Art of Biblical Narrative* (New York: Basic Books, 1985); idem, *The World of Biblical Literature* (New York: Basic Books, 1992); Meir Sternberg, *The Poetics of Biblical Narrative* (Bloomington: Indiana University Press, 1985); Adele Berlin, *Poetics and Interpretation of Biblical Narrative* (Sheffield: Almond, 1983); Phyllis Trible, *Rhetorical Criticism: Context, Method, and the Book of Jonah* (Minneapolis: Augsburg Fortress, 1994). Two recent collections of literary essays should not be overlooked: Robert Alter and Frank Kermode (eds.), *The Literary Guide to the Bible* (Cambridge: Harvard University Press, 1987); Leland Ryken and Tremper Longman III (eds.), *A Complete Literary Guide to the Bible* (Grand Rapids: Zondervan, 1993).

---

34. D. W. Gooding, "The Composition of the Book of Judges," *Eretz-Israel* 16 (1982) 70*–79*; Parunak, *Structural Studies in Ezekiel*; J. Cheryl Exum, "A Literary and Structural Analysis of the Song of Songs," *Zeitschrift für die alttestamentliche Wissenschaft* 85 (1973) 47–79; William H. Shea, "The *Qinah* Structure of the Book of Lamentations," *Biblica* 60 (1979) 103–7.

35. So Alter in 1985 (*Art of Biblical Narrative*, 12–13), and it is still the case today.

36. My reasons for focusing on the final form of each book and setting aside controversial issues involving the prehistory of the text are twofold. First, the final form of these books is all we have. Second, the final form of each book is certainly worthy of study in and of itself, regardless of its prehistory and regardless of whether it was put together by an original author or by a later editor who wove various earlier sources into the book we now have. Moreover, study of the final form of the biblical books may shed additional light on issues regarding composition. For example, structural study may help account for peculiarities and unevennesses in a text in a way that refocuses the question of the text's prehistory. In the end, of course, everyone is working toward a common goal, namely, to discover the best way to account for the text as we now have it.

2
Literary Units

The first step in analyzing the structure of an Old Testament book is to identify its constituent units.[1] In some books, such as the Book of Psalms, the constituent units are obvious. The Psalter comprises 150 individual psalms, mostly well delineated by titles, superscriptions, etc. These psalms are then organized into five "books," each closed by a refrain (Ps. 1–41, 42–72, 73–89, 90–106, 107–50). Similarly, Lamentations is composed of five easily identifiable units (corresponding to the chapter divisions), each unit except the last forming a self-contained acrostic ("A to Z") poem.

Unfortunately, most books in the Old Testament do not have such well-marked units. For instance, the constituent units of the Song of Songs are notoriously difficult to delineate, and modern attempts to identify the extent and number of units diverge widely—anywhere from four to forty-four units.[2] Similarly, books like Isaiah, Hosea, and many of the other prophetic books seem to have few clear indicators of the boundaries of their units, and modern efforts to identify these are often forced—and mutually contradictory.

The goal of structural analysis is to identify the units that the biblical author designed and intended as units, rather than to impose artificial schemes on the text. In order to do this, it is first necessary to learn how Hebrew authors generally delineated their units.

Ancient writers, as previously noted, normally did not use visual, graphic cues to mark off their units (such as the indentation that marks the beginning of this paragraph or the prominently set-off title at the beginning of this chapter). Like the modern orator, biblical authors used verbal techniques to delineate their units, so that their listening audience could follow the presentation, point by point.

There are only three verbal ways for an author to mark a literary unit:

1. mark the unit's beginning
2. mark the unit's end
3. shape the unit into a cohesive whole so that its parts are bound together to form an independent, complete, self-contained "package"

The biblical writers (like other ancient writers) utilized all three of these methods, often in combination, to delineate units both large and small.

Beginning Markers

In modern oral presentations, speakers frequently indicate the parameters of their successive units by using beginning markers such as, "A second topic I would like to discuss today is . . ."; or, "Now let us consider the second question."

In the Hebrew Bible, beginning markers are probably used more than any other method to delineate units. For example, Amos marks off the eight parts of his introductory message (Amos 1–2) by beginning each with the same introductory formula: "for three transgressions of nation x, even for four, I will not turn back my anger," which is then followed by a detailing of that nation's sins (1:3, 6, 9, 11, 13; 2:1, 4, 6).

There are various categories of beginning markers in the Hebrew Bible. The following is a

---

1. Regarding the identification of units on the smaller level, Muilenburg, "Form Criticism and Beyond," *Journal of Biblical Literature* 88 (1969) 8–9, states: "The first concern of the rhetorical critic, it goes without saying, is to define the limits or scope of the literary unit, to recognize precisely where and how it begins and where and how it ends. . . . An examination of the commentaries will reveal that there is great disagreement on this matter, and . . . more often than not, no defense is offered for the isolation of the pericope."

2. For an illuminating survey of modern attempts to analyze the Song of Songs, see Marvin H. Pope, *Song of Songs* (Anchor Bible 7c; Garden City: Doubleday, 1977), 40–55; for a listing of these attempts, see the chapter devoted to the Song of Songs below.

partial list of beginning markers (the examples provided are not exhaustive):

1. title (Prov. 25:1; Isa. 13:1; Hab. 3:1)
2. introductory formula
   a. "there are three things . . . , four things . . ." (Prov. 30:15, 18, 21, 29; cf. Amos 1–2)
   b. "these are the generations of *x*" (frequently in Genesis)
3. common beginning word or phrase[3]
   a. "thus says Yahweh" (*kōh ʾāmar yhwh* or variations)—very common throughout the prophets (Isa. 50:1; Amos 1:3; 2:1)
   b. "hear!" (*šimʿû* or *šĕmaʿ*)—very common throughout the prophets (Isa. 1:2; 49:1; Hos. 4:1; 5:1; Amos 3:1; 4:1; 5:1; Mic. 3:1)
   c. "behold" (*hinnēh* or *hēn*)—common in prophets (Isa. 19:1; 24:1; 52:13; 59:1)
   d. "woe!" (*hôy*, etc.)—common in prophets (Isa. 28:1; 29:1; 30:1; 55:1)
   e. "therefore" (*lākēn*)—often introducing a conclusion (Zeph. 3:8)
   f. "and now" (*wĕʿattâ*) or "now" (*ʿattâ*)—introducing a summation or concluding unit; common in prophets (Mic. 4:9, 11)
   g. "in that day" or variations ("in those days," "the days are coming," etc.)—common in prophets (Joel 3:1 [4:1]; Amos 9:11; Obad. 8; Mic. 4:1)
   h. "for" or "surely" (*kî*)[4] (Joel 3:1 [4:1])
4. vocative—frequent in poetry and prophets (Ps. 8:1 [8:2]; 21:1 [21:2]; 22:1 [22:2])[5]
5. rhetorical question (Ps. 2:1; Nah. 2:11 [2:12]; Isa. 63:1; Jer. 49:1, 7)[6]
6. imperative (other than "hear!")—common in poetry and prophets (Ps. 95:1; 98:1; 100:1; Isa. 40:1; 47:1; 52:1; 54:1; 60:1)
7. orientation—one or more clauses setting the stage for the upcoming narrative (Josh. 1:1a; Ruth 1:1–2) or instructions to a prophet about the delivery of the message that follows (Jer. 7:1–2; 17:19)[7]
8. "abstract"—one or more narrative clauses summarizing the whole upcoming story (Gen. 1:1; 18:1; 22:1)[8]

9. first part of an "inclusio" or a chiasmus—recognizable to the audience, of course, only in retrospect (Ps. 103; 104)[9]
10. shift in time (Gen. 17:1; 1 Sam. 6:1)[10]
11. shift in place (Num. 20:1)
12. shift in characters or speaker (Job 4:1; 6:1)
13. shift in theme or topic (Isa. 40:1)[11]
14. shift in genre (e.g., the narrative in 1 Chron. 10:1 following genealogical lists)[12]
15. shift in narrative technique (or "discourse genre")—shift from dialogue to narration, summary, etc.[13]
16. shift in speed of action (Ruth 1:6)[14]
17. shift from prose to poetry or vice versa (Isa. 36:1; 40:1)
18. shift in tense, mood, or person of the verbs (Lam. 1:1–11, 12–22)[15]

The beginning of a new unit may be indicated by a combination of several such markers. For example, the beginning of the new unit in 1 Chronicles 10 features at least five shifts: genre, time, characters, place, and topic.[16] Most of the techniques listed here may be used to mark the beginning of both larger and smaller units. For example, "woe" (*hôy*) in Isaiah 28:1 marks the beginning of a major part of the Book of Isaiah (the collection of woe oracles in chaps. 28–33); but the same word also marks the beginnings of several individual woe oracles within this collection (e.g., 29:1; 30:1; 31:1; 33:1). Accordingly, this list should be kept in mind when identifying primary-level, secondary-level, or even tertiary-level units.

---

3. Most of the beginning words and phrases listed here are mentioned in Muilenburg, "Form Criticism and Beyond," 14–15.

4. See James Muilenburg, "The Linguistic and Rhetorical Usages of the Particle *Kî* in the Old Testament," *Hebrew Union College Annual* 32 (1961) 135–60.

5. Muilenburg, "Form Criticism and Beyond," 16; Wilbur Pickering, *A Framework for Discourse Analysis* (Arlington: Summer Institute of Linguistics/University of Texas at Arlington Press, 1980), 279.

6. Pickering, *Framework for Discourse Analysis*, 279.

7. Adele Berlin, *Poetics and Interpretation of Biblical Narrative* (Sheffield: Almond, 1983), 102–3.

8. Ibid., 102.

9. Pickering, *Framework for Discourse Analysis*, 280.

10. For utilization of shifts in time, place, characters, and theme, see ibid., 279–80.

11. See John Beekman, John Callow, and Michael Kopesec, *The Semantic Structure of Written Communication* (Dallas: Summer Institute of Linguistics, 1981), 73.

12. Beekman, Callow, and Kopesec (ibid., 118) write: "Our studies have shown that, in general, a group of paragraphs—for example, a section, episode, scene—shares the same discourse genre, so that genre change will often mark a high-level boundary."

13. Ibid., 118; S. Bar-Efrat, "Some Observations on the Analysis of Structure in Biblical Narrative," *Vetus Testamentum* 30 (1980) 158.

14. Bar-Efrat, "Analysis of Structure in Biblical Narrative," 159–60.

15. Pickering, *Framework for Discourse Analysis*, 280.

16. The observation of Beekman, Callow, and Kopesec (*Semantic Structure of Written Communication*, 134) is pertinent here: "Of particular relevance in a narrative is the time and location of the episode. A chain of stimuli and responses are joined together because they are actions that involve the same participants, occur at the same place, and happen during a single period of time and within the same general set of circumstances. Therefore, whenever there is a change in time or place or participants, this often indicates a break within the chain and indicates the start of a new unit at one level or another."

End Markers

A second (less common) way biblical writers delineated their units was to utilize end markers, much as we do when we conclude our fairy tales with the common ending, "And they lived happily ever after." Several categories of end markers can be identified in the Hebrew Bible. The following is a partial list of end markers (the examples provided are not exhaustive):

1. concluding formula
    a. "and it was evening, and it was morning, the *n*th day" (six times in Gen. 1)
    b. "and the land had peace for *x* years" (Judg. 3:11, 30; 5:31; 8:28; see also 1 Kings 14:19–20)
2. poetic refrain (the recurring refrain that closes the three parts of Ps. 42–43; cf. Amos 4:6–11 ["yet you did not return"]; Song 2:6–7)
3. summary (Ezra 6:13–14; the closing summaries of the judges' rules throughout the Book of Judges)
4. conclusion: resolution of tension, completion of action, death of central character, final outcome, etc. (Josh. 6:27; Judg. 4:23–24; the conclusions of each king's reign in Kings and Chronicles)
5. last part of inclusio or chiasmus (Ps. 8:9 [8:10])[17]
6. flashback (1 Sam. 25:43–44)[18]
7. linkage with audience's own time—concluding a story with a statement about the significance or consequences of the story in the audience's own time, often including the phrase "to this day"[19] (Ruth 4:17b; Josh. 7:26; 8:29; 9:27)
8. poetic climactic or ballast lines[20] or concluding exclamation, analogous to a grand finale (Ps. 103:20–22; 106:48; Song 4:16–5:1; the common "hallelujah" closing in Ps. 115–17; 146–50)
9. "says Yahweh" (*nĕʾum yhwh*, *ʾāmar yhwh*, *yhwh dibbēr*, etc.)—often closing prophetic discourses or subunits of discourses (Isa. 21:17; 22:25; Jer. 29:32; Amos 2:16; 3:15; 5:27; 9:15)

As with beginning markers, a combination of these end markers may be used to conclude units. For example, the stories of most of the judges in the Book of Judges close with a combination of conclusion, summary, and concluding formula. Also like beginning markers, end markers can be used to conclude both larger and smaller units.

Techniques for Creating Internal Cohesion

The third way an author can delineate a unit is by shaping the unit into a cohesive whole so that its parts relate to one another to form a complete, independent, self-contained "package." Literary units are generally recognizable because their parts "hang together"; that is, their parts are bound together in some obvious way to form an interrelated whole.[21] For example, Psalm 25 forms a self-contained "package" bound together by the unifying technique of an acrostic poem; each line serves an integral role in the formation of the acrostic. Similarly, the story of Ehud in Judges 3:12–30 forms a unit bound together by its singular focus on Ehud, Israel's second judge. All the sentences and paragraphs in 3:12–30 relate to this single topic, whether they introduce it, develop it, or conclude it.

Various techniques are employed in the Hebrew Bible to create complete, self-contained literary packages. Some of these (with selected examples) are the following:

1. sameness of time (Josh. 1–12 is entirely set in the time of the conquest of Canaan under Joshua)
2. sameness of place (the giving of the law at Mount Sinai in Exod. 19:3–Num. 10:10; the story of David and Abigail at Maon in 1 Sam. 25)
3. sameness of participant(s) (the story of the naive youth and the adulteress in Prov. 7:6–23; the reign of Josiah in 2 Kings 22:1–23:30)
4. sameness of topic or theme[22] (the flood story in Gen. 6:9–9:19; the portrayal of the suffering servant in Isa. 52:13–53:12)
5. sameness of genre (the narrative account in Isa. 36–39, surrounded by prophetic discourses; the genealogies in 1 Chron. 1–9)

---

17. Muilenburg, "Form Criticism and Beyond," 9.
18. Bar-Efrat, "Analysis of Structure in Biblical Narrative," 160–61.
19. Berlin, *Poetics and Interpretation of Biblical Narrative*, 107.
20. Muilenburg, "Form Criticism and Beyond," 9.

21. Beekman, Callow, and Kopesec, *Semantic Structure of Written Communication*, 21 (cf. pp. 20–23), state that a key feature of a semantic unit is coherence or "compatibility." They define "coherence" this way: "In general by coherence is meant that the constituents of a unit will be semantically compatible with one another. Corresponding to the three subclasses of constituents of a unit, it is expected that a well-formed unit will have referential coherence, situational coherence, and structural (relational) coherence."
22. Beekman, Callow, and Kopesec (ibid., 21) call this "referential coherence."

6. sameness of narrative technique (the recorded speech in 2 Chron. 6:14–42 followed by the narration in 7:1–10)

7. sameness of speed of action (Ruth 1:1–5 [rapid, spanning a number of years] and 1:6–18 [slow, covering a single conversation])

8. sameness of literary form (prose, poetry) (the prose interlude in Isa. 36–39; the poetic interlude in Judg. 5)

9. sameness of grammatical/syntactic forms (third-person feminine singular in Lam. 1:1–11 and first-person singular in 1:12–22)

10. inclusio ("sandwich structure," beginning and ending a unit on the same note) (Ps. 8; 146–50)

11. chiasmus (tying an entire unit together structurally by a symmetric arrangement of the parts; e.g., a-b-c-c'-b'-a') (the chiastically arranged narrative of Solomon's reign in 2 Chron. 1–9)

12. keyword[23] (frequent repetition of the same word throughout the unit) ("holy" [*qādôš*] in Lev. 19–26; "pure" [*ṭāhôr*] and "impure" [*ṭāmēʾ*] in Lev. 11–18)

13. patterned repetition of information (Judg. 3:6–16:31; Amos 1–2)[24]

14. recurring motif[25] (dreams and bowing in the Joseph story in Gen. 37–50)

---

23. Muilenburg, "Form Criticism and Beyond," 17, states: "It is the key word which may often guide us in our isolation of a literary unit, which gives to it its unity and focus, which helps us to articulate the structure of the composition." Robert Alter, *The Art of Biblical Narrative* (New York: Basic Books, 1985), 94, writes of the keyword: "This sort of literary mechanism, at once a unifying device and a focus of development in the narrative, will be recognizable to anyone familiar with, say, Shakespeare's elaboration of the multiple implications of the word *time* in *Henry IV*" (see further Alter's discussion on pp. 92–93 of the definition and functions of "keyword" [*Leitwort*]). H. Van Dyke Parunak, "Some Axioms for Literary Architecture" (paper read at the Midwest Regional Meeting of the American Oriental Society and the Society of Biblical Literature at Ann Arbor, Mich., 23 Feb. 1981), 7 n. 16, states: "Strictly, the term 'keyword' applies only to a repeated lexical item used as a structuring device. We will use the term more broadly to refer to any repeated linguistic feature which characterizes a literary unit and marks it as distinct from its context." On pp. 7–8 he writes: "As long as a keyword persists, we know that we are still in the same literary unit. When one keyword disappears or another appears, we recognize a structural division." On keywords as structure markers, see also Umberto Cassuto, "The Sequence and Arrangement of the Biblical Sections," *World Congress of Jewish Studies 1947* (Jerusalem: Magnes, 1952), 1.165–69; reprinted in *Biblical and Oriental Studies*, trans. Israel Abrahams (Jerusalem: Magnes, 1973), 1.1–6.

24. Beekman, Callow, and Kopesec, *Semantic Structure of Written Communication*, 115. An additional example may be drawn from 2 Baruch, where each of the five central units features (1) prayer or lament by Baruch, (2) dialogue between Baruch and God, and (3) an address, usually by Baruch to the people; see F. J. Murphy, *The Structure and Meaning of Second Baruch* (Atlanta: Scholars Press, 1985), 11–13.

25. Alter, *Art of Biblical Narrative*, 95.

Identifying Literary Units

Although subjectivity cannot be entirely eliminated in identifying units, several guidelines can help minimize the problem:

1. *Objective markers*: greater weight should be given to objective markers (such as titles, introductory or concluding formulas, and shifts in time or place) than to more subjective ones (such as shifts in theme).[26]

2. *External cues and internal cohesion*: unit identification that is supported by both external cues (beginning markers and/or end markers) and internal cohesion is more likely to be legitimate than one supported by only one of these. For example, the genealogy of Shem in Genesis 11:10–26, with its conspicuous beginning marker (11:10) and its internal cohesiveness, is obviously a unit. In contrast, it is less clear that Genesis 5:1–6:8 is a unit; while it is introduced and in fact framed by the "these are the generations of *x*" formula (5:1; cf. 6:9), the section lacks an obvious internal unity.

3. *Multiple indicators*: the more indicators there are (internal and external), the more likely the identification. For example, the numerous signals delineating the Ehud story in Judges 3:12–30 give clear evidence that it is a self-contained unit: its beginning is marked by at least five cues: orientation, formulaic introduction, shift in time, shift in place, and shift in participants; its end is marked by a conclusion and by a closing formula ("and the land had rest for *x* years"); and the material between the opening and closing forms a cohesive whole, tied together by sameness of place (region of Benjamin), time (during Ehud's judgeship), topic (Ehud's victory over Eglon), and participants (Ehud, Eglon, etc.), as well as a symmetric design.

---

26. Bar-Efrat ("Analysis of Structure in Biblical Narrative," 169–70) warns: "Since themes or ideas are not stated overtly, but have to be extracted by means of interpretation, one should exercise a good deal of self-restraint and self-criticism before proceeding to the delineation of thematic or ideational structures. Even when dealing with phenomena that are objectively present in the narrative text a certain amount of subjectivity is involved when pointing out structures. This is due to the necessity to single out among a multitude of diverse phenomena those elements with which a significant structure can be realized. The subjective factor increases considerably when the ingredients of the structure are themselves the product of the rather subjective process of interpretation. So in order to steer clear of undue arbitrariness themes and ideas should be borne out by the facts of the narrative as clearly and unambiguously as possible. Also, vague and general formulations should be avoided."

4. *Bracketing*: the bracketing of a proposed unit by two other well-marked units (e.g., Ps. 107; 118; 137; cf. Judg. 3:12–30) lends added weight to its identification.

5. *Perceptibility to ancient audience*: unit boundaries that an ancient audience could have easily perceived should be given more weight than boundaries that would have been more difficult for them to discern. This is a subjective consideration, but it is nevertheless an important one. For example, an audience could hardly miss the unit boundaries in Genesis 1—the six successive days of creation; but the identification of the beginning of the Isaac story as Genesis 21:8 that will be proposed in chapter 6 below is more tenuous, because an ancient audience would not as easily have perceived the unit's boundary here.

6. *Compatibility in overall context*: it is more likely that a unit has been correctly identified if it functions logically and compatibly in its overall structural context. For example, the identification of the Abimelech story (Judg. 8:33–9:57) as a major unit in the Book of Judges is supported by its filling a key slot in the seven-part symmetric layout of the main body, chiastically matching the story of Deborah and Barak.

After a unit has been tentatively identified on the basis of these considerations, the validity of its identification should be tested by rereading the entire context (preferably in Hebrew) as if for the first time by the original audience, and then asking, "Would people in the original audience have perceived the same unit boundaries that I identified?" If the answer to this admittedly subjective query is not a fairly strong affirmative, the identification should be reevaluated.[27]

Length and Number of Units in Biblical Texts

Based on the following chapters, a few general observations can be made about units in the Hebrew Bible. With regard to length, the typical major literary unit in the Hebrew Bible is about fifteen to twenty pages of Hebrew text in BHS—the length of Genesis 1–11, Ecclesiastes, Song of Songs, Isaiah 1–12, and Amos—and would take around half an hour to read to an audience. Secondary units are typically about the size of an average chapter in our modern Bibles—about one or two pages of Hebrew text—and would take an average of five minutes to read. Tertiary-level units range in size from a single sentence or poetic verse to several paragraphs or poetic stanzas.

Seven is the typical number of units that comprise a larger unit in the Old Testament. The frequency of sevenfold structuring is remarkable. Many of the books in the Hebrew Bible exhibit seven-part arrangements—for example, Ruth, Samuel, Kings, Chronicles, Ezra–Nehemiah, Job, Ecclesiastes, Song of Songs, Isaiah, Jeremiah, Ezekiel, and most of the Minor Prophets. Many of the larger units in these books, in turn, comprise seven smaller parts; and many of these smaller units have seven tertiary-level units. The convention of sevenfold structuring appears to have been highly popular in ancient Israel—as it apparently was in surrounding lands.[28]

One common variation of this pattern is the thirteen-part arrangement, which features the seventh part at the center, found in Lamentations, Esther, the stories of Abraham (Gen. 12:1–21:7), Isaac (21:8–28:4), and Jacob (28:5–37:1), the story of the wilderness journey to the plains of Moab (Num. 10:11–21:20), the story of Israel's sojourn in the plains of Moab (Num. 21:21–Deut. 3:29), and Joshua 13–24. Another popular variation is the fourteen-part structure (7 x 2), found in the Joseph story (Gen. 37–50), the exodus account (Exod. 1:1–13:16), Joshua 1–12, and the introduction to Proverbs (Prov. 1:8–9:18). Five-part (e.g., Haggai, Psalms, and the primary structuring scheme of Lamentations) and three-part (e.g., Judges and the Book of the Law) arrangements also occasionally appear, and various other configurations are found from time to time. All of these patterns will be identified and discussed as they occur in the chapters that follow.

---

27. The importance of three personal qualities cannot be overestimated in this process: commonsense, intellectual integrity, and a hardy aversion to imposing one's own scheme on the text.

28. See, e.g., the illustration of "Ishtar's Descent into Hades" (3.1) and the numerous examples of sevenfold (or fourteenfold) structuring in the Sumerian, Akkadian, Ugaritic, and Egyptian texts found in J. B. Pritchard (ed.), *Ancient Near Eastern Texts* (3d ed.; Princeton: Princeton University Press, 1969).

3
Arrangement of Units

The second task in analyzing the structure of an Old Testament book, after the units have been identified, is to consider the arrangement of the units. (It goes without saying that if one has failed to identify a composition's units correctly, an analysis of their arrangement will be skewed.) There are various arrangement schemes that a writer might use in laying out a composition. In our own literary tradition, compositions often follow a simple linear scheme: a-b-c-d-e etc. But other schemes are possible. For example, there is a "sandwich" structure, also called inclusio,[1] in which a composition begins and ends on the same note (as in an a-b-c-d-a' pattern). The inclusio pattern is popular in modern poetry, songs, anecdotes, sermons, plays, television shows, movies, and so forth. Hymns that begin and end with the same stanza follow this arrangement pattern.

To create an inclusio structure in a speech about speed limits, we might begin with a series of questions:

Why should the government regulate how fast we drive? Why do we need speed limits? Why, when our time is valuable and we own cars capable of speeds of over 100 miles per hour, must we creep along at 65 miles per hour on open highways?

Then, after a series of units on the history of speed regulations, the evidence of statistics, and the weaknesses of arguments for deregulation, we might close with a concluding unit in which we repeat one or more of the opening questions, followed by a succinct, climactic answer:

Why should the government regulate how fast we drive? Why do we need speed limits? Because there are no safe alternatives!

By echoing the introduction we are signaling to the listeners that we are concluding the speech. Moreover, the inclusio provides an artistic touch that an audience will appreciate, since humans enjoy a touch of symmetry.

An inclusio, and indeed any pattern other than a linear one, can only be created by use of repetition. Repetition breaks up the strictly linear progression and creates a beat-counterbeat effect, linking two units that share the repetition. In the above inclusio, a link or "echo" between the opening and closing parts is created by repeating in the closing something that was said in the opening. It is not be necessary to repeat the entire opening to create the echo, but there must be enough of a repetition for an audience or reader to catch the echo and appreciate it. (For instance, repeating a single, relatively common phrase from the introduction in the above example, such as "speed limits," would not be enough.)

Repetition can be used to create a wide variety of nonlinear arrangement patterns: a-b-a'-b' or a-b-c-a'-b'-c' or a-b-b'-a'. All possible arrangement schemes fall into one of three basic categories (or combinations of these):

linear	a-b-c
parallel	a-b-c-a'-b'-c'
symmetric	a-b-c-b'-a'

Numerous varieties are possible. For example, a typical inclusio (a-b-c-d-e-a') combines linear and symmetric patterns. An a-b-c-d-b'-c'-a' pattern is a modified symmetry—a combination of symmetric and parallel patterns. An a-a'-b-b'-c-c'-d-d' (pairing) arrangement combines linear and parallel schemes. Many such schemes can be created by varying the type of pattern and the number of constituent parts. Moreover, it is possible for a composition to have two or more schemes simultaneously. For example, a chronologically linear arrangement (a-b-c-d-e) might exhibit a

---

1. This structural pattern was first identified by D. H. Müller, *Die Propheten in ihrer ursprünglichen Form* (Vienna: Hölder, 1896). H. Van Dyke Parunak, *Structural Studies in Ezekiel* (Ph.D. diss., Harvard University, 1978), 16, defines inclusio as a "the device of beginning and ending a stanza with the same or similar words, concepts, or constructions."

secondary symmetric touch. That is, episode d, while following c chronologically, might also exhibit an obvious similarity to b; and e, while chronologically following d, might also have a striking resemblance to a. The result: a secondary a-b-c-b'-a' pattern.

All three basic patterns—linear, parallel, and symmetric, as well as numerous combinations of these—occur throughout the Hebrew Bible.

Linear Patterns

The most common arrangement scheme in the Old Testament is probably the linear pattern, in which the units follow one another in a non-repeating fashion: a-b-c-d-e. This pattern is the one most easily grasped by modern readers because it is most familiar to us. It was probably the most comfortable scheme for ancient listeners as well. The pattern has the advantage of being the easiest to follow; it requires no extra attentiveness on the part of the audience to remember earlier material and listen for repetitions. By its very nature it suits genres such as narrative and procedural instruction where a linear order is most natural.

Chronological Linear Schemes

There are various types of linear schemes. The most common is chronological, in which units are arranged in a chronologically sequential order. The Book of Kings, for example, is basically arranged in this manner, beginning with what happened first, followed by what happened next, and so forth, until the final unit, which recounts what happened last. Stories, narratives, parables, etc., favor this scheme.

In a chronologically linear arrangement there is normally some "unevenness" in the flow of action. Successive episodes can exhibit a variety of chronological relationships, some not strictly sequential. The various types of chronological linear schemes include the following:[2]

1. *Sequential*: a happened, then b happened. For example, 2 Kings 22–25 recounts in chronological order the successive reigns of Josiah, Jehoahaz, Jehoiakim, Jehoiachin, and Zedekiah.
2. *Overlapping*: a and b partially overlap; that is, before a was over, b had begun. For example, in 2 Kings 14:23–15:7 the entire long reign of Jeroboam II is recounted first, followed by an account of the reign of Azariah of Judah, who began his rule in Jeroboam's twenty-seventh year and continued after Jeroboam's death.
3. *Inclusive*: b, an event of short duration, occurs during the span of a, an event of longer duration. For example, in 1 Kings 15:9–31 the entire long reign of King Asa of Judah is recounted, followed by an account of the two-year reign of Nadab of Israel, who began and ended his reign while Asa continued to rule in Judah.
4. *Simultaneous*: a and b happened at the same time. For example, according to 2 Kings 11:3: "[Josiah] remained hidden with his nurse at the temple of Yahweh for six years, while Athaliah ruled the land."

A chronologically arranged narrative also normally includes material that is "off the timeline"—that is, material that stands outside the linear succession of events.[3] Off-the-timeline material, such as asides and flashbacks, generally interrupts the flow of the action (unless it comes at the beginning or end) in order to supply information that is deemed important for the story and its meaning. Material that is off the timeline may include categories such as the following:

1. *Orientation*: setting the stage for the upcoming story. For example, Genesis 2:5–6 sets the stage for the action that begins in 2:7 (see also 1:2; 3:1a; 16:1).
2. *Explanation (or comment)*: pausing in the action to provide some explanatory material designed to shed light on the story at this point. For example, 2 Kings 17:7–23 interrupts the story of the history of Israel to explain why Yahweh let the northern kingdom fall. And in Genesis 2:24, the author pauses in the creation narrative to comment, "For this reason a man will leave his father and his mother" (see also Josh. 2:6; 3:15a; 5:4–7; 7:1).

---

2. These various relationships are discussed by Barbara Hollenbach, "A Preliminary Semantic Classification of Temporal Concepts," *Notes on Translation* 47 (1973) 2–8; Robert Longacre, *The Grammar of Discourse* (New York: Plenum, 1983); and John Beekman, John Callow, and Michael Kopesec, *The Semantic Structure of Written Communication* (Dallas: Summer Institute of Linguistics, 1981), 81. Kathleen Callow, *Discourse Considerations in Translating the Word of God* (Grand Rapids: Zondervan, 1974), 40–41, divides these types into two categories: "Events on the time-line (excluding summaries, explanations, etc.) are either successive or simultaneous. . . . There are also distinctions between different kinds of simultaneous events." These include (1) completely overlapping, (2) beginning and ending together, and (3) a momentary event occurring within the time span covered by a process-type event (p. 42).

3. See, e.g., the discussion by Callow, *Discourse Considerations in Translating the Word of God*, 38–42.

3. *Parenthetical information (or aside)*: pausing in the action to provide information of peripheral interest. For example, in Genesis 22:20–24 the author interrupts the narrative to give some details about what was happening with Abraham's Mesopotamian relatives.

4. *Flashback*: pausing in the action to recount an event that happened at a time previous to the present story. For example, Judges 11:1–3 interrupts the story to supply the audience with some pertinent background information about what happened to Jephthah years earlier.

5. *Flash forward*: pausing in the action to recount an event that will happen at a time after the present story. For example, both Genesis 10 and 36 interrupt the narrative to trace the descendants of the people just mentioned to a time hundreds of years later (the audience's own time).

6. *Summary*: pausing to sum up what has happened to this point or what will happen next. For example, Judges 2:10–3:6 summarizes the entire period of the judges; then 3:7–16:31 traces the period, judge by judge. And in Genesis 35:23–26, the author pauses to review for the audience the names of the twelve sons who have been born to Jacob.

Nonchronological Linear Schemes

Although the chronological scheme is one of the most common types of linear arrangements, it is by no means the only one.[4] Other types of nonchronological linear schemes include the following:

1. *Spatial*: an arrangement according to a spatial rather than temporal scheme. For example, Joshua 15:21–62 describes in a succession of geographically ordered units the southern, western, central, and eastern subdistricts of Judah.

2. *Logical*: an arrangement according to logical argumentation or reasoning, in which each successive unit furthers the discussion by expressing such things as purpose, reason, means, condition, grounds, result, and consequence (e.g., Prov. 2:1–8).

3. *Degree*: an arrangement following an order of degree, such as largest to smallest, most important to least important, best to worst,

oldest to youngest, most holy to least holy, etc. For example, the description of the tabernacle in Exodus 25:10–27:19 starts with the most holy item, the ark, followed by items increasingly less holy: table, lampstand, tabernacle, altar, and courtyard. And in Genesis 49, Jacob's blessings are arranged from the oldest to the youngest son.

4. *List (or parts of the whole)*: an arrangement featuring a series of items, in no particular order, which make up a larger whole (perhaps the laws in Lev. 19).

5. *Collection*: an arrangement of independently composed pieces, such as prophetic messages, songs, proverbs, etc., that have been gathered and placed together in no particular order by an editor (perhaps the psalms in Ps. 1–72 or the proverbs in Prov. 10–22).

6. *Structural*: an arrangement according to some mechanical structural scheme, such as the arrangement according to the Hebrew alphabet in the acrostic poems of Lamentations 1–4 (cf. the Koran, in which the suras are arranged from the longest to the shortest).

7. *Pearling (or catchword bonding)*: an arrangement according to the linking of topics (or words) from one unit to the next. For example, b develops a topic introduced in a; c then develops a topic introduced in b; etc. It could be argued that Psalms 1–5 are so arranged.

Parallel Patterns

In one respect all compositions are arranged linearly, since every composition is made up of a series of units occurring one after another in a linear progression of some sort. The composition will be heard (or read) linearly, unit after unit, so that the succession of units must have some kind of continuity and order; otherwise, the composition will be unintelligible. Nevertheless, a composition can be configured so that, in addition to its primary linear order, it also exhibits a secondary structural scheme created by repetition. As already mentioned, two of the basic schemes are fashioned by repetition: parallel and symmetric patterns.

Parallel arrangements are relatively common in the Hebrew Bible.[5] They generally feature two

---

4. Beekman, Callow, and Kopesec provide an excellent survey of nonchronological relationships in *Semantic Structure of Written Communication*, 78–116; see also Ernst R. Wendland (ed.), *Discourse Perspectives on Hebrew Poetry in the Scriptures* (New York: United Bible Societies, 1994), 52.

5. Parallelism is referred to by H. Van Dyke Parunak ("Oral Typesetting: Some Uses of Biblical Structure," *Biblica* 62 [1981] 155) as "alternation" and by Müller (*Die Propheten in ihrer ursprünglichen Form*) as "responsion," from the model of the Greek chorus echoing back and forth the same essential elements; cf. Parunak, *Structural Studies in Ezekiel*, 15.

sets (or panels)[6] of units, in which the units of the first set are matched in the same order by those of the second set (a-b-c ‖ a′-b′-c′ or variations). When a parallel scheme has an odd number of units, the unmatched unit can be placed at the end (a-b-c ‖ a′-b′-c′ ‖ d), center (a-b-c-d-a′-b′-c′), or (more rarely) beginning (a-b-c-d ‖ b′-c′-d′).

Parallelism frequently occurs in Hebrew poetry. Note, for example, the a-b-c ‖ a′-b′-c′ pattern in Psalm 19:1–2 [19:2–3]:

---

a the heavens
  b tell of
    c God's glory
a′ the sky
  b′ proclaims
    c′ his handiwork

a day by day
  b they pour forth
    c speech
a′ night by night
  b′ they declare
    c′ knowledge

The pattern can also be found in larger units. For example, the creation story in Genesis 1:1–2:4, although primarily linear (first day, second day, etc.), exhibits a secondary parallel pattern (a-b-c ‖ a′-b′-c′ ‖ d):

---

a light
  b sea and sky
    c dry land
a′ lights
  b′ fish and birds
    c′ land animals and humans
      d Sabbath

Whole books may likewise be arranged in this way. The seven parts of Jonah are primarily linear in arrangement (following a chronological order), but also exhibit a secondary parallel pattern (a-b-c ‖ a′-b′-c′ ‖ d):

---

a Jonah's commissioning and disobedience (1:1–3)
  b Jonah and pagan sailors: Yahweh is merciful (1:4–16)
    c Jonah's response to Yahweh's mercy: praise (1:17–2:10 [2:1–11])
a′ Jonah's recommissioning and obedience (3:1–3a)
  b′ Jonah and pagan Ninevites: Yahweh is merciful (3:3b–10)

---

6. The term *panel* as used here seems to have been first adopted by Nils W. Lund, *Chiasmus in the New Testament* (Chapel Hill: University of North Carolina Press, 1942); for a formal definition, see Parunak, *Structural Studies in Ezekiel*, 62. In the present study, I try to avoid using technical terms where possible and so use "set" for "panel."

    c′ Jonah's response to Yahweh's mercy: resentment (4:1–4)
      d Yahweh's lesson (4:5–11)

Parallel arrangements are not as easy to perceive as simple linear patterns because the listener has to remember earlier points in order to catch the repeating pattern. But it is a pleasing and satisfying arrangement. When it is used, an audience experiences a feeling of pleasure and satisfaction when they grasp the repeating pattern and can begin to anticipate the repetitions.

In our own culture, children delight in listening to stories laid out in parallel patterns. "The Three Little Pigs," "Henny Penny," and "Goldilocks and the Three Bears," for example, all feature patterned repetitions that children can grasp and begin to anticipate as the story proceeds. By the time the wolf in "The Three Little Pigs" arrives at the second pig's house, we can guess what he will do and in what order; and certainly by the time he reaches the third pig's house we know precisely what to expect (which provides the author the opportunity to surprise us with a contrasting outcome). "Goldilocks and the Three Bears" features a parallel a-b-c ‖ a′-b′-c′ ‖ a″-b″-c″ pattern: Goldilocks sees Father Bear's x, she tries it, and it is too y; she sees Mother Bear's x, she tries it, and it is too z [the opposite of y]; she sees Baby Bear's x, she tries it, and it is "just right"; and so forth. As we hear the story, the pattern becomes easier and easier to follow because of the cadenced repetition.

There are several advantages to the parallel pattern. One is that its repetitiveness makes it easier to remember, both for the speaker and for the audience. Another advantage is that its repetitions provide an opportunity to do such things as compare, contrast, reiterate, emphasize, explain, and illustrate. For example, the parallel arrangement in the Book of Jonah compels us to compare the prophet's resentful prayer in 4:1–3 (prayed in response to Yahweh's sparing of Nineveh) with his earlier, grateful prayer in 2:2–9 [2:3–10] (prayed in response to his own rescue), which should cause us to perceive Jonah's first prayer as hypocritical, his second as selfish and mean-spirited. Rather than pedantically and overtly moralizing, the author utilizes the structuring pattern to make his point in a more elegant and engaging fashion.

Parallel patterns come in many variations. For example, a pairing pattern (a-a′-b-b′-c-c′ etc.) is featured in the Joseph story of Genesis 37–50, which contains two successive stories of the brothers' conflict with Joseph; two stories about Jacob's sons dealing with sexual tempta-

3.1 Ishtar's descent into Hades

```
a   Ishtar reaches the first gate and takes off her great crown
  b   Ishtar reaches the second gate and takes off her earrings
    c   Ishtar reaches the third gate and takes off her necklaces
      d   Ishtar reaches the fourth gate and takes off her breast ornaments
        e   Ishtar reaches the fifth gate and takes off her birthstone girdle
          f   Ishtar reaches the sixth gate and takes off her bracelets
            g   Ishtar reaches the seventh gate and takes off her breechcloth
              h   Ishtar enters Hades and dies
              h'  Ishtar comes alive and exits Hades
            g'  Ishtar comes to the seventh gate and puts on her breechcloth
          f'  Ishtar comes to the sixth gate and puts on her bracelets
        e'  Ishtar comes to the fifth gate and puts on her birthstone girdle
      d'  Ishtar comes to the fourth gate and puts on her breast ornaments
    c'  Ishtar comes to the third gate and puts on her necklaces
  b'  Ishtar comes to the second gate and puts on her earrings
a'  Ishtar comes to the first gate and puts on her great crown
```

tions; two stories of Joseph's interpreting dreams; two stories of Joseph's brothers coming down to Egypt; etc.

An a-b-a'-b'-a''-b'' pattern governs the layout of Ezra 1–Nehemiah 6:

a   return under Zerubbabel (Ezra 1–4)
  b   main accomplishment (Ezra 5–6)
a' return under Ezra (Ezra 7–8)
  b' main accomplishment (Ezra 9–10)
a'' return under Nehemiah (Neh. 1:1–2:16)
  b'' main accomplishment (Neh. 2:17–6:19)

The most common parallel pattern is probably the seven-part scheme already mentioned: a-b-c ‖ a'-b'-c' ‖ d, in which d generally functions as a climax, high point, or resolution.

Symmetric Patterns

The symmetric (or chiastic[7] or introverted) pattern is also relatively common in the Hebrew Bible.[8] Symmetry generally features two sets of units, in which the units of the second set match in reverse order the units of the first set: a-b-c ‖ c'-b'-a'. There is often an unmatched central unit linking the two matching sets: a-b-c-b'-a' (sometimes called "uneven chiasmus"). An example of a simple chiasmus from English literature is Pope's line: "A wit with dunces, and a dunce with wits."[9]

The chiastic scheme was popular in ancient times.[10] The Babylonian story of Ishtar's descent into Hades, for example, features an easily followed symmetric arrangement (3.1).

In our modern Western literary culture, symmetry is less common than it was in ancient times. Extended symmetries are particularly rare, but simple a-b-a' symmetries frequently occur. For example, many compositions feature an overall a-b-a' pattern, with an introduction, a body, and a conclusion (or an opening, a body, and a closing that echoes the opening).

Some readers may recall the old "Dragnet" series on television. Most episodes opened with the two detectives, Joe and Frank, involved in

---

7. The term *chiasm* or *chiasmus* derives from the crisscross shape of the Greek letter *chi* (X). Lund (*Chiasmus in the New Testament*, 31) defines chiasmus as "a literary figure, or principle, which consists of 'a placing crosswise' of words in a sentence. The term is used in rhetoric to designate an inversion of the order of words or phrases which are repeated or subsequently referred to in the sentence. The simplest application of the principle is found in structures of only *four* terms." S. Bar-Efrat ("Some Observations on the Analysis of Structure in Biblical Narrative," *Vetus Testamentum* 30 [1980] 170) distinguishes between ring (a-b-a'), chiastic (a-b-b'-a'), and concentric (a-b-c-b'-a') patterns. Following popular convention, I use the term *chiasmus* to refer to any symmetric configuration.

8. Symmetric structuring is variously called *epanodos*, introverted parallelism, extended introversion, concentrism, the *chi*-form, palistrophe, envelope construction, recursion, etc. For full survey and bibliography, see J. W. Welch (ed.), *Chiasmus in Antiquity: Structures, Analyses, Exegesis* (Hildesheim: Gerstenberg, 1981), 9–16. For a brief history of the study of chiasmus in the Bible, see ibid., 9; and Parunak, *Structural Studies in Ezekiel*, 7–22.

9. This quotation is taken from H. L. Yelland, S. O. Jones, and K. S. W. Easton, *A Handbook of Literary Terms* (New York: Philosophical Library, 1950), 32, who define chiasmus as "a passage in which the second part is inverted and balanced against the first. Chiasmus is thus a type of antithesis." They also offer an example from Coleridge: "Flowers are lovely, love is flowerlike."

10. Chiastic structures in Sumerian, Akkadian, Ugaritic, Aramaic, talmudic, Old Testament, New Testament, Classical Greek, Latin literature, and the Book of Mormon can be found in Welch, *Chiasmus in Antiquity*, 287–352. J. Myres, "The Last Book of the 'Iliad,'" *Journal of Hellenic Studies* 52 (1932) 264–96, proposes that the twenty-four books of the *Iliad* are arranged symmetrically, suggesting that such symmetry reflects an editorial technique that had its conceptual origin in the bilateral symmetry of late Minoan pottery decoration. More recently C. Whitman, in *Homer and the Heroic Tradition* (Cambridge: Harvard University Press, 1958), esp. chap. 11, supporting Myres's analysis, proposes that such symmetry can also be found within the subunits of these books.

some trivial dialogue, perhaps sitting in a restaurant discussing the acceptability of pickles on peanut butter sandwiches. Then came the call and they were off to solve the case, which would take most of the rest of the program. After the case was solved, however, the final scene would always feature Joe and Frank doing whatever they were doing at the beginning of the show—in this instance back at the restaurant, continuing the discussion about the acceptability of pickles on peanut butter sandwiches. With the return to the restaurant scene, the audience knew the story had reached its conclusion.

In the Hebrew Bible, symmetry occurs on all levels. For example, the pattern can be seen on the verse level:

```
a   he shall open
  b   and no one will shut
  b'  he shall shut
a'  and no one will open
                                    —Isaiah 22:22
a   whoever sheds
  b   the blood
    c   of a human
    c'  by human
  b'  that person's blood
a'  will be shed
                                    —Genesis 9:6
```

Whole sections or books are also frequently arranged in a symmetric configuration or with a symmetric touch. For example, the Book of Judges (which is of course primarily linear) is designed with a secondary symmetric scheme, in which the introduction (1:1–3:6) is matched by the conclusion (17:1–21:25); and the body itself presents the seven major judges in an order that has a conspicuous touch of symmetry:[11]

```
a   Othniel and his good wife (3:7–11; cf. 1:11–15)
  b   Ehud and the victory at the Jordan fords (3:12–31)
    c   Deborah: enemy's skull crushed by woman (4:1–5:31)
      d   Gideon: turning point (6:1–8:32)
    c'  Abimelech: judge's skull crushed by woman (8:33–10:5)
  b'  Jephthah and civil war at the Jordan fords (10:6–12:15)
a'  Samson and his bad wives (13:1–16:31)
```

The symmetric pattern has several compelling advantages:

1. *Beauty*: humans appreciate the esthetic quality of a balanced presentation, whether it be in art, music, architecture, or literature.

2. *Coherence*: a symmetry's tight configuration reinforces its unity.

3. *Sense of completeness*: the audience can recognize when the composition is "winding down," and they know it has concluded when it echoes its beginning. A symmetrically arranged piece "comes full circle," ending where it began.

4. *Central pivot*: in a more extensive symmetry with an uneven number of units (e.g., a-b-c-d-c'-b'-a'), the central unit is the natural location for the turning point, climax, high point, or centerpiece, since it marks the point where the composition reverses its order. Both halves of the symmetry look toward the center unit, making it the natural focal point. In the story of the judges, for example, the rule of Gideon represents the story's turning point. Until Gideon's rule, Israel did well under the judges; with Gideon's rule, however, things deteriorated, and from his time to the end of the period, Israel experienced a succession of bad rulers and civil wars.

5. *Memory aid*: both speaker and audience can remember the successive points of a speech more easily with the aid of the symmetric organization.

6. *Opportunities to exploit the repetitions*: as with the parallel pattern, repetitions provide opportunity to do such things as compare, contrast, reiterate, emphasize, explain, and illustrate.

The disadvantage of the symmetric pattern, particularly an extended symmetry, is that it is more demanding on an audience, since they must remember not only what was previously said so that they can catch the repetitions, but they must do so without the advantage of the rhythmic cadence of a parallel scheme. The pattern also calls for more work on the part of the author. To write a straightforward, linear narrative, for example, an author can simply recount the events as they occurred, giving no heed to such subtleties as foreshadowing, repetitions, echoes, and so on. But to compose a narrative with a more intricate structure, the writer must give additional thought to the final shape of the work. The process does not require fabricating or skewing the recounted events; but it does require additional attention to choices of selection, emphases, and wording.

For example, to accurately retell the story of the Battle of Gettysburg with a symmetric touch, an author/narrator might first analyze the battle

11. See D. W. Gooding, "The Composition of the Book of Judges," *Eretz-Israel* 16 (1982) 70*–79*.

to determine when its turning point occurred. This moment (say the Union victory on Little Round Top on day 2) would then become the center of the account. The author would then recount the events leading up to and following this turning point, selecting, highlighting, and wording the material to create a nicely balanced presentation with the desired symmetric touch. The final presentation might look something like this:

---

a armies gather: missed opportunities by the South
   b first day's battle: Confederates' first major miscalcula-tion: Ewell's fateful decision not to attack the Union forces while they were vulnerable; Southern failure in the assault of Culp's Hill
      c TURNING POINT: assault of Little Round Top on day 2; the tide turns
   b′ last day's battle: Confederates' second major miscalcula-tion: Lee's fateful decision to attack the Union forces when they were invulnerable; failure of the Southern assault of Seminary Ridge
a′ armies disperse: missed opportunities by the North

This recounting would faithfully relate the details of the battle, but the artful balance also gives the account an elegant and engaging touch otherwise lacking in a straightforward linear presentation.

Despite, however, the extra effort required in creating and listening to symmetrically arranged compositions, ancient writers and audiences seem to have appreciated the pattern immensely, if its frequency in ancient literature is any indication. The most common symmetric scheme in the Hebrew Bible is the seven-part symmetry: a-b-c-d-c′-b′-a′. A number of whole books exhibit this organization (e.g., Song of Songs, Jeremiah, and Amos), as do numerous smaller units within books.

There are several popular varieties of the symmetric scheme in the Hebrew Bible. In the thirteen-part chiasmus, the seventh part functions as the climax or turning point: a-b-c-d-e-f-g-f′-e′-d′-c′-b′-a′. The stories of Abraham, Isaac, and Jacob follow this pattern. Fourteen-part symmetries also occur: a-b-c-d-e-f-g-g′-f′-e′-d′-c′-b′-a′. The story of Joseph in Genesis 37–50 and the exodus story in Exodus 1:1–13:16 both have this design. The inclusio, or sandwich structure (a modified chiasmus), frequently appears as well (Ps. 8; 103; 104).

Techniques for Linking Units

All parallel and symmetric patterns have one important feature in common: their structures are created by the matching of units. The ques-

tion is, how do authors make their matching units match? Repetition, of course, is the *sine qua non* of matching: something from one unit must be repeated in the another unit to make the two units match (or echo or correspond to) one another. Moreover, there must be enough of a repetition for the audience to catch it, and the repetition must be unique to those two units. If an author were to try to create a match between two units by including the same key sentence in each, but chose a sentence that had also occurred in several other units, no one would perceive the intended match.

Any sort of repetition can link matching units[12] as long as the repetition is enough for the audience to catch and is unique to the two matching units. In the Hebrew Bible, techniques used to link matching units include the following categories:

1. verbatim repetition (the first and last verses in Ps. 8)
2. near-verbatim repetition (the two commissioning units in Jon. 1:1–3 and 3:1–3a)
3. sameness of place (Bethel links the two episodes in Gen. 28 and 35; the Beersheba well links the episodes in Gen. 21 and 26)
4. sameness of participant(s) (Ishmael links Gen. 16:1–16 and 17:20–27; Lot links Gen. 13 and 19; and Abimelech links Gen. 21 and 26)
5. sameness of time (nighttime links the beginnings of the two units in Song 3:1–5 and 5:2–7:11 [5:2–7:10])
6. sameness of genre (Jonah's two prayers in 2:2–9 [2:3–10] and 4:1–3 are linked by their common genre; they are the only prayers in the book)
7. sameness of speed of action (the opening and closing units of the Book of Ruth echo one another by the speed of action [both cover years of time in a few sentences]; Nah. 2:2b–10 [2:3b–11] and 3:1–7 echo one another by their rapid-fire, staccato speed of action, not found elsewhere in the book)
8. sameness of literary form (prose or poetry) (poetry links Isa. 1–35 with Isa. 40–66 and separates these sections from the prose section in the middle of the book [Isa. 36–39])
9. sameness of atmosphere (happy, somber, tense, etc.) (the joyful atmosphere of the vi-

---

12. Parunak, *Structural Studies in Ezekiel*, 64, states: "Correspondence may be coded between pairs of items using virtually every linguistic category at the language's disposal. For convenience of summary, these may be described in three categories." The three categories are lexical (recurrence of same words), grammatical (recurrence of similar grammatical or syntactic patterns), and rhetorical (correspondence based on cause-effect, symbol and interpretation, and other "logical" or "paradigmatic" connections) (pp. 65–68).

sions of future restoration in Isa. 2:2–5 and 4:2–6 link these two units and set them apart from the somber messages of condemnation that lie between them; likewise Isa. 8:19–9:7 [8:19–9:6] and 11:1–9)

10. sameness of topic or theme[13] (Ruth 1:6–18 and 4:1–12 are linked by a common theme: both units feature two of Naomi's relatives considering whether to support her, with only one choosing to do so; similarly, the two brothers' responses to a seductress create an intentional echo in Gen. 38–39)

11. sameness of beginnings (Jonah's two prayers are introduced in Jon. 2:1 [2:2] and 4:2 by the same clause)

12. repetition of keywords, phrases, or clauses[14] (the first and last units of Amos [1:1–2:16 and 8:4–9:15] share a number of identical words and phrases found nowhere else in the book)

13. recurrence of synonyms[15] (cf. Amos 4:1–13 and 5:18–6:14)

14. repetition of a key motif (the motif of bowing in Gen. 37, 42–44 and 48; the reversal of the elder and younger sons, involving the switching of hands, connects Gen. 38:1–30 and 47:27–49:32)

15. structural similarity, such as similar length of the matching units in contrast to other units, or similar internal structures (the

first and last units of the Song of Songs correspond in their internal structures: each is constructed as a seven-part dialogue between the young man and young woman, with the young woman introducing and concluding each)

How much repetition between units is enough to create a match? Is a single word, for example, enough to connect two nonadjacent units? Possibly—if the word is a striking term that carries some thematic weight in both passages and occurs nowhere else in the context. The determining question must always be this: could the ancient audience have perceived and appreciated the echo?

Analyzing the Arrangement of Units

The problem of subjectivity in analyzing the arrangement of units is even more serious than in the initial identification of units. The danger, in fact, is profound. In my opinion, the great majority of so-called chiasmuses and parallel schemes supposedly found in various parts of the Hebrew Bible or in other ancient literature are forced and unconvincing (including some of my own earlier analyses, I regret to say).

Three common methodological errors are generally found in forced chiasmuses and parallel schemes (which are usually accompanied by misidentifications of units).

The first methodological error might be called *creative titling*, whereby units are made to match by the imaginative wording of their assigned titles. For instance, one might try to make Psalm 1 and Psalm 23 match by titling them "Yahweh cares for his people like tended trees" and "Yahweh cares for his people like tended sheep." By this sort of adroit titling one could make any two units in the Hebrew Bible match, even ones from different books!

The second methodological error could be termed *illegitimate word-linking*, whereby units are seen to match based on the insignificant occurrence of one or more relatively common words in both units—words that may also occur elsewhere in the context. Biblical Hebrew is relatively limited in vocabulary, so that there is a high probability that several words in any given chapter will also occur in any other given chapter of the Old Testament.

To demonstrate this, take two familiar—and very different—chapters chosen at random: Genesis 3 and Psalm 1. An examination of the two passages reveals that at least seven Hebrew words occur in both passages:

---

13. Bar-Efrat, "Analysis of Structure in Biblical Narrative," 168, distinguishes between "theme" and "idea" in the correspondence of units: "Analysis . . . is based on the themes of the narrative units or the ideas contained therein. Themes and ideas are closely related. But themes are usually formulated in the form of short phrases, ideas in the form of complete sentences. Themes define the central issues of the narrative. They are embodied in the various narrative elements discussed before and serve as their focal point and as a unifying and integrating principle. Ideas are the meanings and lessons contained in the narratives, their message or 'philosophy.' In the majority of cases neither the theme nor ideas are stated explicitly. They are implied in the narrative and have to be abstracted by interpretation."

14. Parunak, *Structural Studies in Ezekiel*, 70, writes: "But two paragraphs at opposite ends of a corpus may correspond through shared lexical items that occur nowhere else in the book." William L. Holladay, "Recovery of Poetic Passages in Jeremiah," *Journal of Biblical Literature* 85 (1966) 408–9, includes in this category the recurrence of words that, though not identical, share the same root. Robert Alter, *The Art of Biblical Narrative* (New York: Basic Books, 1985), 94, states: "Word-motifs are . . . used . . . in larger narrative units . . . to establish instructive connections between disparate episodes."

15. Parunak, *Structural Studies in Ezekiel*, 77, agrees with John Jebb's caveat that correspondences are more often approximate than exact. Parunak calls this correspondence by "varied repetition" and adds: "A correspondence may consist of two sentences, each containing basically the same words in similar syntactic structures. . . . However, it is not uncommon for nouns to exchange modifiers or modifying phrases, or for verbs to exchange objects, between the two occurrences" (p. 79).

yhwh ("Yahweh")
yôm ("day")
hālak ("to walk")
ʿēṣ ("tree")
rûaḥ ("wind")
derek ("way")
ʾîš ("man")

One could propose that these so-called lexical repetitions show that Genesis 3 and Psalm 1 match in some concocted structural scheme encompassing Genesis and Psalms. But the truth is, almost any two chapters chosen at random from the Old Testament will share a number of lexical items.[16]

A third methodological error could be called *illegitimate theme-linking*, whereby two units are artificially linked by "discovering" in both units a significant mutually shared theme (or motif) that in reality is either concocted or else insignificant because of its commonality (occurring elsewhere in the surrounding context or frequently throughout biblical literature).

Illegitimate theme-linking is remarkably easy to do. One could easily use it to "prove" that the entire English Old Testament forms one grand chiasmus. Genesis 1 and Malachi 4 could be "linked" by the central theme of God's "day" (Gen. 1:5; cf. 2:1–3; Mal. 4:1, 5) and by the contrasting themes of God's blessing the earth in Genesis 1 and his cursing the earth in Malachi 4. Note also that in Genesis 1 God creates life; but in Malachi 4 he destroys it.

Genesis 2 could similarly be shown to "match" Malachi 3. In Genesis 2 God provides humans with bounteous food, whereas in Malachi 3, humans provide God with skimpy, inferior food (3:8–10). In Genesis 2 God gives humans fruit to eat, and in Malachi 3 God promises once again to provide humans with fruit to eat (3:11). On and on we could go, establishing so-called chiastic matchings of Genesis 3–4 with Malachi 1–2.[17] Or, if we prefer, we could show that Genesis 1–4 matches Malachi 1–4 in parallel order:

Genesis 1 corresponds to Malachi 1, and so forth.[18]

By such methodology one could find matches between any two units from anywhere in the Bible, or, for that matter, between any unit in the Bible and any paragraph in yesterday's newspaper. Several guidelines can help minimize the problem of subjectivity inherent in this methodology:

1. *Objective links*: objective links should be given preference over subjective ones. Objective links include verbatim or near-verbatim repetition and matching of place, time, characters, genre, narrative technique, speed of action, and literary form. More subjective echoes (which are vulnerable to abuse and therefore require greater caution) include matching of theme or topic, repetition of a key motif, matching of atmosphere, repetition of theme words, and matching based on synonyms. An example of an objective link is the almost verbatim repetition of Jonah's commissioning and recommissioning in Jonah 1:1–3 and 3:1–3a. A more subjective correspondence is the one between the story of Othniel (and his good Israelite wife, who inspired him to conquer new territory for Israel) and the story of Samson (and his bad Philistine wives, who led him to intermarriage and settlement among the enemy). One should be particularly circumspect in linking units based on theme or topic. S. Bar-Efrat's warning is appropriate here: "Since themes or ideas are not stated overtly, but have to be extracted by means of interpretation, one should exercise a good deal of self-restraint and self-criticism before proceeding to the delineation of thematic or ideational structures. . . . So in order to steer clear of undue arbitrariness themes and ideas should be borne out by the facts of the narrative as clearly and unambigu-

---

16. For another example: someone could argue that Psalms 1, 11, and 31 were intended to match, since all of them contain the Hebrew terms for "Yahweh," "wicked," and "righteous" (or "right"). But all the other psalms in Psalms 1–31 also contain the name "Yahweh," and most have "wicked" or "righteous" or both.

17. One could continue in this vein: in Genesis 3 Adam breaks faith with God; whereas in Malachi 2, Israel breaks faith with God. Both passages feature the theme of the breakdown of the marriage relationship (the first because of woman's failure, the second because of man's). Both Genesis 4 and Malachi 1 focus on the theme of unacceptable sacrifices (Cain's and Israel's).

18. To concoct a parallel relationship between Genesis 1 and Malachi 1, one could point out that Genesis 1 recounts how God created humans and provided bounteous food for them; whereas Malachi 1 develops the theme of their spurning God and giving him inferior and skimpy food. Genesis 2 deals with the creation of the marriage union, while Malachi 2 deals with its destruction. Genesis 3 and Malachi 3 share themes of sin, God's coming (to the garden and to earth), God's punishment (of Adam and of Judah), and the motif of testing (God tests humans in the garden, humans are invited to test God in Mal. 3). And in Genesis 4 the wicked person rises up and triumphs over the righteous (Cain and Abel); while in Malachi 4 the righteous will rise up and "trample" the wicked. One could go on and on creating such matches!

ously as possible. Also, vague and general formulations should be avoided."[19]

2. *Prominent links*: echoes established by features that are prominent in both units (as in the two matching stories of Abraham's lying about Sarah in Gen. 12:10–20 and 20:1–18) should be preferred over echoes suggested by features that are secondary in one or both units (as in Gen. 38:1–30 and 47:27–49:32, both of which feature—though not prominently—the theme of the reversal of the younger and older son).

3. *Multiple links*: linkages that are established by several different shared elements (as in the two matching stories of treaties with Abimelech and his general Phicol at Beersheba in Gen. 21:22–34 and 26:1–33, featuring various types of correspondences) should be given greater weight than linkages created by a single connection (as in the tenuous match that will be suggested subsequently between Gen. 22:1–19 and 25:19–34).

4. *Unique links*: echoes created by features that are unique to the two units and not found in the surrounding units (as in the two matching units about the Ziphites' betraying David in 1 Sam. 23:19–24:22 [23:19–24:23] and 26:1–25) should be preferred over echoes created by elements that are found elsewhere in the context (e.g., using the theme of the curse to connect Gen. 2:4–3:24 and 9:20–29 is unconvincing by itself, since the same theme occurs elsewhere in Gen. 1–11).

5. *Easily perceived links*: a link that an ancient audience could have easily perceived is more likely than one that would have been more difficult for them to catch. Although this is itself a subjective consideration, it is an important one. For example, an audience could hardly miss the almost verbatim repetition of Jonah's commissioning (Jon. 1:1–3) and his recommissioning (3:1–3a); on the other hand, the correspondence between his two prayers (2:2–9 [2:3–10]; 4:1–3) would have been less conspicuous to an audience.

6. *Author's agenda*: a match furthering the author's agenda (such as the matches among the major judges in the Book of Judges, whose correspondences help convey the author's dominant theme of Israel's religious and political deterioration) is more convincing than a match having no apparent impact on the furtherance of the author's agenda (as in the tenuous correspondence between the account of Moses' return to Egypt in Exod. 4:18–31, and the first cycle of plagues in 7:14–8:19).

7. *Danger of forcing loose ends*: loose ends should not be forced into a perceived pattern. If a particular unit does not fit, so be it. Perhaps one's identified structure is incorrect. By resisting the temptation to force a unit to fit, the originally intended structure might be discovered (and the odd unit might even be the key to it all!).

8. *Danger of rearranging the text*: texts should not be rearranged to make a passage fit one's proposed structural scheme. If a particular segment of a text seems to be out of order, possibly the "order" that it is "out of" has itself been wrongly understood. Rather than proposing textual emendations to make the anomalous segment fit, it is better to reexamine the unit's overall structure.

9. *Danger of reductionism*: care should be taken to avoid reductionism. That is, avoid the tendency to reduce all units to the same structural pattern—to expect, look for, and (naturally) find the same scheme over and over again.

10. *Analyses of other scholars*: the analyses of other scholars should be considered. It is particularly important to determine whether the patterns and repetitions that others have discovered in the text are accounted for and better explained by one's own analysis.

After the arrangement of a composition has been analyzed, its validity should be tested by rereading the text as if for the first time and asking, "Would people in the original audience (upon the first or first few readings) have perceived its arrangement as I have analyzed it?" If the answer to this question is uncertain, the analysis should be reevaluated.

---

19. Bar-Efrat, "Analysis of Structure in Biblical Narrative," 169–70.

4

Structure and Meaning

The third task in studying the structure of an Old Testament book is to consider the relationship of the book's structure to its meaning. The connection between a composition's structure and its message is well known. J. T. Walsh suggests: "The 'meaning' of a work of literature is communicated as much by the structure of the work as by surface 'content.' "[1] "Structure," as S. Bar-Efrat notes, "has rhetorical and expressive value: it is one of the factors governing the effect of the work on the reader and in addition it serves to express or accentuate meaning."[2]

Modern writers often utilize structure to help convey meaning. A scholar, for example, would most likely use a strictly linear arrangement for a carefully reasoned journal article, because this particular structure would help convey the logical progression, in which each step builds on the one before. The parallel structure used in "The Three Little Pigs," on the other hand, enables the storyteller to highlight the contrast between the consequences of folly (exemplified by the first two pigs) and wisdom (as exemplified by the third pig):

---

a first little pig constructs his <u>shoddy</u> house
a second little pig constructs his <u>shoddy</u> house
  b third little pig constructs his <u>well-built</u> house
a first little pig's house <u>falls down</u> and the wolf eats him
a second little pig's house <u>falls down</u> and the wolf eats him
  b third little pig's house <u>does not fall down</u>; he is safe

---

This parallel layout makes it easier for listeners to catch the contrast and get the point. The audience would be less likely to get the point if the story were structured without the parallel structure, as in the following hypothetical arrangement:

---

a introduction
b the house that the second little pig built
c the houses that the third and first little pigs built
d the wolf's visits to the first two little pigs' houses
e flashback about the second little pig's experiences in building his house
f the wolf's visit to the third little pig's house
g flashback about how the second little pig's house actually fell down

---

Had the story been structured according to this latter scheme, some perceptive listeners might, in retrospect, surmise the author's point. But the tight parallel structure that we find in the traditional story helps all of us catch what the author is trying to say.

Structure conveys meaning in three primary ways: through (1) the composition's overall structure, (2) structured repetition, and (3) positions of prominence. Hebrew writers used all three of these methods to help communicate their messages.

Overall Structure

In order to convey meaning, biblical authors selected structural schemes that helped them communicate their messages.[3] For example, the author of Kings used a chronologically linear arrangement to trace Israel's rebellious history from its first sinful king to its last. The linear structure helped the author develop and establish his point: Israel's (and Judah's) revolt was not an isolated incident, but was a long and

---

1. John T. Walsh, "Gen 2:4b–3:24: A Synchronic Approach," *Journal of Biblical Literature* 96 (1977) 172; see also René Wellek and Austin Warren, *Theory of Literature* (3d ed.; Harmondsworth: Penguin, 1963), 139–41.

2. S. Bar-Efrat, "Some Observations on the Analysis of Structure in Biblical Narrative," *Vetus Testamentum* 30 (1980) 172. David N. Freedman, "Pottery, Poetry, and Prophecy: An Essay on Biblical Poetry," *Journal of Biblical Literature* 96 (1977) 6–7, writes of Hebrew poetry (and the same applies to prose): "The form and style, the selection and order of words, all play a vital role in conveying content, meaning, and feeling. In poetry, the medium and message are inseparably intertwined to produce multiple effects at different levels of discourse and evoke a whole range of response: intellectual, emotional, spiritual."

3. See Bar-Efrat, "Analysis of Structure in Biblical Narrative," 173, for examples of this in the stories of creation and of David and Bathsheba.

sustained rebellion, spanning hundreds of years—and all in the face of Yahweh's repeated demonstrations of his power, kindness, and mercy (especially through the ministries of Elijah and Elisha).

The Book of Lamentations represents another example of utilizing the overall arrangement scheme to convey meaning. Before the modern reader can understand this example, however, a particular Hebrew literary technique must be explained. Hebrew eulogies generally feature a peculiar verse structure. Whereas regular poetry is made of balanced couplets (verses) with three stresses per line (a-b-c ‖ a'-b'-c'), the verses in a eulogy are generally constructed in an unbalanced 3+2 pattern, with the second line of each verse cut short in an a-b-c ‖ a'-b' scheme. This so-called *qinah* ("lament") or "dying out" pattern presumably communicates the idea that the loved one's life has been tragically and prematurely cut short before its anticipated full duration—an example of how structure can convey meaning at the verse level.

To communicate the sense of grief over Jerusalem's fall, the writer of Lamentations has, not surprisingly, used this *qinah* pattern in verse after verse of the eulogy. But he has also gone a step farther and arranged the overall structure of the entire eulogy in a 3+2 *qinah* pattern:

a three long poems (chaps. 1–3)
  (1) long acrostic poem: 66 lines
  (2) long acrostic poem: 66 lines
  (3) long acrostic poem: 66 lines
b two shorter poems (chaps. 4–5)
  (4) shorter acrostic poem: 44 lines
  (5) even shorter poem, not acrostic: 22 lines

The rhetorical and emotive impact of the eulogy's 3+2 structure is powerful, reinforcing on a grand scale the sense of grief that pervades the content of the lament. The scheme would not have been lost on an ancient audience, who would have been touched by the power of this structurally conveyed message. In sum, it is important to remember that the overall layout of a biblical book reveals a great deal about the author's message and offers insights about the book's larger purpose and agenda.

Structured Repetition

Second, biblical authors employed structured repetition to convey meaning. As noted in chapter 3, both parallel (a-b-c ‖ a'-b'-c') and symmetric (a-b-c ‖ c'-b'-a') arrangement patterns are created by structured repetition, the matching of units. This matching provides the author with an opportunity to achieve various effects.[4]

Of course, the matching of units is not always utilized for the purpose of conveying meaning. Sometimes authors create echoes and balancing purely for the sake of artistic beauty or to provide a second opportunity to further develop or complete a topic. Categories of such matching include the following:

1. *Structural*: matching mainly functions to help create the structural scheme of the composition. For example, the repetition of the list of Noah's three sons at the beginning and end of the flood story in Genesis 6:9–10 and 9:18–19 creates a touch of balance and serves to bracket the story.
2. *Elaboration*: the second unit of the matched pair simply elaborates on, "fleshes out," or further develops the topic introduced in the first unit. For example, Genesis 28:6–9 introduces Esau's wives; its matching unit in Genesis 36 traces the rest of Esau's family and descendants.
3. *Second perspective*: the second unit simply views the same topic or event from a different vantage or reviews or summarizes it. For example, the two matching units recounting the Jordan crossing provide the audience with two glimpses of the same event, one from the east, as the crossing begins and is being completed (Josh. 3:9–17), the other from the west, as it proceeds and is completed (4:10–13).

On the other hand, the matching of units is often utilized to convey meaning. The author of the Book of Jonah uses the matching of Jonah's two prayers (2:2–9 [2:3–10]; 4:1–3) to draw attention to Jonah's hypocrisy and to communicate the author's own views about God and his ways.

The advantage of using structured repetition to communicate meaning is that it enables an author to make a point subtly, without explicitly saying it, and such subtlety is appreciated by an audience. Most people do not like to be preached at, and they quickly tire of pontifications. But conveyance of meaning subtly is less obtrusive and more enjoyable. It involves the listeners in the discovery of meaning, inviting them to participate, to think. This, in turn, makes the listening process more interesting, pleasurable, and in the end more effective.

---

4. See J. Cheryl Exum, "Aspects of Symmetry and Balance in the Samson Saga," *Journal for the Study of the Old Testament* 19 (1981) 18–25.

Think how pedantic the story of "The Three Little Pigs" would be if the storyteller were to begin by explicitly stating that this story illustrates that it is foolish to do things shoddily and wise to do things with industry and prudence. By being so explicit the author would ensure that the audience would get the point (how could they not?). But the magic would be gone. The story would no longer hold its charm. It would no longer be engaging or entertaining or (as a result) particularly effective.

Hebrew writers utilized the opportunity created by the matching of units to convey or reinforce meaning in various subtle ways:

1. *Emphasis*: matching can emphasize a point by reiterating it.[5] An example is Daniel's matching visions of the rise and fall of the four earthly kingdoms (chaps. 2, 7). The matched repetition drives home the point that human kingdoms will rise, but they will fall—and in the end only Israel's God and his kingdom will stand triumphant. So God's people should remain faithful to Yahweh—even in the midst of persecution—for the present hostile human powers are temporary and will fall at Yahweh's command. Another example of emphasis through structured repetition is the matching stories of Abraham's lying about Sarah (Gen. 12:10–20; 20:1–18), which draws attention to the helplessness of Israel's ancestors and Yahweh's grace and power to protect them.

2. *Highlighting a pattern*: an author may utilize matching to establish and draw attention to a particular pattern (especially a behavior pattern). For example, the author of Jonah recounts two matching episodes about Jonah and pagans (1:4–16; 3:3b–10). Jonah, the pagans, and God do the same thing in each episode: Jonah reluctantly tells the pagans of Yahweh's intentions against them; the pagans (from the leader down), when they hear Jonah's words, appeal to Yahweh for mercy; and Yahweh relents from his judgment. Once might be considered incidental or insignificant; but with two occurrences, the audience begins to perceive the behavioral patterns: Jonah seems to have an attitude problem; pagan people (unlike Israel!) always seem to respond appropriately to Yahweh's threatened judgment; and

Yahweh always seems to relent from his judgment when people appeal to him for mercy. Similarly, in providing matching stories about David's sparing Saul (1 Sam. 23:19–24:22 [23:19–24:23]; 26:1–25) the author establishes his point that David was "a man after God's heart" and a loyal servant to King Saul. Had David spared Saul once, the audience might think that it was a special situation and not instructive; but twice establishes and draws attention to the pattern. The audience begins to see that David would have spared the life of Saul over and over again if additional opportunities arose.

3. *Comparison*: two or more units may be matched in order to draw out the similarity of two things not readily seen as similar. For example, the parallel treatment of each of the foreign nations and then Israel itself in Amos 1–2 insinuates that Israel is no better than its pagan neighbors and—like them—will be punished for its sins.

4. *Contrast*: conversely, matching may highlight the contrast between two things that are in some respects alike.[6] The matched episodes involving Judah and Joseph in Genesis 38 and 39 are alike in various ways: both involve a son of Jacob; both recount how the son is confronted by the illicit sexual invitation of a woman (invitations that involve secrecy and deceit); and in both stories the temptress keeps a token of the man to produce later as evidence against him. But the similarity of these two juxtaposed stories highlights the stark contrast between them: Judah shamefully yields to the temptation—and he prospers as a result; Joseph admirably resists the temptation—but he suffers for it (which prepares the audience to appreciate the end of the story). Compare also the ironic contrast highlighted in the matched episodes of Hezekiah's reception of the Assyrian and Babylonian envoys in Isaiah 36 and 39.

5. *Reversal*: matching may highlight the reversal or undoing of something. The Book of Kings, for example, begins with a unit featuring the establishing of Solomon's majestic kingdom and his building of the temple

---

5. Repetition as a means of emphasis is suggested in Joseph's statement to pharaoh in Genesis 41:32: "The reason the dream was given to pharaoh in two forms is that the matter is firmly established by God." Repetition is often used in our literature for this purpose.

6. This function of repetition is, of course, well known on the Hebrew verse level, where it is called "antithetic parallelism"; for example, "Yahweh knows the way of the righteous, / but the way of the wicked will perish" (Ps. 1:6). The second line echoes the first (both speak of what happens to the "way" of specific behavioral patterns), but the echo highlights the contrast between the consequences of the two behavioral patterns; see further H. Van Dyke Parunak, *Structural Studies in Ezekiel* (Ph.D. diss., Harvard University, 1978), 46–47.

(1 Kings 3–11), whereas the matching unit (2 Kings 18–25) recounts the reversal: the end of Solomon's kingdom and the destruction of the temple. The unit telling of Israel's arrival in Egypt as a small group of seventy individuals and of its enslavement (Exod. 1) is matched by the unit in Exodus 12:1–13:16, which recounts Israel's departure from Egypt as a freed and numerous people. Similarly, Joseph's enslavement to an Egyptian in Genesis 39 is matched by Joseph's enslavement of the entire Egyptian population in 47:13–26 (see also Exod. 2:1–10 ‖ 11:1–10).

6. *Reciprocity*: an author may highlight the reciprocity of two actions by featuring the reciprocal actions in matching units. For example, the writer of the Song of Songs reinforces the mutual love of the two lovers by repeatedly placing their reciprocal speeches or actions in matching units: the young man's invitation to the young woman to join him in the countryside is matched by her similar invitation to him to join her in the countryside (2:8–17; 7:11–8:4 [7:12–8:4]); and her praise of his body, from the head down (including ten body parts) is matched by his praise of her body, from the feet up (including ten body parts) (Song 5:9–16; 6:13–7:7 [7:1–8]).

7. *Resolution (or fulfillment)*: an author may highlight the close connection between a story's opening tension, suspense, or prediction and its closing resolution or fulfillment, by placing the two in matching positions at the beginning and end of the story. For example, the problem of Abram and Sarai's childlessness in Genesis 12:1–9 is resolved with the birth of Isaac in the matching unit in 21:1–7. Deborah's prediction in Judges 4:4–9 is matched by its fulfillment in 4:17–22. Joseph's dream and its fulfillment are matching episodes in Genesis 37, 42–44 and 50.

8. *Totality*: matching units may convey the idea of the totality of a phenomenon by featuring both halves of a merism (day and night, man and woman, etc.).[7] For example, Isaiah 2:10–22 proclaims the future humiliation of the proud men of Judah, and the matching unit in 3:16–17 portrays the future humiliation of the proud women of Judah. Together they function to communicate the idea that the entire population is haughty and will be humbled by Yahweh. Similarly, Amos has matching units condemning wealthy Israelite women (4:1–3) and men (6:1–7).

In summary, when studying a text arranged in a parallel or symmetric scheme, it is worthwhile to consider the functions of the various matchings, since the ancient author may well have planned the matchings to help convey meaning.

Positions of Prominence

Finally, biblical authors utilized positions of prominence to reinforce or convey meaning.[8] Modern storytellers generally place a story's most important moment in the next-to-last unit, because in modern literary tradition this is the

---

7. W. G. E. Watson, "Chiastic Patterns in Biblical Poetry," in *Chiasmus in Antiquity*, ed. J. W. Welch (Hildesheim: Gerstenberg, 1981), 147, notes this function of matching on the verse level.

8. For a good discussion of prominence in discourse, see John Beekman, John Callow, and Michael Kopesec, *The Semantic Structure of Written Communication* (Dallas: Summer Institute of Linguistics, 1981), 24–26, 110–11, who state (p. 24): "Prominence is simply making one or more parts of a unit more important than the other parts. Any well-formed discourse will do this. Otherwise, it just goes on monotonously and nothing is highlighted. The difference between a politician and a good teacher is probably along this line. The politician may not want to make any promise or pledge stand out, in order that he not be held accountable for it. So he may talk very fluently for half and hour without ever highlighting anything. You then go home and talk to someone else, and he asks, 'Well, what did he say?' You reply, 'Well, he spoke very fluently, and it was very impressive, and he really carried people with him.' 'But what did he actually say?' You cannot remember because nothing was made prominent. . . . Some sermons are like that, too. You get a very rosy impression, but you cannot actually remember what was said. That is usually because prominence features are either deliberately or inadvertently omitted so that the point was not put across. A good teacher, on the other hand, takes pains to make sure that the important points are made clear to his students; so he relies heavily on the features of prominence and the inventory of devices his particular language uses to manifest them." Linda K. Jones, *Theme in English Expository Discourse* (Edward Sapir Monograph Series in Language, Culture, and Cognition 2; Lake Bluff, Ill.: Jupiter, 1977), 2–3, states: "Theme, I believe, is basic to being human. When we do something we thereby do not do something else: one thing is important, the other is less important. We consciously or unconsciously assign importance to certain actions in our lives, and less importance to others. . . . Theme is thus deeply rooted in our very perception of the world around us. The human mind is incapable of assigning equal importance to all the data it receives from its sensory sources, probably because it is incapable of paying equal attention to all the data at once. When we look at a picture, we never perceive all its details simultaneously. There are certain parts of the picture that we notice immediately, while the rest we do not. Always in human perception there are foreground and background, figure against ground, important and not important, theme and not-theme (or background)." See also the discussion of R. E. Longacre (ed.), *Discourse Grammar: Studies in Indigenous Languages of Colombia, Panama, and Ecuador*, part 1 (Dallas: Summer Institute of Linguistics and University of Texas at Arlington, 1976), 10.

position of prominence in stories, the place for the climax (the final unit serving as the denouement). Hebrew literary tradition also had standard positions of prominence for various structural schemes, and Hebrew authors exploited these positions to highlight their most important material. The position of prominence in linear and parallel schemes, for example, is generally the final unit. This is presumably due to the final unit's strategic position as the culmination of the composition's forward development. Moreover, it is the last word the author will leave with the audience. In narratives such as the Book of Kings, the final unit generally features highlighted material such as the climax, resolution, outcome, conclusion, or surprise ending of the story.[9]

In parallel schemes with an odd number of units, the final unit's strategic position is further accented when it is the composition's only unmatched unit (a-b-c ‖ a'-b'-c' ‖ d). In the parallel arrangement of the Book of Jonah, the final, unmatched unit (4:5–11) features Yahweh's lesson for Jonah: the book's concluding argument and main point.

In a symmetric scheme, on the other hand, the center is normally the natural position of prominence—as is true of symmetric works of art.[10] When the symmetry has an odd number of units, the central unit is further accented because it is the only unmatched unit.[11] H. Van

Dyke Parunak observes: "Chiastic structures frequently have a unique center item. . . . The uniqueness of this location makes it suitable for emphasizing whatever is placed there. This method of emphasis uses the intrinsic shape of the structure to focus the reader's (or hearer's) attention on the item of interest."[12] In the Hebrew Bible, the central units of symmetric schemes are employed for various important roles:

1. *Turning point*: in chiastically arranged narratives, the movement toward the center in the narrative's first half is reversed on the other side of the center, which makes the central unit a natural position for the story's turning point. The story of Ehud, for example, is designed with a symmetric touch. The first three units (Judg. 3:12–19) feature episodes occurring while Israel is subservient to the enemy (ending at the lowest point of Israel's abject servitude). In the fourth unit (3:20–22) the tide turns when Ehud succeeds in killing the enemy king. The last three units (3:23–30) then trace Israel's ascendancy and ultimate victory. Many of the symmetrically structured stories in the Book of Judges are similarly arranged, as is the entire book. The center of the Book of Judges is Gideon's story. It represents the book's turning point: before Gideon the judges did well; afterward the judges did badly; and Gideon's rule is the turning point—both beginning well and ending badly. Other symmetrically arranged books likewise utilize the central unit for the book's turning point (e.g., Ruth and Esther), as do numerous stories within books (e.g., the story of Jacob's journey to Paddan-aram, with the central unit being the episode of Jacob's departure to return to Canaan in Gen. 31).

2. *Climax*: in symmetrically structured narratives, the central unit can also serve as the story's climax, its point of highest tension.[13] For example, the center of the Ehud story is

---

9. Beekman, Callow, and Kopesec, *Semantic Structure of Written Communication*, 135, state: "Since the final response in a chain usually represents the Resolution or Outcome to the story, there is a movement from the information with lesser prominence to that with more prominence or significance, from the standpoint of the author's purpose. . . . The final response(s) of an episode are thus the most prominent units within the episode." Similarly, Parunak, *Structural Studies in Ezekiel*, 45–46, states: "An example of the use of structure in coding argument can be seen in Galbiati's seventh canon, 'the series leading to a final impression.' Either an alternation (as he describes) or a chiasmus leads to a certain expectancy. Once we see the pattern forming, we anticipate the outcome. An author may heighten the dramatic value of a point by completing the structure with just the opposite of what he has led us to expect." This is of course what occurs in the story of the three little pigs.

10. The importance of the central unit in chiastic structures is observed by many scholars: David N. Freedman, "Preface," in *Chiasm in Antiquity*, ed. J. W. Welch (Hildesheim: Gerstenberg, 1981), 7; H. Van Dyke Parunak, "Oral Typesetting: Some Uses of Biblical Structure," *Biblica* 62 (1981) 165–66; Beekman, Callow, and Kopesec, *Semantic Structure of Written Communication*, 120; L. F. Bliese, "Symmetry and Prominence in Hebrew Poetry: With Examples from Hosea," in *Discourse Perspectives on Hebrew Poetry in the Scriptures*, ed. Ernst R. Wendland (New York: United Bible Societies, 1994), 67–94 ; Ernst R. Wendland, "The Discourse Analysis of Hebrew Poetry: A Procedural Outline," in *Discourse Perspectives on Hebrew Poetry in the Scriptures*, ed. Ernst R. Wendland (New York: United Bible Societies, 1994), 15–16.

11. So Beekman, Callow, and Kopesec, *Semantic Structure of Written Communication*, 120.

12. Parunak, "Oral Typesetting," 165.

13. According to Beekman, Callow, and Kopesec, *Semantic Structure of Written Communication*, 138–39 (see also R. E. Longacre, *An Anatomy of Speech Notions* [Lisse: de Ridder, 1976], 217–28): "*Climax* is generally associated with the build up of *tension* in plot narratives. Frequently, the tension begins with a statement of the problem which then becomes more entangled and involved as complications to that problem are introduced. The climax would occur at the point where the tension is the greatest and the release of that tension begins—i.e. at the *turning point*. . . . This surface-structure phenomenon is referred to as the (grammatical) *peak*."

not only the story's turning point, but also its climax (the turning point and climax of a story frequently occur together); the rest of the story is denouement. Likewise, in most of the symmetrically structured stories in the Book of Judges, the central unit features the climax as well as the turning point. The placement of the climax at the center of a story may seem a bit odd to modern readers, who are accustomed to finding the climax near the story's end.

3. *Centerpiece*: in nonnarrative compositions with a symmetric structure, the central unit often represents the highlight, centerpiece, or most important point, much like the center of a symmetrically arranged work of art. For example, in the Song of Songs, which has an overall symmetric structure, the central unit (3:6–5:1) features the majestic wedding. In Chronicles, a book focused on the temple and its personnel, the center of the symmetrically structured book is the unit devoted to Solomon, the temple builder (2 Chron. 1–9); and at the center of that symmetrically arranged unit stands the grand dedication of the temple (5:2–7:10). In Amos and Zephaniah, both of which exhibit symmetric arrangements, the central unit is the prophet's all-important call to repentance (Amos 5:1–17; Zeph. 2:1–3).

4. *Significant pause (or interlude)*: in some symmetries the central unit features a poignant, conspicuous pause in the action or argument of the composition, an interlude that allows the author to develop a highly significant point. The central unit of the Book of Kings (2 Kings 2:1–8:6) represents a pause in the otherwise relentless, almost uninterrupted parade of sins of the successive Israelite and Judean kings. This pause features the remarkable ministry of the prophet Elisha, whom the author presents as a wonderful representative of Yahweh (in contrast to Israel's kings). Similarly, at the center of Lamentations (3:21–32) the poet pauses in an otherwise relentlessly tragic eulogy to ponder serenely the profound love of Yahweh (cf. also the central unit of Nahum, 2:11–13 [2:12–14]). The center of the symmetry in the Book of Job is an interlude featuring the poem about wisdom (Job 28).

The place of prominence in an even-numbered symmetry (e.g., a-b-c-c'-b'-a') is generally at the beginning and end rather than in the middle.[14] For example, the collection of case laws in Exodus 21:2–22:27 [21:2–22:26] features ten symmetrically arranged units. The most important units are the outer ones (21:2–17; 22:18–27 [22:17–26]), dealing with capital offenses and kindness to the poor, and not the central ones (21:33–22:9 [21:33–22:8]), which deal with more mundane cases involving loss of property. In compositions framed by an inclusio (e.g., a-b-c-d-e-a'), the two halves of the inclusio often serve as the two highlighted positions of the composition, as in the beginning and end of Psalm 8 and Psalm 103.[15]

In summary, structural analysis should seek to identify the positions of prominence in a text and then consider the possible significance of those highlighted positions.

---

14. This is also noted by Beekman, Callow, and Kopesec, *Semantic Structure of Written Communication*, 120. John Jebb, *Sacred Literature* (London: Cadell & Davies, 1820), 60–63, argues that the emphasis normally lies on the outermost positions of a chiastic structure—but this was clearly an overstatement; cf. also John Forbes, *The Symmetrical Structure of Scripture* (Edinburgh: Clark, 1854), 45, 58.

15. Beekman, Callow, and Kopesec, *Semantic Structure of Written Communication*, 120.

5
Value of Structural Analysis

Studying the literary structure of Old Testament texts can provide many insights into a text and its meaning. The following are some of the potential contributions of this discipline.[1]

Appreciation of Literary Artistry

At the very least, the rediscovery of a well-conceived, thoughtful arrangement of a particular Old Testament text enables the modern reader to appreciate the artistic skill and care that went into the composition of that text. A book that initially seems chaotically arranged may turn out to be, upon further study of its internal structure, a masterpiece of literary architecture. The Song of Songs, for example, is often faulted for its rambling disorganization, its so-called charming confusion.[2] Careful analysis of the book's structure, however, reveals an elegant arrangement that is worthy of our admiration.

Identification of Unit Boundaries

A unit of biblical text can be better interpreted if it is correctly delineated. Structural analysis helps identify the parameters of units, which leads, in turn, to a clearer understanding of the text. For example, structural analysis of Samuel and Kings suggests that the material in 1 Kings 1–2 originally concluded the Book of Samuel. Accordingly, these two chapters should be read as the conclusion to Samuel rather than as the introduction to Kings. Similarly, the books of Ezra and Nehemiah appear to form a structural unit (and in fact they are one book in the Hebrew Bible) and should be so studied.

Structural study of the Pentateuch and Joshua strongly suggests that these were originally designed to function as a single composition, beginning in Genesis 1 and ending in Joshua 24. The majestic story of the Pentateuch was never intended to end with Deuteronomy, with Israel *almost* home, and with the story *almost* complete. Rather, the composition was designed to conclude with the grand finale of the Book of Joshua. Accordingly, Joshua should be read as the *end* of the story, not as a story in and of itself.

Discovery of the Rationale behind a Unit's Overall Layout

Another benefit of structural analysis is that it can lead to a better understanding of the rationale behind the general arrangement of an Old Testament text. With the discovery of a text's organizational scheme comes a better understanding of the placement of the parts within that unit. For example, in the story of Abraham (Gen. 12:1–21:7), the two stories of Abraham's lying about his wife may be positioned where they are for purposes of symmetry, as are the two promises regarding Ishmael and the two migrations of Lot's family. Likewise, the story of Hezekiah's illness and the visit of the Babylonian envoys (Isa. 38–39) are out of chronological order in order to accommodate the symmetric presentation developed in chapters 36–39.

In the Song of Songs the wedding does not occur until the fourth unit (3:6–5:1), causing modern readers to be surprised by the lovers' physical intimacy in the units preceding the wedding. Does the book feature premarital sex? The discovery of the symmetric structure of the book probably answers this question. The poet has placed the wedding unit in its present position, not because the wedding represents the fourth scene in a chronologically arranged story, but because the unit stands at the highlighted center of the song's seven-part symmetry, serving as the poem's majestic centerpiece, with concentric circles radiating out from this center.

---

1. For an earlier discussion of the value of surface-structural analysis in the Old Testament, see David A. Dorsey, "Can These Bones Live? Investigating Literary Structure in the Bible," *Evangelical Journal* 9 (1991) 11–25.

2. Paul Haupt, "The Book of Canticles," *American Journal of Semitic Languages and Literature* 18 (1902) 205.

Similarly, the call of Isaiah is probably placed in chapter 6 rather than at the beginning of the book because the author wished to place the account in a position of prominence. Since the book opens with a symmetric, seven-part unit (chaps. 1–12), Isaiah's call was placed at the highlighted center of this opening symmetry.

Clarification of the Relationship of the Parts to the Whole

The importance of context in interpretation is well known. Studying the literary structure of a text helps readers avoid the danger of "not seeing the forest for the trees," since it forces the reader to consider the big picture and the relationship of the parts to the whole. Structural analysis of the Book of Isaiah may, for example, help explain the reciprocal functions of chapters 28–35 and 40–48, as well as the thematically pivotal role of the narrative (chaps. 36–39) positioned between these two units. In similar fashion, the rebuilding role of the final three parts of the Book of Ecclesiastes (following the philosophical demolition carried out in the book's first three units) may be clarified. Identifying the predominantly negative roles played by certain parts of Kings and Judges and the predominantly positive roles served by certain units within the Book of Chronicles helps us better understand the function and intention of the constituent units of these books.

Accounting for Repetitions

There is a great deal of seemingly unnecessary repetition in Old Testament texts, which often confuses modern readers. Structural analysis, however, underscores the point that much of this repetition serves vital rhetorical and structural functions (like Martin Luther King's repeated line, "I have a dream!"). Repetition helps listeners perceive literary structure. The repeated formula "for three transgression of x, even for four, I will not turn back my wrath" would have helped Amos's audience discern the beginnings of each of his seven messages against the foreign nations (Amos 1–2). The formula "and it was evening and it was morning, the nth day" signals for the listener the conclusion of each unit in Genesis 1. Moreover, symmetric and parallel schemes of arrangement require repetition to establish correspondences, and much of the repetitiveness in biblical literature serves to create such structural schemes (e.g., the two listings of Noah's sons in Gen. 6:10 and 9:18–19; the two episodes involving the crossing of the Jordan in Josh. 3–4).

Accounting for Apparently Misplaced Units

A number of isolated passages in the Old Testament seem misplaced. In some instances this may be due to errors in textual transmission. But more often than not, an analysis of the overall arrangement of a book reveals that the problematic unit is appropriately placed after all. Genesis 38, the story of Judah and Tamar, seems to be intrusive in the Joseph story and has been considered a "stray boulder" by various commentators; but structural study suggests that the episode fills several vital structural functions in the organizational scheme of Genesis 37–50 and plays a key role in the development of some of the unit's main themes. Judah's sexual indiscretion in chapter 38 stands in bold contrast to Joseph's righteousness regarding sexual temptation in the adjacent, matching unit in chapter 39. The audience notes the contrast and senses the unfairness: Judah's sin results in prosperity (he has twins, a blessing in ancient families), while Joseph's righteousness results in imprisonment. But the story is not over yet. These two episodes are structurally matched by the episodes at the end of the Joseph narrative, when God rights the wrongs, removing Judah from the position of firstborn and giving the leadership of Israel, along with the double portion, to Joseph.

Clarification of a Unit by Comparison with Its Match

Structural analysis provides another useful tool for illuminating obscure passages. In chiastic and parallel structural patterns, the meaning or function of one unit may be clarified by comparison with its match (this is already a common practice on the poetic verse level). Jonah's pious prayer in Jonah 2 nicely illustrates this. Structural analysis suggests that the author balanced Jonah's psalm of thanksgiving (for his own deliverance) with Jonah's angry and resentful complaint at the deliverance of Nineveh. In light of this matching, it appears that the author intends the reader to notice the stark contrast between the two prayers, with the result that Jonah's pious prayer in chapter 2 will be seen as mean-spirited and hypocritical. Similarly, the structure of the Book of Job suggests that Elihu is in the same category as Job's other three friends and is not intended by the author to function as "the spokesperson for God."

A Check on Redaction-Critical Theories

Modern scholars sometimes question the integrity of books or passages within the Hebrew

Bible on the basis of what seems to be chaotic organization or unevenness in the text (e.g., the intrusive story about Judah and Tamar in Gen. 38), explaining the unevenness with theories involving long, complex processes of accretions, insertions, careless editing, and the like. Structural analysis may sometimes reveal an alternate and more plausible explanation for this so-called unevenness. For instance, the apparent structural chaos of Canticles has led many to consider the book a hodgepodge of lover lyrics collected and loosely woven together over a period of centuries. But several structural studies suggest that Canticles exhibits an overall highly artistic design, a factor that leads some scholars to reconsider the possibility of the book's single authorship.

Discovery of a Unit's Main Point

When we read an Old Testament book, we often have difficulty identifying the author's main point, central purpose, or theme. One reason is that Hebrew writers often highlighted important material and underscored particular themes with techniques that are different from our own. Because biblical authors often emphasized material by placing it in positions of prominence, we must identify these in order to ascertain the author's emphases and his intended central point. Yehuda Radday, while perhaps overstating the case, describes the importance of paying attention to the key role played by the central unit of a chiasmus:

> For instance, we know nothing of the reasons which induced an anonymous writer to write the Book of Samuel. Is it an autobiography, a court chronicle, or a treatise disguised as story? If the importance of the central passage is properly recognized, however, all we have to do in order to find the answer to this question is open the book to its middle and read. This reveals the book's focal concepts. As soon as the fundamental purpose of the book is known, all the rest of it will become readily comprehensible.[3]

A good example of this can be found in Chronicles. Structural analysis suggests that the Chronicler organized most of his material in symmetric configurations that feature the center as the position of prominence. In most of the central slots the Chronicler placed material about the temple, priests, or Levites, which sug-

gests that these themes are central to his purpose. Likewise, Amos and Zephaniah arrange the seven units of their books in a symmetry, with the center unit presenting their call to repentance. In both cases, structural analysis suggests that the call to repentance is the book's central message. On the other hand, in the parallel (a-b-c ‖ a'-b'-c' ‖ d) pattern featured in Jonah, the final unit is highlighted, indicating that God's lesson to Jonah about his mercy and kindness is the book's central message.

Discovery of a Composition's Theme

Sometimes an author's main theme is developed through the composition's overall structure, and in the process of analyzing this structure, the composition's theme is revealed, or clarified. For example, the strong anti-idolatry theme in the account of the treaty at Sinai (Exod. 19:3–Num. 10:10) comes into focus through analysis of the entire composition. Likewise, study of the overall structure of the Song of Songs reveals that one of its intentionally highlighted themes is the reciprocity of the two lovers' love. Study of Judges helps identify that book's double theme of Israel's spiritual decline and God's gracious care for his people despite their unfaithfulness.

Scope of the Following Study

The following chapters will consider the literary structure of each book in the Old Testament, from Genesis to Malachi, together with the implications of the book's structure for its meaning and its message.[4] Several "books" in our English Bible were not originally written as independent books at all, but were parts of larger books. These larger, originally self-contained books, such as the Book of the Law of Moses, Samuel, Kings, and Chronicles, will be treated as single books in the present study.

Each structural analysis has three goals: (1) to identify the book's constituent units, (2) to study the arrangement of those units, and (3) to consider the relationship of the book's structure to its meaning.

3. Yehuda T. Radday, "Chiasmus in Hebrew Biblical Narrative," in *Chiasmus in Antiquity*, ed. J. W. Welch (Hildesheim: Gerstenberg, 1981), 51.

4. I have chosen to follow the canonical order of the English Bible in order to make the study as user-friendly as possible. My decision to deal with every book of the Old Testament may appear either presumptuous or foolhardy; but it reflects my interest in providing a useful resource for readers. In order to be comprehensive, I have sacrificed depth for breadth of coverage, sometimes neglecting more extensive interaction with valuable secondary literature. For this, I apologize.

Book of the Law of Moses

6

Book of the Law: Historical Prologue

Genesis 1:1–Exodus 19:2

The Old Testament comprises a number of "books": thirty-nine in our modern Bibles or twenty-two by early Jewish reckoning (which counted as one book each Judges–Ruth, Samuel, Kings, Chronicles, Ezra–Nehemiah, Jeremiah–Lamentations, and "The Twelve" [the minor prophets]). These books date from various periods and represent a remarkable variety of literature, including historical narrative, eulogy, legal instruction, philosophical treatise, and collections of prayers and proverbs.

As previously noted, some books in the English Old Testament were not originally independent compositions, but were segments of larger books. At some stage in their manuscript history these originally longer books were split into two or more parts to accommodate the limited length of scrolls. The Book of Chronicles, for example, was too long to fit on a single scroll and so was split, for scribal convenience, into two halves. The division eventually became fixed, and today these two halves are reckoned as two separate books in modern versions of the Bible—First Chronicles and Second Chronicles—although all agree that these two books are actually two halves of one original book. In light of the ancient author's writing and designing the whole of Chronicles to function as a single, self-contained book, structural analysis should treat the entirety of Chronicles as one book.

A similar situation presents itself when we turn to the first "book" of the Old Testament. Genesis was not written as an independent composition but was the first section of a larger book, called in ancient sources the "Book of the Law" (also "Book of the Law of Moses," "Book of Moses," "Torah," or "Pentateuch"). This larger book is traditionally identified as encompassing Genesis through Deuteronomy; but not everyone agrees that the book ended with Deuteronomy. Some argue that it also included Joshua (forming a "Hexateuch").[1] Others extend the work through Samuel (an "Octateuch") or Kings (an "Enneateuch")—omitting Ruth. Still others suggest the work included only Genesis through Numbers (a "Tetrateuch").[2]

In order to properly analyze the internal arrangement scheme of this first book of the Bible, we need to know its parameters—where it begins and ends. And since the endpoint is debated, we are confronted with a procedural dilemma: how do we analyze the overall structure of a composition whose extent is uncertain? A logical procedure is to begin with Genesis 1 and follow the structural scheme as it unfolds throughout the Pentateuch, watching for its natural point of structural closure. This procedure provides some compelling support for an original Hexateuch. The evidence for this conclusion will be presented in subsequent chapters; but for the moment it will simply be asserted that structural considerations favor the inclusion of Joshua in the Book of the Law.

The Book of the Law focuses on the great treaty that Yahweh made with Israel at Mount Sinai. The work contains three major parts:

---

a historical introduction to the treaty (Gen. 1:1–Exod. 19:2)
b the treaty (Exod. 19:3–Num. 10:10)
c historical conclusion to the treaty (Num. 10:11–Josh. 24)

Chapters 6–8 will each examine one of these three large units in turn; and chapter 9 will consider the structure and unity of the entire Book of the Law. The purpose of the present chapter is to study the literary architecture of the histori-

---

1. See, e.g., S. R. Driver, *An Introduction to the Literature of the Old Testament* (9th ed.; Edinburgh: Clark, 1913), 116–59; Robert H. Pfeiffer, *Introduction to the Old Testament* (New York: Harper, 1948), 129–30; 293–412.

2. For a summary of views, see Brevard S. Childs, *Introduction to the Old Testament as Scripture* (Philadelphia: Fortress, 1979), 119–28.

cal introduction to the Sinai treaty, Genesis 1:1–Exodus 19:2.[3]

First, a word about the function of this historical introduction. The central unit of the Book of the Law, Exodus 19:3–Numbers 10:10, presents the "treaty" (*bĕrît*) that Yahweh made with Israel at Sinai. This treaty is similar in many respects to secular "vassal" (or "suzerainty") treaties of the ancient Near East. Of particular significance here is the fact that secular treaties open, not with a body of stipulations, but with a historical prologue. These historical prologues are designed to survey past relations between the two covenanting parties—the suzerain and the vassal king—with the aim of engendering gratitude, respect, and trust on the part of the vassal toward the suzerain. For example, in the treaty between the great King Murshilis of Hatti and his vassal King Duppi-Teshub of Amurru, the historical prologue surveys past relations between the two countries, recounting acts of benevolence that King Murshilis and his family had shown to Duppi-Teshub and his family over the years—including their choosing Duppi-Teshub to be the new king of Amurru despite his being "weak and ailing."[4]

Genesis 1:1–Exodus 19:2 serves a similar function: it is the historical prologue to Yahweh's great treaty with Israel. As such, it traces past relations between the two covenanting parties, Yahweh and Israel, with the purpose of engendering gratitude, respect, and trust on the part of vassal Israel toward their suzerain, Yahweh. It begins at the beginning, with creation, and surveys the historical relations between Yahweh and Israel from the earliest times until Israel's arrival at Mount Sinai.[5]

This prologue is quite lengthy and has accordingly been "packaged" into more manageable literary units, each unit with its own focus and internal structure:

---

a   Yahweh and Israel's pre-Abrahamic ancestors (Gen. 1:1–11:32)
b   Yahweh and Abraham (Gen. 12:1–21:7)
c   Yahweh and Isaac (Gen. 21:8–28:4)
d   Yahweh and Jacob (Gen. 28:5–37:1)
e   Yahweh and Joseph (Gen. 37:2–50:26)
f   Yahweh and the exodus (Exod. 1:1–13:16)
g   Yahweh and the wilderness journey (Exod. 13:17–19:2)

Primeval History: Yahweh and Israel's Most Ancient Ancestors (Genesis 1–11)

The first unit deals with Yahweh's relations with Israel's most ancient ancestors. It begins with creation and ends with a brief introduction to Abraham, who will be the focus of the next unit.[6] This opening unit spans thousands of years in eleven chapters.

The internal organization of Genesis 1–11 is conspicuously marked by the recurring formula *ʾēlleh tôlĕdôt* ("these are the generations of *x*"; 2:4; 5:1 [modified]; 6:9; 10:1; 11:10, 27), which the author uses to introduce each new unit.[7] In each instance, *x* is a person or entity that has already been introduced to the audience in the preceding unit; the material that follows deals with the descendant(s) of or subsequent developments from *x*.[8] This formula delineates seven units in Genesis 1–11.

The Creation Story (Genesis 1:1–2:3)

The first unit, the creation story, is self-contained and highly structured. It is divided into seven constituent parts, corresponding to the seven days of creation. Each part (except the seventh) exhibits the same structural design, beginning with the clause "and God said," followed by a jussive verb ("let there be . . ."), and

---

3. Another problem one immediately faces in the Pentateuch (and Joshua) is the question of its composition. Most readers are aware of the controversy regarding the prehistory of the Pentateuch. The most popular view among modern scholars is the "Documentary Hypothesis" (or "JEDP Theory"), which proposes that the Pentateuch (and perhaps Joshua) was compiled over a period of centuries from four main sources, abbreviated J, E, D, and P. Varieties of this theory, as well as radically different views, are also proposed. The focus of the present study, however, will be on the final product. We will set aside for the moment the question of prehistory and simply analyze the text in its present form. Regardless of one's view, the final design of the Pentateuch (and Joshua) is certainly worthy of investigation in its own right. Moreover, structural analysis of the final product may provide new insights regarding the work's composition.

4. J. B. Pritchard (ed.), *Ancient Near Eastern Texts* (3d ed.; Princeton: Princeton University Press, 1969), 203–5.

5. The historical prologue concludes in Exodus 19:2 with the arrival of Israel at Sinai; and 19:3 introduces the book's next major unit, the account of the treaty itself. The beginning of the new unit is marked for the audience by shifts in speed of action (from rapid, covering thousands of years in

less than seventy chapters, to very slow, with the next nearly sixty chapters covering a single year), genre (from narrative prose to compilations of legal instructions), and topic (from Israel's past history to the legal details of the treaty).

6. C. Westermann, *Genesis 1–11: A Commentary*, trans. J. J. Scullion (Minneapolis: Augsburg, 1984), 2.

7. Driver, *Introduction to the Literature of the Old Testament*, 6–7; Westermann, *Genesis 1–11*, 13; and numerous other scholars, identify this recurring formula as an device employed to create the basic literary framework of Genesis 1–11. See Robert L. Cohn, "Narrative Structure and Canonical Perspective in Genesis," *Journal for the Study of the Old Testament* 25 (1983) 3–16.

8. Genesis 2:4 need not be taken as exceptional by special pleading; the audience, hearing this material linearly, would understand the formula in 2:4 as introducing the material that follows (as it does everywhere else).

ending with the conclusion: "And it was evening and it was morning, the [first, second, etc.] day."

Several structuring patterns are discernible. The story is designed so that the descriptions of the creative days grow progressively longer. The first two days are briefly recounted (with 31 and 38 words respectively). The next three days (days 3, 4, and 5) are approximately double that length (69, 69, and 57 words, respectively); and the account of the final creative day (day 6) is doubled again (149 words). This structuring technique conveys the impression of ever-increasing variety and profusion.

While the creation story is primarily linear in its arrangement (day 1, day 2, etc.), it also exhibits a secondary parallel structure (a-b-c ‖ a′-b′-c′ ‖ d), as Umberto Cassuto shows.[9] On the first three days God creates the three spheres or worlds of life: (a) light, (b) sea and sky, and (c) dry land. On the next three days he returns to each of these respective spheres and fills them with living/moving things: (a′) luminaries, (b′) fish and birds, (c′) land creatures, including humans. On the seventh, unmatched day he rests.[10] This structural design conveys a sense of orderliness:

a	light
	b sea and sky
	c dry land
a′	luminaries
	b′ fish and birds
	c′ land animals and humans
	d Sabbath

In both the linear and parallel structures, the Sabbath day stands in the position of emphasis: it culminates the linear arrangement; and it stands as unique and unmatched (and thus highlighted) in the parallel scheme. Its highlighting foreshadows its future importance.

The Sins of Adam and His Offspring (Genesis 2:4–4:26)

The second unit delineated by the *tôlĕdôt* formulas is linked to the preceding one by the technique of "pearling": it picks up a topic introduced near the end of the first unit— "humankind" (*ʾādām*)—and makes it the new central focus.[11] The beginning of this unit is marked for the audience in several ways:

1. The *tôlĕdôt* formula in 2:4 suggests a new beginning.
2. The account of the seventh day of creation in 2:1–3 heralds the end of a unit in that the number *seven* generally represents completeness.
3. The content of 2:1–3 declares the completion of the creative task recounted in 1:1–31.
4. Genesis 2:4–25 neither presents an eighth day nor further describes the seventh, signaling that the series that began in 1:3 is finished.
5. The shift in divine name, from "Elohim" to "Yahweh Elohim," in 2:4–25 suggests a new unit.
6. Shifts in topos (now Eden), characters (now Adam and his family), mood (from tranquillity to discord), storytelling technique (from narrative with no dialogue to narrative carried mainly by dialogue), etc., likewise signal the initiation of a new literary unit.

Unlike the first unit, which was entirely positive, this second unit is predominantly negative. The author uses this positive-negative layout to underscore a theme that will dominate the Book of the Law: human disobedience results in the forfeiture of God's blessings. The unit is composed of three sections that trace the ever-deepening disobedience and the progressive loss of divine blessing: (1) the sin of Adam and Eve (2:4–3:24), (2) the worse sin of Cain in the second generation (4:1–16), and (3) the even worse depravity of Lamech, who culminates Cain's line (4:17–24).[12] The bad-to-worse layout conveys the idea of humankind's steadily deteriorating condition and worsening situation.

The internal structures of the first two stories serve to underscore the destructive role of human disobedience in its worsening state. Both stories comprise seven narrative units. Each story begins well, with humans in happy circumstances, and closes badly, with humans forfeiting this previous happy state and receiving God's punishment. The story of Adam's sin is

---

9. Umberto Cassuto, *A Commentary on the Book of Genesis*, vol. 1: *From Adam to Noah* (Jerusalem: Magnes, 1961), 1–17. See also Michael Fishbane, *Text and Texture: Close Readings of Selected Biblical Texts* (New York: Schocken, 1979), 10–11, who accepts Cassuto's analysis here.

10. Fishbane, *Text and Texture*, 7, notes that 1:1 and 2:4 form an inclusio framing the creation story.

11. G. J. Wenham, *Genesis 1–15* (Word Biblical Commentary 1; Waco: Word, 1987), 156, also notes this editorial technique. The technique of pearling will be used throughout the Pentateuch and Joshua (e.g., Gen. 5:32–6:9).

12. Wenham (ibid., 156) notes: "It is characteristic of the editor's method to bring together a variety of stories under the opening rubric 'This is the family history of. . . .' Thus the story of Cain and Abel (chap. 4) supplements the garden of Eden story in chaps. 2–3, and the divine-human marriage topic (6:1–4) supplements the genealogy of Adam in chap. 5."

6.1 Humankind's first sin (Genesis 2:4–3:24)

a **creation of man**: his happy relationship with the earth and his home in the garden, where he has freely growing food and access to the tree of life (2:4–17)

  b **creation of woman**: her happy relationship with man (2:18–25)

    c **serpent**, in conversation with woman, tempts her (3:1–5)

      d **CENTER: the sin** and God's uncovering of it (3:6–13)

    c′ **punishment of serpent**: its spoiled relationship with woman (3:14–15)

  b′ **punishment of woman**: her spoiled relationship with man (3:16)

a′ **punishment of man**: his spoiled relationship with the earth and expulsion from his home in the garden; he will now have to toil to secure food and will no longer have access to the tree of life (3:17–24)

6.2 Cain's sin (Genesis 4:1–16)

a **Cain's happy beginning**: birth of Cain and Abel (4:1–2)
- Cain's job of "working the <u>soil</u> (ʾădāmâ)"
- (living with his family)

  b **Cain's resentment** of God's rejection of his offering (4:3–5)

    c **God's kind response**: sympathetically reasons with Cain (4:6–7)

      d **CENTER: Cain's sin** and God's uncovering of it (4:8–10)

a′ **Cain's sad ending** (4:11–12)
- he is now cursed "from the <u>soil</u> (ʾădāmâ)"
- banished from living with his family

  b′ **Cain's resentment** of God's punishment (4:13–14)

    c′ **God's kind response**: provides for Cain's protection (4:15–16)

designed with a symmetric touch. The tragic role of Adam's sin is highlighted by its placement at the center, where it functions as the story's turning point (6.1).[13] The structure of the story of Cain's sin, apparently a modified symmetric layout, also highlights the pivotal role of sin by a similar placement of the sin as the story's turning point (6.2).[14]

The structural similarity of these two stories draws attention to humankind's worsening disobedience as well as its deteriorating situation. In the first story, the serpent tempts Eve to do wrong, and she somewhat naively follows its advice; in the second, God himself encourages Cain to do right, and Cain blatantly disobeys, despite God's warning. In the first, the sin was eating forbidden fruit; in the second it is murder! Cain's punishment is parallel to Adam's but more severe. Adam is . . .

1. driven from the garden, to settle in a new home east of Eden
2. forced to till the soil to get food
3. separated from the source of perpetual life (the tree of life)

while Cain is . . .

1. driven out, doomed to wander forever, with no permanent home
2. not even able to till the soil for his food
3. hounded by death (would-be killers) wherever he goes

The third narrative segment (4:17–24) relates the continued deterioration of subsequent generations. This segment comprises a seven-part genealogy, designed in a chronologically linear

---

13. John T. Walsh, "Gen 2:4b–3:24: A Synchronic Approach," *Journal of Biblical Literature* 96 (1977) 161–77, argues that the story of the fall unfolds in a series of seven scenes that can be delineated by the shifts in *dramatis personae* and literary form and that these seven scenes are arranged in a concentric pattern: (a) 2:4b–17, (b) 2:18–25, (c) 3:1–5, (d) 3:6–8, (c′) 3:9–13, (b′) 3:14–19, (a′) 3:22–24. Careful reading of the episode suggests that this analysis begins correctly but perhaps should be modified at the end.

14. The structure of the story of Cain's sin mirrors somewhat that of the story of Adam's sin. In both stories the first two parts set the stage for the sin. In both, the third pericope presents an outside party (the serpent or God) reasoning with the potential sinner: the serpent attempts, successfully, to persuade Eve to do what she shouldn't; God attempts, unsuccessfully, to persuade Cain not to do what he is about to do. The center of both stories is an account of the sin, told with striking brevity, and God's uncovering of the sin, including two questions posed by God: "Where . . . ?" and "What have you done?" Both stories conclude with resultant punishments. In the first, the three participants each receive a punishment. In Cain's story, however, there is only one sinner to be punished; so to match the first story's pattern, the punishment is broken into a three-part discourse. Both episodes are closed by a statement about the expulsion of the sinner(s). Other links connecting the two episodes include the following: (1) the presence of Adam and Eve (cf. 4:1, 25); (2) the virtually identical enigmatic expression in 3:16 and 4:7; (3) the "voice" (qôl) that is heard (3:8, 10; 4:10); (4) the curse affecting the relationship between the offender(s) and the earth (3:17–18; 4:11–12); (5) the idea of hiding from the face of

Yahweh (3:8; 4:14); and (6) Yahweh's driving the offender(s) away, in both cases east of Eden (3:22–24; 4:14–16).

6.3 From creation to Noah (Genesis 1:1–6:8)

a **God's creation** of the world and humans (1:1–2:3)

  b **Adam and Eve,** the first couple; their sin and God's pronouncement of judgment regarding the length of their lives (2:4–3:24)

    c **birth of Adam's first sons;** Cain's murder of Abel (4:1–16)

      d **CENTER: Cain's sinful descendants** (4:17–24)

    c′ **birth of Adam's son Seth** (replacing murdered Abel; 4:25), and genealogy from Adam to Noah (5:1–32)

  b′ **marriage of sons of God and "daughters of men"**; God's pronouncement of judgment regarding the length of their lives(?) (6:1–4)

a′ **God's decision to destroy** the world and humans (6:5–8)

---

fashion that features a natural—and intentional—emphasis on the final, seventh member, the haughty murderer Lamech. Lamech culminates the degeneration of Adam's line through Cain. The loss of blessed tranquillity and subsequent plunge into rebellious discord is possibly communicated structurally in Genesis 2:4–4:24 by the shift from the unified, orderly, cadenced structure of 1:1–2:3, to the more discordant structure of 2:4–4:24, comprising three somewhat disparate parts.

The unit ends on a note of hope (4:25–26), with the birth of Seth and the statement that "at that time people began to call on the name of Yahweh"—which prepares the audience for the more positive unit to follow. The theme of God's grace despite human disobedience has begun.

Human History from Adam to Noah (Genesis 5:1–6:8)

The next unit marked off by the *tôlĕdôt* formulas recounts human history from Adam to Noah. The unit is linked to the previous unit by pearling: the previous unit ended with a note about Adam and his son Seth; the new unit opens with Adam and his son Seth. As with the previous unit, this one is also composed of three parts:

---

a genealogy from Adam to Noah (5:1–32)

b sons of God and "daughters of men" (6:1–4)

c Yahweh's decision to annihilate sinful humankind (6:5–8)

The boundaries of this unit are marked not only by the two *tôlĕdôt* formulas in 5:1 and 6:9, but also by the inclusio formed by the unit's introductory and concluding statements, both of which refer to God's "creating" (*bārā'*) and "making" (*'āśâ*) "humankind" (*'ādām*) (5:1–2; 6:6–7).

The first segment of this unit, the genealogy from Adam to Noah, is highly structured, in stark contrast to the more informally structured genealogy of Cain's descendants. It exhibits a linear, ten-part arrangement. Each of the ten generations from Adam to Noah is presented in identical format:

When *a* had lived *x* years, he became the father of *b*; *a* lived *y* years after the birth of *b* and had other sons and daughters. Thus all the days of *a* were *x* + *y* years; and he died.

This cadenced structuring helps convey a sense of order and well-being (as it did in the creation story). The sense of renewed hope and well-being is also communicated by the positive notes framing the genealogy (4:26b; 5:29) and by the upbeat note about Enoch in the seventh unit: a man who "walked with God." Human obedience results in the restoration of divine blessing (as indicated by the exceedingly long lives enjoyed by these patriarchs).

Alas, this sense of well-being is short-lived. Following the genealogy, two episodes recount the confusion and degeneration characterizing the rest of humankind: (1) an enigmatic story about the sons of God indiscriminately cohabiting with the "daughters of men" (6:1–4), and (2) Yahweh's decision, in light of humankind's continued moral decay, to annihilate the entire human race (6:5–8). But as in the previous unit, this one also closes with a note of hope—"Noah found favor in the eyes of Yahweh" (6:8)—which sets the stage for the next unit.

It is probably not coincidental that these first three units of Genesis comprise a total of seven constituent parts, which exhibit what might be a lightly developed (or fortuitous) symmetric touch (6.3).

Noah and the Flood (Genesis 6:9–9:29)

The fourth unit set off by the *tôlĕdôt* formulas comprises two stories about Noah: the flood (6:9–9:19) and Noah's nakedness (9:20–29). The literary structure of the flood story has received a great deal of attention in recent years. Everyone seems to agree that the story is symmetrically arranged, although they disagree on the number and identification of the parts.[15] Care-

---

15. Umberto Cassuto (*A Commentary on the Book of Genesis*, vol. 2: *From Noah to Abraham* [Jerusalem: Magnes, 1964], 30–32) and Bernard W. Anderson ("From Analysis to Synthesis: The Interpretation of Genesis 1–11," *Journal of Biblical Lit-*

6.4 The flood (Genesis 6:9–9:19)

a **genealogical note** (6:9–10)
  - Noah's three sons enumerated
  - Noah's righteousness

  b **God sees (rāʾâ) that the earth (hāʾāreṣ) is ruined (šāḥat) (6:11–12)***
  - all flesh (kol-bāśar) has ruined (šāḥat) its way

    c **God's instructions to Noah** in light of his coming destruction of life on earth (6:13–22)
  - directions regarding food (ʾoklâ) that they may eat (ʾakal)

      d **they enter the ark** at God's command (7:1–9)
  - Noah takes "clean animals and [clean] birds"

        e **flood begins, ark is closed** (7:10–16)
  - after seven days
  - forty days

          f **waters rise** (7:17–20)
  - series of clauses depicting prevailing waters
  - mountains (hehārîm) are covered and ark is borne over them

            g **CLIMAX: all life on land dies;** only Noah and those with him are spared (7:21–24)

          f' **waters recede** (8:1–5)
  - series of clauses depicting receding waters
  - mountains (hehārîm) are uncovered and ark rests on one of them

        e' **flood ends, ark's window is opened** (8:6–14)
  - after seven days
  - forty days

      d' **they exit the ark** at God's command (8:15–22)
  - Noah takes some "clean animals and clean birds" and offers them to God

    c' **God's instructions to Noah** in light of his renewal of life on earth (9:1–7)
  - directions regarding food (ʾoklâ) that they may eat (ʾakal)

  b' **God promises to never again ruin (šāḥat) the earth (hāʾāreṣ) (9:8–17)†**
  - God will never again ruin (šāḥat) all flesh (kol-bāśar)
  - God will see (rāʾâ) the rainbow

a' **genealogical note** (9:18–19)
  - Noah's three sons enumerated

*Unit b is tied together by the repetition of ʾet and the fourfold repetition of hāʾāreṣ.
†Unit b' is tied together by the fourfold repetition of ʾet and the fourfold repetition of hāʾāreṣ.

6.5 Noah's nakedness (Genesis 9:20–9:29)

a **Noah becomes drunk** and falls asleep (9:20–21)
    b **Ham, Canaan's father, acts shamefully** (9:22)
      c **Shem and Japheth act righteously** (in contrast to Ham) (9:23)
        d **CENTER: Noah discovers what has happened** (9:24)
    b' **Canaan, Ham's son, is cursed** (9:25)
      c' **Shem and Japheth are blessed** (in contrast to Ham's son) (9:26–27)
a' **Noah dies** (9:28–29)

ful attention to structural signals marking beginnings and ends of paragraphs, internal cohesion of individual paragraphs, inclusios, and other structural clues suggests that the story comprises thirteen chiastically arranged parts (6.4), with the seventh (central) part representing the climax: the complete destruction of life on earth (except for Noah and those with him).

The story's symmetric structure emphasizes the highlighted center, which recounts the annihilation of all life on earth.[16] This suggests that the central point of the story—its bottom line—is God's reversal of his creation.

The episode of Noah's nakedness functions as an epilogue to the flood story, presumably included as a foreshadowing of the conquest of Canaan in Joshua (i.e., Canaan, the ancestor of the Canaanites, is cursed). This story appears to be arranged in a seven-part modified symmetry (6.5). The story's arrangement is similar to that of the previous sin stories: (1) setting, (2) sin,

erature 97 [1978]: 23–29) see twelve (different) parts. And Gordon J. Wenham ("The Coherence of the Flood Narrative," *Vetus Testamentum* 28 [1978]: 336–48; cf. *Genesis 1–15*, 155–58) sees thirty-one. Cf. R. E. Longacre, "The Discourse Structure of the Flood Narrative," *Journal of the American Academy of Religion* 47 supplement (1979) 89–133; I. M. Kikawada and A. Quinn, *Before Abraham Was* (Nashville: Abingdon, 1985), 83–106.

16. I owe this insight to Kathi Kunkel (private correspondence).

6.6 Tower of Babel (Genesis 11:1–9)

a **introduction:** <u>all the earth</u> had one language (11:1)

  b **people settle** together in Shinar (11:2)

    c **resolution of the people:** "<u>come</u> (*hābâ*), let us ..." (11:3–4)

      d **CENTER: Yahweh discovers the plot** (11:5)

    c′ **resolution of Yahweh:** "<u>come</u> (*hābâ*), let us ..." (11:6–7)

  b′ **people disperse** from Shinar (11:8)

a′ **conclusion:** <u>all the earth</u> now has many languages (11:9)

---

(3) discovery of the sin (the center and turning point of the story), and (4) curse.

The Dispersing of Humankind (Genesis 10:1–11:9)

The next unit set off by the *tôlĕdôt* formula comprises two parts: the table of nations and the story of the tower of Babel, both of which feature the theme of the dispersing of Noah's descendants throughout the earth.

The table of nations traces the descendants of Noah's three sons. The structuring of this material is dominated by seven-part configurations (perhaps to aid in memory):

1. The list traces the descendants of Noah's seven grandsons: Gomer (10:3), Javan (10:4), Cush (10:7–12), Egypt (10:13–14), Canaan (10:15–19), Aram (10:23), and Arpachshad (10:24–30).
2. Japheth's genealogy (10:2–5) lists seven sons and seven grandsons.
3. Ham's genealogy (10:6–20) lists seven descendants of Cush (10:7), seven cities controlled by Nimrod (10:10–12), and Egypt's seven sons (10:13–14).
4. The entire list includes seventy nations that descended from Noah's three sons.

The story of the tower of Babel exhibits a seven-part symmetric structure, with the center featuring Yahweh's uncovering of humankind's sin (6.6).

Both the table of nations and the tower of Babel stories focus on human dispersion throughout the earth. Both use the key term *pûṣ* ("to scatter"). The first describes humankind's scattering (10:18) and mentions the various languages of the earth (10:5, 20, 31). The second explains, retrospectively, how human scattering (11:4, 8, 9) and language diversity came about (cf. 11:1, 6, 7, 9). Why the dischronologization? David Clines suggests:

> If the material of Genesis 10 had followed the Babel story, the whole table of nations would have to be read under the sign of judgement; where it stands it functions as the fulfillment of the divine command of 9:1, "be fruitful and multiply, and fill the earth,"

the final author understands that the dispersal of the nations may be evaluated both positively (as in chap. 10) and negatively (as in chap. 11).[17]

There may also be a simple, surface-structure explanation: the two units have to follow one another in their present order to fit the overall structural scheme of Genesis 1–11 (see discussion of overall layout below).

Genealogy from Shem to Abraham (Genesis 11:10–26)

The next unit set off by the *tôlĕdôt* formula is the genealogy from Noah to Abraham. Like the genealogy from Adam to Noah, this one also features ten generations and is highly structured, using precisely the same formulaic language as the earlier genealogy except that it omits the concluding formula, "and all the days of *a* were $x + y$ years, and he died." The cadenced, highly structured format again communicates a sense of restored order, in contrast to the structurally (and thematically) fractured preceding unit. This sense of well-being is confirmed by the unit's positive conclusion: the birth of Abraham, Israel's revered ancestor.

The number seven plays a prominent role in both ten-part genealogies (again, perhaps to assist memory). In the Adam-to-Noah genealogy, the seventh son, Enoch, is singled out as special; while in this genealogy, the seventh from the end is special: Eber is apparently the forefather of the "Hebrews" (cf. 10:21, 24–25). Moreover, in the combined genealogies, Eber represents the fourteenth generation (7×2) from creation, and Abraham is twenty-first (7×3).[18]

As with the first three units of Genesis 1–11, the second three units also comprise a total of seven component literary segments. Like the

---

17. David J. A. Clines, *The Theme of the Pentateuch*, rev. ed. (Journal for the Study of the Old Testament Supplement 10; Sheffield: JSOT Press, 1997), 74.

18. According to the Masoretic Text, Abram is reckoned as seventh from Eber, while in the Septuagint he is placed in the twenty-first slot (3×7) since creation; see J. M. Sasson, "Generation, Seventh," in *Interpreter's Dictionary of the Bible: Supplementary Volume*, ed. Keith R. Crim (Nashville: Abingdon, 1976), 354–56.

6.7 From Noah to Abram (Genesis 6:9–11:26)

- a **the flood**: <u>begins</u> with Noah, a <u>righteous man</u> with whom Yahweh makes a covenant and through whom humankind is saved (6:9–9:19)
  - b **sin story**: Noah's nakedness and the curse upon Canaan (9:20–29)
    - c **descendants of good Japheth**, the youngest son (10:1–5)
      - d **CENTER: descendants of bad Ham**: the cursed line, linked with the two sin stories (chaps. 9, 11) (10:6–20)
    - c′ **descendants of good Shem**, the eldest son (10:21–32)
  - b′ **sin story**: tower of Babel (in Shinar); punishment (11:1–9)
- a′ **ten generations from Shem to Abram**: <u>ends</u> with Abram, a <u>righteous man</u> with whom Yahweh will make a covenant and through whom all humankind will be blessed (11:10–26)

6.8 Introduction of Abram and Sarai (Genesis 11:27–32)

- a **introduction**: Terah and his offspring (11:27)
  - b **the family lives in <u>Ur of the Chaldeans</u>**; Haran dies (11:28)
    - c **Abram <u>takes</u> (*lāqaḥ*) Terah's daughter <u>Sarai</u> as his <u>wife</u>**; Nahor marries Milcah, <u>whose father is Haran</u> (11:29)
      - d **CENTER: Sarai is barren**; she has no children (11:30)
    - c′ **Abram is <u>taken</u> (*lāqaḥ*) by <u>Terah</u>**, along with Abram's <u>wife Sarai</u> and Lot, <u>whose father is Haran</u> (11:31a)
  - b′ **the family leaves <u>Ur of the Chaldeans</u>** and settles in Haran (11:31b)
- a′ **conclusion**: summary of Terah's life; his death (11:32)

---

first set, these have a light symmetric touch and also feature the nonchosen and sinful line (Ham ‖ Cain) at the center (6.7).

Introduction of Abram and Sarai (Genesis 11:27–32)

The final unit in Genesis 1–11 to be introduced by the *tôlĕdôt* formula is the brief unit about Abram's family. This unit's boundaries are marked by the *tôlĕdôt* formula ("these are the generations of Terah") at its beginning (11:27) and by the formulaic summary of Terah's life and his death at the end (11:32). The unit's coherence is achieved by its single topic—Terah's life and his family—and by the symmetric touch of its layout (6.8).

The statement of Sarai's barrenness stands, with foreshadowing significance, at the highlighted center of the unit. Her barrenness will create the tension that will dominate the next unit, the story of Abraham.

Genesis 11:27–32 serves at least two structural functions in its context: (1) it completes the structural scheme of the first unit of Genesis, and (2) it creates a link (through pearling) with the next unit by introducing Abram and Sarai, who will be the central figures of that unit.[19]

Overall Layout of Genesis 1–11

Although the seven units comprising Genesis 1–11 follow a chronological order, they also exhibit a conspicuous parallel (a-b-c ‖ a′-b′-c′ ‖ d) arrangement similar to that of the creation story (6.9).

In this parallel scheme, the first unit, the creation story, is echoed by the fourth unit, the flood story. The flood is God's reversal of creation.[20] In the flood, God destroys the creation, then reestablishes a new world. As in the original creation, dry land once again appears from a watery chaos. Echoing the creation story, God sends out from the ark "every living thing . . . of all flesh, birds and animals and every creeping thing that creeps on the earth, that they may . . . be fruitful and multiply upon the earth" (8:17; cf. 1:20–26). God's blessing upon the first humans (1:28–30) is repeated almost verbatim in his blessing upon the second father of the human race (9:1–3, 7). Numerous keywords and phrases link the two stories.

The second unit, the story of the rebellion and expulsion of Adam and Eve and Cain and the genealogy of the nonchosen line of Adam through Cain, is matched by the fifth unit, featuring the genealogy of the nonchosen descendants of Noah and the story of the rebellion and scattering of Noah's descendants. Both units focus on human disobedience. In both, God resolves to deal with the problem using the first-person plural ("let us"; "like one of us"; 3:22; 11:7). In both units, scattering is part of the solution; and in both units the descendants of those outside God's chosen line are delineated in similar terminology and style (cf. 4:17–22; 10:1–32).

---

19. That this brief unit is part of Genesis 1–11, rather than what follows, is supported by its—like the preceding literary units of Genesis 1–11 and unlike the units of the subsequent section—beginning with "these are the generations of *x*" (11:27).

20. See Clines, *Theme of the Pentateuch*, 80–82.

6.9 Arrangement of the seven main units of Genesis 1–11

a **creation**: God creates the world and humankind—a beginning (1:1–2:3)
- <u>dry land appears</u> out of the watery chaos
- animals: <u>every living thing</u>, <u>birds</u>, every animal that <u>creeps</u> (*remeś*) on the ground; <u>male and female</u> (*zākār ûněqēbâ*); <u>after their kind</u> (*lěmînâ*)
- divine <u>blessing on animals</u>: "be fruitful and multiply upon the earth"
- Yahweh <u>blesses the first people</u>: "be fruitful, multiply, fill the earth"
- instructions regarding <u>food</u> that humans may eat (plants)

b **humankind's degeneration: sin and scattering of first people** (Adam, Eve, Cain); nonchosen line of Adam through Cain (2:4–4:26)
- stories about humankind's <u>sins</u>
- God deliberates in <u>first-person plural</u> over human sin (3:22)
- punishment by <u>banishing</u>, <u>scattering</u> sinner

c **ten generations** from Adam to Noah (5:1–6:8)

a′ **flood**: God destroys the world and humankind—a new beginning (6:9–9:29)
- <u>dry land appears</u> out of the watery chaos
- animals: <u>every living thing</u>, <u>birds</u>, every animal that <u>creeps</u> (*remeś*) on the ground; <u>male and female</u> (*zākār ûněqēbâ*); <u>after their kind</u> (*lěmînâ*)
- divine <u>blessing on animals</u>: "be fruitful and multiply upon the earth"
- Yahweh <u>blesses the new first people</u>: "be fruitful, multiply, fill the earth"
- instructions regarding <u>food</u> that humans may eat (now they may eat animals)

b′ **humankind's degeneration: sin and scattering of new first people** (Noah's descendants); nonchosen lines of Noah's sons (10:1–11:9)
- story about humankind's <u>sin</u>
- God deliberates in <u>first-person plural</u> over human sin (11:7)
- punishment by <u>banishing</u>, <u>scattering</u> sinners

c′ **ten generations** from Shem to Abram (11:10–26)

d **conclusion**: Abram (11:27–32)

6.10 Arrangement of the fourteen main units of Genesis 1–11

section 1: Genesis 1:1–6:8

a **creation story**: first <u>beginning</u>, divine blessing (1:1–2:3)

b <u>sin</u> **of Adam**: <u>nakedness</u>, seeing/covering nakedness; curse (2:4–3:24)

c **younger righteous son** Abel murdered (no descendants) (4:1–16)

d **descendants of** <u>sinful son</u> Cain (4:17–26)

e **descendants of** <u>chosen son</u> Seth (5:1–32)

f **divine** <u>judgment</u> **on unlawful(?) unions** (6:1–4)

g **brief introduction of Noah**, through whom God will bless humankind (6:5–8)

section 2: Genesis 6:9–11:26

a′ **flood story**: reversal of creation; <u>new beginning</u>, divine blessing (6:9–9:19)

b′ <u>sin</u> **of Ham**: <u>nakedness</u>, seeing/covering nakedness; curse (9:20–29)

c′ **descendants of** <u>younger righteous son</u> Japheth (10:1–5)

d′ **descendants of** <u>sinful son</u> Ham (10:6–20)

e′ **descendants of** <u>chosen son</u> Shem (10:21–32)

f′ **divine** <u>judgment</u> **on human attempt to stay together** (11:1–9)

g′ **brief introduction of Abram**, through whom God will bless humankind (11:10–26)

The third unit, tracing the ten generations from Adam to Noah, is obviously echoed by the sixth unit, which traces the ten generations from Noah's son Shem to Abram. Both begin with a paragraph setting the temporal stage for the genealogy (5:1–3; 11:10); both include ten generations; and both present the ten generations in a highly structured style that employs virtually identical terminology.

This leaves the seventh unit, the introduction of Abram and his family, as the unmatched final unit. This concluding unit, like that featuring the Sabbath day in the similarly structured creation account, stands in the position of (foreshadowing) emphasis.

Another structuring scheme also ties the material of these chapters together. The first three and second three units in Genesis 1–11 each comprise a total of seven individual episodes (or narrative units). The author apparently designed these with a parallel correspondence between these two sets of seven units (6.10).

In conclusion, Genesis 1–11 is structured to draw attention to and reinforce themes that will

6.11 Abraham and the promise of a son (Genesis 12:1–21:7)

  a **introduction**: journey to Canaan and the <u>promise of descendants</u> (12:1–9)
    b **Abram lies about Sarai** in Egypt; <u>God protects her</u> in foreign king's court (12:10–20)
      c **Lot settles in <u>Sodom</u>** (and Abram settles in Hebron) (13:1–18)
        d **Abram intercedes** for <u>Lot and Sodom</u> militarily (14:1–24)
          e **promise of a son**: from Abram himself (15:1–21)
            f **<u>Ishmael's</u> birth**; promise to him (16:1–16)
              g **CENTER: Yahweh's covenant**: Abram's and Sarai's names changed; circumcision instituted; promise of a son reiterated (17:1–21)
            f′ **<u>Ishmael</u> and Abraham circumcised** (promise to Ishmael) (17:22–27; cf. 17:18, 20)
          e′ **promise of a son**: from Sarah herself (18:1–15)
        d′ **Abraham intercedes** for <u>Sodom and Lot</u> in prayer (18:16–33)
      c′ **Lot flees <u>Sodom</u>**, which God destroys; settles in Moab (19:1–38)
    b′ **Abraham lies about Sarah** in Gerar; <u>God protects her</u> in foreign king's court (20:1–18)
  a′ **conclusion**: <u>birth of Isaac</u> (and tension resolved) (21:1–7)

continue throughout the Pentateuch and Joshua. Of these, the following themes are especially important:

1. Yahweh's desire to bless his people (creation; new plans after the flood)—a central theme of the Sinai treaty
2. the danger of humankind's forfeiture of Yahweh's blessings through disobedience—a theme reiterated throughout the treaty, especially in Deuteronomy
3. Yahweh's mercy and grace, which he extends to humans despite their disobedience
4. Yahweh's use of particular individuals or people for the restoration of blessing—which will be a central theme in the rest of the Pentateuch[21]
5. Yahweh's awesome power as the only God—whose power extends over all creation and humankind (as demonstrated and emphasized in the matching creation and flood stories, Yahweh's scattering of all humankind, etc.)

Abraham and the Promise of a Son (Genesis 12:1–21:7)

Genesis 12 marks the beginning of the second major unit in Genesis. To this point the recounting of human history has proceeded at a relatively rapid pace, covering many hundreds of years in the space of eleven chapters. In Genesis 12 the progression of history slows nearly to a halt. The next ten chapters trace events that occurred during a brief twenty-five-year period in the life of a single individual, Abraham. Several signals indicate the beginning of a new unit

here. The *tôlĕdôt* formulas that punctuated the previous section now cease. The focus also shifts from the entire human race to a single individual and from the entire earth to Canaan. There are also shifts in theme and topic.

The new unit extends to 21:7 and is tied together by the central figure of Abraham and by Yahweh's promise of offspring. This promise is made to Abraham in 12:1–3, creating suspense for the audience, who already know (from the highlighted center of the preceding unit) that Sarah is barren and the couple childless. The suspense builds as Abraham and Sarah continue childless and grow steadily older. The promise is seriously threatened by two episodes in which Sarah is taken by a foreign ruler; and it is further complicated by the birth of Ishmael. The suspense is maintained as Yahweh thrice reiterates the promise, and as Abraham's nephew Lot begins his own family. The tension is finally resolved when Yahweh causes Sarah to conceive and give birth to the long-promised son, Isaac. The coherence and extent of the unit is also communicated to the audience by means of its symmetric arrangement (which we will illustrate shortly).

The individual literary units of the section are not marked in so formal a manner as those in Genesis 1–11. Virtually all the units, however, are self-contained stories delineated by shifts in scene, person, and time. Most are introduced by stage-setting clauses with subject and verb reversed, by *wayĕhî* ("and it was"), and by temporal clauses (12:10; 13:2; 14:1; 15:1; 16:1; 17:1; 21:1). As in the flood story, there are a total of thirteen units in Genesis 12:1–21:7 (6.11). These thirteen units are arranged in a conspicuous symmetric pattern,[22] with Yah-

---

21. The pattern of surveying the nonchosen line first before focusing on the chosen line will also be repeated throughout the rest of Genesis; cf. Nahor and Abraham, Ishmael and Isaac, Esau and Jacob, etc.

22. I partly owe this insight to my student David Carr (private communication).

6.12 Isaac (Genesis 21:8–28:4)

a **Yahweh's choice of the younger son Isaac** (21:8–19)
- family rift involving <u>elder son</u> Ishmael and <u>younger son</u> Isaac
- to protect favored younger son, <u>matriarch proposes that elder son should leave</u>
- she appeals to husband
- blessing and promise of great progeny given to banished son

b **marriage of nonchosen elder son Ishmael (an archer) to foreign woman** (21:20–21)

  c **strife with King Abimelech of Gerar over Abraham's wells** (21:22–34)
- treaty at <u>Beersheba</u> with Abimelech, involving general <u>Phicol</u>
- unlike previous time at Gerar, matriarch is not taken by king
- naming of "Beersheba"

  d **risking everything for the covenant** (22:1–19)
- Abraham's willingness to give up everything, even the <u>life</u> of his beloved son, for Yahweh's covenant

    e **nonchosen genealogy: family of Nahor** (22:20–24)

      f **death of Sarah**, Abraham's wife (23:1–20)
- her burial in the <u>cave of Machpelah</u>

        g **CENTER: Yahweh selects Rebekah** as chosen matriarch and Jacob's wife (24:1–67)

      f′ **death of Abraham**; Abraham's second wife (25:1–10)
- his death and burial in the <u>cave of Machpelah</u>

    e′ **nonchosen genealogy**: family of Ishmael (25:11–18)

  d′ **scorning the covenant** (25:19–34)*
- Esau's <u>life</u> is more important to him than the covenant; he shows contempt for his birthright (and his part in the covenant?): it is no more important than a bowl of beans: "What do I care? I am about to die!"

  c′ **strife with King Abimelech of Gerar over Abraham's wells** (26:1–33)
- treaty at <u>Beersheba</u> with Abimelech, involving general <u>Phicol</u>
- like Abraham's first time at Gerar, matriarch is taken by king
- naming of "Beersheba"

b′ **marriage of nonchosen elder son Esau (an archer) to foreign women** (26:34–35);

a′ **Yahweh's choice of the younger son** (27:1–28:4)
- family rift involving <u>elder son</u> Esau and <u>younger son</u> Jacob
- to protect favored younger son, <u>matriarch proposes that younger son should leave</u>
- she appeals to husband
- blessing and prayer for great progeny given to banished son

*Unit d′ exhibits no strong link to unit d.

---

weh's great covenant with Abraham and Sarah standing strategically at the center, in the seventh position.

The symmetric design of this section accounts for much of the repetition and the otherwise puzzling positioning of episodes; for example, the two accounts of Abraham lying about his wife; the three lengthy promises regarding a son; and the two accounts focusing on Lot and Sodom.[23] The repetitions serve to establish patterns. For example, the repetition of the scenario of Abraham's lying about Sarah draws attention to the weakness of Israel's ancestors and the contrasting power of Yahweh, who is able, even in foreign lands like Egypt or Philistia, to protect his people, and who alone is responsible for the birth of the nation of Israel. Standing in the position of greatest emphasis, in the center and seventh position, is God's great covenant of circumcision, accompanied by his changes of Abram's and Sarai's names and his assurance that the promised son will indeed be through Sarah.

23. Kikawada and Quinn, *Before Abraham Was*, 95, note the symmetry in Genesis 12–20.

The Life of Isaac: Strife between Older and Younger Brothers (Genesis 21:8–28:4)

With the birth of Isaac in 21:1–7 the suspense of the previous unit is finally resolved, and Genesis 21:8 opens a new unit with a shift to a major new focus: Isaac. While Abraham and Sarah will continue to appear for a few more chapters, the central focus of the next several chapters is Isaac. The unit begins with Isaac as an infant and ends with him so old that he can no longer see.

The constituent episodes and narrative segments of this unit are relatively easy to delineate, most having well-marked introductions and conclusions. As in the previous unit, the beginnings of episodes and narrative segments are here marked by *wayĕhî* (or *wayyihyû*), usually followed by a temporal clause (21:20, 22; 22:1, 20; 23:1; 25:11–12, 19–20; 26:1, 34; 27:1) and shifts in time (21:8; 24:1) or person (24:1). Like the previous unit, this one contains thirteen parts arranged in a conspicuous symmetry (6.12) with the structurally highlighted central, seventh episode featuring God's gracious

6.13 Jacob (Genesis 28:5–37:1)

a **Jacob's exile begins (28:5)**
   - Jacob leaves for Paddan Aram, sent off by father Isaac
b **Esau's family (28:6–9)**
c **stop at Bethel (28:10–22)**
   - God appears to Jacob; his promise to Jacob
   - sets up memorial stone to commemorate God's appearance
   - names the place El-Bethel ("God of the house of God")
      d **departure from Canaan and arrival at Paddan-aram (29:1–30)**
         - Laban's treachery with marriage agreement
         - deceitful reassurance: "you are my bone and my flesh!"
         - Jacob loves (ʾāhēb) Rachel, willing to pay any price
      e **Jacob's family becomes large (29:31–30:24)**
         - tension between elder and younger wife finally resolved
         f **Jacob's scheming (30:25–43)**
            - involving positioning of flocks
            - use of his name Jacob
            - result: gains many flocks
            g **TURNING POINT: Yahweh enables Jacob to escape** and depart for home (31:1–55 [31:1–32:1])
         f´ **Jacob's scheming (32:1–32 [32:2–33])**
            - involving positioning of flocks
            - changes Jacob's name
            - result: loses many flocks
      e´ **Jacob introduces his large family** to Esau (33:1–17)
         - tension between him (younger) and Esau (elder) finally resolved
      d´ **arrival back in Canaan from Paddan-aram (33:18–34:31)**
         - sons' treachery with marriage agreement at Shechem
         - deceitful reassurance: "we . . . will be one people!"
         - Shechem loves (ʾāhēb) Dinah, willing to pay any price
c´ **stop at Bethel (35:1–29)**
   - God appears to Jacob; he kept his promise!
   - sets up memorial stone to commemorate God's appearance
   - names the place El-Bethel ("God of the house of God")
b´ **Esau's family (36:1–43)**
a´ **Jacob's exile ends (37:1)**
   - Jacob settles "where his father had lived, in . . . Canaan"

and sovereign selection of the chosen couple—here again with an emphasis on the wife.[24] The divine choice of the new couple is bracketed by the deaths of the previous divinely selected couple.

As in the Abraham unit, the symmetric scheme of this section helps explain much of the repetition and positioning of episodes, such as (1) the two accounts of treaties with King Abimelech of Gerar and Phicol, involving Abraham's wells and the town of Beersheba; (2) the two brief notes about the marriages of the non-favored elder son to foreign women; and (3) the two tragic stories of family strife that resulted in the expulsion of one of the two sons in the family. Structurally highlighted themes in this unit include the following:

1. Yahweh's power over foreign monarchs (as reinforced in the matching stories involving

Abimelech)—a key theme throughout the Book of the Law

2. importance of commitment to Yahweh's covenant

3. Yahweh's sovereign determination of who will be his chosen people (Isaac not Ishmael; Rebekah; Jacob not Esau)

4. Yahweh's choice of the younger over the older—foreshadowing his choice of the younger nation, Israel, over the older nations of the earth

Jacob's Exile and God's Protection and Blessing (Genesis 28:5–37:1)

The next major section begins in Genesis 28:5. Here the focus shifts and narrows to Jacob alone, the next chosen patriarch, and the story of his exile. The new section begins with young Jacob, unmarried and without possessions, leaving his father Isaac to flee to Paddan-aram to escape the murderous anger of Esau (28:5). It ends with the reversal of all of this: Jacob re-

24. The chiastic structure of this section was first pointed out to me by my student David Carr (private communication).

6.14 Parallel pattern in the Joseph story (Genesis 37:2–50:26)

a **trouble between Joseph and his brothers** (37:2–11)
   - they hate him

a' **more trouble between Joseph and his brothers** (37:12–36)
   - they dispose of him

b **sexual temptation involving Judah** (38:1–30)
   - Tamar successfully entices Judah to have sex with her
   - she keeps his ring and staff to produce as condemning evidence later

b' **sexual temptation involving Joseph** (39:1–23)
   - Potiphar's wife unsuccessfully tries to seduce Joseph
   - she keeps his cloak to produce as condemning evidence later

c **Joseph interprets two dreams of prison mates** (40:1–23)

c' **Joseph interprets two dreams of pharaoh** (41:1–57)

d **brothers come to Egypt for food** (42:1–38)
   - they bow to Joseph
   - Joseph fills sacks with grain, money
   - Reuben offers his sons as surety for Benjamin

d' **brothers again come to Egypt for food** (43:1–44:3)
   - they bow to Joseph
   - Joseph fills sacks with grain, money
   - Judah offers himself as surety for Benjamin

e **Joseph has some of his family brought to him** (44:4–45:15)
   - including all his brothers
   - weeping
   - joyful reunion

e' **Joseph has all of his family brought to him** (45:16–47:12)
   - including all his brothers, their families, and his father
   - weeping
   - joyful reunion

f **prospering in Egypt: Joseph in ascendancy** (47:13–26)
   - Joseph prospers in his rule over all Egypt
   - Egyptians are impoverished and enslaved to him
   - Joseph gives Egyptians provisions

f' **prospering in Egypt: blessings on Jacob's sons** (47:27–49:32)
   - Joseph's family prospers and flourishes (cf. 47:27)
   - Jacob's blessings upon sons

g **death of patriarch: Jacob** (49:33–50:14)
   - Jacob dies

g' **death of patriarch: Joseph** (50:15–26)
   - Joseph dies

---

turns home years later, married, with many children and possessions, reconciled with Esau (cf. 35:27–37:1). The cohesion of the unit is partly created by its single theme: Jacob's exile and how God graciously protected and blessed him.

Most of the constituent units of this section are well marked, generally introduced by shifts in person (28:6, 10; 29:31; 31:3; 34:1; 36:1; 37:1), place (28:10; 29:1; 32:1 [32:2]; 35:1), or time (30:25). As with the previous two major sections, this one also contains thirteen units arranged with a touch of symmetry (6.13). Hints of a symmetric arrangement are abundant,[25] including the inclusio of Jacob's departure from home and

his return (a and a'; cf. 35:27); the two units about Esau's family, one positioned immediately after the beginning of Jacob's journey, the other immediately before its end (b and b'); the two stops at Bethel, one on the departing journey, the other on the return trip (c and c'); and the two instances of treachery regarding the promised giving of a girl in marriage (d and d'). The center of the story and its turning point is unit g, in which Jacob decides to leave Paddan-aram and sets out on his journey back to Canaan.

The arrangement of this section serves to highlight two main themes: (1) Yahweh's gracious protection of Israel's weak and scheming ancestor, emphasized by the matching of Yahweh's two gracious appearances to Jacob at Bethel and by Yahweh's key role in Jacob's escape at the story's center, and (2) the chaos caused by family strife

---

25. Fishbane, *Text and Texture*, 42, senses symmetry in this section of Genesis, although his analysis differs from the one presented here (he extends the symmetry from 25:19 through 35:22, with 30:1–43 at the center).

6.15 Symmetry of the Joseph story (Genesis 37:2–50:26)

a **introduction:** beginning of Joseph story (37:2–11)
- Joseph's dream that brothers will <u>bow down</u>
- brothers <u>hate</u> Joseph
- they cannot <u>speak kindly</u> to him
- Joseph's age

b **grievous mourning in Hebron** (37:12–36)
- Jacob weeps over "death" of Joseph in Hebron when brothers take Joseph's cloak back to Jacob
- Jacob refers to his own future death
- <u>Joseph goes from Canaan to Egypt</u> (not back to father in Hebron)

c **reversal of elder and younger sons** of Judah as "firstborn" (38:1–30)
- despite string tied to <u>hand</u> (*yād*)

d **Joseph's enslavement to Egyptian** (39:1–23)
- he is <u>sold</u> (*mākar* in 37:27–28), <u>purchased</u> (*qānâ*), becomes a <u>servant</u> (*ʿebed*) to an Egyptian
- <u>finds favor in the eyes of</u> (*māṣāʾ ḥēn bĕʿênāyw*) his <u>master</u> (*ʾădōnāyw*)
- he is <u>second only to</u> his master
- in charge of Egyptian's <u>bread</u> (*leḥem*)

e **disfavor at pharaoh's court** (40:1–23)
- dishonoring and expulsion of Egyptian servants
- imprisonment
- <u>life and death</u>

f **Joseph's revelation of pharaoh's dreams** (41:1–57)
- promotion to <u>second to pharaoh</u>
- gives God credit

g **CENTER: brothers come to Egypt for food** (42:1–38)

g′ **CENTER: brothers come to Egypt for food** (43:1–44:3)

f′ **Joseph's revelation of his identity** to brothers (44:4–45:15)
- he is <u>second to pharaoh</u>
- gives God credit

e′ **favor at pharaoh's court** (45:16–47:12)
- honoring and reception of Joseph's family into court
- granted good place to live in Goshen
- <u>life and death</u>

d′ **Joseph's enslavement of Egyptians** (47:13–26)
- they are <u>sold</u> (*mākar*), <u>purchased</u> (*qānâ*) by him, and become his <u>servants</u> (*ʿebed*)
- seek to <u>find favor in the eyes of</u> (*māṣāʾ ḥēn bĕʿênayim*) Joseph their <u>master</u> (*ʾădōnî*)
- he is <u>second only to</u> pharaoh
- in charge of Egyptians' <u>bread</u> (*leḥem*)

c′ **reversal of elder and younger sons** of Joseph (47:27–49:32)
- despite Joseph's trying to uncross Jacob's <u>hands</u> (*yād*) when blessing his sons: reversal of Judah (elder) and Joseph (younger) as firstborn

b′ **grievous mourning near Hebron** (49:33–50:14)
- Joseph weeps over death of Jacob near Hebron when he and brothers take Jacob's body back to Hebron
- Jacob's <u>death</u>
- <u>Joseph goes from Canaan back to Egypt</u>

a′ **conclusion:** end of Joseph story (50:15–26)
- Joseph's brothers <u>bow down</u> before him
- fear that he will <u>hate</u> them
- he <u>speaks kindly</u> to them
- Joseph's final age, and death

and social disorder (through the repetition of matching stories of strife and disorder).

Joseph and His Brothers (Genesis 37:2–50:26)

Scholars generally acknowledge that Genesis 37–50 forms a single literary unit (although chap. 38 is often considered intrusive). The central focus on Joseph and his brothers ties these chapters together. The unit opens by introducing to the audience the young boy Joseph; it closes with Joseph's death many years later. The intervening story is one of the best told stories in all of literature.

One of the most striking features of the Joseph story is its well-designed structure. Few compositions show such sophisticated literary architecture. It is made up of fourteen episodes or narrative segments, all of which are well

6.16 Symmetry of the first half of the Joseph story (Genesis 37–42)

a **Joseph dreams** (37:2–11) that his family will <u>bow</u> (*hištaḥăwâ*) to him
  - brothers <u>see</u> (*rāʾâ*) him and cannot <u>speak</u> (*dibber*) kindly to him

b **brothers' cruel treatment of Joseph** because of <u>his dreams</u> (37:12–36)
  - they cast him into a <u>pit</u> (*bôr*), then bring him up <u>from the pit</u> (*min-habbôr*), <u>strip off his garment</u> of honor
  - he is sold to <u>Potiphar</u>

  c **Tamar languishes in father's house** (38:1–30)
    - her <u>plight is forgotten</u> as she <u>waits in vain</u> for help from one morally obliged (Judah)
    - her fate is intertwined with two men who displeased God
    - she is <u>falsely accused of sexual immorality</u> by guilty party
    - theme: <u>putting to death and sparing</u>
    - in the end she is vindicated, given a family of two sons

    d **CENTER: Joseph's integrity and success in Egypt**, in the midst of adversity "Yahweh was with Joseph" (39:1–23)

  c′ **Joseph languishes in prison** (40:1–23)
    - his <u>plight is forgotten</u> as he <u>waits in vain</u> for help from one morally obliged (cupbearer)
    - his fate is intertwined with two men who displeased pharaoh
    - he had been <u>falsely accused of sexual immorality</u> by guilty party
    - theme: <u>putting to death and sparing</u>
    - (in the end he is vindicated, given a family of two sons)

b′ **pharaoh's kind treatment of Joseph** when he interprets <u>his dreams</u> (41:1–57)
  - Joseph was in a <u>pit</u> (*bôr*), pharaoh brings him <u>from the pit</u> (*min-habbôr*), frees him, exalts him, and <u>gives him new garments</u>
  - he is given the daughter of <u>Potiphera</u> as a wife

a′ **Joseph's dream comes true** (42:1–38)
  - his brothers come to Egypt and <u>bow</u> (*hištaḥăwâ*) to him
  - Joseph <u>sees</u> (*rāʾâ*) his brothers and <u>speaks</u> (*dibber*) harshly to them

---

6.17 Symmetry of the second half of the Joseph story (Genesis 43–50)

a **brothers return to Egypt from Canaan and bow to Joseph** (43:1–44:3)
  - they <u>fear</u> that Joseph will make them his <u>slaves</u> (*ʿăbādîm*)
  - Joseph <u>speaks kindly</u> to them; reassures them, <u>don't be afraid</u> (*ʾal-tîrāʾû*); provides for them; <u>weeps</u>

b **Joseph's great weeping** when he hears Jacob is <u>alive</u> (44:4–45:15)
  - Joseph <u>weeps</u> a long time over Benjamin and brothers and <u>kisses</u> them, weeping so loud that the <u>Egyptians</u> hear him
  - when he hears that Jacob is still alive he gives instructions to bring Jacob from Hebron to Egypt

  c **Jacob comes down to Egypt with all twelve sons** (<u>listed in order of birth</u>) (45:16–47:12)
    - Jacob joyous; having thought Joseph dead, he sees Joseph alive!
    - he declares he can now <u>die</u> in peace

    d **CENTER: Joseph's exaltation over all Egypt** and his successful administration during the famine (47:13–26)

  c′ **Jacob blesses all twelve sons in Egypt** (<u>blessed in order of birth</u>) (47:27–49:32)
    - Jacob joyous: "I never expected to see you [Joseph] again, and now I see your sons too!"
    - he is about to <u>die</u>

b′ **Joseph's great weeping** when Jacob <u>dies</u> (49:33–50:14)
  - Joseph <u>weeps</u> over his father and <u>kisses</u> him
  - Joseph gives instructions to take Jacob's body from Egypt to Hebron for burial
  - <u>Egyptians weep</u> a long time in Canaan

a′ **brothers return to Egypt from Canaan and bow to Joseph** (50:15–26)
  - they <u>fear</u> Joseph and say, "We are your <u>slaves</u> (*ʿăbādîm*)"
  - Joseph <u>speaks kindly</u> to them; reassures them, <u>don't be afraid</u> (*ʾal-tîrāʾû*); promises to provide for them; <u>weeps</u>

---

marked by shifts in scene, characters, time, and place. The fourteen constituent units are designed and arranged to serve four different organizational schemes simultaneously:

1. linear: in chronological order
2. parallel: in pairs: a-a′ ‖ b-b′ ‖ c-c′ ‖ d-d′ ‖ etc. (6.14)
3. symmetric #1: fourteen-part symmetry spanning the entire story (6.15)
4. symmetric #2: seven-part symmetry in each half of the story (6.16, 6.17)

Apart from the straightforward linear scheme, the story's parallel pattern would have been the easiest one for an audience to follow and appreciate. The parallel scheme was created by designing the units to function as pairs (6.14).[26] The

26. Even on a smaller scale the story is characterized by pairing: Joseph's two dreams, Judah's two slain sons, Judah's twin sons through Tamar, two temptation scenes with Potiphar's wife, two dreams of two prison mates, two dreams of pharaoh, Joseph's two sons, etc. The predilection for pairs in the Joseph story is observed by Jacob Licht, *Storytelling in the Bible* (Jerusalem: Magnes, 1978), 142.

6.18 Joseph sold into slavery (Genesis 37:12–35)

a **introduction** (37:12–14a)
- Jacob concerned in Hebron: worried about Joseph's brothers, sends him to determine their welfare and reassure him of their well-being

b **Joseph leaves Jacob in Hebron** (37:14b–17)
- go find (*māṣāʾ*) your brothers

c **Reuben attempts to rescue Joseph from brothers' plot** (37:18–24)
- Reuben convinces them to just throw him into pit (he plans to rescue him later)

d **CENTER: Joseph is sold into slavery** (37:25–28)

c′ **Reuben discovers that he has failed to save Joseph from his brothers** (37:29–30)
- Reuben returns to pit to rescue Joseph, but is too late

b′ **brothers return to Jacob in Hebron** (37:31–33)
- they happened to find (*māṣāʾ*) Joseph's garment and give it to Jacob

a′ **conclusion** (37:34–35)
- Jacob distraught in Hebron: mourns Joseph's "death" and refuses to be comforted by Joseph's brothers

6.19 Jacob and his family come to Egypt (Genesis 45:16–47:12)

a **pharaoh's invitation and generosity to Joseph's family** (45:16–20)
- they are invited to dwell in Egypt, in the best of the land

b **Joseph's instructions to brothers** about journey home (45:21–24)

c **Jacob is told that Joseph is alive** (45:25–28)
- Jacob's joyous response: "My son Joseph is still alive! I will go and see him before I die!"

d **CENTER: Jacob and entire family come to Egypt** (46:1–27)

c′ **Jacob sees Joseph alive** (46:28–30)
- Jacob says, "Now let me die, since I have seen your face and know that you are still alive"

b′ **Joseph's instructions to brothers** about meeting with pharaoh (46:31–34)

a′ **pharaoh's reception of, and generosity to, Joseph's family** (47:1–12)
- they are invited to dwell in Egypt, in the best of the land

6.20 Jacob's blessings on his sons (Genesis 47:27–49:33)

a **summary of Jacob's life** (47:27–29a)
- nearing death

b **Jacob charges Joseph to bury him in Hebron** (47:29b–31)

c **Jacob blesses Joseph's two sons**, who have equal status with his own twelve sons (48:1–20)

d **CENTER: Jacob blesses Joseph** (48:21–22)

c′ **Jacob blesses his twelve sons** (49:1–28)

b′ **Jacob charges his sons to bury him in Hebron** (49:29–32)

a′ **summarizing statement** (49:33)
- Jacob's death

story's overall symmetric scheme (6.15) draws attention to the dramatic reversals that occur in the saga (note especially units a and a′, c and c′, and d and d′). The story's first half exhibits its own self-contained symmetry that begins and ends with the theme of the brothers bowing to Joseph and centers on the story of Joseph's integrity and success (6.16). The second half of the story also opens and closes with the theme of the brothers bowing to Joseph. It centers on Joseph's exaltation over all of Egypt (6.17).

Even on a smaller scale the structural architecture in Genesis 37–50 is remarkable. Most of the units are themselves organized in seven-part symmetries. While there is not enough room to give every unit's structure, the episodes of Joseph's being sold into slavery (6.18), Jacob's arrival in Egypt (6.19), and Jacob's blessings on his sons (6.20) provide typical examples.

Analysis of the structure of the Joseph story helps explain the function and design of various parts and features of the story. For example, it clarifies the function of Genesis 38, a unit generally considered a "stray boulder" in the story because it appears to completely interrupt the story line. The analysis offered here suggests that Genesis 38 plays at least three key roles in the artful architecture of the Joseph story by matching (1) the episode of Joseph and Potiphar's wife, (2) the episode of Joseph's imprisonment, and (3) Jacob's blessings. The matching of Genesis 38 and 39 is particularly striking. Both episodes appear to be arranged in a similar seven-part symmetric scheme. The story of Judah and Tamar centers on the seduction of Judah (6.21), while the story of Joseph and Potiphar's wife centers on the failed seduction by Potiphar's wife (6.22).

6.21 Judah and Tamar (Genesis 38)

a **Judah's children** by his first wife (38:1–5)
  b **Tamar's husbands killed** for their (sexual) wickedness (38:6–10)
    c **Judah's promise** to Tamar unfulfilled (38:11–12a)
      d **CENTER: Tamar seduces Judah**; he lays with her (38:12b–18)
    c′ **Judah's promise** of payment to Tamar unfulfilled(?) (38:19–23)
  b′ **Tamar to be killed** for her apparent sexual wickedness(?) (38:24–26)
a′ **Judah's children** by Tamar, his second "wife" (38:27–30)

6.22 Joseph and Potiphar's wife (Genesis 39)

a **Joseph prospers in bondage** (39:1–6a)
    • Yahweh is with him
    • master's trust
  b **Potiphar's wife tries to seduce Joseph** (39:6b–10)
      • his loyalty to Potiphar
    c **she falsely accuses Joseph** to servants (39:11–15)
      d **CENTER: fails to seduce him**, so she lays with his cloak (39:16)
    c′ **she falsely accuses Joseph** to her husband (39:17–18)
  b′ **Potiphar believes wife** (39:19–20)
    • Joseph's loyalty rewarded with imprisonment
a′ **Joseph prospers in prison** (39:21–23)
    • Yahweh is with him
    • prison master's trust

In both episodes a woman entices the main character to have intercourse with her, with exactly opposite results: Judah succumbs, Joseph admirably resists. In both stories the woman retains tokens of the man to produce later as condemning evidence. In both stories the innocent person (Tamar, Joseph) is falsely accused of sexual misconduct. At the center of the first story Judah lays with Tamar; at the center of the second, Potiphar's wife, failing to seduce Joseph to lie with her, lays with the only thing she could get from Joseph, his cloak. The irony of the matchup is highlighted in the conclusions of each story: Judah's sexual license results in an expanded family; while Joseph's righteousness results in undeserved imprisonment.

But of course this is not the end of the story. The symmetric layout of the entire Joseph story invites the audience to consider how the story turns out in the two matching units at the end. Genesis 39, the story of Joseph's integrity, is matched by the unit in 47:13–26, which relates how Joseph is exalted over all of Egypt, second only to pharaoh, and all Egyptians become his slaves (47:13–26). Genesis 38, the story of Judah's failure, is matched by the unit recounting Jacob's blessings, in which Joseph's two sons, not Judah's, receive the blessing of the firstborn. The message is clear: obedience to God's ways will be rewarded in the end, although for a time it may appear otherwise. In the end, God will right all wrongs (and therefore it pays to be faithful to him).

Other themes highlighted by the layout of the Joseph story include the following:

1. Yahweh's power to bless and protect his people, even in foreign lands
2. Yahweh's protection of the disadvantaged (Joseph, Tamar)
3. Yahweh's choice of the younger over the older (Joseph over his brothers)
4. Yahweh's pattern of having his people wait for a long time before helping them or granting their desires (Joseph, Tamar, Jacob)—foreshadowing Israel's sojourn in Egypt

The Exodus from Egypt (Exodus 1:1–13:16)

The next unit of the historical prologue to the Book of the Law is the story of the exodus from Egypt. The beginning of the new unit in Exodus 1 is signaled for the audience by several cues:

1. deaths in Genesis 50 of the two characters who have dominated the final half of the Book of Genesis—Jacob and Joseph
2. recapitulation of the members of Jacob's family (Exod. 1:1–5)
3. shift in time: to a period several hundred years after Jacob and Joseph (cf. 1:6–7)
4. shift in characters: from Jacob and Joseph to Moses
5. shift in topic: from the story of Joseph to the story of Yahweh's rescue of the Israelites from Egyptian slavery

6.23 Preparation for the exodus (Exodus 1:1–6:13)

a **oppression by pharaoh** who did not know Joseph (1:1–22)
- Israelites are subjected to <u>heavy work</u> (*siblôt*), <u>toil</u> (*ʿăbōdâ*), and making <u>bricks</u> (*lĕbēnîm*)
- <u>intensification of persecution</u>; harsh <u>commands</u> (*ṣiwwâ*) of pharaoh
- <u>taskmasters set</u> (*śîm*) over the Israelites
- pharaoh says, "Behold, the <u>people</u> (*ʿam*) are too <u>many</u> (*rab*)"

b **Moses comes to pharaoh's house** as baby (2:1–10)
- daughter of pharaoh <u>sends</u> (*šlḥ*) her maiden to take Moses from water

c **Moses departs from Egypt** (2:11–25)
- Moses <u>sees</u> (*rāʾâ*) a <u>kinsman</u> (*ʾāḥ*) being beaten
- he <u>kills</u> the Egyptian; pharaoh <u>hears</u> of it and <u>seeks</u> (*biqqēš*) to <u>kill</u> (*hārag*) Moses
- Moses is rejected by fellow Israelites
- flees to Midian <u>from Egypt</u>, marries <u>Zipporah</u>; <u>Gershom</u> born

d **TURNING POINT: call of Moses** (3:1–4:17)

c′ **Moses returns to Egypt** (4:18–31)
- Moses wants to return to <u>see</u> (*rāʾâ*) how his <u>kinsmen</u> (*ʾāḥ*) are doing
- <u>hears</u> that pharaoh who <u>seeks</u> (*biqqēš*) him is dead; God's message for pharaoh: "I will <u>kill</u> (*hārag*) your firstborn"; God <u>seeks</u> (*biqqēš*) to kill Moses on way
- Moses is accepted by fellow Israelite
- returns <u>to Egypt</u> from Midian with <u>Zipporah and Gershom</u>

b′ **Moses comes to pharaoh's house** as adult (5:1–4)
- demands that pharaoh <u>send</u> (*šlḥ*) Israelites into wilderness; pharaoh refuses to <u>send</u> (*šlḥ*) them

a′ **worse oppression by pharaoh** who did not know Joseph (5:5–6:13)
- Israelites are subjected to <u>heavier work</u> (*siblôt*), <u>toil</u> (*ʿăbōdâ*), and making <u>bricks</u> (*lĕbēnîm*)
- <u>intensification of persecution</u>; harsh <u>commands</u> (*ṣiwwâ*) of pharaoh
- <u>taskmasters set</u> (*śîm*) foremen over the Israelites
- pharaoh says, "Behold, the <u>people</u> (*ʿam*) are too <u>many</u> (*rab*)"

The exodus story extends from Exodus 1:1 to 13:16, its boundaries marked by the matching of its opening and closing units:

1. The story opens with a statement about the Israelites' arrival in Egypt (1:1–5) and closes with their departure (12:41, 51; 13:3–16).[27]
2. The story begins with a statement of the Israelites' population when they arrived in Egypt (70 persons; 1:5) and ends with a statement of their population when they left (600,000 men; 12:37–38).
3. The story opens with the Egyptians' attempt to kill all the male Israelite babies ("let they escape from the land"; 1:10) and concludes with Yahweh's killing all the firstborn sons of the Egyptians in order to enable the Israelites to escape from the land (12:1–13:16).
4. Joseph's request that the Israelites take his bones with them when they leave Egypt (Gen. 50:24–25) immediately precedes the introduction to the exodus story; the fulfillment of his request immediately follows the account of their departure (Exod. 13:19).

Analysis of the exodus story suggests that it, like the Joseph story, is composed of two symmetrically arranged sections, each section com-

prising seven units. The first section (6.23) sets the stage for the story by recounting the Egyptian oppression of Israel, the call of Moses, and pharaoh's refusal to let the Israelites leave. The section is framed by units featuring accounts of oppression, each involving the production of bricks. The section begins and ends with units highlighting Israel's dire circumstances; it closes with Israel worse off than ever, despite Yahweh's promise that he is going to deliver them. This structural design causes the audience to sense Israel's helplessness. The section goes full cycle, from oppression, to hope and promise, to even worse oppression. This layout serves to highlight the theme that God sometimes makes his people wait. Standing at the highlighted center of this symmetry is the episode of Moses' call at the burning bush and Yahweh's assurance of deliverance, structurally underscoring the point that it was Yahweh who initiated Israel's rescue from Egypt. Here, in the midst of Israel's hopelessness, Yahweh calls Moses and sets in motion Israel's freedom by commissioning Moses to lead Israel out of Egypt.

The second section of the exodus story recounts the actual deliverance (6.24). The battle lines have been drawn; pharaoh has stubbornly refused to let Israel go and has intensified their persecution. The audience can now more fully appreciate the awesome power by which Yah-

---

27. From 13:17 onward the Israelites have left Egypt and are in the "wilderness"; cf. 13:18; 14:3, 11–12.

6.24 Yahweh rescues his people from Egypt (Exodus 6:14–13:16)

a **Yahweh promises to rescue his people from Egypt**; the recommissioning of Moses and Aaron (6:14–7:7)
  - Yahweh will <u>bring them out</u> (*hôṣîʾ*) from Egypt by their hosts (*ʿal-ṣibʾōtām*); to <u>bring out</u> (*hôṣîʾ*) from Egypt his <u>hosts</u> (*ṣĕbāʾôt*), the Israelites
  - "Moses and Aaron did so; as Yahweh had commanded them, so they did"
  - chronological note: ages of Moses and Aaron

b **Yahweh's power to create life** (7:8–13)
  - initial <u>sign</u> (*môpēt*) to pharaoh: Aaron's rod becomes a snake

c **opening cycle of three plagues** (7:14–8:19 [7:14–8:15])
  - each introduced by Yahweh's instructing Moses/Aaron to stretch forth his hand with rod, followed by statement that Moses/Aaron does so, initiating plague

d **CENTRAL CYCLE of three plagues:** Yahweh begins plagues without hand and rod of Moses/Aaron (8:20–9:12 [8:16–9:12])

c′ **closing cycle of three plagues** (9:13–10:29)
  - each introduced by Yahweh's instructing Moses/Aaron to stretch forth his hand with rod, followed by statement that Moses/Aaron does so, initiating plague

b′ **Yahweh's power to terminate life** (11:1–10)
  - final <u>sign</u> (*môpēt*) declared: death of firstborn

a′ **Yahweh rescues his people from Egypt**; commemorative institutions (12:1–13:16)
  - Yahweh <u>brings them out</u> (*hôṣîʾ*) from Egypt by their hosts (*ʿal-ṣibʾōtām*); "the hosts (*ṣĕbāʾôt*) of Yahweh <u>went out</u> (*yāṣāʾ*) from the land of Egypt"
  - "the people did so; as Yahweh had commanded Moses and Aaron so they did"
  - chronological note: length of years of sojourn in Egypt

weh will rescue Israel. The opening of the new section is signaled by the genealogy of Moses and Aaron (6:14–27).

Various scholars recognize that the plagues form three cycles of three plagues each, plus the tenth plague, which stands alone.[28] Each cycle follows the same pattern:

1. The first plague in each cycle is introduced by Yahweh's instructions to Moses to go and "stand before" (*hityaṣṣēb* and *niṣṣab*) pharaoh "in the morning" (*babbōqer*; 7:14–15; 8:20 [8:16]; 9:13).
2. The second plague in each cycle is introduced simply by "Yahweh said to Moses, 'Go in to pharaoh' (*bōʾ ʾel-parʿōh*)" (8:1 [7:26]; 9:1; 10:1).
3. The third plague in each cycle has no instructions by Yahweh to go and warn pharaoh; rather, Moses is instructed to begin the plague by a symbolic action (8:16 [8:12]; 9:8; 10:21).

The three cycles are structured to form an overall symmetry. The first and last cycles match in that each plague in these two cycles is initiated by Yahweh's instructing Moses/Aaron to stretch forth his hand with the rod, followed by a statement that Moses/Aaron stretched forth his hand with the rod and the plague began. The three plagues in the central unit, however, are

initiated differently: in the first two, Yahweh simply has Moses warn pharaoh, then causes the plague to begin; and in the third he has Moses cast ashes into the air to initiate the plague.

A structural pause follows the ninth plague. The tenth plague is not recounted immediately after the ninth. Instead, tension is built through a lengthy introduction to the upcoming plague. This structuring strategy serves not only to heighten (and sustain) the suspense, but to highlight this final plague. This introduction offers an echo of the episode about Aaron's rod, which immediately preceded the plagues. The sign of Aaron's rod becoming a snake demonstrated Yahweh's power to create life. This final plague will demonstrate his power to destroy life. In both units, and nowhere else in the intervening narrative, the signs are called "wonders" (*môpēt*; 7:9; cf. 7:3; 11:9, 10).

This entire section is framed by matching introductory and concluding units. The opening unit features the genealogy of Moses and Aaron (heightening the anticipation that these two men are going to play a key role in the upcoming events). Yahweh recommissions them for the task of leading Israel from Egypt. They are to "bring out" (*hôṣîʾ*) the Israelites from Egypt "by their hosts" (*ʿal-ṣibʾōtām*). Yahweh promises, "I will lay my hand upon Egypt and bring forth (*hôṣîʾ*) my hosts (*ṣĕbāʾôt*) . . . from the land of Egypt by great acts of judgment"; and "Moses and Aaron did so; as Yahweh had commanded them, so they did" (7:6). This introduction is echoed in the concluding unit, which recounts

28. See, e.g., Umberto Cassuto, *A Commentary on the Book of Exodus* (Jerusalem: Magnes, 1967), 92–93.

6.25 Yahweh rescues his people from Egypt (Exodus 12:1–13:16)

a **instructions for preparing for plague on firstborn** (12:1–13)
  - lamb sacrificed (so Yahweh will not slay firstborn Israelites as he will firstborn Egyptians)
  b **memorial** of eating of unleavened bread (12:14–20)
  c **Passover meal instructions** (12:21–28)
  - Moses gives instructions to the people regarding the Passover meal (*pesaḥ*)
  - ends: "the Israelites did as Yahweh commanded Moses and Aaron; thus they did (*kēn ʿāśû*)"
    d **CENTER: the exodus and tenth plague** (12:29–42)
  c′ **additional Passover meal instructions** (12:43–50)
  - Yahweh gives further instructions regarding the Passover meal (*pesaḥ*)
  - ends: "all the Israelites did as Yahweh commanded Moses and Aaron; thus they did (*kēn ʿāśû*)"
  b′ **memorial** of eating of unleavened bread (13:3–10)
a′ **instructions for memorial of redeeming of firstborn** (13:11–16)*
  - redemption of firstborn by lamb to commemorate slaying of firstborn Egyptians and sparing of firstborn Israelites
  *Cf. 13:1–2, which may be misplaced in the present text.

---

the fulfillment of all that was promised in the introduction. The concluding unit then recounts the tenth plague and the exodus from Egypt and contains numerous correspondences with the introduction:

1. "The people of Israel did so; as Yahweh had commanded Moses and Aaron, so they did" (12:28; cf. 12:50).
2. "I brought out (*hôṣîʾ*) your hosts (*ṣĕbāʾōt*) from the land of Egypt" (12:17).
3. "The hosts (*ṣĕbāʾōt*) of Yahweh went out (*yāṣāʾ*) from the land of Egypt" (12:41).
4. "Yahweh brought out (*hôṣîʾ*) the Israelites from the land of Egypt by their hosts (*ʿal-ṣibʾōtām*)" (12:51).
5. The term *ṣĕbāʾōt* ("hosts"), which occurs in both of these units, occurs nowhere else in the Book of Exodus.

Incidentally, Exodus 12:1–13:16 is a surprisingly lengthy and composite section of material to function as a single unit. The greater length, however, is best explained as editorial highlighting: the unit represents the climactic conclusion of the entire story of the exodus. As often occurs in climaxes, the speed of action slows significantly to help convey the importance of the event. The coherence of 12:1–13:16 is reinforced by its symmetric arrangement (6.25). At the center of the symmetry stands the climactic event itself—the exodus and the tenth plague. The additional material of the unit forms concentric circles around this center, which accounts for what otherwise might appear to be careless organization and repetition.

In addition to the internal symmetries of the two sections of the exodus story, the entire story exhibits a conspicuous and revealing overall symmetry (6.26; the only units that do not conspicuously match are units c–e and c′–e′; but

even they exhibit subtle correspondences). The story opens with the Israelites arriving in Egypt few in number. They are enslaved by the Egyptians, and pharaoh tries to decimate their population by killing their male babies. In the story's conclusion all this is reversed: the Israelites depart from Egypt, now a very numerous people; they are freed from Egyptian slavery; and Yahweh decimates the Egyptian population by killing all firstborn males.

The overall symmetric structure highlights several themes. The matching of the first and last units underscores the magnitude of the reversal of Israel's fortunes (this emphasis is designed to engender Israel's gratitude to Yahweh). The matching of the second and next-to-last units underscores the theme of Yahweh's righting of wrongs. In the second unit baby Moses, an Israelite male child, is providentially spared from pharaoh's plot to kill all male Israelite children and grows up, ironically, in pharaoh's own palace. In the next-to-last unit this same Moses, now grown up, announces to pharaoh that Yahweh will kill pharaoh's own firstborn son and all firstborn sons in pharaoh's palace and Egypt (sparing only the Israelites). The double account of Yahweh's commissioning Moses and Aaron, and the positioning of this double commissioning at the story's center and turning point, emphasizes that it was by Yahweh's initiation and power that Israel was rescued from slavery.

The Wilderness Journey (Exodus 13:17–19:2)

This final unit of the historical introduction traces Israel's journey from Egypt to Mount Sinai. A single focus ties it together: Yahweh's guidance, care, and protection of the Israelites as they journey to Sinai. The unit's beginning is heralded by the completion of the symmetric presentation of the previous unit and by a shift

6.26 Symmetric arrangement of the entire exodus story (Exodus 1:1–13:16)

a **enslavement and attempted decimation of Israelites in Egypt** (1:1–22)
  - pharaoh's plot to kill Israelite male babies, etc., to control population
  - new king arose (*wayyāqom*)
  - small total number of Israelites who came down to Egypt: seventy people

  b **Moses, an Israelite male child, escapes death from pharaoh** (2:1–10)
    - Moses grows up (*gdl*) as a son in pharaoh's house

    c **Egyptian strikes (*nākâ*) an Israelite; Moses strikes down (*nākâ*) Egyptian** (2:11–22)

      d **call of Moses: standing on holy ground** (3:1–4:17)
        - distinction between holy and common: ground (*ʾădāmâ*) Moses stands on (*ʿāmad ʿal*) is holy
        - topics: sign (*ʾôt*) (3:12), Israel's three-day journey (3:18)

        e **Moses returns to Egypt** (4:18–31)
          - "bridegroom of blood"

          f **brief encounter with pharaoh** (5:1–5)
            - Moses and Aaron spurned

            g **CENTER: commissioning of Moses and Aaron** (5:6–6:13)
              - promise to deliver Israel from Egypt with mighty hand (*yād*) and mighty acts of judgment
              - people doubt Moses

            g′ **CENTER: commissioning of Moses and Aaron** (6:14–7:7)
              - promise to deliver Israel from Egypt by his hand (*yād*) and mighty acts of judgment
              - Moses' self-doubts

          f′ **brief encounter with pharaoh** (7:8–13)
            - Moses and Aaron spurned

        e′ **first cycle of plagues** (7:14–8:19 [7:14–8:15])
          - Nile turned to blood

      d′ **second cycle of plagues** (8:20–9:12 [8:16–9:12])
        - Yahweh distinguishes between his holy people and Egyptians; afflicts one, not other!
        - begins: Yahweh will distinguish between Egyptians and Israelites (cf. flies, plague on livestock), not afflicting land on which you stand (*ʿāmad ʿal*), only land (*ʾădāmâ*) of the Egyptians (8:21–23 [8:17–19])
        - topics: sign (*ʾôt*) (8:23 [8:19]), Israel's three-day journey

    c′ **third cycle of plagues: Egyptians are struck down!** (9:13–10:29)
      - begins: Yahweh warns that he has not yet struck (*nākâ*) Egyptians themselves, but now he will strike (*nākâ*) them (9:14–15); hail strikes down (*nākâ*) Egyptians, flocks, crops (9:25–33)

  b′ **Yahweh will kill Egypt's firstborn males** (11:1–10)
    - Moses, who has become great (*gdl*) in Egypt, announces that Yahweh will kill all firstborn Egyptian sons, including pharaoh's; only Israelite firstborn will escape being killed

a′ **freedom of Israelites from Egyptian slavery and increased population** (12:1–13:16)
  - Yahweh decimates Egyptian population by killing Egyptian firstborn males
  - pharaoh arises (*wayyāqom*) to mourn decimation of Egyptian people
  - large total number of Israelites leaving Egypt: 600,000 men

in setting. From Exodus 1:1 to the closing story in 13:16, Israel had been in Egypt, sedentary and enslaved. From 13:17 onward they are in the wilderness, a free people on the march, following Yahweh to Mount Sinai. The unit ends in 19:2, with Israel encamped before Sinai at the end of her journey.

Like Genesis 1–11, this final unit has seven constituent parts. Also as in Genesis 1–11, the last part of this unit introduces the topic that will become the theme of the new section that follows: the law (Jethro's advice includes a suggestion that Moses give the people statutes and laws, preparing the audience for what will follow; cf. Gen. 11:27–32, which introduces Abraham, preparing the audience for the story of Abraham that will follow).

The internal structure of the wilderness journey features some important symmetric touches

(6.27). Certainly the two episodes of God's providing water mirror one another; and the victory over the Amalekites as Moses raises his rod may echo the victory over the Egyptians, when Moses lifted his rod over the Sea. If the memorial songs in 15:1–21 are part of the crossing of the Suph (or "Red" or "Reed") Sea story, and if the reception and guidance of Jethro upon Israel's arrival at Sinai corresponds to the episode of Israel's departure from Egypt and Yahweh's guidance (which is not entirely certain), then the wilderness journey could be analyzed as a seven-part symmetry.

This symmetric configuration seems to highlight several key themes. First, the placement of stories involving Israel's complaining in matching positions, as well as at the center of the symmetry, underscores Israel's unworthiness. In these same three units, the recounting of divine

---

6.27 The wilderness journey (Exodus 13:17–19:2)

   a **introduction: departure from Egypt** (13:17–22)
     b **victory over the Egyptians** at the Suph Sea (14:1–15:21)
         • Moses lifts his hand
         • ends: two memorial songs
      c **Yahweh provides the Israelites with water** at Marah (15:22–27)
       d **CENTER: Yahweh provides manna and quail** (16:1–36)
      c′ **Yahweh provides the Israelites with water** at Rephidim (17:1–7)
     b′ **victory over the Amalekites** (by the water) at Rephidim (17:8–16)
         • Moses lifts his hands
         • ends: two memorials
   a′ **conclusion: arrival at Sinai** (18:1–19:2)

---

provisions—in the face of Israel's complaining and lack of faith—emphasizes Yahweh's grace and mercy toward this undeserving people. Finally, the inclusion of two matching stories that illustrate Yahweh's awesome power to achieve military victory for Israel (at the Suph Sea and against the Amalekites) serves to reinforce the truth that Israel's God is able to rescue the nation from mighty foreign enemies. The repetition is also undoubtedly designed to heighten Israel's gratitude to Yahweh.

Overall Layout of Genesis 1:1–Exodus 19:2

While the arrangement of the historical introduction to the Sinai treaty in Genesis 1:1–Exodus 19:2 is primarily linear, following a chronological order from creation to Mount Sinai, there are strong indications that the units are designed to form a secondary symmetric scheme.

Correspondence of the Primeval History (Genesis 1–11) and the Wilderness Journey (Exodus 13:17–19:2)

At first blush, the opening and closing units of the historical prologue seem to have little in common. Nevertheless there are some significant points of correspondence, especially between the Suph Sea story and the creation and flood stories. For example:

1. Both the Suph Sea miracle and the creation and flood stories demonstrate Yahweh's mighty power over the "sea" (*yām*).
2. The miracle at the Suph Sea begins with the "wind" (*rûaḥ*) of God blowing on the sea all night (Exod. 14:21). The creation story begins with the "wind"/"spirit" (*rûaḥ*) of God blowing(?) over the water of the sea in the darkness (Gen. 1:2).
3. In both the Suph Sea and flood stories, God dries the land for his people by a "wind"

(*rûaḥ*) that he causes to blow (Gen. 8:1 ‖ Exod. 14:21).
4. In the creation story, God divides the waters, so that the "atmosphere" (*rāqiaʿ*) is "between" (*bĕtôk*) the waters (Gen. 1:6–8). In the Suph Sea story, God divides the waters so that his people can walk "between" (*bĕtôk*) the waters (Exod. 14:22).
5. In all three stories, God creates "dry land" (*yabbāšâ*) in the midst of the sea (Gen. 1:9–10; 8:14; Exod. 14:16, 22).
6. In both the flood and Suph Sea stories, God uses the waters of the sea to destroy his enemies but spares his chosen people from the same destructive waters.

There are other possible thematic correspondences between the two units: God's feeding his people (in the garden, before and after the flood, in the wilderness), water (in the creation and flood stories, in the Suph Sea story, and in Exod. 15 and 17, where Yahweh provides water in the desert), the Sabbath (which occurs only in these two units of the historical prologue; Gen. 2:1–3; Exod. 16), and supernatural food (fruit of the tree of life in Gen. 2–3; manna from heaven in Exod. 16)—although this last correspondence is probably fortuitous.

Correspondence of the Story of Abraham (Genesis 12:1–21:7) and the Exodus (Exodus 1:1–13:16)

There are more obvious points of correspondence between the Abraham story and the exodus story. Most conspicuous is the connection created by Abraham's "exodus" from Egypt in Genesis 12:10–20, which echoes (and foreshadows) Israel's exodus in various ways. Note these points of similarity:

1. Abram, like Israel, migrates from Canaan to Egypt because of a famine (Gen. 12:10).

2. Abram's wife Sarai is taken and wrongfully retained by pharaoh, just as the Israelites would later be.

3. God brings great plagues upon pharaoh's house to secure Sarai's release (Gen. 12:17), as he later does to secure Israel's release.

4. In Abram's story, pharaoh's resolve is broken because of Yahweh's plagues upon him and his house, and he summons Abram in order to get relief from the plagues (Gen. 12:17–18). The same scenario is repeated with Moses and pharaoh.

5. The exasperated pharaoh gives orders to Abram: "Go (lĕk)!" (Gen. 12:19). Pharaoh similarly orders Moses: "Go (lĕkû)!" (Exod. 8:25 [8:21]; 10:8, 24).

6. Abram is enriched by the Egyptians, leaving Egypt with much newly acquired wealth (Gen. 12:16; 13:2). The Israelites are similarly enriched by the Egyptians as they leave Egypt (Exod. 12:35–36).

There are other correspondences that link the two units for the audience:

1. God promises Abram in Genesis 15:13–14: "Your descendants will be strangers in a country not their own, and they will be enslaved and mistreated four hundred years. But I will punish the nation they serve as slaves, and afterward they will come out with great possessions." This is all fulfilled, of course, in the exodus story, after the Israelites have lived in Egypt for 430 years (Exod. 12:40–41).

2. The story of Abram begins and is dominated by God's promise that he will make Abram's descendants numerous ("a great nation" [Gen. 12:1–2]; "like the dust of the earth" [13:16]; "like the stars" [15:5]). The exodus story begins and ends with units that draw attention to the fulfillment of that promise: "The Israelites were fruitful and multiplied greatly and became exceedingly numerous . . . and multiplied and spread . . . and increased and became even more numerous" (Exod. 1:7; cf. 1:12, 20); "and there were about 600,000 men on foot, besides the women and children" (Exod. 12:37).

3. Both stories (and no others in the historical prologue) feature the topic of circumcision (Gen. 17; Exod. 4:24–26).

4. Both stories feature God's punishing a wicked people (Egypt, Sodom and Gomorrah) by causing natural disasters to fall upon their land, while protecting his own people who live in that land (the Israelites; Lot and his family).

Correspondence of the Stories of Isaac (Genesis 21:8–28:4) and Joseph (Genesis 37:2–50:26)

It is more difficult to see any signs of deliberate linkage between the Isaac and Joseph stories. There are, however, some:

1. Both stories are dominated by strife between older and younger brothers. The Isaac story begins with strife involving Isaac and Ishmael; and it ends with strife between Jacob and Esau. The story of Joseph begins, ends, and features throughout, the strife between Joseph and his older brothers. In both stories, the tension between younger and older brothers always ends with the expulsion of one of the brothers. In each case the younger brother is chosen by God; yet in each case God also blesses the expelled brother.

2. Both stories feature episodes involving a father's deep love for his son (Abraham and Isaac, Isaac and Esau, Jacob and Joseph).

3. In both stories, the issue of birthright plays a prominent role. And in each, the birthright goes, unexpectedly, to the younger son (Jacob, Joseph, Perez, Manasseh).

4. In both stories, the patriarchal blessing is a key topic. And in each, the favorable blessing goes, unexpectedly, to the younger rather than the older son (Jacob and not Esau, Joseph and not Judah, Manasseh and not Ephraim).

5. In both stories, the rejected elder son marries Canaanite women (Esau in Gen. 26:34–35; 28:1, 6–8; Judah in 38:2).

6. Both stories feature prominently the burials in the cave of Machpelah in Hebron (Gen. 23; 50).

The Central Unit—the Jacob Story (Genesis 28:5–37:1)—and the Overall Layout of Genesis 1:1–Exodus 19:2

At the center of the historical introduction to the Sinai treaty in Genesis 1:1–Exodus 19:2 stands, significantly, the Jacob story, where the nation of Israel (with its twelve tribes) is born. Themes from other matchups find their counterparts in this central unit as well: servitude in foreign land under a hard taskmaster, strife between younger and older, reversal of fortunes, and God's protection of his chosen people. The entire historical prologue in its symmetric arrangement centers on the story of Jacob (6.28).

6.28 Book of the Law: Historical Prologue (Genesis 1:1–Exodus 19:2)

a **primeval history: Yahweh's power in creation and the flood** (Gen. 1–11)
- Yahweh's mighty power over the sea (*yām*) in creation and flood stories
- God uses wind (*rûaḥ*) over waters to begin creation and to dry the land from flood
- God creates dry land (*yabbāšâ*) in the midst of the sea, in creation, flood stories
- God drowns wicked and saves chosen from water in flood story
- God provides food for his people in the garden and during and after the flood
- creation of Sabbath (2:1–3): rest (*šabbāt*), holy (*qādôš*), seventh day (*yôm šebîʿî*)

b **Abraham: Yahweh promises numerous descendants and an exodus** (Gen. 12:1–21:7)
- Abraham in Egypt, because of famine; Sarah wrongfully retained by pharaoh
- God sends great plagues on pharaoh's house; pharaoh lets her go; leave enriched
- prediction of 400-year sojourn in foreign land, enslavement, punishment of that nation, and exodus "with great possessions" (15:13–14)
- promise that Abraham's descendants will be numerous (12:2; 13:16; 15:5)
- circumcision of Abraham and sons (17:1–27)
- God punishes Sodom and Gomorrah by natural disasters, sparing righteous

c **Isaac: strife between brothers; triumph of younger** (Gen. 21:8–28:4)
- strife between Ishmael/Isaac; Esau/Jacob; younger chosen by God
- strife ends with expulsions of Ishmael and Jacob
- younger son (Isaac, Jacob) gets blessing and birthright unexpectedly
- elder son (Esau) marries Canaanite women
- first use of cave of Machpelah: Abraham buys it, buries Sarah in it

d **CENTER: Jacob and birth of twelve tribes of Israel** (Gen. 28:5–37:1)

c′ **Joseph: strife between brothers; triumph of younger** (Gen. 37:2–50:26)
- strife between Joseph and older brothers; Joseph chosen by God
- strife ends with expulsion of young brother, Joseph
- younger son (Joseph) gets blessing, birthright, unexpectedly
- elder son (Judah) marries Canaanite woman
- final use of cave of Machpelah: Joseph buries Jacob in it

b′ **exodus: Yahweh increases Israel and delivers them from Egypt** (Exod. 1:1–13:16)
- Israel in Egypt, because of famine, is wrongfully retained by pharaoh
- God sends great plagues on Egypt; pharaoh lets them go; leave enriched
- 400-year sojourn; enslavement, punishment of Egypt; exodus, enrichment
- Israel becomes numerous: population grows from 70 people to 600,000 men!
- circumcision of Moses and son(?) (Exod. 4)
- God punishes Egypt by natural disasters, sparing his people

a′ **wilderness journey: Yahweh's power in the desert** (Exod. 13:17–19:2)
- Yahweh's demonstrates his mighty power over the sea (*yām*) in Suph Sea crossing
- God uses wind (*rûaḥ*) over waters to dry Suph Sea so Israel can cross
- God creates dry land (*yabbāšâ*) in the midst of the Suph Sea
- God drowns Egyptians and saves Israelites from water in Suph Sea story
- God provides food for his people in the wilderness
- first use of Sabbath (Exod. 16): rest (*šabbāt*), holy (*qādôš*), seventh day (*yôm šebîʿî*)

Conclusion

The foregoing analysis offers several insights regarding the form and message of Genesis 1:1–Exodus 19:2. The overall symmetric arrangement of the section reinforces the possibility that it was designed to function as a single unit—a grand, unified historical prologue. The chronological order of the material, moving period by period from creation to Sinai, helps convey the impression of a thoroughgoing, complete historical introduction to the treaty. The important points in Yahweh's past relations with Israel and its ancestors are presented here in a methodical, comprehensive format.

The choice of introducing the historical survey with a unit about Yahweh's relations with Israel's very distant ancestors—including the creation of the first human beings—reveals the author's blatantly anti-idolatrous agenda. This structuring design allows the author to quietly assert that Israel's God Yahweh is none other than the creator of heaven and earth, who orchestrated the flood, and who established all the nations and peoples of the earth. If Yahweh is indeed such a God, he is worthy of Israel's trust. He will be powerful enough to keep his part of the agreement, whether Israel is in Egypt, Sinai, Canaan, or anywhere else in his world.

A structuring pattern found throughout Genesis is the technique of first introducing the "big picture" (all creation, all humankind from Adam's two sons, all humankind from Noah's three sons, all of Shem's descendants, all of Abraham's sons, both of Isaac's sons, all of Jacob's sons) and then backtracking to pick up a single, divinely chosen strand: humans (not other creatures), Seth (not Cain), Shem (not his brothers), Abraham (not his brother), Isaac (not Abraham's other children), Jacob (not Esau), Joseph (not his brothers). This structuring technique helps convey the author's theme that, while Yahweh has dealt graciously with all creation and with all humanity, his pattern is to choose a particular line through whom he will work in a special way. This technique provides the historical precedent for what will happen at Sinai, when Yahweh enters into a unique, unparalleled treaty relationship with one particular nation among all the nations of the earth.

The placement of Jacob's story at the center of the historical prologue is logical enough, since it is here that Israel as a nation is born. On the other hand, this highlighted story is also the most embarrassing, marked by moral and ethical failure, deceit, cowardice, greed, murder, and deep family rifts. This is probably not coincidental, and it serves to reinforce another major theme found throughout the Book of the Law—that Yahweh has chosen Israel in spite of its unworthiness and weakness (Exod. 31–34; Deut. 4–11). Standing at the very center of the historical introduction—a center that could have been filled with a glowing account of Israel's ancestor Jacob and his courage and faithfulness—is the presentation of Jacob as a man of weaknesses and failures, who is graciously helped and protected by Yahweh despite his unworthiness. The implied message here is that it is Yahweh, not Israel's ancestors, who deserves Israel's admiration and gratitude as the hero of its history.[29]

The theme of Israel's unworthiness is further developed by the structural matching of the Isaac story, marked by the conniving and deceit of Israel's ancestor Jacob, with the Joseph story, featuring the deceit and treachery of Jacob's sons (ancestors of the Israelites). The repeated coverage of such behavior draws attention to the moral weakness of Israel's ancestors. The same theme is highlighted by the structure of the wilderness journey. It is undoubtedly significant that the story of Yahweh's gracious treaty with Israel is immediately preceded by a unit filled with Israel's complaining, murmuring, and unbelief. His selection of Israel was based on divine grace, not human merit.

The theme of the reversal of fortunes, particularly the exaltation of the weak and the humbling of the strong, is reinforced structurally throughout the historical introduction. This theme is effectively communicated by the pairing of the story of Abraham, featuring the elderly and childless couple Abram and Sarai, with the exodus story, in which the descendants of Abraham and Sarah become a great nation. This theme is highlighted by the layout of the Joseph story, which begins with Joseph weak and helpless in the hands of his powerful older brothers and concludes with the tables dramatically turned, as the brothers fearfully bow before Joseph, now the powerful ruler over Egypt. It is also underscored by the arrangement of the story of Jacob, in which Jacob begins as a poor fugitive and ends as the prosperous patriarch of a large clan, and by the structure of the exodus story, which opens with the people of Israel sojourning in Egypt, vulnerable, seventy in number, and reduced to cruel slavery, and ends with Israel leaving the devastated land of Egypt a freed and powerful nation numbering in the millions.

The interplay of Israel's weakness and Yahweh's strength is a theme developed structurally throughout the prologue. In the Abraham story, Abraham is frequently portrayed as vulnerable and weak. He lies about his wife twice (in matching units, to reinforce the point). He is unable to protect himself or his wife in Egypt, or even in the small town of Gerar. In the exodus account, which matches Abraham's story, the helplessness of the Israelites in Egypt is emphasized throughout, as the people are reduced to ever-worsening conditions of servitude. In both stories, Yahweh's mighty power contrasts the conspicuous weakness of those he rescues. The repetition of this theme in matching units serves to underscore the point that it is not by Israel's strength but by Yahweh's power that Israel is a freed people. He is the one who has repeatedly protected and rescued them; and the same power he demonstrated in Egypt against mighty pharaoh will continue to be available to his people when they find themselves in other vulnerable circumstances. All this is designed to accomplish the key purpose of the historical prologue: to engender a sense of gratitude, respect, and trust on the part of vassal Israel toward their new suzerain, Yahweh.

---

29. This recalls the gracious selection of Duppi-Teshub, a "weak and ailing" vassal, by the great King Murshilis (see discussion at the beginning of this chapter).

7

Book of the Law: Treaty at Sinai

Exodus 19:3–Numbers 10:10

The account of the treaty between God and Israel at Mount Sinai is one of the most intriguing stories in the Bible. It forms the second major unit of the Book of the Law. The author took sixty-eight chapters to prepare the audience for this treaty. He now takes nearly as much space—about fifty-nine chapters—to present the agreement.

The new unit extends from Exodus 19:3, when Israel arrives at Mount Sinai, to Numbers 10:10, when the nation departs. The unit is tied together by many factors, including (1) its single topic: the Sinai treaty, (2) its genre: primarily legal and procedural regulations, and (3) the singularity of its time and place: the events of the unit take place at one place, Mount Sinai, during one year.

The structure of this unit is well planned. The stipulations of the treaty are grouped according to topic. Most of these groups are framed by narrative interludes, generally episodes involving displays of Yahweh's glory ("theophanies") or stories of Israel's disobedience. The entire unit comprises seven larger units (7.1).

The narrative episodes not only mark the beginnings and ends of units; they also break up what otherwise would be an exceedingly long, tedious, and uninterrupted compilation of laws, giving the audience periodic relief from potential boredom.

Ten Commandments (Exodus 19:3–20:21)

The first unit of the Sinai treaty records the giving of the Ten Commandments. The unit is framed by two narratives about Yahweh's awesome presence on Mount Sinai and the importance of the people respecting his holiness by keeping at a safe distance.

The first of these narratives (19:3–25) emphasizes Yahweh's awesome "holiness" (*qōdeš*). Yahweh offers to make Israel his "holy" (*qādôš*) nation. He invites them to come before his "holy" (*qādôš*) mountain. They must prepare themselves by taking three days to "be made holy" (*qādaš*)—ceremonially fit to approach his holy presence. Only then may they approach the mountain (19:7–20); and only the priests may actually approach Yahweh—after they are "made holy" (*qādaš*; 19:21–25). The narrative is arranged in a seven-part scheme (7.2), each paragraph introduced by Moses' movements.

The narrative serves to establish that the God with whom Israel is dealing is an awe-inspiring being whose terrifying presence commands complete respect. He is all powerful, he is dangerous, and he is not to be trifled with. The narrative lends a sense of gravity to the opening group of stipulations. The Ten Commandments serve as the treaty's overarching stipulations (overarching laws generally preceded the more detailed stipulations in ancient secular treaties). They appear to be arranged in a 3+7 (or 4+6) scheme (7.3).[1]

The arrangement of these laws into two sections—responsibilities to Yahweh and responsibilities to one another—introduces a central theme of the treaty: the people of Israel are to love and obey Yahweh, and they are to love one another. The treaty requirements will be bidirectional.

Civil Laws (Exodus 20:22–24:11)

The second literary unit in the Sinai treaty presents the treaty's civil laws.[2] The new unit is framed by narrative material. The unit begins in 20:22 with a narrative (or reported instructions) dealing with the altar to be built for the upcom-

---

1. The Sabbath commandment involves responsibilities to both Yahweh (honoring his "day," in memory of his creation) and others (being kind to one's family members, servants, aliens, and animals). If the Sabbath is understood primarily as a duty to God, the Ten Commandments would then take on a 4+6 scheme.

2. Little work has been done on the structure of this section of Exodus; see Nahum Sarna, *Exodus* (JPS Torah Commentary; Philadelphia: Jewish Publication Society, 1990), 117–18; J. Durham, *Exodus* (Word Biblical Commentary 3; Waco: Word, 1987), xxx.

7.1 Seven major units of the treaty at Sinai (Exodus 19:3–Numbers 10:10)

a **Ten Commandments** (Exod. 19:3–20:21)
  (1) narrative introduction: theophany on Sinai; people to keep distance (19:3–25)
    (2) <u>laws</u> (20:1–17)
  (1´) narrative conclusion: theophany on Sinai; people keep distance (20:18–21)
b **judicial laws** (Exod. 20:22–24:11)
  (1) narrative introduction: God has no form; altar for treaty ceremony (20:22–26)
    (2) <u>laws</u> (21:1–23:33)
  (1´) narrative conclusion: treaty ceremony, with altar; leaders "see" God (24:1–11)
c **instructions for building tabernacle and dedicating priests** (Exod. 24:12–34:28)
  (1) narrative introduction: Moses ascends Mount Sinai to receive tablets of stone; tells others to wait; Aaron put in charge; Moses stays forty days (24:12–18)
    (2) <u>laws</u> (25:1–31:17)
  (1´) narrative conclusion: Moses receives stone tablets; but while he is on Mount Sinai forty days, Aaron and people sin with golden calf (31:18–34:28)
d **building the tabernacle** (Exod. 34:29–40:38)
  (1) narrative introduction: Moses' face shines from God's glory (34:29–35)
    (2) <u>laws followed</u>, detail by detail: tabernacle constructed (35:1–40:33)
  (1´) narrative conclusion: theophany at tabernacle; God's glory so intense that even Moses cannot enter tabernacle (40:34–38)
e **sacrificial laws and dedication of the priests** (Lev. 1–10)
  (1) "narrative" introduction: Yahweh summons Moses at tabernacle (1:1)
    (2) <u>laws for sacrifices</u>; priests dedicated (1:2–9:24)
  (1´) narrative conclusion: sin of Nadab and Abihu at tabernacle (foreshadows need for next two sections) (10:1–20)
f **purity laws** (Lev. 11–18)
g **holiness laws** (Lev. 19:1–Num. 9:14)
  • narrative conclusion: theophany and marching orders (Num. 9:15–10:10)

7.2 Yahweh's holiness (Exodus 19:3–25)

a **Yahweh offers Israel a treaty relationship** (19:3–6)
  • begins: "Moses <u>went up</u>"
b **Israel accepts Yahweh's offer** (19:7–8a)
  • begins: "Moses <u>went back [down]</u>"
c **Yahweh invites people to come before him**, after "consecrating" themselves (19:8b–13)
  • begins: "Moses <u>brought back [up]</u> their answer to Yahweh"
d **Moses instructs the people to "consecrate" themselves** for the meeting (19:14–15)
  • begins: "Moses <u>went down</u>"
e **Yahweh's glory descends on Mount Sinai**; consecrated people approach; Yahweh speaks to Moses in the hearing of the people and invites him alone to come up (19:16–20b)
  • begins: "Moses <u>led the people out</u> to meet God"
f **Yahweh instructs Moses to warn the people** to keep at a distance; and to have only the priests approach him on the mountain (19:20c–24)
  • begins: "Moses <u>went up</u>"
g **Moses goes down and speaks to the people** (19:25)
  • begins: "Moses <u>went down</u>"

ing treaty ceremony, with a reminder that they are to have no idols, in light of what they "saw" (*rāʾâ*) when God spoke to them from "heaven" (*haššāmayim*) (20:22–26). This episode is matched by the narrative account of the treaty ceremony at the conclusion of the unit, where the altar plays a key role (24:4–6) and in which the leaders "see" (*rāʾâ*) God, under whose feet is something that looks "like . . . sapphire, clear as heaven (*haššāmayim*)" (24:10, 11).

The intervening collection of civil laws (7.4) comprises two sections: (1) a section of so-called case laws (or casuistic laws), which are introduced by "if" (*kî* or *ʾim*; 21:2–22:27 [21:2–22:26]), and (2) a section of imperatival (or apodictic)

laws, that is, stipulations expressed as commands (e.g., "you are not to . . ."—as in the Ten Commandments; 22:28–23:19 [22:27–23:19]). Each section has its own symmetric arrangement: the first is, like the Ten Commandments, composed of ten parts; the second has seven.

The structures of these two sections reveal some surprising emphases. In even-numbered symmetries such as that of the first section, the outer units tend to carry the emphasis, and this appears to be true here. The legal cases at the center (involving loss of property, etc.) are less serious, and the cases become progressively more serious (such as capital offenses) as one works outward. Accordingly, the laws with

7.3 The Ten Commandments (Exodus 20:3–17)

a **responsibilities to Yahweh**

    (1) they are to have him as their only God (20:3)

    (2) they are not to make idols (representing God) (20:4–6)

    (3) they are not to misuse God's name (20:7)

b **responsibilities to each other**

    (4) they are to rest on the Sabbath day and allow others to rest (20:8–11)

    (5) they are to honor their parents (20:12)

    (6) they are not to murder (20:13)

    (7) they are not to commit adultery (20:14)

    (8) they are not to steal (20:15)

    (9) they are not to give false testimony (20:16)

    (10) they are not to covet what belongs to others (20:17)

7.4 Civil laws (Exodus 21:2–23:19)

section 1: case ("casuistic") laws (21:2–22:27 [21:2–22:26])

a   **kindness to servants** (21:2–11)

  b   **capital offenses:** <u>surely he will die</u> (*môt yûmāt*) (21:12–17)

    c   **noncapital bodily assaults** (21:18–27)

      d   **death or injury** of person by animal (21:28–32)

        e   **loss of property** due to accident (21:33–36)

        e′   **loss of property** due to theft (22:1–9 [21:37–22:8])

      d′   **death, injury,** or loss of animal by person (22:10–15 [22:9–14])

    c′   **noncapital bodily offense:** seduction of virgin (22:16–17 [22:15–16])

  b′   **capital offenses:** <u>surely he will die</u> (*môt yûmāt*) (22:18–20 [22:17–19])

a′   **kindness to aliens, widows, orphans, poor** (22:21–27 [22:20–26])

section 2: imperatival ("apodictic") laws (22:28–23:19 [22:27–23:19])

a   **responsibilities to God** (22:28–30 [22:27–29])

    • <u>tribute</u> from crops, herds

    • <u>no other gods</u>

  b   **do not eat meat torn by wild animals** (22:31 [22:30])

      • <u>give it to dogs</u> (do not scrounge for food—God will provide for you, his holy people)

    c   **justice,** especially for poor (23:1–3)

      • <u>in his case</u> (*běrîbô*)

      d   **CENTER: kindness to personal enemies** (23:4–5)

    c′   **justice,** especially for poor (23:6–9)

      • <u>in his case</u> (*běrîbô*)

  b′   **do not eat sabbatical year produce** (23:10–12)

      • <u>leave it for wild animals</u>; Sabbath rest (do not be tightfisted; God will provide for you)

a′   **responsibilities to God** (23:13–19)

    • <u>tribute</u> from crops, herds

    • <u>no other gods</u>

greatest structural emphasis are those at the beginning and end—the laws about kindness to the disadvantaged and poor. This suggests that the treaty considers kindness to the poor and disadvantaged as an even more important issue than the capital offenses (which are treated in the second and next-to-last positions). This remarkable emphasis on kindness to the poor will be reiterated throughout the treaty.

In an odd-numbered chiasmus such as that in the second section, the highlighted position is either the center or, less often, the beginning and end. In this section the lengthy first and last units, which deal with Israel's responsibilities to God, seem to have the greatest prominence. But the central unit also carries a natural emphasis,

suggesting that kindness to personal enemies is viewed here as a key requirement. The repetition of the call to kindness to the poor in the matching units c and c′ serves to reinforce this theme.

Instructions for Building the Tabernacle and Dressing and Dedicating the Priests (Exodus 24:12–34:28)

The third section of the Sinai treaty shifts to the topic of Yahweh's temple and his priests.[3] If Yahweh is to be their "god," he will require a "sanc-

---

3. The surface structure of this material has been given little attention; see Durham, *Exodus*, 350–53; Umberto Cassuto, *A Commentary on the Book of Exodus* (Jerusalem: Magnes, 1967), 319–451.

7.5 Tabernacle instructions (Exodus 24:12–34:28)

a **narrative introduction** (24:12–18)
- Moses goes up to receive stone tablets
- accompanied by Joshua, Moses tells others to wait
- Aaron in charge
- Moses stays forty days

b **instructions for building tabernacle, I** (25:1–27:19)
- no accompanying instructions for using items
- items in order from most holy to least holy:
  (1) materials (25:1–9)
  (2) ark (25:10–22)
  (3) table (25:23–30)
  (4) lampstand (25:31–40)
  (5) tabernacle (26:1–37)
  (6) bronze altar (27:1–8)
  (7) courtyard (27:9–19)

c **regular (tāmîd) maintenance of lamps** (27:20–21)
- before Yahweh
- from evening to morning

d **CENTER: priestly garments and dedication** (28:1–29:37)

c′ **regular (tāmîd) maintenance of daily sacrifices** (29:38–46; conclusion: 29:44–46)
- before Yahweh
- evening and morning

b′ **additional instructions for building and maintaining tabernacle** (30:1–31:17)
- instructions involve warnings
- regulations for priests and people:
  (1) altar of incense (30:1–10)
  (2) atonement money (30:11–16)
  (3) wash basin (30:17–21)
  (4) anointing oil (30:22–33)
  (5) incense for incense altar (30:34–38)
  (6) supervision by Bezalel and Oholiab (31:1–11)
  (7) no work on Sabbath (31:12–17)

a′ **narrative conclusion** (31:18–34:28)
- Moses receives stone tablets
- while he stays forty days on mountain with Joshua, people tire of waiting
- Aaron, whom Moses left in charge, leads Israel in sin with the golden calf

---

tuary," so that he "may dwell among them" (Exod. 25:8); and he will also require priests to serve him there.

The section is arranged in a seven-part symmetry (7.5), with the center (d) treating the consecration of Yahweh's chosen priests, Aaron and his sons. The section is framed by matching episodes (a and a′) that focus, ironically, on Israel's sin with the golden calf idol, led by none other than Aaron himself, the future priest. The symmetric scheme may help explain why the instructions about the tabernacle are presented in two separate segments. Segment b records instructions for making the various parts of the tabernacle, with no accompanying explanations about the function of these parts. This segment is made up of seven smaller units, arranged in the order from most holy (the ark) to least holy (the courtyard). Matching segment b′ deals with aspects of the tabernacle and its service that call for comment (or cautions) for priests or people. This part is also probably made up of seven units (if 30:22–33 comprises one unit), apparently arranged in a simple linear scheme.

The structural design of this third section of the treaty may offer several new insights. Perhaps the most important is the intentionality of the anti-idolatrous theme here. In Israel's idolatrous world, the design and construction of a temple would be the responsibility of knowledgeable priests, who would not only oversee the temple's construction, but would also make, dress, and consecrate the idol in a special ceremony. In the present unit this expectation is turned on its head. It is Israel's God, not its priests, who oversees the design and construction of his temple. And at the very center of the unit (d), in precisely the place where the audience might expect a structurally highlighted description of the making, dressing, and consecrating of the god, we find precisely the opposite: Yahweh's own instructions regarding how he wants his priests to be chosen, dressed, and con-

7.6 Aaron's sin and Moses's intervention (Exodus 31:18–34:28)

  a **Moses receives two stone tablets** inscribed by God (31:18)
  b   **Aaron's foolish idolatry** (32:1–10)
       • Yahweh's determination to destroy Israel
       • Aaron <u>sees</u> (*rāʾâ*) the idol he fashions; Yahweh <u>sees</u> (*rāʾâ*) their sin
    c   **Moses intercedes:** do not destroy Israel! God agrees (32:11–15)
      d   **CENTER: Moses deals with the sin;** <u>two stone tablets</u> are broken; God refuses to
           go to Canaan with them; <u>people repent</u> (32:16–33:6)
    c′   **Moses intercedes:** do not abandon Israel! God agrees (33:7–17)
  b′   **the majestic and living God** (33:18–34:26)
       • Yahweh's renewed covenant with Israel: warning—no idolatry!
       • Moses <u>sees</u> (*rāʾâ*) Yahweh's presence and awesome glory
  a′ **Moses receives two new stone tablets** inscribed by God (34:27–28)

secrated! The divine instructions for the priestly garments and consecration are full of irony; they are parodies (or at least echoes) of how priests would normally dress and consecrate an idol.[4]

This theme is underscored by the unit's narrative frame. This narrative, enclosing Yahweh's instructions for his temple and priests, recounts the story of Israel's idolatrous debauchery, led by Aaron himself. The implication is clear: Israel's system of temple worship was not the invention of Israel's priests. To the contrary, as the framing story illustrates, Israel and its priests were involved in foolish idolatry at the very time Yahweh was giving instructions for Israel's dignified, monotheistic system of worship. Israel's system of worship was given to Israel by Yahweh in spite of the unworthiness of his idolatry-bent people and their priest.

The final narrative conclusion of this unit is arranged in a seven-part symmetry (7.6) that highlights the contrast between Aaron's foolish idolatry (b) and Moses' dignified and marvelous worship of Yahweh, the living God (b′). It also underscores, through balanced repetition, the theme of Yahweh's grace and mercy to his disobedient people.

Yahweh agrees to tabernacle among his people Israel, not because of their special wisdom and righteousness, but in spite of their foolishness and "stubbornness of heart." He is a gracious God, who chooses to live among this sinful people because they have asked for, and received, his forgiveness.

Building of the Tabernacle (Exodus 34:29–40:38)

The fourth section of the Sinai treaty is a narrative account of the actual construction of the tabernacle and the making of the priestly gar-ments. The unit is framed by two narrative segments whose correspondence is instructive. The introductory narrative (a) tells how Moses' face would shine after being in God's presence on Mount Sinai, so much so that the people were unable to approach Moses unless he veiled himself. The concluding narrative (a′), which follows the account of the building of the tabernacle, tells how the completed tabernacle was filled with God's glory, a glory so brilliant that even Moses could not approach it. God's presence had moved from the mountain to the tabernacle and was more awesome and glorious than ever!

The intervening accounts of the construction of the tabernacle and the making of the priestly garments are arranged in a symmetric scheme, with the climax in this case at the end. The result is an overall seven-part symmetry (7.7).

Sacrificial Regulations (Leviticus 1–10)

The fifth section of the treaty deals with Israel's sacrificial system (7.8).[5] The unit opens with a one-verse introduction, in which Yahweh summons Moses and speaks to him from the tabernacle—his new abode. This is followed by a collection of regulations for Israel's sacrifices (a). The collection is arranged in a ten-part scheme (like the Ten Commandments and civic laws), in which the five types of sacrifices are treated two times, once as they pertain to the people (unit a-(1)) and a second time as they pertain to the priests (unit a-(2)).[6] In the second series, the five types of sacrifices are arranged from most

---

4. This point is further emphasized by the conspicuous absence of an idol in the throne room (i.e., the Holy of Holies), which has the expected footstool for the seated deity (i.e., the ark), with cherubim flanking its throne (as cherubim often did in the ancient world)—but no throne, and no idol!

5. For a brief discussion of the surface structure of Leviticus, see J. E. Hartley, *Leviticus* (Word Biblical Commentary 4; Dallas: Word, 1992), xxx–xxxv. See also scattered discussions throughout J. Milgrom, *Leviticus 1–16: A New Translation with Introduction and Commentary* (Anchor Bible 3; New York: Doubleday, 1991). Using a thematically based structural analysis, Erhard S. Gerstenberger, *Leviticus*, trans. D. W. Stott (Old Testament Library; Louisville: Westminster/ John Knox, 1996), 17–19, identifies eight units in the Book of Leviticus.

6. See, e.g., Hartley, *Leviticus*, 3–5.

7.7 Building the tabernacle (Exodus 34:29–40:38)

a **introduction:** Moses' face shines from <u>God's glory</u> on Mount Sinai (34:29–35)
  - glory so intense, people cannot approach Moses unless he veils himself

b **opening convocation** (35:1–36:7)
  - Moses assembles people and instructs them about properly making tabernacle and priestly garments
  - <u>people bring to Moses all the materials</u> for tabernacle and priests' garments

c **people carry out work** (36:8–38:20)
  - seven parts of the tabernacle, arranged from most holy to least holy:
    (1) tabernacle (36:8–38)
    (2) ark (37:1–9)
    (3) table (37:10–16)
    (4) lampstand (37:17–24)
    (5) altar of incense (37:25–29)
    (6) bronze altar and basin (38:1–8)
    (7) courtyard (38:9–20)

d **CENTER: materials used for making tabernacle and priestly garments** (38:21–31)

c′ **people carry out work** (39:1–31)
  - priestly garments, arranged in seven(?) parts, perhaps moving from most holy to least holy:
    (1) ephod (39:2–7)
    (2) breastpiece (39:8–14)
    (3) gold chains and rings (39:15–21)
    (4) robe (39:22–26)
    (5) tunic (39:27)
    (6) undergarments, etc., of linen (39:28–29)
    (7) diadem for turban (39:30–31)

b′ **closing convocation** (39:32–40:33)
  - <u>people bring to Moses all the completed work</u>
  - Moses inspects and approves their work, and he sets up the tabernacle and dresses Aaron in priestly garments

a′ **CLIMAX: tabernacle filled with <u>God's glory</u>** (40:34–38)
  - glory so intense, even Moses cannot approach it (supersedes glory on Sinai)

7.8 Sacrificial regulations (Leviticus 1–10)

introduction: Yahweh speaks to Moses from the tabernacle (1:1)

a **sacrificial regulations** (1:2–7:38)
  (1) **instructions for the people** (1:2–6:7 [1:2–5:26])
    - begins: <u>speak to the Israelites and say to them</u>
    (a) whole burnt offering (1:2–17)
    (b) grain offering (2:1–16)
    (c) peace offering (3:1–17)
    (d) sin offering (4:1–5:13)
    (e) guilt offering (5:14–6:7 [5:14–26])
  (2) **instructions for the priests** (6:8–7:36 [6:1–7:36])
    - begins: <u>give Aaron and his sons these instructions</u>
    (f) whole burnt offering (6:8–13 [6:1–6])
    (g) grain offering (6:14–23 [6:7–16])
    (h) sin offering (6:24–30 [6:17–23])
    (i) guilt offering (7:1–10)
    (j) peace offering (7:11–36)
  (3) **climactic conclusion to sacrificial instructions** (7:37–38)

b **dedication of priests for sacrifices and tabernacle work** (8:1–9:24)
  (1) assembly and priests' consecration ceremony (8:1–36)
  (2) priests begin their ministries by supervising the sacrifices (9:1–22)
  (3) Yahweh's approval: his fire consumes the sacrifices (9:23–24)

c **concluding narrative:** sin and death of two priests: Nadab and Abihu (10:1–20)

---

holy (whole burnt offering) to least holy (fellowship)—a natural order for priestly instructions. In the first series, however, which is addressed to the people, the peace offering, the most common type of sacrifice for the people, stands at the center.

The collection of sacrificial regulations is followed by an account of the consecration of the priests, who must be properly ordained in a special ceremony before the Israelites can begin bringing their regular sacrifices (b). The climax of this account comes at the close of the ordina-

7.9 Purity regulations (Leviticus 11–18)

a **main collection of ritual purity laws** (11:1–16:34)
  (1) ritual impurity from eating or touching the carcasses of animals classified as repulsive (*šeqeṣ*) to eat (11:1–47)
  (2) ritual impurity from (repulsive) childbirth discharges (12:1–8)
  (3) ritual impurity from (repulsive) "leprosy" on skin and fabrics (13:1–59)
  (4) rectification of ritual impurity from (repulsive) "leprosy" on skin (14:1–32)
  (5) ritual impurity from (repulsive) "leprosy" on walls of house (14:33–57)
  (6) ritual impurity from (repulsive) bodily discharges (15:1–33)
  (7) Day of Atonement, when all ritual impurity is rectified (16:1–34)

b **additional—and more serious—purity laws** (17:1–18:30)
  (1) offensive behavior in eating sacrifices (17:1–16)
  (2) offensive moral behavior that defiles (*ṭāmēʾ*), including incest, adultery, child sacrifice, homosexual behavior, bestiality, and any other "detestable practices" that have "defiled" the Canaanites—because of which "the land is vomiting them out"; and if Israel does these same things, the land will likewise "vomit them out" (18:1–30)

tion ceremony, when fire blazes forth from Yahweh's presence to consume the priests' offerings, indicating Yahweh's approval of their ordination and their right to offer sacrifices. Israel's joyful sacrifices may now begin.

The unit closes, however, on a negative note, with the story of the sin and punishment of Aaron's two priestly sons, Nadab and Abihu (c). The placement of this embarrassing story here, directly after the story of the ordination of the priests, is probably not coincidental. The story stands as a warning and as a reminder that Israel's system of worship was designed and instituted by Yahweh, not Israel's priests. Yahweh is in charge; and the priests must follow his instructions. (It will be recalled that the other negative story about priests in this treaty—Aaron's sin with the golden calf in Exod. 32–33—closed the unit that provided Yahweh's instructions for the priests' ordination ceremony.)

Purity Regulations (Leviticus 11–18)

The sixth section (7.9) of the Sinai treaty presents regulations for the maintenance of ritual purity at the tabernacle, so that the holiness of Yahweh's sanctuary may be respected and not violated (as it was in the preceding story of Nadab and Abihu in Lev. 10:10). The keywords of this section that unite the material are "impure" (*ṭāmēʾ*) and "pure" (*ṭāhôr*). In order to respect the sanctity of Yahweh's tabernacle (cf. 15:31), the Israelites are to be "pure" when they come to participate in tabernacle services.

The main collection of regulations for ritual purity (a) comprises a series of seven units, organized by topic. Each unit is introduced by "Yahweh said to Moses" (11:1; 12:1; 13:1; 14:1, 33; 15:1; 16:1) and concludes with a summary statement that begins "this is the law concerning (*zōʾt tôrat*) . . ." (11:46–47; 12:7; 13:59; 14:32;

14:54–56; 15:32) or "this (*zōʾt*) will be for you a lasting ordinance" (16:34). The series culminates with a unit about the Day of Atonement, when all violations of ritual purity from the previous year are forgiven.

Following this main collection is a second section made up of two additional collections of laws dealing with other acts that cause impurity (b). That these two chapters are part of the purity regulations (and not the holiness laws that follow, as commonly supposed) is suggested from the continued occurrence of the term "impure" (*ṭāmēʾ*) through chapter 18 (cf. 17:15; 18:19, 20, 23, 24, 25, 27, 28, 30).

The first additional collection (unit b-(1)) deals with improper behavior in eating sacrifices, including eating sacrifices in places other than the tabernacle, eating blood or fat, or eating anything found dead or torn by wild animals, by which the people will become ritually "impure" (*ṭāmēʾ*). The second collection (unit b-(2)) deals with morally offensive behavior that will make the people and their land "impure" (*ṭāmēʾ*), such as incest, adultery, child sacrifice, and bestiality—all affronts to the sanctity of Yahweh's presence.

The concluding position of Leviticus 17–18 carries structural emphasis. Here a significant bridge is made between ritual and moral impurity. In Leviticus 11–16 Israel is taught that they must not violate the sanctity of Yahweh's tabernacle by coming to it in a state of ritual impurity. The ritual sanctity and holiness of Yahweh's presence requires ritual purity, as dictated by Yahweh; and ritual impurity (though morally innocuous) results in being barred from ritual tabernacle services. In Leviticus 17–18, particularly chapter 18, Israel is taught that, analogous to ritual impurity, there is moral impurity. There are morally offensive practices (incest, child sacrifice, etc.) that defile those who do them.

7.10 First section of laws pertaining to holiness (Lev. 19:1–26:46)

a **moral holiness of people in everyday life** (Lev. 19)
- Sabbath theme: <u>observe my Sabbaths and respect my sanctuary</u> (19:30)
- prohibition against making <u>idols</u> (19:4)
- kindness to <u>slaves, aliens, poor, disadvantaged</u> (19:10–15, 20–22, 32–34)
- theme of <u>crops</u>: planting, reaping, and leaving for the poor (19:9–10, 19, 23–25)

b **serious violations of moral holiness** requiring <u>death</u> (*môt yûmāt*) (Lev. 20)
- cursing parents, adultery, incest, etc.
- <u>any Israelite or alien</u>

c **priestly holiness** (Lev. 21–22)
- <u>eating</u> of holy sacrifices

d **CENTER: seven holy times in calendar**—all involving priestly sacrifices at tabernacle (Lev. 23): Sabbath, Passover, Firstfruits, Weeks, Trumpets, Day of Atonement, Tabernacles

c′ **priests' tending of lamps** (Lev. 24:1–9)
- <u>eating</u> holy bread from table

b′ **serious violations of moral holiness** requiring <u>death</u> (*môt yûmāt*) (Lev. 24:10–23)
- blasphemy, murder
- <u>same law for the alien and native</u>

a′ **moral holiness in people's everyday lives** and during the sabbatical year and year of Jubilee (Lev. 25:1–26:2)
- Sabbath theme: <u>observe my Sabbaths and respect my sanctuary</u> (26:2)
- prohibition against making <u>idols</u> (26:1)
- kindness to <u>slaves, aliens, poor, disadvantaged</u> (25:6–55)
- theme of <u>crops</u>: planting, reaping, and leaving for the poor (25:3–22)

interlude: covenantal blessings and curses (Lev. 26:3–46)

Like ritual impurity, moral impurity is offensive and spoils fellowship with God. But moral defilement is profoundly offensive to God, and the resulting spoiled fellowship is far more serious. Unlike ritual impurity, the Israelites are to avoid moral impurity at all costs, because its defilement will lead Yahweh to punish them severely: they will be expelled from his presence and driven from the land, like the Canaanites before them.

Holiness Laws (Leviticus 19:1–Numbers 10:10)

The final unit of the Sinai treaty deals with laws pertaining to "holiness" (*qōdeš*). Everything that belongs to a deity is "holy" (*qādôš*). And what belongs to the deity must, of course, be accorded special status and treated with special care and respect, so as not to show disrespect for the deity and incur his displeasure.

This section covers a wide range of topics, since Yahweh has identified so many areas of Israel's life as belonging to him. Everything identified as holy is subject to rules involving special care and caution: tabernacle furniture (Num. 4), days of the calendar (Sabbath, Passover, etc.; Lev. 23), sacrifices (Lev. 22), gifts dedicated to Yahweh (Lev. 27; Num. 7), Nazirites (Num. 6), Levites (Num. 8), priests (Lev. 21–22), and most interestingly the entire nation—every individual (Lev. 19–20). The material of this unit is tied together by the keyword *qādôš* ("holy"), which suddenly begins to occur with frequency in Le-

viticus 19 and continues without significant break through Numbers 8.[7]

The unit is divided into two larger sections separated by a climactic centerpiece—the blessings and curses in Leviticus 26:3–46.[8] The unit is concluded by a unit featuring preparations to leave Sinai (Num. 9:15–10:10). These two larger sections are each arranged in seven-part symmetries (7.10 and 7.11).[9]

As might be expected, both of these larger sections are arranged so that the degree of holiness increases as one moves toward the center. In both, the outer units deal with holiness issues involving all the people; the centers deal with the most holy people—the priests—and in the second section, the intermediate units deal with the Levites, who have an intermediate level of holiness.

As in the collection of the purity laws in Leviticus 17–18, so in this collection the author uses

---

7. Occurrences of *qdš* ("holy") after Leviticus 26 include Lev. 27:3, 9, 10, 14, 15, 16, 17, 18, 19, 21, 22, 23, 25, 26, 28, 30, 32, 33; Num. 3:28, 32, 38, 47, 50; 4:4, 12, 15, 16, 19, 20; 5:9, 10, 17; 6:5, 8, 11, 20; 7:1, 9, 13, 19, 25, 31, 37, 43, 49, 55, 61, 67, 73, 79, 85; 8:17, 19.

8. Leviticus 26:3–45 comprises two parts: promises (26:3–13) and warnings (26:14–45) The latter features a series of six ever-worsening punishments (26:14–17, 18–20, 21–22, 23–26, 27–35, 36–39) followed by a seventh and final unit that constitutes a surprise ending: even after all this rebellion and series of punishments, if the remnant of the punished people repent, Yahweh will relent and forgive them (26:40–45)!

9. The use of chiastic (e.g., a-b-c-x-c′-b′-a′) patterns on the smaller level in Leviticus is pointed out by Milgrom, *Leviticus 1–16*, 39–42, etc.

7.11 Second section of laws pertaining to holiness (Lev. 27:1–Num. 10:10)

  a **vows and modifications,** because of timing of Jubilee (Lev. 27)

    b   **Levites:** census (Num. 1:1–5:4)

       • maintenance of holy encampment

       • special status of Levites, who are <u>substitutes for Israel's firstborn males</u>

      c **special situations involving gifts** to <u>tabernacle</u> (Num. 5:5–6:21)

        d **CENTER: priestly, Aaronic blessing** (Num. 6:22–27)

      c´ **special tribal gifts** to <u>tabernacle</u> (Num. 7:1–89)*

    b´ **Levites:** special status of Levites (Num. 8:5–26)†

       • Levites are <u>substitutes for Israel's firstborn males</u>

       • maintenance of ritual purity

  a´ **Passover and modification,** because of timing of Passover (Num. 9:1–14)

    addendum: instructions for marching (Num. 9:15–10:10)

*Numbers 8:1–4 is puzzling here.

†Jacob Milgrom, *Numbers* (JPS Torah Commentary; New York: Jewish Publication Society, 1990), xxiv, identifies 8:5–22 as a self-contained, symmetrically arranged unit.

---

structure to bridge the span between what is primarily a ritual concept (ritual holiness) and the moral extension of the concept. In the case of the collection of purity laws, the moral implications were presented at the end (chap. 18), whereas here the moral and ethical implications are declared from the outset: "Be holy, because I, Yahweh your God, am holy. Respect your mother and father" (19:2–3). The moral implications of holiness are highlighted by their placement in four matching units; namely, in the opening two (a-b) and closing two (b´-a´) units of the first section.

Overall Layout of Exodus 19:3–Numbers 10:10

Several observations can be made about the overall organization of the Sinai treaty in Exodus 19:3–Numbers 10:10 (7.12). First, its seven sections are arranged in an order of increasing holiness, beginning with laws for all the people (Ten Commandments, civil laws) and proceeding to matters of increasing holiness: the tabernacle and its construction (more holy, but built by lay people), the sacrifices, the purity laws, and the holiness laws.

Second, the six sections of laws (the section recounting the construction of the tabernacle is narrative) are arranged in order from shorter to longer (page count from BHS):

---

  a Ten Commandments: about 1 page

  b civic laws: about 6 pages

  c tabernacle instructions: about 13 pages

 (d tabernacle building: narrative only)

  e sacrificial laws: about 15 pages

  f purity laws: about 16 pages

  g holiness laws: about 39 pages

This arrangement is reminiscent of the creation story in Genesis 1, where the six successive cre-

ative days likewise increase in descriptive length. The impression this structural design creates (as in the creation story) is one of ever-increasing variety and grandeur.

Finally, the seven units of the law appear to be arranged with a symmetric touch, with the narrative of the building of the tabernacle standing at the center. The first three sections (Ten Commandments, civil laws, tabernacle instructions) are matched in reverse order by the last three sections (sacrificial, purity, holiness laws)—although the connection between the civil and purity laws is weak.

Correspondence of the Ten Commandments (Exodus 19:3–20:21) and Holiness Laws (Leviticus 19:1–Numbers 10:10)

The Ten Commandments (with its narrative frame) and the holiness regulations conspicuously match. As noted earlier, the main theme of the narrative frame of the Ten Commandments (Exod. 19:3–25; 20:18–21) is holiness. Yahweh will make Israel his "holy" (*qādôš*) nation, a kingdom of priests (19:3–6). He invites the people to come before his "holy" (*qādôš*) mountain; but they must respect his holiness, upon pain of death. They must "make themselves holy" (*qādaš*), and only then will they be permitted to approach the mountain (19:7–20); and only the priests will be permitted to actually approach Yahweh, and even they must "be made holy" (*qādaš*) in order to do so (19:21–25). This emphasis on holiness foreshadows the holiness laws, which will focus on Yahweh's holiness, the people's holiness, the holiness of Yahweh's abode, and the special holiness of his priests.

Moreover, nearly all the Ten Commandments are reiterated in the holiness unit. For example, the latter opens with five of the ten: honoring one's mother and father, keeping the Sabbath,

7.12 The Sinai treaty (Exodus 19:3–Numbers 10:10)

a Ten Commandments—and holiness on Mount Sinai (Exod. 19:3–20:21)
- begins: <u>Israel arrives at Mount Sinai</u>
- date (19:1–2)
- Yahweh's glory on Sinai like <u>cloud</u> (ʿānān; 19:9) and <u>fire</u> (ʾēš; 19:18)
- begins: Yahweh's presence on Sinai sounds like <u>trumpets</u> (19:16–19)
- theme: <u>holiness</u> (qōdeš; 19:3–25; cf. 20:18–21)
- commandments about idolatry, misusing Yahweh's name, Sabbath, honoring parents, murder, stealing, adultery, perjury, etc.

b civil laws—moral, ethical purity (Exod. 20:22–24:11)
- focus on moral, ethical behavior
- prohibition against <u>bestiality</u>, <u>"following the practices"</u> of Canaanites
- prohibition against eating meat of animal torn by wild beasts
- use of blood, fat in sacrifices; sprinkling blood for ritual cleansing

c tabernacle instructions—sacrificial altar (Exod. 24:12–34:28)
- instructions for altar, for all sacrifices
- climax: <u>priests' ordination prescribed</u> (28:1–29:46)
- concluding narrative: <u>sin of Aaron</u> and golden calf (32:1–33:23)
- Israel's idolatrous, debauched sacrificing, with <u>drunkenness</u> (32:1)

d CLIMAX: tabernacle built and filled with Yahweh's glory! (Exod. 34:29–40:38)
- summary in 40:36–38

c′ sacrificial instructions—for sacrificial altar (Lev. 1–10)
- instructions for sacrifices to be offered on altar
- climax: <u>priests' ordination described</u> (Lev. 8–9)
- concluding narrative: <u>sin of Aaron's sons</u>, Nadab and Abihu (Lev. 10)
- Israel's sacrificing to be dignified, monotheistic; <u>no drunkenness</u>

b′ purity laws—ritual, moral purity (Lev. 11–18)
- moral, ethical behavior (Lev. 17–18)
- prohibition against <u>bestiality</u>, <u>"following the practices"</u> of Canaanites
- prohibition against eating meat of animal torn by wild beasts
- use of blood, fat in sacrifices; sprinkling blood for ritual cleansing

a′ holiness laws—most of Ten Commandments repeated (Lev. 19:1–Num. 10:10)
- ends: Israel <u>departs from Mount Sinai</u>
- date (Num. 10:11)
- Yahweh's glory on tabernacle like <u>cloud</u> (ʿānān; Num. 9:15–22) and <u>fire</u> (ʾēš; 9:15–16)
- ends: silver <u>trumpets</u> sound orders from Yahweh's tabernacle (Num. 10)
- theme: <u>holiness</u> (qōdeš) throughout
- commandments about idolatry, misusing Yahweh's name, Sabbath, honoring parents, murder, stealing, adultery, perjury, etc.

not making idols, not stealing, and not swearing falsely (Lev. 19:3–4, 11–12). The reference in Leviticus 19:12 to profaning Yahweh's name may echo the third commandment (see also the case of the blasphemer in Lev. 24). The Sabbath is a frequent topic in the holiness unit (19:30; 23:3; 26:2). There are also additional prohibitions against idolatry (cf. 26:1), adultery (20:10), and murder (24:17–22). Even reminiscences of the tenth commandment can be found in such passages as Leviticus 19:16b–18.

There is another clear link between the opening and closing units of the law: the narrative introducing the Ten Commandments is mirrored by the concluding narrative of the holiness laws, creating a frame for the entire corpus. The first narrative begins with Israel arriving at Sinai (Exod. 19:1–2), and the second concludes with Israel leaving Sinai (Num. 10:11). In both, dates are provided (Exod. 19:1; Num. 10:11). In the first, Yahweh's glory is manifest on Mount Sinai, in the form of a "cloud" (ʿānān; Exod. 19:9) and "fire" (ʾēš; 19:18). In the second, his glory is manifest in the tabernacle, likewise in the form of a "cloud" (ʿānān; Num. 9:15–22) and "fire" (ʾēš; 9:15–16). In the first, Yahweh's presence on Sinai is heralded by what sounds like trumpets (Exod. 19:16–19); and the Israelites must wait until they hear the ram's horn before they approach the mountain (19:13). In the final narrative, as the Israelites leave Mount Sinai they are instructed to make trumpets (Num. 10) for signaling from the tabernacle, Yahweh's new abode.

Correspondence of the Civil Laws (Exodus 20:22–24:11) and Purity Laws (Leviticus 11–18)

The correspondence between the units of civil and purity laws is tenuous. Shared topics include the following:

1. bestiality (Exod. 22:19 [22:18]; Lev. 18:23)
2. prohibition against eating animal meat torn by wild beasts (Exod. 22:31 [22:30]; Lev. 17:15)

3. sprinkling blood for ritual cleansing (Exod. 24:6–8; Lev. 14:51–52, etc.)

4. proper use of blood and fat in sacrifices (Exod. 23:18; Lev. 17:6–14)

5. prohibition against "following the practices" of the Canaanites (Exod. 23:24; Lev. 18:3)

Correspondence of the Tabernacle Instructions (Exodus 24:12–34:28) and Sacrificial Instructions (Leviticus 1–10)

The link between the tabernacle and sacrifices units is obvious. The tabernacle unit deals with the construction of the tabernacle and its altar; and the sacrifices unit deals with the primary activity of the tabernacle: the offering of sacrifices on the altar. The first unit features, at its highlighted center, instructions for the priests' ordination (Exod. 28–29); the second unit features, at its highlighted conclusion, the account of the priest's ordination (Lev. 8–9). Exodus 29:1–37 mirrors Leviticus 8:1–36, detail for detail. The tabernacle unit closes with a narrative about the sin of Aaron (Exod. 32–33); and the sacrificial laws conclude with a narrative about the sin of Aaron's two sons (Lev. 10).

Conclusion

The foregoing analysis suggests a number of insights about the Sinai treaty in Exodus 19:3–Numbers 10:10. The arrangement of the laws according to topic (civil laws, tabernacle instructions, sacrificial laws, purity laws, holiness regulations, etc.) makes the collection easier to follow (cf. Deut. 30:11–14)—which reveals the author's desire to make the collection understandable and practical.

The arrangement of topics in order of increasing holiness, beginning with the Ten Commandments and civil laws and culminating in the purity and holiness laws, reflects the idea that Yahweh is raising his people from their common status to a special position of remarkable dignity and holiness. He begins with rudimentary laws for their moral, ethical, and societal behavior (Ten Commandments, civil laws). He then honors them with the privilege of building a holy sanctuary for him, so that he may dwell among them, of all the peoples of the earth (Exod. 25–40). This honor, in turn, requires special new rules for respect, etiquette, and dignity on the occasions when they appear before him at his sanctuary to bring him sacrifices (Lev. 1–18). The holiness laws (Lev. 19:1–Num. 10:10) culminate the exaltation. The entire nation, including all its members from greatest to least, is now to be considered holy. The people are sacred because Yahweh has taken up his abode among them. As such, they are to regulate their lives in a manner befitting a sacred people (cf. Lev. 26:11–13).

The symmetric arrangement of the corpus places special emphasis on the central unit, the account of the building of the tabernacle (Exod. 34:29–40:38). This suggests that the centerpiece of the entire Sinai treaty, its climax, is Yahweh's gracious act of taking up his abode among his people. The climax of this central unit—the climax of the climax—is its grand finale, when Yahweh's glory fills the completed structure:

> And so Moses finished the work. Then the cloud covered the tent of meeting, and the glory of Yahweh filled the tabernacle. Moses could not enter the tent of meeting because the cloud had settled upon it, and the glory of Yahweh filled the tabernacle.
>
> —Exodus 40:33b–35

The placement of this tabernacle unit at the highlighted center of the symmetry underscores the tabernacle's key role in the treaty. Israel's life, its calendar, its camp, its order of march—everything—will now center around Yahweh's sanctuary. Yahweh's sacred presence is the reason for Israel's special status among the nations; and it is the focus of all its laws.

The structural positioning of the two sin stories (Exod. 31:18–34:35; Lev. 10) reinforces one of the treaty's central themes. The first story, Aaron's sin with the golden calf, immediately follows Yahweh's instructions for the priests' clothing and ordination. The second story, the sin of Aaron's two sons, immediately follows the ceremony in which the priests are clothed and ordained. The blatant structural strategy here is to underscore the point that Israel's system of worship is not (in contrast pagan systems) the invention of its priests, but was given to Israel directly from Yahweh, despite the wicked behavior and unworthiness of the priests.

The layout of the tabernacle unit (Exod. 24:12–34:28) reinforces this theme. Yahweh's instructions for his dignified, monotheistic-based sanctuary are framed by two narratives that recount Israel's plunge into foolish, chaotic idolatry (24:12–18; 31:18–34:28). This structural scheme helps underscore the point that Yahweh's tabernacling among his people is Yahweh's idea from beginning to end. It is not their idea; for while he is giving these instructions to Moses on Mount Sinai, the Israelites are busy setting up their own pagan idol and its makeshift altar. This layout also reinforces a related point: Yahweh's choice to dwell among his people is based on divine grace and forgiveness rather than on human merit. He has chosen to live among his people despite their unworthiness (a theme developed throughout the Book of the Law).

The author's strong anti-idolatry agenda is reinforced by the symmetric arrangement of the tabernacle instructions in Exodus 24:12–34:28. As already noted, an ancient audience would have every reason to expect, at the highlighted center of such a unit, priestly instructions about how the sanctuary's central focus, the idol, should be clothed (with breastpiece, robe, tiara, etc.) and dedicated by the priests in a special ceremony. This anticipation is turned on its head, and instead the highlighted center (28:1–29:46) features God's own instructions for the clothing of his priests (with breastpiece, robe, tiara, etc.) and for their dedication in a special ceremony!

Another theme emphasized by structure is the mandate to be kind to the poor and disadvantaged (including the widow, orphan, alien, servant, blind, deaf, elderly, etc.). The first section of civil laws opens and closes with this theme, drawing attention to the topic by its repetition and by its placement in the unit's two positions of emphasis (Exod. 21:2–11; 22:21–28). In the second section of civil laws the theme reappears, this time in the three highlighted central positions (23:1–3, 4–5, 6–9—if one counts the call to kindness to one's personal enemies); and again the theme is reinforced by its repetition. In the treaty's final unit, the holiness laws, the theme is once more featured; and again it is emphasized by its double coverage in the unit's introductory and concluding sections (Lev. 19; 25:1–26:2). Kindness to the poor and disadvantaged is a key stipulation—perhaps the key stipulation—in this treaty. The Israelites should understand the plight of the powerless better than most, since they were rescued by Yahweh from slavery in a foreign land: "Do not mistreat an alien or oppress him, for you were aliens in Egypt" (Exod. 22:21). "Do not oppress an alien; you yourselves know how it feels to be aliens, for you were aliens in Egypt" (23:9). "Treat the alien as one of your native-born. Love him as yourself, for you were aliens in Egypt" (Lev. 19:33–34). This theme of kindness to the disadvantaged pervades the treaty and affects nearly every aspect of it. The people whom Yahweh freed from slavery and oppression are to be forever kind to the poor. In this most basic mandate, the Israelites can express their gratitude to their suzerain, loving others as Yahweh has loved them. And in so doing they behave and look like him.

8.2 Victory in the Plains of Moab (Numbers 21:21–Deuteronomy 3:29)

a **victory over Sihon and Og**: Israel settles in these lands (Num. 21:21–35)
- story preceded by Israel's arrival in the <u>valley</u> (*gayĕʾ*) of Moab

b **Yahweh stops Moab from harming Israel** (Num. 22:1–24:25)
- Balaam <u>blesses</u> Israel
- at first Yahweh <u>stops Balaam from coming</u> to Moab (from south?)
- when Yahweh allows Balaam to come to Moab, he is not to curse Israel

c **Moses <u>takes</u> (*lāqaḥ*) sinful <u>leaders</u> (*roʾšîm*) who worship Baal, to kill them** (Num. 25:1–18)
- Moses <u>delegates</u> this task to Israel's <u>judges</u> (*šōpĕṭîm*)

d **lists**: census figures for <u>twelve tribes</u> (Num. 26:1–27:11 [25:19–27:11])
- for <u>allotment of land</u>
- <u>Levites</u>
- <u>Zelophehad's daughters</u>
- division by <u>lot</u>
- larger tribes get larger lands

e **Joshua and Eleazar to lead Israel into Canaan** (Num. 27:12–23)

f **offerings and gifts to Yahweh** (Num. 28–29)*

g **CENTER: victory over Midian** (Num. 31:1–24)

f′ **offerings and gifts to Yahweh** from war spoils (Num. 31:25–54)

e′ **Transjordanian tribes to go into Canaan with Joshua and Eleazar** (Num. 32:1–42)

d′ **lists**: forty-two stages of journey (Num. 33:1–36:13)
- Canaan's boundaries
- representatives of <u>twelve tribes</u>
- forty-two <u>levitical</u> cities
- <u>allotment of land</u>
- <u>Zelophehad's daughters</u>
- division by <u>lot</u>
- larger tribes get larger lands

c′ **Moses <u>takes</u> (*lāqaḥ*) wise <u>leaders</u> (*roʾšîm*) and <u>judges</u> (*šōpĕṭîm*)** (Deut. 1:1–18)
- Moses <u>delegates</u> responsibilities to them

b′ **Yahweh stops Israel from harming Moab and Edom** (Deut. 1:19–2:15)
- Yahweh <u>has blessed</u> Israel
- at first Yahweh <u>stops Israel from coming</u> to Canaan (from the south)
- when Yahweh allows Israel to go through Moab, they are not to attack Moab

a′ **victory over Sihon and Og**: Israel settles in these lands (Deut. 2:16–3:29)
- ends: Israel settles in the <u>valley</u> (*gayĕʾ*) of Moab (3:29)

*An addendum (Num. 30:1–16 [30:2–17]) deals with vows.

people further instructions for their sacrifices and ritual purity (units e and e′)—a structuring touch designed to underscore the point that Yahweh's continued presence among his people is because of his grace, not their worthiness. The structure also reinforces the theme that Israel's system of worship was given by Yahweh himself and was not the invention of Israel (who is busy rebelling against Yahweh and his instructions).

This latter theme is given additional structural emphasis by its repetition in the (highlighted) central three units of the symmetry. The story of Korah's revolt (f) and its matching unit (f′) illustrate the danger of Israel's trying to modify Yahweh's laws; the central unit (g) demonstrates that Israel's system of worship and priests are determined by Yahweh alone. This treaty is Yahweh's idea from beginning to end. It is not Israel's own concoction, subject to capricious human modification.

Victory in the Plains of Moab (Numbers 21:21–Deuteronomy 3:29)

Following this negative unit comes a more upbeat unit recounting Israel's positive experiences upon their arrival at the plains of Moab (8.2). With the passing away of the rebellious generation, the new generation begins to experience God's blessing. The unit recounts Israel's triumphs as it arrives in Transjordan, including its defeat of Sihon and Og, Balaam's failure to curse Israel, and their victory over the Midianites. And now Yahweh begins to make preparations with Israel's new leaders for the invasion and allotment of Canaan.

Both the beginning and end of this unit are somewhat difficult to determine. One could argue that the previous unit does not close until Numbers 22:1, when Israel is said to finally arrive at the plains of Moab. Careful analysis, however, suggests that the previous unit closes with 21:20,

8.3 Exhortation to obey Yahweh (Deuteronomy 4–11)

a **lessons from Yahweh's awesome acts at Mount Sinai (4:1–40)**
- exhortation to obey Yahweh and his laws
- do not be enticed into idolatry
- begins: and now (wĕ'attâ)
- section on blessings and curses (4:25–31)
- themes: awesome signs etc. that Israel saw (rā'â), Israel's love for Yahweh
- reminder of what they saw when Yahweh punished sinners at Baal-peor

b **lessons from the first giving of the tablets (4:41–5:33)**
- remember the first time they were given, with the Ten Commandments
- remember Israel's respect for Yahweh at Sinai—and do not lose that respect for Yahweh!

c **don't forget! lessons from Yahweh's past and future care (6:1–25)**
- when Yahweh has given you Canaan, do not forget: it was Yahweh who rescued you from Egypt and gave you this land
- remember how Yahweh tested you in the wilderness
- description of wonderful land of Canaan: houses filled with good things; vineyards and olive groves
- warning about when they have eaten and are satisfied
- key expression: don't forget (pen-tiškaḥ)
- begins: exhortation parallel to introduction in 8:1 (6:1–2)

d **CENTER: completely destroy the Canaanites!** promise of victory; warning against following their ways (7:1–26)

c' **don't forget! lessons from Yahweh's past and future care (8:1–20)**
- when Yahweh has given you Canaan, do not forget: it was Yahweh who cared for you in the wilderness and gave you this land
- remember how you tested Yahweh in the wilderness
- description of wonderful land of Canaan: fine houses, vines, and olive oil
- warning about when they have eaten and are satisfied
- key expression: don't forget (pen-tiškaḥ)
- begins: exhortation parallel to introduction in 6:1–2 (8:1)

b' **lessons from the second giving of the tablets (9:1–10:11)**
- remember the second time they were given
- remember Israel's sin and disrespect for Yahweh—so that you do not become proud and think Yahweh gave you this land because of your righteousness; you are a stiff-necked people!

a' **lessons from Yahweh's awesome acts in Egypt and wilderness (10:12–11:32)**
- exhortation to obey Yahweh and his laws
- do not be enticed into idolatry
- begins: and now (wĕ'attâ)
- section on blessings and curses (11:13–32)
- themes: awesome signs etc. that Israel saw (rā'â), Yahweh's love for Israel
- reminder of what they saw when Yahweh punished Dathan and other sinners

when Israel arrives at the plains ("valley") of Moab. The author then opens the next unit at 21:21 with the story of Israel's conquest of Sihon and Og, which actually occurred as Israel was arriving at its final destination. This narrating technique of closing one unit at a natural stopping point and then opening the next by backtracking to pick up the action at a point in time before the end of the previous unit, is a favorite structuring technique throughout the Pentateuch and Joshua. The reason for it here is transparent: the author wants to hold the upbeat story of Israel's victory over Sihon and Og for his collection of positive stories in the Plains of Moab unit.

How far does this unit extend? The presence of an overall symmetric arrangement in the unit is most helpful in determining its end. The possibility of an intentional symmetry is suggested by the repetition of material about Zelophehad's daughters (Num. 27; 36). Moreover, nearby are two discussions of the future allotment of Canaan based on the size of the tribes (26:52–56;

33:50–54). There are also two matching accounts of Israel's conquest of Sihon and Og (Num. 21:21–35; Deut. 2:16–3:29). But with this latter matching we face a problem. It seems unlikely that the unit extended into the Book of Deuteronomy, since Deuteronomy appears to form its own, self-contained unit, with its grand introduction (1:1–5) and its grand conclusion of Moses' death (chap. 34).

There are compelling reasons, however, to suggest that the unit that opens in Numbers 21:21 with Israel's conquest of Sihon and Og closes in Deuteronomy 2:16–3:29, where the same story is repeated in greater detail. The strongest evidence that these two stories frame a self-contained unit is the intervening material's symmetric arrangement.

The theme of divinely aided military victory is structurally highlighted by its treatment in the symmetry's three positions of emphasis: the beginning, the end, and the center. This theme will be reinforced by the layout of Joshua 1–12.

Exhortation to Obey Yahweh (Deuteronomy 4–11)

The third unit of the historical conclusion represents the first major section of Moses' speech to Israel in the plains of Moab (8.3).[2] The speech actually begins in Deuteronomy 1; but as suggested above, the first three chapters, narrative in form, serve to conclude the narrative unit beginning in Numbers 21:21. Deuteronomy 4 introduces a major shift in genre—from predominantly narration to exhortation. Moses now turns to his present audience and delivers an extended exhortation to them to love and obey Yahweh and his laws: "Hear now, O Israel, the decrees and laws I am about to teach you. Follow them" (4:1). The exhortation continues through chapter 11, where it concludes in a grand finale. In chapter 12 there is another shift—from general exhortation to specific laws.

The unity of Deuteronomy 4–11 is suggested by its internal organization. The unit appears to comprise seven parts that are arranged with a symmetric touch.[3] Although all seven units call for Israel's obedience and loyalty to Yahweh and his laws, each has a particular focus or theme. The parts are well delineated, marked off by the interplay of three structuring techniques:

1. narrative interruptions: the intrusive narrative in 4:41–43 concludes a unit, and the narrative in 4:44–49 introduces the next unit
2. formulaic introductions: (a) "these are the laws" followed by "hear, O Israel" (4:45–5:1; 6:1–3) or simply "hear, O Israel" (9:10); (b) "and now (wĕʿattâ), O Israel, hear" (4:1) or simply "and now (wĕʿattâ), O Israel" (10:12)
3. shifts of topic: treatment of the Canaanites (7:1–26); giving of the two tablets of stone (4:44–5:33; 9:1–10:11); idolatry and what Is-

rael saw (4:1–40); remembering (and not forgetting) God's care for Israel in the wilderness and in the new land (8:1–20)

The structural repetitions and matching serve to emphasize the main theme: Israel should learn from what has happened to them and not forget the lessons from their history. This history, including the experiences in the wilderness and at Mount Sinai, should serve as reminders to be loyal to Yahweh alone, to avoid idolatry, to avoid pride, and to be careful to respect the holy presence of Yahweh. These exhortations center around the structurally highlighted central unit, which features the promise of victory over the Canaanites and the warning not to follow any of their evil ways. Israel's difficult circumstances are about to permanently change for the better; but they must always remember what they have learned from their experiences in the wilderness.

Laws for Israel's Life in Canaan (Deuteronomy 12–26)

A new unit begins in Deuteronomy 12, with the conspicuous shift from general exhortations to an extended review of the specific laws by which Israel is to regulate its life in Canaan. The unit contains no narrative. The laws are organized according to topic, and they are reviewed without significant break from Deuteronomy 12 through Deuteronomy 26. Moses is never referred to in the third-person here (unlike in Deut. 4–11); the unit is entirely in the form of direct speech. This lengthy review finally ends in 27:1, with a shift back to narrative and references again to Moses in the third-person.

The structure of Deuteronomy 12–26 is somewhat complex, but perhaps recoverable.[4] The material appears to be organized in three sections, each with its own focus and self-contained structure:

a Israel's duties to Yahweh at "the place Yahweh will choose" (12:1–17:7)
b laws pertaining to Israel's leadership (17:8–19:21)
c various laws dealing with warfare, legal issues, marriage and family, everyday life, and kindness to the poor and disadvantaged (20:1–26:19)

2. The structure of Deuteronomy has not been successfully analyzed; see Moshe Weinfeld, *Deuteronomy: A New Translation with Introduction and Commentary* (Anchor Bible 5; New York: Doubleday, 1991), 2–12; Eugene H. Merrill, *Deuteronomy* (New American Commentary; Nashville: Broadman, 1994), 27–32; Christopher J. H. Wright, *Deuteronomy* (New International Biblical Commentary; Peabody, Mass.: Hendrickson, 1996), 1–5. Duane Christensen, *Deuteronomy 1–11* (Word Biblical Commentary 6a; Dallas: Word, 1991), xli, identifies symmetric arrangements throughout the Book of Deuteronomy, on both larger and smaller levels, and sees the whole book arranged in a five-part chiasmus: (a) chaps. 1–3, (b) chaps. 4–11, (c) chaps. 12–26, (b') chaps. 27–30, (a') chaps. 31–34.

3. Symmetry in this section is observed by F. Garcia López, "Analyse Littéraire de Deutéronomie v–xi," *Revue Biblique* 84 (1977) 481–522, who analyzes Deuteronomy 5–11 as a five-part chiasmus.

4. The most detailed work on the structure of Deuteronomy 12–26 may be found in G. Braulik's publications: "The Sequence of the Laws in Deuteronomy 12–26 and in the Decalogue," in *A Song of Power and the Power of Song*, ed. Duane L. Christensen (Winona Lake, Ind.: Eisenbrauns, 1993), 313–35; *Die deuteronomische Gesetze und der Dekalog* (Stuttgarter Bibelstudien 145; Stuttgart: Katholisches Bibelwerk, 1991); *Die Mittel deuteronomischer Rhetorik* (Analecta Biblica 68; Rome: Pontifical Institute, 1978).

8.4 Israel's duties to Yahweh (Deuteronomy 12:1–17:7)

a **worship and bring offerings to Yahweh alone at chosen place** (12:1–31)
  - theme: eating (ʾākal) "at the place Yahweh will choose"
  - "there rejoice before Yahweh your God, you, your sons and daughters, your menservants and maid-servants, and the Levites"—twice repeated
  - prohibition against Asherah poles, standing stones, improper sacrifices

b **death to those who encourage worshiping other gods** (12:32–13:18 [13:1–19])
  - "if it is true and has been proved that this detestable thing was done"
  - stoning of guilty person; "then all Israel will hear and fear"
  - "you must purge the evil from among you"
  - begins: if (kî) . . . in your midst (qirběkā)

c **eating clean animals; eating firstborn and tithes at chosen place** (14:1–29)
  - unacceptable things that may not be eaten

d **CENTER: kindness to poor** (15:1–18)

c′ **eating acceptable sacrifices and firstborn at chosen place** (15:19–23)
  - unacceptable things that may not be eaten

a′ **worship and bring offerings to Yahweh alone three times a year at chosen place** (16:1–17:1)
  - theme: eating (ʾākal) "at the place Yahweh will choose"
  - "there rejoice before Yahweh your God, you, your sons and daughters, your menservants and maid-servants, and the Levites" twice repeated
  - prohibition against Asherah poles, standing stones, improper sacrifices

b′ **death to those who worship other gods** (17:2–7)
  - "if it is true and has been proved that this detestable thing was done"
  - stoning of guilty person; "then all Israel will hear and fear"
  - "you must purge the evil from among you"
  - begins: if (kî) . . . in your midst (qirběkā)

8.5 Israel's leadership (Deuteronomy 17:8–19:21)

a **judicial leadership: court of highest appeal** (17:8–13)*
  - in "the place Yahweh will choose"
  - "you must purge the evil from Israel; all the people will hear and be afraid and will not be contemptuous again"

b **king to be unlike those of other nations** (17:14–20)
  - begins: when you enter the land
  - he will be from among your brothers

c **Levites: next-to-most holy** (18:1–2)

d **CENTER: priests—most holy** (18:3–5)

c′ **Levites: next-to-most holy** (18:6–8)

b′ **prophet to be unlike those of other nations** (18:9–22)
  - begins: when you enter the land
  - he will be from among your brothers

a′ **judicial leadership: courts of higher appeal** (19:1–21)
  - at cities of refuge
  - "you must purge the evil from Israel; all the people will hear and be afraid and will not be contemptuous again"

*Deuteronomy 16:18–20 might belong in this section.

Israel's Duties to Yahweh at "the Place Yahweh Will Choose" (Deuteronomy 12:1–17:7)

The first section in Deuteronomy 12–26 is organized into seven units, arranged in a modified symmetry (8.4), at the center of which stands a structurally highlighted, passionate call for kindness to the poor (unit d). The duplication and matching of units (a and a′) focusing on instructions about "the place Yahweh will choose" underscores the importance of maintaining a single place of worship. The danger of following other gods is also emphasized by structured repetition (units b and b′).

Regulations Pertaining to Israel's Leadership (Deuteronomy 17:8–19:21)

The second section in Deuteronomy 12–26 deals with Israel's secular and religious leadership (8.5). The material is arranged in a seven-part symmetry reflecting degrees of holiness. The least holy leadership positions are treated in the symmetry's outer slots (units a and a′, b and b′), the Levites (with their intermediate holiness) are dealt with on either side of the center (units c and c′), and the most holy leader—the priest—is the focus of the central unit (d).

8.6 Miscellaneous laws (Deuteronomy 20–26)

a **rules of warfare** (20:1–20)
  b **kindness to poor and unfortunate** (as well as civic issues) (21:1–22:12)
    • protection of women in vulnerable marriage circumstances
    • sensitivity to animals (ox, birds)
    • sensitivity regarding criminals (treating hanged bodies with respect)
    c **marriage violations and issues** (22:13–30)
      d **treatment of foreign groups**: Ammonites, Moabites, Edomites, Egyptians (23:1–14)
        • topic: emasculation
  b′ **kindness to poor and unfortunate** (as well as civic issues) (23:15–25:4)
    • wives in vulnerable marriage circumstances
    • animals (ox)
    • criminals (sensitivity in flogging)
    c′ **marriage violations and issues** (25:5–10)
      d′ **treatment of foreign group**: Amalekites (25:11–19)
        • topics: emasculation, integrity
conclusion (26:1–19)

8.7 Moses' final words (Deuteronomy 27–34)

a **Moses' instructions about the twelve tribes reciting the blessings and curses**; the <u>blessings</u> of the covenant (27:1–26)
  b **curses of the covenant**: drought, crop failure, disease, wild animals, military defeat, exile, death, etc. (28:15–68)
    c **reassurance of victory**, as with <u>Sihon and Og</u> (29:1–30:10 [28:69–30:10])
      • exhortation to obey this law
      d **CENTER: call to obedience** (30:11–20)
    c′ **reassurance to Joshua of victory**, as with <u>Sihon and Og</u> (31:1–13)
      • exhortation to obey this law
  b′ **curses of the covenant** in form of song: drought, crop failure, disease, wild animals, military defeat, exile, death, etc. (31:14–32:47)
a′ **Moses' <u>blessings</u> upon the twelve tribes** (32:48–33:29)
epilogue: Moses' death on Mount Nebo (34:1–12)

Miscellaneous Laws (Deuteronomy 20–26)

The third section in Deuteronomy 12–26 deals with various issues involving proper conduct in warfare, civil cases, family and marriage, everyday life, and kindness to the poor and disadvantaged. In contrast to the previous two sections, the laws here are generally shorter in length, cover a wider variety of topics, and are more in number. The arrangement of this section is by far the most difficult of the three to analyze. The analysis in 8.6 represents the tentative proposal that the section is laid out in a seven-part parallel scheme.

Three themes of this section are particularly highlighted by their repetition or structural positioning: (1) love for the poor and disadvantaged, (2) fairness and justice in marriage issues, and (3) sensitivity in warfare.

Moses' Final Words and Exhortations and His Death (Deuteronomy 27–34)

The fifth unit in the historical conclusion presents a collection of Moses' final words and exhortations to Israel, concluded with the account of his death. The unit features an impassioned call to obedience, with a strong emphasis on the blessings that Israel will experience if they are faithful to Yahweh, and the curses that they will experience if they rebel. The unit appears to be arranged in a seven-part symmetry plus an epilogue recounting Moses' death (8.7).

The unit's structure highlights the climactic call to obedience in 30:11–20. The matched warnings of curses that will result from disobedience and the matched reassurances of victory that will result from obedience underscore the importance of these two related themes.

Conquest of Canaan (Joshua 1–12)

The sixth unit in the historical conclusion of the Book of the Law is the account of the conquest of Canaan in Joshua 1–12.[5] This unit recounts how Yahweh enabled Joshua and the Israelites to conquer Canaan, as he had promised their ancestors. The unit concludes with a summary of the conquest (Josh. 12), and 13:1 shifts to a new topic: the dividing up of Canaan and the

---

5. The surface structure of the Book of Joshua has received little attention in scholarly literature; see J. Alberto Soggin, *Joshua: A Commentary* (Old Testament Library; Philadelphia: Westminster, 1972), 2–3; Richard D. Nelson, *Joshua: A Commentary* (Old Testament Library; Louisville: Westminster/John Knox, 1997), 12–14.

8.8 Israel's initial success in entering Canaan (Joshua 1–8)

a **opening focus on "Book of the Law of Moses"** (1:1–18)
- Joshua encouraged to follow all the law that Moses gave
- he is to meditate in this Book of the Law day and night and is not to let it "depart out of your mouth"
- Joshua gives orders to Israelites

b **encouragement from a believing Canaanite: Rahab hides spies** (2:1–24)
- Rahab secretly hides (ṭāman) the spies in her respect for Yahweh's power
- her life is to be spared for her act of faith in Yahweh
- good result from Rahab's report—Joshua is encouraged: "Yahweh has given into our hands (nātan bĕyād) the whole land; all the people are melting (mûg) in fear because of us!" (2:24); from Rahab's report: when we heard (šāmaʿ), our hearts (lēbāb) melted (māsas) (2:11)

c **Jordan "stands up"! Yahweh miraculously enables Israel to cross the Jordan to enter Canaan** (3:1–4:24)
- Yahweh gives Joshua puzzling marching orders, with promise of success—then delivers miracle at the perfect time
- people follow the priests carrying the ark, who play key role
- miracle involves Yahweh's removing a barrier—Jordan River (by earthquake?), which "stands up" so Israelites can enter Canaan

d **CENTER: Israel worships Yahweh in promised land**: Canaanites are disheartened; circumcision; Passover; arrival of the "commander of Yahweh's army"; manna ceases; Israel eats produce of Canaan for first time; they are now "on holy ground"! (5:1–15)

c′ **Jericho falls down! Yahweh miraculously enables Israel to cross over walls to enter and conquer Jericho** (6:1–27)
- Yahweh gives Joshua puzzling marching orders, with promise of success—then delivers miracle at the perfect time
- people follow the priests carrying the ark, who play key role
- miracle involves Yahweh's removing a barrier—a city wall (by earthquake?), which "falls down" so Israelites can enter Jericho

b′ **discouragement from a faithless Israelite: Achan hides plunder** (7:1–8:29)
- Achan secretly hides (ṭāman) the plunder in disrespect of Yahweh's orders
- he is put to death for his act of unfaithfulness against Yahweh
- bad result from Achan's sin—Joshua is discouraged: now Yahweh "has given us into the hands of (nātan bĕyād) the Amorites"; the Israelites' hearts (lēbāb) melted (māsas); and now "when the Canaanites and the other people . . . hear (šāmaʿ)," they will come and defeat Israel

a′ **closing focus on "Book of the Law of Moses"** (8:30–35)
- Joshua leads ceremony at Mount Ebal, according to what is written in the book of the law of Moses (repeated)
- copies on stones the law of Moses
- afterward "Joshua read all the words of the law . . . just as it is written in the law"

---

record of the tribal allotments, which will be the focus of Joshua 13–24.

The story of the conquest falls into two sections: (1) Israel's initial success in entering Canaan, closed by the ceremony at Mount Ebal (Josh. 1–8), and (2) Israel's conquest of the rest of Canaan (Josh. 9–12). Each section contains seven units, all well marked by shifts in time, place, characters, etc. And each section has been arranged with a symmetric touch.

The first section (8.8) begins and ends with units that focus on the central importance of the Book of the Law of Moses (a and a′), which serves to underscore this theme. The central unit (d) represents an important (and structurally highlighted) pause in the conquest, when Israel worships Yahweh at Gilgal in grateful celebration of their arrival in the new land—which reinforces the point that it was only by Yahweh's enabling that Israel began the conquest of Canaan.

The second section (8.9) recounts Israel's conquest of the rest of Canaan. This section begins and ends with a focus on "all the kings west of the Jordan" who opposed the Israelites. In unit a, "all the kings" gather to fight against Joshua

in "one (ʾeḥād) accord"; in unit a′, "all the kings" have been defeated. Their unity has been broken, and they are listed separately, one by one, with the word "one" (ʾeḥād) listed after each name. This odd use of ʾeḥād may reflect the point that while these kings began by opposing Joshua as one body (9:1–2), Yahweh shattered their unity, so that each was separately conquered by Joshua, one by one (a possible example of structure clarifying a difficulty). The theme of Israel's God-given victory over "all the kings" is also the focus of the center unit (d).

To further tie together the entire conquest story (Josh. 1–12), the author designed the material so that the seven units of the first section are matched in parallel order by the seven units of the second section (8.10). This extended structural design is intriguing. The sparing of the Canaanite woman Rahab (b) is matched by the sparing of the Canaanite people of Gibeon (b′); Joshua's putting to death faithless Achan (f) is paralleled by his putting to death the hardened Canaanites (f′); the great nature miracle of the "stopping" (ʿāmad) of the Jordan (c) is matched by the great nature miracle of the "stopping" (ʿāmad) of the sun (c′); the conquest

8.9 Israel's conquest of the rest of Canaan (Joshua 9–12)

a **all the kings of Canaan oppose Joshua as one (9:1–2)**
  - includes kings west of the Jordan, as far as Lebanon, highlands, Shephelah, etc.
  - image of kings gathering to oppose Joshua as one (ʾeḥād) (cf. together, yaḥdāw)

b **mercy for a believing remnant: Israel makes peace with Gibeonites (9:3–27)**
  - they come in submission—compelled by their respect for Yahweh—and are spared
  - the Hivites . . . living in Gibeon make a treaty of peace with the Israelites
  - the believing Gibeonites are spared

c **defeat of southern coalition, led by king of Jerusalem (10:1–15)**
  - begins: "when King Adoni-zedek of Jerusalem heard (šāmaʿ) . . . he sent to (šālaḥ ʾel) . . ."—followed by a list of kings of coalition
  - kings "gather together . . . to fight (lĕhillāḥēm) Israel"
  - Yahweh reassures Joshua: do not be afraid of them (ʾal-tîrāʾ mēhem); I will give them into your hands (nātan bĕyad)
  - Joshua and the entire army with him (wĕkol-ʿam hammilḥāmâ ʿimmô) carry out surprise attack (pitʾōm) against enemy
  - Israel struck (nākâ) the enemy and pursued them (wayyirdĕpēm) as far as (ʿad) [name] and as far as (wĕʿad) [name]

d **CENTER: ritual ceremony at Makkedah** and conquest of seven cities (and "all the kings") of the south (10:16–43)

c′ **defeat of northern coalition, led by king of Hazor (11:1–15)**
  - begins: "when King Jabin of Hazor heard (šāmaʿ) . . . he sent to (šālaḥ ʾel) . . ."—followed by a list of kings of coalition
  - kings "gather together (yaḥdāw) . . . to fight (lĕhillāḥēm) Israel"
  - Yahweh reassures Joshua: do not be afraid of them (ʾal-tîrāʾ mippĕnêhem); I will give them into your hands (nātan bĕyad)
  - Joshua and the entire army with him (wĕkol-ʿam hammilḥāmâ ʿimmô) carry out surprise attack (pitʾōm) against enemy
  - Israel struck (nākâ) the enemy and pursued them (wayyirdĕpûm) as far as (ʿad) [name] and as far as (wĕʿad) [name]

b′ **no mercy for hardened Canaanites: Israel makes peace with none but Gibeonites (11:16–23)**
  - all others come against Israel in hardness of heart—compelled by Yahweh in order to annihilate them—and are destroyed
  - the Hivites living in Gibeon . . . made a treaty of peace with the Israelites
  - the hardened Canaanites are all put to death

a′ **all the kings of Canaan whom Joshua conquered are listed one by one (12:1–24)**
  - includes kings west of the Jordan, from valley of Lebanon, in the highlands, Shephelah, land of the Hittites
  - image of kings conquered by Joshua as shattered forces, falling to the Israelites one (ʾeḥād) by one (ʾeḥād); the term is repeated thirty-one times, once after each king

and burning of the city of Jericho (e) is matched by the conquest and burning of Hazor (e′). And the story of the ceremonies at Gilgal (d) may possibly be matched by the story of the ceremony at Makkedah (d′).

Many of the subunits in the conquest story are themselves arranged in seven-part schemes, some of which are chiastic. The unit about Rahab (8.11), for example, is so arranged (with her agreement at the center). The story of the Jordan crossing (8.12) follows a similar structure, centering—significantly—around the erection of the memorial stones.[6]

The story of Achan's sin and the conquest of Ai (8.13) also forms a seven-part chiastic arrangement, with the episode about the rectification of Achan's sin at the highlighted center.

The structural design of Joshua 1–12 draws attention to several themes. The structure helps reinforce the point that Israel was able to conquer Canaan only because of Yahweh's initiation, guidance, help, and miraculous intervention (highlighted by the matchup of narratives that share this theme). The matching of chapters 1 and 8, which open and close the first section, underscores the importance of obedience to the law. The importance of acknowledging Yahweh's leadership is emphasized by the positioning of the two accounts of religious ceremonies in the highlighted central and concluding positions of the first section of the conquest narrative. The matching of the two units featuring Rahab and the Gibeonites may imply that Yahweh had a pattern of sparing believing Canaanites, one way or the other. The arrangement of the Achan story highlights the importance of obeying Yahweh. If Israel disobeys Yahweh it will no longer be able to win battles; only by confessing and rectifying its sin will it begin to experience God's blessing again. The layout of this story also reinforces the theme that the conquest of Canaan was possible only by Yahweh's empowerment.

Allotment of Land of Canaan (Joshua 13–24)

The final unit of the historical conclusion is the story of the allotment of Canaan. This unit is probably designed to comprise thirteen smaller units, each focusing on a single topic or event (8.14). These thirteen units appear to be arranged in a symmetry, with the opening and closing units (a and a′) introduced with state-

---

6. The framing of this unit and its coherence are discussed by N. Winther-Nielsen, "The Miraculous Grammar of Joshua 3–4," in *Biblical Hebrew and Discourse Linguistics*, ed. R. D. Bergen (Dallas: Summer Institute of Linguistics/Winona Lake, Ind.: Eisenbrauns, 1994), 300–319.

8.10 Conquest of Canaan (Joshua 1–12)

a **introduction to first phase** (1:1–18)
- no one will be able to oppose Joshua
- all land west of Jordan will be given to Joshua; <u>the Great Sea</u>, <u>Lebanon</u>, <u>land of Hittites</u>

  b **believing Canaanite is spared: Rahab** (2:1–24)
- Rahab sides with Israel, against own people; <u>makes agreement with Israel</u>
- Rahab's act of faith <u>involves deception</u>; she is spared
- her testimony: <u>we have heard</u> about what Yahweh did in "<u>Egypt</u> . . . to <u>Sihon</u> and <u>Og</u>, the two kings of the Amorites east of the Jordan"

    c **miracle of the <u>stopping</u> (ʿāmad) of the Jordan River** (3:1–4:24)

      d **ceremonies at Gilgal,** after Jordan <u>stopped</u> (5:1–15)
- <u>evening</u> (ʿereb) ceremony; Yahweh's commander and Joshua's <u>feet</u> (regel)
- kings' "hearts melted and they had no courage to face Israel"
- Israel's humiliation is <u>rolled away</u> (gālal)

        e **conquest and burning of city of Jericho** (6:1–27)

          f **faithless Israelite, Achan, put to death** (7:1–8:29)
- Achan secretly takes forbidden <u>plunder</u>
- <u>hearts of Israelites</u> melted; Canaanites may attack
- Israel allowed to take plunder and livestock at Ai

            g **conclusion to first phase:** assembly of twelve (victorious) Israelite tribes (8:30–35)

a′ **introduction to second phase** (9:1–2)
- kings of all the land west of the Jordan join to oppose Joshua
- from along <u>the Great Sea</u>, <u>Lebanon</u>, including <u>the Hittites</u>

  b′ **believing Canaanites are spared: Gibeonites** (9:3–27)
- Gibeonites side with Israel, against own people; <u>make agreement with Israel</u>
- Gibeonites' act of faith <u>involves deception</u>; they are spared
- their testimony: <u>we have heard</u> about what Yahweh did "in <u>Egypt</u> . . . and to the two kings of the Amorites east of the Jordan, <u>Sihon</u> . . . and <u>Og</u>"

    c′ **miracle of the <u>stopping</u> (ʿāmad) of the sun** (10:1–15)

      d′ **ceremony at Makkedah,** after sun <u>stopped</u> and victory achieved (10:16–31)
- <u>evening</u> (ʿereb) ceremony; Joshua's commanders and <u>feet</u> (regel)
- "the five kings hid in a cave"
- stones <u>rolled</u> (gālal) to seal in kings

        e′ **conquest and burning of city of Hazor** (11:1–15)

          f′ **hardened Canaanites put to death** (11:16–23)
- Israelites now allowed to take <u>plunder</u> and livestock
- <u>hearts of Canaanites</u> are hardened; must attack

            g′ **conclusion to conquest:** list of thirty-one conquered Canaanite kings (12:1–24)

8.11 Rahab (Joshua 2)

a **spies depart from Joshua** at camp in Transjordan to get report of land (2:1a)

  b **spies arrive at Rahab's house** (2:1b–6)
- she sends <u>king's soldiers</u> toward Jordan while <u>hiding</u> spies on roof

    c **Rahab asks for sign** (2:7–13)
- asks spies to protect <u>her family</u> when Jericho is captured

      d **CENTER: agreement:** Rahab helps spies escape (using rope that will be sign); they promise to spare her (2:14–16)

    c′ **spies designate rope as sign** before they leave (2:17–21a)
- spies reassure her that she and <u>her family</u> will be protected

  b′ **spies leave Rahab's house** (2:21b–22)
- she sends spies out (in opposite direction from Jordan, to <u>hide</u> in hills)
- <u>king's soldiers</u> search for spies in vain

a′ **spies return to Joshua** at camp in Transjordan with report (2:23–24)

ments about Joshua's old age (13:1; 23:1) and the land that remains to be conquered, which Yahweh will help them conquer. Other match-ups suggest themselves: the private inheritances of the two heroes of Kadesh (Caleb in d and Joshua in d′), the Transjordanian tribes (b and b′), the Levites (c and c′), and the Rachel tribes (Joseph in f and Benjamin in f′). And at the cen-

ter (g) is the account of the casting of lots before Yahweh at Shiloh to divide up the remaining land. The highlighted position of this central unit underscores the point that it was Yahweh himself who directed the allotment of the land.

The only real difficulty in this analysis is the matchup of the description of Judah's allotment (e) with the descriptions of the allotments of the

8.12 Crossing the Jordan (Joshua 3–4)

a **in camp on east side of Jordan** (3:1–5)
- Joshua promises that Yahweh will do great deed

  b **Joshua instructs priests to carry ark down to Jordan** (3:6–8)
- Joshua instructs priests to carry ark before people (3:6)
- Yahweh instructs Joshua that priests should carry ark down to Jordan, promises to <u>magnify</u> Joshua (3:7–8)

    c **Yahweh stops Jordan and people begin to cross** (3:9–17)
- <u>Levites</u>, with ark, remain <u>in middle of Jordan</u>

      d **CENTER: erection of memorial stones** (4:1–9)

    c′ **people finish crossing while Jordan is stopped** (4:10–13)
- <u>Levites</u>, with ark, remain <u>in middle of Jordan</u>

  b′ **Joshua instructs priests to carry ark up out of Jordan** (4:14–18)
- Yahweh <u>magnifies</u> Joshua; instructs him to command priests to carry ark up out of Jordan (4:14–16)
- Joshua instructs priests to carry ark out of Jordan (4:17–18)

a′ **in camp on west side of Jordan** (4:19–24)
- Joshua recounts mighty acts that Yahweh has done, memorialized by stones

8.13 Achan and Ai (Joshua 7:1–8:29)

a **Ai defeats Israel**: people of Ai pursue Israelites and defeat them (7:1–5)

  b **Joshua lies prostrate until evening** before the Lord (7:6–9)

    c **God's directions** for rectifying sin (7:10–15)

      d **CENTER: Achan's sin exposed and punished** (7:16–26)

    c′ **God's directions** for conquering Ai (8:1–2)

  b′ **Joshua spends two nights** in valley as he prepares attack (8:3–9)

a′ **Israel defeats Ai**: people of Ai pursue Israelites, but this time are defeated (8:10–35)

8.14 Allotment of land of Canaan (Joshua 13–24)

a **introduction** (13:1–7)
- Yahweh's challenge to Joshua, when he is old, to divide the land
- theme: <u>the land that remains</u>—whose inhabitants Yahweh will <u>drive out</u>

  b **Transjordanian tribes** (13:8–33)
- their allotments outside of Canaan

    c **Levites** (14:1–5)
- they will have no territory, only towns in other tribes

      d **personal allotment** for <u>hero of Kadesh</u>: Caleb (14:6–15)

        e **non-Rachel** tribal allotment: <u>Judah</u> (15:1–63)

          f **Rachel** tribal allotment: <u>Joseph</u> (16:1–17:18)

            g **CENTER: allotment at Shiloh**: seven tribes receive land by Yahweh's lot (18:1–10)

          f′ **Rachel** tribal allotment: Benjamin—next to <u>Joseph</u> (18:11–28)

        e′ **non-Rachel** tribal allotments: Simeon (inside <u>Judah</u>) and others (19:1–48)

      d′ **personal allotment** for <u>hero of Kadesh</u>: Joshua (19:49–50)
- conclusion of Shiloh allotments (19:51–52)

    c′ **Levites** (20:1–21:45)
- their towns in other tribes and their cities of refuge

  b′ **Transjordanian tribes** (22:1–34)
- their return to their allotments outside of Canaan, and their memorial altar to commemorate their share with the tribes in Canaan

a′ **conclusion** (23:1–24:33)
- Joshua's closing challenge to Israel, when he is old
- theme: <u>the land that remains</u>—whose inhabitants Yahweh will <u>drive out</u>

six smaller tribes (e′). The two units are about equal in length. Perhaps the connection between the two is found in the introduction to the group of six, where Simeon, the first tribe, receives an inheritance "within the territory of Judah" (19:1) and whose land "was taken from the share of Judah, because Judah's portion was more than they needed. So the Simeonites received their inheritance from the territory of Judah" (19:9).

The organization of Joshua 13–24 highlights several themes:

1. the challenge to continue the conquest, emphasized by its focus in the introductory and concluding units (a and a′)
2. the emphasis on the inclusion of the Transjordanian tribes among the Israelites, highlighted by its double coverage in matching units (b and b′)

8.15 Numbers 10:11–Joshua 24:33

a **wilderness journey: only Caleb and Joshua are faithful** (Num. 10:11–21:20)
- only <u>Caleb and Joshua</u> are faithful to Yahweh; only they will enter Canaan
- at <u>Kadesh</u>, Caleb gave good report; he <u>followed Yahweh wholeheartedly</u>; promised he would inherit area he explored (<u>Hebron area</u>) (14:24)
- brief <u>historical note</u> about Hebron (13:22); home of Anakites
- <u>men from each tribe</u> sent out to explore Canaan, including Caleb and Joshua

b **conquest of Transjordan under Moses** (Num. 21:21–Deut. 3:29)*
- topic: <u>war spoils</u> (Num. 31:1–54)
- <u>Transjordanian tribes</u> must go with brothers into Canaan (Num. 32:1–42)
- victories take place from main camp at Shittim, opposite Jericho
- almost entirely <u>upbeat</u>; isolated failure (Baal-peor) quickly remedied

c **Moses' exhortations to serve Yahweh, in light of lessons from Yahweh's past blessings and punishments** (Deut. 4–11)
- <u>narrative</u>; Moses transfers leadership to Joshua
- <u>blessings and curses</u>; <u>Mount Ebal and Mount Gerizim</u>
- Moses not allowed to enter Canaan; will die "in this land" (4:21–22); to <u>view land from Pisgah</u> (cf. 3:23–28)

d **CENTER: laws for life in Canaan** (Deut. 12–26)

c′ **Moses' exhortations to serve Yahweh, in light of the prospects of Yahweh's future blessings or punishments** (Deut. 27–34)
- <u>narrative</u>; Moses transfers leadership to Joshua
- <u>blessings and curses</u>; <u>Mount Ebal and Mount Gerizim</u>
- Moses not allowed to enter Canaan; dies on Mount Nebo, after <u>viewing land from top of Pisgah</u> (34:1–12)

b′ **conquest of Canaan under Joshua** (Josh. 1–12)
- topic: <u>war spoils</u> (7:1–8:35; 11:1–23)
- <u>Transjordanian tribes</u> go with brothers into Canaan
- victories take place from main camp at Gilgal, near Jericho
- almost entirely <u>upbeat</u>; isolated disobedience (Achan) quickly remedied

a′ **allotment of Canaan: only Caleb and Joshua are rewarded with their own allotments** (Josh. 13–24)
- <u>Caleb and Joshua</u> are only two individuals to receive personal allotments
- Caleb recalls experience at <u>Kadesh</u>, his good report, and that he <u>followed Yahweh wholeheartedly</u>; promise of inheriting Hebron area; he is given Hebron as the first allotment given in Canaan (14:6–15)
- brief <u>historical note</u> about Hebron (14:15); home of Anakites
- <u>men from each remaining tribe</u> sent out by Joshua to explore and divide up remaining land of Canaan

*Numbers 32–35 also corresponds to the allotment in Joshua 13–24.

---

3. the central role played by Yahweh in the allotment of the land to the tribes, underscored by the central position of the account of the divinely directed allotment of Canaan at Shiloh (g)

Overall Layout of Numbers 10:11–Joshua 24:33

To reinforce the unity of the historical conclusion to the Sinai treaty in Numbers 10:11–Joshua 24:33, its seven constituent units have been designed and arranged to form an overall symmetry, with Moses' grand review of the law (Deut. 12–26) at its center (8.15).

Conclusion

Numbers 10:11–Joshua 24:33 functions as a historical conclusion to the great treaty at Sinai. The main themes of this conclusion are highlighted in part by its structure. For example, the central importance of the law for Israel's success in the land is emphasized by the placement of Moses' grand review of the law (Deut. 12–26) at the center of the symmetric arrangement. The

positioning of this unit at the center reinforces the view (expressly stated throughout Deuteronomy and elsewhere) that the laws are central to Israel's future prosperity.

The importance of obeying Yahweh and his laws is reinforced by the double coverage of this theme in matching units on either side of the center. The first unit (Deut. 4–11) is Moses' introductory appeal to Israel to love and obey Yahweh and keep his laws based on lessons from the past. Israel's unique relationship with Yahweh has repeatedly made it the recipient of God's great acts of salvation in the past (rescue from Egypt, care in the wilderness, the revelation of his power at Sinai); but disobedience (complaining in the wilderness, idolatry with the golden calf, rebellion at Kadesh) has always resulted in punishment. Israel should learn from its past and humbly and gratefully continue to obey Yahweh and his laws (for its own sake!). In the matching unit in Deuteronomy 27–34, on the other hand, Moses calls Israel to obedience primarily in light of the future. Israel should obey Yahweh because its future blessing depends upon it. If Israel obeys Yahweh and refrains from rebellion, it will continue to experience Yahweh's gracious care and blessing; but if it rebels against Yahweh, it will be punished. Moses offers two possible futures for Israel ("I set before you two ways"): wonderful blessings if obedient or terrible curses if disobedient.

The theme of obedience and its rewards is further emphasized by the structural pairing of the wilderness journey (Num. 10:11–21:20) and the allotment of Canaan (Josh. 13–24). In the wilderness, the whole nation (including Moses, Aaron, Miriam, Korah, and all the people) rebelled—with the prominent exceptions of Caleb and Joshua. As a result, that whole generation perished in the wilderness—all, that is, except Caleb and Joshua. In the matching unit, the account of the tribal allotments, the obedient new generation is allotted the newly conquered land, and faithful Caleb and Joshua are rewarded for their faithfulness in the wilderness with special, private allotments (14:6–15; 19:49–50).

Finally, the promise of divine blessing (particularly in military conflicts) as a reward for obedience is underscored by the structural pairing of two outstanding examples of how Israel was blessed when it obeyed Yahweh. The first (Num. 21:21–36:13) recounts how an obedient generation of Israelites experienced victory and Yahweh's blessings under Moses' leadership in Transjordan, conquering the lands of the Amorites. The matching unit in Joshua 1–12 tells a similar story: how this same obedient generation of Israelites experienced Yahweh's mighty victories under Joshua's leadership in Canaan, conquering the lands of the Canaanites. The great military success in Transjordan under Moses' leadership and the even greater military success in Canaan under Joshua, are credited throughout to Yahweh whose blessing was upon this faithful new generation of Israelites as long as they refrained from rebellion. The exceptions (such as Israel's sin at Baal-peor and Achan's at Jericho) serve to prove the rule. Israel can expect Yahweh's continued blessings and help in the land if they remain obedient to him.

9
Book of the Law: Structural Unity

The foregoing analysis suggests that the first book in the Hebrew Bible is not Genesis through Deuteronomy, but Genesis through Joshua.[1] The design of the plot line that begins in Genesis and continues through Deuteronomy supports this conclusion. This plot line is filled with foreshadowings, predictions, instructions, commands, promises, introductions, and preparatory actions that do not find their fulfillments, completions, or conclusions until the story's grand finale in Joshua. Only in Joshua are all the loose ends of the story finally tied together for the audience. For example, Yahweh's promise to Abraham that the land of Canaan will be given to Abraham's descendants four centuries later creates a tension that is developed, intensified, and sustained throughout Genesis, Exodus, Leviticus, Numbers, and Deuteronomy. The suspense is finally resolved in Joshua.

Such interrelated, interwoven lines of suspense multiply as the story progresses, creating an ever-intensifying anticipation of the story's conclusion. Will Yahweh keep his repeated promises to Abraham, Isaac, and Jacob that their descendants will be given the land of Canaan? Will Israel be able to drive out the Canaanites as it has been promised repeatedly, beginning in the Book of Exodus? Will Yahweh keep his promises to the Israelites and go with them and ahead of them as they conquer the land? Will Caleb inherit Hebron, as God promised at Kadesh (Num. 14–15)? Will Joshua erect the altar on Mount Ebal as he was directed (Deut. 27)? Will the Israelites divide up the land in the manner that Yahweh has instructed (Num. 34)? What about the ceremony that Israel is to have at Shechem after it conquers the land (Deut. 11; 27)? Will Joshua establish cities of ref-

uge and levitical cities as he had been directed? Will the tribe of Joseph be given a double portion? Will Joseph's territory be in the Shechem area as promised? Will the Transjordanian tribes participate in the conquest of Canaan, as Moses instructed?

Dozens of such lines of suspense are developed as the story unfolds from Genesis through Deuteronomy. And as the story approaches its conclusion, the audience begins to anticipate the grand finale, the climax, when all the lines of suspense will finally be resolved and everything wrapped up. Such development and resolution of suspense is the very essence of good literature; it is what makes a good story so enjoyable and engaging. Without the Book of Joshua, the Book of the Law, which begins in Genesis 1 and builds and maintains suspense through Exodus, Leviticus, Numbers, and Deuteronomy, has no ending. This alone suggests that the Book of the Law of Moses was designed to close, not with Deuteronomy, but with Joshua.

The overall structure of Genesis through Joshua strongly supports this conclusion. I have already suggested that the material from Genesis 1 through Joshua 24 comprises three major units. These three units create a symmetry focusing on the Sinai treaty:

---

a historical introduction to the Sinai treaty
  (Gen. 1:1–Exod. 19:2)
  b Sinai treaty (Exod. 19:3–Num. 10:10)
a′ historical conclusion to the Sinai treaty
  (Num. 10:11–Josh. 24)

This sense of balance is reinforced by the similar structural design of the three units. Each is composed of seven symmetrically arranged parts. Without Joshua the final section of the Pentateuch would comprise only five parts, making both the historical conclusion and the entire Pentateuch oddly unbalanced and structurally incomplete. Moreover, careful examina-

---

1. For a recent argument for the Hexateuch, including a brief structural analysis of its symmetric arrangement (differing somewhat from the one proposed here), see J. Milgrom, *Numbers* (JPS Torah Commentary; Philadelphia: Jewish Publication Society, 1990), xiii–xix.

tion of the layout of the Pentateuch and Joshua suggests that, with the inclusion of Joshua, the entire composition forms an overall twenty-one-part symmetry. The seven parts of the historical introduction (Gen. 1:1–Exod. 19:2) appear to be matched in chiastic order by the seven parts of the historical conclusion (Num. 10:11–Josh. 24); and at the center is the treaty itself (Exod. 19:3–Num. 10:10), which forms its own sevenfold symmetry.

Correspondence of the Primeval History (Genesis 1–11) and the Allotment of Canaan (Joshua 13–24)

At first blush there would seem to be little in common between the primeval history and the allotment of Canaan. There may, however, be a very significant and intentional connection. Genesis 1–11 recounts, among other things, how all the peoples of the earth came to live in their respective "lands" ('ereṣ)—all the peoples, that is, except the descendants of Abraham. The various peoples spread out "into their lands" (bĕ'arṣōtām) "according to their families" (lĕmišpĕḥōtām) (Gen. 10:5). The Canaanites, for example, settled in Canaan; and their "territory" (gĕbûl) and its boundaries are described: "And the territory of the Canaanites extended (wayĕhî gĕbûl) from (min) Sidon . . . as far as ('ad) Gaza" (10:19). Thus all the peoples of the earth settled in their respective "lands" (bĕ'arṣōtām) "according to their families" (lĕmišpĕḥōtām). Conspicuous by its absence, of course, is the audience's own nation: Israel.

Israel finally receives its "land" ('ereṣ) in Joshua 13–24. In that unit, in language reminiscent of Genesis 10, Israel is allotted its land. Israel's tribes are allotted their "territories" (gĕbûl) "according to their families" (lĕmišpĕḥōtām) (Josh. 15:1–2; 19:32–33; etc.). The expression "and their territory extended (wayĕhî gĕbûl) from (min) . . . as far as ('ad)" (and variations) occurs throughout the tribal allotment descriptions in Joshua 13–21 (13:30; 19:10; etc.).

There are other significant points of contact between Genesis 1–11 and Joshua 13–24. The first unit concludes with the introduction of Israel's ancestors: Terah and his two sons, Abraham and Nahor (Gen. 11:27–32). The last unit concludes with Joshua's farewell address, in which he refers back to the time when Israel's ancestors lived "beyond the River," mentioning Terah, Abraham, and Nahor by name:

Long ago your ancestors, including Terah the father of Abraham and Nahor, lived beyond the River. . . .

But I took your father Abraham from the land beyond the River. . . . Throw away the gods your ancestors worshiped beyond the River . . . and serve Yahweh . . . Choose this day whom you will serve, whether the gods your ancestors served beyond the River. . . .

—Joshua 24:2–3, 14–15

Terah is mentioned nowhere else in the Pentateuch or Joshua—or in fact anywhere else in the entire Hebrew Bible (except once in Chronicles).[2] With Joshua 24 we come full circle.

Correspondence of the Stories of Abraham (Genesis 12:1–21:7) and the Conquest of Canaan (Joshua 1–12)

The story of Abraham is filled with foreshadowings and predictions that find their fulfillment in the story of the conquest. The most obvious of these is Yahweh's repeated promise to Abraham that his descendants would be given the land of Canaan. This promise is first made to Abram in Genesis 12:6–7 and then repeated in Genesis 13:14–17:

Lift up your eyes from where you are and look north and south, east and west. All the land that you see I will give to you and your offspring forever. . . . Go, walk through the length and breadth of the land, for I am giving it to you.

In Genesis 15:13–21 Yahweh promises Abram:

Your descendants . . . will be strangers in a country not their own, and they will be enslaved and mistreated four hundred years. . . . But in the fourth generation your descendants will come back here, for the sin of the Amorites is not yet full. . . . To your descendants I will give this land . . . the land of the . . . Perizzites . . . Amorites, Canaanites, Girgashites and Jebusites.

This promise is reiterated to subsequent generations (Gen. 26:2–5; 28:13; 35:12); but it is the promise to Abraham that is repeated. This is seen in the promise to Isaac:

To you and your descendants I will give all these lands and will confirm the oath I swore to your fa-

---

2. It may also be significant that in Genesis 12:6–7 (i.e., in the paragraph immediately following the close of Gen. 1–11), Abram arrives in Shechem from Mesopotamia, having recently buried his father and having left his brother Nahor behind. In Shechem he is told: "To your descendants I will give this land" (12:6–7). In Israel's final assembly in the Book of Joshua (Josh. 24), the story comes full circle: Abraham's descendants have become many (cf. Gen. 12:2) and have been given this land; they now assemble at Shechem and listen to Joshua's farewell address, in which he refers to their ancestors who lived in Mesopotamia, including Abraham and his father Terah and his brother Nahor.

ther Abraham . . . I will give them all these lands . . . because Abraham obeyed me and kept . . . my laws.

—Genesis 26:3–5

Yahweh's promise to Abraham (cf. also Gen. 17:8) is finally fulfilled in Joshua 1–12, when Yahweh actually "gives" (*nātan*) the land of Canaan to Israel (cf. 1:3, 15; 2:9, 14, 24). Joshua 1–12 opens with Yahweh's promise to Joshua that he is about to "give" (*nātan*) Canaan to Israel (1:3), which is followed by the account of how Yahweh gave the land to Israel, victory by victory, "giving" (*nātan*) city after city into the hands of the Israelites (6:2; 10:8, 29–30, 32; 11:6, 8). The unit closes with the land now in Israel's hands, including "the lands of the Hittites, Amorites, Canaanites, Perizzites, Hivites, and Jebusites" (Josh. 12:7–8; cf. Gen. 15:16). God's ancient promise to Abraham was finally fulfilled!

There are other touch points between the two units that an audience would appreciate. Abram's arrival and activities in Canaan foreshadows the events of the conquest in Joshua 1–12. For example, when Abram first enters Canaan he builds an altar at Shechem—his first altar in the land (Gen. 12:6–7). When Israel enters Canaan, the nation assembles at Shechem and builds an altar there—also their first altar in the land. Abram's second stop is between Bethel and Ai, where he builds his second altar (Gen. 12:8). Israel's second battle in Canaan takes place near Ai, with Israel camping "between Bethel and Ai" (Josh. 8:12). Abram eventually settles in Hebron, where he builds his third altar (Gen. 13:18; cf. 14:13; 18:1). Joshua's third battle involves Hebron (Josh. 10:3, 5); and his southern campaign results in the conquest of Hebron (10:36–37). In Abram's only military campaign, he and his small force attack and defeat a northern enemy (by night and presumably by surprise), having pursued them "as far as Dan" (Gen. 14:14–15). This foreshadows Joshua's fourth battle, in which he conducts a surprise attack against the northern Canaanite enemy and pursues them "as far as the valley of Mizpah"—in the region of Dan (Josh. 11:7–8).

Correspondence of the Story of Isaac (Genesis 21:8–28:4) and Moses' Final Exhortation and Death (Deuteronomy 27–34)

The story of Isaac has several possible links with the final chapters of Deuteronomy, although this match is weak. One of the most prominent developments in the Isaac story is the death of Abraham (and Sarah), with the emphasis on their place of burial in the cave of Machpelah

(Gen. 23, 25). Perhaps an echo of this is the account of Moses' death and burial (Deut. 34), in which his burial place stands in contrast to that of Abraham: "No one knows where his grave is" (34:6). The contrast of their burials may be fortuitous; but certainly Abraham and Moses are the two dominant figures in the Pentateuch and Joshua; and here, in the composition's third and third-to-last units, are the accounts of their final words, deaths, and burials.

The theme of life and death may also tie these two units together. This theme is emphasized in Deuteronomy 27–34. For example, in 30:19–20 Moses exhorts Israel:

> I have set before you life and death. . . . Choose life, so that you and your children may live. . . . For Yahweh is your life, and he will give you many years in the land he swore to give to your fathers, Abraham, Isaac, and Jacob.

Abraham is willing to obey God even if it means the death of his beloved son Isaac (Gen. 22); while Esau, in contrast, scorns the birthright (and his part in God's blessing?) because, he claims hyperbolically, he is "about to die" (25:19–34).

Correspondence of the Story of Jacob (Genesis 28:5–37:1) and Moses' Review of the Law (Deuteronomy 12–26)

The story of Jacob and Moses' review of the laws in Deuteronomy 12–26 may have an interesting link. The story of Jacob is dominated by societal discord: family, marital, sibling, and community strife; mistreatment of aliens (Jacob); treachery (Laban, Jacob, Rachel; Jacob's sons at Shechem); murder; dishonesty; theft (Rachel); favoritism; and so forth. These themes completely dominate the narrative; there is hardly an episode that does not revolve around the theme of societal and family discord and strife.

Whether coincidental or not, Moses' survey of the laws that are to govern Israel's life in Canaan, in Deuteronomy 12–26, represents the antithesis of this theme. His survey focuses on the laws that will regulate society and family so that there will be peace and justice rather than chaos and wrongdoing. The laws deal with many of the very problems that are illustrated in the story of Jacob, especially family and marital strife, strife among siblings, community strife, dishonesty, murder, and the mistreatment of aliens and the disadvantaged.

Several links are particularly striking. First, the plight of the younger versus the older son (Jacob and Esau) and the plight of the unloved versus the loved wife and their children (Leah and Rachel) are treated in Deuteronomy 21:15–17. Second, the giving of the birthright to the younger son rather than to the elder son (Jacob and Esau) is discussed—and forbidden—in the same passage. Third, the theme of Jacob's mistreatment as an alien and a hired hand in a foreign land is echoed in Deuteronomy 12–26, which deals extensively with the call to kindness to the alien and the hired hand (cf. 24:14, 17). Lastly, the regulations about a hired worker's wages and about letting servants go in the seventh year, not "empty-handed," but supplying them liberally "from your flock," recalls Jacob's plight with Laban, who withheld or changed Jacob's wages, would not let him go after seven or even twenty years, and tried to send him away "empty-handed" (cf. Gen. 31:6–7, 38–42; Deut. 15:12–18; 24:14–15).

Correspondence of the Story of Joseph (Genesis 37–50) and Moses' Introductory Exhortation to Obey Yahweh (Deuteronomy 4–11)

The story of Joseph and Moses' introductory exhortation may have an important connection. Joseph's story remarkably exemplifies what Moses declares in Deuteronomy 4–11, that Israel's history teaches that obedience brings blessing and disobedience brings punishment. In Deuteronomy 4–11, Moses bases his call to love and obey Yahweh on the lessons from Israel's history. He points out that when Israel remained obedient to Yahweh, it was blessed; but when it disobeyed, it was punished. These lessons should teach Israel that it should obey Yahweh; for in the end, it pays.

The story of Joseph is a classic illustration of this truth from Israel's history. Joseph's brothers sinned: they plotted Joseph's death, sold him as a slave, and lied to their father. In contrast, Joseph remained faithful to God, even in the midst of adversity and suffering. In the end the older brothers are punished: they are brought to their knees, humiliated, judged for their wrongdoing; and Judah forfeits his status as firstborn. Joseph, however, is exalted and rewarded, blessed by Yahweh and made a great ruler over Egypt. He is elevated over his brothers and reckoned as Jacob's firstborn.

Correspondence of the Stories of the Exodus (Exodus 1:1–13:16) and Israel's Sojourn in Transjordan (Numbers 21:21–Deuteronomy 3:29)

The exodus story and the story of Israel's sojourn in the plains of Moab have many points of correspondence connecting them. The most obvious is the similarity of Israel's circumstances and Yahweh's protection. These two units recount the two times in the Book of the Law when the nation of Israel sojourned in a foreign nation and was protected by Yahweh against that nation's hostile intentions. In Egypt, Yahweh protected Israel from pharaoh, even though the king called in magicians to oppose Moses and the Israelites. In Moab, Yahweh protected Israel from that land's monarch, even though the king called in a magician to curse Israel. In both stories the king is driven by fear of Israel (Exod. 1:10; Num. 22:2–3). Israel's troubles with pharaoh begin when he expresses his fear that the Israelites might be dangerous, because "the people (ʿam) are too numerous for us (rab wěʿāṣûm mimmennû)" (Exod. 1:9). Israel's troubles with Balak begin when Balak expresses a very similar fear: "The people (ʿam) are numerous (rab)" and "the people (ʿam) are too numerous for me (ʿāṣûm hûʾ mimmennî)" (Num. 22:3, 6). In both stories, the monarch and his hired magician(s) are powerless against Yahweh (cf. 23:23).

There are other ties between these two accounts. Balaam's oracles refer twice to Israel's exodus from Egypt (Num. 23:22; 24:8). In both stories Yahweh uses ordinary animals in miraculous ways (snakes turning to sticks, donkeys talking) to stop Israel's opponents. Both stories emphasize Israel's numerous population, reckoning it at about 600,000 men (Exod. 12:37; Num. 26). Both stories tell of Israel's departure from Rameses the day after the Passover celebration, while the Egyptians were mourning and burying their dead firstborn, which is described in both units as a judgment upon Egypt's gods. And both mention the journey from Rameses to Succoth (Exod. 11:1–13:16 [esp. 12:37]; Num. 33:3–5).

Correspondence of the Two Stories of Israel's Wilderness Journeys (Exodus 13:17–19:2; Numbers 10:11–21:20)

The two accounts of Israel's journey through the wilderness correspond in too many ways to list. They are obviously alike in that they recount the two times in which the nation is in migration. Both are journeys through the "wilderness." One ends with Israel's arrival at Sinai; the other begins with Israel's departure from Sinai. The first closes with the date of their arrival at Sinai (Exod. 19:1) and the second opens with the date their departure (Num. 10:11). The first features Moses meeting and speaking with his father-in-

9.1 Book of the Law (Genesis 1–Joshua 24)

a **primeval history**: the nations <u>receive their allotted territories</u> (Gen. 1–11)
- nations' <u>territory</u> (*gĕbûl*) <u>according to their families</u> (*lĕmišpĕḥōtām*)
- topic: introduction of Israel's ancestors in Mesopotamia: <u>Terah, Nahor, Abraham</u>

  b **Abraham** (Gen. 12:1–21:7)
  - <u>Yahweh's promise</u> to <u>give</u> (*nātan*) Canaan to Abraham's descendants
  - Abraham <u>builds altar in Shechem</u>; lives in area <u>between Bethel and Ai</u>; <u>Hebron</u>
  - military victory against enemy from north; sudden attack, pursuit past Dan

    c **Isaac** and <u>death of Israel's founding father</u>, Abraham (Gen. 21:8–28:4)
    - themes: <u>death</u> (Sarah, Abraham, Ishmael, Isaac [on Moriah; nearing death]), <u>blessings</u> (Abraham, Ishmael, Isaac, Jacob, Esau)

      d **Jacob**: a story illustrating <u>evils of social and family discord</u> (Gen. 28:5–37:1)
      - story of social and family strife, murder, lying, theft, abuse of aliens, etc.
      - plight of <u>unloved wife</u>, hired man; <u>younger and older siblings</u>; birthright

        e **Joseph**: a story of how God <u>rewards faithful obedience</u> (Gen. 37:2–50:26)
        - themes: <u>faithfulness rewarded</u>, disobedience punished

          f **exodus from Egypt** (Exod. 1:1–13:16)
          - <u>Yahweh saves Israel in foreign land</u>
          - host king fears Israel is <u>too numerous</u>; calls <u>magicians</u> to oppose; fails

            g **failure and divine grace in the wilderness** (Exod. 13:17–19:2)
            - <u>nation in migration</u>
            - ends: arrival at Sinai
            - date: third new moon
            - <u>meeting Jethro</u>
            - <u>complaining</u> (*lûn*); provision of <u>water</u> from rock; <u>manna</u>; quail

              CENTER: treaty at Sinai (Exod. 19:3–Num. 10:10)

            g′ **failure and divine grace in the wilderness** (Num. 10:11–21:20)
            - <u>nation in migration</u>
            - begins: departure from Sinai
            - date: second year, second month, twentieth day
            - <u>meeting Jethro</u>
            - <u>complaining</u> (*lûn*); provision of <u>water</u> from rock; <u>manna</u>; quail

          f′ **victory in Moab** (Num. 21:21–Deut. 3:29)
          - <u>Yahweh saves Israel in foreign land</u>
          - host king fears Israel is <u>too numerous</u>; calls <u>magician</u> to oppose; fails

        e′ **call to obedience**; based on lessons from history (Deut. 4–11)
        - history teaches that <u>faithfulness is rewarded</u>, disobedience punished

      d′ **laws for stability and justice** in society and families (Deut. 12–26)
      - laws to counter <u>social and family strife</u>, murder, lying, theft, abuse of aliens, etc.
      - laws for <u>unloved wife</u>, hired man; <u>younger and older siblings</u>; birthright

    c′ **Moses' final words** and <u>death of Israel's other founding father</u>, Moses (Deut. 27–34)
    - themes: <u>death</u> and life (in following the covenant), <u>blessings</u>

  b′ **conquest of Canaan** (Josh. 1–12)
  - <u>promise to Abraham is fulfilled</u>: Yahweh <u>gives</u> (*nātan*) Canaan to Abraham's descendants
  - <u>Shechem altar</u>; battle in area <u>between Bethel and Ai</u>; <u>Hebron</u> conquered
  - military victory against enemy from north; sudden attack, pursuit past Dan area

a′ <u>allotment of land</u> of Canaan to Israel (Josh. 13–24)
- Israel's tribal <u>territories</u> (*gĕbûl*) <u>according to their families</u> (*lĕmišpĕḥōtām*)
- topic: Israel's ancestors in Mesopotamia: <u>Terah, Nahor, Abraham</u> (24:1–33)

---

law as Israel arrives at Mount Sinai; the second features Moses meeting and speaking with his father-in-law as Israel departs. Other shared themes include the following:

1. Israel's "complaining" (*lûn*) about the lack of food and water (Exod. 15–17; Num. 11; 21; "murmur" [*lûn*] is a keyword in both stories [cf. Exod. 16:7–8; 17:3; Num. 14:27, 36; 16:11; 17:5 [17:20]], and the complaints in both contain wishes to return to Egypt and memories of the better food they had there)

2. Moses' bringing forth water from a rock by striking it with his rod (Exod. 17; Num. 20)

3. the miraculous provision of manna—which both stories describe "like coriander seed" that came down with the night dew and could be collected in the morning (Exod. 16; Num. 11)

4. the miraculous provision of quail that "covered the ground" (Exod. 16; Num. 11)

Conclusion

The intricate and overarching symmetric scheme spanning Genesis through Joshua strongly suggests that the final product was designed to function as a single composition (9.1). This grand symmetric plan, together with the prolific use of various peculiar structuring techniques throughout (e.g., thirteen-part and fourteen-part symmetries, the frequent use of addenda) suggests, but does not demand, a single author/editor.[3]

The immediate framing of the treaty with two condemnatory units about Israel's troubled journeys from Egypt to Sinai (g) and from Sinai to the plains of Moab (g′) is certainly intentional. The point is clear: Yahweh's covenant with Israel was not based on Israel's righteousness, since Israel rebelled and sinned all along the journey to and from Sinai. The agreement, rather, was based on divine grace; it was given despite the lack of, rather than because of, Israel's worthiness. The internal structures of these two wilderness stories reinforce this theme of divine grace. They recount, in matched duplication (for emphasis), how Yahweh provided his rebellious people with food and water despite their sin and complaining.

The pairing of the Joseph story (e), which teaches that righteousness is rewarded, and Moses' introductory exhortation to obey Yahweh (e′) underscores the importance of obedience and faithfulness to Yahweh. Moreover, the pairing of the unit about Abraham (b)—including

---

3. This analysis does not necessarily rule out the Mosaic authorship of Genesis through Deuteronomy. One could speculate that Moses laid out the overall plan of the Book of the Law, completed all but its final sections (leaving unfinished the end of Deuteronomy and the Book of Joshua), and directed a successor such as Phinehas to complete the book's unfinished final sections after his death, following Israel's successful conquest and allotment of Canaan.

Yahweh's promise that Abraham's descendants would inherit the land—with the unit in which Yahweh keeps his promise and enables Israel to conquer the land (b′) highlights the themes of Yahweh's trustworthiness and his mighty power. Yahweh is worthy of Israel's devotion. It was he who promised to make them a nation and give them a land; and it is only by Yahweh's grace and initiative that Israel is a nation and has its own divinely granted land.

The matching of the stories of the miraculous exodus (f) and the victories in the plains of Moab (f′) reinforces the theme of Yahweh's great power, which is evidenced even in foreign lands (Egypt, Moab) and against the supernatural forces of magic (Egyptian magicians, Balaam) and pagan gods. Yahweh is worthy of Israel's obedience and trust. He has demonstrated that he can protect them if they trust him (as he can punish them if they rebel).

The most conspicuous point of the overall structure of the Book of the Law is the central position of the Sinai treaty. The treaty stands at the center of the entire composition, and both the historical introduction and the historical conclusion support it. The symmetric scheme helps convey the profound, central importance of this treaty and its laws for the nation of Israel. At the center of the treaty itself stands the account of the construction of the tabernacle, climaxed by the glory of God's entering and filling the sanctuary. Yahweh's remarkable act of tabernacling among his people, then, represents the climax of the climax. It is the central point, the bottom line, of the entire Book of the Law. Almighty God has taken up his abode among humankind, among the people of Israel. All else in the book and in Israel's history leads toward or derives from this central truth.

Unit 3
Historical Books

10

Judges

Israel's Downward Spiral

The Book of Judges tells the story of Israel's religious and political disintegration during the period of the judges. The casual reader may mistake the book as a collection of hero stories; but a closer reading reveals that it is a condemnatory treatise, depicting the period of the judges as one of failure and portraying most of the judges as antiheroes. The book's only real hero is Israel's God, Yahweh, who continued to graciously help Israel despite its repeated unfaithfulness and despite the failures of its judges—particularly the later judges. The book's structure is designed on both larger and smaller levels to convey the author's two main themes: Israel's spiritual and political decline and Yahweh's gracious and repeated deliverance of Israel.

The Book of Judges (like the Book of the Law) is composed of three major parts, each well delineated by various structuring techniques:[1]

a prologue (1:1–3:6)
b main body (3:7–16:31)
c epilogue (17:1–21:25)

Prologue (Judges 1:1–3:6)

The prologue sets the stage for the main body. It comprises two parts: (1) a review of the territorial successes and failures of the various tribes after Joshua's death (1:1–2:5), and (2) a summary and theological interpretation of the period of the judges (2:6–3:6).[2]

Failure of Israel's Conquest of Canaan (Judges 1:1–2:5)

The first section of the prologue tells how the conquest of Canaan faltered after the time of Joshua. The symmetric (a-b-a′) structure of this section reinforces the sense of failure (10.1). Both the opening and closing episodes feature all-Israel assemblies (a and a′). Both assemblies involve communication between Israel and Yah-

---

1. For example, Carl F. Keil, *Biblical Commentary on the Books of Joshua, Judges, Ruth* (Edinburgh: Clark, 1868), 237; George F. Moore, *Judges* (International Critical Commentary; Edinburgh: Clark, 1895), xiii–xv; Karl Budde, *Das Buch der Richter* (Leipzig/Tübingen: Mohr, 1897), vii–viii; J. Alberto Soggin, *Judges: A Commentary*, trans. John Bowden (Old Testament Library; Philadelphia: Westminster, 1981), 4 (Moore, Budde, and Soggin all begin the main body with 2:6); D. W. Gooding, "The Composition of the Book of Judges," *Eretz-Israel* 16 (1982), 72*; Barry G. Webb, *The Book of Judges: An Integrated Reading* (Sheffield: Sheffield Academic Press, 1987), 81, 181–82. This three-part arrangement has been created by designing the main body with an unmistakable internal coherence that unifies it into a self-contained whole and separates it from what precedes and follows. A tripartite arrangement is quite useful to a storyteller and satisfying to an audience: the introduction allows the storyteller to set the stage for his upcoming story, orienting the audience and arousing their interest; and after the story, a conclusion or epilogue not only gives the audience a chance to "unwind," but it gives the storyteller an opportunity to enhance the story's effect by drawing out its significance or by augmenting it in such a way as to reinforce its message. The three-part arrangement of Judges serves these ends. The book's prologue prepares the audience for the upcoming story by setting its stage, by summarizing it in advance, and by explaining why the story will develop the way it does. In so doing, it piques the listener's interest. The main body tells the story; and the epilogue augments the story with two anecdotes designed to reinforce the story's message.

2. For example, Keil, *Judges*, 237–66; Moore, *Judges*, xiii–xv; G. W. Thatcher, *Judges and Ruth* (New York: Oxford University Press, 1904), 4–5; C. F. Burney, *The Book of Judges* (2d ed.; London: Rivington, 1920; repr. New York: Ktav, 1966), xxxiv–xxxv; John Gray, *Joshua, Judges, Ruth* (New Century Bible; London: Nelson, 1967; repr. Grand Rapids: Eerdmans, 1986), 194–97; Soggin, *Judges*, 4, 17–44; Gooding, "Composition of the Book of Judges"; Webb, *Judges*, 81–122. Of these, Thatcher, Moore, and Soggin (all following Budde) see 1:1–2:5 as the introduction to the whole book and 2:6–3:6 as the introduction to the main body. The break between the two parts is marked by the structural fissure at 2:6. After reviewing a series of events that occurred after Joshua's death (1:1–2:5), the author returns in 2:6 to a time before Joshua's death, recounting the leader's death again and then reviewing another series of events that occurred after his death (2:6–3:6). This dischronologization creates a major break in the flow of the narrative and effectively divides the prologue into two halves. The author then reinforces this two-part arrangement by designing each part with a self-contained, coherent internal configuration (see below). The only real question here is how to understand the structural place of 2:1–5. Although there is virtual consensus that it functions as the conclusion of the unit beginning in 1:1, this episode could be either understood as standing on its own as a third unit in the book's introduction or—less likely—seen as the introduction

---

10.1 Failure to conquer Canaan (Judges 1:1–2:5)

a **optimistic opening assembly** (at Gilgal?) (1:1–2)
- tribal conquests begin
- obedient Israelites initiate positive communication with Yahweh
- tribes set out to take land, with Yahweh's blessing and direction

b **failure of the tribes to take their lands** (1:3–36)
- (1) Judah: more positive
- (2) Benjamin: negative
- (3) Joseph: negative
- (4) Zebulun: negative
- (5) Asher: negative
- (6) Naphtali: negative
- (7) Dan: very negative

a´ **disheartening closing assembly** at Bokim (2:1–5)
- conquest ends in failure and divine condemnation
- Yahweh initiates negative communication with disobedient Israelites
- Yahweh will no longer help tribes take their land

---

weh, deal with the issue of the conquest of Canaan, and twice employ the verb "go up" (ʿālâ). The author uses their corresponding themes to highlight the decline that occurs in the period between them.[3]

The material enclosed between these two assemblies (b) is structured to reinforce this sense of decline. This seven-part survey of the victories and defeats of seven Israelite tribes is arranged from positive to negative. It begins with a relatively positive section about Judah's exploits (1:3–20) and is then followed by five sections, each almost entirely negative, recounting the failures of five other tribes (Benjamin, Joseph, Zebulun, Asher, Naphtali) to take various Canaanite cities. The survey concludes with the worst case of all, the failure of Dan: "The Amorites forced the Danites to remain in the high-

lands, not permitting them to come down into the valley" (1:34).

The author's preference for seven-part presentations is evident on a microstructural level throughout 1:1–2:5. For example, the review of the tribes' accomplishments achieves a seven-part presentation by omitting Reuben, Levi, Gad, and Issachar and placing Simeon within the story of Judah's conquest.[4] The Judah unit (1:3–20) likewise has a septenary configuration; it is composed of seven episodes (arranged geographically from north to south) plus a summary:

---

a victory at Bezek (1:3–7)
b conquest of Jerusalem (1:8)
c conquest of Hebron (1:9–10)
d conquest of Debir (1:11–15)
e settlement of the Arad area by the Kenites (1:16)
f conquest of Hormah (1:17)
g failure to conquer Philistia (1:18, reading with the Septuagint)
   summary (1:19–20)

The story of the Joseph tribes (1:22–29) is structured in seven symmetric parts, beginning and ending with Ephraim's territory, with events in Manasseh's territory in between:

---

a Ephraim's success in conquering Bethel (1:22–26)
   b Manasseh's failure to conquer Beth-shean (1:27)
   c Manasseh's failure to conquer Taanach (1:27)
   d Manasseh's failure to conquer Dor (1:27)
   e Manasseh's failure to conquer Ibleam (1:27)
   f Manasseh's failure to conquer Megiddo (1:27–28)
g Ephraim's failure in conquering Gezer (1:29)

---

to the material of 2:6–3:6. Webb (pp. 102–3) points out that 2:1–5 is connected with what precedes by the recurrence of the keyword ʿlh ("to go up"). He argues that 2:1–5 reviews and evaluates the events in chap. 1. Moore (pp. 56–57) argues similarly. Robert G. Boling, *Judges: A New Translation with Introduction and Commentary* (Anchor Bible 6a; Garden City: Doubleday, 1975), 36, suggests that chap. 1 functions as an exegesis "by anticipation" of the angel's speech in 2:1–5. By so organizing the prologue, the author is able to set the stage for the upcoming story in two phases: historically, by reviewing the Israelite tribes' activities in the conquest of Canaan after Joshua's time (1:1–2:5); then ideologically, by summarizing the upcoming story from a theological perspective (2:6–3:6)—which has the additional effect of creating a sense of anticipation for the listener.

3. The first assembly is optimistic: the nation initiates communication with Yahweh; they ask Yahweh which tribe should lead the conquest; and Yahweh's answer ("Judah") is entirely positive. The second assembly is a negative echo of the first: now it is Yahweh, disappointed with his disobedient people, who initiates the communication. His message is condemnatory: because of their disobedience, the tribes will no longer be able to successfully go up against the Canaanites. The assembly ends with the Israelites weeping (2:4–5). What began well ends badly.

4. It should be noted that the order of the seven tribes is geographic, from south to north (with Dan in its proper position according to events that will be narrated at the end of the book)—an arrangement that would have been appreciated by Israelite listeners familiar with the land.

10.2 Israel's pattern of decline (Judges 2:6–3:6)

a **positive beginning**: during lifetime of Joshua and elders, Israelites set out to take their inheritances and they <u>serve</u> (*wayyaʿabdû*) Yahweh (2:6–9)

b **sin of next generation** (2:10–13)
- contrasted with their <u>fathers</u> (*ʾabôt*)
- <u>served</u> (*ʿbd*) the Baals; <u>worshiped</u> (*wayyištaḥăwû*) other gods
- <u>went after other gods</u> (*wayyēlĕkû ʾaḥărê ʾĕlōhîm ʾăḥērîm*)
- occurred once; and they had an excuse ("they did not know")

c **judgment**: military defeat from surrounding nations (2:14–15)
- begins: <u>Yahweh was angry with Israel</u> (*wayyiḥar-ʾap yhwh bĕyiśrāʾēl*)

d **CENTER: Yahweh's gracious intervention** (2:16)

b′ **worse sins of each successive generation** (2:17–19)
- contrasted with their <u>fathers</u> (*ʾabôt*)
- <u>served</u> (*ʿbd*) the Baals; <u>worshiped</u> (*lĕhištaḥăwôt*) other gods
- <u>went after other gods</u> (*lāleket ʾaḥărê ʾĕlōhîm ʾăḥērîm*)
- not just once, but repeatedly; and no excuse given

c′ **worse judgment**: Yahweh will no longer enable Israel to take their own land (2:20–3:4)
- begins: <u>Yahweh was angry with Israel</u> (*wayyiḥar-ʾap yhwh bĕyiśrāʾēl*)

a′ **disheartening conclusion**: Israelites, having failed to take their land, settle among the Canaanites, intermarry, and <u>serve</u> (*wayyaʿabdû*) their gods (3:5–6)

Finally, a seven-part presentation is found in the brief Asher unit, which features a list of seven unconquered cities (1:31–32): Acco, Sidon, Ahlab, Achzib, Helbah, Aphek, Rehob.

Israel's Decline during the Period of the Judges (Judges 2:6–3:6)

The second section of the prologue offers a theological explanation and an overview of the entire period of the judges. The author's view presented here is that Israel went from bad to worse—in a downward spiral—during the period; and this view is reinforced by the section's structure.[5] The section comprises seven paragraphs arranged in a modified (a-b-c-d-b′-c′-a′) symmetry (10.2). The last three paragraphs match the first three, but describe situations worse than those of the first three. The center (d) describes Yahweh's gracious, successive acts of intervention: "Yahweh raised up judges, and they delivered them from their plunderers." By positioning the paragraph about Yahweh's help at the center of this bad-to-worse symmetry, the author suggests that Yahweh's gracious help had little moral effect on Israel, who became even worse despite his help.

Main Body (Judges 3:7–16:31)

The main body of the Book of Judges recounts, in chronological order, the stories of the successive judges that ruled over Israel during the period of the judges. There were thirteen judges to review, but the author creates a seven-part scheme by singling out seven judges (the "major judges") to cover in detail, while merely summarizing the other ("minor") judges in two or three verses each.[6] The seven resulting units of the main body are the following:

---

a Othniel (3:7–11)
b Ehud (3:12–30)
c Deborah and Barak (4:1–5:31)
d Gideon (6:1–8:32)
e Abimelech (8:33–9:57)
f Jephthah (10:6–12:7)
g Samson (13:1–16:31)

Each of these units is clearly delineated for the audience by the highly structured manner in which the unit is introduced, developed, and concluded. Each unit follows the same basic pattern of presentation consisting of eleven elements, with minor variations:

a. beginning
1. introductory statement about Israel's lapse into evil: "And the Israelites again did evil in the eyes of Yahweh" (*wayyōsipû*

---

5. It is noteworthy that both sections of the prologue (1:1–2:5; 2:6–3:6) are organized according to a similar structural plan. Both begin optimistically with the tribes' setting out to possess their inheritances and Israel's serving Yahweh; and both end negatively, with the disintegration of the conquest and allusions to Israel's idolatry. In both, the intervening paragraphs are arranged in a bad-to-worse order, reinforcing the theme of Israel's decline. The emphasis on Israel's failure is unmistakable.

6. The six minor judges are Shamgar (3:31), Tola (10:1–2), Jair (10:3–5), Ibzan (12:8–10), Elon (12:11–12), and Abdon (12:13–15).

10.3 Othniel (Judges 3:7–11)

a **beginning of oppression** (3:7–8)
- Israel sins and Yahweh sells them into the <u>hand</u> (*bĕyăd*) of Cushan-rishathaim
- subjugation for eight years

b **TURNING POINT: Yahweh intervenes** and raises up Othniel, who rescues Israel (3:9)

a′ **end of oppression** (3:10–11)
- Yahweh delivers Cushan-rishathaim into the <u>hand</u> (*bĕyăd*) of Othniel
- the land has rest for forty years

---

bĕnê yiśrā'ēl la'ăśôt hāra' bĕ'ênê yhwh) or a slight variation (3:7, 12; 4:1; 6:1; 10:6; 13:1)[7]

2. details of the evil (3:7b; 8:33b–34; 10:6)
3. statement about Yahweh's anger (3:8a; 10:7)
4. statement about Yahweh's "giving," "selling," etc., Israel to their enemies (3:8; 3:12; 4:2; 6:1; 10:7; 13:1b)
5. details of the oppression, usually including number of years Israel served the oppressor (3:8, 13–14; 4:2–3; 6:1b–5; 10:8–9; 13:1b)
6. statement about Israel's "cry" (*z'q*) to Yahweh for help (3:9, 15; 4:3; 6:7; 10:10)
7. statement or narrative about Yahweh's raising up a deliverer (3:9, 15; cf. 4:4–7; 6:8–40; 13:2–25; etc.)

b. story proper

8. story proper, recounting the activity of the judge
9. summary statement of the victory, following the general pattern: "So on that day Yahweh gave [enemy's name] into the hand of [judge's name]" (3:10, 30a; 4:23–24; 8:28a; 11:33; cf. 9:56–57; 16:30c)

c. conclusion

10. concluding chronological statement in the form "and the land had peace *x* years" or "and [judge's name] ruled *x* years" (3:11, 30b; 5:31c; 8:28; 12:7; 16:31; cf. 9:22)
11. account of the death (and sometimes burial) of the judge (3:11; 4:1; 8:32; 9:55–10:1; 12:7; 16:30–31)[8]

This highly repetitive pattern would have helped the ancient audience more easily follow the author's organization when moving from one story to the next.

The internal structures of these stories are remarkably similar. All but one are designed in

7. Moreover, 8:33 has "and the Israelites again prostituted themselves to the Baals."

8. The units about Othniel and Jephthah contain all eleven elements, Ehud and Gideon have nine, Deborah has eight, Samson seven, and Abimelech six.

seven-part symmetries (Othniel's story is arranged in a three-part symmetry). In all seven, the central episode represents the story's turning point. In all but one (Samson) the turning point features Yahweh's gracious intervention. The author utilizes the symmetric scheme in the first three stories (Othniel, Ehud, Deborah) to underscore the point that it was Yahweh's intervention—occurring at the midpoint of each story—that reversed Israel's bad fortunes and brought her deliverance. In the final four stories (Gideon, Abimelech, Jephthah, Samson) the symmetric arrangement is employed to emphasize Israel's deterioration.

Othniel (Judges 3:7–11)

The brief story of Othniel, the first judge, exhibits a three-part symmetric layout designed to convey the theme that Israel's calamity was reversed by Yahweh's intervention (10.3).

Ehud (Judges 3:12–30)

The Ehud story has seven constituent paragraphs, delineated primarily by scene changes (10.4). These paragraphs are arranged to form a symmetry that carries the story's movement forward from disaster to restoration. As in the Othniel story, the opening and closing paragraphs frame the story with a negative introduction (a) and positive conclusion (a′). At the center (d) stands the turning point: Ehud's "message from God" and his killing of the enemy king.

Deborah (Judges 4–5)

The story of Deborah and Barak exhibits a similar seven-part design, with each episode (or paragraph) delineated primarily by scene changes (10.5). As in the previous two stories, the first and last paragraphs here (a and a′) frame the story with a sad beginning (Jabin's oppression and a negative chronological note) and a happy ending (the end of Jabin's oppression and a positive chronological note). The second paragraph (b) introduces Deborah, who predicts that Yahweh will give Sisera into the hands of a woman. This paragraph finds its match in

10.4 Ehud (Judges 3:12–30)

a **beginning of oppression** (3:12–14)
  - Moab (crosses the Jordan and) <u>smites</u> (*wayyak*) Israel
  - <u>negative chronological note</u>
  - result: humiliation

b **Ehud's first trip down to Jericho** (3:15–17)
  - appeal to Yahweh
  - Ehud sent to Moabite king with a gift <u>in his hand</u> (*bĕyādô*)
  - result: humiliation

c **Ehud leaves palace after giving Eglon tribute** (3:18–19)
  - passes place called <u>The Idols</u> (*happĕsîlîm*)
  - palace servants asked to give king <u>privacy</u>
  - result: humiliation

d **TURNING POINT: Yahweh gives victory** (cf. 3:28); Ehud's "message from God":
    he kills the enemy king (3:20–22)

c′ **Ehud leaves palace after killing Eglon** (3:23–26)
  - passes place called <u>The Idols</u> (*happĕsîlîm*) again
  - palace servants give king <u>privacy</u>
  - result: triumph

b′ **Ehud's second trip down to Jericho** (3:27–28a)
  - Ehud goes down to Jericho again, this time leading Israel's army in attack
  - "Yahweh has given them <u>into your hand</u> (*bĕyedkem*)"
  - result: triumph

a′ **end of oppression** (3:28b–30)
  - Israel <u>smites</u> (*wayyakkû*) Moab, driving Moabites back across Jordan
  - <u>happy chronological note</u>
  - result: triumph

10.5 Deborah (Judges 4–5)

a **beginning of oppression** (4:1–3)
  - Israel sins and is <u>oppressed</u> by <u>King Jabin of Canaan</u>
  - <u>negative chronological note</u>: oppression lasts twenty years

b **Deborah's prediction about a woman killing Sisera** (4:4–9a)
  - interaction between a brave woman (Deborah) and a weak military man (Barak)

c **troops gather** (4:9b–13)
  - Barak <u>goes up</u>, with his troops <u>at his feet</u> (*bĕraglāyw*)
  - Sisera gathers his troops for battle

d **TURNING POINT: Yahweh gives victory** (4:14–15a)

c′ **troops disperse** (4:15b–16)
  - Sisera <u>goes down</u> from his chariot and flees <u>on foot</u> (*bĕraglāyw*)
  - Barak pursues fleeing enemy troops

b′ **Deborah's prediction comes true: Jael kills Sisera** (4:17–22)
  - interaction between a brave woman (Jael) and a weak man (Sisera)

a′ **end of oppression** (4:23–24)
  - God ends the oppression of <u>King Jabin of Canaan</u>, and Israel <u>oppresses</u> and finally destroys Jabin
  - <u>positive chronological note</u>: land rests forty years

interlude: Song of Deborah (5:1–31)

the story's next-to-last paragraph (b′), which recounts the fulfillment of Deborah's prediction: Sisera is killed by Jael, a woman. Both episodes feature conversations between a brave, strong woman (Deborah, Jael) and an apparently weak military man (Barak, Sisera).

In the third paragraph (c) the armies gather for battle; in the third-to-last paragraph (c′) they disperse following the battle. In both, Barak and Sisera are the two main participants, and they appear in chiastic order: Barak–Sisera–Sisera–Barak. Another possible echo between the two units occurs when Barak "goes up" (*ʿālâ*) onto Mount Tabor, and his forces "go up at his feet" (*wayyaʿal bĕraglāyw*); in the matching scene, Sisera "gets down" (*wayyēred*) out of his chariot and flees "on foot" (*bĕraglāyw*).

The fourth, central paragraph (d) represents, again, the story's turning point, in which Yahweh gives the Israelites victory.

The Song of Deborah in chapter 5 serves as an interlude that breaks up the patterned succession of stories and allows the audience to relax a moment. This interlude creates anticipation

10.6 Gideon (Judges 6:1–8:32)

a **beginning of oppression** by Midianites (6:1–10)
  - negative chronological note

b **Gideon's divine call; his destruction of idolatry at Ophrah** (6:11–40)
  - Gideon's family's good involvement
  - Gideon's fleece laid on the ground to collect dew (which encourages Gideon to lead Israel to victory)
  - Gideon pleases Yahweh, opposes the people
  - good results: Yahweh in control

c **troops gather for the battle** (7:1–14)
  - army is made smaller, "that Israel may not <u>boast</u>"
  - intertribal cooperation assumed
  - good results: Yahweh in control

d **TURNING POINT: Yahweh gives victory** (7:15–22)*

c′ **troops disperse after the battle** (7:23–8:21)
  - the pursuit; attempt to enlarge the army; <u>boasting</u>
  - intertribal bickering
  - tragic results: Yahweh not in control

b′ **Gideon's call by Israelites and his lapse into idolatry at Ophrah** (8:22–27)
  - Gideon's family's bad involvement
  - Gideon's garment spread out (on the ground) to collect spoils (which leads to idolatry)
  - Gideon cooperates with the people, displeases Yahweh
  - tragic results: Yahweh not in control

a′ **end of oppression** by Midianites (8:28–32)
  - positive chronological note

*Alternatively, the central unit could be construed as 7:9–22.

---

that a new phase of the book is about to begin, which is indeed the case.[9]

Gideon (Judges 6:1–8:32)

Now begins the downward plunge (10.6). Like the preceding stories, Gideon's story opens with a unit recounting Israel's sin and resultant oppression (a), including a negative chronological note, and it closes with an antithetically matching unit (a′), which summarizes the reversal of the oppression, with a positive chronological note. Also as in the previous stories, the central unit (d) recounts the story's turning point: Yahweh gives Israel victory in the battle.

But here the similarities end. Unlike the earlier stories, in which the suspenseful prebattle units are symmetrically matched by positive postbattle units, here the two prebattle units are matched by two tragic postbattle units. The second and next-to-last units (b and b′) are parallel in several ways: they both recount events that take place in Gideon's home town of Ophrah (unlike the other episodes of the story), and they share the theme of Gideon's involvement in the issue of idolatry. But they stand in stark—and significant—contrast: the first is a positive, upbeat episode about Gideon's divine call and his commendable destruction of the idolatry at

Ophrah;[10] the second recounts how Gideon receives an unholy call to kingship from disobedient Israelites, and how he reestablishes idolatry in Ophrah.

In the story's third unit (c), Gideon gathers his troops at En-harod in preparation for the battle. Here Yahweh instructs Gideon to reduce the size of his army, "lest Israel boast . . . : 'My own hand has delivered me.' " The tribes are working together. One would expect the third-to-last scene (c′) to relate the reversal of the third scene, the scattering and pursuit of the troops after the battle. But the echo is disheartening: Israel's army becomes huge and falls into envy, boasting, and strife. Tragic civil war breaks out (8:1–17) in place of the earlier tribal cooperation. This third-to-last unit is arranged in a modified chiasmus (10.7).

In each of the first four units Yahweh was in charge, and all went well. In the second half of the story Yahweh no longer seems to be involved, and all goes badly. Despite Israel's downward spiral, however, Yahweh's grace continues. The central unit of the Gideon story recounts, as in the previous stories, the story's turning point: Yahweh gives Israel victory.

---

9. The author includes the song within the story of Deborah and Barak by placing the standard closing refrain, "and the land had rest forty years," at the end of the song (5:31c).

10. This three-part unit begins (6:11–24) and ends (6:33/36–40) with interaction between Gideon and Yahweh, in each case accompanied by signs; these units frame the central episode of Gideon's destruction of Baal's altar in Ophrah (6:25–32).

10.7 Civil war (Judges 7:23–8:21)

a   **two Midianite captains killed** and strife with Ephraimites (7:23–8:3)

  b   **Succoth refuses to help Gideon** (8:4–7)

    c   **Penuel refuses to help Gideon** (8:8–9)

      d   **CENTER: Gideon's victory** (8:10–12)

  b′   **Succoth punished by Gideon** (8:13–16)

    c′   **Penuel punished by Gideon** (8:17)

a′   **two Midianite kings killed** (8:18–21)

10.8 Abimelech (Judges 8:33–9:57)

a   **introduction:** Israel's sin (8:33–35)

    • anticipates Israel's sin against Gideon's family

  b   **Gideon's seventy sons killed by Abimelech** (9:1–6)

    • setting: <u>town north of Shechem</u>

    • killing involves a <u>stone</u> (and presumably a sword)

    • <u>sons of Gideon killed</u> by fellow Israelites

    c   **Jotham's curse upon Shechem and Abimelech** (9:7–21)

      • calls for <u>strife between Abimelech and Shechem</u>

      • prominence of <u>trees</u> (ʿēṣîm)

      • speaks from <u>top of the mount</u> (rōʾš har) (Gerizim)

      • calling for <u>fire</u> (ʾēš) to come out from Abimelech and consume lords of Shechem

      d   **TURNING POINT: God intervenes to help**; summary of Abimelech's rule (9:22–25)

    c′   **Jotham's curse upon Shechem fulfilled:** Shechem destroyed by Abimelech (9:26–49)

      • <u>strife</u> breaks out <u>between Abimelech and Shechemites</u>

      • <u>trees</u> or <u>wood</u> (ʿēṣîm) used against Shechem

      • <u>tops of mountains</u> (rōʾšê hehārîm)

      • <u>fire</u> (ʾēš) used by Abimelech to destroy Shechemites

  b′   **Gideon's son, Abimelech, is killed** (9:50–55)

    • setting: <u>town north of Shechem</u>

    • killing involves a <u>stone</u> and a sword

    • <u>son of Gideon killed</u> by fellow Israelite

a′   **conclusion** (9:56–57)

    • looks back on how God punished Shechem and Abimelech for their sin against Gideon's family

---

Abimelech (Judges 8:33–9:57)

The layout of the Abimelech story underscores the story's tragedy and irony (10.8). Like the previous units, this unit (1) forms a seven-part symmetry, opening (unit a) with Israel's lapse into idolatry and closing (unit a′) with a summary statement about the end of the oppression; (2) features at its center (unit d) the turning point in which Yahweh intervenes and turns the tide of the oppression; and (3) utilizes the matching of the units b and c with units c′ and b′, to move the story from tension to resolution, from Israel's oppression to its relief. The difference, however, is disheartening. In this story, Israel's oppressor is none other than Israel's own judge! And this time the turning point comes when Yahweh graciously intervenes by instigating a deadly plot against this judge.

The opening paragraph (unit a) sets the stage by recounting Israel's lapse into idolatry and alluding to the upcoming mistreatment of Gideon's family. The concluding paragraph (unit a′) looks back on the story, in part summarizing what happened: Yahweh punished Israel and its judge for mistreating Gideon's family. The second unit (b) recounts the atrocity against Gideon's family: Abimelech kills Gideon's seventy sons and Israel proclaims Abimelech king. This is matched by the next-to-last episode (b′), in which Abimelech's crime is requited: Abimelech himself is killed. Both episodes take place in towns north of Shechem. In both, sons of Gideon are killed. In both, the killing involves a stone and a sword (expressly in the second story, presumably in the first). The story's third unit (c) is Jotham's parable, which he delivers to the rulers of Shechem from atop Mount Gerizim. He curses them for what they did to his brothers: "Let fire (ʾēš) come out from Abimelech, and devour the rulers of Shechem . . . and let fire (ʾēš) come out from the rulers of Shechem . . . and devour Abimelech" (9:20; cf. 9:15). Jotham's parable finds its fulfillment in the third-to-last episode (c′), which recounts the fulfillment of his curse in the civil war between Abimelech and the rulers of Shechem, a war in which "fire" (ʾēš) from Abimelech literally breaks out upon the rulers of Shechem. These

---

10.9 Jephthah (Judges 10:6–12:7)

a **introduction:** Israel's oppression and cry for help (10:6–16)
  - chronological note
b **diplomacy in response to Ammonite threat** (10:17–11:28)
  - begins: Ammonites <u>called to arms</u> (*wayyiṣṣāʿăqû*)
  - Ammonites cross over to Gilead <u>to fight</u> (*lĕhillāḥēm*; 11:12)
  - <u>why have you come against me to fight against my land?</u> (11:12)
  - <u>Jephthah first resorts to diplomacy</u>, which fails
  c **Jephthah's vow** (11:29–31)
    d **TURNING POINT:** Yahweh gives victory (11:32–33)*
  c′ **Jephthah's vow sadly fulfilled** (11:34–40)
b′ **diplomacy in response to Israelite threat; tragic civil war** (12:1–6)
  - begins: Ephraimites <u>called to arms</u> (*wayyiṣṣāʿēq*; 12:1)
  - Ephraimites cross over to Gilead <u>to fight</u> (*lĕhillāḥēm*)
  - <u>why have you come up against me today to fight against me?</u> (12:3)
  - <u>Jephthah first resorts to diplomacy</u>, which fails
a′ **conclusion:** summary of Jephthah's rule; his death and burial (12:7)
  - chronological note
*Notice the new beginning in 11:32.

---

two units are also linked by the prominence of "trees" (*ʿēṣîm*; 9:8–15; 9:48–49) and by references to the "tops of mountains" (9:7, 25, 36). The central unit in the story (d) represents the turning point: God turns the tide by sending an evil spirit to undo Abimelech and his allies. The summary statement in 9:22 supports the identification of this unit as the story's center.

Jephthah (Judges 10:6–12:7)

The layout of Jephthah's story, a seven-part symmetry, likewise helps convey the theme of Israel's deterioration (10.9). The author balances the positive episode of Jephthah's prebattle dispute with Moab (b)[11] with the negative episode of his postbattle dispute with fellow-Israelites (b′).[12] And the promising episode involving Jephthah's vow (c), immediately preceding the

central unit, is matched by the story of its tragic fulfillment immediately following the central unit (c′). Again, the center (d) of the story features Yahweh's gracious intervention.

Samson (Judges 13–16)

The Samson saga comprises seven fairly well-delineated episodes, all of which are marked off by geographical shifts of scene (10.10). These seven episodes form a symmetry that draws attention to Israel's ever-worsening condition. Rather than simply conveying movement from positive to negative, the chiastic layout here presents movement from negative to negative. The story is all bad (after the introductory unit), with each embarrassing episode matched by another equally embarrassing episode. With Samson, Israel's situation has utterly deteriorated.

The symmetry here is relatively clear. The first episode (a) recounts Samson's birth, with a reference to the "day of his death" (13:7). Samson's father Manoah is mentioned several times; and the episode closes with a reference to Samson's home "between Zorah and Eshtaol." In the last episode (a′), Samson dies and his body is returned to his home and buried "between Zorah and Eshtaol, in the tomb of Manoah his father" (16:31; Manoah's name occurs nowhere else in

---

11. The structure of the Jephthah story is somewhat baffling. The difficulty involves 10:17–11:28. Were this section a single unit, the entire Jephthah story would exhibit a seven-part, symmetric configuration, with 10:17–11:28 functioning as the second part of the story. The story would then have the same general layout as the stories of Ehud, Deborah and Barak, and Gideon, with the victorious battle episode at the center (11:32–33). But it appears as though 10:17–11:28 comprises, not one, but two self-contained units: Jephthah's selection as Gilead's ruler (10:17–11:11) and Jephthah's correspondence with the king of Ammon (11:12–28)—each of which is in some way paralleled by the next-to-last part (12:1–6; see below). Since this yields eight parts to the Jephthah story and an otherwise unattested a-b-b′-c-d-c′-b″-a′ design, I assume that 10:17–11:28 is to be considered a single, self-contained unit describing Jephthah's preparations for war. I treat this passage accordingly, but am not entirely certain of this.

12. The echoes connecting the two stories are unmistakable, forcing the audience to compare them and sense the deterioration. Both begin with a statement that the antagonists (Ammonites, Ephraimites) are "called to arms" (*wayyiṣṣāʿăqû/wayyiṣṣāʿēq*; 10:17; 12:1). In both, the antagonists cross over to Gilead "to fight" (*lĕhillāḥēm*; 11:12; 12:3). In both, Jephthah confronts the antagonists by asking why they have come "to fight against me/my land" (11:12; 12:3), to

which the antagonists respond (11:13; 12:1). In both, Jephthah first resorts to diplomacy by answering the charges and giving his own account of the circumstances leading to the crisis (11:15–22; 12:2–3), mentioning Yahweh's involvement in both (11:21; 12:3). Both feature the theme of receiving permission to cross over/through, employing the keyword "pass over/through" (*ʿbr*; 11:17, 19, 20; 12:1, 3, 5). Both result in Jephthah's victory over the antagonists. That these two episodes match so closely invites comparison; and the comparison underscores the point that what began so well, with Israel opposing a foreign enemy, ends badly, in bloody civil war.

10.10 Samson (Judges 13–16)

a **Samson's birth** (13:1–25)
- chronological note
- his parents <u>see</u> God and do not <u>die</u>; reference to "day of his [Samson's] death"
- Samson grows up <u>between Zorah and Eshtaol</u>; mention of <u>Manoah</u>

b **Samson betrays his secret to his Philistine wife** (14:1–20)
- begins: Samson <u>falls in love</u> with woman in Sorek Valley
- Philistines threaten to burn woman's house down if she will not <u>entice</u> (*pth*) Samson to betray secret
- woman <u>initially fails</u>; but when she questions his love for her, he finally reveals his secret to her; and <u>she tells the Philistines</u>
- keyword: <u>tell</u> (*lĕhaggîd*)
- setting: <u>Sorek Valley</u> (Timnah)

c **Samson visits wife at Timnah** (15:1–8)
- angered by Philistines and destroys town's fields
- begins: Samson <u>goes</u> (*bwʾ*) to visit his wife
- ends: Samson goes down to Etam

d **TURNING POINT: Samson kills one thousand Philistines** with jawbone of ass; fellow Israelites reject Samson's leadership and Philistines begin to take the initiative against him (15:9–20)
- summary of years of Samson's judgeship

c' **Samson visits prostitute at Gaza** (16:1–3)
- opposed by Philistines and destroys town's gates
- begins: Samson <u>goes</u> (*bwʾ*) to the Gaza prostitute
- ends: Samson takes the Gaza gates up to Hebron

b' **Samson betrays his secret to Delilah** (16:4–22)
- begins: Samson <u>falls in love</u> with Delilah in Sorek Valley
- Philistines offer Delilah gifts to <u>entice</u> (*pth*) Samson to betray secret
- Delilah <u>initially fails</u>; but when she questions his love for her, he finally reveals his secret to her; and <u>she tells the Philistines</u>
- keyword: <u>tell</u> (*lĕhaggîd*)
- setting: <u>Sorek Valley</u> (Delilah's home)

a' **Samson's death** (16:23–31)
- chronological note
- Samson cannot <u>see</u>, and he <u>dies</u>
- he is buried <u>between Zorah and Eshtaol</u>; mention of <u>Manoah</u>

the Samson saga). The first episode begins with a chronological note ("Yahweh gave them into the hands of the Philistines forty years"); and the last episode ends with a chronological note ("he judged Israel twenty years"). The correspondence between these units reinforces the sense of tragedy, beginning with the birth of a promising new judge and ending with his tragic death at the hands of the enemies.

In episodes b and b', Samson falls in love with a woman in the Sorek valley (the Timnite, Delilah). In both, the woman is secretly approached by the Philistines, who ask her to "entice" (*pth*) Samson to betray his secret (the answer to the riddle, the source of his strength) to her (14:15; 16:5). In both cases the Philistines offer the woman incentives. In both cases the woman pleads with Samson, at first unsuccessfully, to betray his secret. In both cases the woman uses the ploy of questioning his love for her by protesting, "You have not told me" (*wĕlî lōʾ higgadtâ*, 14:16; *wĕlōʾ-higgadtā lî*, 16:15). In both cases the woman persists, over a period of days, until Samson finally gives in "and tells her" (*wayyagged-lāh*; 14:17; 16:17). In both stories the woman then tells the secret to the Philistines.

Both betrayals result in the Philistines' temporarily getting the better of Samson. And in both stories, the keyword is "tell" (*lĕhaggîd*), occurring twelve times in the Timnite story and seven times in the Delilah story.

Episodes c and c' also match, although not as obviously. Both begin with Samson's going to visit a woman (the Timnite, the Gaza prostitute). In each instance he is thwarted by the Philistines: in Timnah he is not allowed to go to the woman; in Gaza he is not allowed to leave the town after he has visited the woman. And in both episodes he reacts angrily by recklessly destroying the town's property (burning the town's fields with the help of three hundred foxes, ripping the town's gates down and carrying them on his shoulders up to Hebron).

Overall Layout of Judges 3:7–16:31

The stories of the seven judges in the main body of the Book of Judges are arranged with a conspicuous symmetric touch (10.11).[13] The first judge, Othniel (a), is matched by the last

---

13. The chiastic arrangement of the main body is convincingly demonstrated by Gooding's excellent article: "Composition of the Book of Judges."

10.11 Seven judges (Judges 3:7–16:31)

a **Othniel** (3:7–11; 1:11–15)
- evaluation: positive
- procures a <u>good Israelite wife</u> by obeying Yahweh
- drives Canaanites from the land and settles there
- <u>wife presses him</u> for a good thing: to extend their territory
- <u>good</u> judge, leading a <u>united</u> Israel
- blessed by his brave <u>Israelite father-in-law</u>

b **Ehud** (3:12–30)
- evaluation: positive
- <u>Transjordanian king</u> oppresses Israel <u>eighteen years</u>; occurs in <u>Benjamin</u>
- Ehud has a secret <u>message</u> and <u>message</u> from God for enemy king
- <u>captures fords of Jordan</u> and with help of <u>Ephraimites</u> kills thousands of enemies attempting to cross
- Israelites united

c **Deborah and Barak** (4:1–5:31)
- evaluation: positive
- <u>woman crushes Sisera's skull</u> in a careless moment
- Israelites united

d **TURNING POINT: Gideon** (6:1–8:32)
- evaluation: positive/negative
  - (1) Gideon's stand <u>against idolatry</u> at Ophrah (6:1–32)
    - (2) Gideon's battle against Midianites (6:33–7:25)
    - (2') Gideon's battle against Israelites (8:1–21)
  - (1') Gideon's lapse <u>into idolatry</u> at Ophrah (8:22–32)

c' **Abimelech** (8:33–9:57)
- evaluation: negative
- <u>woman crushes Abimelech's skull</u> in careless moment
- Israelites fragmented; civil war

b' **Jephthah** (10:6–12:7)
- evaluation: negative
- <u>Transjordanian king</u> oppresses Israel <u>eighteen years</u>; occurs in <u>Benjamin</u>
- Jephthah sends <u>messages</u> twice to enemy king
- <u>captures fords of Jordan</u> and kills thousands of <u>Ephraimites</u> who cross
- Israelites fragmented; civil war

a' **Samson** (13:1–16:31)
- evaluation: negative
- procures <u>bad wives</u> from Canaan's native population, disobeying Yahweh
- settles among the pagan inhabitants of Canaan
- wives <u>press him</u> for bad things: to betray his secrets
- <u>bad</u> judge, <u>fragmenting</u> Israel
- betrayed by his cowardly pagan <u>father-in-law</u>

judge, Samson (a'); likewise, Ehud (b) matches Jephthah (b'); Deborah and Barak (c) match Abimelech (c'); and Gideon stands at the center (d) as the pivotal judge. The author does not simply match these judges for artistic balance but also utilizes the correspondences to reinforce the sense of Israel's spiritual and political decline. The final three judges are made to correspond to their earlier counterparts in ways that highlight Israel's deterioration.

Othniel and Samson

The stories of the first and last judges, Othniel and Samson, have striking points in common that link them together and set them apart from the other five major judges. The parallels mostly have to do with the prominent role played by their wives, a theme not found in the stories of the other judges (the material about Othniel and his wife comes from the prologue, 1:11–15). For example, their stories relate how the judges procure their wives, how their wives make key requests of them, how those requests are obtained, and the impact of the judges' fathers-in-law on their lives.[14] But these very points of correspondence serve to highlight the sense of decline. Othniel's wife is a good Israelite woman; Samson's wives are treacherous pagan women. Othniel gets his wife in a commendable way, by driving the Canaanite inhabitants from Israel's territory—as Yahweh had commanded. In con-

14. Another possible link (which may be merely fortuitous): Samson's strength is, of course, central to his story (16:5, 6, etc.); but the idea of exerting strength also occurs in Othniel's story: "his hand was strong" (*tāʿāz*) against his enemy (3:10).

trast, Samson gets his wives by settling among Canaan's pagan inhabitants and intermarrying with them—actions forbidden by Yahweh according to the book's prologue.[15] Othniel's Israelite wife "entices" (sût) him (or "pleads" with him) in order to get a good thing, an expansion of their territory; Samson's pagan wives plead with him too, but for wrongful things, namely, the betrayal of his secrets (14:15–17; 16:15–17). Othniel's brave Israelite father-in-law, Caleb, gives Othniel his daughter and generous gifts; Samson's treacherous pagan father-in-law gives him no gifts and even reneges and takes his daughter back and gives her to another (this is a pitiful scene: Israel's mighty judge humiliated, in his disobedience, by a commoner among Canaan's pagan population).

In addition, Othniel delivers Israel from the hands of its enemy; Samson falls into the hands of Israel's enemies and is imprisoned and humiliated by them (3:10; 16:23–24). The Israelites are apparently united under Othniel's leadership, but fragmented under Samson; in fact, the Israelites betray Samson to the enemy. Othniel appears to be a good judge; Samson is a bad judge and a sinner: he blatantly scorns his Nazirite vow at every turn (touching a lion's carcass, the corpses of slain Philistines to strip off their clothes, and the "fresh" jawbone of an ass, etc.). The happy statement at the end of Othniel's story, "the land had rest forty years," has no parallel at the end of Samson's story.

What began well with Israel's first judge—good Othniel—ends in disaster with Israel's final judge—foolish Samson. The story ends with Israel in defeat and with Israel's final, disobedient judge dying as a captive in enemy hands. The story's direction is decidedly downward.

Ehud and Jephthah

The same sort of positive-to-negative movement occurs between the second and next-to-last judges, Ehud and Jephthah. In both stories a Transjordanian king oppresses Israel for eighteen years (3:14; 10:8). In both, the enemy crosses the Jordan and acts hostilely toward Benjamin (3:13; 10:9). Both judges have messages for the enemy king (3:19–20; 11:12, 14). And both

judges capture the fords of the Jordan River with the prominent involvement of the Ephraimites.

The author uses this last parallel to highlight the theme of political disintegration. In Ehud's story, Ehud captures Jordan's fords with the help of the Ephraimites, and together they cut down thousands of Moabite enemies attempting to cross the river. It is a scene of admirable tribal cooperation. In striking contrast, Jephthah captures the Jordan fords as an act of hostility against the Ephraimites; and he kills thousands of Ephraimites attempting to cross the river. The contrastive echo draws the audience's attention to the deterioration: in place of the intertribal cooperation at the beginning of the period of the judges, Israel plunges into bloody civil war near the end of the period.

The story of Ehud ends on a happy note, with eighty years of peace (3:30). In contrast, the story of Jephthah ends in civil war and the backfiring of Jephthah's vow; there is no mention of the land having rest.

Deborah and Abimelech

The matching of the stories of Deborah and Abimelech also serves to underscore the sense of decline. Both stories recount how a woman killed Israel's archenemy. In the story of Deborah, she predicts that a woman will kill Israel's enemy Sisera (4:8–9). The suspense created by this prediction continues until the very end of the story, when finally a woman named Jael crushes Sisera's skull in an unsuspecting moment with her hammer and a tent stake.

In the Abimelech story, Jotham calls down a deadly curse upon Israel's archenemy. The suspense created by this curse continues until the very end of the story, when again a woman kills Israel's enemy (9:50–57), here also by crushing his skull in a careless moment. The echo, however, is full of irony. In this latter instance Israel's slain archenemy is none other than Israel's own judge, wicked Abimelech. Moreover, in place of the tribal cooperation in Deborah's story, the Abimelech story features bloody civil war. And unlike Deborah's story, Abimelech's has no happy closing statement about the land's rest.

Gideon—the Central and Pivotal Judge

What, then, is the function of the central story, that of Gideon? D. W. Gooding proposes that Gideon's story falls into four chiastically arranged parts, creating a good-to-bad configuration that makes Gideon's reign the book's turning point:[16]

---

15. Note the question of Samson's parents: "Isn't there an acceptable woman among your relatives or among all our people?" (14:3). The audience senses the tragedy of this since the author has explained in the prologue that Israel's deterioration was caused by settling among the Canaanites and intermarrying with them (3:5–6). Othniel, with his own exemplary marriage, was an appropriate choice to be God's first judge for Israel. Samson's marriages stand in stark and sad contrast. Israel got off to a good start and deteriorated because of its disobedience, as exemplified by its judges.

16. Gooding, "Composition of the Book of Judges," 74*.

10.12 Idolatry at Dan (Judges 17–18)

a **Micah sets up an <u>idolatrous shrine</u> for his private use** (17:1–6)
   - Micah makes an <u>idol</u> (*pesel*) and cultic objects for his <u>shrine</u> (*bêt ʾĕlōhîm*)
   - result: peaceful

b **Micah secures services of Levite** (17:7–13)
   - Levite arrives at Micah's home
   - "live with me <u>and be my father and priest</u> (*wehyēh-lî lĕʾāb ûlĕkōhēn*)"; states benefits of the job; Levite agrees
   - result: peaceful

c **Danite spies visit Micah's house in peace** (18:1–6)
   - begins: they <u>set out from Zorah and Eshtaol</u>
   - result: peaceful

d **TURNING POINT: Danites carry out their mission** and return to propose hostility (18:7–10)

c′ **Danite spies visit Micah's house in hostility** (18:11–17)
   - begins: they <u>set out from Zorah and Eshtaol</u> again, this time with an army, confiscate Micah's idols and kidnap his priest
   - result: hostile

b′ **Micah loses services of Levite** (18:18–26)
   - Danites take Levite from Micah's home to serve as their priest
   - "come with us <u>and be our father and priest</u> (*wehyēh-lānû lĕʾāb ûlĕkōhēn*)"
   - result: hostile

a′ **Danites set up an <u>idolatrous shrine</u> to serve their entire tribe** (18:27–31)
   - Danites use Micah's <u>idol</u> (*pesel*) in their <u>shrine</u> (*bêt ʾĕlōhîm*)
   - Levite's identity finally given: Moses' grandson!
   - result: hostile

---

a Gideon's stand against idolatry (6:1–32)
  b Gideon's battle against Israel's enemy (6:33–7:25)
  b′ Gideon's battle against fellow-Israelites (8:1–21)
a′ Gideon's lapse into idolatry (8:22–32)

Gideon's story, like the book's main body, begins well and ends disastrously. Gideon's stand against idolatry in the beginning contrasts with his lapse into idolatry at the end; the cooperation among the Israelite tribes in the battle against the Midianites contrasts with the ugly account of Gideon's intertribal warfare. From Gideon to the end, Israel and its judges will experience repeated civil war; and the phrase "and the land had rest x years" (3:11, 30; 5:31; 8:28) will not be used of any judge after Gideon.

Epilogue (Judges 17–21)

With the notice of Samson's death and the summary of his judgeship in 16:31, the audience would now expect the introduction of the next judge. Instead, 17:1 has none of the standard features that the author has used to mark the beginnings of the stories about individual judges. The audience is given no chronological framework, nor any clue as to how to connect the new story with the events that have preceded. Consequently, a sense is conveyed that the chronologically ordered parade of judges is over and a new part of the book is beginning.

What follows are two stories that take place sometime early in the period of the judges, each introduced by *wayĕhî* ("and it happened"; 17:1;

19:1). The stories are punctuated by the recurring line "in those days Israel had no king, and all the people did as they saw fit" (17:6; 21:25) or its shortened form without the second clause (18:1; 19:1). These two stories serve as parade examples of Israel's moral and political decline during the period of the judges. In addition, the structure of each story reinforces the theme of Israel's degeneration.

Moses' Descendants and the Idolatry at Dan (Judges 17–18)

The first story recounts how Moses' own grandson and descendants set up and ran the idolatrous cult center at Dan (10.12). The story contains seven episodes, arranged so that the last three episodes chiastically match, in a bad-to-worse fashion, the first three episodes. The first and last episodes feature the setting up of idolatrous shrines, both of which contain Micah's idols. But the correspondence serves to convey the sense of deterioration. The first shrine is set up by a private individual—which is bad enough—but the second is set up by an entire tribe! The peaceful mood of the first episode also stands in contrast to the (intentionally repugnant?) violence surrounding the second episode. In the story's second episode a Levite (Moses' grandson!) moves from his home and becomes Micah's private idolatrous priest. Though reprehensible, at least the transaction is peaceful and, again, involves only one individual. In the next-to-last episode the Levite moves again, this time being hostilely forced to move,

---

10.13 Rape of the Levite's concubine (Judges 19)

a **concubine leaves her home in Ephraim** and goes to her father's home (19:1–2)

  b **happy negotiations for the woman (19:3–4)**
- Levite comes and speaks kindly to his concubine and her father, and he wins her back
- <u>tranquil scene</u> of father and husband peaceably conversing (about concubine?)

    c **hospitality in Bethlehem (19:5–9)**
- the Levite is detained extra days by his hospitable host

      d **TURNING POINT: Levite begins journey home;** ironically refuses to stay overnight in Jebus, because it is "a town of foreigners" (19:10–13)

    c′ **inhospitality in Gibeah (19:14–21)**
- local people do not take the Levite and his concubine in; finally taken in by an outsider, who fears for their safety

  b′ **terrible negotiations for the woman (19:22–26)**
- evil men of Gibeah come and speak hostilely to the old man who is hosting the Levite and his concubine; they prevail and rape the concubine
- <u>tense scene</u> of old man and interested male parties discussing the concubine's fate

a′ **concubine is brought back to her home in Ephraim—dead (19:27–30)**

---

and becomes an idolatrous priest for an entire Israelite tribe. In the third episode the Danite spies make a peaceful visit to Micah's home on their way to Laish, and they have a friendly conversation with the Levite. It is a happy and peaceful episode. In the third-to-last episode the Danite spies and their compatriots return to Micah's home, this time not in peace, but hostilely, to plunder Micah's shrine and to kidnap his Levite priest. The center of the story (18:7–10) is the turning point, when the action turns from peace to hostility.

Atrocity at Gibeah and the Ensuing Civil War (Judges 19–21)

The second story of the epilogue recounts the rape and death of a Levite's concubine in Gibeah and the ensuing war of retribution. Structurally, the material of this story is organized in two sections: (1) the rape of the concubine at Gibeah and (2) the war of retribution. Both are structurally designed to reinforce the author's agenda.

Rape of the Levite's Concubine at Gibeah (Judges 19)

The first section of the story of the atrocity at Gibeah is arranged in seven, symmetrically ordered episodes, structured to underscore the sense of deterioration (10.13). The first episode, in which the Levite's concubine leaves her home in Ephraim for a new life with her father (a), has its sad echo in the final episode (a′), in which she is brought back, dead, to her Ephraimite home. In the second episode (b) the Levite goes to Bethlehem to woo his concubine back. He talks to her hospitable, agreeable father, and he wins her back. All seems well. This has a terrible echo in the next-to-last episode (b′), where the woman is again at the center of negotiations involving the elderly owner of the house. But this time it is not her husband, but wicked men, who

are negotiating for her; and this time the outcome is horrific: she is mass raped, and she dies.

In the third episode (c) the Levite decides to leave his gracious host in Bethlehem, to be on his way. But the hospitality of the father-in-law results in his being detained there a few more days. The unit seems to have no other function than to emphasize the father-in-law's admirable hospitality. In the third-to-last episode (c′) we have the sad echo: the Levite and his concubine arrive in inhospitable Gibeah and no one takes them in, until finally an elderly man, himself an outsider, finds them in the town square and takes them in.

The center of the story (d) represents the turning point: the Levite and his concubine finally leave Bethlehem and set out for home. The unit's central position serves to highlight the terribly ironic statement of the Levite, that they should not spend the night in the pagan town of Jebus because it is "a city of foreigners, who do not belong to the people of Israel" (19:12). The irony here, as subsequent events will show, is that Israel has become more wicked than even the native pagans of Canaan.

The War of Retribution (Judges 20–21)

The story of Israel's response to the atrocity is arranged in a seven-part symmetry, and once again the parallels between matching units are utilized to reinforce the sense of Israel's downward plummet (10.14). In the first episode (a) the tribes assemble at Mizpah and hear how the Benjaminites forcibly took the Levite's concubine. They declare they will not return home until the crime is punished. This has its terrible echo in the last episode (a′), when the tribes arrange for the surviving Benjaminites (some of whom could have been the original culprits!) to forcibly take two hundred innocent young

10.14 War against Benjamin (Judges 20–21)

a **first all-Israel assembly (20:1–11)**
- tribes hear about atrocity in which concubine was forcibly taken and raped by Benjaminites
- they vow, "none of us will return to his home" until justice is achieved

b **second all-Israel assembly, immediately preceding the war (20:12–17)**
- Israel, enraged at the atrocity, sent men through all the tribe of Benjamin demanding that the culprits be turned over
- Benjaminites refuse to turn over to the Israelites the men who violently took and raped the concubine

c **Israel defeated by Benjaminites (20:18–25)**
- two battles, each concluded with tally of casualties

d **TURNING POINT: Yahweh promises victory (20:26–28)**

c′ **Israel defeats Benjaminites (20:29–48)**
- two phases of the battle, each concluded with tally of casualties

b′ **next-to-last all-Israel assembly, immediately following the war (21:1–15)**
- Israelites pity surviving Benjaminites; they sent word to the Benjaminites and proclaim peace; Israelites attack Jabesh-gilead and slaughter all the inhabitants, saving alive four hundred virgins, whom they give to Benjaminites
- Israelites violently capture and turn over to Benjaminites four hundred innocent young women

a′ **last all-Israel assembly (21:16–25)**
- tribes condone Benjaminites' forcibly taking for themselves two hundred women at Shiloh
- then they return, "each to his own tribe and family"

women for themselves at Shiloh. The tribes then return to their homes.

The second episode (b) features the Israelites' diplomatic efforts immediately before the war, in which they "sent men through all the tribe of Benjamin" (20:12) with the message to give up the culprits "that we may put them to death and put away evil from Israel" (20:13). In the next-to-last episode (b′), occurring immediately after the war, the Israelite tribes once again send a message to the Benjaminites, this time a message of peace. In antithetic parallelism, Israel's earlier outrage has turned to compassion (21:6). But here again the echo is terrible: Israel now sends men to commit an atrocity that in some respects supersedes that of the Benjaminites. They attack and slaughter the entire population of Jabesh-gilead, including hundreds of men, women, and children and forcibly take for the Benjaminites (again, some of whom could have been the criminals of Gibeah!) four hundred virgins. The original crime of Gibeah is dwarfed by this greater act of villainy.

The third episode (c), recounting the series of defeats Israel experienced against the Benjaminites in this bloody civil war, is matched in antithetic parallelism by the third-to-last episode (c′), their victory over the Benjaminites. The central episode and the turning point of the story (d) is the all-Israel assembly at Bethel, in which Yahweh intervenes and assures the despondent Israelites that their fortunes will turn the next day. As in the tragic stories of Abimelech and Samson, the center here is marked by a chronological note about Israel's leader: Phinehas, grandson of Aaron (20:28).

Correspondence of Prologue and Epilogue

The two-part prologue and the two-part epilogue of the Book of Judges not only form the frame of the book; they also chiastically match in such a way as to underscore the book's main themes (10.15).[17]

The first part of the prologue (a) and the last part of the epilogue (a′) have a number of significant correspondences that link them together and invite comparison:

1. Both stories involve all the Israelite tribes.
2. Both feature all the Israelite tribes involved in military activity.
3. Both feature all-Israel assemblies.
4. In both, the Israelite tribes inquire of Yahweh, "Who will go up for us first against the Canaanites/Benjaminites, to fight against them?"; and in both, Yahweh responds, "Judah" (1:1–2; 20:18).
5. Both feature the assembled Israelites' weeping and offering sacrifices (2:1–5; 20:23–26).
6. Both feature the theme of procuring wives (1:11–15; 19:1–30; 21:1–25).
7. Bethel and Jerusalem (Jebus) figure prominently in both (1:7–8, 21–26; 19:10–14; 20:18–28).

The author utilizes all these points of correspondence to underscore the sense of Israel's decline. In the first unit, Israel's assemblies, its military activity, the inquiring of Yahweh, the weeping, and the offering of sacrifices are all part of the divinely ordered conquest of Ca-

---

17. See Gooding, "Composition of the Book of Judges," 75*–77*.

10.15 Correspondence of prologue and epilogue (Judges 1:1–3:6; 17:1–21:25)

prologue: Judges 1:1–3:6

  a **Israel's holy war against the Canaanites** (1:1–2:5)

- evaluation: mostly bad
- two all-Israel assemblies, involving the conquest of Canaan
- military activity of Israelite tribes in conquest of Canaan
- "the Israelites asked Yahweh, 'Who shall go up for us first against the Canaanites, to fight against them?' and Yahweh said, 'Judah shall go up' " (1:1–2)
- Israelites weep and sacrifice before Yahweh (2:1–5)
- Othniel wins his wife by capturing Canaanite town (1:11–15)
- the Benjaminites fail to drive the Jebusites from Jebus (1:21)
- Bethel captured from the Canaanites

  b **Israel's cyclical, idolatrous decline, generation after generation, during the period of the judges** (2:6–3:6)

- evaluation: bad
- children are worse than parents (2:10, 17, 19)
- importance of obedience to law of Moses (3:4)
- cyclical lapsing into idolatry (2:11–13, 19)
- Sidonians left in land by Yahweh to test Israel's obedience

epilogue: Judges 17:1–21:25

  b' **Israel's permanent idolatrous revolt at Dan, under Moses' own grandson and descendants** (17:1–18:31)

- evaluation: worse!
- parent encourages son to become idolatrous
- disobedience to Moses' law supervised by Moses' own grandson and descendants
- permanent establishment of idolatry
- Sidonians exterminated by wicked, idolatrous Israelites

  a' **Israel's (unholy) civil war against wicked Benjaminites** (19:1–21:25)

- evaluation: worse!
- several all-Israel assemblies, involving civil war
- military activity of Israelite tribes against Benjamin
- "the Israelites . . . asked Yahweh, 'Who will go up for us first to battle against the Benjaminites?' and Yahweh said, 'Judah shall go up first' " (20:18)
- Israelites weep and sacrifice to Yahweh during civil war
- men of Gibeah forcibly take and rape Levite's concubine; then Benjaminites, with cooperation of other tribes, forcibly take hundreds of women by slaughtering Israelite inhabitants of the entire town of Jabesh-gilead and by mass kidnapping women at Shiloh
- Levite refuses—tragically—to stay overnight with the Jebusites
- tribes assemble at Bethel in civil war

naan; in the second, these same elements are part of Israel's terrible civil war. In the former, the procuring of wives is a positive theme: Othniel wins his wife by a courageous victory over the Canaanites; in the latter, the procuring of women is a very negative theme, featuring rape, mass kidnapping, etc. In the former, the Benjaminites fail to drive out the Jebusites from Jebus (1:21); in the latter, the Levite avoids pagan Jebus and seeks hospitality instead among fellow Israelites in Benjamin's tribe, ironically suffering an outrage far worse than he presumably would ever have experienced at Jebus. (There is little doubt that the inclusion of 1:21 in the prologue is to enable this irony to be created.) The reader is now forced to wonder, why should God help the Benjaminites drive out the Jebusites? They have become worse than the Jebusites! What began with optimism, with the tribes' jointly fighting against the wicked Canaanites, ends with the terrible story of Israel's own unspeakable wickedness and its own bloody civil war.

Similarly, the first part of the epilogue (b') contains ironic echoes of the last part of the prologue (b). The topic of idolatry is central in both; and in both there is the interwoven themes of parents, children, and idolatry. But the difference is significant. In the former, children reject the more obedient examples of their parents and turn to idols (2:10, 17, 19); in the latter, parents encourage their children to become idolatrous. In the former, the idolatry is sporadic or cyclical; in the latter, idolatry becomes a permanent institution. In the former, Yahweh leaves some of the pagan peoples of Canaan, including the Sidonians (3:3), to test Israel to see if Israel will be faithful to him; in the latter, idolatrous and treacherous Israelites attack and exterminate a town of peaceable and unsuspecting Sidonians. No wonder—the reader realizes—Yahweh is no longer blessing Israel's conquest of Canaan. The Israelites have become worse than the Canaanites! In the former, obedience to Moses' law is key to Israel's prosperity (3:4); in the latter, an entire Israelite tribe not only spurns Moses' law, but hires Moses' own grandson and Moses' descendants, generation after generation, to oversee their idolatrous rebellion!

Conclusion

Structural designs on both large and small levels reinforce the author's two main themes in the Book of Judges. The first theme—that Yahweh's gracious help alone saved Israel in its successive crises—is underscored by the author's utilizing the fourth, central position (the position of prominence) in the symmetries to record Yahweh's gracious intervention in Israel's successive plights, which always serve as the story's turning point.

To communicate the second theme—Israel's moral and political deterioration—the author exploits the symmetric matches to create good-to-bad (or bad-to-worse) echoes. Again and again the audience hears stories that begin well and end badly. This relentless structuring pattern reflects the author's determination to emphasize the theme that the period of the judges was a bad time for Israel. Israel's behavioral pattern during the period was not merely cyclical (apostasy, oppression, deliverance by a judge, judge's death, apostasy) but a downward spiral, with the Israelites becoming worse with every cycle. As the author states in the beginning, "When the judge died, they turned back and acted more corruptly than their fathers" (2:19).[18]

All this suggests that the book may have been written to counter the popular view current in the author's day (perhaps the early united monarchy) that the period of the judges was "the good old days," when Israel's heroes of old led the nation to glorious victories, when "there was no [oppressive] king" over the land, and when each person could do as he or she saw fit. The author retells the story of this period, selecting and structuring the material to show that it was a shameful period in Israel's history; that Israel was in religious and political decline; that Israel's judges had feet of clay; and that Yahweh, and Yahweh alone, was the hero of the period, who graciously and repeatedly saved Israel, despite their persistent unfaithfulness.

---

18. Ibid., 72*.

11

Ruth

The Power of Kindness

The Book of Ruth tells the story of the tragedy and subsequent restoration of a family from Bethlehem during the period of the judges. Like most modern stories, the tale has an introduction (the misfortune that befalls Naomi's family; 1:1–5), body (the events that eventually reverse Naomi's fortunes; 1:6–4:12), and conclusion (the restoration of Naomi's family; 4:13–22). The story is moderate in length (approximately five pages in most English and Hebrew editions), but long enough to expect some structural "packaging" for the benefit of the audience. Careful analysis suggests that the story is made up of a series of seven major narrative units or episodes, each set off by shifts in scene, time, characters, speed of action, topic, etc.:[1]

a	Naomi loses her family (1:1–5)
b	Ruth chooses to stay with Naomi (1:6–19a)
c	Naomi and Ruth arrive in Bethlehem, destitute (1:19b–22)[2]
d	Ruth and Boaz meet (2:1–23)
e	Ruth proposes to Boaz (3:1–18)
f	Boaz redeems Naomi's property and marries Ruth (4:1–12)
g	Naomi's family is restored (4:13–22)

Naomi Loses Her Family (Ruth 1:1–5)

The first unit sets the stage for the story. In a few brief strokes the narrator recounts the mis-

fortune that occurs in Naomi's family. The successive blows to her family are recounted in a parallel pattern (11.1).

Ruth Chooses to Stay with Naomi (Ruth 1:6–19a)

Following the introduction, the first scene of the story takes place somewhere along the road back to Judah. Several shifts signal a new unit in 1:6:

1. speed of action (from rapid [the events of more than a decade are summarized in five verses] to very slow [thirteen verses recount a single conversation])
2. time
3. place
4. storytelling technique (from narrative to primarily dialogue)
5. characters (from all the family members in 1:1–5 to the three surviving female members in 1:6–19a)

In a seven-part chiasmus, the new unit presents a conversation between Naomi and her two daughters-in-law (11.2). The conversation is introduced in 1:6–7, recounted in 1:8–17, and concluded in 1:18–19a. The entire episode is tied together by the repetition of the keyword šûb ("return"), which occurs nine times, and by the episode's symmetric structure.

There is a significant shift in main character in this unit. The first half of the conversation is dominated by Naomi, whose passionate speeches take up most of the dialogue (over a dozen clauses), while the terse protest of her daughters-in-law (only four words) places them in the background. In the second part, however, the roles are reversed. Naomi's speech is terse (only ten words) as she urges her remaining daughter-in-law, Ruth, to go back (1:15). In contrast, Ruth's passionate speech is not only unexpected but much longer (about ten clauses)

---

1. This analysis is supported by Nancy M. Tischler, "Ruth," in *A Complete Literary Guide to the Bible*, ed. Leland Ryken and Tremper Longman III (Grand Rapids: Zondervan, 1993), 151–64, who analyzes Ruth as comprising these same seven units (pp. 152–53). For an excellent study of the structure of Ruth, which differs only slightly from the one presented in the present work, see Victor M. Wilson, *Divine Symmetries: The Art of Biblical Rhetoric* (New York: University Press of America, 1997), 137–46.

2. It could be argued that 1:19b–22 does not form a separate unit or episode but simply closes the unit that begins in 1:6. The previous unit, however, seems to conclude with 1:18, with the resolution of the tension introduced in 1:6–8. Moreover, 1:19b–22 shifts in scene (from Moab to Bethlehem), characters (from Naomi and her two daughters-in-law to Naomi, Ruth, and the women of Bethlehem), and topic (from the issue of who will return with Naomi to the reception Naomi received when she and Ruth arrived in Bethlehem).

121

11.1 Naomi loses her family (Ruth 1:1–5)

a **tragedy**: famine and family's emigration to Moab (1:1)
  b **respite**: names of family members; sojourn in Moab (1:2)
a′ **worse tragedy**: Elimelech dies, leaving Naomi with her sons (1:3)
  b′ **respite**: sons' marriages; names of wives; continued sojourn in Moab (1:4)
a″ **even worse tragedy**: Naomi's sons die, leaving Naomi with no family (1:5)

11.2 Ruth stays with Naomi (Ruth 1:6–19a)

a **introduction** (1:6–7)
  • Naomi begins journey to Judah
  • daughters-in-law <u>go with</u> (hālak + ʿimmâ) her
  b **Naomi's short speech: "return home!"** (1:8–9a)
    c **both daughters-in-law refuse** (1:9b–10)
      • Naomi <u>kisses</u> them good-bye
      • they <u>weep</u>
      • they <u>refuse</u> to leave
      d **CENTER: Naomi's sad speech**: no hope of marriage (1:11–13)
    c′ **one daughter-in-law refuses, the other agrees** (1:14)
      • they <u>weep</u>
      • Orpah <u>kisses</u> Naomi good-bye
      • Ruth <u>refuses</u> to leave
  b′ **Naomi's short speech: "return home!"** (1:15)
a′ **climactic conclusion** (1:16–19a)
  • Ruth's passionate speech of loyalty
  • Ruth is determined to <u>go with</u> (hālak + ʾittâ) Naomi, and the two recommence the journey together

11.3 Naomi and Ruth arrive in Bethlehem (Ruth 1:19b–22)

a **narrative**: <u>arrival</u> of the two women in <u>Bethlehem</u> (bwʾ + bêt leḥem) (1:19b)
  b **dialogue** between Naomi and the townspeople (1:19c–21)
a′ **narrative**: <u>arrival</u> of the two women in <u>Bethlehem</u> (bwʾ + bêt leḥem) (1:22)

(1:16–17). With this speech, Ruth captures center stage, where she will remain for the rest of the story.

Naomi and Ruth Arrive, Destitute, in Bethlehem (Ruth 1:19b–22)

Ruth 1:19b introduces the story's next scene, the arrival in Bethlehem. The beginning of the new episode is marked by shifts in

1. location (from Moab to Bethlehem)
2. character (from the three widows to Naomi, Ruth, and the people of Bethlehem)
3. time
4. topic

The episode is bracketed by two statements of their "arrival" (bwʾ) in Bethlehem (1:19b, 22). The word bwʾ ("come") occurs twice in the introduction and once in the conclusion, in each instance followed by "Bethlehem."

The episode briefly relates the sad arrival of the two widows in Bethlehem and features a brief, poignant exchange between Naomi and the townspeople (11.3). The episode is composed of three parts, symmetrically arranged.

Ruth and Boaz Meet (Ruth 2)

With the fourth episode we reach the story's turning point. The previous three episodes featured the disintegration of Naomi's family and the two sad scenes of her departure from Moab and arrival in Bethlehem. The audience is ready for a turn of events. Listeners are led to anticipate a hopeful new development by the introduction of the new unit in 2:1: "Now Naomi had a relative . . . named Boaz."

The beginning of this unit is marked not only by this stage-setting clause but also by shifts in time (sometime after their arrival in Bethlehem), place (the women's living quarters and Boaz's field), and characters (Ruth and Boaz are now the main characters, with minor roles played by Naomi and the reapers). As this episode opens, the audience senses that Naomi's family is near extinction, and that a turning point is needed if the family is to survive. Since the opening unit there has been a steady decline in Naomi's family. Six family members were mentioned in the first unit (Elimelech, Naomi, their two sons, two daughters-in-law); three in the next (Naomi and her two daugh-

11.4 Ruth and Boaz meet (Ruth 2)

---

a **introduction**: Ruth tells <u>Naomi</u> her plans to glean (an activity of the destitute) (2:1–2)

  b **Ruth goes out and gleans (2:3)**
- without apparent plan or guarantee of safety
- she <u>begins working in morning</u> (cf. 2:7), happening upon Boaz's field

    c **Boaz arrives and hears about Ruth (2:4–7)**
- "from morning until now she <u>sat</u> (*yšb*) only for a little" (presumably <u>eating a little, by herself</u>)
- <u>time reference</u>

      d **TURNING POINT: Ruth and Boaz meet;** Boaz's kindness and generosity to Ruth (2:8–13)

    c′ **Boaz invites Ruth to join him and his harvesters for a bountiful meal (2:14)**
- she <u>sits</u> (*yšb*) with them and <u>eats, with food left over</u>
- <u>time reference</u>

  b′ **Ruth arises and gleans again in Boaz's field (2:15–17)**
- enjoys Boaz's full protection and assistance
- she <u>works until evening</u>

a′ **conclusion**: Ruth returns to <u>Naomi</u> and joyfully tells her all that has happened (2:18–23)

---

ters-in-law); two in the third unit (Naomi and Ruth); and primarily one in the fourth unit: Ruth.

The episode comprises a series of seven paragraphs designed to form a symmetry, with the dramatic meeting of Ruth and Boaz serving as the turning point (11.4).

The turning point and climax of the episode (d) is unmistakable. Up to the point that Boaz and Ruth meet, the audience watches this poor but determined young woman laboring to support herself and her destitute mother-in-law as she gleans in unknown fields, alone, unprotected, and uncertain. Her pluck (no pun intended) and diligence are admirable; but the outcome of her efforts remains in question. With the arrival of Boaz, particularly with his friendliness and apparent devotion to Yahweh, the audience has reason to hope that he will be kind to Ruth. But we cannot be sure. Then, when Boaz and Ruth meet in 2:8–13, the direction of the entire book changes. Up to this point the narrative has been heavy with hopelessness and destitution. After the meeting, the narrative exudes hope.

In this particular episode the theme of the reversal of Ruth's fortunes is reinforced through the structure. The episode's symmetry allows the author to contrast the destitution and despair of the first three paragraphs with the hope and plenty of the final three paragraphs. The episode begins with Ruth's resolving to venture out (in the morning) to glean wherever she can find permission, uncertain as to where to go, not knowing whether she will succeed or fail (a). Naomi gives her assent but offers no words of hope. The story ends with Ruth's joyful return to Naomi that evening with happy news and abundant food and with Naomi's excited reaction (a′).

The second paragraph (b) features Ruth's going out to glean, proceeding tentatively (from field to field?) and happening upon the field of Boaz—the consequences of which are uncertain both to her and to the audience. In the next-to-last paragraph (b′) we find her once again going out to glean; but what a difference! This time she gleans with the owner's unqualified, enthusiastic blessing and protection (cf. 2:8–9). Now the owner even instructs his workers to see that she is allowed to gather extra grain normally not permitted to gleaners (2:15–16). Her fortunes have certainly turned!

The third scene (c) portrays Ruth, a foreign woman, gleaning alone all morning, "sitting down" (*yšb*) only for a little, presumably to eat what little she has brought along, and presumably eating alone. In the third-to-last scene (c′) she again "sits down" (*yšb*); but how things have changed! Now she sits because she is invited by the wealthy owner of the land to eat with him and his coworkers, and he provides her not only with as much food as she can eat, but so much that she has extra for Naomi (cf. 2:18).

Ruth's report to Naomi (2:18–23) is itself arranged in a sevenfold symmetry (11.5), with Naomi's joyful exclamation at the center (d). The end of this unit, like the end of the previous ones, is marked by a temporal clause involving the barley harvest: "until the end of the barley and wheat harvests" (2:23), which compares favorably with the end of the previous unit: "they came to Bethlehem at the beginning of the barley harvest" (1:22).

Ruth Proposes to Boaz at the Threshing Floor (Ruth 3)

A number of rhetorical indicators signal that a new episode begins in 3:1. The beginning of the new episode is marked by shifts in . . .

11.5 Ruth's report to Naomi (Ruth 2:18–23)

  a **narrative:** Ruth returns to her <u>mother-in-law</u> (*ḥămôtâ*) from gleaning (2:18)

    b **Naomi's delighted question: where did you work?** (2:19a)

      c **Ruth's response** (2:19b)

        d **CENTER: Naomi's joyful praise of Yahweh** (2:20)

      c′ **Ruth's response continued** (2:21)

    b′ **Naomi's advice about where Ruth should work in the future** (2:22)

  a′ **narrative:** Ruth regularly gleans and returns daily to her <u>mother-in-law</u> (*ḥămôtâ*) (2:23)

11.6 Ruth proposes to Boaz (Ruth 3)

  a **Naomi's instructions** to Ruth at their home (3:1–5)
- tension level: suspense introduced

    b **Ruth leaves Naomi and goes to the threshing floor;** there she follows Naomi's instructions (3:6–7)
- tension level: suspense grows

      c **Boaz awakens and finds Ruth <u>lying at his feet</u>;** her proposal (3:8–9)
- tension level: suspense reaches zenith

        d **CLIMAX: Boaz accepts her proposal!** (3:10–13)

      c′ **Boaz and Ruth awaken in the morning,** with Ruth <u>still lying at his feet</u>; his gift (3:14–15c)
- tension level: tranquillity

    b′ **Ruth leaves the threshing floor and goes back to Naomi;** there she reports what happened (3:15d–17; cf. BHS)
- tension level: tranquillity

  a′ **Naomi's optimistic instructions** to Ruth at their home (3:18)
- tension level: tranquillity

11.7 Boaz marries Ruth (Ruth 4:1–12)

  a **the elders assemble at the city gate** to hear Boaz's case involving Ruth (4:1–2)
- tension

    b **Boaz introduces the case:** he presents the kinsman with the opportunity to redeem Naomi's estate (4:3–4b)
- more tension

      c **kinsman's first, positive response:** "I will redeem it" (4:4c)
- even more tension

        d **CLIMAX: Boaz's declaration** that the redemption of Naomi's estate includes marrying Ruth the Moabitess (4:5)
- most tension: Boaz places everything on the line

      c′ **kinsman's second, negative response:** "I cannot redeem it" (4:6–8)
- relief! Now Boaz is free to marry Ruth

    b′ **Boaz concludes the case:** he redeems Naomi's estate and marries Ruth (4:9–10)
- greater relief! Boaz chooses to marry her

  a′ **the elders at the city gate** give their blessing on the marriage agreement (4:11–12)
- sense of joy and well-being: townspeople approve

1. time (the harvest is now over and the time of winnowing has arrived)
2. topic (from the procurement of food to the procurement of a husband for Ruth)
3. place (from Boaz's fields to the town's threshing floor)

This episode, like the previous one, features seven paragraphs arranged with a symmetric touch (11.6). The arrangement is designed to build tension in the first three paragraphs, reach the turning point and climax in the fourth paragraph, and then wind down through the happy denouement in the three final paragraphs that chiastically match the opening three.

Boaz Redeems Naomi's Estate and Marries Ruth (Ruth 4:1–12)

The beginning of the next episode is marked by shifts in location (now the action takes place at the city gate), participants (Boaz, the kinsman, the ten elders, the people of Bethlehem), and time (the next day). This episode recounts the legal procedure that takes place at the city gate involving Boaz and the unnamed kinsman. The unit is structured in a sevenfold symmetry (11.7). The same use of suspense found in the previous two episodes is also found here.

The audience would have perceived the complicating factor of the kinsman as a threat to the

> **11.8 Marriage of Boaz and Ruth and restoration of Naomi's family (Ruth 4:13–22)**
>
> a **Boaz and his son** (4:13)
> - <u>Boaz</u> marries Ruth, and they have a <u>son</u>
>
> b **women bless child** (4:14)
> - "may his <u>name be called</u> (*qrʾ*) (great) in Israel!"
>
> c **Naomi** (4:15a)
> - women bless <u>Naomi and child</u>
> - "may he bring you renewed life, and may he care for you in your old age"
>
> d **CENTER: praise of Ruth** (4:15b)
>
> c′ **Naomi** (4:16)
> - <u>Naomi takes child</u> and suckles him (renewing his life)
> - she becomes his foster-mother, taking care of him in her old age
>
> b′ **women name child** (4:17)
> - "and they <u>called his name</u> (*qrʾ*) Obed"
>
> a′ **Boaz and his son** (4:18–22)
> - the place of <u>Boaz and his son</u>, Obed, in the line of David

hoped-for marriage of Ruth and Boaz. What if the kinsman agrees to marry Ruth? We do not know what kind of person he is; but we know (through earlier speeches) that Boaz is a good man and that Naomi is excited that Ruth might be able to procure such a fine husband.

The suspense is maintained as long as possible. Boaz begins by deferring to the nearer kinsman (b), and to our dismay the kinsman accepts the right of redemption (c). At the center of the episode (d), Boaz reveals his "ace in the hole": he points out to the kinsman that redemption involves marrying "Ruth the Moabitess, the widow of the dead, in order to restore the name of the dead to his inheritance." The suspense peaks here, at the center of the episode. All is on the line. What will the kinsman choose?

The tension breaks in the fifth paragraph: the kinsman refuses to accept the responsibility and relinquishes his rights to Boaz (c′). The rest is happy denouement.

Conclusion: Marriage of Boaz and Ruth and Restoration of Naomi's Family (Ruth 4:13–22)

The story ends as it began, with a tersely told narrative recounting in broad strokes (covering years, rather than moments or days) the subsequent history of Naomi's family. The beginning of this unit is signaled by shifts in mood and speed of action, from the tense legal proceedings at the city gate to the celebrative survey of Naomi's later family history (spanning a period of many years). There is also a shift in participants: the previous scene at the gate was dominated by the male population of Bethlehem; this unit, except for its frame, belongs to the women.

The unit could be analyzed as comprising either five or seven parts (if the threefold blessing of the women be taken as three separate parts). The seven-part design is more likely, since with this design the unit exhibits a conspicuous symmetric scheme (11.8).

The introductory and concluding genealogical (father-son) paragraphs (a and a′), featuring Boaz and his son, frame five joyous central parts involving Naomi and the women of Bethlehem. In the second and next-to-last parts (b and b′), the women of Bethlehem are the speakers; and in both, the women's words focus on the "calling" (*qārāʾ*) of the boy's "name" (*šĕmô*). The third and third-to-last parts (c and c′) address the mutually beneficial relationship between the new baby and Naomi. At the center (d) stands the splendid praise of Ruth, the one who (humanly speaking) enabled this happy ending to happen.

The structure of the genealogy in 4:18–22 is similar to that of the genealogies in Genesis 5 and 11 in several respects: (1) it begins with *ʾēlleh tôlĕdôt* ("these are the generations of *x*"); (2) it features ten generations; (3) the final, tenth generation is the most important (David; as are Noah and Abraham in the Genesis genealogies); and (4) the seventh generation here (Boaz) is special (cf. Enoch in Gen. 5).

Overall Layout of the Book of Ruth

A symmetric touch in the overall layout of the Book of Ruth has been sensed by others, although with mutually conflicting analyses.[3] The

---

3. See Robert Alter, *The Art of Biblical Narrative* (New York: Basic Books, 1985), 58–60; F. B. Huey Jr., "Ruth" (Expositor's Bible Commentary 3; Grand Rapids: Zondervan, 1992), 512; S. Bar-Efrat, "Some Observations on the Analysis of Structure in Biblical Narrative," *Vetus Testamentum* 30 (1980) 156–57; S. Bertman, "Symmetrical Design in the Book of Ruth," *Journal of Biblical Literature* 84 (1965) 165–68; M. Gow, "The Significance of Literary Structure for the Translation of the Book of Ruth," *Bible Translator* 35 (1984) 309–20; A. B. Luter and Richard O. Rigsby, "An Adjusted Symmetrical Structuring of Ruth," *Journal of the Evangelical Theological Society* 39 (1996) 15–28.

11.9 The Book of Ruth

a **introduction: devastation of Naomi's family** (1:1–5)
- Naomi's family is lost; Elimelech's line is ended
- Ruth's tragic marriage to Naomi's son: he is sickly and dies; no children
- both of Naomi's sons die
- past events set the stage for the story
- economy of words

b **two of Naomi's relatives deliberate whether to support her** (1:6–19a)
  - both initially agree
  - one turns back when marriage is mentioned
  - one chooses to stay with Naomi, in an admirable speech
  - a blessing is uttered for Ruth
  - decision to support Naomi means that Ruth will probably not remarry

c **return to Bethlehem in emptiness and hopelessness** (1:19b–22)
  - setting: "at the beginning of the barley harvest"
  - surprised question of identity: "is this Naomi?"
  - "I left full, but Yahweh has brought me back empty (rêqām)"
  - Naomi and Ruth come into (bwʾ) Bethlehem in despair

d **TURNING POINT: meeting of Ruth and Boaz** (2:1–23)

c′ **Ruth's appeal at the threshing floor and her return to Bethlehem in fullness and hope** (3:1–18)
  - setting: when the people were "winnowing barley"
  - surprised question of identity: "who are you?"
  - Ruth left empty; she returns with six measures of barley: "you must not go back empty-handed (rêqām)" (3:17)
  - Ruth comes into (bwʾ) Bethlehem with good news and hope

b′ **two of Naomi's relatives deliberate whether to support Naomi** (4:1–12)
  - both initially agree
  - one turns back when marriage is mentioned
  - one chooses to help Naomi, in an admirable speech
  - a blessing is uttered for Ruth
  - decision to support Naomi means that Ruth will be remarried

a′ **conclusion: restoration of Naomi's family** (4:13–21)
- Naomi's family is restored; Elimelech's line is raised up again
- Ruth's happy marriage to Naomi's relative: he is wealthy and robust (note etiologies of names); they are blessed with a son
- "your daughter-in-law . . . is more to you than seven sons!"
- future events provide broader significance of story
- economy of words

---

book is most likely designed to form a seven-part symmetry (11.9).

Correspondence of the First and Last Units (Ruth 1:1–5; 4:13–22)

The correspondence between the book's introduction and conclusion is obvious. The introduction sets the stage for the story by recounting in striking brevity the tragedy of Naomi's family; the conclusion relates in similar brevity the final outcome of the story (this sort of economy of words is not found elsewhere in the book). The introduction provides necessary background details for the story; the conclusion surveys future events that place the story into the larger framework of Israel's history. The decimation of Naomi's family in the introduction is reversed in the conclusion. The death of Naomi's sons in the first unit is counterbalanced by the birth of the son ("to Naomi") in the last unit. The apparent termination of Elimelech's family line in the beginning is reversed in the conclusion by

the restoration of his line, which will culminate in King David.

Moreover, in place of the earlier famine, exile in a foreign land, dying, and a sense of despair, the story's conclusion has the family back home, in prosperity, with the beginning of new life and an atmosphere of rejoicing. In the opening unit Naomi lost her only two sons; now the women of Bethlehem declare, "Your daughter-in-law . . . is more to you than seven sons!" (4:15). In the introduction Ruth is married by Naomi's poor (and sickly, according to the meaning of Mahlon's name) son and then is left a widow. Now Ruth is remarried to a wealthy (and robust, by Boaz's name) kinsman of Naomi. In the first unit Ruth had no children; in the last, the Lord opens her womb and she bears a son who will have significance for all Israel.

Correspondence of the Second and Next-to-Last Units (Ruth 1:6–19a; 4:1–12)

The second and next-to-last units likewise correspond in a way that would not have been lost on an ancient Hebrew audience. In both, two relatives of Naomi are confronted with a choice of helping her (Orpah and Ruth, Boaz and the kinsman). In each episode, both relatives are equally willing to help at first and agree to do so: Orpah and Ruth state that they will remain with Naomi; both Boaz and the kinsman are willing to redeem Naomi's estate. But in both episodes, one relative relents when the issue of marriage is mentioned. In both episodes, the committed relative's determination to help is presented as admirable. In both episodes, Ruth is given a blessing, in the first by her mother-in-law, in the second by the women of Bethlehem.

Some of these points of similarity help draw out the wonderful reversal of fortunes that Ruth and Naomi experience. In the earlier episode the two widowed daughters-in-law are considering whether to return with their destitute, widowed mother-in-law to a life of poverty and probably permanent widowhood. Ruth's tenacious decision to support her aging mother-in-law is a bittersweet decision. In contrast, the latter episode involves a happy decision. Now two wealthy male relatives consider which of them will support Naomi, redeem her estate, marry Ruth, and restore life and posterity to Naomi's lost family.

Correspondence of the Third and Third-to-Last Units (Ruth 1:19b–22; 3:1–18), and the Book's Overall Layout

The third unit briefly recounts the journey of Naomi and Ruth to Bethlehem and their arrival there "at the beginning of the barley harvest." It is a sad episode. Naomi hears the townswomen ask in surprise and disbelief, "Is this Naomi?" She responds in bitterness that she left Bethlehem full and is returning empty.

The third-to-last episode recounts the story of Ruth's going to Boaz at the threshing floor to make her appeal to him. Although the contents of this episode are very different from that of Ruth and Naomi's arrival in Bethlehem, there appear to be several intentional editorial touches that create points of correspondence between the two otherwise dissimilar units. In 3:9 Boaz asks in surprise, "Who are you?" which may possibly be a happy echo of the similar question the surprised townspeople ask of Naomi in the third episode, "Is this Naomi?" (1:19). The third episode takes place "at the beginning of the barley harvest" (1:22), normally a time of scarcity, since the harvest is just beginning; the third-to-last episode occurs when the people were "winnowing barley . . . at the

threshing floor" (3:2), a traditional time of great celebration because of the plenteous harvest that has been secured for the coming year. In the third episode Naomi and Ruth "come into" (bwʾ) Bethlehem in bitterness (1:22); in its counterpart, Ruth, who has spent the night outside the city, now again "comes into" (bwʾ; cf. BHS) Bethlehem, this time with joyful news and hope (3:15). In the former episode Naomi says despairingly as she comes into the city, "I went away full, and the Lord has brought me back empty (rêqām)" (1:21); in the latter, Ruth (who had left the city empty-handed the previous evening) is given six measures of barley by Boaz, who says, "You must not go back empty-handed (rêqām) to your mother-in-law" (3:17). Thus, as in the other matched units, here too the correspondences all serve to highlight the change of fortunes and the new hope that began with the story's turning point.

The central literary unit (chap. 2) is, appropriately, the turning point of the entire story; it is here that Ruth and Boaz meet, and from that moment on the lives of Naomi and Ruth are filled with ever-increasing hope.

There is one main difficulty with the foregoing analysis. Two of the units that should not match (chaps. 2 and 3) obviously do. The threshing-floor story and the gleaning story correspond in many details. Both stories are suspenseful episodes about Ruth's venturing out into the fields of Bethlehem to procure help. Both begin and end with Ruth and Naomi's talking at home. Both end with Ruth's returning to Naomi to tell her the good news, and with Ruth's bringing home to Naomi a plentiful supply of grain that she has procured through Boaz's generosity. In both, the first three paragraphs are full of suspense and uncertainty; neither the audience nor Ruth knows whether her adventure will succeed. In both, the central, fourth paragraph represents the turning point of the story. In both, the turning point features a kind speech by Boaz to Ruth in which he offers her his full and enthusiastic support. And in both, the final three parts are full of hope and good news. Indeed, the match between these two stories is far better than that between the threshing-floor story and the story of Naomi's and Ruth's arrival in Bethlehem in 1:19b–22. Moreover, it could be argued that the rather brief scene in 1:19b–22 is not even a separate episode at all, but the conclusion of the episode of Naomi's journey back to Bethlehem. If this were the case, the Book of Ruth might be analyzed as comprising six, not seven, chiastically matching units (11.10).

11.10 Alternative analysis of the Book of Ruth

a **introduction**: devastation of Naomi's family (1:1–5)
  b **Naomi's two relatives deliberate whether to support her** (1:6–22)
    c **Ruth goes out to Boaz's field**: Boaz's support and generosity (2:1–23)
    c′ **Ruth goes out to threshing floor**: Boaz's support and generosity (3:1–18)
  b′ **Naomi's two relatives deliberate whether to support her** (4:1–12)
a′ **conclusion**: restoration of Naomi's family (4:13–22)

This is a legitimate alternative analysis of the book's structure, supported especially by the strong, obvious correspondences between the six matched units. On the other hand, it is very difficult to see 1:19b–22 as simply the conclusion of the episode of 1:6–19a and not a separate unit (see above). Also, there is the obvious appeal of an analysis proposing a more conventional seven-part symmetric scheme, particularly when the central part of the symmetry turns out to be the story's unmistakable turning point. Which analysis is correct? I tentatively favor the seven-part analysis in 11.9.

Conclusion

The structure of the Book of Ruth may reveal several insights about the book and its message. First, it is noteworthy that the book begins with three episodes marked by tragedy, despair, and hopelessness and ends with three episodes that feature ever-increasing hope and, ultimately, triumph. This suggests that the composition was intended to be an uplifting story, designed to encourage and inspire the audience.

The book's layout is also obviously intended to create and retain tension and suspense. The entire book is structured so that even at the end of the third unit the audience still remains in suspense as to how the widows' dire situation can be rectified. Moreover, the individual episodes

(e.g., Ruth's gleaning, her proposal to Boaz, the legal procedure at the city gate) are designed to create and maintain suspense for as long as possible. This interest in creating suspense (and thereby holding the audience's attention) reveals that one of the purposes of the composition is to entertain (in the best sense of the word)—to function as a good story.

The book's layout may also reveal one of the primary morals of the story. The book is structured so that the meeting of Ruth and Boaz is the turning point of the story. Their meeting "happens" in the central episode of the book—and in the highlighted center of that episode. Before this meeting, the audience has little reason to hope for a reversal of Naomi's misfortunes. After Ruth and Boaz meet, hope is born anew, and the chain of events set in motion by their meeting leads step by step to the wonderful restoration of Naomi's family. And since the success of this meeting is the result of Ruth's loyalty, diligence, and determination to support her aging mother-in-law, combined with Boaz's kindness and generosity, the audience is left with the central moral of the story: the admirable qualities exhibited by Ruth and Boaz can be used by God to reverse the fortunes of a whole family; or even the fortunes of a whole nation, as shown by the final outcome of this story—the Davidic dynasty.

12
Samuel

David—a Man after God's Heart

The Book of Samuel (in the Hebrew Bible, 1 Samuel and 2 Samuel are a single book) might be better entitled "The Book of David," since its main character is David, not Samuel. The book tells the story of David's life, with the purpose of demonstrating that David was a man after God's heart and the rightful choice for Israel's throne. It is composed of a series of larger sections, each focusing on one era or theme in David's life. The number of such sections is generally seen as a half dozen or so.[1] Further structural analysis suggests, however, that the book comprises seven well-defined units, each with its own artful internal layout:

a birth and rule of Samuel (1 Sam. 1–7)
b Saul's reign, failure, and rejection by God (1 Sam. 8–15)
c David in Saul's court (1 Sam. 16–20)
d David as a political fugitive (1 Sam. 21–31)
e David as king over Israel and his kindness to Saul's family (2 Sam. 1–8)
f David's failure and its dreadful consequences (2 Sam. 9–20)
g David's final years and Solomon's accession (2 Sam. 21–1 Kings 2)[2]

---

1. Otto Kaiser, *Introduction to the Old Testament: A Presentation of Its Results and Problems*, trans. John Sturdy (Minneapolis: Augsburg, 1975), 153, analyzes the major literary divisions of the Book of Samuel as follows: (a) Eli and Samuel (1 Sam. 1–7), (b) Samuel and Saul (1 Sam. 8–15), (c) Saul and David (1 Sam. 16–2 Sam. 1), (d) David and his kingdom (2 Sam. 2–12), (e) David and his succession (2 Sam. 13–20), (f) additions (2 Sam. 21–24). Brevard S. Childs, *Introduction to the Old Testament as Scripture* (Philadelphia: Fortress, 1979), 267–68, is reticent to accept the entirety of Kaiser's analysis for at least two reasons: (1) the few obvious summaries of literary sections (1 Sam. 7:15–17; 14:47–52; 2 Sam. 8:15–18; 20:23–26) do not completely coincide with Kaiser's divisions (the second and third are problematic); and (2) the introductory formula in 1 Samuel 13:1 shows that a major division begins there. Childs attributes these problems partially to editorial processes spanning many years.

2. For the rationale of including 1 Kings 1–2 in the analysis of the Book of Samuel, see the discussion below.

Birth and Rule of Samuel (1 Samuel 1–7)

The book opens with the story of Samuel, the prophet who would play a key role in David's rise to power. This unit begins with the narrative of Samuel's birth and ends with the summary of his rule: "So Samuel judged Israel all the days of his life" (7:15–17). The unit is composed of seven chronologically arranged episodes or narrative units, designed to form a symmetry, with Samuel's call at the highlighted center (12.1).

Some of the smaller units in 1 Samuel 1–7 exhibit this same structure. For example, the narrative of Samuel's birth is so arranged (12.2). This story's layout underscores the theme of the reversal of fortunes, a theme that will dominate the Book of Samuel. Notice that the turning point, the birth of Samuel, is placed at the center. On the other hand, the next unit, about Eli's wicked sons, has a layout that utilizes the matchups to highlight the contrast between Samuel and the wicked sons of Eli (12.3).

Saul's Reign, His Failure, and His Rejection by God (1 Samuel 8–15)

The second major unit in Samuel is the story of the establishment of Saul's kingship and his failure and rejection by God (12.4).[3] The story begins with Yahweh's choosing Saul to be Israel's king (a), and it closes with Yahweh's rejecting Saul as Israel's king (a'). The unit is organized in a positive-to-negative fashion, beginning with the good stories about Saul (culminating in Saul's great victory over the Ammonites), fol-

---

3. Joel Rosenberg, "1 and 2 Samuel," in *The Literary Guide to the Bible*, ed. Robert Alter and Frank Kermode (Cambridge: Harvard University Press, 1987), 122–45, identifies this unit as including only chaps. 8–12; but see Victor M. Wilson, *Divine Symmetries: The Art of Biblical Rhetoric* (New York: University Press of America, 1977), 116–18.

12.1 Birth and rule of Samuel (1 Samuel 1–7)

a **introduction: Samuel's birth and lifelong dedication to Yahweh** (1:1–2:11)
- born in <u>Ramah</u>
- Samuel's family goes up from Ramah to Shiloh <u>from year to year</u>
- ends: <u>Elkanah went home to Ramah</u>

b **Eli's wicked sons show contempt for Yahweh at the tabernacle** (2:12–26)
- Israel's priests disrespect Yahweh's tabernacle and Yahweh's offerings

c **prophecy that Eli's sons will be killed on one day** (2:27–3:1a)

d **TURNING POINT: Samuel's call** (3:1b–4:1a)

c′ **prophecy about Eli's sons comes true: their deaths** (4:1b–22)

b′ **travels of the ark; Philistines show respect for Yahweh's ark** (5:1–7:1)
- Philistine priests respect Yahweh's ark and honor him with offerings

a′ **conclusion: Samuel's victory and lifelong rule over Israel** (7:2–17)
- lives in <u>Ramah</u>
- Samuel goes <u>from year to year</u> to various centers, then returns to Ramah
- ends: <u>Samuel always went home to Ramah</u>

12.2 Samuel's birth (1 Samuel 1:1–2:11)

a **Elkanah and his family go** yearly from Ramah to <u>Shiloh</u> (1:1–8)

b **Hannah's sad prayer** (1:9–11)

c **sad conversation** between Hannah and Eli (1:12–18)

d **TURNING POINT: birth of Samuel** (1:19–23)

c′ **happy conversation** between Hannah and Eli (1:24–28)

b′ **Hannah's happy prayer** (2:1–10)

a′ **Elkanah goes home to Ramah**, but Samuel remains in <u>Shiloh</u> (2:11)

12.3 Eli's wicked sons (1 Samuel 2:12–26)

a **introduction**: Eli's sons do not know Yahweh (2:12)

b **wickedness of Eli's sons** (2:13–17)

c **Samuel** ministers <u>before Yahweh</u> (2:18)

d **CENTER: Hannah has more children** (2:19–21b)

c′ **Samuel** grows up <u>before Yahweh</u> (2:21c)

b′ **wickedness of Eli's sons** (2:22–25)

a′ **conclusion**: Samuel grows in favor with Yahweh (2:26)

---

lowed by stories about Saul's failures and rejection by God. The symmetric arrangement scheme is designed to highlight the reversal of Saul's fortunes, with the central episode being Samuel's farewell address.

Young David—a Man after God's Heart (1 Samuel 16–20)

The third unit in Samuel is the story of young David's rise to fame and his life in Saul's court. Like the previous unit, this one is also arranged in a positive-to-negative order. It opens with the positive episodes of David's anointing by Samuel, his victory over Goliath, his popularity in Saul's court, and his friendship with Jonathan. Following the centrally positioned high point, David's fortunes turn, with three stories (that chiastically match the first three, to heighten the change in fortune) recounting Saul's murderous jealousy of David and his attempts to kill the young hero. The layout of this unit is similar to the others (12.5).

David's Life as a Political Fugitive (1 Samuel 21–31)

The fourth major unit in Samuel tells the story of David's life as a political fugitive. The unit is arranged in a well-crafted seven-part symmetry (12.6). The author has deliberately selected stories that address questions about David's character (e.g., why did David defect to the Philistines?) and that demonstrate that David was a man after God's heart, whom God repeatedly protected from Saul's misdirected jealousy. The unit represents the turning point of the book, beginning as it does with King Saul's seeking to kill David and concluding with Saul's death, which opens the way for David to become the new king.

This central unit of the Book of Samuel opens with a symmetrically arranged account of David's initial escape from Saul (12.7), framed by episodes involving the priests at Nob, and closes with a surprisingly long, symmetrically arranged account of Saul's death at the battle of Gilboa (12.8).

12.4 Saul's reign and rejection by God (1 Samuel 8–15)

a **God chooses Saul when Israel demands a king at Ramah** (8:1–10:16)
- evaluation: good
- begins: Israel comes to Samuel in Ramah
- God chooses Saul and Samuel declares this choice to Saul
- Saul protests that he is insignificant and therefore not the right choice (9:21)
- "as Saul turned to go, God changed his heart" (10:9)
- Samuel will offer sacrifices at Gilgal (10:8)
- ends: Saul went to his home in Gibeah (10:9–16)

b **Saul chosen by casting of lots at Mizpah** (10:17–27)
- evaluation: good
- lots work well for Samuel, identifying Saul as rightful king

c **story of war preparations and victory over Ammonites** (11:1–13)
- evaluation: good
- Saul is able to gather a huge army (330,000 soldiers)
- Saul succeeds in gathering many troops by slaughtering two oxen
- seven-day wait results in victory

d **CENTER: Samuel's farewell address** (11:14–13:1)
- ends: summary of Saul's reign

c′ **story of war preparations against Philistines** (13:2–15)
- evaluation: bad
- Saul gathers a pathetically small army (only 600 soldiers)
- Saul fails to keep troops with him by sacrificing (oxen?)
- seven-day wait results in God's condemnation

b′ **Saul's tainted victory at Michmash with the casting of lots** (13:16–14:52)
- evaluation: bad
- lots do not work well for Saul, identifying Jonathan as the culprit to be killed when Jonathan is actually the hero

a′ **God rejects Saul; Saul's sin in Amalekite war** (15:1–35)
- evaluation: bad
- ends: Samuel returns to Ramah never to see Saul again
- God rejects Saul, and Samuel declares this choice to Saul
- Saul's insignificance in his own eyes (15:17)
- "as Samuel turned to go, Saul caught hold of . . ." (15:27)
- Saul intended to disobey God by offering sacrifices at Gilgal (15:21)
- ends: Saul went to his home in Gibeah

12.5 Young David in Saul's court (1 Samuel 16–20)

a **Samuel leaves Ramah to anoint David in Bethlehem, fearing that Saul will kill him** (16:1–13)
- evaluation: good

b **happy story of David's playing harp for Saul when evil spirits trouble him** (16:14–23)
- outcome: Saul loves David
- evaluation: better

c **David's victory over Goliath** (17:1–58)
- evaluation: even better
- Goliath's spear intended to be used against David
- David slays the Philistine giant and keeps his head as a trophy
- Goliath intends to kill David; his plan fails

d **CENTER: David's successes at Saul's court** (18:1–6)
- evaluation: best
- Jonathan loves David; people are pleased with him

c′ **Saul's jealousy over song about David's victory over Goliath** (18:7–30)
- evaluation: bad
- Saul takes his spear and nearly kills David
- David slays two hundred Philistines and keeps their foreskins as bride-price for Michal
- Saul intends to kill David through the Philistines; his plan fails

b′ **sad story of David's playing harp for Saul when evil spirits trouble him** (19:1–17)
- outcome: Saul is jealous and sends assassins to kill David; Michal saves him
- evaluation: worse

a′ **David flees to Samuel at Ramah, fearing that Saul will kill him;** Samuel and Jonathan save David; David leaves Saul's court forever, becoming a fugitive (19:18–20:42)
- evaluation: worst

12.6 David's life as a political fugitive (1 Samuel 21–31)

a **David flees; Saul has Yahweh's priest Ahimelech and family killed** (21:1–22:23)
- David seeks help and inquires of Yahweh from Yahweh's high priest (cf. 22:15)
- Yahweh's priest gives hungry David bread from Yahweh's own table
- David is given Goliath's sword, which he had used to decapitate the Philistine
- Israelites begin to gather and join David
- David is dismissed from the presence of King Achish of Gath

   b **David saves the Judean town** of Keilah from Philistines (23:1–18)

      c **Ziphites betray David; David spares Saul's life** (23:19–24:22 [23:19–24:23])
- begins: "the Ziphites went up to Saul at Gibeah and said, 'Is not David hiding . . . on the hill of Hachilah, south of Jeshimon?' "
- David refrains from killing unsuspecting Saul; takes a token
- "Saul recognized David's voice and said, 'Is that your voice, David my son?' " (24:16 [24:17]); Saul admits guilt and goes home
- ends: Saul returned home, and David went to the stronghold

         d **CENTER: death of Samuel; David and Abigail** (25:1–44)
- Abigail's speech about David's future kingship

      c′ **Ziphites betray David; David spares Saul's life again** (26:1–25)
- begins: "the Ziphites went to Saul at Gibeah and said, 'Is not David hiding on the hill of Hachilah, opposite Jeshimon?' "
- David refrains from killing unsuspecting Saul; takes tokens
- "Saul recognized David's voice and said, 'Is that your voice, David my son?' " (26:17); Saul admits guilt and goes home
- ends: David went on his way, and Saul returned home

   b′ **David protects Judean towns**, while "protecting" Philistines (27:1–12)

a′ **Yahweh has Saul and his sons killed at battle of Gilboa** (28:1–31:13)
- Saul unsuccessfully inquires of Yahweh (he had killed Yahweh's priests!); then he inquires of a witch (something Yahweh had forbidden); meanwhile, David successfully inquires of Yahweh from Abiathar, sole priestly survivor of Saul's slaughter of the priests of Nob (30:7–8)
- witch gives hungry Saul a feast
- Saul is decapitated by Philistine swords
- Israelites of Saul's army scatter; Israelites in Transjordan flee
- David is dismissed from the presence of King Achish of Gath and Philistines

---

12.7 Early period of David's fugitive life (1 Samuel 21–22)

a **Ahimelech, priest at Nob, helps David**, and Doeg the Edomite sees it (21:1–9 [21:2–10])

   b **David flees Judah** and is spared at Gath (21:10–15 [21:11–16])

      c **David hides near Adullam;** family joins him for their safety (22:1)

         d **TURNING POINT: four hundred fighting men join him** (22:2)

      c′ **David takes his family to Moab for safety** (22:3–4)

   b′ **David returns to Judah;** Forest of Hereth (22:5)

a′ **Ahimelech, priest at Nob**, and all the priestly families at Nob, are betrayed by Doeg the Edomite; Saul has Doeg kill them all (Abiathar escapes) (22:6–23)

12.8 Saul's death (1 Samuel 28–31)

a **introduction:** setting for battle (background information) (28:1–4)

   b **prediction of witch of Endor:** Saul and sons will die next day (28:5–25)

      c **David returns to Ziklag;** families have been captured (29:1–30:6)

         d **TURNING POINT: David's victory over Amalekites** (Yahweh promises David victory) (30:7–25)

      c′ **David returns to Ziklag** with rescued families (30:26–31)

   b′ **prediction of witch of Endor comes true:** Saul and sons are killed (31:1–7)

a′ **conclusion:** aftermath of battle: recovery of bodies of Saul and sons (31:8–13)

It is curious that the story of Nabal and Abigail falls at the center of this section of Samuel.[4]

4. Rosenberg, "1 and 2 Samuel," 137, also identifies the story of Nabal and Abigail as the center of a symmetry, with chaps. 24 and 26 matching. His overall analysis, however, differs significantly from the one presented here; he sees the entirety of 1 Samuel 13–31 as forming a grand symmetry. See also Robert P. Gordon, "David's Rise and Saul's Demise: Narrative Analogy in 1 Sam. 24–26," *Tyndale Bulletin* 31 (1980) 37–64, who likewise identifies 1 Samuel 25 as serving a central role in the narrative, enclosed by stories of David sparing Saul. He argues that Saul does not vanish from view in 1 Samuel 25; rather, Saul is Nabal's alter ego.

The story seems an unlikely center, since it does not seem to represent a high point, turning point, or climax of any sort. There are, however, at least two points that support its centrality and importance: (1) it opens with the death of Samuel (25:1), which certainly marks a significant turning point in the book, and (2) some of the most important themes in the entire Book of Samuel are verbalized here in Abigail's remarkable speech: (a) David's refraining from avenging himself with his own hands (25:26,

12.9 David becomes king (2 Samuel 1–8)

> **part 1: David becomes king over Judah** (2 Sam. 1–4)
> a **David kills the man who claims to have killed Saul,** Israel's king (1:1–16)
> > b **David's lament** over Saul and Jonathan (1:17–27)
> > > c **David made king of Judah** and expresses gratitude to people who properly buried bodies of Saul and Jonathan (2:1–7)
> > > > d **TURNING POINT: rivalry between north and south**; David's kingdom prevails; closed by list of David's sons (2:8–3:5)
> > > c´ **Abner comes to make David Israel's king**; he is assassinated without David's approval or knowledge (3:6–27)
> > b´ **David's lament** over Abner (3:28–39)
> a´ **David kills people who killed Saul's son** Ish-bosheth, Israel's king (4:1–12)
> **part 2: David establishes his rule over all Israel** (2 Sam. 5–8)
> a **David becomes king over Israel;** summary of reign; conquest of Jerusalem (5:1–16)
> > b **military victories** over Philistines (5:17–25)
> > > c **David "danced before Yahweh"** in joy as he brings the ark up to Jerusalem (6:1–23)
> > > > d **CLIMAX: promise of David's everlasting dynasty** (7:1–17)
> > > c´ **David "sat before Yahweh"** in joy when he prays before the ark, thanking God for the promise (7:18–29)
> > b´ **military victories** over Philistines and others (8:1–14)
> a´ **summary of David's reign** (8:15–18)

31), (b) David's innocency of wrongdoing (and the wish that it will continue his whole life; 25:28), (c) God's protection and blessing of David (25:29), and (d) God's intention to make David Israel's king and to make David's dynasty Israel's permanent ruling dynasty (25:28, 31).

David Becomes King over Israel and His Kindness to Saul's Family (2 Samuel 1–8)

The book's fifth major section tells the story of how David became king over all Israel after Saul's death. One of the main themes of this section is the mercy and kindness David showed to members of Saul's family. The section falls into two parts, each organized in a standard seven-part symmetry (12.9). The first part recounts David's rule over Judah and his expressions of grief over the deaths of members of Saul's family and court; while the second part tells the story of how David became king over all Israel and surveys the successes of his reign.

David's Sin and Its Consequences (2 Samuel 9–20)

The book's sixth major unit tells the story of David's sin with Bathsheba and its terrible consequences. The story is introduced by a brief episode about Mephibosheth (2 Sam. 9), which provides background information without which the audience will not understand some of the events of the story. The story proper comprises two long sections, each laid out in the standard sevenfold symmetry (12.10): the first recounts David's sin, the second traces its consequences. The first is told in the context of David's war against the Ammonites, while the second involves David's war against his own son in Transjordan.

The echoes between the two parts serve to highlight David's tragedy. For example, both wars take place in Transjordan; but the second is a tragic civil war. In both wars, David stays home, waiting for word from the front lines (which in both stories would be terrible news). In both wars, Joab leads David's troops in victory; the second war unfortunately involves the death of David's own son. In both wars, David waits with anxiety to hear if Joab has carried out his orders regarding a specific warrior: Uriah in the first, Absalom in the second. In the first war David instructs Joab to kill Uriah, the innocent husband of Bathsheba (Joab obeys, to David's satisfaction); in the second war David instructs Joab not to kill Absalom, a person who is truly a traitor (this time Joab disobeys and David is deeply distraught). In both stories David grieves over the loss of his sons (Amnon, Bathsheba's first son, Absalom). In both parts, Israel's leader commits adultery: in the first part, David has intercourse with Uriah's wife; in the second, Absalom sleeps with David's concubines.

Conclusion of David's Reign (2 Samuel 21–1 Kings 2)

The concluding unit of the Book of Samuel presents the final details of David's reign and the story of Solomon's succession. That this unit includes the first two chapters of 1 Kings is indicated by at least two considerations. First, a grand biography of King David would not likely have ended with the incident of the plague in 2 Samuel 24, since that would have left the audience hanging. The storyteller would certainly have recounted the end of the story, David's death (which we have in 1 Kings 1–2). Second,

12.10 David's sin and its consequences (2 Samuel 9–20)

> **part 1: David's sin** (2 Sam. 9:1–12:31)
> > • background information: Mephibosheth and Ziba (9:1–31)
> > a **war with the Ammonites** (10:1–19)
> > > b **David's sin with Bathsheba; she conceives a child** (11:1–5)
> > > > c **David covers up his guilt** (11:6–27)
> > > > > d **TURNING POINT: God uncovers David's sin** (12:1–12)
> > > > c′ **David admits his guilt** (12:13–15a)
> > > b′ **Bathsheba's child dies**; her next, Solomon, lives (12:15b–25)
> > a′ **victory over the Ammonites** (12:26–31)
> **part 2: consequences of David's sin** (2 Sam. 13:1–20:22)
> > a **Absalom's revolt** (13:1–15:16)
> > > • Joab and wise woman cooperate to help the traitor Absalom
> > > b **David's flight from Jerusalem** (15:17–17:29)
> > > > • <u>Shimei</u> curses David; <u>Abishai urges David to let him kill Shimei</u>; David strongly rebukes Abishai
> > > > • <u>Mephibosheth</u> ignores David's plight; <u>Ziba and Barzillai</u> offer help
> > > > c **David remains at gate of Mahanaim to await news of battle** (18:1–5)
> > > > > d **CLIMAX: Absalom is defeated and killed** (18:6–18)
> > > > c′ **David at gate of Mahanaim hears news of battle and Absalom's death;**
> > > > he mourns bitterly over Absalom's death (18:19–19:8c [18:19–19:9c])
> > > b′ **David's return to Jerusalem** (19:8d–43 [19:9d–44])
> > > > • <u>Shimei</u> begs for mercy; <u>Abishai urges David to let him kill Shimei</u>; David strongly rebukes Abishai
> > > > • <u>Mephibosheth</u> is rebuked; David shows gratitude to <u>Ziba and Barzillai</u>
> > a′ **Sheba's revolt** (20:1–22)
> > > • Joab and wise woman cooperate to help the traitor Absalom
> > > • end marker: list of members of David's cabinet (20:23–26)

12.11 End of David's reign (2 Samuel 21–1 Kings 2)

> a **famine caused by Saul's war against Gibeonites** (2 Sam. 21:1–14)
> > • ends: <u>then Yahweh answered prayer in behalf of the land</u> (21:14)
> b **David's heroes** (21:15–22)
> > • how they defeated great Philistine warriors
> > c **David's song of praise** (22:1–51)
> > c′ **David's last words** (23:1–7)
> b′ **David's heroes** (23:8–39)
> > • including how they defeated Philistines in battle
> a′ **plague caused by David's census** (preparing for wrongful war?) (24:1–25)
> > • ends: <u>then Yahweh answered prayer in behalf of the land</u> (24:25)
> > > d **conclusion:** David's death and Solomon's succession (1 Kings 1:1–2:46)
> > > > • ends: so the kingdom was firmly established in Solomon's hands (2:46)

the final outcome of the stories of a number of characters introduced in the Book of Samuel (Mephibosheth, Joab, Shimei, Abiathar, Zadok, Benaiah) is not recounted until 1 Kings 1–2. It is only in 1 Kings 1–2 that all the plot lines are resolved.[5] Evidently a later scribal or editorial decision moved the story of David's death and Solomon's succession from the end of the Book of Samuel to the beginning of the Book of Kings, where it served to introduce the reign of the first king of that book, Solomon.

The organization of 2 Samuel 21–1 Kings 2 is unusual (12.11). It has seven units (which supports the inclusion of 1 Kings 1–2 in this analysis of the Book of Samuel); but these seven units are not arranged with the typical symmetric scheme. Instead, the first six units form a symmetry,[6] while the seventh unit (1 Kings 1–2) stands alone (and is thus highlighted), exhibiting its own modified chiastic pattern (12.12).

Overall Layout of the Book of Samuel

The material of the Book of Samuel is primarily arranged in a chronologically linear order, but

5. Many scholars identify 1 Kings 2 as the close of the Samuel narrative; see, e.g., Jan P. Fokkelman, *Narrative Art and Poetry in the Books of Samuel: A Full Interpretation Based on Stylistic and Structural Analysis* (4 vols.; Studia Semitica Neerlandica; Assen: Van Gorcum, 1981–93); R. N. Whybray, *The Succession Narrative: A Study of II Samuel 9–20 and I Kings 1 and 2* (London, 1968); A. A. Anderson, *2 Samuel* (Word Biblical Commentary 11; Dallas: Word, 1989), xxviii–xxxiv.

6. The symmetric configuration of chaps. 21–24 is also noted by Rosenberg, "1 and 2 Samuel," 138–39.

12.12 Solomon's accession (2 Kings 1–2)

a **Adonijah plots to become king** (1:1–11)

  b **Adonijah's plot foiled**; Solomon spares Adonijah (1:12–53)

    c **David's charge to Solomon**, including instruction to kill Joab and Shimei (2:1–9)

      d **CENTER: David's death** (2:10–12)

a′ **Adonijah plots again to become king** (2:13–22)

  b′ **Adonijah's plot fails**; Solomon puts Adonijah to death (2:23–25)

    c′ **Solomon puts Joab and Shimei to death** and banishes Abiathar (2:26–46)

12.13 The Book of Samuel

a **Samuel succeeds elderly Eli and rules over all Israel** (1 Sam. 1–7)

- Hannah's song: my horn, my rock, grave, death, thundered against them from heaven, exalt, armed with strength, darkness, feet, anointed one, he gives the king, humble, proud; God's uniqueness; etc.
- theme: fall of Eli's priestly line
- Yahweh's plagues and human efforts that stopped them (4:1–6:21)
- people offer up the two cows pulling the ark's cart, as burnt offerings (after plagues ceased), using wood of cart as fuel, setting ark on rock

  b **Saul's failure** (1 Sam. 8–15)

- war against King Nahash of Ammon, triggered by Nahash's threatened humiliation of Israelites in Transjordan
- Saul's sins and their uncovering and condemnation by prophet Samuel
- Saul's response: he makes excuses

    c **David's initial rise to popularity in Saul's kingdom** (1 Sam. 16–20)

- Saul initially accepts David, then turns against him
- David is anointed by Samuel; Michal's marriage to David
- theme: members of Saul's family were kind to David

      d **TURNING POINT: Yahweh reverses fortunes of Saul and David**; Saul seeks to kill David but is himself killed (1 Sam. 21–31)

    c′ **David's initial rise to power over all Israel** (2 Sam. 1–8)

- Saul's kingdom initially opposes David, then accepts him
- David is anointed by Judah; Michal's remarriage to David
- theme: David was kind to members of Saul's family

  b′ **David's failure** (2 Sam. 9–20)

- war against King Nahash of Ammon, triggered by Nahash's humiliation of David's ambassadors in Transjordan
- David's sin and its uncovering and condemnation by prophet Nathan
- David's response: he repents

a′ **Solomon succeeds elderly David; David's final years** (2 Sam. 21–1 Kings 2)

- David's song (obviously echoing Hannah's): my horn, my rock, grave, death, thundered against them from heaven, exalt, armed with strength, darkness, feet, anointed one, he gives the king, humble, proud; God's uniqueness; etc.
- themes: fall of Eli's priestly line; Zadok replaces Abiathar, "fulfilling the word Yahweh had spoken at Shiloh about the house of Eli" (1 Kings 2:27)
- Yahweh's plagues and human efforts that stopped them (2 Sam. 21, 24)—one plague involves place where ark would rest
- David offers the two oxen pulling the threshing sledge as burnt offerings (after plague ceased), using wood of sledge as fuel (ark will rest on this rock)

there is a secondary symmetric scheme here as well (12.13).[7]

Conclusion

At the least, the foregoing analysis of the Book of Samuel helps account for the presence and position of a number of repetitions in the book, many of which serve important roles in symmetric designs (e.g., the matched stories of the wickedness of Eli's sons, the two stories of the Ziphites' betraying David, the paired stories of David's sparing Saul's life).

Particular themes are reinforced by structure. For example, the surprising number of matched stories about David's kindness to Saul and his family serves to highlight this theme. Apparently one of the book's purposes was to address the accusation (probably rife during the early years of Solomon's reign) that David was a traitor and an enemy of Saul and his family. Likewise, the strategically placed stories illustrating how Saul's own children loved David underscore David's innocence in Saul's court. The book serves, in part, as an apology, or defense, seeking to demonstrate that David was indeed a man after God's heart and Israel's rightful king.

Of particular interest are the parallel stories of David's kindness to personal enemies, includ-

7. The chiastic analyses of 1 Samuel and 2 Samuel by Yehuda Radday, "Chiasm in Samuel," *Linguistica Biblica* 9–10 (1971) 21–31, appear to be forced.

ing Saul, members of Saul's family and court, and Shimei. The number of such matched stories draws attention to this admirable quality in David's life. Moreover, the central episode of the entire book is the story of how David was mercifully prevented from taking vengeance upon Nabal. The point is clear: the person after God's heart does not seek vengeance against personal enemies but entrusts that responsibility to an all-knowing and just God (cf. 2 Sam. 16:12).

Another important point is underscored by the repetition of matched units focusing on the disastrous sins of Saul and David. Both units recount the sin, God's exposure and condemnation of the sin, and the sin's terrible consequences (Saul lost his kingdom and his life, David's family was torn apart). This repetition emphasizes the importance of Israel's leaders (and people) obeying God and his laws. In addition, the contrasted responses of Saul and David carry the message that when a person sins, he or she should sincerely repent (as David did) and not just give excuses (as Saul did).

Other themes are developed and reinforced by repetition, including the importance of seeking direction from Yahweh and the importance of obedience even in the midst of adversity (the matching stories of David helping Judean towns in the midst of his own dangerous situation).

One of the most important themes in the book is that God will, in the end, right all wrongs, punishing the wicked and rewarding the righteous. While the wicked may flourish for a season (Samuel's sons, Saul), God will surely punish them. Conversely, even though righteous people may suffer terribly, God will remain with them during their suffering, protecting and guiding them. This point is emphasized, for example, by the matched stories about how God enabled David to escape from wicked king Saul. God will surely protect and help the person whose heart is right with him. The book is written to inspire the audience to follow God and obey his laws, because in the end God will reward those who obey him and will punish those who turn from him and flaunt his laws.

13

Kings

Israel's Revolt against God

The Book of Kings (in the Hebrew Bible, 1 Kings and 2 Kings are one book) recounts the history of Israel from the time of Solomon to the Babylonian exile. Written during the exile, the book addresses the burning theological question of the day: Has God failed? Was Yahweh not powerful enough to protect his people and his temple from the mighty forces of Mesopotamia? The author's answer is a thundering "No! God has not failed! It is Israel who has failed; and here is the record of its failure for which it is being punished." The book appears to comprise seven well-defined parts, each with its own self-contained internal arrangement:[1]

a reign of Solomon (1 Kings 3:1–11:43)[2]
b birth of the northern kingdom and its first seven kings (1 Kings 12:1–16:34)
c Elijah and Israel's Omride dynasty (1 Kings 17:1–2 Kings 1:18)
d Elisha's ministry during the Omride dynasty (2 Kings 2:1–8:6)
e Elisha and the rise of the early Jehu dynasty (2 Kings 8:7–13:25)
f final seven kings of the northern kingdom and its fall (2 Kings 14:1–17:41)
g final seven kings of the southern kingdom and its fall (2 Kings 18:1–25:30)

Solomon's Reign (1 Kings 3–11)

The account of Solomon's reign is laid out in an obvious symmetry, beginning and ending with details of Solomon's government, wisdom,

wealth, and marriages, with the building of the temple at the center.[3] There are a total of thirteen parts, with the account of the dedication of the temple standing at the unit's center, in the seventh position (13.1).

The author's agenda is immediately suggested in this unit's structure. Although inspiring stories about King Solomon could have been used to open and close the unit, the author instead frames the unit with negative material about Solomon's marriages to foreign women. This book is going to have a condemnatory focus. At the same time, the central importance of the temple is reinforced by the placement of the story of its building and dedication in the center units (f, g, and f'). The seventh and central unit in chapter 8, which recounts the temple's dedication, is itself arranged in a carefully designed seven-part symmetry (13.2).

Establishment of the Northern Kingdom: Its First Seven Kings (1 Kings 12–16)

The book's second major unit recounts the story of the birth and troubled early years of the rebellious northern kingdom of Israel. The unit is framed by the conclusion of Solomon's reign and his death, on the one side, and the introduction to Elijah's ministry on the other (17:1). The material between forms a seven-part structure of sorts by its central focus on the northern kingdom and that kingdom's first seven kings (13.3). On the other hand, in order to maintain the book's chronological order, the author must deal with three contemporary Judean kings who reigned during this period; and these are inserted at an appropriate point in the narrative—after Jeroboam (14:21–15:24).

---

1. For discussion of the arrangement of the Book of Kings, see S. R. Driver, *An Introduction to the Literature of the Old Testament* (9th ed.; Edinburgh: Clark, 1913), 186–203; Otto Eissfeldt, *The Old Testament: An Introduction*, trans. Peter R. Ackroyd (New York: Harper & Row, 1965), 283–301; P. R. House, *1, 2 Kings* (New American Commentary; Nashville: Broadman, 1995), 58–61; George Savran, "1 and 2 Kings," in *The Literary Guide to the Bible*, ed. Robert Alter and Frank Kermode (Cambridge: Harvard University Press, 1987), 148.

2. See the previous chapter on Samuel for a discussion of 1 Kings 1–2.

3. Amos Frisch, "Structure and Its Significance: The Narrative of Solomon's Reign (1 Kings 1–12.24)," *Journal for the Study of the Old Testament* 51 (1991) 3–14, analyzes this section as comprising nine units, with 6:1–9:9 as the central unit and focus of the entire section.

13.1 Solomon's reign (1 Kings 3–11)

a **Solomon's marriage to Egyptian princess** (3:1–3)
- his love of Yahweh

b **Solomon's request for wisdom; will receive great wealth and wisdom** (3:4–15)

c **two women come to Solomon** (3:16–28)
- his wisdom in justice
- people see

d **overview of government** (4:1–34 [4:1–5:14])
- officials, forced labor, horses, etc.

e **Hiram of Tyre** provides supplies for Solomon (5:1–18 [5:15–32])

f **Solomon builds Yahweh's temple and palace** (6:1–7:51)

g **CLIMAX: temple dedication** (8:1–66)

f′ **Yahweh's approval of temple** (9:1–9)
- "after Solomon had finished building the temple and palace"

e′ **Hiram of Tyre** is paid for supplies (9:10–14)

d′ **overview of government** (9:15–28)
- officials, forced labor, horses, etc.

c′ **queen of Sheba comes to Solomon** (10:1–13)
- his wisdom and justice
- she sees

b′ **Solomon's great wisdom and wealth** (10:14–29)

a′ **Solomon's marriages to foreign women** (11:1–43)
- his love of them; his sin and punishment

13.2 Dedication of the temple (1 Kings 8)

a **introduction** (8:1–2)
- all the people of Israel assemble
- chronological reference

b **dedication** (8:3–13)
- sacrifices and installation of ark

c **Solomon blesses people** (faces people) (8:14–21)
- praise be to Yahweh

d **CENTER: Solomon's dedicatory prayer** (8:22–54)

c′ **Solomon blesses people** (faces people) (8:55–61)
- praise be to Yahweh

b′ **dedication** (8:62–64)
- sacrifices

a′ **conclusion** (8:65–66)
- all Israel are dismissed
- chronological reference

13.3 First kings of the northern kingdom (1 Kings 12–16)

a **Jeroboam and the birth of the northern kingdom** (12:1–14:20)
- three contemporary Judean kings (14:21–15:24)
  (1) Rehoboam (14:21–31)
  (2) Abijah (15:1–8)
  (3) Asa (15:9–24)

b **Nadab** (15:25–32)

c **Baasha** (15:33–16:7)

d **Elah** (16:8–10)

e **Zimri** (16:11–20)

f **Omri** (16:21–28)

g **Ahab** (16:29–34), who is worse than even Jeroboam and all the preceding kings and will be the villain of the next unit

A linear layout, like that found in this section, generally features an emphasis on the end or beginning or both; and there appears to be an emphasis here on both the opening and closing units—the particularly wicked reigns of Jeroboam and Ahab. The author especially highlights the first unit, Jeroboam's reign and his idolatry at Bethel and Dan, by its greater length. The "sin of Jeroboam" will follow Israel throughout its history and will eventually lead to its downfall.

13.4 Elijah (1 Kings 17–2 Kings 1)

a **Elijah and Ahab**: drought and <u>fire from heaven</u> (1 Kings 17:1–18:46)
- king <u>seeks Baal instead of Yahweh for help</u>
- Yahweh <u>demonstrates his power</u> with <u>fire</u> that <u>falls</u> upon the offerings and <u>consumes</u> them

b **Yahweh encourages Elijah in Sinai** (19:1–21)
- faithful remnant: Elisha
- bright spot in narrative: focus on righteous people

c **war between Israel and Aram** (20:1–43)
- Ahab wins; Ben-hadad not killed
- other prophets (not Elijah) <u>predict Ahab's victories</u>

d **CENTER: Naboth's vineyard and the sin of Ahab and Jezebel** (21:1–29)
- <u>summary</u> of Ahab's sinfulness

c′ **war between Israel and Aram** (22:1–40)
- Ahab loses and is killed
- another prophet (not Elijah) <u>predicts Ahab's defeat</u>

b′ **reign of Jehoshaphat** (22:41–50 [22:41–51])*
- he is a faithful king; activity in Sinai
- bright spot in narrative: focus on righteous king

a′ **Elijah and Ahaziah**: king's sickness and <u>fire from heaven</u> (1 Kings 22:51–2 Kings 1:18 [1 Kings 22:52–2 Kings 1:18])
- king <u>seeks Baal-zebub instead of Yahweh for help</u>
- Yahweh <u>demonstrates his power</u> with <u>fire</u> that <u>falls</u> upon the soldiers and <u>consumes</u> them

*Unit b′ is an admittedly weak match with unit b.

13.5 Elijah and the drought (1 Kings 17–18)

a **introduction**: Elijah's declaration: <u>there will be no rain!</u> (17:1)

b **Yahweh keeps his prophet alive** at the <u>brook</u> (*naḥal*) Cherith (17:2–6)

c **Elijah demonstrates Yahweh's power in Phoenicia** (17:7–24)
- themes: extravagant use of meager supplies before God's miraculous provision, prophet's action repeated "three times"

d **CENTER: contest between Yahweh and Baal proposed** (8:1–19)

c′ **Elijah demonstrates Yahweh's power in Israel** (18:20–39)
- themes: extravagant use of meager supplies before God's miraculous provision, prophet's action repeated "three times"

b′ **Baal's prophets are killed** at the <u>brook</u> (*naḥal*) Kidron (18:40)

a′ **conclusion**: Elijah's declaration: <u>rain is coming now!</u> (18:41–46)

Elijah's Ministry (1 Kings 17–2 Kings 1)

The book's third unit tells the story of Elijah's ministry. It begins with Elijah's appearance in 1 Kings 17:1 and ends with his departure from the earth in 2 Kings 2 (the departure account actually functions as the first episode in the Elisha cycle; see below). The unit has seven parts, arranged with a chiastic touch (13.4). The two great demonstrations of Yahweh's power to Israel's kings are highlighted by their placement in the unit's opening and closing positions. Furthermore, the matching stories featuring Yahweh's power in the midst of the Israel-Aram conflicts emphasize his control of international events. The author underscores the guilt of Israel's leadership by placing the condemnatory story about King Ahab and Naboth's vineyard at the center of the unit.

The first story, Elijah and the drought, has its own symmetric configuration, which serves to highlight Yahweh's power over all nature, and in all nations (13.5).

Elisha and His Miracles (2 Kings 2:1–8:6)

At the very center of the book stands a delightful centerpiece comprising a collection of inspiring stories about the miraculous works of the prophet Elisha. Elisha's miracles are less grandiose than Elijah's, mostly private, quiet miracles helping the poor and unfortunate. In this central unit, politics recede into the background: no king's reign is traced, and most of the stories do not even involve a king. Elijah's ominous warning about the end of the Omride dynasty is held in suspense for the moment. The unit represents the eye of the storm, with Yahweh's admirable prophet Elisha quietly doing what pleases Yahweh, Israel's rightful king (in contrast to Israel's evil human kings)—helping the poor and helpless.

There are fourteen episodes in the unit, exactly twice the number of the Elijah cycle—which is at least curious in light of the reference to Elisha's "double portion." The fourteen episodes fall into two groups, each ending with a story about the

13.6 Elisha (2 Kings 2:1–8:6)

first group of miracles (2:1–4:37)
- theme: death

a   **power over death** (2:1–12a)
- Elijah <u>departs</u> to heaven

   b   **Elisha and sons of prophets after a <u>death</u>** (2:12b–18)
- Elisha parts the Jordan; response of sons of prophets to Elijah's <u>death</u>

      c   **water sweetened** at Jericho (2:19–22)
- no more <u>death</u> in it

         d   **death of the mocking boys at Bethel** (2:23–25)

      c′ **water provided** during Moabite campaign (3:1–27)
- redness of water mistaken to be from <u>death</u> of slain Israelites

   b′ **Elisha and sons of prophets after a <u>death</u>** (4:1–7)
- one of sons of prophets <u>dies</u>; widow's oil multiplied

a′ **power over death** (4:8–37)
- Elisha raises son of Shunamite woman from the <u>dead</u>

second group of miracles (4:38–8:6)
- theme: helping those in distress

a   **poisonous pottage made harmless** <u>during the famine</u> (4:38–41)

   b   **miraculous multiplication of the loaves** of <u>barley</u> (4:42–44)

      c   **Elisha heals the Syrian soldier,** Naaman, of leprosy (5:1–27)
- the Israelite king does not know what to do with him

         d   **lost axhead restored** (6:1–7)

      c′ **Elisha blinds the Syrian soldiers**—and then spares them (6:8–23)
- the Israelite king does not know what to do with them

   b′ **miraculous provision of fine meal** and <u>barley</u> during the siege of Samaria (6:24–7:20)

a′ **Shunamite woman helped** <u>during the famine</u> (8:1–6)
- she tells to the king her story of her son's raising from the dead

---

Shunamite woman (4:8–37; 8:1–6). Each group of seven is arranged in a loose symmetry (13.6).

Elisha and the Establishment of Jehu's Dynasty (2 Kings 8:7–13:25)

The book's fifth unit returns to the story of Israel's political history. National developments and the successive reigns of kings come into focus again. The unit's boundaries are well defined, framed with an inclusio involving Hazael of Damascus. The unit opens with Elisha's anointing Hazael and predicting his victories over Israel (a); and it closes with a sweeping six-verse grand finale (a′) that includes a summary of Hazael's victories over Israel and his death, Elisha's death, and a theological summary of God's dealings with Israel. (Such theologizing occurs only twice in the book: here and at the end of the next literary unit in 2 Kings 17.) To create a seven-part arrangement in this unit, the author organizes his material around the reigns of seven kings who ruled during this era, including three kings of Israel, three kings of Judah, and (oddly) one king of Aram:

a   Hazael of Aram (8:7–15)
b   Jehoram of Judah (8:16–24)
c   Ahaziah of Judah (8:25–29)
d   Jehu of Israel (9:1–10:35)

e   Joash of Judah (and his queen mother Athaliah) (11:1–12:21 [11:1–12:22])
f   Jehoahaz of Israel (13:1–9)
g   Jehoash of Israel (13:10–25)—with a grand conclusion, including Hazael's death and a theological statement

The unit also exhibits certain symmetric features in its overall layout (13.7). It opens with Hazael's rise to power (a) and closes with his fall from power and death (a′). It has at the center the momentous story of Jehu's revolt (d), which would profoundly affect Israel's history. As the sin of Ahab's family in the affair with Naboth's vineyard formed the highlighted center of the book's third unit, Yahweh's punishment of Ahab's family for their sin forms the highlighted center of this third-to-last unit.

Final Years of the Northern Kingdom (2 Kings 14–17)

The sixth unit of the book covers the period from Elisha's death and the reign of Jeroboam II (Israel's last powerful king) to the fall of the northern kingdom. Reminiscent of the book's second unit, the author again creates a seven-part scheme of sorts, this time by focusing on the end of the northern kingdom, with its seven final kings (13.8). Again, the accounts of con-

13.7 Establishment of Jehu's dynasty (2 Kings 8:7–13:25)

a **Hazael anointed king of Aram**: he will devastate Israel (8:7–15)
  - begins: Ben-hadad suffers from illness (he will not recover)

b **Jehoram of Judah** (8:16–24)
  - his chariots
  - military defeats

c **Ahaziah of Judah** (8:25–29)
  - introduction to Athaliah

d **CENTER: Jehu's coup and fall of Omride dynasty**; deaths of Jezebel and Ahab's entire family; sin involving Naboth's vineyard avenged! (9:1–10:35)

c′ **Joash of Judah** (11:1–12:21 [11:1–12:22])
  - Athaliah's wicked rule

b′ **Jehoahaz of Israel** (13:1–9)
  - his chariots
  - military defeats

a′ **Jehoash of Israel**: he defeats Hazael (13:10–25)
  - ends: Elisha suffers from terminal illness
  conclusion: Elisha's death and Hazael's reign and death

13.8 Final seven kings of the northern kingdom (2 Kings 14–17)

(1) Amaziah of Judah (14:1–22)

a **Jeroboam II—Israel's last great king** (14:23–29)

(2) Uzziah of Judah (15:1–7)

b **Zechariah** (15:8–12)

c **Shallum** (15:13–16)

d **Menahem** (15:17–22)

e **Pekahiah** (15:23–26)

f **Pekah** (15:27–31)

(3) Jotham of Judah (15:32–38)

(4) Ahaz of Judah (16:1–20)

g **CLIMAX: Hoshea** and the fall of the northern kingdom (17:1–41)
summary and theological explanation for fall of the northern kingdom (17:7–23)

---

temporary Judean kings are inserted at appropriate places.

The striking absence of a prophetic witness characterizes the unit. God has apparently given up; his silence is obvious and the effect is a sense of hopelessness. The successive reigns of the kings in this unit are recounted in a negative, staccato, relentlessly linear fashion. There are no interruptions, no hopeful pauses in this downward plunge to destruction. Even the interruptive accounts of the kings of Judah offer no hope—they are equally short, generally negative, and devoid of promise. The last episode, standing in the highlighted position, is the unit's climactic grand finale: the fall of Samaria and the end of the northern kingdom.

Final Years of Judah (2 Kings 18–25)

The seventh and final unit of the book is the story of Judah's final years. It is a well-defined unit, bracketed by the fall of the northern kingdom on the one end and the fall of Judah on the other (13.9). There were eight kings from Hezekiah to Zedekiah. In order to achieve a seven-part arrangement, the author divides the unit into two sections of approximately equal length. The first section, arranged in a seven-part symmetry, recounts the reign of Hezekiah. The second section traces Judah's final seven kings.[4] Their reigns are recounted in a more perfunctory manner (good King Josiah is given slightly more space), and the arrangement here is linear, creating the sense of an uninterrupted plummeting toward the terrible end, Judah's fall. The final episode, the fall of Jerusalem, is structurally highlighted and serves as the climax of this entire unit. But the highlighted center of the Hezekiah story—Yahweh's rescue of Jerusalem when good King Hezekiah prayed—suggests what Yahweh could have done for Jerusalem if the people had only repented and turned back to him.

Functioning in a manner similar to that of Hezekiah's, the longer account of Josiah's reign (part 2, unit c) suggests what Judah should have been doing instead of following the evil ways of the northern kingdom. This account is arranged

---

4. One could argue that the author achieved seven parts in the unit by bracketing Zedekiah's artificial reign with accounts of King Jehoiachin, as if the latter was considered Judah's final king.

13.9 Judah's final years (2 Kings 18–25)

part 1: Hezekiah's reign (18:1–20:21)

a   **summary of Hezekiah's reign** and reference to the fall of the northern kingdom (18:1–12)

b   **arrival of hostile emissaries and troops from Assyrian king** (18:13–19:13)
  - they come with threatening <u>message</u> and hostile intentions
  - Hezekiah does not allow them into the city and fears them
  - Isaiah reassures: these Assyrians <u>will not destroy Jerusalem</u>!

c   **Hezekiah prays** for rescue from Assyrians (19:14–34)
  - <u>Isaiah's reassurance</u> that prayer will be answered

d   **CLIMAX: Yahweh delivers Jerusalem!** (19:35–37)

c′ **Hezekiah prays** for rescue from death (20:1–11)
  - <u>Isaiah's reassurance</u> that prayer will be answered

b′ **arrival of friendly emissaries from Babylonian king** (20:12–19)
  - they come with <u>message</u> and gifts of peace
  - Hezekiah welcomes them into the city and trusts them
  - Isaiah warns: these Babylonians <u>will destroy Jerusalem</u>!

a′ **summary of Hezekiah's reign** (20:20–21)

part 2: final seven kings of Judah (21:1–25:30)

a   **Manasseh** (21:1–18); prediction of Judah's destruction and exile

b   **Amon** (21:19–26)

c   **Josiah** (22:1–23:30)

d   **Jehoahaz** (23:31–35)

e   **Jehoiakim** (23:36–24:7)

f   **Jehoiachin** (24:8–17)

g   **CLIMAX: Zedekiah** (24:18–25:30) and the fall and exile of Judah

---

13.10 Josiah (2 Kings 22:1–23:30)

a   **introductory summary** of Josiah's reign (22:1–2)

b   **Hilkiah discovers law book** (22:3–20)
  - inevitability of judgment because of disobedience of fathers (Josiah will be spared)

c   **assembly in Jerusalem** for covenant renewal (23:1–3)

d   **CLIMAX: Josiah's reforms** (23:4–20)

c′ **assembly in Jerusalem** for Passover (23:21–23)

b′ **Josiah fully obeys the law book that Hilkiah discovered** (23:24–27)
  - inevitability of judgment because of sins of fathers

a′ **concluding summary** of Josiah's reign (23:28–30)

---

in a seven-part chiasmus that places structured emphasis on Josiah's religious reforms (13.10).

Overall Layout of the Book of Kings

The Book of Kings exhibits two interwoven arrangement schemes. The first is a linear layout, in which the book's units are arranged in chronological order, from the reign of Solomon in the tenth century B.C. to the fall of Jerusalem in the sixth century B.C. In addition, the book's arrangement exhibits a symmetric touch (13.11).[5] This is particularly apparent in the Elijah-Elisha cycles, where, for example, the predictions about the fall of the Omride dynasty and the upcoming punishment of Jezebel, which are pronounced in the third unit of Kings, are held in suspense throughout the book's central unit and are fulfilled in the third-to-last unit. Similarly,

the second unit relates the birth of the northern kingdom and its first seven kings, while the next-to-last unit tells the story of the demise of the northern kingdom and its last seven kings. In the first unit the temple is built and Solomon reigns in Jerusalem; in the last unit the temple is destroyed and Solomon's dynasty in Jerusalem ends. At the center of the book stands the story of Elisha and his miracles.

Conclusion

The chronologically linear layout of the Book of Kings draws attention to the book's concluding unit (the final unit in a linear scheme is the natural point of emphasis). This ending, or actually double ending, features the disastrous fall of the northern and southern kingdoms. Its highlighted position as the book's grand finale suggests that Israel's and Judah's fall is what the Book of Kings is about. The book's successive units build toward this conclusion and function to establish the reason for it. Each successive

---

5. A seven-part symmetric layout of Kings is proposed by Savran, "1 and 2 Kings": (a) 1 Kings 1:1–11:25, (b) 1 Kings 11:26–14:31, (c) 1 Kings 15:1–16:22, (d) 1 Kings 16:23–2 Kings 12:23 [1 Kings 16:23–2 Kings 12:22], (c′) 2 Kings 13:1–16:20, (b′) 2 Kings 17:1–41, (a′) 2 Kings 18:1–25:30.

13.11 The Book of Kings

a **Solomon's reign in Jerusalem; Jerusalem's wealth; temple is built** (1 Kings 3:1–11:43)
  - highlighted position (center): Solomon builds the temple
  - making of temple's bronze and gold articles, bronze pillars and Sea, etc.

  b   **rise of northern kingdom:** its first <u>seven</u> kings (1 Kings 12:1–16:34)
    - first unit is the longest
    - focus: <u>birth of the northern kingdom</u>

    c   **prophet Elijah and early Omride dynasty** (1 Kings 17:1–2 Kings 1:18)
      - central unit: <u>Jezebel kills Naboth</u> for his vineyard
      - prediction: <u>dogs</u> will lick up <u>Jezebel's blood</u> in Naboth's vineyard
      - prediction: <u>annihilation of Ahab's family</u> in his son's day
      - establishment of Baal worship
      - instructions to <u>anoint Jehu and Hazael</u> as new kings

      d   **CENTERPIECE: Elisha's miracles of kindness** (2 Kings 2:1–8:6)

    c′ **prophet Elisha and end of Omride dynasty** (2 Kings 8:7–13:25)
      - central unit: <u>Jezebel is killed</u> for sin against <u>Naboth</u>
      - fulfillment: <u>dogs</u> lick up <u>Jezebel's blood</u> in Naboth's vineyard
      - fulfillment: <u>annihilation of Ahab's family</u> in his son's day
      - removal of Baal worship
      - Elisha <u>anoints Jehu and Hazael</u> as new kings

  b′ **fall of northern kingdom:** its last <u>seven</u> kings (2 Kings 14:1–17:41)
    - last unit is longest
    - focus: <u>fall of the northern kingdom</u>

a′ **Solomon's dynasty in Jerusalem ends; fall of Jerusalem and destruction of Solomon's temple** (2 Kings 18:1–25:30)
  - highlighted position (end): Solomon's temple destroyed
  - plunder of temple's gold and bronze articles, bronze pillars and Sea, etc.

---

unit reinforces God's case against Israel and Judah and demonstrates why he finally punished them. Here is the carefully documented and chronologically arranged record of Israel's and Judah's revolt against Yahweh, generation after generation, king after wicked king.

The symmetric scheme reinforces several themes. For example, it serves to underscore the theme of Yahweh's power and his control over the events of history—even Israel's disastrous fall. The book's first two units demonstrate that it was Yahweh who established Solomon's and Jeroboam's kingdoms; and the matching final two units declare that it was Yahweh who destroyed those same two kingdoms. Israel and Judah did not fall because Yahweh could not protect his own people. To the contrary, their fall, like their establishment, was orchestrated by his almighty power and decree.

The balancing of the unit featuring the sinful Omride dynasty with the unit recounting Yahweh's punishment of that dynasty draws attention to the theme that Israel's disasters were the result of its sins against Yahweh and his laws. Yahweh is just; and while his punishment is sometimes delayed (as in the case of Ahab and Jezebel's sin against Naboth), it nevertheless comes.[6] The same thematic balancing occurs in the matching of the unit recounting Israel's religious revolt under Jeroboam I and the unit recounting the fall of Israel. The issue of theodicy is developed in part through the composition's structure.

The placement of the collection of Elisha's miracles at the center of the book is most curious. Why is this collection in the book at all? And why at the center of the book, in the position of emphasis in the book's symmetric layout? The unit may serve to illustrate—and underscore—the kind of righteous leadership that Yahweh wanted Israel's kings to practice—defending and helping the poor and weak, as Elisha, Yahweh's representative, did so admirably, and as Israel's evil kings failed to do (cf. Ahab's treatment of Naboth). The unit may also serve as a key piece of evidence against Israel. It recounts Yahweh's many miracles through Elisha, which amply demonstrated Yahweh's power, his love for his people, and his disapproval of their disobedience—so that even foreigners like Naaman the Aramean were moved to respect Israel's God. Israel was without excuse in its rejection of Yahweh.

Most important, for the exiled Jews in Babylonia the Book of Kings served as an encouraging reminder that Yahweh was not just a weak local deity who had failed to protect his people against the forces of Mesopotamia. The book's structure emphasizes that Yahweh is almighty,

---

6. It should also be observed that the main focus of the author's condemnation is Israel's political leadership. It is the kings (not the priests or false prophets or people) who are primarily evaluated by the author.

and that their nation had fallen because Yahweh had decreed that it fall as an act of divine punishment for their disobedience. The layout reinforces the theme that Yahweh is worthy of their respect, their trust, and their obedience. Not only is he all powerful, as the stories of Elijah and Elisha show; but he also loves his people and is able and willing to help them, even in the worst of times and even in foreign lands, as those same stories (and others in the book) show. The Judean exiles in Babylonia needed to know these truths if they were to continue to place their trust in the God who had destroyed their land.

14

Chronicles

Encouraging Stories from Israel's History

The Book of Chronicles (in the Hebrew Bible, 1 Chronicles and 2 Chronicles are one book) is an inspiring account of Israel's history from the time of King Solomon to the return from exile in the reign of Cyrus. Chronicles is not a superfluous repetition of the Book of Kings, although both books cover the same period of Israel's history. Chronicles has an entirely different agenda from that of Kings. Written more than a century after Kings, the purpose of Chronicles was to provide the postexilic community with hope and a desperately needed sense of identity and direction. The tiny, chastened Jewish community and its religious leaders needed to hear, not words of condemnation (as in the Book of Kings), but a message that would inspire them to get back on track and regroup around the focal point of the temple, with its priests and Levites who could teach and lead them according to God's laws. The author wanted to demonstrate that the key to Israel's success, past and future, lay with the temple and its servants.

Accordingly, both the content and structure of Chronicles are quite different from Kings.[1] The Chronicler's presentation is loosely based on the account from Kings; but the material from Kings is thoroughly recast and augmented with much new material, mostly inspirational stories involving the temple, priests, and Levites. The Chronicler has completely reorganized the material on both smaller and larger levels to develop his main theme—the central importance of the temple, priests, and Levites for the well-being of Israel. The book appears to have seven major parts, each with its own carefully designed and self-contained internal arrangement:

a genealogies (1 Chron. 1:1–9:44)
b establishment of David's kingdom (1 Chron. 10:1–22:1)
c David's preparations for Solomon's building of the temple (1 Chron. 22:2–29:30)
d reign of Solomon (2 Chron. 1:1–9:31)
e group of four kings: Rehoboam to Jehoshaphat (2 Chron. 10:1–20:37)
f group of seven kings: Jehoram to Ahaz (2 Chron. 21:1–28:27)
g Judah's final kings (2 Chron. 29:1–36:23)

Genealogies (1 Chronicles 1–9)

The book's first major unit is a collection of genealogies, set apart from the rest of the book by its genre. The arrangement of the genealogies underscores the theme that will be developed throughout the book. Even though there are twelve tribes to cover, the author has arranged and designed the material to create a seven-part, symmetric scheme, with the tribe of Levi at the highlighted center (14.1). This structuring pattern, a seven-part symmetry with the temple or priests and Levites featured at the center, will be utilized throughout Chronicles to emphasize the importance of these institutions.

The genealogies open with a unit (a) devoted not to a tribe, but to the ancestors of the Israelites from Adam to Jacob. The second unit (b) presents the tribe of Judah, with King David's line at the center (3:1–24). Presumably Judah is the first tribe because of its royal status and because it was the dominant tribe in the postexilic community. Next comes a brief unit (c; about half the length of b) surveying a group of peripheral tribes: Simeon, Reuben, Gad, and half-Manasseh.

---

1. The literary structure of the Book of Chronicles has received little attention by scholars. Most commentators are content simply to list the book's contents with little regard for the Chronicler's literary efforts. J. M. Myers, *1 Chronicles* (Anchor Bible 12; Garden City: Doubleday, 1965), xli–xlv, is typical; after admitting that "one of the most vexing problems of almost every Old Testament book . . . has to do with sources and literary structure," he offers no analysis of the book's literary structure but instead simply lists the general content of Chronicles, arranged into four parts: (1) genealogies (1 Chron. 1–9), (2) David, the book's central character (1 Chron. 10–29), (3) Solomon (2 Chron. 1–9), (4) story of Judah (2 Chron. 10–36). Other commentators and introductions also exhibit a lack of interest here, offering similar, mostly four-part, analyses.

These first three units are followed by the center of the presentation: a unit treating the tribe of Levi (d). This lengthy central unit is itself arranged symmetrically, with the all-important priestly families at the center (6:49–60). The priests, then, stand at the center of the entire genealogy of 1 Chronicles 1–9.

To balance the third unit, the third-to-last unit briefly surveys another group of peripheral tribes (c′): Issachar, Benjamin, Naphtali, half-Manasseh, Ephraim, and Asher. Next, to balance the royal tribe of Judah, the next-to-last unit presents the other royal tribe, Benjamin, tracing in particular the line of King Saul (b′). (Also, Benjamin was the other main tribe of the postexilic community.) Finally, the seventh unit (a′), like the first, is not devoted to a tribe at all. Complementing the first unit, which traces Israel's roots back to Adam, the last unit focuses on the present. It is a registry of the families that have returned to Jerusalem from exile. Having opened with Israel's most distant past, the author then closes with its most immediate present.[2]

This arrangement highlights the central importance of the Levites and priests in Israel. The priests and Levites have played—and must continue to play—the key role in God's kingdom.

Establishment of David's Kingdom (1 Chronicles 10:1–22:1)

Following the genealogies come two lengthy sections about David. One might assume that these sections comprise a single unit since they are tied together by its central figure, David. They fall, however, into two distinct parts: (1) an overview of the events of David's reign (10:1–

22:1) and (2) David's preparations for the building of the temple (22:2–29:30). Each part exhibits its own self-contained, independent structure and comprises a distinct unit.

First Chronicles 10:1–22:1 is framed by two stories that account for the temple's location: David's accession to the throne and his capture of Jerusalem, the city where the temple would be located (a), and David's census and his acquisition of Aruna's threshing floor on the northern edge of Jerusalem, where the temple would actually be constructed (a′).[3]

The Chronicler organized the material of this section into seven chiastically arranged units, with the centerpiece being David's transportation of the ark to Jerusalem, accompanied by the ministry of the priests and Levites (14.2). The unit's overall symmetric arrangement serves to highlight the central importance of the temple. While David's other accomplishments are also recounted in the unit, David's activities involving the temple are emphasized by being placed at the beginning, in the middle, and at the end. This structural design reflects the author's agenda—to encourage the postexilic community to pay attention to the temple as King David did.

David's Preparations for Solomon's Building of the Temple (1 Chronicles 22:2–29:30)

There are several indications that 1 Chronicles 22:2 introduces a new literary unit. One is the abrupt appearance of a new main character, Solomon. From this point on, Solomon will figure prominently (though passively) throughout chapters 22–29.[4] Another indicator is the shift

2. For a virtually identical analysis of this unit, see William Johnstone, "Guilt and Atonement: The Theme of 1 and 2 Chronicles," in *A Word in Season: Essays in Honour of William McKane*, ed. James D. Martin and Philip R. Davies (Journal for the Study of the Old Testament Supplement 42; Sheffield: JSOT Press, 1986), 125–38.

3. In both cases the Chronicler places the acquisition of the holy site immediately after a punitive national disaster brought upon Israel by Yahweh (the defeat of Israel by Philistia, the plague); in both cases the holy site is a former "Jebusite" place.

4. The expression "his/my/your son Solomon" occurs some fifteen times in these chapters; and he is referred to numerous other times.

14.2 Establishment of David's kingdom (1 Chronicles 10:1–22:1)

a **David becomes king and captures Jerusalem (where the future temple will be) from the Jebusites** (10:1–11:9)
  - prominent role played by <u>Joab</u>
  - follows a national disaster: defeat by Philistines
  b **military exploits of David and his soldiers** (11:10–12:40 [11:10–12:41])
    c **David wishes to bring Yahweh's ark to Jerusalem but is prevented** (13:1–14:17)
      - instead builds his <u>house</u> (*bayit*) and becomes firmly established in Jerusalem
        d **CENTER: ark brought to Jerusalem; role of <u>Levites and priests</u> in the celebration** (15:1–16:43)
    c′ **David wishes to build Yahweh's <u>house</u> (*bayit*) in Jerusalem but is prevented** (17:1–27)
      - instead Yahweh will build David an eternal <u>house</u> (*bayit*)
  b′ **military exploits of David and his soldiers** (18:1–20:8)
a′ **David acquires the future temple mount from Aruna the Jebusite** (21:1–22:1)
  - prominent role played by <u>Joab</u>
  - follows a national disaster: plague

14.3 Preparations for building the temple (1 Chronicles 22:2–29:30)

a **David assembles people** and gives speech to Solomon and people concerning the temple (22:2–19)
  - instructions about <u>gathering of materials</u> and support of Solomon
  - "Solomon my son . . . is <u>young and inexperienced</u>"
  - David's <u>review</u> of his desire to build the temple, Yahweh's rejection of his request, Yahweh's reason, and the decision to have Solomon build it instead (22:7–10)
  b **civil ruler:** David's appointment of Solomon as king (23:1)
    c **Levites:** their duties assisting the priests (23:2–32)
      d **CENTER: priests and their duties** (24:1–19)
    c′ **Levites:** their duties as musicians and gatekeepers (24:20–26:32)
  b′ **civil rulers:** David's appointment of government officials (27:1–34)
a′ **David assembles people** and gives speech to Solomon and people concerning the temple; David's death (28:1–29:30)
  - instructions about <u>gathering of materials</u> and support of Solomon
  - "Solomon my son . . . is <u>young and inexperienced</u>"
  - David's <u>review</u> of his desire to build the temple, Yahweh's rejection of his request, Yahweh's reason, and the decision to have Solomon build it instead (28:2–6)

in focus. Chapters 10–21 provide an overview of David's entire reign; in chapters 22–29, the focus shifts to a single aspect of that reign: David's preparations for Solomon's building of the temple. The speed of action also shifts. With chapter 22 the action slows almost to a halt, reminiscent of chapters 1–9. Chapters 22–29 have virtually no action. The entire section appears to transpire in the context of two or three assemblies at Jerusalem and is composed mostly of speeches.

The unit (14.3) is framed by matching accounts (a and a′) of David's assembling the people to address them (and Solomon) about the temple's construction. In both assemblies, David encourages the people to support and help Solomon, reminding them that, "Solomon my son . . . is young and inexperienced" (22:5; 29:1). In both, David addresses Solomon separately, with similar words in each speech.[5] In both units, David recounts, in virtually identical words, his

initial desire to build the temple, God's negative response, God's explanation for the rejection, and the promise that Solomon his son would be the one to build it (22:7–10; 28:2–6). Numerous additional lexical correspondences could also be noted in these parallel stories.

Like previous units, this one comprises seven parts, symmetrically arranged, with the center (d) focusing, as expected, on the priests. The two units (c and c′) flanking this center deal with the roles of the Levites; and the two units (b and b′) outside these deal with David's establishment of Israel's civil rulers. There is one structural peculiarity here. The Chronicler appears to employ a single verse (23:1) as an entire unit (b): David's appointment of Solomon as king balances the much more extensive unit of David's appointment of Israel's other government officials (b′). This need to balance the material in chapter 27 explains the otherwise inexplicable occurrence of the one-sentence unit, detached from what precedes and what follows, in 23:1. Again the author underscores the importance of the temple, priests, and Levites by structuring the entire unit so that it begins, ends, and centers on this theme.

5. For example, the words "Yahweh be with you. . . . Be strong and of good courage. Fear not; be not dismayed" (22:11–13), are echoed in 28:20: "Be strong and of good courage. . . . Fear not, be not dismayed; for Yahweh . . . is with you."

14.4 Reign of Solomon, the temple builder (2 Chronicles 1–9)

a **Solomon's wisdom and wealth** (1:1–17)
- "the king made <u>silver</u> . . . as common in Jerusalem as stone, and he made <u>cedar</u> as plentiful as the sycamore of the Shephelah"
- <u>trade in horses</u>: "12,000 horsemen, whom he stationed in the chariot cities and with the king in Jerusalem"

b **Solomon's foreign relations with Hiram of Tyre** (2:1–18 [1:18–2:17])
- Hiram's <u>admiration of Solomon's wisdom</u>
- Solomon's use of <u>foreigners</u> in his building projects
- Hiram: "because Yahweh <u>loves his people</u> he has made you king over them . . . <u>blessed be Yahweh</u> God of Israel."

c **Solomon builds the temple** (3:1–5:1)
- begins: "then Solomon <u>began</u> to build Yahweh's temple"

d **CLIMAX: dedication of the temple** (5:2–7:10)

c′ **God accepts the temple** (7:11–22)
- begins: "thus Solomon <u>finished</u> the temple of the Lord"

b′ **Solomon's foreign relations with Hiram of Tyre and queen of Sheba** (8:1–9:12)
- queen of Sheba's <u>admiration of Solomon's wisdom</u>
- Solomon's use of <u>foreigners</u> in his building projects
- queen of Sheba: "because your God <u>loves Israel</u> . . . he has made you king over them"; "<u>blessed be Yahweh</u> your God"

a′ **Solomon's wisdom and wealth** (9:13–28)
- "the king made <u>silver</u> as common in Jerusalem as stone, and <u>cedar</u> as plentiful as the sycamore of the Shephelah"
- <u>trade in horses</u>: "12,000 horsemen, whom he stationed in the chariot cities and with the king in Jerusalem"
conclusion: Solomon's death (9:29–34)

14.5 Dedication of the temple (2 Chronicles 5:2–7:10)

a **ark dedicated with countless sacrifices** (5:2–10)
- begins: people are <u>assembled</u>

b **glory of God fills temple** (5:11–14)
- "for he is good; his love is forever"

c **Solomon's prayer** (6:1–2)

d **CENTER: Solomon's dedicatory speech** (6:3–11)

c′ **Solomon's prayer** (6:12–42)

b′ **glory of God fills temple** (7:1–3)
- "for he is good; his love is forever"

a′ **temple, court, and altar dedicated with multitude of sacrifices** (7:4–10)
- ends: people are <u>dismissed</u>

Reign of Solomon, the Temple Builder (2 Chronicles 1–9)

The fourth unit in Chronicles is the account of Solomon's reign. The parameters of this unit are well marked: the previous unit ended with a formulaic summary of David's reign, death, and burial, with a reference to further written sources about David (1 Chron. 29:26–30); and a similar formulaic summary of Solomon's reign, death, and burial, with a reference to further written sources about Solomon, marks the end of the account of Solomon's reign (2 Chron. 9:29–31). These summaries serve to frame the entire unit.

The presentation of Solomon's reign is organized in a seven-part symmetry, arranged so that Solomon's dedication of the temple is featured in the highlighted center (14.4).[6]

6. For a similar analysis of the Solomon narrative, see Raymond B Dillard, "The Literary Structure of the Chronicler's Solomon Narrative," *Journal for the Study of the Old Testament* 30 (1984) 85–93, who analyzes the unit as containing eight parts chiastically arranged: (a) 1:1–17, (b) 2:1–16, (c) 2:17–5:1, (d) 5:2–7:10, (d′) 7:11–22, (c′) 8:1–16, (b′) 8:17–9:12, (a′) 9:13–28.

The temple's central importance is highlighted by the placement of Solomon's construction of it at the center—in fact, in the unit's three central positions (c, d, c′). Solomon may have been fabulously wealthy and wise; but his most important accomplishment was what he did for the temple—which is intended as an inspiring example for the postexilic community to follow.

The central episode of this unit, the dedication of the temple, is itself organized in a sevenfold symmetry (14.5), with Solomon's dedicatory speech at the center, flanked by the two dedicatory prayers of Solomon.

Judah's Kings from Rehoboam to Good King Jehoshaphat (2 Chronicles 10–20)

The rest of the Book of Chronicles recounts the reigns of Judah's remaining nineteen kings. Two repeating structuring devices seem to tie the entirety of 2 Chronicles 10–36 into a single unit: (1) the similar formulaic introductions that begin most of the kings' reigns[7] and (2) the similar formulaic conclusions that end most of the kings' reigns.[8] In light of these recurring formulas and the lack of any major interruptive breaks in the presentation of these nineteen kings, it might appear that the entirety of 2 Chronicles 10–36 forms a single, extraordinarily long unit—the book's fifth and last. Certainly a reader would sense no major breaks as obvious as those encountered earlier in the book.

There are indications, however, that the Chronicler structured this lengthy section into three parts, using the exceptionally lengthy treatments of Jehoshaphat and Hezekiah as division markers. The accounts of these two exemplary kings are highlighted by their remarkable length, comprising 101 and 117 verses respectively, compared with an average length of only 23 verses for each of the other kings. The audience would certainly sense a pause, a lingering over these two good kings, presumably for the purpose of viewing in some detail their commendable reigns. The two accounts are also exceptional in another respect. Instead of the overall symmetric arrangement used in the stories of virtually every other king, the accounts of these two kings are structurally complex, each containing not one, but four, symmetrically arranged units.

---

7. The introductory formula includes (1) king's name, (2) age at accession, (3) length of reign in Jerusalem, (4) mother's name, and (5) a summary evaluation regarding his obedience/disobedience to the Lord, usually in the form "he did what was right/evil in the eyes of the Lord" and sometimes with an additional line, "he walked in the ways of x," or yet another line illustrating or qualifying the evaluation. The introduction to Jotham's reign is typical: "Jotham was twenty-five years old when he began to reign, and he reigned sixteen years in Jerusalem. His mother's name was Jerushah the daughter of Zadok. And he did what was right in the eyes of the Lord" (27:1–2). The first four kings are exceptional: the statements about Rehoboam and Jehoshaphat are placed at the conclusions of their accounts (12:13–14; 20:31–33), while the introductions to Abijah (13:1–2) and Asa (14:1–2) lack various elements: Abijah's age at accession and an evaluation; Asa's age at accession, length of reign, and mother's name. But from the reign of Jehoram, the fifth king, onward, the formulaic introduction is fairly consistent (although in several instances, including the last four, the mother's name is omitted).

8. The concluding formula includes the following elements: (1) written source where "the rest of the acts" of the king are found, usually expressed in the form "now the rest of the acts of [king's name], they are written in [name of source]"; (2) the king's death (if natural, he is said to have "slept with his fathers"); (3) the place of his burial; and (4) the succession, in the form "and x his son reigned in his stead" (although in three cases [2 Chron. 14:1; 17:1; 21:1] this line functions more as a link than as an ending marker). This concluding formula is omitted from the accounts of Amon (33:21–25) and the final four kings: Jehoahaz, Jehoiakim, Jehoiachin, and Zedekiah (36:1–14), although Jehoiakim's account refers to the written source containing the rest of his acts and contains a succession statement (36:8).

It is possible that these two exceptionally long narratives are intended to break up the otherwise uninterrupted survey of the successive kings into three blocks, with the Jehoshaphat narrative culminating Judah's first series of kings (chaps. 10–20), the Hezekiah account introducing the final series of kings (chaps. 29–36), and, standing between these two, a central series of seven kings (chaps. 21–28). This would give the Book of Chronicles seven constituent units of relatively uniform length (approximately 21, 20, 16, 15, 14, 16, and 18 pages respectively in BHS). The intentionality of this design is supported by the fact that each of the three resultant literary units in 2 Chronicles 10–36 exhibits its own self-contained structure, in each case a sevenfold symmetric scheme. We will examine each of these in order.

The author begins his survey of Judah's remaining kings in 2 Chronicles 10–20. In this section he recounts the reigns of four kings, organizing each presentation to draw attention to what the king accomplished with regard to the temple, priests, and Levites. The units about the first three kings—Rehoboam, Abijah, and Asa (14.6)—are structured similarly, in seven-part or five-part chiasmuses (or modified chiasmus) with the central part featuring material (unique to Chronicles) about the temple, priests, and Levites.

The Chronicler's extensive treatment of the reign of good King Jehoshaphat is presented in four larger units. The first unit about Jehoshaphat's reign provides an overview of his rule. It is arranged with a modified chiastic touch (14.7).

The second unit about Jehoshaphat recounts his alliance with Ahab and their joint battle against Syria. It is arranged in a seven-part symmetry, but in this case the Chronicler apparently has no material about the priests, Levites, or temple to place at the center of the story. Instead, he structures the story so that the prophecy of Micaiah takes the central position (14.8).

The third unit about Jehoshaphat (19:4–11) is uncharacteristically short; it is not arranged chiastically or in seven parts, but has only two or three subunits. The entire unit focuses on Jehoshaphat's utilization of the Levites in the country's judicial system—an example the postexilic community might be wise to follow.

The fourth unit, the story of Jehoshaphat's victory over the invaders from Edom, exhibits the conventional sevenfold, symmetric arrangement, with an episode about the key role of the

14.6 Rehoboam to Asa (2 Chronicles 10–16)

first king: Rehoboam (10:1–12:16)
  a **introduction**: revolt of Jeroboam and ten northern tribes (10:1–19)
    b **invasion** of Israel by Judah forbidden (11:1–4)
      • prophecy of Shemaiah
     c **establishment of fortified cities** in Judah (11:5–12)
      d **CENTER: support of priests and Levites** (11:13–17)
     c′ **placement** of princes of Judah **in fortified cities** of Judah (11:18–23)
    b′ **invasion** of Judah by Egypt (12:1–12)
      • prophecy of Shemaiah
  a′ **conclusion**: summary of reign and warfare with Jeroboam (12:13–16)
second king: Abijah (13:1–22)
  a **introductory summary** (13:1–2b)
    b **warfare with Jeroboam** (13:2c–3)
     c **CENTER: Abijah's speech focused on priests and Levites** (13:4–12)
    b′ **warfare with Jeroboam**; Abijah's victory (13:13–19)
  a′ **concluding summary** (13:20–22)
third king: Asa (14:1–16:14 [13:23–16:14])
  a **introductory summary** (14:1–8 [13:23–14:7])
    b **invasion** by Ethiopians (14:9–15 [14:8–14])
      • appeal to Yahweh
      • victory
     c **prophetic message** of approval (15:1–7)
      d **CENTER: religious reforms**: temple refurbished (15:8–19)
    b′ **invasion** by Israel (16:1–6)
      • appeal to Syria
      • victory
     c′ **prophetic message** of disapproval (16:7–10)
  a′ **concluding summary** (16:11–14)

14.7 Overview of Jehoshaphat's reign (2 Chronicles 17)

  a **fortification of the cities of Judah** (17:1–2)
    b **Yahweh establishes Jehoshaphat** (17:3–5a)
     c **gifts from Judah** (17:5b)
      d **CENTER: religious reforms; priests and Levites** (17:6–9)
    b′ **Yahweh protects Jehoshaphat** (17:10)
     c **gifts from Philistia** (17:11)
  a′ **fortification of the cities of Judah** (17:12–19)

14.8 Jehoshaphat's alliance with Ahab (2 Chronicles 18:1–19:3)

  a **Jehoshaphat's alliance** with Ahab (18:1)
    b **Jehoshaphat and Ahab agree to join in battle** against Syria (18:2–3)
     c **false prophets**, including Zedekiah, prophesy (18:4–11)
      d **CENTER: Yahweh's prophet Micaiah prophesies** (18:12–22)
     c′ **false prophet** Zedekiah son of Chenaanah responds (18:23–27)
    b′ **Jehoshaphat and Ahab join in battle** against Syria; Ahab is killed (18:28–34)
  a′ **Jehoshaphat's alliance** with Ahab condemned by prophet (19:1–3)

Levites standing at the highlighted center (14.9).

The entire Jehoshaphat account is then closed by a formulaic summary of his reign (20:31–21:1), with the last verse evidently functioning as the introduction to the next unit.

The seven units in 2 Chronicles 10–20 appear to form a symmetry, with the unit introducing the reign of good King Jehoshaphat and his use of the priests and Levites to teach the people the law at the highlighted center (14.10).

Jehoram to Ahaz (2 Chronicles 21–28)

The Chronicler next presents in rapid-fire manner the reigns of the seven kings who ruled between good kings Jehoshaphat and Hezekiah (14.11). Each king's reign appears to be structured according to a seven-part (or five-part) chiasmus, although the stories of Uzziah and Jotham could be analyzed otherwise. In each account the Chronicler places at the center new material (not found in Kings) about the priests,

14.9 Jehoshaphat's victory over Edom (2 Chronicles 20)

a **three nations invade** Judah; Jehoshaphat is afraid (20:1–3a)
   b **assembly of Judah** (20:3b–4)
      • fasting and petition to Yahweh
     c **Jehoshaphat's prayer** for deliverance (20:5–12)
       d **CENTER: prophecy of Levite;** Levites praise Yahweh (20:13–19)
     c′ **Jehoshaphat's speech** and Yahweh's deliverance (20:20–25)
   b′ **assembly of Judah** (20:26–28)
      • rejoicing and thanksgiving to Yahweh
a′ **no more invasions;** fear of Yahweh falls upon nations (20:29–30)

14.10 Rehoboam to Jehoshaphat (2 Chronicles 10–20)

a **Rehoboam: three nations invade and defeat Judah** (10:1–12:16)
      • three nations, with a vast army, invade Judah from the south, from Egypt
      • Judeans assemble in Jerusalem
      • prophecy of Shemaiah at the assembly: "[Yahweh] will abandon you!"
      • invaders defeat Judah and take great spoils from the temple
   b **Abijah** (13:1–22)
      • king's speech in the hill country of Ephraim condemning Israel for forsaking Yahweh and for rejecting his priests and Levites, which Judah has appointed to be Yahweh's ministers
     c **Asa** (14:1–16:14 [13:23–16:14])
      • interrelations of Judah and Israel
      • Syrians defeat Israel
      • Asa condemned by Hanani the seer for his alliance with Syria, which culminated in the defeat of Israel
       d **CENTER: Jehoshaphat's reign;** priests and Levites appointed to teach the law (17:1–19)
     c′ **Jehoshaphat and his alliance with Ahab** (18:1–19:3)
      • interrelations of Judah and Israel
      • Syrians defeat Israel
      • Jehoshaphat condemned by Jehu the son of Hanani the seer for alliance with Ahab, which culminated in defeat of Israel
   b′ **Jehoshaphat's appointment of the priests and Levites** (19:4–11)
      • king goes out to the hill country of Ephraim, to bring people back to Yahweh
      • he appoints priests and Levites to administer justice in Judah
a′ **Jehoshaphat: three nations invade Judah, but are defeated** (20:1–37)
      • three nations, with a vast army, invade Judah from the south, from Edom
      • Judeans assemble in Jerusalem
      • prophecy of Jahaziel at the assembly: "Yahweh will be with you!"
      • invaders are defeated by Judah; great spoils are brought back to the temple

Levites, or temple; or if he has no such material (as with Jehoram, Amaziah, and Ahaz), he uses an episode involving a prophet of Yahweh as the centerpiece. In the case of Joash, the entire story deals with Joash and the priests; so the Chronicler uses the center position for the turning point of Joash's reign, the death of the priest Jehoiada.

It is noteworthy that most of the stories involving the temple in this unit are negative, recounting what the kings did wrong regarding the temple. The seven kings in this unit are presented as unsuccessful or only moderately successful kings; and the author implies that their failure as kings may be related to their failure with regard to the temple. Each king in this unit, except Jotham, either neglected the temple (as suggested by silence) or committed sacrilege against it. The unit serves as a word of warning to the postexilic community: here is what happened when our leaders in earlier times ne-

glected or violated the temple; let's not repeat their mistakes!

The seven units of this group are also arranged with a symmetric touch (14.12). To highlight the idea that this entire group of inferior kings failed with regard to the temple, the three structurally prominent slots—the introductory, central, and concluding positions—feature kings who did nothing (at least recorded) regarding the temple. Three of the remaining four units (Jotham being the exception) tell stories of how the king violated the temple.

Judah's Final Kings and the Fall of Jerusalem (2 Chronicles 29–36)

The Chronicler seems to have organized the final group of Judah's kings in a manner similar to the first group of Judean kings in chapters 10–20, except in reverse order. There he began with three Judean kings, followed by a lengthy

14.11 Jehoram to Ahaz (2 Chronicles 21–28)

first king: Jehoram (21:1–20)
- a **introduction**: beginning of Jehoram's reign (21:1–3)
  - b **Jehoram kills all his father's sons** so that he alone, the <u>eldest</u>, is left (21:4–7)
    - c **military defeat**: Edom and Libnah revolt against Judah (21:8–10)
      - d **CENTER: letter from the <u>prophet</u> Elijah** (21:11–15)
    - c′ **military defeat**: Philistines and Arabs defeat Judah (21:16–17a)
  - b′ **Jehoram's sons are killed,** except <u>youngest</u> (21:17b; cf. 22:1)
- a′ **conclusion**: end of Jehoram's reign; his death (21:18–20)

second king: Ahaziah and Athaliah (22:1–23:21)
- a **young Ahaziah is made king** (22:1–2)
  - b **bad influence of wicked Athaliah** and her family upon government (22:3–5a)
    - c **bloody coup**: <u>Athaliah puts to death</u> all the members of the royal family—except Joash (22:5b–12)
      - d **TURNING POINT: Jehoiada the <u>priest</u> hides Joash**; <u>priests and Levites</u> anoint Joash to be the new king (23:1–11)
    - c′ **bloody coup**: <u>Athaliah is put to death</u> in takeover led by Joash's counselor Jehoiada (23:12–15)
  - b′ **good influence of godly Jehoiada** the priest upon government (23:16–19)
- a′ **young Joash is made king** (23:20–21)

third king: Joash (24:1–27)
- a **good beginning**: Joash begins his reign, does what is right with Jehoiada's help (24:1–3)
  - b **Joash decides to restore temple**; <u>confronts Jehoiada</u> (24:4–7)
    - c **Joash influences princes**; good result: <u>temple</u> is repaired (24:8–14)
      - d **TURNING POINT: Jehoiada the <u>priest</u> dies** (24:15–16)
    - c′ **princes influence Joash**; bad result: <u>temple</u> is abandoned (24:17–19)
  - b′ **Joash <u>confronted by Zechariah</u>** son of Jehoiada; Joash kills Zechariah (24:20–22)
- a′ **bad ending**: Joash is killed because of his sin of killing Jehoiada's son (24:23–27)

fourth king: Amaziah (25:1–28)
- a **introduction**: Amaziah becomes king; <u>kills assassins</u> of his father (25:1–4)
  - b **listens to prophet's warning**: do not join forces with Israel! (25:5–10)
    - c **victory!** (25:11–13)
      - d **TURNING POINT: Amaziah's idolatry**; rejects <u>prophet's</u> warning (25:14–16)
  - b′ **doesn't listen to Jehoash's warning**: do not fight with Israel! (25:17–20)
    - c′ **defeat!** (25:21–24)
- a′ **conclusion**: Amaziah <u>is assassinated</u> (25:25–28)

fifth king: Uzziah (26:1–23)
- a **introductory summary**: after the king <u>slept with his fathers</u> (26:1–3)
  - b **good beginning**: early years of godliness and resulting prosperity (26:4–5)
    - c **Uzziah's successes** (26:6–15)
      - d **TURNING POINT: Uzziah's pride**; enters <u>temple</u> to usurp <u>priests'</u> work (26:16)
    - c′ **Uzziah's disaster**: he is struck with leprosy (26:17–20)
  - b′ **bad ending**: final years of shame, because of his sin (26:21)
- a′ **concluding summary**: Uzziah <u>slept with his fathers</u> (26:22–23)

sixth king: Jotham (27:1–9)
- a **introductory summary**: <u>age</u> at accession and <u>length</u> of reign (27:1)
  - b **Jotham's godliness** (27:2)
    - c **CENTER: activities of Jotham**, including building <u>temple</u> gate (27:3–5)
  - b′ **Jotham's godliness**: the reason for Jotham's success (27:6)
- a′ **concluding summary**: <u>age</u> at accession and <u>length</u> of reign (27:7–9)

seventh king: Ahaz (28:1–27)
- a **introductory summary** (28:1a)
  - b **Ahaz's evil practices** (28:1b–4)
    - c **military disasters** because of Ahaz's wickedness (28:5–8)
      - d **CENTER: Judah spared through a <u>prophet's</u> message** (28:9–15)
    - c′ **military disasters** because of Ahaz's wickedness (28:16–21)
  - b′ **other evil practices of Ahaz** (28:22–25)
- a′ **concluding summary** (28:26–27)

account of good King Jehoshaphat. Here he opens with a lengthy account of good King Hezekiah, followed by three units tracing Judah's final kings.

Good King Hezekiah (2 Chronicles 29–32)

The four units comprising the Jehoshaphat account appear to be matched, in parallel order, by the four units comprising the Hezekiah ac-

14.12 Jehoram to Ahaz (2 Chronicles 21–28)

a **Jehoram** (21:1–20)
- slaughters his brothers (ʾaḥîm)
- center: condemnation of slaughter by prophet (of northern kingdom)
- Edom revolts; Shephelah town of Libnah revolts (joins Philistia, presumably)

b **Ahaziah/Athaliah** (22:1–23:21)
- war with Syria, eastern neighbor, leads to king's death
- warning against anyone except priests and Levites entering temple
- Athaliah enters temple; is killed

c **Joash:** priest confronts Joash for wrongdoing (24:1–27)
- Joash spurns priest's warning, dies as Yahweh's punishment
- reign begins well, ends badly

d **Amaziah:** no mention of temple, priests, Levites (25:1–28)

c′ **Uzziah:** priest confronts Uzziah for wrongdoing (26:1–23)
- Uzziah spurns priest's warning, Yahweh punishes with leprosy
- reign begins well, ends badly

b′ **Jotham** (27:1–9)
- war with Ammon, eastern neighbor, is successful
- he did not enter Yahweh's temple

a′ **Ahaz** (28:1–27)
- Israelites slaughter Judeans, their brothers (ʾaḥîm)
- center: condemnation of slaughter by prophet (of northern kingdom?)
- Edom defeats Judah; Philistia captures several Shephelah towns

---

14.13 Parallel presentations of the reigns of Jehoshaphat and Hezekiah (2 Chronicles 17–20; 29–32)

Jehoshaphat (17:1–20:37)
a **Jehoshaphat becomes king** and mobilizes the priests and Levites (17:1–19)
b **Jehoshaphat and his alliance** with the northern kingdom (18:1–19:3)
c **religious reforms** extend into highlands of Ephraim; establishes order of priests and Levites (19:4–11)
- not a seven-part chiasmus
d **invasion** from Edom **miraculously stopped** in response to Jehoshaphat's prayer (20:1–37)

Hezekiah (29:1–32:33)
a′ **Hezekiah becomes king** and mobilizes the priests and Levites (29:1–36)
b′ **Hezekiah calls for northern tribes** to join in Passover celebration (30:1–27)
c′ **religious reforms** extend into Ephraim and Manasseh; establishes order of priests and Levites (31:1–21)
- not a seven-part chiasmus
d′ **invasion** from Assyria **miraculously stopped** in response to Hezekiah's prayer (32:1–33)

14.14 Hezekiah's restoration of the temple (2 Chronicles 29)

a **initiation of temple restoration** immediately upon Hezekiah's accession (29:1–3)
b **exhortation to priests and Levites** to sanctify themselves and temple (29:4–11)
c **Levites and priests** sanctify themselves and temple (29:12–19)
d **CENTER: Hezekiah's grand dedication of temple** (29:20–30)
c′ **Levites and priests,** now sanctified, offer sacrifices (29:31–33)
b′ **exhortation for additional priests** to sanctify themselves; Levites help (29:34–35a)
a′ **conclusion of temple restoration,** which came about suddenly (29:35b–36)

---

count (14.13). It is also interesting that the third unit in each is different from the others in that it is not symmetrically arranged.

The first unit about Hezekiah's reign recounts how Hezekiah mobilized the priests and Levites in the restoration of the temple. Its symmetric arrangement draws attention to the grand dedication of the temple at its center (14.14).

The second unit about Hezekiah tells the story of Hezekiah's great Passover celebration. Its symmetric arrangement centers on the climactic celebration itself (14.15).

The third unit (chap. 31) focuses on Hezekiah's contributions to the temple and his assignment of duties to the priests and Levites. The material of this unit appears to have a simple linear arrangement.

The fourth unit recounts how Yahweh delivered Hezekiah from the Assyrians and from a serious illness. Its chiastic structure centers on Yahweh's great deliverance of Jerusalem (14.16).

Manasseh (2 Chronicles 33)

The story of Manasseh's reign is also pre-

14.15 Passover (2 Chronicles 30)

  a **introduction**: invitation to <u>all Israel and Judah</u> to come to the temple for Passover (30:1)

    b **agreement to modify** date of the Passover (30:2–5)

      c **Hezekiah's plea** to <u>northern kingdom tribes</u> (including the promise of Yahweh's forgiveness) (30:6–12)

        d **CLIMAX: Passover celebration at the temple** (30:13–17)

      c′ **Hezekiah's prayer** for those from <u>northern kingdom tribes</u> who are unclean ("may Yahweh forgive them") (30:18–22)

    b′ **agreement to modify** length of time of the Passover (30:23–24)

  a′ **conclusion**: summary of joyous celebration of <u>all Judah and Israel</u> (30:25–27)

14.16 Deliverance from the Assyrians (2 Chronicles 32)

  a **invasion of the Assyrians**; its intended purpose (32:1)

    b **Hezekiah's building activities** to prepare for the Assyrian invasion, including the <u>tunnel from the Gihon spring</u> (32:2–8)

      c **first crisis, from without: Sennacherib's invasion** (32:9–19)

        d **TURNING POINT: Hezekiah and the <u>prophet</u> Isaiah cry out to Yahweh**; Yahweh saves Jerusalem! (32:20–23)

      c′ **second crisis, from within: Hezekiah's illness and pride** (32:24–26)

    b′ **Hezekiah's building and other activities**, including the <u>tunnel from the Gihon spring</u> (32:27–30)

  a′ **visit of the Babylonians**; its intended purpose (32:31)

    conclusion: Hezekiah's death (32:32–33)

14.17 Manasseh (2 Chronicles 33)

  a **introductory summary** (33:1)

    b **examples of Manasseh's wicked practices** (33:2–9)

      c **God speaks to Manasseh** (33:10–11)

        • king <u>does not hear</u>

        • result: Manasseh imprisoned

        d **TURNING POINT: Manasseh's repentance** (33:12)

      c′ **Manasseh speaks to God** (33:13)

        • God <u>hears</u>

        • result: Manasseh freed

    b′ **examples of Manasseh's righteous deeds** (33:14–17)

  a′ **concluding summary** (33:18–20)

    addendum: Manasseh's son Amon was like wicked Manasseh (33:21–25)

14.18 Josiah (2 Chronicles 34–35)

  a **Josiah goes through north**, purging it from idolatry (34:1–7)

    • ends: <u>and he returned to Jerusalem</u>

    b **restoration of the temple** (34:8–13)

      • <u>oversight by priests and Levites</u>

      • levitical <u>musicians</u>

      • help from <u>northern</u> as well as southern tribes

      c **discovery of the law book; reading of the book to Josiah** (34:14–19)

        • Josiah's repentance in response to the book

        d **CLIMAX: message from Hulda the prophetess** (34:20–28)

      c′ **reading of the law book by Josiah** (34:29–33)

        • Josiah leads a covenant renewal ceremony in response to the book

    b′ **Passover at the temple** (35:1–19)

      • <u>oversight by priests and Levites</u>

      • levitical <u>musicians</u>

      • participation by <u>northern</u> as well as southern tribes

  a′ **Josiah goes north** to fight Pharaoh Necho; Josiah is mortally injured (35:20–27)

    • ends: <u>Josiah brought back to Jerusalem to die</u>

sented in a seven-part chiasmus, with an addendum (14.17). Uncharacteristically for the Book of Chronicles, the center has nothing to do with priests, Levites, temple, or prophets, but represents the turning point of the story, the repentance of Manasseh.

Josiah (2 Chronicles 34–35)

The Josiah story focuses on his religious reforms involving the temple, priests, and Levites. The center is the episode about Hulda the prophetess (14.18).

14.19 Judah's final four kings (2 Chronicles 36)

a **Jehoahaz taken captive to Egypt** (36:1–4)

b **Jehoiakim taken captive to Babylon**; <u>temple</u> plundered (36:5–8)

c **Jehoiachin taken captive to Babylon**; <u>temple</u> plundered (36:9–10)

d **Zedekiah taken captive to Babylon**; punishment because <u>temple</u> defiled (36:11–14)

e **Israel's sin**—involving the <u>temple</u> (36:15–16)

f **Israel's punishment**: captivity and destruction of Jerusalem and <u>temple</u> (36:17–21)

g **CONCLUSION**: Cyrus's proclamation to Jews to return and rebuild the <u>temple</u>! (36:22–23)

14.20 Judah's final kings (2 Chronicles 29–36)

a **Hezekiah's cleansing of temple** and temple <u>vessels</u> (29:1–36)
  - restoration of temple services
  - because of <u>desecration of temple</u> and spurning of Yahweh, "our fathers have fallen by the sword and our sons and our daughters . . . are in <u>captivity</u> for this" (29:6–9)
  - begins: in <u>first year of his reign</u> Hezekiah calls for purifying of defiled temple

b **Hezekiah's great Passover celebration** (30:1–27)

c **Hezekiah purges land** (31:1–21)
  - organization of Levites and priests
  - destroys pagan <u>Asherim</u>, <u>high places</u>, and <u>altars</u>

d **CENTER: Yahweh saves Hezekiah and Jerusalem!** (32:1–33)

c′ **Manasseh reverses Hezekiah's purge** (33:1–25)
  - restores pagan <u>Asherim</u>, <u>high places</u>, and <u>altars</u> "that his father Hezekiah had broken down"

b′ **Josiah and his great Passover celebration** (34:1–35:27)

a′ **final four kings of Judah and their captivity** (36:1–23)
  - <u>destruction and plundering of temple and vessels</u>
  - <u>captivity</u> of the people
  - ends: in <u>first year of his reign</u>, Cyrus calls for rebuilding of destroyed temple

14.21 The Book of Chronicles

a **beginning**: genealogies from Adam to the <u>Babylonian exile and return</u> (1 Chron. 1:1–9:44)
  - topics: Babylonian <u>exile</u> and <u>return</u>

b **establishment of David's kingdom** (1 Chron. 10:1–22:1)
  - <u>promise to David</u> that his dynasty would continue forever (17:1–27)
  - David's defeat of <u>Syria</u>, <u>Ammon</u>, <u>Moab</u>, <u>Edom</u> (in the <u>Valley of Salt</u>), <u>Philistia</u> (on numerous occasions)
  - David's <u>intrusion</u> into the priestly/levitical sphere of duty in the transportation of the ark (13:5–14; 15:12–15)

c **David assembles all Israel** to make preparations for Solomon's building of the temple (1 Chron. 22:2–29:30)
  - themes: <u>unity of all Israel</u>, sense of happy <u>cooperation</u>

d **CENTER: Solomon, the temple builder** (2 Chron. 1:1–9:31)

c′ **division of Israel; Judean kings from Rehoboam to good King Jehoshaphat** (2 Chron. 10:1–20:37)
  - themes: the <u>disintegration of all Israel</u>, <u>strife</u>

b′ **seven kings: Jehoram to Ahaz** (2 Chron. 21:1–28:27)
  - three crises threatening the <u>promise to David</u> of an eternal dynasty (cf. 21:7; 21:16–22:1; 22:10–11; 23:3)
  - warfare with the neighboring nations: <u>Syria</u>, <u>Ammon</u>, <u>Moab</u>, <u>Edom</u> (in the <u>Valley of Salt</u>), <u>Philistia</u> (on numerous occasions)
  - theme: <u>intrusion</u> into the priestly/levitical sphere of duty (23:6; 26:16–21; 27:2)

a′ **end**: Judah's final kings: good King Hezekiah to the <u>Babylonian exile</u>, and a note about <u>the return</u> (2 Chron. 29:1–36:23)
  - Judah's <u>exile</u> and a reference to the <u>return</u>

Judah's Final Four Kings (2 Chronicles 36)

The last unit presents in quick succession the captivity of Judah's final four kings, the plundering and destruction of the temple and Jerusalem, the captivity of the people, and Cyrus's decree to the Jews in captivity. Each episode except the first features the topic of the temple; and all except the last are negative.

A linear arrangement is employed here (14.19), which places significant emphasis on the final episode: Cyrus's decree inviting Jewish people to return to Jerusalem and rebuild the temple.

Overall Layout of 2 Chronicles 29–36

The seven units in 2 Chronicles 29–36 exhibit a conspicuous symmetric scheme of arrangement, with the central unit being Yahweh's deliverance of Hezekiah (14.20).

Overall Layout of the Book of Chronicles

Although the Book of Chronicles is primarily linear in arrangement (following a chronological order), there are indications that the book's seven constituent units have also been designed to form a symmetry (14.21). The genealogies at the beginning (a) trace Israel's tribes and families down to the time of the Babylonian exile and to the return under Cyrus,[9] listing various individuals who went into exile or returned to Jerusalem as a result of Cyrus's edict.[10] This links the book's beginning with its end (a'), which also features the Babylonian captivity and the return—bringing the book full circle.

The story of the establishment of David's kingdom (b) corresponds in several respects to the second cycle of Judah's kings (b'). First, the promise to David that his house and throne would be established forever (1 Chron. 17) is echoed in the three stories where David's line is nearly extinguished but is preserved because of God's promise to David (cf. 2 Chron. 21:7; 23:3).[11] Second, David's military conquests, including defeat of Philistia (14:8–17; 18:1; 20:4–8; cf. 10:1–12), Moab (18:2), Syria (18:3–8), Edom (18:12–13), and Ammon (19:11–20:3), find their echoes in the later accounts of warfare with these same neighboring countries.[12] Lastly, the theme of wrongful intrusion into the priestly/levitical duties is introduced with David's trans-

porting the ark to Jerusalem (1 Chron. 13:5–14; 15:12–15), and it is further developed in the second cycle of Judean kings, which documents three analogous intrusions (2 Chron. 23:6; 26:16–21; 27:2).

The book's third and third-to-last units are possibly intended to echo one another in matching contrast. The account of David's preparations for the building of the temple portrays Israel as a happy unified nation (c). The action takes place almost entirely at harmonious assemblies of "all Israel."[13] The book's third-to-last unit (c') traces the unraveling of this unity; the episodes in this unit focus on the disintegration of Israel's unity.[14] Admittedly, this is a weak connection.

---

9. The final chapter of the genealogies, which lists those who returned from exile to settle in Jerusalem, begins with a summary statement about the exile and return: "And Judah was taken into captivity in Babylon because of their unfaithfulness (ma'al). Now the first to dwell again in their possessions in their cities were . . . ; and some of the people of Judah, Benjamin, Ephraim, and Manasseh settled in Jerusalem" (1 Chron. 9:1–3).

10. References to the Babylonian exile and the return occur within the genealogies: "the sons of [King] Jeconiah the captive" (3:17); "they dwelt in their place until the exile" (5:22); "so the God of Israel stirred up . . . King Tiglath-pileser of Assyria, and he carried them away" (5:26); "the sons of Ehud . . . were carried away into exile to Manahath" (8:6).

11. The first three Judean kings in 2 Chronicles 21–28 demonstrate the validity of the great covenant that Yahweh made with David regarding his descendants in 1 Chronicles 17: (1) After Jehoram slew all the descendants of David except himself, the Chronicler adds: "Yet Yahweh would not destroy the house of David, because of the covenant that he had made with David, and since he had promised to give a lamp to him and to his sons for ever" (2 Chron. 21:7)—an obvious link to 1 Chronicles 17. (2) The Philistine and Ethiopian invaders slew all the sons of Jehoram except one, Ahaziah (21:16–22:1), as a punishment from "Yahweh the God of David your father" (21:12). (3) Upon Ahaziah's death Athaliah slew all the sons of Ahaziah except one, baby Joash ("and the house of Ahaziah had no one to rule the kingdom") (22:9–11). When the remaining descendant of David is presented, Jehoiada declares, "Behold, the king's son! Let him reign, as Yahweh spoke concerning the sons of David" (23:3).

12. See, e.g., warfare involving Edom (2 Chron. 21:8–10a; 25:5–13; cf. 1 Chron. 18:12–13), Philistia (2 Chron. 26:6–7; cf. 1 Chron. 18:1; 20:4–8; 28:5–29), Syria (2 Chron. 22:5–7; 24:23–25), and Ammon (2 Chron. 26:8; 27:5). References to warfare with Syria, Ammon, Moab, Edom, and Philistia are concentrated almost entirely in these two units in Chronicles. No warfare with these nations occurs anywhere else in the entire book, with the single exception of the story of Jehoshaphat's (non)battle with the invaders from Edom (2 Chron. 20).

13. "All Israel" gathers and joins with David in covenant in the cooperative effort to begin preparations for the temple. A major theme is the unity of "all Israel" in this cooperative effort: in his first assembly David exhorts "all the leaders of Israel" to help Solomon (22:17); in the second assembly David "assembled all the leaders of Israel" (23:2) and instructs them regarding all the duties of the priests and Levites (23:1–26:32). He continues by appointing military and civil officials over all of Israel, over each of the Israelite tribes (27:1–34). In the third assembly David gathers "all the officials of Israel" and instructs them to help Solomon (1 Chron. 28–29). Phrases and clauses used in recounting this third assembly emphasize Israel's unity under David: "king over all Israel" (28:4), "in the sight of all Israel" (28:8), "all the people" (28:21), "all the assembly" (29:1, 10, 20), "[all] the leaders of the tribes" (29:6, 9), "all Israel" (29:23), and "all the leaders . . . pledged their allegiance to King Solomon. And Yahweh gave Solomon great repute in the sight of all Israel" (29:24–25).

14. The account of Rehoboam begins with an assembly of "all Israel" for the purpose of making Rehoboam, Solomon's son, king (2 Chron. 10:1) Thus this unit begins on a note reminiscent of David's assembling all Israel to make Solomon his son king. But the outcome is dramatically different: Israel is torn apart and most of "all Israel" revolts against David's house. In the account of Abijah's reign (2 Chron. 13) another all-Israel assembly of sorts takes place—again in striking contrast to David's. This time the two factions of divided Israel gather to fight one another. While in David's assembly David appointed the priests and Levites to their various duties (1 Chron. 23–26), now in Abijah's speech to the assembled tribes he accuses Israel with regard to the priests and Levites ("you have driven out the priests of Yahweh, the sons of Aaron, and the Levites"; 2 Chron. 13:9) and goes on to point out how only Judah has the priests and Levites in their proper services (13:10–12). Asa, the third Judean king (14–16) also calls an assembly, gathering "all Judah and Benjamin, and those from Ephraim, Manasseh, and Simeon who were sojourning with them, for great numbers had deserted to him from Israel" (15:9). Here is an echo of the former unity of all Israel under the house of David. In both this and David's final assembly, the people "rejoice" (śmḥ) greatly (1 Chron. 29:9; 2 Chron. 15:15); in both, the king and people offer numerous sacrifices to Yahweh (1 Chron. 29:21–22; 2 Chron. 15:11). But in the account of Asa's reign is also another episode of civil war (16:1–6). Here, in contrast to David's donating vast sums of gold and silver to the treasury for the building of the temple, Asa takes gold and silver from the temple treasury to aid his war effort against Israel. The account of Jehoshaphat includes an episode in which he attempts to reestablish a unity between the rebellious northern tribes and Judah, but is con-

At the center (d) stands the story of Solomon the temple builder, creating an overall seven-part symmetry that places the temple's construction and magnificent dedication in the position of greatest prominence.

Conclusion

The linear arrangement of the Book of Chronicles places emphasis on the final unit, an ending that is significantly different from Kings. The Book of Kings, it will be recalled, culminates with the destruction of Jerusalem and the Babylonian exile, reflecting the book's interest in this terrible disaster and its cause. In contrast, Chronicles closes with Cyrus's invitation to return to Jerusalem and rebuild the temple, reflecting a more positive purpose to encourage the postexilic community. The book seeks to inspire Jews of the Diaspora and those living in Israel to rediscover the key role of the temple for the future prosperity of the restored community.

Identification of the Chronicler's favorite structuring scheme helps account for many of the differences between Kings and Chronicles. Throughout Chronicles, material from Kings is augmented with new material about the temple, priests, Levites, or (rarely) a prophet and then reorganized into symmetric presentations centering around the new material (e.g., Rehoboam, Abijah, Asa, Jehoshaphat [first and last units], Ahaziah, Joash, Uzziah, Jotham, Hezekiah [first and second units]). There are at least seventeen instances where this pattern of reorganization can be seen. For example, the account of the reign of Uzziah (Azariah) in 2 Kings 15:1–7 is arranged in a somewhat linear fashion:

a overview of his reign (15:1–4)
b leprosy (cause not given) (15:5)
c formulaic conclusion (15:6–7)

The Chronicler expands this account and redesigns its structure so the central episode features a story unique to Chronicles: Uzziah's un-

lawful entry into the temple—the cause of his leprosy:

a introductory summary: after the king <u>slept with his fathers</u> (26:1–3; cf. 25:28)
  b good beginning: early years of godliness and resulting prosperity (26:4–5)
    c Uzziah's successes (26:6–15)
      d TURNING POINT: Uzziah's pride; enters <u>temple</u> to usurp <u>priests</u>' work (26:16)
    c' Uzziah's disaster: he is struck with leprosy (26:17–20)
  b' bad ending: final years of shame, because of his sin (26:21)
a' concluding summary: Uzziah <u>slept with his fathers</u> (26:22–23)

Five of the book's seven major units (genealogies, David's reign, David's preparation for the building of the temple, Solomon's reign, first collection of Judean kings) are similarly structured. Moreover, the entire book is arranged according to the same scheme. The Chronicler entirely reorganized the presentation of Israel's history as it appears in Kings, so that the new center features the reign of Solomon the temple builder. Furthermore, the kings of the northern kingdom are omitted since they completely abandoned Yahweh's temple (and the priests and Levites) and therefore were of only peripheral interest to the book's agenda. The Chronicler likewise omits extensive material in Kings about the ministries of Elijah and Elisha, at least in part because these prophets had little to do with the temple, priests, or Levites. They were prophets in the northern kingdom, where these institutions were gone.

This structural highlighting of stories about the temple and its servants helps the Chronicler establish and emphasize the pattern that throughout history, when Israel did right with regard to the temple, priests, and Levites, it always prospered; conversely, when it did wrong in these areas, it always suffered. The Book of Chronicles is written and structured to demonstrate that Israel's well-being, past and future, has depended and will continue to depend on its obedience in these areas. The encouragement to the postexilic audience—particularly to the priests and Levites themselves—is to give heed to these lessons from history and carefully follow all God's laws with regard to his temple and its servants. Only then will the postexilic community experience God's full blessings upon their land and their lives.

demned by God for it (18:1–19:3); the unity that was exemplified under David is gone, even prevented by God himself. There are several other echoes linking these two parts of Chronicles, but they are less obvious and perhaps fortuitous: the musical duties of the Levites (1 Chron. 25; 2 Chron. 20:21–22); the establishment of the responsibilities of the priests and Levites (1 Chron. 23–26; 2 Chron. 17:7–9; 19:8–11); the recurring promise, prayer, etc., "Yahweh be with you" (or the like) (1 Chron. 22:11, 16; 28:20; 2 Chron. 15:2; 17:3; 20:17); and other similar examples (cf. 1 Chron. 28:9; 2 Chron. 15:2–3).

15
Ezra–Nehemiah

God's People Return to Jerusalem

The books of Ezra and Nehemiah tell the intriguing story of how Jewish exiles returned from Babylonia to resettle in the land of Judah. Although Ezra and Nehemiah are two books in the English Bible, they are generally reckoned as one book in Hebrew Bibles. Structural analysis supports their compositional unity.[1] The combined work comprises seven well-defined units that form a structural whole:

a Zerubbabel's return (Ezra 1–2)
b Zerubbabel's accomplishment (Ezra 3–6)
c Ezra's return (Ezra 7–8)
d Ezra's accomplishment (Ezra 9–10)
e Nehemiah's return (Neh. 1–2)
f Nehemiah's accomplishment (Neh. 3:1–7:3)
g final reforms and lists (Neh. 7:4–13:31)

Zerubbabel's Return (Ezra 1–2) and the Rebuilding of the Temple (Ezra 3–6)

Ezra–Nehemiah opens with two units about the successful return and work of Zerubbabel, a leader from the royal line of David. The first of these units recounts Zerubbabel's return with a group of Jewish exiles from Babylonia, inspired by King Cyrus's decree. The unit falls into three parts, arranged in a simple linear pattern, with a natural structural emphasis on the final unit, the list of returnees (suggesting the importance of the individuals who chose to return):

a Cyrus's decree (1:1–4)
b valuables and gifts collected for the new temple (1:5–11)
c list of those who returned with Zerubbabel (2:1–70)

1. For brief discussions of the arrangement of Ezra–Nehemiah, see S. R. Driver, *An Introduction to the Literature of the Old Testament* (9th ed.; Edinburgh: Clark, 1913), 540–51; Otto Eissfeldt, *The Old Testament: An Introduction*, trans. Peter R. Ackroyd (New York: Harper & Row, 1965), 542–52; H. G. M. Williamson, *Ezra–Nehemiah* (Word Biblical Commentary 16; Waco: Word, 1985), xxi–xxxv; Rolf Rendtorff, *The Old Testament: An Introduction* (Philadelphia: Fortress, 1986), 277–82.

This is followed by a unit that tells the story of the temple's rebuilding by Zerubbabel and the Jews who returned with him (15.1). This unit is laid out in a seven-part symmetry, framed by structurally highlighted episodes involving religious assemblies (Feast of Booths and Passover)—perhaps to underscore the importance of observing these festivals. The theme of enemy opposition is emphasized by its repetition in matching units (c and c'). At the center (d) stands the turning point of the story: the ministry of the prophets Haggai and Zechariah, who inspired the dispirited people to start building the temple again. The placement of their ministry here, as the story's turning point, reinforces the point that it was through divine encouragement that the temple was finally completed.

Ezra's Return (Ezra 7–8) and Accomplishments (Ezra 9–10)

The third and fourth units of Ezra–Nehemiah focus on a second figure: Ezra. The third unit recounts how Ezra returned with a group of Jews some eighty years after Zerubbabel. This unit, like the previous one, is structured in a seven-part symmetry whose highlighted center provides the list of names of those who returned with Ezra, underscoring the importance of the individuals who returned (15.2).

The fourth unit recounts how Ezra dealt with the problem of racial/religious intermarriage among the Jews in Judah. The story is arranged in a seven-part symmetry that serves to highlight the central episode, the people's agreement to resolve the problem (15.3).

Nehemiah's Return (Nehemiah 1–2) and Work (Nehemiah 3:1–7:3)

The fifth and sixth units in Ezra–Nehemiah focus on a third figure: Nehemiah. The fifth unit recounts Nehemiah's return to Judah and is possibly arranged with a symmetric touch, al-

15.1 Rebuilding of temple (Ezra 3–6)

a **religious celebration** before temple is built: Feast of Booths (3:1–6)
- priests and Levites involved in proper sacrifices (with altar properly built)

  b **building of the temple begins** (3:7–13)
- date mentioned

    c **opposition:** hostile correspondence, and work stops (4:1–24)
- copies of enemies' letter to king and king's negative reply

      d **TURNING POINT: prophets Haggai and Zechariah encourage the people** to continue the work (5:1–2)

    c′ **opposition:** hostile correspondence, and work begins again! (5:3–6:12)
- copies of enemies' letter to king and king's positive reply

  b′ **building of the temple is completed** (6:13–15)
- date mentioned

a′ **religious celebration** after temple is built: Feast of Passover (6:16–22)
- priests and Levites involved in proper sacrifices

15.2 Ezra's return (Ezra 7–8)

a **Ezra's return** to Jerusalem with Jews (7:1–10)

  b **king's blessing on trip:** gifts of gold, silver, etc., for temple (7:11–26)

    c **Ezra gathers the people** to return (7:27–28)

      d **CENTER: list of returnees** (8:1–14)

    c′ **Ezra gathers the people** to return (8:15–21)

  b′ **Jews ask God's blessing on trip:** care of king's gifts of gold, silver, etc., for temple (8:22–30)

a′ **Ezra's return** to Jerusalem with Jews; sacrifices [of gratitude] (8:31–36)

15.3 Ezra deals with the problem of intermarriage (Ezra 9–10)

a **problem of intermarriage introduced** (9:1–2)

  b **people gather about Ezra,** who sits in distress over problem (9:3–4)

    c **Ezra kneels in prayer** at temple in self-abasement (9:5–15)

      d **CLIMAX: people agree to resolve problem!** (10:1–4)

    c′ **Ezra arises from prayer** at temple (still) in self-abasement (10:5–6)

  b′ **Ezra gathers people;** they sit in distress; representatives sit and deal with problem (10:7–15)

a′ **problem of intermarriage resolved;** list of those guilty (10:16–44)

15.4 Nehemiah's return (Nehemiah 1–2)

a **Nehemiah hears report** of the problem (1:1–3)
- topics: trouble ($r\bar{a}^{\varsigma}\hat{a}$), disgrace ($herp\hat{a}$), gates burned with fire, walls broken down

  b **Nehemiah sits down** and mourns some days (1:4–11)

    c **Nehemiah's request** to king to let him go to Jerusalem (2:1–5)

      d **TURNING POINT: request granted!** (2:6)

    c′ **Nehemiah's request** to king to give him letters for governors (2:7–10)

  b′ **Nehemiah arises,** goes to Jerusalem, and remains there three days (2:11–16)

a′ **Nehemiah gives own report** of the problem; responses from Jews and enemies (2:17–20)
- topics: trouble ($r\bar{a}^{\varsigma}\hat{a}$), disgrace ($herp\hat{a}$), gates burned with fire, walls broken down

though the correspondences are not strong and a linear pattern may be all that is intended. The possible symmetric configuration (as shown in 15.4) would highlight the king's granting Nehemiah permission to return as the story's turning point.

The sixth unit recounts how Nehemiah directed the rebuilding of the walls and gates of Jerusalem amid much opposition. The unit's symmetric design underscores the theme of enemy opposition by its repetition in matching episodes (15.5). Similar repetition emphasizes the value of prayer in the face of opposition. At the center of the unit stands the episode about Nehemiah helping the poor—a structurally highlighted reminder of the importance of kindness to the poor.

Concluding Lists and Final Reforms (Nehemiah 7:4–13:31)

The final unit of Ezra–Nehemiah at first glance seems to be a hodgepodge of material, including events from various times in the ministries of Zerubbabel, Ezra, and Nehemiah. But this final unit is tied together by its modified chiastic structure (a-b-c-d-a′-b′-c′; see 15.6). The unit functions as the book's grand finale, pulling together and structurally highlighting main themes from the previous units: the importance of the individuals

15.5 Rebuilding Jerusalem amid opposition (Nehemiah 3:1–7:3)

a **walls begun:** list of builders (3:1–32)

  b **verbal opposition:** ridicule; Nehemiah's <u>prayer</u> and response (4:1–6 [3:33–38])

    c **plot to kill workers:** <u>prayer</u> and solution (4:7–23 [4:1–17])

      d **CENTER: Nehemiah helps poor** (5:1–19)

    c′ **plot to kill Nehemiah:** solution and <u>prayer</u> (6:1–9)

  b′ **verbal opposition:** intimidation; Nehemiah's response and <u>prayer</u> (6:10–14)

a′ **walls completed:** doors put in place, guards stationed (6:15–7:3)

15.6 Grand finale (Nehemiah 7:4–13:31)

a **list of returnees under Zerubbabel** (7:4–73)

  b **Ezra assembles people** before <u>Water Gate and Ephraim Gate</u>; law is read; celebration of Feast of Booths (8:1–18)

    c **reforms:** confession of sin, sealed by list of names (9:1–10:39 [9:1–10:40])

      • topics of resolutions: <u>Sabbath</u>; <u>purity of priests, Levites, and temple</u>; <u>intermarriage</u>

    d **CENTER: list of names** of new residents of Jerusalem chosen (11:1–36)

a′ **list of priests and Levites returning under Zerubbabel** (12:1–26)

  b′ **Nehemiah assembles people** before <u>Water Gate</u>, <u>Ephraim Gate</u>, and other city gates; new wall is dedicated (Ezra involved) (12:27–47)

    c′ **reforms:** Nehemiah's final reforms (13:1–31)

      • topics of reforms: <u>Sabbath</u>; <u>purity of priests, Levites, and temple</u>; <u>intermarriage</u>

15.7 Paired parallel pattern in Ezra–Nehemiah

a <u>Zerubbabel's</u> return (Ezra 1–2)

a′ <u>Zerubbabel's</u> accomplishment (Ezra 3–6)

  b <u>Ezra's</u> return (Ezra 7–8)

  b′ <u>Ezra's</u> accomplishment (Ezra 9–10)

    c <u>Nehemiah's</u> return (Neh. 1–2)

    c′ <u>Nehemiah's</u> accomplishment (Neh. 3:1–7:3)

      d final reforms and lists (Neh. 7:4–13:31)

15.8 Alternating parallel pattern in Ezra–Nehemiah

a **Zerubbabel's** <u>return</u> (Ezra 1–2)

  b **Zerubbabel's** <u>accomplishment</u> (Ezra 3–6)

a′ **Ezra's** <u>return</u> (Ezra 7–8)

  b′ **Ezra's** <u>accomplishment</u> (Ezra 9–10)

a″ **Nehemiah's** <u>return</u> (Neh. 1–2)

  b″ **Nehemiah's** <u>accomplishment</u> (Neh. 3:1–7:3)

    c final reforms and lists (Neh. 7:4–13:31)

who returned, the city's new walls and gates, the temple, priests, and Levites, and the issue of intermarriage.

Overall Layout of the Book of Ezra–Nehemiah

In addition to the primarily chronological arrangement scheme of the Book of Ezra–Nehemiah, there are at least three structural patterns operating simultaneously: paired parallel (15.7), alternating parallel (15.8), and symmetry (15.9).[2]

2. A partially symmetric arrangement of the book is also suggested by William Johnstone, "Guilt and Atonement: The Theme of 1 and 2 Chronicles," in *A Word in Season: Essays in Honour of William McKane*, ed. James D. Martin and Philip R. Davies (Journal for the Study of the Old Testament Supplement 42; Sheffield: JSOT Press, 1986), 134–35 n. 2. Johnstone likewise identifies seven constituent units in Ezra–Nehemiah: Ezra 1:1–4:5; 4:6–23; 4:24–6:22; 7:1–10:44; Neh. 1–7; 8–10; 11–13.

Conclusion

The structure of Ezra–Nehemiah helps clarify a number of questions about the book. First, structural analysis strongly supports the compositional unity of these two books. That the two books together have seven parts would by itself support their unity. The interlacing parallel and symmetric structuring schemes that tie the two books together seem to seal the argument.

The work's structure also helps explain the presence and location of anomalous sections. For example, the interruptive account of Nehemiah's kindness to the poor (Neh. 5) serves a critical structural role as the centerpiece of the story of his rebuilding the city's walls (3:1–7:3). Likewise, the puzzling repetition of the list of the returnees under Zerubbabel (Ezra 2; Neh. 7) functions structurally to connect the beginning

15.9 Symmetry in Ezra–Nehemiah

a **Zerubbabel's return and list of returnees** (Ezra 1–2)
- list of returnees, gold, silver, priestly garments (2:1–70)

  b **building of temple and opposition from enemies** (Ezra 3–6)
- themes: <u>opposition</u>, the story of the Jews' success

    c **Ezra's return** (Ezra 7–8)
- <u>dealings with king</u>
- orders from king to Transeuphrates <u>governors to assist Jews</u>
- recounted in <u>first-person</u>

      d **CENTER: purification of people** (Ezra 9–10)

    c′ **Nehemiah's return** (Neh. 1–2)
- <u>dealings with king</u>
- orders from king to Transeuphrates <u>governors to assist Jews</u>
- recounted in <u>first-person</u>

  b′ **building of walls and opposition from enemies** (Neh. 3:1–7:3)
- themes: <u>opposition</u>, the story of the Jews' success

a′ **Zerubbabel's return and list of returnees; final reforms** (Neh. 7:4–13:31)
- list of returnees, gold, silver, priestly garments (7:4–73)

and end of the work and to reinforce its symmetric design (and to draw attention to the importance of the people who returned).

Analysis of the work's literary architecture helps identify the author's emphases. For example, the author's theme of enemy opposition is highlighted by its matched repetition not only within the story of Zerubbabel's building of the temple and within the story of Nehemiah's building of the walls, but also by its use in connecting larger units in the book. One occurrence of opposition in the story might seem coincidental, unique to that event; but the fourfold repetition serves to create a pattern. God's people may often experience opposition when they attempt to carry out his work; but through prayer and God's gracious help they can succeed in their work despite the opposition.

Other themes are emphasized by repetition:

1. the importance of individual people who participate in God's work, as shown, for example, by repetition of the lists of names of specific people who returned with Zerubbabel[3]

2. the central role of the priests and Levites in the life of the postexilic community (structural repetitions throughout the book are too numerous to list)

3. the key role of prayer in carrying out God's work and in facing difficulties (emphasized by the repetition of this theme in matching units in Ezra 9–10 and Neh. 4–6)

4. the importance of repentance and fasting (e.g., through the repetition of Ezra's self-abasement in Ezra 9:5–15 and 10:5–6)

5. the importance of obedience regarding three particular issues for the well-being of the postexilic community: Sabbath observance, avoidance of intermarriage with non-Jews, and the purity of the priests, Levites, and temple services (cf. Neh. 9–10 and 13)

The most obvious theme highlighted by the work's structure is returning to the homeland. Three times in the structured parallel pattern of Ezra–Nehemiah the audience hears how godly Jews dared to leave their comfortable homes in the Diaspora to return to Judah and how, despite hardship and opposition, God was with them, blessing their efforts and their lives, and answering their prayers.

---

3. See Tamara C. Eskenazi, "The Structure of Ezra–Nehemiah and the Integrity of the Book," *Journal of Biblical Literature* 107 (1988) 641–56, who observes how the structure of Ezra–Nehemiah is shaped by the lists of people. These lists underscore a major theme: the shift away from isolated heroes to the importance of all the people.

16

Esther

Divine Providence Protects God's People

The Book of Esther tells the story of how the Jewish Feast of Purim was instituted, when a Jew named Mordecai and his niece Esther saved the Jewish people during the reign of the Persian King Xerxes. The story comprises a series of episodes arranged to maximize suspense and to create surprises and ironies for the enjoyment of the audience.[1]

Shifts in time, place, character, and topic delineate most of the episodes; and a banquet or fast marks the conclusion of a number of episodes. Careful analysis of the story suggests that it is made up of thirteen episodes, primarily arranged in a chronologically linear pattern, with the final three episodes climaxing the story (the triumph of the Jews over their enemies and the establishment of the Feast of Purim). In addition to the linear scheme, the thirteen episodes also form a conspicuous symmetry, with the seventh, center episode functioning as the story's turning point (16.1).[2]

There is another prominent structural scheme in the Book of Esther. Each half of the story forms its own symmetry: the first seven episodes form a seven-part chiasmus, and the last seven episodes also form a seven-part chiasmus (the book's central episode in chap. 6 serves double duty). The symmetric design of the first half of Esther centers around Haman's evil plot (16.2), while the symmetric design of the second half of Esther centers on the foiling of his plot (16.3).

The structure of the Book of Esther offers several insights about its function and meaning. One obvious point is that the story's layout is designed to entertain the audience by creating and holding suspense for as long as possible. For example, the tension created by Haman's terrible edict is introduced early in the story (chap. 3), but the audience is kept in suspense until near the end, when we finally learn how this terrible scheme was neutralized (chaps. 8–9). Likewise, the audience must wait in suspense to learn whether Esther's attempt to save her people will work. We assume that the turning point will occur when Esther boldly approaches the king in 5:1–4 to beseech his help for the Jews. But the storyteller prolongs the suspense. When Esther succeeds in approaching the king, she defers her request until her private dinner for the king and Haman; then she postpones it again until a second private dinner for the two men. Finally, when the suspense can be held no longer, she springs her trap!

The story's structure also reinforces the author's use of irony. For example, the irony involving Haman's gallows is highlighted by structurally matching the episode of Haman's building of the gallows with the episode in which he is hanged on it. The irony in chapter 6 is classic: Haman enthusiastically advises the king how the king might honor an unnamed man (whom Haman, in his self-importance, assumes is himself), only to discover that the man to be so rewarded is his despised enemy Mordecai; even more ironically, Haman's suggestion that "one of the king's most trusted nobles" be chosen to assist in the honoring backfires on him: the king chooses Haman to assist in honoring Mordecai! The irony is made even more obvious for the audience by placing the ironic (and

---

1. Carey A. Moore, *Esther: Introduction, Translation, and Notes* (Anchor Bible 7b; Garden City: Doubleday, 1971), x, divides the book into thirteen units: 1:1–22; 2:1–18; 2:19–23; 3:1–15; 4:1–17; 5:1–8; 5:9–14; 6:1–13; 6:14–7:10; 8:1–17; 9:1–19; 9:20–32; 10:1–3. See also Athalya Brenner, "Esther in the Looking-Glass: On Symmetry and Duplication in the Scroll of Esther," *Beth Miqra* 86 (1981) 267–78 [in Hebrew].

2. See Yehuda Radday, "Chiasm in Joshua, Judges, and Others," *Linguistica Biblica* 27–28 (1973), 9, for an analysis of the book in seven parts: 1; 2–3; 4–5; 6:1 (the center); 6–7; 8–9; 10. Jon Levenson, *Esther: A Commentary* (Old Testament Library; Louisville: Westminster/John Knox, 1997), 5–12, sees the book as containing ten parts arranged with a symmetric touch and based on the book's ten banquets. In addition, Levenson notices a second structuring scheme: a fifteen-part (loosely speaking) chiastic scheme, with chap. 6 at the center.

16.1 The Book of Esther

a **king's proud feast** (1:1–22)
- king <u>deposes Queen Vashti</u>
- <u>letters sent</u> throughout empire

b **Esther becomes queen** (2:1–18)
- king gives <u>feast in her honor</u>
- <u>gives gifts</u>

c **king's life is saved** (2:19–23)
- those <u>plotting to kill</u> the king <u>are killed</u>

d **Haman's plot:** Haman convinces king to send royal edict to kill Jews on Adar 13 (3:1–4:3)
- Haman to destroy: "if it please the king, let it be written"
- <u>destroy, kill, and annihilate</u> Jews; <u>plunder their goods</u>
- edict in all languages, sealed with king's signet, sent by couriers
- ends: Susa distressed at edict; Mordecai dresses in sackcloth

e **Mordecai learns of Haman's plot** and money involved; appeals to Esther to risk all to stop Haman (4:4–17)

f **Esther invites king and Haman** to her <u>first banquet</u> (5:1–14)
- <u>Haman builds gallows</u> to hang Mordecai
- <u>king asks Esther:</u> "What is your petition?"
- "it will be given you, even <u>up to half my kingdom</u>"

g **TURNING POINT: Haman's fortunes turn;** he honors Mordecai the Jew! (6:1–14)

f′ **Esther invites king and Haman** to <u>second banquet</u> (7:1–10)
- <u>Haman hanged on gallows</u> he built for Mordecai
- <u>king asks Esther:</u> "What is your petition?"
- "it will be given you, even <u>up to half my kingdom</u>"

e′ **Mordecai and Esther given Haman's estate** (8:1–2)*

d′ **Haman's plot foiled:** Esther convinces king to send second royal edict to allow Jews to kill enemies on Adar 13 (8:3–17)
- Esther to king: "if it please the king . . . let it be written"
- <u>destroy, kill, and annihilate</u> enemies; <u>plunder their goods</u>
- edict in all languages, sealed with king's signet, sent by couriers
- ends: Susa rejoices at edict; Mordecai dresses royally; joy

c′ **Jews' lives are saved** (9:1–10)
- those <u>plotting to kill</u> Jews <u>are killed</u>

b′ **Esther wins second day for Jews in Susa** (9:11–19)
- another <u>feast day</u> instituted because of Esther (annual <u>feast will perpetually honor Esther!</u>)
- <u>giving of gifts</u>

a′ **Jews' Feast of Purim** (9:20–10:3)
- king <u>promotes Mordecai</u>
- <u>letters sent</u> throughout empire

*Unit e′ is an admittedly weak match of unit e.

16.2 Haman's evil plot hatched (Esther 1–6)

a **Queen Vashti deposed** (1:1–22)
- king asks advice from advisors: <u>what ought to be done</u> to disobedient queen?
- advisors <u>give king advice,</u> which he follows
- <u>example made</u> of queen: here is what happens to a disrespectful woman!

b **Esther goes to king** (2:1–18)
- he is <u>pleased</u> and makes her his new queen
- king gives Esther a <u>banquet</u> (*mišteh*)

c **Mordecai learns of plot to kill king** and contacts Esther so she will tell king (2:19–23)

d **CENTER: Haman's plot** (3:1–15)

c′ **Mordecai learns of plot to kill Jews** and contacts Esther so she will appeal to king (4:1–17)

b′ **Esther goes to king** (5:1–14)
- he is <u>pleased</u> and asks her request
- Esther gives king a <u>banquet</u> (*mišteh*)

a′ **Mordecai honored** (6:1–14)
- king asks advice from Haman: <u>what ought to be done</u> to someone the king wishes to honor?
- Haman <u>gives king advice,</u> which he follows (to Haman's chagrin!)
- <u>example made</u> of Mordecai: here is what happens to a man the king wishes to honor!

16.3 Haman's evil plot foiled (Esther 6–10)

a **Mordecai is honored** (6:1–14)
  • begins: king reads the <u>royal records</u> about <u>Mordecai's deeds</u>
  b **king asks Esther for her request** on <u>second day</u>, at her second banquet (7:1–10)
    • <u>Esther requests</u> that Jews not be killed
    • result: <u>Haman hanged</u>
    c **Mordecai's new prominence in palace** (8:1–2)
      • he is given king's signet ring and appointed over Haman's estate
      • all that was supposed to be Haman's (including king's signet ring used in plot to kill Jews) is given to a Jew
      d **CENTER: Haman's plot foiled** (8:3–17)
    c′ **Mordecai's new prominence in the palace** (9:1–10)
      • Jews kill those intending to kill them
      • all that was supposed to be done to Jews by their enemies, the Jews do to them
  b′ **king asks Esther for her request**; Esther's request for <u>second day</u> (9:11–19)
    • <u>Esther requests</u> that Jews be allowed to kill enemies one more day
    • result: bodies of <u>Haman's sons are hanged</u> and second day of Purim banquet
a′ **Mordecai is honored, promoted to be second to the king** (9:20–10:3)
  • ends: statement that <u>Mordecai's deeds</u> are recorded in <u>royal records</u>

humorous) backfiring of Haman's self-serving advice directly after his advice, so that even children in the audience would not miss it.

Several matchups in the story serve to highlight the theme of just retribution against the enemies of God's people. The episodes recounting the evil plots against the Jews are matched by episodes recounting the backfiring of those plots, in which the very evils devised against the Jews end up falling upon those who devised them. The repetition of this theme suggests its importance to the author. The lesson: whatever our enemies plot against us will, in the end, miscarry and fall upon them. This message would provide encouragement and reassurance to Jewish people living in a hostile world, whether in the Diaspora or in the land of Judah.

It is significant that the turning point of the story (chap. 6) does not involve the brave actions of either Mordecai or Esther (although we have every reason to expect this), but rather an ironic twist of fate in which the fortunes of wicked Haman begin to turn. Up to this point in the story everything has gone well for Haman, and his schemes against Mordecai and the Jews appear to be working without hitch. This episode, in which Haman's advice to the king backfires on him, marks the turning point of Haman's success. From this point on, his schemes begin to unravel. By designing the story with this episode as the turning point, the author implies that the real reason the Jews were saved

was (divine) providence. Granted, by all appearances it was the brave actions of two Jews that saved God's people. But the real turning point of the story was a triumph caused neither by Mordecai nor Esther, but by an ironic twist of fate and a combination of providential coincidences: the king just *happened* to be sleepless that night; he *happened* to ask for the royal records to be read; the section read *happened* to be about Mordecai's good deed; Haman *happened* to be in the palace the next day; Haman *happened* to misread the king's intentions; etc. The author's moral: the security of God's people is ultimately in the hands of God himself. As Mordecai says to Esther: "If you remain silent at this time, relief and deliverance for the Jews will arise from another place. . . . Who knows but that you have come to your royal position for such a time as this" (4:14).

The placement of the institution of Purim in the final position, a position of prominence, indicates that the explanation for how Purim came about is the focal point of this story and may be the primary reason the story was composed. That the story moves from despair to hope, from disaster to triumph, ending in victory and festivity, indicates that the story is designed to inspire and encourage the audience. The message of the book is an uplifting one: things may be bad; but God has a way of righting all wrongs. Everything will work out in the end for God's people.

Unit 4
Poetic Books

17
Job
Where Can Wisdom Be Found?

The Book of Job deals with one of the classic problems faced by adherents of monotheism: if God is indeed good, all powerful, and in control, why do bad things happen in this world? The book tackles this subject by examining the case of Job, a righteous man whom God allowed to suffer undeservedly. Analysis of the book's structure helps clarify the function and position of some of its constituent parts;[1] and it may also help clarify the author's answer to the book's central question.

Prologue (Job 1–2)

The Book of Job opens with a narrative introduction, or prologue, that sets the stage for the discussions that follow. The prologue recounts how Job, a righteous and prosperous man, was allowed by God to undeservedly suffer a series of terrible disasters. The narrative is organized in a seven-part parallel fashion (a ‖ b-c-d ‖ b'-c'-d') that reinforces the pattern: Satan's accusation—Job's sufferings—Job's righteous response (17.1).

The parallel scheme allows the author to establish a pattern that stresses several important points through repetition. First, God is pleased with Job and considers him more righteous than any other person. Second, the immediate cause of Job's suffering is Satan's instigation, not Job's sin. Third, God allows Job to suffer, but

with apparent reluctance and with restrictions. Last, Job remains righteous despite his suffering, proving Satan wrong.

Job's Curse upon the Day of His Birth (Job 3)

Job's opening monologue appears to be a self-contained unit separate from the dialogue that follows.[2] Its introduction suggests that it is an independent unit: "After this, Job opened his mouth and cursed the day of his birth" (3:1). The speech is a monologue with a specified purpose: to curse the day he was born. Although it leads naturally into the dialogue that follows, it has a certain separateness that the audience would perceive. The speech falls into two parts: (1) a series of wishes, expressed with the Hebrew jussive ("may that day . . ."; 3:3–10) and (2) a series of questions ("why . . . ? 3:11–26).

Dialogue between Job and His Three Friends (Job 4–27)

After Job's curse upon the day of his birth comes a lively dialogue between Job and his three friends. This dialogue is arranged in three larger cycles, each cycle following the same parallel pattern:[3]

---

1. Throughout his excellent commentary, N. C. Habel attempts to analyze the surface structure of each literary unit of the book (*The Book of Job* [Old Testament Library; Philadelphia: Westminster, 1985]). Arguing for the integrity and unity of the book, Habel observes (p. 46) that the author of Job often uses the palistrophe (chiasmus) in his arrangement of the larger literary units, with a key line or passage frequently located at the pivot point. The most typical palistrophe in Job is the a-b-c-d-c'-b'-a' pattern (e.g., 14:13–17; 19:6–12; 19:21–29; 23:2–17; 25:2–14; 33:1–33; 34:2–37). A number of other patterns are also occasionally found, including a-b-c-b'-a' (e.g., 16:9–14) and a-b-c-d-a'-b'-c'-d' (e.g., 15:2–16). Unfortunately Habel does not attempt to analyze the macrostructure of the book.

2. See Otto Eissfeldt, *The Old Testament: An Introduction*, trans. Peter R. Ackroyd (New York: Harper & Row, 1965), 456; and C. Westermann, *The Structure of the Book of Job* (Philadelphia: Fortress, 1981), 18–19. Francis I. Andersen, *Job* (Tyndale Bible Commentary; Downers Grove, Ill.: Inter-Varsity, 1976), 22, seems to favor this view, pointing out an interesting result: "By separating off chapter 3 as an opening statement, we leave Eliphaz to commence the debate in chapter 4. Job replies to this, and so it goes on. This implies that the dynamics of the dialogue is a succession of attacks by Job upon the statements of his friends, rather than criticisms of Job's words by each of his friends in turn." Weighing against this is the introduction in 2:11–13 of the three friends who will be participating in the dialogue, which might suggest that the dialogue with the friends begins with 3:1.

3. In the third cycle, the third friend, Zophar, does not have a speech; but 27:13–23 may be his third speech, its introduction having been lost.

17.1 Prologue (Job 1–2)

a **introduction** (sets the stage): Job's righteousness and prosperity (1:1–5)
  b **Satan's first challenge** (1:6–12)
    • begins: "One day the sons of God came . . . and Satan also came with them. Yahweh said to Satan, . . . 'Have you considered my servant Job? There is no one like him.' "
    • Satan accuses Job and proposes suffering; God grants permission, with restrictions
    • ends: <u>and Satan went out from Yahweh's presence</u>
    c **suffering befalls Job**: loss of wealth and family (1:13–19)
      d **Job's first righteous response** (1:20–22)
        • Job's act of <u>self-abasement</u> and declaration of faith in God
        • conclusion: "in all this, Job <u>did not sin</u>"
  b' **Satan's second challenge** (2:1–7a)
    • begins: "One day the sons of God came . . . and Satan also came with them. Yahweh said to Satan, . . . 'Have you considered my servant Job? There is no one like him.' "
    • Satan accuses Job and proposes suffering; God grants permission, with restrictions
    • ends: <u>and Satan went out from God's presence</u>
    c' **more suffering befalls Job**: loss of health (2:7b)
      d' **Job's second righteous response** (2:8–10)
        • Job's act of <u>self-abasement</u> and declaration of faith in God
        • conclusion: "in all this, Job <u>did not sin</u>"

---

a Eliphaz
   • Job's response
b Bildad
   • Job's response
c Zophar
   • Job's response

The dialogue's parallel pattern is partly designed for the enjoyment of the audience, who would perceive the pattern early on and could begin to anticipate each successive speaker. What will Bildad say next, in light of Job's stinging response to Eliphaz? How will Job respond now to Zophar's outlandish accusation? And so on.

Job's speeches are given about twice as much space as those of his friends, perhaps because their speeches serve primarily as foils, expressing repeatedly the same banal view that God always operates according to a principle of exact individual retribution: x amount of suffering is the result of x amount of sin, and therefore Job is suffering so much because he has sinned so much. The audience already knows that this view is incorrect (and of course is reminded over and over again, with each friend's speech, of the danger of applying this misguided theology to anyone who suffers). The friends' wrongheaded speeches provide the audience with the opportunity to hear what is far more important to the author: the responses of a man who, though suffering terribly, is highly esteemed by God and who "speaks rightly" of God. It is Job's speeches that the author wants the audience to hear, for they exemplify how a truly righteous person responds (with qualities such as integrity, honesty about one's feelings,

etc.) to suffering, heartbreak, false accusations, confusion, and apparent abandonment by God himself.

Poem about Wisdom (Job 28)

A poem about wisdom is the book's fourth literary unit. With no introduction, the poem at first seems to be the continuation of Job's (or Bildad's) speech in chapter 27. But the singularity of its theme (wisdom) and its remarkably tranquil mood set the poem apart from its turbulent surroundings. Some commentators consider the poem intrusive.[4] F. I. Andersen is more likely correct in arguing that the poem properly belongs where it is and that it functions as a restful interlude at a transition point in the book:

> Chapter 28 is best explained as a kind of coda between the main dialogue and Job's final word, but not as a part of Job's own thought at this stage. It is a comment by the author, and the speaker is the person telling the story, not one of the characters in the story.[5]

N. C. Habel agrees, suggesting that chapter 28 is an "authorial comment" that differs significantly from the speeches that precede and follow and that it functions to mark a transition in the movement of the book.[6]

---

4. For example, J. Alberto Soggin, *Introduction to the Old Testament: From Its Origins to the Closing of the Alexandrian Canon*, trans. John Bowden (3d ed.; Louisville: Westminster/ John Knox, 1989), 388.
5. Andersen, *Job*, 53.
6. Habel, *Job*, 38–39, 392.

Final Summations for the Defense and Prosecution (Job 29–37)

Following the interlude in chapter 28 we come to a monologue by Job. Job 29:1 introduces this lengthy monologue: "And once again Job took up his speech (*mĕšālô*) and said. . . ." And 31:40b closes it: "The words of Job are ended."[7] Job's speech comprises two parts, which sum up his position:

---

a summary of Job's suffering (29:1–30:31)
b Job's final oath of innocence (31:1–40)

This monologue is followed by the statement, "So these three men gave up trying to answer Job, because he was righteous in his own eyes" (32:1), which is followed, in turn, by the monologue of a fourth friend, Elihu, who now speaks up because "he was angry that the three friends had been unable to refute Job" (32:3). Elihu had not participated in the earlier dialogue because of his youth (32:4). But now that the three friends had failed to refute Job, "his anger was aroused" (32:5). He recasts and reinforces the three friends' case against Job in a final argument aimed to succeed where theirs had failed. He begins by referring to their failure to refute Job (32:6–16) and then proceeds to offer a series of quotations by Job (33:9–11; 34:5–6, 9; 35:2–3), following each quotation with an exposé of the error of Job's words. If Job was not guilty before, he is now because of his wicked words! Elihu's monologue comprises four speeches, each separately introduced (chaps. 32–33; 34; 35; 36–37).

The monologues of Job and Elihu are possibly intended as two parts of a single structural unit, analogous to the collection of speeches of Job and his other friends in chapters 4–27. The two constituent speeches would serve, then, as the final summations for the defense and the prosecution.[8]

---

7. Various scholars (including Eissfeldt, *Old Testament: An Introduction*, 456; Habel, *Job*, 71; and Andersen, *Job*, 22) identify Job's monologue in chaps. 29–31 as a unit separate from the dialogue and from the poem about wisdom in chap. 28.

8. Andersen, *Job*, 40–51, argues that Elihu is an adjudicator, not a protagonist. Habel, *Job*, 36–37, proposes a similar understanding for Elihu: "As part of the narrative design, Elihu presents the case of the earthly arbiter, the answer of orthodoxy given in a trial situation. And as E. Kraeling rightly observes, Elihu's words would provide an appropriate termination of the book if it were not for the intervention of Yahweh. . . . Elihu's speeches are designed to provide an orthodox ending and a plausible resolution of the earthly dispute. That ending, however, is overridden by an answer from Yahweh that lies beyond the canons of orthodoxy. . . . As elsewhere in the narrative plot of the book, the author has introduced an apparent resolution of the conflict which is exposed as such

God's Speeches (Job 38:1–42:6)

Following Job's and Elihu's final speeches, God himself appears and speaks to Job. God's speech is composed of two parts, each introduced by the expression "and Yahweh answered Job" and each closed by a response from Job (the significance of these divine speeches will be considered shortly):

---

a God's first speech (38:1–39:30)
   • Job's response (40:1–5)
b God's second speech (40:6–41:34 [40:6–41:26])
   • Job's response (42:1–6)

Epilogue (Job 42:7–17)

The book closes as it opens, with a narrative. This time the narrative recounts the reversal of Job's misfortunes that occurred in the book's introduction. The epilogue is laid out in a three-part linear scheme:

---

a Yahweh honors Job by having him pray for his three misguided friends (42:7–9)
b Yahweh restores Job's prosperity and family (42:10–15)
c conclusion: happy summary of the rest of Job's long and prosperous life (42:16–17)

Overall Layout of the Book of Job

The Book of Job exhibits a primarily linear arrangement based on chronological order. But it also has a symmetric structure (17.2). The book's symmetry is most obvious in the correspondence of the prologue and epilogue. Alan Cooper notes that the prologue and epilogue are structurally designed so that the elements making up the prologue are matched in chiastic order by the constituent parts of the epilogue (17.3).[9]

Also, the collection of speeches by Job and his older three friends in chapters 4–27 is balanced by the collection of speeches by Job and his younger friend in chapters 29–37. These two cycles of speeches obviously echo one another. In both cycles, Job speaks of his suffering and maintains his innocence, while his friends argue that his suffering is due to his sin. The audience hears both positions once in the opening dialogue, then a second time in the closing summations and final arguments.

---

by subsequent events. Thus the Elihu speech is a deliberate foil and anti-climax which retards the plot and heightens the surprise appearance of Yahweh as a celestial participant."

9. A. Cooper, "Narrative Theory and the Book of Job," *Studies in Religion* 11 (1982) 39–40. The main difference between Cooper's outline and the one presented here is that Cooper sees six elements in each unit, while I see seven, with two elements rather than one involved in the material about Job's three friends.

17.2 The Book of Job

a **prologue: Job's suffering** (1:1–2:13)
- Job's righteousness declared by God
- Job has <u>seven sons and three daughters</u>—all of whom are killed
- Job's <u>flocks</u> are lost: 7,000 <u>sheep</u>, 3,000 <u>camels</u>, 500 <u>yoke of oxen</u>, 500 <u>donkeys</u>
- Job's family members (Job's children, who were <u>brothers and sisters</u>) hold <u>parties</u>; death
- the three friends <u>come to help Job</u>

b **Job's introductory speech**: he wishes his birth had never happened (3:1–26)
- topics: <u>birth</u>, <u>womb</u>, <u>offspring</u>, <u>counting months</u>, <u>day</u>, <u>night</u>, <u>light</u>, <u>darkness</u>, <u>dawn</u>, <u>Leviathan</u>, <u>clouds</u>, <u>freedom</u>, <u>captivity</u>, <u>life</u>, <u>death</u>, <u>awaking</u>, etc.
- there are many tragic "mistakes" in Job's life and in this world: things that should never happen

c **cycle of speeches by Job and his three older friends** (4:1–27:23)
- Job's speeches focus on his terrible suffering and his innocence
- friends' speeches: Job suffers because he has sinned

d **CENTER: poem about wisdom** (28:1–28)
- only God knows why things are the way they are

c′ **cycle of summation speeches by Job and his younger friend** (29:1–37:24)
- Job's speeches focus on his terrible suffering and his innocence
- friends' speeches: Job suffers because he has sinned

b′ **God's closing speech**: birth and all life is under God's good control (38:1–42:6)
- topics: <u>birth</u>, <u>womb</u>, <u>offspring</u>, <u>counting months</u>, <u>day</u>, <u>night</u>, <u>light</u>, <u>darkness</u>, <u>dawn</u>, <u>Leviathan</u>, <u>clouds</u>, <u>freedom</u>, <u>captivity</u>, <u>life</u>, <u>death</u>, <u>awaking</u>, etc.; 60 nouns and verbs, totaling 120 repetitions, are shared with chap. 3
- there are no "mistakes" in this world: everything is under God's good control

a′ **epilogue: Job's suffering reversed** (42:7–17)
- Job's righteousness declared by God
- Job has <u>seven more sons and three more daughters</u>—his new daughters surpassing his first ones in beauty
- Job's <u>flocks</u> are restored: 14,000 <u>sheep</u>, 6,000 <u>camels</u>, 1,000 <u>yoke of oxen</u>, 1,000 <u>donkeys</u>
- Job's family members (his <u>brothers and sisters</u>) hold a <u>party</u>; Job's restoration
- three friends must <u>come to Job for help</u>

17.3 Chiastic matching of the prologue and epilogue of the Book of Job

prologue

a **introduction**: Job lives a righteous life (1:1)

  b **Job's children**: seven sons and three daughters (1:2)

    c **Job's flocks**: 7,000 <u>sheep</u>, 3,000 <u>camels</u>, 500 <u>yoke of oxen</u>, 500 <u>donkeys</u> (1:3)

      d **parties** of Job's family members (they are brothers and sisters) (1:4–5)

        e **Job's afflictions** (1:6–2:10)

          f **three friends** (names listed) come to Job to console him (2:11)

            g **friends are silent** seven days and seven nights (2:12–13)

epilogue

            g′ **friends rebuked** for words; seven bulls and seven rams (42:7–8)

          f′ **three friends** (names listed) come to Job to ask for help (42:9)

        e′ **Job's afflictions** are reversed (42:10)

      d′ **party** of Job's family members (his brothers and sisters) (42:11)

    c′ **Job's flocks**: 14,000 <u>sheep</u>, 6,000 <u>camels</u>, 1,000 <u>yoke of oxen</u>, 1,000 <u>donkeys</u> (42:12)

  b′ **Job's children**: seven sons and three daughters (42:13–15)

a′ **conclusion**: Job dies old and full of days (42:16–17)

The only major problem with the possibility of an overall symmetry is the resultant matchup of the book's second and next-to-last units; that is, Job's introductory curse on the day of his birth in chapter 3 and God's speeches in 38:1–42:6. At first blush these seem to have little in common. Cooper, however, argues that these two units are intended to correspond structurally:

The God speeches set the stage for Job's restoration by forcing him to remove the curse which has hung over the proceedings since chapter 3. Job has placed a curse on his "day," and he has invoked

those who would rouse Leviathan. God summons Job to assume the mantle of divinity, and to see what authority he can exert over the day—or over any other aspect of the cosmos, for that matter (38:12ff.). Job confesses his powerlessness (40:3–5). Then God rouses Leviathan and asks whether Job is prepared to confront him (41:1ff.). Again Job admits his helplessness (42:1–2, 5–6).[10]

Habel likewise sees this connection, noting at least three references in God's speeches to state-

10. Cooper, "Narrative Theory and the Book of Job," 43.

ments made by Job in chapter 3.[11] Closer scrutiny shows that God's speeches are in fact filled with allusions to Job's words in chapter 3, demonstrating that the two units do indeed correspond. Topics shared between God's speeches and Job's words include the following:

1. birth (*yld*): 3:1–12 ‖ 38:21, 28–29; 39:1–4; cf. 38:8
2. offspring and young: 3:12, 16 ‖ 38:32, 41; 39:4, 16, 30, etc.
3. day (*yôm*): 3:1, 3, 4, 8 ‖ 38:12, 21, etc.
4. light (*ʾôr*): 3:9, 16, 20 ‖ 38:15, 19, 24
5. darkness (*ḥōšek*): 3:4, 5, cf. 3:9 ‖ 38:19, cf. 38:2
6. leviathan (*liwyātān*): 3:8 ‖ 41:1–34 [40:25–41:26]
7. doors (*delet*): 3:10 ‖ 38:8, 10; 41:14 [41:6]
8. stars (*kôkāb*): 3:9 ‖ 38:7
9. womb (*reḥem*): 3:11 ‖ 38:8
10. belly (*beṭen*): 3:10 ‖ 38:29; 40:16
11. coming out (*yāṣāʾ*): 3:11 ‖ 38:8, 29, 32; 39:4, 21; 41:20, 21 [41:12, 13]
12. clouds (*ʿānān*): 3:5 ‖ 38:9
13. "eyelids of the dawn" (*ʿapʿappê-šāḥar*): 3:9 ‖ 41:18 [41:10]
14. lying down (*škb*): 3:13 ‖ 38:37; 40:21
15. "counting the months" (*sippēr yĕrāḥîm*): 3:6 ‖ 39:2
16. being free (*ḥāpšî*): 3:19 ‖ 39:5
17. being bound (*ʾsr*, etc.): 3:18 ‖ 39:5
18. being hidden (*ṭmn*): 3:16 ‖ 40:13
19. being hidden (*str*): 3:10, 23 ‖ 40:21
20. awaking (*ʿwr*): 3:8 ‖ 41:10 [41:2]
21. death (*mwt*): 3:11 ‖ 38:17
22. rejoicing (*śyś*): 3:22 ‖ 39:21
23. shouting with joy (*rnn*): 3:7 ‖ 38:7; 39:13
24. turmoil (*rōgez*): 3:17, 26 ‖ 39:24
25. fear (*paḥad*): 3:25 ‖ 39:16, 22; 40:17
26. exhaustion/labor (*yĕgîʿîm*): 3:17 ‖ 39:11, 16
27. perishing (*ʾbd*): 3:3 ‖ 39:26
28. deep darkness (*ṣalmāwet*): 3:5 ‖ 38:17
29. strength (*kōaḥ*): 3:17 ‖ 39:11, 21; 40:16
30. servant (*ʿebed*): 3:19 ‖ 39:9; 41:4 [40:28]
31. not hearing the shout of the driver (*nōgēś*): 3:18 ‖ 39:7
32. blocking (*skk*): 3:23 ‖ 38:8

In all, over sixty nouns and verbs in Job's curse are repeated in Yahweh's speeches. In many instances the repetition is multiple, so that the total number of repetitions reaches over 140 (compared with possibly 30 correspondences in Elihu's [much longer] speech in chaps. 36–37 and about 12 in Eliphaz's speech in chap. 22).

Every verse in Job's curse has at least one verbal echo in God's speech, and most verses have multiple echoes. It would appear that Yahweh is responding almost entirely to Job's initial outcry in chapter 3, virtually ignoring the intervening debate.

At the center of the book stands the poem about wisdom, the significance of which will be considered shortly.[12]

Conclusion

Several observations may be made regarding the interplay of structure and meaning in the Book of Job. The author uses the narrative frame to show the audience how to interpret the intervening speeches. The prologue reveals in advance that the accusations of Job's friends (including Elihu) will be unfounded. Job was not suffering because he had sinned. On the other hand, the epilogue tells the audience, in retrospect, that the foregoing speeches of Job rightly represented God, while the speeches of his friends misrepresented God.

The balancing of the speeches of Job and his three friends with the speeches of Job and his other friend suggests that Elihu is to be understood as another misguided friend (and not God's spokesperson, as some suggest). The implication of the book's layout according to the foregoing analysis is that Elihu is just another wrongheaded friend, whose role is like that of a prosecutor, summing up the case against Job in closing arguments.

The matching of Job's initial speech in chapter 3 and God's speech at the end is most revealing. In his curse, Job wished that the day of his birth had never occurred; that he had never lived; that he had never emerged from the womb; and that he had never seen the light of day but had remained in darkness. His birth, his survival, his present life, were tragic mistakes that he wished had never happened. God's speech addresses Job's tormented protests. God proclaims his omniscient and benevolent authority over all the areas that Job considered "mistakes" in his seemingly ill-advised birth, in-

---

11. Habel, *Job*, 51.

12. This analysis is similar to Cooper's ("Narrative Theory," 40), except that he sees the prologue-epilogue frame bracketing seven rather than five parts: (a) the curse (3:1–26); (b) first dialogue (argumentation); (c) second dialogue (accusation); (d) third dialogue (disorder); (c′) Job's self-vindication (accusation); (b′) Elihu (argumentation); (a′) recantation of the curse (38:1–42:6). Cooper's reconstruction is weakened by its dependence on two questionable assumptions: (1) the third dialogue cycle was purposely made to be in disarray by the author, and (2) the first two dialogues can legitimately be distinguished as "argument" and "accusation" respectively and these correspond to Job's and Elihu's monologues.

cluding day, night, light, darkness, birth, the womb, life, death, Leviathan, etc. God asserts that all these areas, as well as various other aspects of his creation that might be deemed "mistakes" (e.g., destructive hail, storms, lightning [which had destroyed Job's flocks], east wind [which had caused the death of his children], silly ostriches, Behemoth, Leviathan), are part of his almighty, all-knowing, all-wise rule of the universe. He and he alone knows all there is to know about his creation and its function. Accordingly, he alone holds the key to Job's question of why? The message to Job is simple: "Job, I alone know all about everything, from beginning to end, including the seemingly mistaken events of your birth, your life, and your present suffering. And everything is ultimately under my good and wise control. Even in regard to your present suffering, I know all about it; I am in control of it; and I intend only good through it. I do not make mistakes."

In the book's overall symmetry, the poem about wisdom stands at the center. It is a quiet interlude positioned between two cycles of heated debates raging on either side of it. It is apparently the author's own comment on the issue at hand. Cooper suspects that the poem is the climax of the entire book.[13] And Habel likewise argues that "28:28 clearly echoes 1:1 and seems to constitute an inclusio which signals a closure at the midpoint of the scenes in the book as a whole."[14] That the author placed his own statement at the midpoint of the composition is in keeping with his organizational scheme in the smaller units of the book. As Habel notes in his analysis of the microstructural patterns in the book: "A key line or passage is often located at the pivot point of the typical a-b-c-d-c-b-a palistrophe [symmetric] pattern."[15] If chapter 28 is the pivot point of the book, a great deal more importance should be placed on it in analyzing the overall message of Job. The poem's message is, in fact, central to the book, for its theme anticipates the divine speeches. Wisdom—the understanding of why things are the way they are (and why things like Job's suffering happen)—cannot be discovered by humans. God alone possesses this knowledge and understanding. For humans, whose knowledge is profoundly limited, the essence of wisdom is to trust ("fear") God, who alone knows all things. Job and his three friends want to understand why Job is suffering; but only God knows why. And he is worthy of Job's honest and tenacious trust.

13. Ibid., 42.

14. Habel, *Job*, 46.
15. Ibid.

18
Psalms

Israel's Hymns and Prayers to God

The Book of Psalms is perhaps the most beloved and widely read book in the Old Testament. It exhibits a timelessness that spans the millenniums, and its constituent prayers and sacred songs have inspired people throughout history. The book is a collection—or collection of collections—of 150 psalms composed during various periods of Israel's history.[1] While there is no rigorous arrangement scheme governing the order of the psalms, the Psalter contains several collections or groupings of psalms. Most prominent are the five collections or "books" that comprise the Psalter:

---
book 1: Psalms 1–41
book 2: Psalms 42–72
book 3: Psalms 73–89
book 4: Psalms 90–106
book 5: Psalms 107–50

The boundaries of these five books are marked by concluding doxologies. Book 1 concludes with the doxology in 41:13 [41:14]:

"Praise be to Yahweh, the God of Israel, from everlasting to everlasting. Amen and Amen." Books 2, 3, and 4 close with similar doxologies (72:18–20; 89:52 [89:53]; 106:48). And book 5 concludes with the doxological Psalm 150, or perhaps with the entire series of final "Hallelujah Psalms"—Psalms 146–50.

Each of the five books has its own distinctives. Nearly all the psalms of book 1 are attributed to David; and the name Yahweh is used almost exclusively when referring to God. Similarly, most of the psalms of book 2 are ascribed to David or to (or for) the sons of Korah; but in this collection, Elohim is normally used rather than Yahweh. Books 3 and 4 are two smaller collections, each containing only seventeen psalms. Most of the psalms of book 3 are ascribed to (or for) Asaph or the sons of Korah and are primarily prayers of the community. The psalms of book 4 are likewise mostly communal prayers, and all are anonymous. Book 5 comprises a wide variety of psalms, mostly anonymous except for two short collections of Davidic psalms.

In addition to these books, the Psalter contains other groupings. For example, several short collections of psalms are grouped together according to ascribed author or recipient:

---
a David: Psalms 3–41, 51–65, 68–70/71, 108–10, 138–45
b sons of Korah: Psalms 42/43–49, 84–85, 87–88
c Asaph: Psalms 73–83

And some psalms are grouped together according to genre or function:[2]

---
a psalms of ascents: Psalms 120–34
b enthronement psalms: Psalms 93, 96–99
c hallelujah psalms: Psalms 146–50

---

1. Regarding the demarcation of the 150 psalms, it must be remembered that the original Hebrew Psalter probably contained no spatial breaks between psalms and that the enumerated titles (Psalm 1, Psalm 2, etc.) were not introduced until the Middle Ages. How, then, could ancient readers know where one psalm ended and the next began? The boundaries of most of the individual psalms are demarcated by introductory titles or superscriptions or both. For example, the psalm known today as Psalm 3 is introduced by its superscription: "A psalm of David, when he fled from his son Absalom." Only thirty-four psalms lack titles or superscriptions (only seventeen in the Septuagint). And a few of these (e.g., Ps. 10, 33, 43, 71) are not titled because they were apparently continuations of the psalms preceding them. Most of the remaining untitled psalms are delineated by introductory or closing exclamations: (1) "hallelujah!" (Ps. 103–6, 111–13, 115–17, 135, 146–50); (2) "Yahweh reigns!" (Ps. 93, 97, 99); and (3) "sing to Yahweh a new song!" (Ps. 96, 98). A few others are set off by self-contained internal structures (Ps. 119, 136) or by being sandwiched between two well-delineated psalms (Ps. 107, 118, 137). Only a few have uncertain parameters. For a fine discussion of these untitled psalms, see Gerald H. Wilson, *The Editing of the Hebrew Psalter* (Society of Biblical Literature Dissertation Series 76; Chico: Scholars, 1985), 173–228.

2. See Gerald H. Wilson, "Evidence of Editorial Divisions in the Hebrew Psalter," *Vetus Testamentum* 34 (1984) 337–52, for a helpful discussion of groupings in the Psalter. For further discussion of issues relating to the Psalter's canonical arrangement, see Wilson's *Editing of the Hebrew Psalter*.

18.1 Psalm 6

a **appeal for help:** "turn, O Yahweh, save my life!" (6:1–4 [6:2–5])
  - "my bones are <u>terrified</u> (*nibhal*) . . . my soul is <u>terrified</u> (*nibhal*)"
  - "<u>turn back</u> (*šûb*), . . . O Yahweh, save my life!"
  b **CENTER: description of despair** (6:5–7 [6:6–8])
a′ **appeal for help answered:** "Yahweh has heard my supplication!" (6:8–10 [6:9–11])
  - "my enemies are <u>terrified</u> (*nibhal*)"
  - "[my enemies] <u>turn back</u> (*šûb*) and are put to shame!"

The most exciting challenge for structural studies in the Psalter is the analysis of the internal arrangements of individual psalms. The surface structures of some of the psalms seem, at first glance, to be easily identifiable. For example, the acrostic psalms (9–10, 25, 34, 37, 111, 112, 119, 145) are arranged according to the order of the Hebrew alphabet; each successive line begins with the appropriate letter of the alphabet. Psalm 119, the most famous of the acrostic psalms, is an intensively developed acrostic. Its 176 verses are arranged in twenty-two stanzas (corresponding to the twenty-two letters of the Hebrew alphabet) of eight verses each, with all eight verses in each stanza beginning with the appropriate letter of the alphabet.

But readers often find the organization of thought within individual psalms, including these acrostic psalms, difficult to follow. The psalmists seem to jump back and forth within a single psalm, from cries for help to reports of victory back to cries for help—or the like. For example, in Psalm 25, an acrostic psalm, the psalmist asks Yahweh to teach him (25:4–5), then prays for forgiveness (25:6–7), then speaks of Yahweh's teaching the humble (25:8–10), then prays for forgiveness again (25:11), and finally returns to the topic of Yahweh's teaching people (25:12–14). While the reader can be inspired by individual verses in this psalm, the psalmist's flow of thought seems disjointed and confusing. In this chapter I will examine the internal organizations of a sampling of psalms from throughout the Psalter. My purpose will be not only to understand the internal organizations of these psalms but also to consider the relationship between their structures and their meanings.

There is a wide variety of structural patterns attested within the Psalms, including symmetric, parallel, and linear configurations. Among the symmetric schemes, three-part, four-part, five-part, and seven-part arrangements are particularly common. Parallel and linear patterns likewise appear in a variety of configurations. In this chapter, I will analyze selected psalms that exhibit various kinds of symmetric, parallel, and linear arrangement patterns:

1. three-part symmetries: Psalms 6, 15, 57, 72, 79
2. four-part symmetries: Psalms 1, 2, 3, 8, 26, 70, 137, 139
3. five-part symmetries: Psalms 22, 27, 51, 54, 56, 58, 67, 71, 106, 135
4. six-part symmetries: Psalm 115
5. seven-part symmetries: Psalms 7, 11, 18, 25, 30, 86
6. parallel patterns: Psalms 44, 100, 126, 130
7. linear patterns: Psalms 148, 150

Three-Part Symmetries

A number of psalms exhibit a three-part symmetric configuration. The structural matching of the opening and closing units provides the psalmist opportunity to underscore certain points or themes, while the unmatched central unit generally carries the psalm's main emphasis.

Psalm 6

In Psalm 6, a prayer for deliverance from grave illness and enemy opposition, the psalmist's appeal to Yahweh for help in the opening stanza is echoed by the joyous report of Yahweh's help in the closing stanza. In the highlighted central stanza the psalmist describes his deep grief over his dire situation, emphasizing the desperation that gives rise to this prayer (18.1).

Psalm 15

Psalm 15 asks, then answers, the question: Who can stand (i.e., be accepted) before Yahweh? The psalm opens with the question and closes with a summary answer. The body, accented by its central position in the symmetric layout, develops the answer more fully, employing an alternating pattern to underscore both the positive and negative aspects of the kind of behavior that Yahweh finds acceptable (18.2).

Psalm 57

In Psalm 57, which praises God for deliverance from enemies, a refrain is utilized to close the introductory and concluding stanzas. The

18.2 Psalm 15

a **brief introductory question:** "who can stand (i.e., be accepted) in Yahweh's presence?" (15:1)

b **CENTER: lengthy answer** (15:2–5b)

(1) positive: those who do three things (15:2)

(2) negative: those who do not do three things (15:3)

(1') positive: those who do three things (15:4)

(2') negative: those who do not do two things (15:5a–b)

a' **brief concluding answer:** "those who do these things shall never be moved!" (15:5c)

18.3 Psalm 57

a **cry to God for help** (57:1–5 [57:2–6])

- prayer that God will send from <u>heaven</u> . . . his <u>love</u> (ḥesed)
- ends with refrain: "be exalted, O God, above the heavens; let your glory be over all the earth"

b **CENTER: report of deliverance** (57:6 [57:7])

a' **praise to God (for his help)** (57:7–11 [57:8–12])

- "your <u>love</u> (ḥesed) is as high as <u>heaven</u>"
- ends with refrain: "be exalted, O God, above the heavens; let your glory be over all the earth"

18.4 Psalm 72

a **prayer for justice, prosperity, and the king's long life** (72:1–7)

- "may he defend the <u>afflicted</u> (ʿānî)"; "may he save the <u>needy</u> (ʾebyôn)"
- "may the <u>mountains</u> yield prosperity"
- "as long as the <u>sun</u> endures"

b **CENTER: prayer for ascendancy** over all the nations (72:8–11)

a' **prayer for justice, prosperity, and the king's long life** (72:12–17)

- "may he deliver the <u>needy</u> (ʾebyôn) . . . and the <u>afflicted</u> (ʿānî); may he pity . . . the <u>needy</u> (ʾebyôn); and may he save the lives of the <u>needy</u> (ʾebyôn)"
- "may there be abundance of grain . . . on the <u>mountains</u>"
- "may his name endure as long as the <u>sun</u>"

18.5 Psalm 79

a **report of harm done to Judah by the nations** (79:1–4)

- the <u>nations</u> (gôyim) have <u>poured out</u> (špk) their <u>blood</u> (dm); they have given the bodies <u>of your servants</u> (ʿăbādêkā) to the birds
- we have become a <u>taunt</u> (ḥerpâ) <u>to our neighbors</u> (liškēnênû)

b **CENTER: prayer for God's help and forgiveness** (79:5–9)

a' **cry for vengeance for harm done to Judah by the nations** (79:10–13)

- the <u>nations</u> (gôyim); let the <u>outpoured</u> (špk) <u>blood</u> (dm) <u>of your servants</u> (ʿăbādêkā) be known among the <u>nations</u> (gôyim)
- repay sevenfold the <u>taunts</u> (ḥerpâ) <u>of our neighbors</u> (liškēnênû)

---

center, the structure's position of thematic accent, reports God's deliverance (18.3).[3]

Psalm 72

The matched repetition in Psalm 72, a prayer on behalf of the king, serves to emphasize the themes of hope for justice, prosperity, and the king's long life. The highlighted central stanza is a prayer that the king be granted dominion over all the nations (18.4).[4]

Psalm 79

Psalm 79 is a prayer for vengeance upon the nations that destroyed Judah. The introductory

report of the harm done to Judah by the nations is balanced by the matching concluding prayer requesting that God repay the nations for what they did to Judah. The structurally highlighted center is a plea for God's help and forgiveness (18.5).

Four-Part Symmetries

Four-part symmetries are common in the Psalter. This structural scheme allows the psalmist to underscore, by matched repetition in units a and a' and in units b and b', particular themes and points. The positions of emphasis in this configuration are generally the opening and closing units.

Psalm 1

Psalm 1, a wisdom psalm, draws a comparison between the righteous and the wicked, par-

---

3. H. Möller, "Strophenbau der Psalmen." *Zeitschrift für die alttestamentliche Wissenschaft* 50 (1932) 17–19, offers an identical analysis.

4. Verses 18–20 serve as the editorial closing to book 2 of the Psalter and thus are not included in the analysis of Psalm 72.

18.6 Psalm 1

a **righteous keep separate from the wicked** (1:1–2)
  - righteous <u>do not stand</u> in the <u>assembly</u> (reading *baʿǎdat;* cf. order in Syriac) of wicked
  - righteous avoid the "<u>way</u> (*derek*) of the wicked" (cf. BHS)

b **fruitful, secure state of righteous** (1:3)
  - righteous compared to well-watered, permanent, green, fruitful trees

b′ **barren, insecure state of wicked** (1:4)
  - wicked compared to dry, wind-driven, brown, useless chaff

a′ **wicked will be kept separate from the (blessed) righteous on judgment day** (1:5–6)
  - wicked <u>will not stand</u> in the <u>assembly</u> (*baʿǎdat*) of righteous
  - "<u>way</u> (*derek*) of the wicked" will perish, in contrast to the "<u>way</u> (*derek*) of the righteous"

18.7 Psalm 2

a **frightening counsel of mighty kings of the earth** who plot against Yahweh and his anointed (2:1–3)
  - <u>kings</u> (*mlk*) of the <u>earth</u> (*ʾrṣ*)

b **declaration of Yahweh** about his appointment of his king in Zion (2:4–6)

b′ **declaration of Yahweh's king** about his appointment by Yahweh: all the nations of the earth are to be his inheritance! (2:7–9)

a′ **joyful counsel for the now helpless kings of the earth**: serve Yahweh in joy and fear (2:10–12)
  - <u>kings</u> (*mlk*), rulers of the <u>earth</u> (*ʾrṣ*)

ticularly regarding their contrasting fates. The opening section declares that the righteous keep separate from the wicked; while the matching, closing section declares that the wicked will be kept separate from the righteous in the time of judgment. The psalm's second section likens the successful lives of the righteous to well-watered, fruitful trees; while the psalm's next-to-last section compares the futile lives of the wicked to dry, useless chaff. The structure serves to draw out the contrast between the blessed state of the righteous and hapless state of the wicked (18.6).[5]

Psalm 2

While Psalm 2 exhibits a number of interpretive difficulties, it is clear that the poem depicts a reversal of fortunes between the pagan kings and Israel's king. The psalm is structured in a four-part symmetry that emphasizes the striking reversal of fortunes described in the psalm. The psalm's opening stanza features the frightening scene of (apparently powerful) pagan rulers plotting against Yahweh and his anointed; while in the closing stanza the tables are turned: now the pagan kings, apparently defeated and helpless, are exhorted to serve Yahweh with fear, lest he be angry. The two central stanzas recount, first in Yahweh's words and then in the words of Israel's king, how Yahweh foiled the intentions of the pagan kings by appointing his own king in

Zion and by giving to him all the nations of the earth as an inheritance (18.7).[6]

Psalm 3

In Psalm 3, a prayer for help in the face of great danger from enemies, the psalmist's description of his plight in the opening unit is balanced by his appeal for help from his plight in the closing unit. The intervening two units, which declare the psalmist's confidence in Yahweh, provide the bridge between his description of his plight and his appeal to Yahweh for help (18.8).[7]

Psalm 8

The writer of Psalm 8 expresses his wonder that Yahweh designed such a marvelous creation and honored humble humankind by appointing them to rule over all his work. The psalm is framed by an inclusio that serves to emphasize the psalmist's admiration of Yahweh (18.9).[8]

Psalm 26

Psalm 26 appeals to Yahweh for vindication. Its structure underscores the psalmist's integrity

---

5. See similar analyses in Robert L. Alden, "Chiastic Psalms: A Study in the Mechanics of Semitic Poetry in Psalms 1–50," *Journal of the Evangelical Theological Society* 17 (1974) 14; and Nils W. Lund, "Chiasmus in the Psalms," *American Journal of Semitic Languages and Literature* 49 (1932–33) 294. Lund labels 1:3d and 1:4a as two separate, matching central units.

6. See H. Möller, *Strophenbau der Psalmen* (Ph.D. diss., 1931), 40–41, for an identical analysis. Alden, "Chiastic Psalms," 14, breaks the psalm into the same a-b-b′-a′ units, but further divides each unit.

7. Lund, "Chiasmus in the Psalms," 298–99, offers an almost identical analysis (the only difference is that he identifies the third and fourth units as 3:5–7a and 3:7b–8a). Cf. N. H. Ridderbos, *Die Psalmen: Stilistische Verfahren und Aufbau, mit besonderer Berücksichtigung von Ps 1–41* (Beiheft zur Zeitschrift für die alttestamentliche Wissenschaft 117; Berlin: de Gruyter, 1972), 37, 60–61.

8. On the use of inclusions, see Victor M. Wilson, *Divine Symmetries: The Art of Biblical Rhetoric* (New York: University Press of America, 1997), 38–39.

18.8 Psalm 3

a **enemies have arisen!** (3:1–2 [3:2–3])
- many have <u>arisen</u> (*qûm*) against me
- many say, "There is not <u>salvation</u> (*yĕšûʿâ*) for him in God"

b **statement of trust**: Yahweh is a surrounding shield (3:3–4 [3:4–5])

b′ **statement of trust and confidence**: I am not afraid of surrounding foes (3:5–6 [3:6–7])

a′ **O Yahweh, arise!** (3:7–8 [3:8–9])
- <u>arise</u>! (*qûm*), O Yahweh!
- "<u>save</u> (*yšʿ*) me, O my God! . . . <u>salvation</u> (*yĕšûʿâ*) belongs to Yahweh"

18.9 Psalm 8

a **refrain**: "O Yahweh, our Lord, how majestic is your name in all the earth!" (8:1a [8:2a])

b **question**: in light of Yahweh's <u>glory</u> (*hôd*) in his creation of the heavens and in the <u>works</u> (*maʿăśê*) <u>of your fingers</u>, of what value is humankind to Yahweh? (8:1b–4 [8:2b–5])

b′ **answer**: humankind is valuable because Yahweh has given them <u>glory</u> (*kābôd*) and has put them in charge of "the <u>works</u> (*maʿăśê*) <u>of your hands</u> (8:5–8 [8:6–9])

a′ **refrain**: "O Yahweh, our Lord, how majestic is your name in all the earth!" (8:9 [8:10])

18.10 Psalm 26

a **introductory declaration of (past) integrity** (26:1–3)
- <u>I have walked in my integrity</u> (*ʾănî bĕtummî hālaktî*)

b **description of innocence** (26:4–7)
- "<u>I hate</u> the company of evildoers"
- "I wash my <u>hands</u> in innocence"

b′ **description of innocence**, contrasted with guilt of the sinners (26:8–10)
- "Yahweh, I <u>love</u> the house in which you dwell"
- "sinners . . . in their <u>hands</u> are wicked schemes; their right <u>hands</u> are full of bribes"

a′ **concluding declaration of (future) integrity** (26:11–12)
- <u>I will walk in my integrity</u> (*ʾănî bĕtummî ʾēlēk*)

18.11 Psalm 70

a **opening appeal to God for help**: "deliver me, O God; <u>hasten</u> (*ḥûšâ*) to <u>help</u> (*ʿzr*) me" (70:1 [70:2])

b **ill wishes for enemies** (70:2–3 [70:3–4])

b′ **good wishes for those who seek God** (70:4 [70:5])

a′ **closing appeal to God for help**: "<u>hasten</u> (*ḥûšâ*), O God; you are my <u>help</u> (*ʿzr*)" (70:5 [70:6])

---

and innocence by means of matched repetition (18.10).

Psalm 70

In Psalm 70, a short prayer for help, the opening and closing verses present matching appeals to God for help, underscoring the urgency of the appeal. The two central units detail the psalmist's specific requests, presenting two sides of the same coin: the first expresses ill wishes toward the psalmist's enemies; the second, good wishes for those who seek God (18.11).[9]

Psalm 137

Psalm 137 laments the fall of Jerusalem. Writing in exile, the psalmist prays for vengeance against the Babylonians and Edomites, who brought suffering upon Jerusalem. The chiastic structure is used to connect the present sorrow of the Jewish exiles with the wished-for sorrow of Babylon and to link the psalmist's vow to remember Jerusalem with the prayer that Yahweh would remember the evil the Edomites did against Jerusalem (18.12).[10]

Psalm 139

In light of Yahweh's omniscience and omnipresence, Psalm 139 requests that Yahweh search the psalmist's heart to see that he is indeed innocent of the malicious accusations leveled against him. The psalm's layout functions to highlight the theme of Yahweh's omniscience and to emphasize the psalmist's plea for exoneration (18.13).

---

9. Robert L. Alden, "Chiastic Psalms (II): A Study in the Mechanics of Semitic Poetry in Psalms 51–100," *Journal of the Evangelical Theological Society* 19 (1976) 196, offers an identical analysis of Psalm 70.

10. Robert L. Alden, "Chiastic Psalms (III): A Study in the Mechanics of Semitic Poetry in Psalms 101–150," *Journal of the Evangelical Theological Society* 21 (1978) 208, analyzes Psalm 137 as a six-part chiasmus: (a) 1a, (b) 1b–2, (c) 3, (c′) 4, (b′) 5–7, (a′) 8–9.

18.12 Psalm 137

a **present sorrow of exiled Jews in <u>Babylon</u>** (137:1–4)
- wretchedness of Jewish captives in Babylon; they weep and cannot sing for their captors

b **vow to <u>remember Jerusalem</u>** (137:5–6)
- <u>may I exalt</u> Jerusalem <u>above</u> my highest joy!

b′ **may Yahweh <u>remember</u> the evil Edom did against <u>Jerusalem</u>** (137:7)
- they said, "<u>Tear it down</u>! <u>Tear it down</u> to its foundations!"

a′ **future blessedness of those who bring evil upon <u>Babylon</u>** (137:8–9)
- blessedness of those who pay back Babylon for what it did to the Jews

18.13 Psalm 139

a **Yahweh, you have searched and known all about me** (139:1–6)
- "you have <u>searched</u> (*ḥqr*) me and <u>known</u> (*ydʿ*) me; you <u>know</u> (*ydʿ*) when I sit and when I rise . . . ; you discern all <u>my ways</u> (*drk*) . . . ; you <u>know</u> (*ydʿ*) my every word"

b **Yahweh's omnipresence: you fully know wherever I go—you know about all my activity** (139:7–12)

b′ **Yahweh's omniscience: you fully know my innermost being—you know all about every part of me, inside and out** (139:13–18)

a′ **Yahweh, search and know me!** (139:19–24)
- "<u>search</u> (*ḥqr*) me and <u>know</u> (*ydʿ*) my heart! test me and <u>know</u> (*ydʿ*) my thoughts! see if there is any wicked <u>way</u> (*drk*) in me, and lead me in the <u>way</u> (*drk*) everlasting."

18.14 Psalm 22

a **introductory complaint: God does not hear my cries for help!** (22:1–8 [22:2–9])

b **appeal for help** (22:9–11 [22:10–12])
- "<u>do not be far</u> (*ʾal-tirḥaq*) from me . . . for there is none to <u>help</u> (*ʿzr*)!"

c **CENTER: description of dire situation** (22:12–18 [22:13–19])

b′ **appeal for help** (22:19–21 [22:20–22])
- "<u>do not be far</u> (*ʾal-tirḥaq*) from me . . . hasten to <u>help</u> (*ʿzr*)!"

a′ **concluding praise: God has heard my cry for help!** (22:22–31 [22:23–32])

Five-Part Symmetries

Like the three-part chiasmus, the five-part symmetric configuration allows the psalmist to emphasize particular ideas and themes through matched repetition and to highlight the main point by placing it in the central position of the symmetry. This configuration appears to be the most popular of all arrangement schemes in the Psalter.

Psalm 22

Psalm 22 is a prayer for deliverance in the face of serious illness and ruthless enemies. The psalm's symmetric scheme is utilized by the psalmist to emphasize by repetition his appeal to God for help and to draw out the contrast between his initial plight and his final deliverance. The description of the psalmist's desperate situation is accentuated by its placement at the center (18.14).[11]

Psalm 27

In Psalm 27, a prayer for deliverance, the psalmist's cry for help stands in the position of emphasis at the center of the chiastic arrangement (18.15).[12]

Psalm 51

A penitential psalm, Psalm 51 is structured in a five-part chiasmus plus an addendum. The psalm's structure places emphasis on the seven-verse central plea for forgiveness, at the center of which stands the structurally highlighted central plea: "Hide your face from my sins, and blot out all my iniquities." The grounds for hope of divine forgiveness are emphasized by repetition in matching units at the psalm's beginning and end (18.16).

Psalm 54

A prayer for help against enemies, Psalm 54 opens with an introductory plea for deliverance and closes with a matching report of deliverance. The description of the threat of enemy aggression is balanced by the prayer that God will destroy the enemies. The psalm's structurally highlighted center presents the psalmist's statement of trust in God (18.17).

---

11. Möller, *Strophenbau der Psalmen*, 30–36, sees this psalm as a seven-part chiasmus (Hebrew verse numbers): (a) 2–6, (b) 7–11, (c) 12–14, (d) 15–19, (c′) 20–22, (b′) 23–27, (a′) 28–32.

12. Alden, "Chiastic Psalms," 20, analyzes this psalm as a twelve-part symmetry. Wilson, *Divine Symmetries*, 52, also considers this psalm to be chiastically arranged.

18.15 Psalm 27

a **introductory declaration of trust and lack of fear** (27:1–3)
  - "my _heart_ (_lb_) shall not fear"; "I trust [Yahweh]!"
  - "may _my adversaries_ (_ṣāray_) stumble"
b **I seek to live in Yahweh's house; may he hide me!** (27:4–6)
  - "I will _seek_ (_ʾăbaqqēš_) . . . to live in Yahweh's house"
  - "may he _hide_ (_str_) me in the _hiding place_ (_str_) of his tent"
c **CENTER: cry for help** (27:7)
b′ **I seek Yahweh's face; may he not hide from me!** (27:8–10)
  - "come, _seek_ (_baqqěšû_) his face; your face, O Yahweh, do I _seek_ (_ʾăbaqqēš_)"
  - "do not _hide_ (_str_) your face from me"
a′ **concluding exhortation to trust and not fear** (27:11–14)
  - "let your _heart_ (_lb_) take courage; wait upon Yahweh!"
  - "do not abandon me to the desire of _my adversaries_ (_ṣāray_)"

18.16 Psalm 51

a **grounds for requesting forgiveness**: God's mercy and love (51:1–2 [51:3–4])
b **confession of transgressions and sins** (51:3–5 [51:5–7])
c **CENTER: plea for forgiveness and restoration** (51:6–12 [51:8–14])
  - center of center: "hide your face from my sins, and blot out all my iniquities!"
b′ **vow to confess Yahweh's ways to transgressors and sinners** and to praise God (51:13–15 [51:15–17])
a′ **grounds for forgiveness**: not sacrifices but a broken spirit (51:16–17 [51:18–19])
addendum: (51:18–19 [51:20–21])—probably added later to correct the potential impression that sacrifices are no longer necessary

18.17 Psalm 54

a **plea to God for help** (54:1–2 [54:3–4])
  - "_save me_, O God, by _your name_ (_šimkā_)"
b **report that the enemies seek to kill the psalmist** (54:3 [54:5])
c **CENTER: statement of trust**: "God is my help!" (54:4 [54:6])
b′ **wish that God would kill the psalmist's enemies** (54:5 [54:7])
a′ **report of God's help and vow to praise** (54:6–7 [54:8–9])
  - "I will give thanks to _your name_ (_šimkā_) . . . for he has _delivered me_"

18.18 Psalm 56

a **opening appeal to God for help** (56:1–2 [56:2–3])
b **statement of trust**: "in God, whose word I praise; in God I trust; I am not afraid; what can flesh do to me?" (56:3–4 [56:4–5])
c **CENTER: complaint and appeal for deliverance** (56:5–9a [56:6–10a])
b′ **statement of trust**: "in God, whose word I praise; in God I trust; I am not afraid; what can flesh do to me?" (56:9b–11 [56:10b–12])
a′ **vow to praise God because of his help** (56:12–13 [56:13–14])

Psalm 56

In Psalm 56, a prayer for help against one's enemies, the opening appeal for help is echoed by the closing vow to praise God for his help. Two statements of trust, accented by repetition, are positioned in the second and next-to-last lots, linked by the refrain "in God, whose word I praise." The central unit presents the psalm's central point: the psalmist's complaint and his appeal for help (18.18).

Psalm 58

Psalm 58 calls upon God to judge the wicked. The opening condemnation of the injustice of the wicked leaders ("gods") is matched by the contrastive closing unit, which declares that God judges righteously. The complaint in the second unit that the wicked are like deadly poisonous snakes is echoed in the next-to-last unit by the wish that the wicked become like melting snails. The highlighted central unit presents the psalmist's central prayer that God might break the power of the wicked (18.19).[13]

Psalm 67

The structure of Psalm 67, a hymn of praise, serves to emphasize the prayer, positioned at the center, that all peoples might praise God. The psalmist's wishes that God might bless Is-

---

13. Alden, "Chiastic Psalms (II)," 192, analyzes Psalm 58 as an eight-part chiasmus, with the double center being 58:6a and 58:6b. Lund, "Chiasmus in the Psalms," 309, sees a nine-part chiasmus (eliminating 58:9), with the center at 58:6.

18.19 Psalm 58

a **wicked leaders(?) do not judge righteously** (58:1–2 [58:2–3])
- keywords: judge (*špṭ*), in the earth (*bāʾareṣ*), humankind (*ʾādām*), righteous (*ṣdq*)

b **description of wicked**: they sin from birth; they are like the "burning" (i.e., venom) of serpents (58:3–5 [58:4–6])

c **CENTER: plea to break the power of the wicked** (58:6 [58:7])

b′ **curse upon the wicked**: may they be like an untimely birth; like the snail that dissolves; may they be for "burning" (58:7–9 [58:8–10])

a′ **God judges righteously!** (58:10–11 [58:11–12])
- keywords: judge (*špṭ*), in the earth (*bāʾareṣ*), humankind (*ʾādām*), righteous (*ṣdq*)

18.20 Psalm 67

a **prayer that God will bless us** (67:1–2 [67:2–3])
- "may God bless us (*yĕbārĕkēnû*)"; may all nations know God's power

b **refrain**: "let the peoples praise you, O God; let all the peoples praise you" (67:3 [67:4])

c **CENTER: call to the nations to praise God** (67:4 [67:5])

b′ **refrain**: "let the peoples praise you, O God; let all the peoples praise you" (67:5 [67:6])

a′ **prayer that God will bless us** (67:6–7 [67:7–8])
- "may God bless us (*yĕbārĕkēnû*)"; may all the ends of the earth fear God

---

18.21 Psalm 71

a **plea to God for help** (71:1–4)
- "let me not be put to shame (*bôš*); save me!"

b **statement of trust** (71:5–9)
- "you have been my hope from my youth (*minnĕʿûrāy*)"
- "in you is my praise (*hll*) continually (*tāmîd*)"
- "even to old age (*ziqnâ*) . . . do not forsake me (*ʾal-taʿazbēnî*)"

c **CENTER: prayer for help from the enemies** (71:10–13)

b′ **statement of trust** (71:14–19)
- "you have taught me from my youth (*minnĕʿûrāy*)"
- "in you I will hope continually (*tāmîd*); I will praise (*hll*) you evermore"
- "even to old age (*ziqnâ*) . . . do not forsake me (*ʾal-taʿazbēnî*)"

a′ **vow to praise God for his help** (71:20–24)
- my enemies "have been put to shame (*bôš*); you have redeemed me!"

---

rael and that the nations might praise God are underscored by matched repetition (18.20).[14]

Psalm 71

Psalm 71, a prayer for deliverance structured much like Psalm 56, opens with a plea for help and closes with a matching vow to praise God for the help he has given. The psalmist's trust in God is highlighted by its repetition in the second and next-to-last stanzas; and the structurally emphasized central unit represents the main point of the psalm: the psalmist's plea for help (18.21).[15]

Psalm 106

Psalm 106 requests that God show mercy to his rebellious, exiled people and regather them from the nations. At the accented central position of the psalm stands the confession that Is-

rael has continuously rebelled against God and has received God's just punishment. The psalmist traces Israel's pattern of rebellion, in chronological order from the exodus to the exile, illustrating how Israel repeatedly sinned against God, each time suffering punishment as a consequence. But the psalmist finds hope in two examples in which God showed mercy to his rebellious people: the Red Sea (b) and the current exile (b′). It is apparently in light of these merciful acts that he is moved to petition God to once again show them mercy and regather them from the nations. The psalm's chiastic structure serves to link and emphasize God's past and recent acts of mercy (18.22).[16]

Psalm 135

Extolling Yahweh's mighty power, the psalmist utilizes the structure of Psalm 135 to underscore the contrast between Yahweh and worthless idols. The psalm's opening and closing stanzas are joyous calls to praise; the second

---

14. Both Lund, "Chiasmus in the Psalms," 289, and Möller, *Strophenbau der Psalmen*, 20–22, analyze Psalm 67 this way. Alden, "Chiastic Psalms (II)," 194–95, however, sees it as arranged in a nine-part chiasmus, with the central three units being lines 4a, 4b, and 4c.

15. Alden, "Chiastic Psalms (II)," 197, analyzes the psalm as comprising ten chiastically arranged parts, with the double center being 71:12a and 71:12b.

16. Verse 48 serves as the editorial closing to book 4 of the Psalter and thus is not included in the analysis of Psalm 106.

18.22 Psalm 106

a **opening prayer** (106:1–5)
  - "give thanks! (hôdû) . . . declare his praise (tĕhillâ) . . . remember me when you save (yšʿ) your people"

  b **past example of God's mercy to his rebellious people:** the Red Sea (106:6–12)

  c **CENTER: Israel's history of rebellion and punishment,** with seven examples listed (106:13–43)

    (1) sin of complaining in the wilderness (106:13–15)
      - punishment: wasting disease

    (2) sin of Dathan and Abiram (106:16–18)
      - punishment: swallowed by earth; fire

    (3) sin of making the golden calf at Sinai (106:19–23)
      - punishment: God's determination to destroy the people

    (4) sin at Kadesh-barnea (106:24–27)
      - punishment: people died in the wilderness

    (5) sin at Baal-peor (106:28–31)
      - punishment: plague

    (6) sin at Meribah (106:32–33)
      - punishment: trouble for Moses

    (7) culmination: sin in Canaan (106:34–43)
      - punishment: defeat and suffering

  b′ **recent example of God's mercy to his rebellious people:** the exile (106:44–46)

a′ **closing prayer** (106:47)
  - "save (yšʿ) us . . . that we may give thanks (hôdû) . . . and glory in your praise (tĕhillâ)"

18.23 Psalm 135

a **call to priests and Levites to praise Yahweh** (135:1–4)
  - begins: hallelujah!
  - fourfold exhortation to praise Yahweh!
  - exhortation to those who serve Yahweh, who stand in his temple and in his courts (i.e., the house of Aaron and the Levites), to praise Yahweh
  - repetition of "house (bêt) of Yahweh"

  b **superiority of Yahweh over all gods** (135:5–7)
    - "whatever Yahweh wishes, he does (ʿśh) in heaven and on earth . . . he makes (ʿśh) lightning"

    c **CENTER: Yahweh's power demonstrated in Israel's history** (135:8–14)

  b′ **inferiority of idols** (135:15–18)
    - "the idols are the work (ʿśh) of human hands; . . . those who make (ʿśh) them shall be like them"

a′ **call to priests, Levites, and all Israel to bless Yahweh** (135:19–21)
  - ends: hallelujah!
  - fourfold exhortation to bless Yahweh!
  - exhortation to the house of Aaron and the Levites to bless Yahweh
  - repetition of house (bêt)

---

and next-to-last stanzas contrast Yahweh's power with the uselessness of the idols; and the central stanza, in the position of emphasis, celebrates Yahweh's power as illustrated in Israel's history. The entire psalm is enclosed by the inclusio "hallelujah!" (18.23).[17]

Six-Part Symmetries

I have found only one clear example of a psalm arranged in a six-part chiasmus. This structural scheme, like the four-part chiasmus, offers no central position of emphasis but allows for the reiteration of important points through the repetition in matching units.

Psalm 115

The six-part structure of Psalm 115 draws out the contrast between Yahweh, the God who protects and helps Israel, and the useless idols of the pagan nations (18.24).[18]

Seven-Part Symmetries

Seven-part symmetric schemes, so common elsewhere in the Hebrew Bible, are relatively scarce in the Psalter. There are, however, a few clear examples of this configuration. Like three-part and five-part chiasmuses, seven-part symmetries allow for emphasis through matched

---

17. Alden, "Chiastic Psalms (III)," 207, suggests a four-part chiasmus: (a) 1–4, (b) 5–14, (b′) 15–18, (a′) 19–21.

18. Alden, "Chiastic Psalms (III)," 205, analyzes Psalm 115 similarly (the final three units are identified as vv. 9–14, 15–16, and 17–18).

18.24 Psalm 115

- a **introductory call to praise** (115:1)
  - b **nations' taunt**: where is Israel's God? (115:2–3)
    - • answer: "our God is in the <u>heavens</u>!"
    - c **pagans trust in useless idols that can do nothing** (115:4–8)
      - • the folly of all those who <u>trust</u> (*bṭḥ*) in them
    - c′ **let Israel trust in Yahweh, its help and shield!** (115:9–11)
      - • repeated exhortation to <u>trust</u> (*bṭḥ*) in Yahweh
  - b′ **response to taunt**: Yahweh is creator of <u>heaven</u> and earth; may he bless Israel! (115:12–16)
    - • "the <u>heavens</u> are Yahweh's <u>heavens</u>!"
- a′ **concluding call to praise** (115:17–18)

18.25 Psalm 7

- a **opening plea** (7:1–2 [7:2–3])
  - b **innocence of psalmist** (7:3–5 [7:4–6])
    - • I am innocent! if I have wronged others, may I be punished!
    - c **request that Yahweh, the divine judge, arise in anger and render judgment** (7:6–8a [7:7–9a])
      - • theme: God's judgment (*mšpṭ*)
      - d **CENTER: plea for justice** (judge me in my righteousness! punish the wicked and reward the righteous!) and statement of trust (7:8b–10 [7:9b–11])
    - c′ **declaration that Yahweh, the righteous judge, will punish in anger the wicked** (7:11–13 [7:12–14])
      - • theme: God a righteous <u>judge</u> (*špṭ*)
  - b′ **guilt of psalmist's enemies** (7:14–16 [7:15–17])
    - • the enemies are guilty! may their wrongdoing be returned on their own heads!
- a′ **closing praise** (7:17 [7:18])

18.26 Psalm 11

- a **opening statement about seeking refuge with Yahweh** (11:1)
  - b **the <u>wicked</u> (*rĕšāʿîm*) fire arrows upon the upright** (11:2)
    - c **question**: what can the <u>righteous</u> (*ṣaddîq*) do in the face of this destruction? (11:3)
      - d **CENTER: statement of confidence**: Yahweh reigns in heaven and sees what everyone does (11:4)
    - c′ **answer**: Yahweh will judge between the <u>righteous</u> (*ṣaddîq*) and the wicked, and he hates the one who loves violence (11:5)
  - b′ **Yahweh will rain coals of fire upon the <u>wicked</u> (*rĕšāʿîm*)** (11:6)
- a′ **closing statement about finding security in Yahweh's presence**: the righteous behold Yahweh's face (11:7)

repetition and through the highlighted central position.

Psalm 7

The symmetric structure of Psalm 7 underscores the contrast between the psalmist's innocence and his enemies' guilt and highlights Yahweh's role as righteous judge. The psalm's center is the thematic center of the psalm: the psalmist's appeal to Yahweh to vindicate him and condemn his wicked enemies (18.25).[19]

Psalm 11

Psalm 11 expresses the belief that Yahweh, in whom the psalmist trusts, is a just, almighty, and all-knowing God who sees everyone's behavior and will punish the wicked and reward the righteous. The theme of God's all-knowing justice is emphasized by its placement in the central position of the psalm's symmetric lay-

out. The depiction of the present evil behavior of the wicked, who aggressively persecute the upright, is set in matched contrast to the description of the future reversal of their fortunes, when Yahweh will aggressively punish them (18.26).[20]

Psalm 18

Psalm 18 celebrates Yahweh's dramatic rescue of the psalmist from his enemies. The opening and closing stanzas of praise echo one another, emphasizing the psalmist's joyous celebration of Yahweh's deliverance. The majestic depiction of Yahweh's spectacular rescue of the psalmist from his enemies is matched by the equally dramatic depiction of the psalmist's spectacular defeat of his enemies with Yahweh's help—which serves to underscore the psalmist's attribution of his deliverance and victory to Yahweh. The

19. Alden, "Chiastic Psalms," 15, analyzes the psalm similarly, but with eight parts: (a) 1–2, (b) 3–7, (c) 8, (d) 9a, (d′) 9b, (c′) 10–11, (b′) 12–16, (a′) 17.

20. Alden, "Chiastic Psalms," 16, offers a similar analysis, with the main difference being his breaking the central unit into two parts (11:4a and 11:4b). Wilson, *Divine Symmetries*, 52, also identifies this psalm as chiastically arranged.

18.27 Psalm 18

a **opening praise** (18:1–3 [18:2–4])
- Yahweh is <u>my rock</u> (*ṣûrî*) and the horn of <u>my salvation</u> (*yišʿî*)
- Yahweh is <u>my deliverer</u> (*mĕpalṭî*), who has rescued me <u>from my enemies</u> (*min-ʾōyĕbay*)

b **Yahweh's spectacular rescue of the psalmist:** majestic, dramatic imagery of Yahweh's rescue of psalmist from his enemies (18:4–19 [18:5–20])
- "I <u>cried</u> (*šiwwaʿ*) to God, and he heard my voice . . . ; my cry reached his ears"
- "he <u>delivered me</u>"; "Yahweh was my <u>support</u>"
- "he brought me out into a <u>broad place</u> (*rḥb*)"
- "he delivered me from <u>my enemy</u> (*ʾōyĕbî*), from <u>those who hated me</u> (*miśśōnĕʾay*)"
- "he sent out his arrows and scattered them; he flashed lightning and routed them"

  c **Yahweh's help came because the psalmist was blameless** (18:20–24 [18:21–25])
- speaking of Yahweh in <u>third-person</u>
- "I have kept the <u>ways</u> (*darkê*) of Yahweh . . . I have been <u>blameless</u> (*tāmîm*)"

    d **CENTER: Yahweh exalts the humble but brings low the proud!** (18:25–29 [18:26–30])
- speaking of Yahweh in <u>second-person</u>

  c′ **Yahweh is blameless, helping those who appeal to him** (18:30–31 [18:31–32])
- speaking of Yahweh in <u>third-person</u>
- "this God—his <u>way</u> (*darkô*) is <u>blameless</u> (*tāmîm*)"

b′ **psalmist's spectacular defeat of his enemies with Yahweh's help:** majestic, dramatic imagery of psalmist's defeat of his enemies (18:32–45 [18:33–46])
- "they <u>cried</u> (*šiwwaʿ*) . . . to Yahweh, but he did not answer them"
- "you <u>delivered me</u> . . . he <u>delivered me</u>"; "your right hand <u>supported</u> me"
- "you gave me a <u>broad place</u> (*rḥb*) for my steps"
- "you turned back <u>my enemies</u> (*ʾōyĕbay*); I destroyed <u>those who hated me</u> (*mĕśanʾay*)" (cf. BHS)
- "I pursued my enemies and overtook them; I did not turn back until they were consumed; I struck them down, so that they were not able to rise; they fell under my feet."

a′ **closing praise** (18:46–50 [18:47–51])
- Yahweh is <u>my rock</u> (*ṣûrî*) and the God of <u>my salvation</u> (*yišʿî*)
- Yahweh is <u>my deliverer</u> (*mĕpalṭî*), who has rescued me <u>from my enemies</u> (*mēʾōyĕbay*)

---

central stanza, which lauds Yahweh's praiseworthy character as champion of the humble and enemy of the wicked, serves as both structural and thematic focal points of this psalm (18.27).[21]

Psalm 25

The primary structure of Psalm 25, a prayer for forgiveness and help, is its acrostic order. In addition, the poem exhibits a secondary seven-part symmetric configuration that features matched sections on forgiveness (c and c′), divine instruction (b and b′), and cries for help (a and a′). These matched repetitions underscore the psalmist's need for divine forgiveness, guidance, and aid. The structurally highlighted central unit declares Yahweh to be a gracious, loving, and forgiving teacher and guide (18.28).[22]

Psalm 30

The structure of Psalm 30 centers on the expression of confidence in Yahweh. The prayer's symmetric configuration serves to underscore the danger of the psalmist's impending death (with repeated references to "the pit") and his appeal to Yahweh for help (18.29).[23]

Psalm 86

Psalm 86 is a prayer for God's help in the face of trouble and dangerous enemies. Its chiastic configuration accents the themes of God's love, the psalmist's need for God's help, and the praiseworthiness of God. The structurally highlighted central unit is a prayer for guidance and help (18.30).[24]

Parallel Structures

There are several clear examples of psalms exhibiting parallel arrangement schemes. A parallel arrangement may be employed to establish

---

21. Möller, *Strophenbau der Psalmen*, 22–29, also analyzes this psalm as chiastic, but with eleven parts (Hebrew verse numbers): (a) 2–3, (b) 4–6, (c) 7–16, (d) 17–21, (e) 22–25, (middle) 26–27, (e′) 28–31, (d′) 32–36, (c′) 37–46, (b′) 47–49, (a′) 50–51.

22. A symmetric configuration of this psalm is noticed by Alden, "Chiastic Psalms," 18–19 (who identifies twenty-two parts) and Möller, "Strophenbau der Psalmen," 252–56 (who analyzes the psalm as comprising eight chiastically arranged parts). Wilson, *Divine Symmetries*, 52, also identifies this psalm as chiastically arranged.

23. Alden, "Chiastic Psalms," 22, sees here a chiasmus of nine parts, with center being 30:6.

24. Pierre Auffret, "Essai sur la Structure Littéraire du Psaume lxxxvi," *Vetus Testamentum* 29 (1979) 385–402, analyzes Psalm 86 as a nine-part chiasmus, identifying the psalm's three main divisions as verses 1–7, 8–13, and 14–17.

18.28 Psalm 25

a   **introductory cry for help** (25:1–3)
- "do not let me be put to shame (*ʾal-ʾēbôšâ*)"
- "do not let those who wait for you (*qwh*) be put to shame"
- "do not let my enemies (*ʾōyĕbay*) triumph over me"

  b   **Yahweh—teach me your ways!** (25:4–5)
- "show me your ways (*drk*), O Yahweh"

    c   **plea for forgiveness** (25:6–7)
- "do not remember . . . my transgressions"
- for the sake of your goodness, O Yahweh (*lĕmaʿan ṭûbĕkā yhwh*)

      d   **CENTER: Yahweh's good and gracious character** (25:8–10)

    c′   **plea for forgiveness** (25:11)
- "pardon my guilt"
- for the sake of your name, O Yahweh (*lĕmaʿan-šimĕkā yhwh*)

  b′   **Yahweh will teach his followers the way** (25:12–14)
- "he will show them the way (*drk*) they should go"

a′   **concluding cry for help** (25:15–21)
- "do not let me be put to shame (*ʾal-ʾēbôš*)"
- I wait for you (*qwh*)
- "consider how many are my enemies (*ʾōyĕbay*)"

addendum (25:22)

18.29 Psalm 30

a   **promise to praise**: because "you have not let my enemies rejoice (*śmḥ*) over me" (30:1 [30:2])

  b   **report of appeal to God and rescue from the pit** (30:2–3 [30:3–4])
- "I cried to you . . . and you brought up my soul from Sheol . . . from among those gone down (*yrd*) to the pit"

    c   **statement of Yahweh's favor** (*birṣônô*) (30:4–5 [30:5–6])

      d   **CENTER: expression of confidence** (30:6 [30:7])

    c′   **statement of Yahweh's favor** (*birṣônô*) (30:7 [30:8])

  b′   **report of appeal to God and plea to rescue from the pit** (30:8–10 [30:9–11])
- "I cried to you . . . 'What profit is there . . . if I go down (*yrd*) to the pit?' "

a′   **promise to praise**: because Yahweh has "clothed me with joy (*śmḥ*)" (30:11–12 [30:12–13])

18.30 Psalm 86

a   **introductory plea for God to be gracious** (86:1–4)
- be gracious to me (*honnēnî*)
- save (*hôšaʿ*) your servant (*ʿabdĕkā*)

  b   **God's love—when facing times of trouble** (86:5–7)
- "for you, O Lord (*ʾattâ ʾădōnāy*), are good and forgiving and abounding in love (*wĕrab-ḥesed*)"

    c   **praise**: God alone is God and Creator; his works are great (86:8–10)
- O Lord (*ʾădōnāy*), the nations will glorify your name (*wîkabbĕdû lišmekā*)

      d   **CENTER: prayer for guidance and help** (86:11)

    c′   **praise**: God has delivered me! (86:12–13)
- O Lord (*ʾădōnāy*), I will glorify your name (*waʾăkabbĕdâ šimkā*)

  b′   **God's love—when facing ruthless enemies** (86:14–15)
- "and you, O Lord (*ʾattâ ʾădōnāy*), are compassionate and gracious and abounding in love (*wĕrab-ḥesed*)"

a′   **concluding plea for God to be gracious** (86:16–17)
- be gracious to me (*honnēnî*)
- save (*hôšîʿâ*) the son of your maidservant

---

or underscore an important pattern in the psalmist's line of reasoning. The repetitions generated by this pattern may also serve to emphasize certain points. If the structure features an unmatched final unit, that unit presents the psalm's main point.

Psalm 44

A prayer for help, Psalm 44 is arranged in a parallel a-a′-b-b′-c pattern. The structure is utilized to develop the psalmist's logical argument

for why God should respond to this appeal for help. The unmatched (and thus emphasized) final stanza presents the psalm's "bottom line"—the appeal for help (18.31).

Psalm 100

Psalm 100 is a brief but majestic praise of Yahweh. It is arranged in an alternating a-b-a′-b′ pattern that emphasizes by matched repetition both the call to praise Yahweh and his praiseworthiness (18.32).

18.31 Psalm 44

a **our ancestors trusted you, God, for victory, and you granted it** (44:1–3 [44:2–4])
- not by their <u>sword</u> (*ḥrb*); their arm did not <u>save</u> (*yšʿ*) them

a′ **we also have trusted you, God, for victory, and you granted it** (44:4–8 [44:5–9])
- my <u>sword</u> (*ḥrb*) will not <u>save</u> (*yšʿ*) me

b **now you have rejected us:** we are <u>like sheep</u> (*kĕṣōʾn*) for the slaughter (44:9–16 [44:10–17])

b′ **but we have not rejected you:** yet we are <u>like sheep</u> (*kĕṣōʾn*) for the slaughter (44:17–22 [44:18–23])

c **conclusion:** rise up! help us! (44:23–26 [44:24–27])

18.32 Psalm 100

a **call to praise:** "make a joyful noise to Yahweh!" (100:1–2)

b **reason for praise:** "<u>for</u> (*kî*) Yahweh is God; he has made us" (100:3)

a′ **call to praise:** "enter his gates with thanksgiving!" (100:4)

b′ **reason for praise:** "<u>for</u> (*kî*) Yahweh is good" (100:5)

18.33 Psalm 126

a **report of past restoration** (126:1)
- <u>when Yahweh restored the fortunes</u> (*bĕšûb yhwh et-šĕbût*; cf. BHS) of Zion

b **report of past resultant joy:** "our mouth was filled with laughter, our tongues with <u>shouts of joy</u> (*rinnâ*)" (126:2–3)

a′ **prayer for present restoration** (126:4)
- <u>O Yahweh, restore our fortunes</u> (*šûbâ yhwh et-šĕbûtēnû*; cf. BHS)

b′ **prayer for present resultant joy:** "may those who sow in tears reap with <u>shouts of joy</u> (*rinnâ*); may . . . they come home with <u>shouts of joy</u> (*rinnâ*)" (126:5–6)

18.34 Psalm 130

a **appeal to Yahweh:** "I cry to you, Yahweh; Lord, hear . . . my supplications!" (130:1–2)

b **theological statement: Yahweh forgives iniquities:** "if you, Yahweh, should mark <u>iniquities</u> (*ʿăwōnôt*), who could stand? but there is forgiveness with you" (130:3–4)

a′ **appeal to Yahweh:** "I wait for Yahweh; my soul waits. . . . O Israel, hope in Yahweh!" (130:5–7a)

b′ **theological statement: Yahweh redeems from iniquities:** "for with Yahweh is love, and with him is the power to redeem; it is he who can redeem Israel from all its <u>iniquities</u> (*ʿăwōnōtāyw*)" (130:7b–8)

18.35 Psalm 148

a **call to everything in the <u>heavens</u> to praise Yahweh** (148:1–6)
- begins: <u>praise Yahweh from the heavens!</u> followed by a series of <u>heavenly entities</u> that are summoned to praise
- ends: <u>let them praise the name of Yahweh</u>

b **call to everything on <u>earth</u> to praise Yahweh** (148:7–13a)
- begins: <u>praise Yahweh from the earth!</u> followed by a series of <u>earthly entities</u> that are summoned to praise
- ends: <u>let them praise the name of Yahweh</u>

c **may Yahweh be the praise of <u>his people Israel</u>!** (148:13b–14)

Psalm 126

Psalm 126 is a prayer requesting that Yahweh restore the fortunes of the people of Judah, as he did in earlier times. The psalm is arranged in an alternating a-b-a′-b′ pattern (18.33), which is utilized by the psalmist to link his request for present restoration and the renewal of joy (a′ and b′) to Yahweh's past restoration of his people and the renewal of their joy (a and b).

Psalm 130

A prayer for forgiveness, Psalm 130 is arranged in a four-part parallel pattern that highlights both the appeal to Yahweh and the theme of Yahweh's forgiveness of iniquities (18.34).

Linear Structures

Some of the psalms appear to exhibit a simple linear configuration, the simplest and most straightforward of arrangements. The development of thought moves forward step by step, generally culminating in a concluding unit that carries the psalm's main emphasis.

Psalm 148

A celebrative psalm, Psalm 148 calls upon all creation to praise Yahweh. It is arranged in three successive stanzas, laid out in an a-b-c pattern and framed by the inclusio "hallelujah!" The psalmist addresses first the heavens, then

18.36 Psalm 150

a **call to praise Yahweh for his mighty deeds and his greatness** (150:1–2)
- <u>what</u> Yahweh is to be praised for

b **call to praise Yahweh with various musical instruments** (150:3–5)
- <u>how</u> Yahweh is to be praised

c **climactic all-inclusive call to praise:** "let all that breathe praise Yahweh!" (150:6)
- <u>who</u> is to praise Yahweh

the earth, then the people of Israel (in an ever-narrowing focus). The arrangement places emphasis on the final unit (18.35).

Psalm 150

Psalm 150 serves as the grand finale of the Psalter, calling upon everyone to praise Yahweh. Framed by the inclusio "hallelujah!" this majestic psalm is arranged (like Ps. 148) in a three-part linear configuration (18.36) that climaxes in the all-inclusive exclamation standing in the structurally highlighted final position: "Let everything that breathes praise Yahweh!"

Conclusion

Analyzing the structures of individual psalms is a challenging but rewarding effort. The discovery of a psalm's internal organization can help clarify the functions of its constituent parts. Such analysis can account for the apparent disorganization and puzzling repetitions that characterize so many psalms. More important, understanding a psalm's scheme of arrangement can enable the reader to more easily identify the psalm's main themes and points of emphasis.

The preceding survey attests to the diversity of structural schemes found in the Psalter. Such diversity also characterizes the contents of the psalms. In typology the psalms range from hymns of praise and joyful songs of trust to agonized pleas for help and prayers for vengeance. The circumstances of their composition are equally diverse. We find psalms born out of triumph and defeat, safety and mortal danger, obedience and abject moral failure. The emotions expressed in the psalms—often underscored by structure—run the full gamut, from ecstatic joy and contentment to anger, loneliness, fear, and despair. The psalms reflect a God who hears the prayers of individuals in whatever circumstances they find themselves. The psalmists understood God to be sympathetic to the plight of the helpless, a protector of the troubled, a companion to the lonely, and a forgiver of the repentant sinner. He is a person's greatest source of hope and joy. Almighty, all-knowing, and altogether good, he is Israel's glorious and eternal king. And he alone is worthy of Israel's trust and praise.

19
Proverbs

Yahweh—the Source of All Wisdom

The Book of Proverbs is undoubtedly the most practical book in the Bible. The work contains collections of proverbs and discourses about how to live wisely. Its sayings and discussions seek to define wise and foolish behavior, to consider the positive and negative consequences of wise and foolish living, and to explore the relationship between wisdom and Yahweh. Its reflections touch on virtually all areas of life, including marital relationships, business dealings, service to God, speech, inner attitudes, treatment of the poor, work habits, making plans, child rearing, interaction with members of the opposite sex, eating and drinking, finances, advice, treatment of enemies, physical appearance, and so forth.

Like the Psalter, the Book of Proverbs is primarily a collection, or a collection of collections. It comprises a variety of separately composed pieces that have been gathered together and published in a single work. The book is composed of seven parts, six of which are introduced by titles (19.1).[1]

It could be argued that these seven parts are arranged with a modest symmetric touch, like this:[2]

```
a  two-part introduction (1:1–7; 1:8–9:18)
  b  Solomon's proverbs—first collection (10:1–22:16)
    c  words of the wise (22:17–24:34)
  b′ Solomon's proverbs—second collection (25:1–29:27)
a′ two-part conclusion (30:1–33; 31:1–31)
```

It seems more likely, however, that these seven parts are arranged in a more or less linear fashion. The prologue and introduction introduce the series of five collections of proverbs that follow in chapters 10–31, and these collections are arranged in order from longest to shortest—with the minor exception of the "words of the wise" in 22:17–24:34, which is slightly shorter than the second Solomonic collection that follows it in chapters 25–29.

It is noteworthy that the book opens, not with the first collection of proverbs, but with an introduction (1:8–9:18) that expounds the value of wisdom. This organizational decision suggests that the editor of the book felt that his readers need to be convinced of the value of wisdom before they will be interested in utilizing the collection of wise sayings. The introduction, then, serves as a "hook."

Little satisfactory work has been done on the internal structures of these seven parts.[3] Two of the sections are rather straightforward in their arrangements. The "words of Lemuel" are structured in a four-part, linear configuration: three short units dealing with womanizing (31:2–3), drinking (31:4–7), and justice (31:8–9), followed by an acrostically arranged poem about the ideal wife (31:10–31). The "sayings of Agur" comprise a series of short units, mostly organized around lists (e.g., 31:7–9, 11–14, 15–16, 18–19, 21–23, 24–28, 29–31).

On the other hand, no arrangement scheme has been discovered in the two lengthy sections of Solomonic proverbs in 10:1–22:16 and 25:1–

---

1. Presumably the short twelve-verse addendum to the "words of the wise," which also has a title, is not intended as a major literary unit. Also, the prologue of the book (1:1–7) could conceivably be intended as part of the introduction, which would account for the lack of a new title after the prologue. But the prologue does seem to be a clearly defined literary unit, laying out the grand purpose and theme of the entire book.

2. The apparent symmetry is probably fortuitous. Not only do the sayings of Agur and Lemuel have no significant correspondence to chaps. 1–9 (except for the reference to the fear of Yahweh in 31:30; cf. 1:7), but it is also hard to see why 22:17–24:34 would have been selected to serve as the centerpiece of an intentional symmetry.

3. An excellent summary of work in the composition and internal organization of the various parts of the book is found in R. N. Whybray, *The Composition of the Book of Proverbs* (Journal for the Study of the Old Testament Supplement 168; Sheffield: Sheffield Academic Press, 1994). See also R. C. Van Leeuwen, *Context and Meaning in Proverbs 25–27* (Atlanta: Scholars Press, 1988); and the discussions throughout Roland E. Murphy, *Proverbs* (Word Biblical Commentary 22; Nashville: Nelson, 1998).

19.1 The Book of Proverbs

a **prologue (1:1–7)**
  - title (1:1)
b **introduction (1:8–9:18)**
  - begins: "listen, my son" (1:8)
c **first collection of Solomonic proverbs (10:1–22:16)**
  - title (10:1)
d **words of the wise (22:17–24:34)**
  - title (22:17; cf. Septuagint; secondary title in 24:23)
e **second collection of Solomonic proverbs (25:1–29:27)**
  - title (25:1)
f **words of Agur (30:1–33)**
  - title (30:1)
g **words of Lemuel (31:1–31)**
  - title (31:1)

29:27. Most likely there is no significant organizational design in either section (although a few smaller groupings of two or more proverbs can be identified).[4] These two collections may simply be that: collections of proverbs to be pondered individually, without regard for context.

One unit that invites analysis is the introduction in 1:8–9:18, because it represents a sustained, connected discussion. Unfortunately, the literary structure of this discussion is difficult to identify. S. R. Driver says of it: "No definite arrangement can be traced in the subjects treated; nor is the argument logically articulated; the discourse flows on till the topic in hand is exhausted, and then it recommences with another."[5] R. B. Y. Scott attempts to explain what appears to be a disturbed composition by positing ten discourses with three longer and three shorter poetic insertions as well as miscellaneous later disruptive additions.[6] R. N. Whybray also identifies ten units.[7] Ernst Sellin and Georg Fohrer attribute the disorganization to "gradual accretion."[8] Franz Delitzsch sees fifteen definable but disorganized discourses: "The fifteen discourses, in which the Teacher appears twelve times and Wisdom three times, are neither of a symmetrically chiseled form nor of internally fashioned coherence."[9]

At first glance one might think the recurring introductory expression "my son ($b\check{e}n\hat{i}$)" (or variations: "listen, my son[s]"; "and now, my son[s]"; etc.) marks the beginning of each new unit, which would create a total of seventeen units (they occur in 1:8, 10, 15; 2:1; 3:1, 11, 21; 4:1, 10, 20; 5:1, 7; 6:1, 20; 7:1, 24; 8:32). Some of these (2:1; 3:1; 4:1; 5:1; 6:1, 20; 7:1) clearly mark the beginnings of units. But three occurrences (5:7; 7:24; 8:32—the three instances of "and now [$w\check{e}\,catt\hat{a}$], my sons") simply introduce the conclusion of a unit; while five (1:10, 15; 3:11; 4:10, 20) mark a minor transition within a unit. Careful study suggests that there are fourteen units in 1:8–9:18, all of which are self-contained and have a single focus:[10]

---

a deadly invitation of criminals (1:8–19)
b life-giving invitation of wisdom (1:20–33)
c exhortation to seek wisdom (2:1–11)
d deadly folly from which wisdom protects a person (2:12–22)
e value of wise behavior (3:1–20)
f examples of wise behavior (3:21–35)
g value of wisdom (4:1–27)
h warning to avoid adultery (5:1–23)
i examples of foolish behavior (6:1–19)
j warning to avoid adultery (6:20–35)
k the loose woman makes her appeal in the streets (7:1–27)
l Lady Wisdom makes her appeal in the streets (8:1–36)
m Lady Wisdom makes her appeal from her home (9:1–12)
n Lady Folly makes her appeal from her home (9:13–18)

There are several clever structuring schemes governing the interrelationships of these fourteen units. For example, the opening four units

---

4. It is possible that the "sayings of the wise" is structured in three parts (22:17–23:11; 23:12–24:12; 24:13–34) of ten units each, with each part introduced by an admonition to be wise (22:17–21; 23:12; 24:13–14). The structural relationship of these three parts and the structural schemes represented within each part remain uncertain.

5. S. R. Driver, *An Introduction to the Literature of the Old Testament* (9th ed.; Edinburgh: Clark, 1913), 395.

6. R. B. Y. Scott, *Proverbs, Ecclesiastes* (Anchor Bible 18; Garden City: Doubleday, 1965), 16.

7. Whybray, *Composition of the Book of Proverbs*, 12–28.

8. Ernst Sellin and Georg Fohrer, *Introduction to the Old Testament* (Nashville: Abingdon, 1968), 319.

9. Franz Delitzsch, *The Proverbs of Solomon* (repr. Grand Rapids: Eerdmans, 1950), 1.12. See also the discussion in Murphy, *Proverbs*, 8–9.

10. The third unit could conceivably extend to the end of chap. 2 (no new beginning markers occur in the chapter). There is a shift in focus, however, in 2:12, and 2:12–22 is possibly intended to function as a fourth unit, dealing with the representatives of folly from which wisdom will protect the wise son.

19.2 Folly and wisdom in Proverbs 1:8–2:31

a **invitation of sinners:** do not listen to it! (1:8–19)
- their <u>way</u> is evil; they <u>hasten to do evil</u>; their <u>end is death</u>

b exhortation to <u>**hear the call of wisdom**</u> (1:20–33)
- she <u>raises her voice</u> (*tittēn qôlāh*) and <u>calls</u> (*tiqrā*ʾ)
- those who reject wisdom will someday <u>seek</u> her but not <u>find</u> (*māṣāʾ*) her
- the foolish do not choose the <u>fear of Yahweh</u> (*yirʾat yhwh*)

b′ exhortation to <u>**call out to wisdom**</u> (2:1–11)
- <u>call</u> (*tiqrāʾ*) and <u>raise one's voice</u> (*tittēn qôlekā*) to her
- <u>seek</u> wisdom, that you may <u>find</u> (*māṣāʾ*) the knowledge of God
- the wise will understand the <u>fear of Yahweh</u> (*yirʾat yhwh*)

a′ **invitation of sinners:** wisdom will protect you from sinners' enticements (2:12–22)
- their <u>way</u> is evil; they <u>delight to do evil</u>; their <u>end is death</u>

19.3 Folly and wisdom in Proverbs 7:1–9:18

a **the available woman makes her appeal in the streets** (7:1–27)
- invitation to come to her <u>house</u> (*bayit*)
- she is called <u>restless</u> (*hōmîyyâ*)
- tragic end of those who go to her—involving death and <u>Sheol</u>
- her appeal is <u>based on deception</u>

b **Lady Wisdom makes her appeal in the streets** (8:1–36)
- invitation extended to the <u>naive</u> (*petî*) from the <u>heights</u> (*mĕrômîm*) in the <u>city</u> (*qeret*)
- <u>rewards</u>: life, etc.

b′ **Lady Wisdom makes her appeal from her home** (9:1–12)
- invitation extended to the <u>naive</u> (*petî*) from the <u>heights</u> (*mĕrômîm*) in the <u>city</u> (*qeret*)
- <u>rewards</u>: life, etc.

a′ **Lady Folly makes her appeal from her home** (9:13–18)
- invitation to come to her <u>house</u> (*bayit*)
- she is called <u>restless</u> (*hōmîyyâ*)
- tragic end of those who go to her—involving death and <u>Sheol</u>
- her appeal is <u>based on deception</u>

---

form a symmetry that serves to reinforce the author's exhortations to avoid the invitations of folly and to respond to the invitations of wisdom (19.2). These four units also exhibit an a-a′-b-b′ scheme of arrangement, since the first two units feature the competing appeals from folly and wisdom, while the last two units focus on the value of wisdom.

The final four units of chapters 1–9 are also arranged symmetrically (19.3). As with the four introductory units, so here the author opens and closes with the appeals of folly and places the two appeals of wisdom in the center. It is interesting to note that in both of these sections the author lets the audience hear the appeal of folly first and last. Wisdom is found, not in ignorance of the (very real) appeal of folly, but in the realization of its ultimate disappointment and destructiveness.

As in the introductory section, this section could also be analyzed as an a-a′-b-b′ scheme of arrangement, since the first two units feature the loose woman and Lady Wisdom making their appeals in the streets and in the last two units Lady Folly and Lady Wisdom make their invitations to their banquets from their own homes (19.4).

Between these four introductory and four concluding sections are six intervening units,

grouped into two sections of three units each. The first section focuses on wisdom and its benefits, the second section on folly and its negative consequences. Each section is arranged in an a-b-a′ pattern, with the central unit in each devoted to practical advice on various areas of life (19.5).

In addition, these six units are arranged with a symmetric touch. The chiasmus they form is part of larger chiastic scheme that encompasses all fourteen units of Proverbs 1–9 (19.6).

The Book of Proverbs represents a sustained argument for the value of living wisely. Both wise and foolish choices present themselves to individuals in all walks of life and in every activity of life; but the only logical alternative is always wisdom. Foolish choices may provide some satisfaction in the short run, but in the long run they are disappointing and deadly. Wise choices, on the other hand, while sometimes difficult in the short run, are ultimately rewarding and life-giving.

The theme of these two competing choices is highlighted in 1:8–9:18 by the matched invitations of wisdom and folly. The appeal of sinners in 1:8–19 is matched by the appeal of wisdom in

19.4 Folly and wisdom in Proverbs 7:1–9:18

a **the available woman's appeal in the streets**, which leads to <u>death</u> (7:1–27)
- "she is in the street, in the squares, at every corner"
- she makes her appeal to <u>one who is simple, who lacked judgment</u>
- giving in to her costs one his <u>life</u>

a′ **Lady Wisdom's appeal in the streets**, which leads to <u>life</u> (8:1–36)
- "she takes her stand on the heights along the road, beside the city gates, at the entrances"
- she makes her appeal to <u>the one who is simple, who is foolish</u>
- "whoever finds me finds <u>life</u>"

b **Lady Wisdom's <u>rich banquet at her home</u>** (9:1–12)
- her appeal: "let all who are simple come in here!" she says to those who lack judgment.
- she is <u>wealthy</u>: she sends her maids to invite people to her banquet
- <u>her house</u> is a splendid home, with its "seven pillars"
- her <u>banquet</u> is sumptuous: at her prepared table <u>are meat and mixed wine</u>

b′ **Lady Folly's <u>paltry banquet at her home</u>** (9:13–18)
- her appeal: "let all who are simple come in here!" she says to those who lack judgment.
- she is <u>poor</u>: she has no maids, simply sits at her door and invites people in
- <u>her house</u> appears to be just a "dive" (no marks of wealth are mentioned)
- the <u>meal</u> she offers is paltry: no table is mentioned, just <u>bread and water</u>

19.5 Wisdom and folly in Proverbs 3:1–6:35

part 1: wisdom and good consequences (3:1–4:27)

a **exhortations to wise living and its benefits** (3:1–20)*
- begins: <u>my son</u>

b **wisdom's benefits and practical advice** on various areas of life (3:21–35)†
- begins: <u>my son</u>

a′ **exhortations to wise living and its benefits** (4:1–27)
- begins: <u>listen, my sons</u>

part 2: folly and its bad consequences (5:1–6:35)

a **warnings against <u>adultery</u> and its negative consequences** (5:1–23)
- begins: <u>my son</u>

b **folly's negative consequences; practical advice** on various areas of life (6:1–19)
- begins: <u>my son</u>

a′ **warnings against <u>adultery</u> and its negative consequences** (6:20–35)
- begins: <u>my son</u>

*Proverbs 3:1–20 comprises seven parts. Each of the first six is a two-verse segment presenting wise behavior and its good consequences. The seventh segment comprises a concluding statement (3:13) and seven supporting assertions (3:14–20).

†Proverbs 3:21–35 presents practical advice for the wise person to follow, featuring seven "don'ts" (ʾal). The aphorisms here focus mainly on wrong behavior that one should avoid.

1:20–33. The solicitation of Lady Folly (the adulteress) in the streets (7:1–27) is matched by the solicitation of Lady Wisdom in the streets (8:1–36). Lady Wisdom's invitation to her banquet (9:1–12) is matched by Lady Folly's invitation to her meal (9:13–18). There are two, and only two, competing alternatives available to a person: the way of wisdom and the way of folly.

Structural matching also serves to underscore the contrast between the negative consequences of foolish choices and the benefits of wise ones. For example, in chapter 7 Lady Folly, in the form of the adulteress, walks the streets looking for victims to lead off to momentary pleasure—and permanent death. She uses deceptive words to capture her prey, and those captured by her will die (7:21–27). In matching contrast, in chapter 8 Lady Wisdom walks the streets looking for people to rescue from death. She uses words that are honest and

true (8:6–9), providing wonderful things to all who follow her, including life, wealth, favor from Yahweh, and understanding that is more valuable than silver and gold (8:10–11, 18, 35). This contrast is further developed through the two invitations to meals in chapter 9. The home to which Lady Wisdom invites the naive is a home of wealth, with its "seven pillars" (9:1), maids (9:3), and a dining room with a banqueting table (9:2). Lady Folly's house, in contrast, appears to be a cheap house, a shack, like the "dive" of a common prostitute. The meal that Lady Wisdom prepared is a banquet; it includes the slaughtering of an animal for the meat serving, the mixing of wine, the setting of her table, and maids (9:2–5). Lady Folly, by contrast, has not even prepared a meal; she simply sits at the front door of her house and invites passersby to come in, because "stolen water is sweet; bread eaten in secret is deli-

19.6 Proverbs 1–9

a **invitation of folly** (1:8–19)
  - wicked invite others to lie in secret to ambush and steal, swallowing the innocent like Sheol
  - but death awaits those who live as they do

b **invitation of wisdom** (*ḥôkmôt*) (1:20–33)
  - she calls (*tiqrāʾ*) to naive (*petî*) and scoffers (*lēṣ*)

c **invitation to call out for wisdom:** call out (*tiqrāʾ*) and cry aloud (*tittēn qôlekā*) (2:1–9)
  - seek her and you will find the knowledge of God
  - she is more valuable than silver (*kesep*), etc.
  - she is from Yahweh

d **the loose woman** (2:10–22)
  - wisdom will protect you from the available woman who makes smooth her words (*mēʾiššâ zārâ minnokrîyyâ ʾămārêhā heḥĕlîqâ*)
  - "house descends to death" and "her paths to the Rephaim"

e **good consequences of wise living** (3:1–20)
  - including riches, honor, favor, health
  - responses to correction (*tôkaḥat*) and discipline (*mûsār*)

f **practical advice** about right social behavior (3:21–35)
  - seven "don'ts"

g **embrace wisdom** (4:1–27)
  - embrace (*ḥibbēq*) her and she will honor you
  - align (*pillēs*) your path (*maʿgāl*)
  - eyes ahead (*nōkaḥ ʿênayim*)

g′ **don't embrace the adulteress** (5:1–23)
  - embrace (*ḥibbēq*) her and you will be shamed
  - she does not align (*pillēs*) her paths (*maʿgāl*)
  - everything is before his eyes (*nōkaḥ ʿênayim*)

f′ **practical advice** about wrong social behavior (6:1–19)
  - seven evils

e′ **bad consequences of adultery** (6:20–35)
  - including poverty, dishonor, disfavor, disease
  - responses to correction (*tôkaḥat*) and discipline (*mûsār*) (6:20–23 echoes 3:1–3)

d′ **the loose woman** (7:1–27)
  - wisdom will protect you from the available woman who makes smooth her words (*mēʾiššâ zārâ minnokrîyyâ ʾămārêhā heḥĕlîqâ*)
  - "her house is the path to Sheol; it descends to . . . death"

c′ **invitation of wisdom who calls out** (*tiqrāʾ*) and cries aloud (*tittēn qôlāh*) (8:1–36)
  - seek her and you will find her
  - choose her above silver (*kesep*), etc.
  - she is created by Yahweh

b′ **invitation of wisdom** (*ḥôkmôt*) (9:1–12)
  - she calls (*tiqrāʾ*) to naive (*petî*) and scoffers (*lēṣ*) to come to her house

a′ **invitation of Lady Folly** to her house (9:13–18)
  - stolen water is sweet
  - bread eaten in secret is delicious
  - but death and Sheol await the one who goes in to her

cious!" (9:17). Her "meal," then, is nothing but bread and water—and she can only make it sound appealing by describing it as "stolen," to be enjoyed "in secret." The matching draws out the contrast and helps convey the idea that folly, while initially exciting because of its forbiddenness and secrecy, in the final analysis is disappointing and deadly.

What is the relation between wisdom and faith in Yahweh? According to the Book of Proverbs the two are intertwined. On the one hand, those who earnestly seek wisdom will grow in their knowledge of Yahweh (2:5), because all wisdom comes from Yahweh (2:6). Conversely, the first and most important step in one's quest for wisdom is to fear Yahweh—that is, to submit to him and obey him. The book's motto, "the fear of Yahweh is the beginning of wisdom," suggests that the very essence of wisdom is to live in obedience to the Lord.

20

Ecclesiastes

God Alone Holds the Key to Life's Meaning

The Book of Ecclesiastes addresses the issue of life's meaning. Why do I exist? What is the purpose of my life? How can I find meaning and significance to my life? What can I do to make my life worthwhile? The author of Ecclesiastes offers some surprising answers to these questions. And he utilizes structure to reinforce his points.

The difficulty in analyzing the structure of the Book of Ecclesiastes is notorious. Roland E. Murphy expresses the sentiments of many: "No one will ever succeed in giving a satisfactory outline of the contents of the book. Any schematic outline superimposes upon the meditation of Coheleth a framework that he certainly never had in mind."[1] Franz Delitzsch (in agreement with Jerome) was equally skeptical: "All attempts to show, in the whole, not only oneness of spirit, but also a genetic progress, an all-embracing plan, and an organic connection, have hitherto failed, and must fail."[2] A. G. Wright lists twenty-three commentators who despair of finding coherence in the book;[3] and his list could be greatly augmented. Many would agree with S. R. Driver's description of the book's disorganization:

The literary form of Qoheleth is imperfect. Except in c. 1–2, where the author is guided by the course of his (real or imagined) experience, the argument

is seldom systematically developed: the connexion of thought is often difficult to seize; the subject is apt to change with some abruptness; and the Book shows no clearly marked subdivisions . . . evidently it reflects the author's changing moods, and these, for some reason, he has presented side by side without always bringing them into logical connexion with each other.[4]

A few scholars attempt to discover some overarching order in Ecclesiastes, none with much success.[5] The best known effort is that of A. G. Wright, who identified twenty units in the book.[6] But neither his nor H. L. Ginsberg's analysis has been well received.[7] M. A. Eaton tenta-

---

1. R. E. Murphy, "The Pensées of Coheleth," *Catholic Biblical Quarterly* 17 (1958) 184–94.

2. Franz Delitzsch, *Commentary on the Song of Songs and Ecclesiastes* (1891; repr. Grand Rapids: Eerdmans, 1982), 188.

3. A. G. Wright, "The Riddle of the Sphinx: The Structure of the Book of Qoheleth," *Catholic Biblical Quarterly* 30 (1968) 313; his list includes George A. Barton, Kurt Galling, Hans W. Hertzberg, R. B. Y. Scott, and others. For an excellent survey of attempts to identify an overall structure in Ecclesiastes, see R. E. Murphy, *Ecclesiastes* (Word Biblical Commentary 23a; Waco: Word, 1992), xxxii–xxxix, and the discussion in C. L. Seow, *Ecclesiastes* (Anchor Bible 18c; New York: Doubleday, 1997), 43–45. Seow favors the analysis of F. J. Backhaus, *"Denn Zeit und Zufall trifft sie alle": Studien zur Komposition und zum Gottesbild im Buch Qohelet* (Bonner biblische Beiträge 83; Frankfort am Main: Hain, 1993), who argues that the body of Ecclesiastes falls into four parts: 1:3–3:22; 4:1–6:9; 6:10–8:17; 9:1–12:8.

4. S. R. Driver, *An Introduction to the Literature of the Old Testament* (9th ed.; Edinburgh: Clark, 1913), 188.

5. See A. Bea; H. L. Ginsberg, "The Structure and Contents of the Book of Koheleth," in *Wisdom in Israel and in the Ancient Near East*, ed. M. Noth and D. W. Thomas (Vetus Testamentum Supplement 3; Leiden: Brill, 1955), 138–49; Otto Zockler; E. Podechard; Denis Buzy, "La Composition Littéraire du Cantique des Cantiques," *Revue Biblique* 49 (1940) 169–84.

6. Wright, "Riddle of the Sphinx," postulates that the eightfold repetition of "vanity and a chase after wind" in 1:12–6:9 marks eight literary units that present Qoheleth's investigation of life in the first half of the book (1:12–15; 1:16–18; 2:1–11; 2:12–17; 2:18–26; 3:1–4:6; 4:7–16; 4:17–6:9). Qoheleth's twin conclusions are then presented in the second half of the book (6:10–11:6): (1) humans cannot find out what is good for them to do (7:1–8:17), in which each of the four subdivisions (7:1–14; 7:15–24; 7:25–29; 8:1–17) is marked at its end by an allusion to one's inability to find sense in the world; and (2) humans cannot know what will come after them, with six subdivisions (9:1–6; 9:7–10; 9:11–12; 9:13–10:15; 10:16–11:2; 11:3–6), each marked at its end by references to human ignorance. The book is framed by two poems (1:2–11; 11:7–12:8) and the title (1:1) and epilogue (12:9–14). In a subsequent article, Wright argues that his analysis is confirmed by numerical patterns in Ecclesiastes (word and letter counts, etc.); see "The Riddle of the Sphinx Revisited: Numerical Patterns in the Book of Qoheleth," *Catholic Biblical Quarterly* 42 (1980) 38–51. Wright's analysis has not been well received, partly because some of his divisions are unlikely (e.g., the breaks at 1:15; 2:17; 7:24; 8:17). Most scholars, moreover, are not willing to grant his methodology of numerical confirmation.

7. Ginsberg's confidence that he has "no hesitation in declaring that there are exactly four main divisions in the book" (p. 138) is not shared by others, particularly in light of his failure to base his analysis on any objective criteria.

20.1 The Book of Ecclesiastes

   title: author mentioned in third-person (1:1)
a **poem about the brevity and insignificance of life** (1:2–11)
   b **wisdom's failure to discover life's meaning** (1:12–2:26)
      c **poem about time** (3:1–15)
         d **CENTER: fear God!** (3:16–6:12)
      c′ **poem about time revisited** (7:1–14)
   b′ **wisdom's failure revisited** (7:15–10:19)
a′ **poem about life's brevity revisited** (10:20–12:8)
   conclusion: author mentioned in third-person (12:9–14)

20.2 Human life is fleeting (Ecclesiastes 1:2–11)

   introductory declaration: "Utterly transitory and insignificant!" says the teacher. "Fleeting and inconsequential! Everything—a human life and all its accomplishments—is fleeting and insignificant!" (1:2)
a **human insignificance**—in light of the ever-continuing <u>earth</u> (1:3–4)
b **human insignificance**—in light of the ever-continuing cycle of the <u>sun</u> (1:5)
c **human insignificance**—in light of the ever-continuing cycle of the <u>wind</u> (1:6)
d **human insignificance**—in light of the ever-continuing cycle of the <u>streams</u> (1:7)
   e **humans cannot even see or hear all** there is to see and hear in this world (1:8)
   f **humans cannot even find significance** to their brief lives by doing something new (1:9–10)
   g **humans will not even be remembered** by future generations (1:11)

---

tively analyzes the book as comprising nine literary units arranged in three major sections, but he admits that there are problems with this analysis:[8]

---

a pessimism: its problems and its remedy (1:2–2:23; 2:24–3:22)
b life "under the sun" (4:1–5:7; 5:8–6:12; 7:1–8:1; 8:2–9:10; 9:11–10:20)
c the call to decision (11:1–12:8) plus the epilogue (12:9–14)

The greatest challenge in analyzing the book's structure is in identifying the book's constituent parts. Careful study of the book's literary architecture suggests that, apart from its introductory title and conclusion, the work is composed of seven major units, arranged symmetrically, each with its own self-contained internal structure (20.1).

Human Life and Work Are Fleeting and Insignificant in Light of Earth's Permanence (Ecclesiastes 1:2–11)

The author begins the Book of Ecclesiastes with three negative units in which he argues that a person's life is inherently insignificant and that the ways humans desperately strive to achieve lasting significance or meaning for their lives

are futile. It is generally agreed that the book's first unit (following the title in 1:1) is 1:2–11. In this opening unit the author begins his philosophical demolition: a person's fleeting life and transitory accomplishments are insignificant in light of the permanence of the earth, with its ever-continuing cycles of nature. A human—even an entire generation—comes and goes, leaving hardly a trace, while the sun, earth, winds, and rivers continue on, unaffected by a person's brief appearance and disappearance on the face of this planet. The unit is organized linearly, with an introductory declaration (the book's motto) followed by a seven-part poem arranged in a 4+3 pattern (20.2).

Human Inability to Discover Meaning in Life, Even through Wisdom (Ecclesiastes 1:12–2:26)

The book's second unit begins with shifts of person (from third-person to first-person) and genre (from poetry to prose autobiography). This autobiographical account continues through 2:26, at which point the author shifts back to poetry. In this unit the author recounts his own exploration of various ways a person might seek purpose or meaning in life. Although the unit's layout is difficult to analyze, due to numerous interpretive uncertainties, I tentatively suggest that it comprises seven parts, in which the author recounts in succession seven dead ends he encountered as he explored possible keys to life's meaning. These seven parts are possibly arranged with a light symmetric touch (20.3).

---

8. M. A. Eaton, *Ecclesiastes: An Introduction and Commentary* (Downers Grove, Ill.: InterVarsity, 1983), 51–53. Eaton expresses caution, however, sensing at least three weaknesses in his analysis: (1) 5:1–7 does not seem to be closely linked with either what precedes or what follows; (2) 3:16–22 does not seem to lead naturally into the problem of suffering in 4:1–3; and (3) There is only a loose coherence in the units of 7:1–8:1 and 8:2–9:10.

20.3 Human inability to discover meaning in life (Ecclesiastes 1:12–2:26)

a **effort #1—the philosopher: discover the big picture** ("all that is done under heaven") in order to see one's place in it **(1:12–15)**
  - <u>disappointment</u>: it is an impossible task ("what is lacking cannot be counted"); the <u>big picture</u> cannot be discovered; a person's life and work can be seen as nothing more than "chasing wind"

b **effort #2—the student: acquire wisdom and knowledge (1:16–18)**
  - <u>disappointment</u>: this effort is like "chasing wind"—it is endless and fruitless; it only makes a person more painfully aware than ever of his or her abysmal ignorance of the point of life
  - keyword: <u>wisdom</u> (ḥokmâ)

c **effort #3—the party animal: just have fun! (2:1–2)**
  - <u>disappointment</u>: fun and laughter provide no meaning to life either; after it is all over, nothing has been gained
  - keyword: <u>pleasure</u> (śimḥâ)

d **effort #4—the alcoholic: escape the pain with wine (2:3)*
  - <u>disappointment</u>: the nagging question of the meaning of life can not be silenced with wine

c′ **effort #5—the workaholic and the aristocrat: accomplish much and become wealthy, filling your life with pleasures (2:4–11)**
  - <u>disappointment</u>: one's accomplishments and wealth, while enjoyable, fail to provide lasting meaning or significance to life
  - keyword: <u>pleasure</u> (śimḥâ)

b′ **effort #6—the puritan: live wisely (2:12–16)**
  - <u>disappointment</u>: wise living, though of some value, fails to provide life with any lasting meaning or significance; the wise, like the fool, dies and is forgotten
  - keyword: <u>wisdom</u> (ḥokmâ)

a′ **(implied) effort #7—the philanthropist: accomplish and acquire much as a legacy for future generations** (i.e., making a difference in the <u>big picture</u>) **(2:17–23)**
  - <u>disappointment</u>: who knows what the next generation or future generations will do with one's accomplishments or gifts? others in the future may even use one's gifts and legacy for folly or evil

conclusion: one can neither discover nor achieve lasting significance for one's life; nor can one discover life's ultimate meaning; so abandon the futile effort and enjoy the gifts and work that God daily gives you. Live in a way that pleases God; enjoy the happiness that comes from him as you live this life, the ultimate purpose of which you cannot perceive **(2:24–26)**.

*I translate 2:3 something like: "I tried dulling my senses with wine and embracing folly, until I thought, 'What good does this do during a person's fleeting days?' "

Poem about Time and Human Inability to See the "Big Picture" (Ecclesiastes 3:1–15)

Following the conclusion of the second unit in 2:24–26, a new unit commences in 3:1. Abrupt shifts in genre (from prose to poetry) and topic (now focusing on the theme of time) mark the new beginning. This unit is structured in an a-b-a′ scheme, comprising an introduction (3:1), poem (3:2–8), and conclusion (3:9–15). The poem itself is composed of fourteen poetic verses that seem to come in pairs[9]—making a total of seven couplets that appear to be arranged in a simple linear scheme. Each verse, and in fact each half of each verse, is introduced by the word "time" (ʿēt); for example, the first couplet (3:2):

a <u>time</u> to be born, and a <u>time</u> to die
a <u>time</u> to plant, and a <u>time</u> to uproot

In this poem and the conclusion that follows, the author makes the point that humans are able to grasp how particular events and activi-

ties in life (weeping and laughing, tearing and mending, etc.) are appropriate at specific times, yet they are unable to comprehend the larger picture. They innately know there is a "big picture" (God has placed the sense of "eternity" [ʿōlām] in their hearts), but they are unable comprehend it, since it has been withheld from them (3:11).

The conclusion in 3:9–15 is similar to, and reinforces, the conclusion of the second unit: you cannot discover the big picture, so abandon the effort and simply obey ("fear") God, who alone knows the big picture, enjoying the gifts God gives you, including your food and work, trusting that God has his perfect purposes in all that happens "from beginning to end" (3:11, 14).[10]

9. Most of these pairs are obviously intended. The exception is 3:7, where the two poetic verses do not seem to form a pair.

10. It could be argued that 3:9–15 belongs with the next unit, since it shares certain characteristics with the following section; particularly the genre of the first-person report ("I have seen"; "I know"; etc.). On the other hand, the theme of "time" (ʿēt) continues through 3:11 and can also be seen in 3:14–15. Further, the grand conclusion in 3:12–13 echoes the grand conclusion of the previous unit (2:24–26) and would be heard by the audience as another conclusion to a unit.

20.4 Moral perplexities (Ecclesiastes 3:16–6:12)

  a **problem: the world is full of injustice** (3:16–22)
- <u>resolution</u>: in the end, God will judge the wicked and the righteous (and will right all wrongs); this is true, although it appears that humans, like animals, simply die and that is the end of it
- key line: <u>all go to the same place</u> (3:20)

  b **problem: life is full of suffering and deprivation** (4:1–6)
- <u>resolution</u>: be satisfied with what God has given you (6:6)

   c **problem: the world is full of dissatisfied people who give their lives to accumulate wealth** (4:7–16)
- <u>resolution</u>: focus on getting good friends and children instead of wealth; a young person living thus is better off than even a <u>king</u> who is alone

    d **CENTER: fear God!** keep your promises to him (5:1–7 [4:17–5:6])

   c′ **problem: the world is full of dissatisfied people who give their lives to accumulate wealth** (5:8–12 [5:7–11])
- <u>resolution</u>: be satisfied with what you have; whoever loves money never has enough; but "the laborer's sleep is sweet"; mention of the <u>king</u> who accumulates wealth

  b′ **problem: life is full of misfortune and deprivation** (5:13–20 [5:12–19])
- <u>resolution</u>: enjoy what God has given you (5:18–20)

  a′ **problem: life is full of injustice and unfairness** (6:1–12)
- <u>resolution</u>: be satisfied with what you have (6:9)
- key line: <u>all go to the same place</u> (6:6)

This World's Moral Perplexities and How to Understand Them and Enjoy Life Despite Them (Ecclesiastes 3:16–6:12)

The conclusion of the previous unit creates the anticipation of another new literary unit, and that expectation is fulfilled in 3:16, with the introduction of a new section featuring a series of mostly prose discussions. Each successive discussion in this new series, except 5:1–7 [4:17–5:6], is introduced by first-person observations beginning with "I have seen" or variations thereof.

In this unit the author considers various phenomena in life that defy reason and imply that there is no overall divine plan, no "big picture," to believe in, including some cruel realities in this world that seem to make it impossible to truly enjoy the life God gives. The author structures most of the discussions in two parts: (1) disturbing observation and (2) considerations that mitigate against despair (or advice in light of the cruel reality). For example, he begins by pointing out that wickedness and injustice often triumph over justice in this life (3:16). He then expresses a belief that keeps him from despair: God will one day judge the wicked and the righteous (3:17).

Though there are many interpretive difficulties in 3:16–6:12, I tentatively suggest that the section comprises seven parts arranged with a symmetric touch (20.4). The center functions nicely as the unit's centerpiece for two reasons: (1) its main point is to "fear God" (an expected central point), and (2) it is highlighted by its different form from the other six units—it consists entirely of admonitions.[11]

Practical Advice in Response to the Poem about Time in 3:1–15 (Ecclesiastes 7:1–14)

A new section is introduced in 7:1; shifts in genre and theme mark its new beginning. In place of the extended, discursive first-person observations of the last unit, Ecclesiastes 7:1 introduces a series of poetic proverbs that continue through 7:14, where they are concluded with a thought, "a person cannot know anything about the future," similar to the ending of the previous unit (6:12).[12]

The fourteen verses of this unit are tied together by the keyword *ṭôb* ("good" or "better"), which occurs eleven times, including twice in the first verse and twice in the last. In this unit the author offers practical advice about the comparative value of various actions and experiences in life.

This unit appears to intentionally echo the poem about time in 3:1–15. Specific echoes and allusions include references to "death," "birth," "mourning," "laughter," "destroying" (*ʾibbēd*), "good times," "bad times," "what God has done" (*maʿăśēh ʾĕlōhîm*), etc. It seems that in 7:1–14 the author is offering practical advice in response to the poem about time. Yes, there is "a time to be born and a time to die" (3:2); but "the day of death is better than the day of birth" (7:1) and "it is better to go to a house of mourning than to go to a house of feasting; for death is the destiny of every person; the living should take this to heart" (7:2). Yes, there is "a time to weep and a time to 'laugh' (*śḥq*), a time to mourn and a time to dance" (3:4); but "sorrow is better than laughter (*śḥq*)" (7:3), "the heart of the wise is in

---

11. Another hint of symmetry is the position of the section's two similar summaries (3:22; 5:18–20 [5:17–19]) at the end of the first unit and before the beginning of the last unit.

12. Wright, "Riddle of the Sphinx," 325, also identifies 7:1–14 as a separate literary unit.

20.5 Practical advice (Ecclesiastes 7:1–14)

a **thinking about the day of death** is <u>better</u> than thinking of the day of birth (7:1–2)
b **sorrow** is <u>better</u> than laughter (7:3–4)
c **listening to painful things** is <u>better</u> than listening to foolish laughter (7:5–6)
d **the final outcome or result of a matter** is <u>better</u> than its beginning (7:7–8)
e **the "good old days"** are <u>not better</u> than the present (7:9–10)
f **wisdom** is <u>better</u> than folly(?) (7:11–12)
g **conclusion:** enjoy the <u>good</u> times, but remember: both good and bad times are from God (7:13–14)

20.6 Practical advice about wise living in this perplexing world (Ecclesiastes 7:15–10:19)

a **though life is not predictable,** <u>live wisely</u>! (and avoid perfectionism) (7:15–22)
   • collection of proverbs (7:19–22)
b **though perfect wisdom is unattainable,** <u>live wisely</u>! (7:23–8:8)
   • collection of proverbs (8:1–8)
c **though the wicked sometimes prosper,** fear God! it will go better for the righteous (8:9–13)
d **though justice miscarries and life is incomprehensible,** enjoy the life and gifts and work that God gives you! (8:14–17)
e **though life is uncertain and fleeting,** live life to the fullest! (9:1–10)
f **though wisdom does not always bring success,** <u>live wisely</u>! (9:11–10:4)
   • collection of proverbs (9:17–10:4)
g **though fools often succeed,** avoid folly and <u>live wisely</u>! a land ruled wisely is blessed (10:5–19)
   • collection of proverbs (10:8–19)

the house of mourning" (7:4), and "like the crackling of thorns under the pot, so is the laughter ($ś\d{h}q$) of fools" (7:6).

As with the earlier poem about time, this unit comprises fourteen poetic verses that appear to form seven smaller units of two verses apiece. Each features proverbs about what is *ṭôb*—"good" or "better" (20.5). These units, like those in the poem about time, appear to be arranged in a simple linear pattern.

Practical Advice about Wise Living in This Perplexing World (Ecclesiastes 7:15–10:19)

A new unit begins when the author returns to extended autobiographical observations and advice, with frequent first-person references (hearkening back to the book's second unit). In this unit, reminiscent of the fourth unit, the author considers cruel truths in this world that would seem to make it impossible to enjoy the life God gives. As in the fourth unit, most points comprise two parts: (1) the disturbing observation and (2) advice in light of the cruel reality. The unit has numerous ties to 1:12–2:26, where wisdom was the theme word. Here the author makes the point that, despite wisdom's being unable to uncover the key to life's meaning and despite its not always leading to success and riches and power, wisdom is still superior to folly and should be followed.

The internal structure of this unit is difficult to determine (20.6). There appear to be seven parts, which may be arranged with at least a touch of symmetry (though not in a strict chiasmus). The center is 8:14–17, which serves nicely as the unit's centerpiece, with its grand conclusion: "So I commend the enjoyment of life, because nothing is better" (8:15). Collections of proverbs conclude the first two parts and the last two parts.

Practical Advice in Light of Life's Brevity and Uncertainty, Echoing the Poem in 1:2–11, and the Conclusion (Ecclesiastes 10:20–12:8)

M. A. Eaton is essentially correct in suggesting that 11:1–12:8 is a literary unit, "bound together by sustained exhortation, indicating that the whole section is concerned with decisive obedience."[13] His identification needs only minor adjustment: the final verse of chapter 10 also belongs to this unit (10:20). The new unit here is marked by a shift in mood. The truisms and philosophical discourses in the previous section now give way to a series of imperatives (don't revile, cast, give, sow, be happy, follow, etc.), with a focus on youth.

The unit consists of three sections: (1) seven wise sayings about living in light of life's uncertainty and unpredictability (10:20–11:6; the seven sayings are 10:20; 11:1, 2, 3, 4, 5, 6); (2) exhortation in light of life's brevity to enjoy life, especially while one is still young—remembering that God will one day judge each person's life (11:7–10); and (3) a poem exhorting young people to remember God before they grow old (12:1–8). This unit mirrors the book's first unit, offering practical advice in light of the realities presented in the first unit. Yes, it is true (as ex-

---

13. Eaton, *Ecclesiastes*, 139.

pressed in the book's first unit) that the brevity of human life on this eternal earth seems to reduce human life to insignificance. Life is fleeting. But this need not lead to despair. Instead, you should "remember your creator in the days of your youth" (12:1) and "be happy, young man, while you are young, and let your heart give you joy in the days of your youth" (11:9). Yes, it is true that the wind follows eternal, cyclical patterns (1:6); but "whoever watches the wind will not plant" (11:4); and "in spite of your not knowing the path of the wind . . . sow your seed in the morning, and at evening let not your hands be idle" (11:5–6).

The author utilizes a number of these echoes to offer advice or to underscore the book's main themes. In the first unit brief human life is contrasted to the sun's eternal cycle (1:5); in the final unit young people are exhorted, "Remember your creator . . . before the sun . . . grows dark [for you]" (12:2; cf. 11:8). In other words, do well and enjoy life while you are alive! The first unit declared that generations come and "go" (*hālak*), while the "earth" (*'ereṣ*) remains "forever" (*lĕʿôlām*) (1:4); in this final unit this idea is reinforced: "All go (*hālak*) to their eternal (*ʿôlām*) home" (12:5), and their "dust returns to the earth (*'ereṣ*) it came from" (12:7). In the first unit the author points out that unlike the brief life of a human, the "wind" (*rûaḥ*) eternally "goes" (*hālak*), "goes about" (*sābab*), and "returns" (*šûb*) (1:6); this thought is reinforced in the last unit, which declares that the "spirit" (*rûaḥ*) of a person "returns" (*šûb*) to God (12:7) and that we "go" (*hālak*) to our eternal home while our mourners "go about" (*sābab*) in the streets (12:5; cf. 11:4–5). In contrast to the picture of continuous, abundant water in the first unit (1:7), the last unit pictures the end of our brief life as water spilled out and gone forever (12:6). In the first unit, humans will not be "remembered" (*zkr*) by future generations (1:11); in the final unit, however, the reader is encouraged to "remember (*zkr*) your creator" (12:1). Lastly, in contrast to the statement in the first unit that "the eye can never see everything" (1:8), in the last unit the author exhorts his readers to "follow . . . whatever your eyes see" (11:9) and to remember their creator before their eyes grow dim (12:2–3). In an obvious touch of symmetry, the book's final unit closes as its first unit opened, with the book's "motto" ("vanity of vanities"; 12:8; cf. 1:2).

Following the motto comes the book's brief conclusion ("now all has been heard; here is the conclusion of the matter"; 12:9–14). This conclusion, like the book's opening two verses, refers to the author in the third-person ("Qoheleth"), creating an inclusio that frames the entire book.

Overall Layout of the Book of Ecclesiastes

In addition to the linear layout of the Book of Ecclesiastes, there are two other conspicuous structural patterns in the book's overall organizational design. First, the book's seven units alternate between short, poetic sections and longer autobiographical prose discussions, in an a-b-a-b-a-b-a pattern. Second, as already suggested, the book's seven constituent units appear to form an overall symmetric arrangement, with the center featuring the call to "fear Yahweh" (20.7).

Conclusion

The symmetric design of the Book of Ecclesiastes may help explain the occurrence of various repeated features throughout the book; for example, the recurrence in 10:20–12:8 of topics such as the sun, earth, wind, cycle of rain, remembering, circling, returning, and eternity; the repetition in 7:1–14 of the themes of birth, death, mourning, laughter, etc.; and the return in 3:16–6:12 to the theme of wisdom. The highlighted position of the central unit exhorting the audience to "fear God" (5:1–7 [4:17–5:6]), together with the equally highlighted position of the final conclusion, which likewise urges listeners to "fear God" (12:9–14), suggests the central importance of this theme to the author.

Also instructive is the author's designing the presentation so that the first three negative units, which demolish all hope of discovering life's ultimate meaning or of achieving any inherent lasting significance in one's life, are matched in the last half of the book by three positive units, which seek to provide practical and encouraging advice for joyfully living this fleeting and incomprehensible life. By using this structural design, moving from the negative to the positive, the author is able to leave the listener with uplifting words of encouragement and hope. The arrangement indicates that the author's purpose is not to dishearten the audience but to encourage and instruct.

It is significant that the author begins with negative units. Demolition of misguided hope must precede rebuilding on firmer ground. He clears away the foolish debris down to bedrock, and only then does he begin to rebuild on a solid foundation. His point is this: although humans innately sense that there is divine order and purpose in this universe ("the big picture"), they are

20.7 The Book of Ecclesiastes

title: author mentioned in third-person (1:1)

a **poem about the brevity and insignificance of life** in light of earth's permanence (1:2–11)
  - short, poetic
  - begins with motto: " 'vanity of vanities,' says the teacher" (1:2)
  - themes: <u>remembering</u> (zākar), <u>earth</u> (ʾereṣ), <u>sun</u> (šemeš), <u>wind</u> (rûaḥ), <u>water cycle</u>, <u>eternity</u> (ʿôlām), <u>going</u> (hālak), <u>circling</u> (sābab), <u>returning</u> (šûb), etc.

  b **wisdom's failure to discover life's meaning** or find ways to achieve meaning for one's life (1:12–2:26)
    - long, prose, autobiographical
    - theme: <u>wisdom</u> (ḥokmâ)

    c **poem about time**, and human inability to see the "big picture" (3:1–15)
      - short, poetic; fourteen-verse poem
      - topics: <u>time, death, birth, mourning, laughter, destroying</u>
      - "a time to be <u>born</u> and a time to <u>die</u>" (3:2)
      - "a time to <u>laugh</u> (śāḥaq), a time to <u>mourn</u>" (3:4)

      d **CENTER: fear God!** learn how to understand this world's moral perplexities and enjoy life despite them (3:16–6:12)

    c′ **poem about time revisited** (practical advice in response to 3:1–15) (7:1–14)
      - short, poetic; fourteen-verse poem
      - topics: <u>time, death, birth, mourning, laughter, destroying</u>
      - "the day of <u>death</u> is better than the day of <u>birth</u>" (7:1; cf. 7:2)
      - "sorrow is better than <u>laughter</u> (śāḥaq)" (7:3; cf. 7:6); "the heart of the wise is in the house of <u>mourning</u>" (7:4)

  b′ **wisdom's failure revisited** (echoing 1:12–2:26): practical advice in light of wisdom's failure to explain life's meaning or its perplexities: guide your life by wisdom, despite wisdom's shortcomings (7:15–10:19)
    - long, prose, autobiographical
    - theme: <u>wisdom</u> (ḥokmâ)

a′ **poem about life's brevity revisited** (echoing the poem in 1:2–11): practical advice about enjoying life and remembering God in one's youth (10:20–12:8)
  - short, poetic
  - ends with motto: " 'vanity of vanities,' says the teacher"
  - themes: <u>remembering</u> (zākar), <u>earth</u> (ʾereṣ), <u>sun</u> (šemeš), <u>wind</u> (rûaḥ), <u>water cycle</u>, <u>eternity</u> (ʿôlām), <u>going</u> (hālak), <u>circling</u> (sābab), <u>returning</u> (šûb), etc.

conclusion: author mentioned in third-person (12:9–14)

unable to comprehend or discover it (cf. Job 28). God has withheld it from them. They are like a horse with blinders, unable to see either to the left or to the right, only what is directly before them. That is the cruel reality, and no amount of effort on their part can either bring about the discovery of the big picture or calm the longing to know it.

The good news is that God knows the big picture. He knows the meaning and significance of everything, from beginning to end (3:11), including the meaning, purpose, and importance of an individual's life and all that occurs in it. Humans cannot discover the key to life's ultimate meaning, but they can trust and obey ("fear") the one who holds that key (12:13). And they can experience joy by living wisely, choosing what is good, and being careful to enjoy the gifts that God has given, such as food, spouse, and work—gifts that God has given for enjoyment during this incomprehensible, difficult, fleeting life "under the sun."

21

Song of Songs

Love—the Flame of Yahweh

The Song of Songs, or "Canticles," is a poetic portrayal of the romantic relationship between a young man and a young woman. It is, without question, one of the most intriguing books in the Bible. The Song's structure is notoriously difficult to analyze.[1] Among those who attempt to delineate the book's constituent units there is little agreement in methodology or results. Marvin Pope provides a useful survey of earlier structural analyses (most of which employ differing criteria for distinguishing units):[2]

Kessler	four units
Robert	five units
Exum	six single acts

Delitzsch	six two-scene acts
Buzy	seven units
Angénieux	eight units
Cannon	thirteen units
Bettan	eighteen units
Schmidt	nineteen units
Jastrow	twenty-three units (and some fragments)
Eissfeldt	twenty-five units
Gordis	twenty-eight units

While the recent trend is to analyze the book as comprising a few larger units, consensus seems far off.[3]

Not only are the Song's constituent speeches and snatches of speeches hard to delineate; but these speeches do not seem to be arranged in easily identifiable "packages" or stanzas. They seem to simply follow one after another in an apparently erratic fashion, alternating between the young woman, the young man, and others, from one end of the book to the other. Many readers can sympathize with Paul Haupt, who concludes that the book is "simply a collection of popular love-ditties, and these erotic songs are not at all complete . . . neither are they given in their proper order."[4]

Examination of the Song's structure, however, reveals a well-conceived layout designed both to achieve esthetic beauty and to reinforce some of the author's main themes.[5] The Song comprises seven larger units, arranged symmetrically, each with its own well-planned internal organization (21.1). Each new unit begins with shifts in scene, perspective, and mood; and each closes

---

1. Important studies of the Song's literary structure include Denis Buzy, "La Composition Littéraire du Cantique des Cantiques," *Revue Biblique* 49 (1940) 169–84, who identifies seven poems, each beginning with the theme of desire and ending with the fulfillment of desire in the mutual possession of the lovers; Roland Murphy, "The Structure of the Canticle of Canticles," *Catholic Biblical Quarterly* 11 (1949) 381–91; J. Angénieux, "Structure du Cantique des Cantiques," *Ephemerides Theologicae Lovanienses* 41 (1965) 96–142; idem, "Les Trois Portraits du Cantique des Cantiques," *Ephemerides Theologicae Lovanienses* 42 (1966) 582–86; idem, "Le Cantique des Cantiques en huit Chants à Refrains Alternants," *Ephemerides Theologicae Lovanienses* 44 (1968) 87–140; R. Kessler, *Some Poetical and Structural Features of the Song of Songs* (Leeds University Oriental Society Monograph 8; Leeds: Leeds University Press, 1957); André Robert, Raymond Tournay, and André Feuillet, *Le Cantique des Cantiques: Traduction et Commentaire* (Études Biblique; Paris: Lecoffre [Gabalda], 1963), 18–57; L. Krinetzki, *Das Hohe Lied: Kommentar zu Gestalt und Kerygma eines alttestamentlichen Liebesliedes* (Kommentare und Beiträge zum Alten und Neuen Testament; Düsseldorf: Patmos, 1964); J. Cheryl Exum, "A Literary and Structural Analysis of the Song of Songs," *Zeitschrift für die alttestamentliche Wissenschaft* 85 (1973) 47–79; William H. Shea, "The Chiastic Structure of the Song of Songs," *Zeitschrift für die alttestamentliche Wissenschaft* 92 (1980) 379–96; E. C. Webster, "Pattern in the Song of Songs," *Journal for the Study of the Old Testament* 22 (1982) 73–93; G. Lloyd Carr, *The Song of Solomon* (Leicester: Inter-Varsity, 1984), 44–49; and D. M. Goulder, *The Song of Fourteen Songs* (Journal for the Study of the Old Testament Supplement 36; Sheffield: JSOT Press, 1986).

2. Marvin H. Pope, *Song of Songs* (Anchor Bible 7c; Garden City: Doubleday, 1977), 40–54.

3. See the recent balanced summary by Roland E. Murphy, *The Song of Songs* (Hermeneia; Minneapolis: Fortress, 1990), 62–67.

4. Paul Haupt, "The Book of Canticles," *American Journal of Semitic Languages and Literature* 18 (1902) 205.

5. See David A. Dorsey, "Literary Structuring in the Song of Songs," *Journal for the Study of the Old Testament* 46 (1990) 81–96.

21.1 The Song of Songs

  a **opening words of mutual love and desire** (1:2–2:7)
    b **young man's invitation to the young woman** to join him in the countryside (2:8–17)
      c **young woman's nighttime search** for the young man (3:1–5)
        d **CENTER: their wedding day** (3:6–5:1)
      c′ **young woman's nighttime search** for the young man, and their speeches of admiration and longing (5:2–7:11 [5:2–7:10])
    b′ **young woman's invitation to the young man** to join her in the countryside (7:12–8:4 [7:11–8:4])
  a′ **closing words of mutual love and desire** (8:5–14)

with a refrain alluding to the lovers' union. Each unit except the last opens with the lovers apart and with a sense of excited tension; and each closes on a note of tranquillity, with the lovers united. And on both smaller and larger levels the Song's structure reinforces the poet's theme of love's reciprocity and mutuality.

Opening Dialogue: The Young Man and Young Woman Express Their Mutual Admiration and Desire (Song 1:2–2:7)

That 1:2–2:7 is designed to function as a literary package is evident from several factors:[6]

1. the symmetry created by its constituent speeches
2. the tight stimulus-response connections linking these speeches
3. the sense of completeness created by progression from tension to resolution
4. the singularity of scene
5. the recurrence of keywords and motifs

The internal structure of the unit is well conceived. To satisfy the ancient audience's preference for seven, the unit comprises seven speeches, alternating between the young woman and the young man:[7]

  a young woman's opening speech (1:2–7)
    b young man's response to her (1:8–11)
  c young woman's response to him (1:12–14)
    d young man's exclamation (1:15)
  e young woman's response to him (1:16–17)
    f young man's response to her (2:1–2)
  g young woman's response to him, and refrain (2:3–7)

The speeches are tightly linked, mainly by stimulus-response connections: each successive speech is a response to the preceding speech, generally echoing one of the lines or themes of the preceding speech, or answering a question posed in the preceding speech ("pearling"). Only the fourth speech (d) is exceptional. It is not linked in any apparent way to the preceding speech and thus stands highlighted.

This tight linking communicates the ardent interaction between the two lovers—one of the Song's main themes. Rather than seven soliloquies, the author provides here a lively dialogue in which each lover is affected by what the other

---

6. The unity and coherence of 1:2–2:7 is defended by a number of scholars: Denis Buzy, *La Cantique des Cantiques* (Paris: Letouzey & Ané, 1950), 20–21; Robert, Tournay, and Feuillet, *Cantique des Cantiques*, 56–57; Murphy, "Structure of the Canticle of Canticles," 384–85; Carr, *Song of Solomon*, 45. Exum, "Literary and Structural Analysis of the Song of Songs," 70–74, identifies 1:2–2:6 as the unit's boundaries (as does Webster, "Pattern in the Song of Songs," 74). Her exclusion of 2:7 from the unit is challenged by Michael V. Fox, *The Song of Songs and the Ancient Egyptian Love Songs* (Madison: University of Wisconsin Press, 1985), 107, and Murphy, "Structure of the Canticle of Canticles," 384–85; *Song*, 63. Rolf Rendtorff, *The Old Testament: An Introduction* (Philadelphia: Fortress, 1986), 262, takes 1:7–2:7 as the unit's boundaries, which is also favored more recently by Murphy, *Song of Songs*, 65.

7. The series begins with a speech by the young woman ("oh that he would kiss me"; 1:2), in which she expresses, in three stanzas (1:2–4, 5–6, 7), her affection and desire for the young man (1:2–7). Her speech ends with a question to the young man ("where do you pasture?" [1:7]). The young man's response (1:8–11) begins with a reply to her last question ("if

you do not know" [1:8]) and then goes on to express his admiration for her, wishing he could make her a costly necklace. Her response (1:12–14) picks up on his thoughts about the front of her neck, wishing that he himself (rather than a necklace) might lie between her breasts. The fourth speech is the young man's brief, seven-word exclamation of his admiration for her beauty (1:15). It is not linked in any apparent way to the preceding speech. The intensity created by its brevity is magnified by the double repetition of the exclamatory *hinnēh* ("behold!"): "Behold, you are beautiful (*hinnāk yāpâ*), my love! Behold, you are beautiful! Your eyes are doves." The young woman's response (1:16–17) echoes his exclamation: "Behold, you (too) are beautiful (*hinnĕkā yāpeh*), my love!" (1:16). The sixth speech should probably be delineated as 2:1–2 and ascribed to the young man (with BHS correcting *ănî* ["I"] in 2:1 to *ʾattĕ* ["you" feminine]). This speech is apparently linked to the young woman's preceding speech by its echo of the metaphorical use of sweet-smelling and beautiful plants. Interestingly, while she used these metaphors to describe the place of intimacy, he employs them to describe her own beauty: "You are a rose of Sharon. . . . Like (*kĕ-*) a lily among brambles, so (*kēn*) is my beloved among the young women (*bēn habbānôt*)" (2:2). The young woman's next speech (2:3–7) begins with an echo of the young man's last line: "Like (*kĕ-*) an apple tree among the trees of the woods, so (*kēn*) is my beloved among the young men (*bēn habbānîm*)" (2:3)—thus linking her speech to his by a tail-head connection; and as in her previous response, her speech moves from the linking echo to focus on the place of their intimacy, with allusions to the intimacy itself (2:3b–7).

21.2 Opening dialogue (Song 1:2–2:7)

a **young woman's** long speech, expressing her desire to be with the young man in his home (1:2–7)
- aside to the <u>daughters of Jerusalem</u>
- "<u>he has brought me into</u> (*hĕbîʾanî*) his chambers"
- keywords: threefold mention of <u>love</u> (*ʾhb*); <u>wine</u> (*yayin*)

  b **young man's** words of <u>admiration</u> for his <u>beloved</u> (*raʿyātî*) (1:8–11)
  - her <u>uniqueness among women</u> (*bannāšîm*)

    c **young woman's** short speech of <u>admiration and desire</u> (1:12–14)
    - theme: <u>fragrance</u> (nard, myrrh, henna blossoms); reference to <u>his bed</u>

      d **CENTER: <u>young man's</u> exclamation** (1:15)

    c′ **young woman's** short speech of <u>admiration and desire</u> (1:16–17)
    - possible theme: <u>fragrance</u> (cedar, pine); reference to <u>our bed</u>

  b′ **young man's** words of <u>admiration</u> for his <u>beloved</u> (*raʿyātî*) (2:1–2)
  - her <u>uniqueness among the young women</u> (*bên habbānôt*)

a′ **young woman's** long speech describing union with the young man in <u>his home</u> (2:3–7)
- aside to the <u>daughters of Jerusalem</u>
- "<u>he has brought me into</u> (*hĕbîʾanî*) the house of <u>wine</u>"
- keywords: threefold mention of <u>love</u> (*ʾhb*); <u>wine</u> (*yayin*)

---

says. Here and throughout the Song, the structure helps convey the idea that the lovers speak to, listen to, affect, react to, and respond to one another. The alternation of speeches also helps convey the idea of the reciprocity, or mutuality, of the two lovers' love. The book could have opened with a unit featuring the pining of one lover for the other; but instead it opens with an fervent exchange in which the two lovers, with equal ardor, interact with one another.

To enhance the unit's artistry, the seven speeches also exhibit a symmetric touch (21.2). This is suggested, for example, by the correspondence of the first (a) and last (a′) speeches. Unlike the other speeches, these two are relatively long, and both are spoken by the young woman. In the first she expresses her desire to be with him in his home; in the last she describes their union in his home. Both contain asides to the "daughters of Jerusalem" (1:5; 2:7), who are not mentioned elsewhere in the unit. In both, the young woman states that "he has brought me into" (*hĕbîʾanî*) his house/chambers (1:4; 2:4). A keyword in both is "love" (*ʾhb*), occurring three times in the first speech, three times in the last, and nowhere else in the unit. "Wine" (*yayin*) is mentioned twice in the first speech (1:2, 4), once in the last (2:4), and nowhere else in the unit. The desires she expresses in the first speech find their fulfillment in the last.

The second (b) and next-to-last (b′) speeches (reading "you [feminine singular] are" in 2:1a, with BHS) also echo one another. Both are speeches by the young man, expressing his words of admiration for the young woman. Both emphasize the uniqueness of her beauty "among women." And both refer to her as "my beloved" (*raʿyātî*).

The brief third (c) and third-to-last (c′) speeches are spoken by the young woman. They are linked by references to the bed (or "couch": *meseb*[8] and *ʿereś*), and perhaps also by the theme of fragrance.

At the center (d) stands the young man's simple exclamation regarding her beauty.

The unit also exhibits a quantitative symmetry. The first speech is the longest, followed by progressively shorter speeches, until we arrive at the central speech, which is the shortest speech of all (seven words). Then the speeches become progressively longer again (except that the fifth and sixth are reversed). This is reflected in the word count:

a 73 words
  b 48 words
    c 20 words
      d 7 words
    c′ 13 words
  b′ 12 words
a′ 49 words

The effect of this quantitative symmetry is that the sense of intensity builds as the exchanges move with escalating speed toward the center, then gradually relaxes as the speeches move away from the center. The audience first feels the crescendo of excitement as the interchange becomes more rapid-fire, then senses the relaxing of tension as the pace slows. This structuring design reinforces the unit's progression from tension to rest.

The end of the unit is well marked. The young woman's speech in 2:3–7 (a′) completes the symmetry begun in 1:2, signaling the unit's comple-

---

8. See Fox, *Song of Songs*, 105; Murphy, *Song of Songs*, 131.

tion; and the declaration "his left hand is under my head," particularly with its climactic ending, "I adjure you, O daughters of Jerusalem" (2:6–7), communicates a sense of closure. The unit began with the lovers apart and yearning for one another, a tension sustained throughout their exchange. The tension is resolved in this final speech, with the lovers united in one another's embrace. The unit proceeds, then, from separation and desire, to union and fulfillment, concluding on a note of rest.[9]

The Young Man Invites the Young Woman to Join Him in the Country (Song 2:8–17)

In the book's second unit, the young woman relates how the young man came to her home and invited her to join him in the countryside.[10] Several signals clearly mark the beginning of the unit:

1. shift in scene: from his house (or palace) in the city to her country home
2. shift in perspective: in the previous unit the young woman yearned to come into his house and be with him; now the young man is outside her house, wishing that she would come out and join him in the countryside
3. shift in mood: from the quiet ambiance of their union to the excited, charged mood of the young man's enthusiastic arrival and invitation
4. shift in genre: from dialogue to a description of an experience
5. the dramatic exclamation "the sound of my beloved! behold he is coming (*hinnēh-zeh bāʾ*)!" (2:8), which has the effect of transporting the audience to this new scene to view, with the young woman, the approaching young man[11]

The unity of 2:8–17 is evident. It comprises a single episode or scene that could be entitled "The young man comes to the young woman's home and invites her to join him in the countryside." Its cohesion is reinforced by its symmetric structure (which will be discussed shortly) and by the sense of completeness achieved by the unit's movement from separation to union, from tension to resolution (2:16–17).

Regarding its internal arrangement, the unit comprises three well-defined parts: (1) the young woman's description of the young man's approach, (2) the young man's invitation to her, and (3) her concluding refrain describing their union. Symmetry once again plays a key role in the design. The unit's three parts form a symmetry based on speaker:

a	young woman (2:8–9)
b	young man (2:10–15)
a′	young woman (2:16–17)

Moreover, the young woman's opening and closing words echo one another by various repetitions, including "my beloved" (*dôdî*), which occurs three times in her first speech (counting her introduction to his speech in 2:10a) and two times in her last; "like a gazelle or like the fawn of a deer" (*dômeh/dĕmēh liṣbî ʾô lĕʿōper hāʾayyālîm*; 2:9, 17); and "upon the mountains" (*ʿal-hehārîm/hārê*; 2:8, 17).

These are more than mechanical repetitions. The poet utilizes these repetitions to help communicate the unit's movement from separation to union. In her introductory speech the young woman uses the picture of "a gazelle or the fawn of a deer" who leaps "upon the mountains" to depict their separation: she is in her home, he is out there (albeit coming!) (2:8–9). In the concluding speech she employs these same words ("be like a gazelle or the fawn of a deer upon the mountains"; 2:17) to allude to their union. The turn of these repetitions poignantly captures the progression from distance to intimacy.

There is also symmetry within the young man's speech (21.3). His speech has two stanzas. The first (b) is framed by the invitation "arise my beloved, my beautiful one!" (2:10, 13) and contains, in an artistic touch, seven clauses (seven subjects and predicates) depicting the arrival of spring.[12] The second stanza (b′) echoes the first with lexical repetitions such as *qôl* ("voice"), *rāʾâ* ("to see"), *šāmaʿ* ("to hear"), *sĕmādar* ("blooms"), and "dove" (*tôr* and *yônâ*).[13] The poet utilizes the

---

9. Buzy ("Composition Littéraire du Cantique des Cantiques") recognizes the importance of this structuring pattern in the layout of the Song; he argues that each of the Song's seven units begins with the theme of desire and ends with the fulfillment of desire in the mutual possession of the lovers.

10. The identification of 2:8–17 forming a coherent unit is proposed by a number of scholars: Buzy, *Cantique des Cantiques*, 20–21; Francis Landy, *Paradoxes of Paradise: Identity and Difference in the Song of Songs* (Sheffield: Almond, 1983), 41–42; Murphy, *Song of Songs*, 65; Goulder, *Song of Fourteen Songs*, 22–25. Others identify the unit as 2:7–3:5: Exum, "Literary and Structural Analysis of the Song of Songs," 53–56 (criticized by Landy, *Paradoxes of Paradise*, 40); Murphy, "Structure of the Canticle of Canticles," 383; Webster, "Pattern in the Song of Songs," 74; Rendtorff, *Old Testament: An Introduction*, 263.

11. The *hinnēh* + *zeh/zōʾt* + participle combination, or part of it, is a common beginning marker in Hebrew literature (see 3:6; 8:5) and often communicates a new beginning.

12. It should also be noted that the young man's entire speech in 2:10–15 contains seven imperatives (arise, come, arise, come, show, cause to hear, catch)—although this might be fortuitous.

13. Fox, *Song of Songs*, 112.

21.3 Young man's invitation (Song 2:8–17)

a **young woman's description of her beloved's approach** (2:8–9)
  - refers to him as <u>my beloved</u> (*dôdî*)
  - portrays him as leaping <u>upon the mountains</u> (*ʿal-hehārîm*), <u>like a gazelle or the fawn of a deer</u> (*dômeh liṣbî ʾô lĕʿōper haʾayyālîm*)
  - <u>relationship</u>: very distant

  b **young man's invitation:** come out with him <u>to see and hear the beauty of nature</u> in the spring (2:10–13)
    - keywords: <u>voice</u> (*qôl*), <u>see</u> (*rāʾâ*), <u>hear</u> (*šāmaʿ*), <u>blooms</u> (*sĕmādar*), <u>dove</u>, focused on <u>nature</u>
    - <u>relationship</u>: less distant

  b′ **young man's more intimate invitation:** he longs <u>to see her beauty and hear her voice</u> (2:14–15)
    - keywords: <u>voice</u> (*qôl*), <u>see</u> (*rāʾâ*), <u>hear</u> (*šāmaʿ*), <u>blooms</u> (*sĕmādar*), <u>dove</u>, focused on <u>her</u>
    - <u>relationship</u>: intimate

a′ **young woman's response: she assents** (2:16–17)
  - refers to him as <u>my beloved</u> (*dôdî*)
  - invites him to intimacy, to be <u>like a gazelle or the fawn of a deer upon the mountains</u> (*dĕmēh . . . liṣbî ʾô lĕʿōper haʾayyālîm*)
  - <u>relationship</u>: very intimate

repetitions to help convey the idea of movement from distance to intimacy. In the first stanza the young man uses these terms to depict the beauty of nature; in the second he uses these same terms to depict the young woman's own beauty and his desire for her.

The unit's structure underscores the theme of mutuality. Although the unit features the young man as the initiator this time, he is not portrayed as pining for a reluctant, less interested partner. The poet designed the unit so that the young woman excitedly introduces the young man's invitation in the beginning and happily assents to his invitation at the end. Her own ardor frames his. The theme of mutuality and reciprocity is also reinforced by the alternation of perspective and primary initiator. In the Song's first unit the young woman is "out there" and desires to come into the young man's home to be with him (1:4, 12, 17; 2:4); in the second, it is the young man who is "out there," and he desires that she come out of her home to join him. In the first instance the young woman is the primary initiator and speaker; in the second, the young man fills that role.

The Young Woman's Nighttime Search for the Young Man (Song 3:1–5)

Next comes a tightly woven unit in which the young woman recounts a nighttime search for her beloved.[14] Her narration forms a simple unity with a beginning, a middle, and an end: she misses him, she seeks him, she finds him. Like the first two units, this one opens with the two lovers apart and closes with them together. Unlike the first two, it features no dialogue between the lovers.

The beginning of the new unit is marked by the shift of scene in 3:1. The previous unit featured the young man's daytime invitation to her to join him in the countryside. This new scene opens with the young woman lying alone in bed at night, missing her beloved. The new unit is also signaled by a shift in mood, from the peaceful ambiance of the lovers' union to the tension now created by the lovers' separation.

The unit's cohesion is achieved by its symmetric arrangement (which will be discussed shortly), by its steady movement from tension to resolution, and by the heavy concentration of verbal recurrences. The expression, "the one whom my soul loves"(*ʾēt šeʾāhăbâ napšî*) occurs in every verse of the unit except the last. It ties the unit together by its rhythmic repetition. Other verbal recurrences include the fourfold repetition of the verb *biqqēš* ("seek"; 3:1a, 1b, 2b, 2c) and the fourfold repetition of the verb *māṣāʾ* ("find"; 3:1, 2, 3, 4).

Regarding internal organization, the unit appears to have seven subunits, through which the poet builds, then relaxes, the tension. The first "episode" (a)—if we can call it such (the young woman is in her bed, misses her beloved, and cannot find him)—introduces the tension. In the second episode (b) she goes out to search for her lover, but fails to find him, creating a deepening sense of suspense. Next, she is found by the city guards (c), generating even more suspense (will she be harmed?). Finally, positioned at the point of highest tension[15] stands the young woman's almost desperate question (d): "Have you seen the one whom my soul loves?" She appears to have exhausted her resources; she may even be in per-

---

14. The unity and coherence of 3:1–5 is noted by a number of scholars: Buzy, *Cantique des Cantiques*, 20–21; Landy, *Paradoxes of Paradise*, 47 (he excludes 3:5); Carr, *Song of Solomon*, 26–27; Murphy, *Song of Songs*, 146.

15. Robert Alter, *The Art of Biblical Narrative* (New York: Basic Books, 1985), 65, calls a similar structural high point in Psalm 13 (v. 3) "the climactic point of desperation"—marked there, as here, by a sudden breaking away of the structural pattern of the unit to this point.

21.4 Young woman's search (Song 3:1–5)

a **in bed, the young woman yearns for her absent lover** (3:1)
- tension: introduced

b **she leaves her home** to search for him (3:2)
- tension: builds

c **she is <u>found</u> (*mṣʾ*) by the guards** (3:3a)
- tension: intensifies from complication

d **CENTER: her desperate question** (3:3b)
- tension: at its peak

c′ **she leaves the guards and <u>finds</u> (*mṣʾ*) her lover** (3:4a)
- tension: resolution begins

b′ **she returns to her home** with him (3:4b)
- tension: resolution deepens

a′ **refrain: the lovers are united, presumably back in her bed** (3:5)
- tension: resolution completed

sonal danger; and she is still separated from the one she loves. We have reached the zenith of suspense and are now ready for the unit's resolution.

In the final three episodes the tension subsides in successive steps. First, she leaves the guards (nothing bad has happened to her) and finds her beloved (c′), causing the audience to feel a sense of relief. Next she takes the young man by the hand and brings him back to her home (b′), further relaxing the tension. Finally, in her joyful refrain, which alludes to their union and intimacy (a′), a sense of complete tranquillity is reached.

The unit exhibits a symmetric touch (21.4). The opening episode, in which the young woman is in her bed and missing her absent lover, finds its matching resolution in the closing refrain, in which the young woman celebrates their happy union and intimacy, presumably back in her bed. The second episode, in which she leaves her home to search for him, is mirrored in the next-to-last episode, in which she returns to her home with him. The third episode, in which the young woman (having failed to find her lover) is "found" (*mĕṣāʾûnî*) by the city guards, finds its echo in the third-to-last episode, when she leaves the guards and "finds" (*māṣāʾtî*) her beloved. At the center stands her poignant question.

The unit's end is signaled by the completion of the symmetry, by the resolution of tension, and by the unit's happy ending (their union), conveyed by the same refrain that closed the Song's first unit:

I adjure you, O daughters of Jerusalem,
by the gazelles or the hinds of the field,
that you stir not up nor awaken love until it please.[16]
—Song of Songs 3:5

The ideal of reciprocity continues to be developed by the alternation of theme and perspective. The Song's previous unit featured the young man yearning for the young woman; this unit now features her yearning for him. In the previous unit he came to her home and invited her to come out and join him; now she leaves her home to find him and bring him into her home. He was the initiator in the first instance; now she is the initiator. In the previous unit he bemoaned her inaccessibility (2:13b–14); now she bemoans his. The poet uses the repetition of lexical items to draw attention to this reciprocity. In the previous unit the young man twice invited her to "arise" (*qûmî*) from her home and come out with him; in this unit she declares that she will "arise" (*ʾāqûmâ*) and go out to search for him. The previous unit closed with the young woman's invitation to the young man to "go around" (*sōb*); now she vows to "go around" (*ʾăsôbĕbâ*) to find him.[17]

Their Wedding Day (Song 3:6–5:1)

The Song's fourth main unit opens with a description of the approaching bridal party, followed by a series of speeches in which the young man praises and expresses his desire for his bride, and concludes with an exchange alluding to their union (4:12–5:1).[18] The beginning of the

---

16. Interestingly, all three closing refrains, or endings, encountered so far feature male or female "gazelles" (*ṣĕbî*) and "deer" (*ʾayil*), alternating between genders (2:4–7, 16–17; 3:4–5).

17. The unit's tight structure may also convey the sense of the young woman's plucky tenacity. The unit's parts are packed together tightly, with no gaps or pauses between the young woman's successive actions, so that she appears to proceed without stop from one frustrated attempt to the next, relentlessly searching until she finds her lover; and then, with equal intensity (again the effect of no pauses or breaks), she does not stop until she has brought him back with her to the safety and privacy of her home.

18. Several scholars identify 3:6–5:1 as a self-contained, coherent unit: Robert, Tournay, and Feuillet, *Cantique des Cantiques*, 56–57; Exum, "Literary and Structural Analysis of the Song of Songs," 61–65; Rendtorff, *Old Testament: An Introduction*, 263; Carr, *Song of Solomon*, 45.

new unit in 3:6 is marked for the audience by several indicators:

1. shift in scene: from the private, nighttime setting in the young woman's home and in the streets of Jerusalem to the public, daytime scene in the wilderness east of Jerusalem
2. shift of perspective: from the young woman's to another's
3. shift in theme: from the young woman's private search to the couple's public wedding
4. shift in dramatic mood: from a troubled, anxious mood to a festive mood
5. the rhetorical question *mî zōʾt ʿōlâ* ("who is this coming up?"), which has the effect of suddenly transporting the audience to the new scene

The beginning of the new unit in 3:6, in fact, echoes that of the second unit (2:8). Both feature an abrupt shift from a scene of private intimacy to a public, eyewitness account of one of the lovers approaching. In both, the opening lines include a series of participles + *zeh/zōʾt* ("this") + *hinnēh* ("look!"). In the earlier unit it was the young man approaching; now it is the young woman—presumably another structuring touch designed to underscore the theme of reciprocity.

The unit's coherence is reinforced by its symmetric arrangement (to be discussed shortly), by the completion of movement from separation to union, and by the inclusio formed by the two speeches of the poet himself (see subsequent discussion). The repetition of keywords also ties the material together: *kallâ* ("bride"), a word that occurs nowhere else in the book, occurs six or seven times in this unit (4:7 [following the Cairo Genizah], 8, 9, 10, 11, 12; 5:1); and *lĕbānôn* ("Lebanon") and *lĕbônâ* ("frankincense"), terms occurring only twice elsewhere in the book (5:15; 7:4 [7:5]), show a sevenfold repetition (3:6, 9; 4:6, 8a, 8b, 11, 15). A thematic unity—their wedding—also ties this section together and sets it apart from the rest of the book. The unit opens with the bridal party approaching. References to the "wedding day" and wedding apparel (3:11), the festive mood, the pomp, allusions to family and the public (3:7–8, 10–11; 5:1c), and the recurrence of the term *kallâ*—all reflect the wedding theme.

The layout of the unit follows the same three-part pattern used in the first three units: (1) introduction, with the lovers apart; (2) body, featuring the lovers admiring/desiring one another; and (3) conclusion, with the lovers united. The

unit opens with a description of an approaching bridal party: "Who is this (*zōʾt*, feminine singular) coming?" (3:6). The pronoun *zōʾt* in all likelihood refers to the young woman, who is approaching in the wedding palanquin, the *ʾappiryôn* (3:9) upon which the Israelite bride, not the groom, rode to the wedding.[19] The groom is apparently awaiting her arrival in Jerusalem. (The speaker here appears to be, not the groom, but the poet himself.) This description is followed by five speeches (4:1–11) in which the young man praises his bride:

a	his lengthy praise of her beauty (4:1–5)
b	his speech of desire (4:6)
c	his exclamation of praise regarding her beauty (4:7)
d	another speech of desire (4:8)
e	speech of praise (4:9–11)[20]

These praise speeches, in turn, are followed by the climactic exchange in 4:12–5:1—a grand finale in which the lovers allude to their union and intimacy. This exchange culminates with the poet's own exclamation: "Eat, O friends, and drink; drink deeply of love!" (5:1c).

Counting the young man's five speeches, this unit has seven parts and exhibits a symmetric structure (21.5). The introductory description of the approaching bride, accompanied by the wafting fragrances of myrrh, frankincense, etc., is mirrored by the description of the bride at the end, which also features wafting fragrances of myrrh, frankincense, etc. In both, "Lebanon" and "wood" (*ʿāṣê*) are mentioned (3:9; 4:14). The first features a description of the fragrant-smelling wedding litter, with seven items mentioned (litter, sedan chair, pillars, base, seat, interior, crown). The second features a description of the bride herself as a fragrant-smelling garden, with probably seven specific fragrant spices mentioned (henna, spikenard, saffron, cane, cinnamon, myrrh, aloes—and possibly "the wood of frankincense").[21] Another important link be-

---

19. Contra Fox, *Song of Songs*, 125–26.

20. It is not entirely clear whether the speech beginning in 4:9 extends to 4:15 (with the young woman's response coming in 4:16) or only to 4:11, with 4:12 introducing the conclusion to the entire unit (4:12–5:1). It seems likely that the poet intends 4:12–5:1 to form the unit's grand finale, tied together by the theme of "garden" (*gan* is mentioned six times in these verses: 4:12a, 12b [following BHS], 15, 16a, 16b; 5:1a) and other lexical links: "myrrh" (*mōr*; 4:14; 5:1), "choice fruits" (*pĕrî mĕgādîm*; 4:13, 16), and "spices" (*bĕśāmîm*; 4:14, 16). In all probability the young man's fifth speech is 4:9–11, with his words in 4:12–5:1 serving as part of the concluding exchange with the young woman.

21. In the young man's acceptance (5:1a–b) he also enumerates seven things he has come into and partaken of (garden, myrrh, spices, honeycomb, honey, wine, milk).

21.5 The wedding day (Song 3:6–5:1)

a **approach of the young woman in the wedding procession** (3:6–11)
  - wafting fragrances, including myrrh, frankincense; mention of wood, Lebanon, and seven items accompanying her
  - poet's own words (3:6–11)

b **young man's lengthy speech of admiration** (4:1–5)
  - review of seven of her body parts: eyes, hair, teeth, lips, cheeks, neck, breasts

c **his short speech of desire** (4:6)
  - he yearns to go to "the mountain (*har*) of myrrh, to the hill of frankincense (*lĕbônâ*)"

d **CENTER: his very short speech of admiration** (4:7)

c′ **his short speech of desire** (4:8)
  - he yearns for her to come with him from the mountains (*har*), from Lebanon (*lĕbānôn*)

b′ **his lengthy speech of admiration** (4:9–11)*
  - review of seven of her body parts: eyes, neck, breasts (with versions), oils, lips, garments

a′ **union of the lovers** (4:12–5:1)
  - wafting fragrances, including myrrh, frankincense; mention of wood, Lebanon, and seven(?) fragrant spices
  - poet's own words (5:1c)

*See note 20.

tween these two units is that in both the poet himself speaks (3:6–11; 5:1c), which happens only here and once at the end of the Song (8:5).

The second and next-to-last parts are longer speeches by the young man. They clearly echo one another. In both, he admires the young woman's physical attributes. In both, he enumerates seven of her features or articles of adornment that he particularly admires, including in each inventory her "eyes" (*ʿênayik*), "lips" (*śiptôtayik*), "neck"/"necklace" (*ṣawwāʾrēk/ṣawwĕrōnāyik*), and "breasts" (*šādayik/daddayik* [cf. versions]). The third and third-to-last parts are the young man's two expressions of desire for the young woman. In both he employs metaphors involving mountains (4:6, 8). At the center stands the young man's exclamation regarding his beloved's beauty, which, as in most of the symmetries in the book, does not function as the unit's climax.[22]

As in the first unit of the book, this unit's seven parts vary markedly in length; and, as in the first unit, their arrangement forms a quantitative symmetry. The first speech is long (sixty-seven words), followed by progressively shorter speeches, until the central speech, which is the shortest of all (six words), after which the speeches become progressively longer again:

a 67 words
  b 56 words
    c 12 words
      d 6 words
    c′ 16 words
  b′ 34 words
a′ 74 words

This structuring technique creates the sense that the unit's intensity builds as the young man's speeches move with quickening speed toward the center, climaxed by his exclamation in 4:7, and then subsides in intensity as his speeches become longer again, until we arrive at the unit's restful conclusion.

The overall layout of this unit again reinforces the theme of reciprocity. Even though the young man's speeches of desire and praise take center stage in the unit, reciprocity is conveyed by having his speeches introduced by the description of the young woman's resplendent approach as his bride-to-be and concluded by her enthusiastic acceptance of his amorous overtures. As in the second unit, her own ardor frames his. The structure of the grand finale in 4:12–5:1 also communicates the mutuality of the lovers' love. The young man's admiration of the young woman as a delightful garden (4:12–15) is followed by her invitation to him to come in and enjoy her garden's fruits (4:16), which is followed in turn by the young man's joyous acceptance of her invitation (5:1a–b).

The alternating scheme of the Song's larger units continues to convey the theme of reciprocity as well. In the preceding unit it was the young man who was "out there," and the young woman went out to find him and bring him home. Now it is the young woman who is "out there," approaching from the wilderness, in-

22. The centers of the chiasmuses in Canticles are not used as points of emphasis, except in the book's overall chiasmus. Of all the units that are chiastically arranged, none of the central speeches could be considered the high point or turning point of its unit. The first and seventh parts of the chiasmus generally carry the dramatic high points (see especially 1:2–2:7; 3:1–5; 3:6–5:1; 5:2–7:11 [5:2–7:10]); although in the book's final unit the third and third-to-last parts (8:6–7, 11–12) appear to be that unit's points of highest emotional intensity. In three units the second and next-to-last slots are used for praises of the lover's body (units a, d, e).

accessible in the mountain heights of Lebanon and Mount Hermon, or in a locked garden; and it is the young man who now yearns to be united with her (see especially 4:8, 12). In the previous unit the audience saw everything through the eyes of the young woman; now they see everything primarily from the young man's perspective. The young woman was the speaker and initiator in the previous unit; now he is the main speaker and initiator.

The Young Woman's Nighttime Search for the Young Man and Their Speeches of Mutual Praise (Song 5:2–7:10 [5:2–7:11])

A fifth literary package—the Song's longest—opens with the young woman recounting another nighttime search for the young man, followed by their speeches of mutual praise, and closed by a stanza alluding to their union.[23] Several rhetorical devices signal the beginning of a major unit at 5:2:

1. shift in scene: from the daytime wedding scene to the nighttime setting, with the young woman lying alone in bed
2. shift in mood: from the festivity of the wedding and union to the tension created by the opening of the new scene, in which the two lovers are separated
3. the young woman's unintroduced exclamation in 5:2, "the sound of my beloved knocking!" (*qôl dôdî* + participle), which transports the audience to the new scene, as did her similar exclamation at the beginning of the second unit in 2:8 ("behold, the sound of my beloved coming, bounding . . . !" [*qôl dôdî* + participles])

The entirety of 5:2–7:10 [5:2–7:11] is tied together by its symmetric design (see subsequent discussion), by the continuity of its thematic development, and by the succession of fairly evenly spaced questions by the women of Jerusalem: "how?" (5:9), "where?" (6:1), "who?" (6:10), and "why?" (6:13 [7:1]). This succession of questions sustains, or periodically recharges, emotional interest throughout the series of longer speeches. These questions not only tie the unit together, but also set it apart from the rest of the Song, since such interaction with these daughters of Jerusalem occurs nowhere else in the Song.[24]

The unit's internal design comprises a series of speeches by the lovers, punctuated by questions from the women of Jerusalem. It begins, as did the third unit, with the young woman recounting that she was alone in her bed (5:2). As in the third unit, she recounts how she went out to search for her lover in the city streets and was found by the city guards. But unlike the third unit, the resolution of the tension (the union of the lovers) is delayed. Receiving no help from the guards (5:7), she asks the daughters of Jerusalem for assistance (5:8). Their counterquestion (5:9) prompts her to describe the beauty of the young man she seeks (5:10–16). Their further query (6:1) leads to her declaration of his whereabouts ("he has gone down to his garden"; 6:2–3). But the series is not yet concluded. Now the young man, without introduction, exclaims his praise of the young woman (6:4–9). The young woman then responds to another question by the daughters of Jerusalem by recounting her descent to the garden where her lover is waiting (6:10–12). Yet another remark and question by the Jerusalemite women (6:13 [7:1]) prompts the young man to describe the beauty of his beloved's body (7:1–7 [7:2–8]). This lively series finally concludes with an exchange between the two lovers that alludes to their union, sealed by the young woman's happy declaration: "I am my beloved's, and his desire is for me" (7:8–10 [7:9–11]).[25]

The unit exhibits a seven-part symmetric arrangement (21.6). The opening speech, the young woman's recounting of the lovers' nighttime separation, parallels the closing stanza celebrating their union. In the first the young man expresses his desire for union, but because of the young woman's hesitation they are separated; in the last, he again expresses amorous desires, and this time her acceptance climaxes their happy union. Both feature references to "sleep" (*yĕšēnâ/yĕšēnîm*; 5:2; 7:9 [7:10]), grasping (5:4–6; 7:8 [7:9]), and sweet aromas (5:5; 7:8 [7:9]).

The second and next-to-last speeches echo one another in strikingly reciprocal fashion. Each speech contains one lover's praise of the

---

23. Shea, "Chiastic Structure of the Song of Songs," 387–95, also proposes the unity of 5:2–7:10 [5:2–7:11].

24. The intensive recurrence of *dôd* ("beloved"), occurring nineteen times, likewise reinforces this unity.

25. Exum, "Literary and Structural Analysis of the Song of Songs," 49, 56–61, identifies the end of the unit as 6:3, "I am my lover's and my lover is mine; he feeds among the lilies," which corresponds to part of the refrain closing the second unit (2:16–17). This line indeed might temporarily suggest to an audience that the unit has come to its end; but that impression fades with the next lines, which do not introduce a new scene but simply continue the series of exchanges with no change of venue (in fact, the discovery in 6:2–3 leads to the action of 6:11–12). Shea, "Chiastic Structure of the Song of Songs," 387–96, sees this unit as extending to 7:10 [7:11], where the young woman's declaration, "I am my beloved's and his desire is for me," marks its end.

21.6 Young woman's search (Song 5:2–7:10 [5:2–7:11])

a **their separation and her nighttime search (5:2–8)**
- his desire to be with her
- her refusal, and their separation and her fruitless search for him
- topics: sleep (yĕšēnâ), grasping, sweet aromas

  b **her praise of his body, from the head down (5:9–16)**
  - ten parts praised, including head (rōʾš), hair, eyes (ʿênayim), belly, legs
  - mention of ivory (šēn), towers (migdal), Lebanon, lilies (šôšannîm), sources of water
  - begins: question by daughters of Jerusalem
  - begins: two lines beginning with Hebrew mah ("how?")
  - ends: summary statement introduced by this (zeh)

    c **her declaration to the daughters of Jerusalem (6:1–3)**
    - her beloved went down (yārad) to his garden (gan)
    - begins: question by daughters of Jerusalem

      d **CENTER: his praise of her unique beauty (6:4–9)**

    c' **her declaration to the daughters of Jerusalem (6:10–12)**
    - she went down (yārad) to the garden (gannâ)
    - begins: question by daughters of Jerusalem

  b' **his praise of her body, from the feet up (6:13–7:7 [7:1–8])**
  - ten parts praised, including head (rōʾš), hair, eyes (ʿênayim), belly, legs
  - mention of ivory (šēn), towers (migdal), Lebanon, lilies (šôšannîm), sources of water
  - begins: question by daughters of Jerusalem
  - begins: two lines beginning with Hebrew mah ("what?"; "how!")
  - ends: summary statement introduced by this (zōʾt)

a' **their union (7:8–10 [7:9–11])**
- his desire to be united with her
- her agreement
- topics: sleep (yĕšēnîm), grasping, sweet aromas

beauty of the other's body. Each speech is prompted by a question or request from the daughters of Jerusalem (5:9; 6:13a [7:1a]). Each speech is introduced by two lines that begin with *mah* ("how!" "what?" 5:9; 6:13b–7:1a [7:1b–2a]). The first speech is the young woman's praise of the young man's body, beginning with his head and proceeding downward; the second is the young man's praise of her body, beginning from her feet and proceeding upward. In both speeches, ten body parts are selected for praise, including, in both, the "head" (*rōʾš*), hair, "eyes" (*ʿênayim*), belly, and legs. Both mention "ivory" (*šēn*; 5:14; 7:4 [7:5]), "towers" (*migdal*; 5:13; 7:4 [7:5]), Lebanon (5:15; 7:4 [7:5]), and "lilies" (*šôšannîm*; 5:13; 7:2 [7:3]). Both speeches allude to sources of water in depicting the other's eyes (5:12; 7:4 [7:5]). Lastly, both descriptions end with a summary statement introduced by "this" (*zeh/zōʾt*; 5:16; 7:7 [7:8]).

The third and third-to-last units consist of brief speeches by the young woman. Each speech is the young woman's response to the Jerusalemite women. A question by these women introduces each speech. In each, the young woman describes a trip taken "down" (*yārad*) to a "garden" (*gan/gannâ*) filled with flowers. In both, the purpose of the descent to the garden is given: "to feed/look" (*lirʿôt/lirʾôt*) among the flowers of the garden (6:2, 11),

The central unit comprises the young man's praise of the young woman's beauty. Unlike the other speeches, this one is not introduced (and is thus highlighted). His speech simply bursts forth with the unintroduced exclamation: "How beautiful you are!"—words that strikingly echo the centers of other units.[26]

The poet continues to structure his material to reinforce the theme of reciprocity. The matching speeches of praise in 5:10–16 and 7:1–7 [7:2–8], as noted, are paradigms of reciprocity: her admiration of his body, from the head down, is echoed by his admiration of her body, from the feet up. This theme also continues to be conveyed by the point-counterpoint arrangement of the Song's larger units. The previous unit featured the young man as the main speaker, praising the young woman's beauty, desiring her, and inviting her. In the first half of this unit the

26. The young man's praise, forming the center of this unit's chiasmus, begins here with his introductory exclamation: *yāpâ ʾattĕ raʿyātî* ("you are beautiful, my beloved!" 6:4). At the center of the first unit is his almost identical exclamation: *yāpâ raʿyātî* ("behold, you are beautiful, my beloved!" 1:15); and the center of the fourth unit is introduced and concluded by the same exclamation (4:1, 7). Even the center of the second unit contains these same terms in the repeated line: "Arise, my beloved, my beautiful one (*raʿyātî yāpātî*)" (2:10, 13). It is also noteworthy that in all but this last citation the exclamation is followed by the young man's praise of the young woman's captivating "eyes" (*ʿênayik*; 1:15b; 4:1b, 9; 6:5).

young woman becomes the main speaker, searching for, yearning for, and praising the beauty of the young man (5:2–6:3; cf. 6:11–12); then, in the second half of the unit, the young man becomes the main speaker, and he reciprocates with speeches expressing his praise for her beauty, his desire for her, and his own words of invitation (6:4–9; 7:1–9 [7:2–10]).

Her Invitation to Him to Join Her in the Country (Song 7:11–8:4 [7:12–8:4])

The book's sixth unit consists entirely of a speech by the young woman, in which she invites the young man to come with her to the countryside, wishes for intimacy with him, and closes with a happy refrain alluding to their union.[27] The unit's beginning is marked for the audience by several techniques:

1. shift in scene: from a nighttime setting and garden imagery to a springtime, countryside setting
2. shift in genre: from exchanges of speeches of admiration to a monologue
3. shift in number of participants: from many to a single one—the young woman
4. the introductory imperative *lekâ dôdî* ("come, my beloved!"; 7:11 [7:12])[28]

The unity of 7:11–8:4 [7:12–8:4] is partially created by the singularity of speaker: the young woman is the sole speaker and initiator throughout (in contrast to the rapid changes of speakers in the previous and following units). The unit is also tied together by its single theme: her yearning for their privacy so that she might give him her love. The recurrence of lexical items such as *nātan* ("to give") and *rimmônîm* ("pomegranates") and the repetition of motifs of fruits and fruit juices also reinforces its cohesion.

The internal organization of the unit is tripartite: (1) her invitation to him to accompany her to the countryside (7:11–13 [7:12–14]), (2) her wish that he were her brother, so that she could kiss him without public disapproval and bring him into her home (8:1–2), and (3) a closing refrain, alluding to their union (8:3–4). The unit does not appear to exhibit a symmetric configuration. It simply moves in linear fashion (a-b-c; or more accurately, a-a'-b) from the young woman's two expressions of her yearning to be alone and intimate with her beloved, to her happy refrain. Like the preceding units, this one moves from separation to union, ending in tranquillity, with a closing refrain quite similar to the closing refrains used to mark the ends of the first and third units.

The author continues to develop the theme of reciprocity. The last part of the previous unit featured the young man as initiator and main speaker, expressing his admiration and longing for the young woman; now the author provides the complement: the young woman is initiator and speaker, expressing her longing for the young man.

Closing Words of Love and Desire (Song 8:5–14)

The book's final unit comprises a series of brief speeches by two or more speakers.[29] Unlike the previous units, this one not only ends, but begins, with the two lovers united. Also unlike the previous units, this one does not develop a sense of tension or suspense generated by the lovers' separation; for now the two lovers are together from the beginning. They are happily united, and their ardent words are spoken in a setting of rest and tranquillity.

The poet helps his listeners know that a new unit begins in 8:5 by using several techniques:

1. shift in scene: from the verdant spring countryside near the young woman's house to the edge of the semibarren wilderness
2. shift in mood: from tranquillity to a sense of excitement and anticipation generated by the rhetorical question in 8:5
3. shift in speaker: from the young woman to a new speaker (the poet?)
4. the rhetorical question in 8:5, "who is this coming up from the wilderness?" which has the effect of transporting the audience to a new scene and which was earlier used to introduce the fourth unit (3:6)

The unit is difficult to exegete, but its constituent parts can be identified with some certainty

---

27. Other scholars identify these verses as forming a cohesive unit: Buzy, *Cantique des Cantiques*, 20–21; Shea, "Chiastic Structure of the Song of Songs," 385–87; Webster, "Pattern in the Song of Songs," 74; and Goulder, *Song of Fourteen Songs*, 60–62.

28. Imperatives often introduce new units in the Hebrew Bible The previous occurrence of an imperative voiced by one of the lovers was in 5:2, which marked the beginning of the previous unit; and the same imperative, *raʿyātî . . . lĕkî* ("my beloved, come!"), also occurred at the beginning of the second unit (2:10), preceded only by the young woman's brief introduction to the unit.

29. Scholars who identify 8:5–14 as the Song's concluding unit include Buzy, *Cantique des Cantiques*, 20–21; Murphy, "Structure of the Canticle of Canticles," 384; Exum, "Literary and Structural Analysis of the Song of Songs," 74–77; Shea, "Chiastic Structure of the Song of Songs," 381–85, who begins the unit with 8:6; Carr, *Song of Solomon*, 45; Webster, "Pattern in the Song of Songs," 74.

21.7 Closing words of love (Song 8:5–14)

a **introductory rhetorical question** (8:5a)
- vision of the young woman coming up from the wilderness, united with her beloved
- lovers are <u>united</u>
- image of <u>travel through rugged terrain</u>
- young woman is leaning <u>upon</u> (*ʿal*) the young man

b **young man's(?) short speech** (8:5b)
- he recounts that he "awakened" her under the apple tree
- image of <u>young woman reposing</u> in verdant scene and young man <u>arousing</u> her

c **young woman's longer speech** (8:6–7)
- themes: <u>ownership</u> (using <u>give</u> [*ntn*]), <u>value</u> and power of love
- she would be a seal upon his heart and arm, showing that he belongs to her
- love is powerful; its value is beyond all financial reckoning

d **CENTER: the brothers and their sister** (8:8–10)

c′ **young woman's longer speech** (8:11–12)
- themes: <u>ownership</u> (using <u>give</u> [*ntn*]), <u>value</u> of vineyards (and love?)
- she would give him one thousand shekels (showing that her "vineyard"—herself—belongs to him?)
- much money is insignificant compared with her love

b′ **young man's short speech** (8:13)
- he yearns for her to respond to him
- image of young woman <u>reposing in garden</u> and young man wishing to <u>arouse</u> her

a′ **concluding refrain** (8:14)
- image of the young man going out upon the spice mountains (united with his beloved)
- lovers are <u>united</u>
- image of <u>travel through rugged terrain</u>
- young man is viewed as <u>upon</u> (*ʿal*) the mountains (an allusion to the young woman?)

(21.7). It begins with the rhetorical question (a), presumably asked by the poet, followed by an enigmatic speech by one lover (b), who recalls to the other lover, "Under the apple tree I awakened you" (8:5b). According to the Masoretic Text, these words are spoken by the young woman. According to the Syriac version and BHS, however, they are the young man's words. The latter seems more likely on the basis of content.

Next comes a speech by the young woman (c), in which she asks that her beloved place her as a seal on his heart and arm and then speaks of love's power. In the following stanza (d), which is apparently an exchange between the young woman and her brothers, the young woman expresses confidence regarding her sexual maturity and her desirability to her lover. The young woman (c′) then speaks about Solomon's vineyard and her own vineyard, the point of which seems to be that her vineyard—herself—belongs to him.

Finally comes a closing request by the young man (b′): "O you who dwell in the gardens, friends listen to your voice; let me (also) hear it!" (8:13). Her joyous response (a′) echoes the closing refrains of the book's first three units: "Make haste, my beloved, and be like a gazelle or a young roe, upon the mountains of spices" (8:14).

Without a clearer grasp of the meaning of these speeches it might be presumptuous to speculate regarding the unit's theme, although

the sense of security and togetherness and the ideals of commitment and the pricelessness of love are certainly present. The unit's cohesion is reinforced by its arrangement: it appears to exhibit a seven-part symmetric configuration. The unit begins with a single question regarding the young woman and her beloved coming up from the wilderness (8:5a). It concludes with a single sentence by the young woman inviting her beloved to "flee" upon "the mountains of spices" (8:14). The first speech refers to the young woman *ʿal* ("upon") her beloved; the last refers to the young man *ʿal* ("upon") the "mountains of spices"—presumably an allusion to the young woman. Both speeches refer to the young woman's "beloved" (*dôd*), a term occurring nowhere else in this unit. Both transport the audience, in their imagination, to view the lovers at a distance, out in nature. If the second unit depicts intimacy through symbolic language, which it almost certainly does, then both allude to the lovers united in intimacy.

The unit's second speech shifts from the (arid, virtually treeless) wilderness, to a more verdant scene, under an apple tree. As already noted, this speech is most likely the young man's. He speaks of "awakening" his beloved under the apple tree. This short speech appears to have as its match the unit's equally short next-to-last speech, where the young man is again the speaker and addresses the young woman in a

21.8 Point-counterpoint in the Song of Songs

  a **young woman initiates:** she is the primary speaker, longing to join the young man in his home (1:2–2:7)
    b **young man initiates:** he is the primary speaker, longing for her to come out of her home and join him in the countryside (2:8–17)
  a **young woman initiates:** she goes out, finds the young man, and brings him to her home (3:1–5)
    b **young man initiates:** he praises and yearns for her (3:6–5:1)
  a **young woman initiates:** she yearns for him and praises him (5:2–6:3)
    b **young man initiates:** he praises her and longs for her (6:4–7:10 [6:4–7:11])
  a **young woman initiates:** she invites him to countryside and longs for him (7:11–8:4 [7:12–8:4])
    c **the two lovers are together:** no predominant initiator (8:5–14)

scene of verdure, "in the gardens." In both scenes the young woman is portrayed as reposing, and in both the young man elicits, or wishes to elicit, a response from her.

The third and the third-to-last speeches are both longer and are spoken by the young woman. In the first speech she asks to be a seal upon his heart and arm, which would mark him as belonging to her (8:6). She speaks of the power of love, which is beyond all financial reckoning (8:7). This is apparently echoed, in another stroke of reciprocity, by the third-to-last speech of the unit, which although somewhat obscure seems to touch on these same points: she would (happily) give to him the sum of a thousand shekels of silver that he collects from all those tending the vineyards he owns, demonstrating that her vineyard—herself—likewise belongs to him. The power of her love surpasses all financial reckoning: she happily would give (and even more, if necessary!) the thousand shekels of silver—an extravagant price—to show that she is his. In the former speech she asks for a token showing that she owns him; in the latter speech she offers a token that shows that he owns her.

The center of this unit is a stanza about a sister and her breasts, presumably a dialogue between the young woman and her brothers. It concludes with her confident assertion of her own sexual maturity and her desirability to her beloved.

As already noted, from a structural perspective this final unit is different from the previous six in that it does not move from separation to union. Instead, the unit both begins and ends with the lovers united. This would appear to be a "highlighting" technique designed to mark this unit as the book's conclusion, bringing the Song to its happy, tranquil closing.

Overall Layout of the Song of Songs

The overall organization of the seven major units in the Song of Songs reflects several structuring patterns. First, the units are de-signed so that each new unit begins with the two lovers apart and concludes with the two united—except the final unit, which begins and ends with the two together. This rhythm ties the entire Song into a cohesive whole with a highlighted conclusion:

  a apart—together
  b apart—together
  c apart—together
  d apart—together
  e apart—together
  f apart—together
    g together—together

Further, a point-counterpoint scheme of arrangement is used in the structuring of the book's units. The units alternate (the extra long fifth unit falls into two parts) between the young woman and young man as main speaker and initiator (21.8).

The poet artfully avoids leaving either the young woman or young man "stranded" at the end (which would have happened, for example, had he featured the young man as the main speaker and initiator in the final unit). The final unit is laid out so that both lovers initiate and neither dominates.

The Song's seven constituent units are arranged with a symmetric touch (21.9).[30] The book's first and last units are obvious matches.[31] The echoes linking the two units are manifold and conspicuous. In both, a sevenfold internal structure is achieved primarily by the alternation of speakers. In both, the exchange is rapid,

30. An overall chiastic structure in the book is proposed by a number of scholars: Exum, "Literary and Structural Analysis of the Song of Songs"; Shea, "Chiastic Structure of the Song of Songs"; Webster, "Pattern in the Song of Songs"; Carr, *Song of Solomon*, 44–47. Each of these arrives at different identifications of the Song's constituent units.

31. The correspondence between 1:2–2:7 and 8:5–14 is noted by Exum, "Literary and Structural Analysis of the Song of Songs," 74–78; Shea, "Chiastic Structure of the Song of Songs," 381–85; Rendtorff, *Old Testament: An Introduction*, 261–62; Norman K. Gottwald, *The Hebrew Bible: A Socio-Literary Introduction* (Philadelphia: Fortress, 1985), 547; Carr, *Song of Solomon*, 45; and others.

21.9 Symmetrical arrangement of the Song of Songs

a **opening words of mutual love and desire** (1:2–2:7)
- seven speeches, alternating between the young woman and the young man
- Solomon mentioned by name
- young woman's vineyard contrasted with brothers'
- brothers mistreat(?) the young woman; her self-assurance regarding her beauty
- apple tree as a place of intimacy
- ends with refrain: his left arm . . .

  b **young man's invitation to the young woman to join him in the countryside**; three stanzas (2:8–17)
- description of the renewal of spring and nature
- flowers and grapevines; vineyards in bloom
- he comes to her home to invite her to come out with him
- ends with refrain: my lover is mine . . .

    c **young woman's nighttime search** for the young man (3:1–5)
- begins: young woman in bed at night, yearning for her absent lover
- she goes out to search for him, but is found by the guards who go about the city
- refrain: my lover is mine . . . (immediately precedes the unit's beginning)

      d **CENTER: their wedding day** (3:6–5:1, framed by poet's words)

    c′ **young woman's nighttime search** for the young man, and their speeches of admiration and longing (5:2–7:10 [5:2–7:11])
- begins: young woman in bed at night, yearning for her absent lover
- she goes out to search for him, but is found by the guards who go about the city
- ends with refrain: I am my lover's . . .

  b′ **young woman's invitation to the young man to join her in the countryside**; three parts (7:11–8:4 [7:12–8:4])
- description of the renewal of spring and nature
- flowers and grapevines; vineyards in bloom
- she would bring him to her home
- refrain: I am my lover's . . . (immediately precedes the unit's beginning)

a′ **closing words of mutual love and desire** (8:5–14)
- seven speeches, symmetrically arranged, alternating mainly between young woman and young man
- Solomon mentioned by name
- her vineyard contrasted with Solomon's others
- brothers belittle(?) the young woman; her self-assurance regarding her beauty
- apple tree as a place of intimacy
- refrain: his left arm . . . (immediately precedes the unit's beginning)

the speeches short. Both contain a speech dealing with the young woman's brothers, who apparently belittle(?) her (1:6; 8:8–9). In both, the young woman expresses self-assurance regarding her beauty (1:5; 8:10; and nowhere else in the book). In both, the young woman's own vineyard and the vineyards of others are compared (1:6; 8:11–12). In both, the apple tree is mentioned as a place of lovemaking (2:3; 8:5; apple trees are mentioned nowhere else in the book). Both mention the young man's "friends" (*ḥăbĕrîm*; 1:7; 8:13), a term occurring nowhere else in the Song. In both, her "breasts" (*šādayim*) are mentioned (1:13; 8:8?, 10). In both, Solomon is mentioned by name (1:5; 8:11; and nowhere else in the book except in its central unit). The identical refrain ("his left arm") marks the end of the first unit and immediately precedes the last.

The second and next-to-last units also obviously correspond.[32] Here the lovers invite one

another to come out into the countryside. In the first, he invites her; in the second she invites him. In both, the countryside is romantically described in terms of flowers, grapevines, and vineyards in bloom (2:12–15; 7:12 [7:13]). The one begins with the young man coming to her home; the other concludes with the young woman wishing to bring him to her home (2:9; 8:2). Unlike the other units of the Song, these two units comprise, not seven, but three stanzas each. Moreover, numerous verbal links connect the two units:

lĕkî/*lĕkâ* ("come!"; 2:10, 13; 7:11 [7:12])
sĕmādar ("blossoms"; 2:13, 15; 7:12 [7:13])
kĕrāmîm ("vineyards"; 2:15; 7:12 [7:13])
gepen/*gĕpānîm* ("vine[s]"; 2:13; 7:12 [7:13])
nātĕnû rêaḥ ("they give fragrance"; 2:13; 7:13 [7:14])

The refrain "his left arm . . ." directly precedes the beginning of the one unit and closes the other. The refrain "my lover is mine and I am

---

32. This correspondence is observed by Shea, "Chiastic Structure of the Song of Songs," 385–87.

his" ends one unit; and the similar refrain, "I am my lover's, and his desire is for me," immediately precedes the beginning of the other unit (2:16; 7:10 [7:11]).

The third and third-to-last units, despite their differences in length,[33] clearly echo one another. Each features the young woman's account of her nighttime loneliness in her bed, her lover's absence, her search for him in the streets, and her being found by the city guards (3:1–4; 5:2–7).[34] Numerous lexical repetitions link the two units:

lêlôt/lāyĕlâ ("night"; 3:1; 5:2)

qûm ("arise"; 3:2; 5:5)

biqqaštîw wĕlōʾ mĕṣāʾtîw/biqqaštîhû wĕlōʾ mĕṣāʾtîhû ("I sought him but I did not find him"; 3:1, 2; 5:6)

mĕṣāʾunî haššōmĕrîm hassōbĕbîm bāʿîr ("the guards who go about in the city found me"; 3:3; 5:7)

The refrain immediately preceding the beginning of the one unit ("my lover is mine . . ."; 2:16) recurs in a modified form as the conclusion of the other (7:10 [7:11]).

This leaves 3:6–5:1, the unit featuring the wedding day and the lovers' exchanges of words of admiration, as the Song's central unit. That this fourth unit is intended to function as the book's climax and centerpiece seems most likely for several reasons. First, unlike the other units, this one begins and ends with the poet's own words, serving to highlight it. Second, the dramatic conclusion in 4:16–5:1, particularly the poet's own exclamation in 5:1c ("eat, O friends, and drink; drink deeply, O lovers!"), serves as an appropriate emotive climax and high point of the book. Third, it would be expected that a symmetrically arranged song celebrating romantic love would have the wedding scene at its center, functioning as the centerpiece of the en-

tire song. Lastly, the name "Solomon," which occurs in the first and last units, occurs elsewhere in the book only here (3:7, 11), reinforcing the Song's symmetry if indeed this unit is the central one.

Conclusion

Although there is room to speculate regarding the prehistory of the various constituent pieces comprising the Song of Songs,[35] the foregoing analysis suggests, at the very least, that the final author intensively reshaped the material of the Song from beginning to end. The sophistication and homogeneity of the Song's surface-structure design strongly suggests a unified poem that was composed by a single author.

The author's structuring designs reinforce and enhance the Song's main themes. The most prominent of these themes is the idea of the reciprocity, or mutuality, of the lovers' love. The carefully designed alternation of speeches, initiations, and invitations underscores the mutuality of the lovers' passion for one another. The theme is also conveyed by the matching of reciprocal expressions of love, such as the matching of his speech admiring her body from the feet up with her speech admiring his body from the head down (both mentioning ten body parts). Similarly, his invitation to her to join him in the countryside is matched by her invitation to him to join her in the countryside. Such matchings of reciprocal speeches occur throughout the Song.

These structuring techniques underscore the point that the two lovers are equally in love, equally adore one another, and are equally ready to initiate, to suggest, to invite. The ideal conveyed by the author's structure (as well as by the contents of the speeches) is an egalitarianism and mutuality in romantic love that is virtually unparalleled in ancient Near Eastern literature. In a world that was strongly patriarchal, where love lyrics often portrayed the man as a "bull" and the woman as something less than his equal, the Song of Songs represents a surprisingly high view of woman and a remarkable vision of the ideal of equality and delightful reciprocity in the marriage relationship.

---

33. See Shea's discussion ("Chiastic Structure of the Song of Songs," 379–80) of the phenomenon in biblical and ancient Near Eastern literature of quantitative unevenness in corresponding units.

34. A number of scholars note the correspondence of these two nighttime search units: Exum, "Literary and Structural Analysis of the Song of Songs, 56–59; Shea, "Chiastic Structure of the Song of Songs," 387–88; Carr, *Song of Solomon*, 45; Murphy, *Song of Songs*, 62–63.

35. See Murphy, *Song of Songs*, 60–62.

Major Prophets

22
Isaiah
Trust in Yahweh Alone

Isaiah began his ministry during the eighth century B.C., at a time when the powerful nation of Assyria was threatening to overwhelm the smaller kingdoms—including Judah—along the eastern Mediterranean coast. Isaiah called the people of Judah to return to Yahweh their God, from whom they had strayed, and to trust in him alone for their ultimate protection. The Book of Isaiah contains some of the most beautiful poetry in all of human literature. The exquisite literary quality of its messages is unsurpassed in the Old Testament. The book's poetic beauty is partially achieved by its many elegant structural schemes.

Before examining the structure of Isaiah, however, we should briefly address the problem of the book's composition. There is general (but not complete) consensus among modern scholars that the book is the work of at least two authors: the prophet Isaiah, who wrote most of chapters 1–39 ("First Isaiah"), and an anonymous prophet living 150 years after Isaiah, who wrote the bulk of chapters 40–66 ("Deutero-Isaiah"). Some suggest that chapters 56–66 came from yet a third author ("Trito-Isaiah") who lived during the time of Ezra and Nehemiah.[1] For purposes of this investigation, the issue of the book's composition will be set aside, and the structure of the book in its final form will be analyzed. The goal of this chapter is simply to study the organizational schemes that were used in shaping the book into its present form, with the hope that such a study might yield fresh insights about the book and its meaning.

Most would agree that the book's final form comprises seven larger units: three introductory collections of messages (chaps. 1–12, 13–27, 28–

35), the historical narrative (chaps. 36–39), and three final collections of messages (chaps. 40–48, 49–54, 55–66).[2]

Introductory Messages of Condemnation, Pleading, and Future Restoration (Isaiah 1–12)

There are compelling indications that chapters 1–12 form the book's first major unit. The varied messages in this section follow one another without significant break through the end of chapter 12 and are concluded, as Norman Gottwald suggests,[3] by the hymn at the end. Chapter

---

1. Some (Bernhard Duhm, Karl Budde, Paul Volz, Otto Eissfeldt, etc.) analyze the book, particularly Trito-Isaiah, as comprising an even greater number of disparate units; see Otto Eissfeldt, *The Old Testament: An Introduction*, trans. Peter R. Ackroyd (New York: Harper & Row, 1965), 303–46, for a survey of views.

2. For example, Eissfeldt states (*Old Testament: An Introduction*, 304) that the Book of Isaiah "divides naturally into three sections": sayings (chaps. 1–35), narratives (chaps. 36–39), and sayings (chaps. 40–66). Certainly the block of historical narratives in Isaiah 36–39 separates the collection of messages in Isaiah 1–35 from that in Isaiah 40–66. Isaiah 1–35 itself is regarded by most scholars (e.g., Franz Delitzsch, *Isaiah* [3d ed.; repr. Grand Rapids: Eerdmans, 1964], 1.56; Brevard S. Childs, *Introduction to the Old Testament as Scripture* [Philadelphia: Fortress, 1979], 331–32; Norman K. Gottwald, *The Hebrew Bible: A Socio-Literary Introduction* [Philadelphia: Fortress, 1985], 382) as comprising three parts: (a) messages of judgment and eschatological redemption (chaps. 1–12); (b) oracles against the nations (chaps. 13–27); (c) messages of woe, ending with future redemption (chaps. 28–35). Bernhard Duhm (see J. Alberto Soggin, *Introduction to the Old Testament: From Its Origins to the Closing of the Alexandrian Canon*, trans. John Bowden [3d ed.; Louisville: Westminster/John Knox, 1989], 257–58) has this analysis with one exception: Isaiah 34–35, he argues, did not come from the same source as Isaiah 28–33 and should be considered a separate unit (Soggin and Robert H. Pfeiffer [*Introduction to the Old Testament* (New York: Harper, 1948), 448] follow Duhm's analysis). S. R. Driver (*An Introduction to the Literature of the Old Testament* [9th ed.; Edinburgh: Clark, 1913], 206) prefers to treat Isaiah 24–27 as a separate unit. Delitzsch (*Isaiah*, 1.55–56), on the other hand, sees the three parts of Isaiah 1–35 as three pairs of units: (a) prophecies founded upon the growing obduracy of the great mass of the people (2–6) and (a') the consolation of Immanuel under the Assyrian oppressions (7–12); (b) predictions of judgment and salvation of the heathen (13–23) and (b') prophecy of judgment of the world and the last things (24–27); (c) revolt from Ashur and its consequences (28–33) and (c') prediction of revenge and redemption (34–35). Finally, in a variation of this scheme, Gottwald (*Hebrew Bible*, 377–86) sees each of the three parts of Isaiah 1–35 as ending with a salvation prophecy or hymn: 11–12, 24–27, 34–35.

3. Gottwald, *Hebrew Bible*, 382–87.

22.1 Call to repentance (Isaiah 1)

a Israel's rebellion (1:2–4)
- they have <u>forsaken</u> (ʿzb) Yahweh, <u>rebelled</u> (pšʿ), and <u>sinned</u> (ḥṭʾ)
- Israel is <u>not like animals</u> (who know their master)!

  b **Israel's present devastation (1:5–9)**

    c **condemnation of Israel:** <u>rulers</u> and <u>murderers</u> (1:10–15)

      d **CENTER: call to repentance (1:16–20)**

    c′ **condemnation of Israel:** <u>rulers</u> and <u>murderers</u> (1:21–23)

  b′ **Israel's present devastation to be reversed! (1:24–27)**

a′ **Israel's rebellion: guilty parties will be punished (1:28–31)**
- those who have <u>forsaken</u> (ʿzb) Yahweh, <u>rebels</u> (pšʿ), and <u>sinners</u> (ḥṭʾ)
- they will be <u>like trees for burning</u>

22.2 Pride and judgment (Isaiah 2–4)

a **future exaltation of Jerusalem**—mountain of Yahweh (2:2–5)

  b **possessions of proud men:** pride and idolatry (2:6–9)

    c **future humiliation of Israel's proud men (2:10–22)**

      d **CENTER: coming judgment upon Jerusalem (3:1–15)**

    c′ **future humiliation of Israel's proud women (3:16–17[?])**

  b′ **possessions of proud women:** list of proud finery to be removed (3:18[?]–4:1)

a′ **future restoration of Jerusalem**—mountain of Zion (4:2–6)

22.3 Song of the vineyard (Isaiah 5)

a **song of the vineyard:** <u>metaphorical portrayal</u> of Israel's <u>coming destruction</u> (5:1–7)

  b **condemnatory <u>woes</u>** (hôy) (5:8–12)
- themes: <u>injustice</u>, <u>drunkenness</u>

    c **verdict:** <u>therefore</u> (lākēn) (5:13–14)
- theme: <u>death</u>

      d **CENTER: humiliation of humankind, exaltation of God (5:15–17)**

  b′ **condemnatory <u>woes</u>** (hôy) (5:18–23)
- themes: <u>injustice</u>, <u>drunkenness</u>

    c′ **verdict:** <u>therefore</u> (lākēn) (5:24–25)
- theme: <u>death</u>

a′ <u>**literalistic portrayal**</u> of the Israel's <u>coming destruction</u> (5:26–30)

---

13 introduces the book's next major unit, the collection of oracles against the nations. The internal organization of Isaiah 1–12 reflects its unity. The unit exhibits an overall three-part scheme similar to that of the entire Book of Isaiah: two collections of messages (chaps. 1–5 and 7–12) separated by a unique, isolated central unit—the account of Isaiah's call (chap. 6). This three-part scheme subdivides into seven units.

The collection's first unit is the message in chapter 1 (2:1 introduces a new message). This message—the book's first—is organized in a seven-part symmetric scheme,[4] with a call to repentance standing at its highlighted center (22.1).

The collection's second unit is introduced by the heading "this is what Isaiah son of Amoz saw concerning Judah and Jerusalem" (2:1). The extent of this unit is somewhat difficult to determine. The breaks at 2:6, 3:1, and 4:2 repre-

sent no greater shifts than some of those within the first message (e.g., 1:10, 21). Isaiah 5:1 should probably be identified as the beginning of the next unit, marked by sudden shifts to first-person singular and to a new genre (song). Supporting this conclusion is the tying together of material in chapters 2–4 by the unifying theme of pride/humiliation and its seven-part symmetric arrangement (22.2).

The third unit of this collection is introduced in 5:1: "I will sing a song. . . ." The unit extends at least to 5:7; but 5:8–30 appears to complete the unit by elaborating on the accusations and threats of 5:1–7. The internal structure of chapter 5, although difficult to analyze, supports its unity. It possibly exhibits a modified chiastic structure (22.3).

The collection's fourth unit is the self-contained account of Isaiah's call in chapter 6. It is arranged in a symmetric configuration that features the actual call at the highlighted center (22.4). The matching draws attention to the contrast between Isaiah's purged lips and the peo-

---

4. The successive paragraphs are introduced by a shift in addressee and the following terms: "hear!" "why?" "hear!" "wash!" "how!" (ʾêkâ) and "therefore" (lākēn).

22.4 Isaiah's call (Isaiah 6)

a **Yahweh's heavenly splendor and glory** (6:1–4)
   - begins: the image of Yahweh sits (yšb) enthroned in his heavenly abode
   - theme: fullness—Yahweh's heavenly abode is filled (with his majesty); the earth (ʾereṣ) is full of his glory

  b **Isaiah's distressed reaction** (6:5a)
   - begins: and I said (waʾōmar)

    c **Isaiah's lips are unclean; but they are purified** (6:5b–7)
   - his sins are forgiven
   - his eyes have seen (rʾh)
   - he lives among a sinful people (ʿam)

      d **CLIMAX: Isaiah's call and acceptance** (6:8)

    c′ **the people's eyes, hearts, ears are sinful** (6:9–10)
   - they will not be forgiven
   - their eyes will not see (rʾh)
   - the people (ʿam) are sinful

  b′ **Isaiah's distressed reaction** (6:11a)
   - begins: and I said (waʾōmar)

a′ **Judah's future devastation and humiliation** (6:11b–13)
   - begins: the image of no one sitting/dwelling (yšb) in the land
   - theme: emptiness—the land/earth (ʾereṣ) will be empty and desolate

---

22.5 Messages about impending invasion (Isaiah 7:1–8:18)

a **introduction**: plot of Syria and Samaria against Judah, and Judah's fear (7:1–2)

  b **prediction of failure of invasion** that presently threatens (7:3–9)
   - topics: Jerusalem's water source; fearing Rezin, son of Remaliah

    c **child Immanuel**: sign of Syria-Samaria failure (7:10–16)

      d **CENTER: coming of greater invasion**: Assyria! (7:17–25)

    c′ **child Maher-shalal-hash-baz**: sign of Syria-Samaria failure (8:1–4)

  b′ **prediction of success of future invasion** from Assyria (8:5–10)
   - topics: Jerusalem's water source; fearing Rezin, son of Remaliah

a′ **conclusion**: don't fear what these people fear; instead, fear Yahweh! (8:11–18)*

*Isaiah 8:19–9:1a [8:19–23a] is difficult to analyze; it may belong to the unit's conclusion.

22.6 Present failure and future restoration of Judah (Isaiah 8:19–11:9)

a **good news! future reign of righteous and just Messiah** (8:19–9:7 [8:19–9:6])*
   - topics: Messiah's childhood and lineage from David

  b **denunciation of pride of threatening invader, Samaria** (9:8–12 [9:7–11])
   - topics: Samaria, arrogance (gōdel lēbāb), felling (gdʿ) cedars (of Lebanon)
   - quotations of Samaria's haughty boasts

    c **condemnation of Israel's leaders** (9:13–17 [9:12–16])
   - themes: widow, fatherless, day of punishment

      d **CENTER: coming destruction of Israel** (9:18–21 [9:17–20])

    c′ **condemnation of Israel's leaders** (10:1–4)
   - themes: widow, fatherless, day of punishment

  b′ **denunciation of pride of future invader, Assyria** (10:5–34)
   - topics: Samaria, arrogance (gōdel lēbāb), felling (gdʿ) Lebanon's trees
   - quotations of Assyria's haughty boasts

a′ **good news! future reign of righteous and just Messiah** (11:1–9)
   - topics: Messiah's childhood ("shoot") and lineage from David

*If Isaiah 8:19–9:1a [8:19–23a] is part of the previous unit, then this unit begins with 9:1b [8:23b].

---

ple's sinful hearts, eyes, and ears and to the contrast between Yahweh's heavenly majesty and Judah's future humiliation and devastation.

Chapter 6 is followed by a longer fifth unit that centers around the Syria-Samaria threat against Jerusalem and the symbolic naming of children. The threat of the invasion is introduced in 7:1–2, and the unit's conclusion comes in 8:11–18, with the first-person summary statement by Isaiah about himself and his children, who have served as signs to Israel. The unit is structured in a seven-part chiasmus (22.5).

Delineation of the sixth unit is difficult. The repeating refrain "yet for all this, his anger is not turned away, his hand is still upraised" (9:12, 17, 21 [9:11, 16, 20]; 10:4) ties together most of chapters 9–10. But the themes introduced in

22.7 Introductory messages (Isaiah 1–12)

a **introduction: Israel's disobedience and resultant devastation** (1:1–31)
 - conquest of Israel by foreign armies
 - theme: <u>unacceptable worship</u> of Yahweh

 b **visions of future restoration of Jerusalem** under rule of Yahweh and his <u>Messiah</u> (2:1–4:6)
 - bracketing <u>denunciations of pride</u> of men and women
 - coming judgment

  c **coming destruction of Judah** ("Song of the Vineyard") by a nation from afar off (5:1–30)
 - vineyard will no longer be <u>hoed</u> (*yēʿādēr*), becoming <u>briars and thorns</u> (*šāmîr wāšāyit*) <u>for trampling</u> (*lĕmirmās*)
 - Yahweh will <u>whistle for</u> (*šāraq lĕ-*) enemies to invade (5:26)
 - <u>arrows and bows</u>; metaphor of attacking lions

   d **CENTER: call of Isaiah** (6:1–13)

  c′ **coming destruction of Judah**, not by neighboring nations, but by (far off) Assyria (7:1–8:18)
 - fields once <u>hoed</u> (*yēʿādērûn*) will become <u>briars and thorns</u> (*šāmîr wāšāyit*) <u>for trampling</u> (*lĕmirmās*) (7:23–25)
 - Yahweh will <u>whistle for</u> (*šāraq lĕ-*) enemies to invade (7:18)
 - <u>bows and arrows</u>; metaphor of attacking flies/bees (7:18–24)

 b′ **visions of future restoration of Israel** under the <u>Messiah</u>'s righteous reign (8:19–11:9)
 - bracketing <u>denunciations of the pride</u> of Samaria and Assyria
 - failure of Israel's leadership
 - coming judgment

a′ **conclusion: Israel's future restoration and obedience** in a reversal of chapter 1 (11:10–12:6)
 - Israel's future conquest of foreign countries
 - theme: future <u>joyous worship</u> of Yahweh

chapter 9 continue on through the beginning of chapter 11. Study of the section's internal structure suggests that it forms a self-contained unit arranged in a seven-part symmetry and bracketed by the matching messages of hope in chapters 9 and 11 (22.6).

The expression "in that day" (*bayyôm hahûʾ*; 11:10; 12:1, 4) punctuates the collection's joyous final unit in 11:10–12:6. This unit envisions the restoration of Judah and Israel to their lands, the reestablishment of peace, and the restoration of their relationship with Yahweh.

The seven units that make up this introductory collection of messages in Isaiah form a symmetry, with the highlighted central unit being, significantly, Isaiah's call in chapter 6 (22.7).

Oracles against the Nations (Isaiah 13–27)

Isaiah 13:1 introduces the beginning of the second major unit in Isaiah: the oracles against the nations. While the oracles themselves end with chapter 23, the message of chapters 24–27 should be included in the collection. This final message echoes the introductory oracle against Babylon and functions as the collection's joyous conclusion (paralleling the conclusion of the first collection).

The internal arrangement of this collection is puzzling. G. A. Smith calls this section a "jungle" or "thicket," containing "a number of long and short prophecies which are a fertile source of perplexity . . . here [the reader] loses himself among a series of prophecies obscure in them-

selves and without obvious relation to one another."[5] One observation that helps clarify the apparent mess is that some of the smaller oracles may not be intended as separate units but may function as component parts of larger units.[6] For example, the final nine verses of chapter 14 (which speak of Assyria and Philistia) may function as the conclusion of the Babylon oracle.[7] Likewise, the disparate material in chapters 17–20 (22.8), though complex,[8] is prob-

5. G. A. Smith, *The Book of Isaiah* (New York: Armstrong, 1888; rev. ed.: New York: Harper, 1927), 1.271–72.

6. Some are too short to function as major literary units: the words about Arabia comprise only five verses (21:13–17), Assyria and Philistia have four verses apiece (14:24–27, 29–32), Damascus possibly only three verses (17:1–3), and Edom only two verses (21:11–12). Moreover, two of these (Assyria and Ethiopia) do not even have introductions, suggesting that they are part of what precedes them.

7. This is suggested by the mention of the Assyrians in 14:24–27, which has no special introduction and continues the theme of the preceding verses—Yahweh's "breaking" the Mesopotamian enemy (cf. 14:5). The four-verse message for Philistia features the warning not to "rejoice" (*śmḥ*) that "the rod (*šēbeṭ*) that smote you is broken (*šbr*)" (14:29), a natural addendum to the Babylon oracle, which declared, "Yahweh has broken (*šbr*) the . . . rod (*šēbeṭ*) of the rulers; . . . the whole earth . . . rejoices (*śmḥ*)" (14:5–8).

8. The unit begins with "an oracle for Damascus" (17:1) but quickly shifts focus to include the northern kingdom of Israel (17:3–11), followed by two sections, neither one introduced, of "woes" (*hôy*) upon "many peoples" (17:12–14) and Ethiopia (18:1–7), which ends with a depiction of the Ethiopians "at that time" bringing gifts to Yahweh in Jerusalem (18:7). Next comes a section entitled "an oracle for Egypt" (19:1–25), which ends with a prophecy of the future conversion of the Egyptians to the worship of Yahweh (19:16–25). And this is followed by a brief message involving Isaiah's going about naked for three years as a sign that Egypt and Ethiopia will be taken into exile by Assyria (20:1–6).

22.8 Oracles against Egypt and Ethiopia (Isaiah 17–20)

a **Syria and Israel will be conquered and depopulated (17:1–3)**
  b **devastated Israel's remnant will turn to Yahweh (17:4–11)**
   - begins and punctuated by phrase <u>in that day</u> (*bayyôm hahû᾿*)
   - four or <u>five</u> remaining "branches"; fate of their "strong <u>cities</u>"
    c **fall of Ethiopia ("rivers," "waters," "Nile") (17:12?–18:3)**
     d **Ethiopian remnant will worship Yahweh in Zion (18:4–7)**
    c´ **fall of Egypt ("rivers," "waters," "Nile") (19:1–15)**
   b´ **devastated Egypt's remnant will turn to Yahweh**, worshiping him together with Israel and Assyria (19:16–25)
   - begins and punctuated by phrase <u>in that day</u> (*bayyôm hahû᾿*)
   - fate of <u>five</u> of the <u>cities</u> of Egypt
a´ **Egypt and Ethiopia will be conquered and exiled (20:1–6)**

22.9 Oracles against the nations (Isaiah 13–27)

a **fall of Babylon and Judah's restoration (13:1–14:32)**
   - <u>darkening of sun and moon</u>; shaking, trembling of earth
   - permanent desolation of Babylon; it <u>struck</u> (*nkh*) others, it will be struck; Yahweh will <u>bring it down</u>
   - their agony compared to that of a <u>woman giving birth</u>
   - kings of the earth together in the <u>pit</u> (*bôr*), Sheol
   - Yahweh will show <u>compassion</u> (*rḥm*) to Jacob (and not Babylon)
   - ends: <u>Jews will find refuge</u> in Jerusalem
  b **oracle about Judah's neighbor, Moab (15:1–16:14)**
   - themes: <u>wailing</u> (*yll*), <u>weeping</u>, <u>cessation of rejoicing</u>, <u>singing</u>, playing the <u>harp</u> (*kinnôr*), <u>water and sea</u>
   - ends: <u>three years</u> relating to coming punishment
    c **oracles mostly concerning Egypt and Ethiopia (17:1–20:6)**
   - key phrase: <u>in that day</u> (*bayyôm hahû᾿*)
   - foreigners will come to Jerusalem to worship in future
   - <u>punishment and future restoration</u> of Israel
     d **CENTER: fall of Babylon (and Edom and Arabia) (21:1–17)**
    c´ **oracle concerning Jerusalem and Egyptian(?) Shebna (22:1–25)**
   - key phrase: <u>in that day</u> (*bayyôm hahû᾿*)
   - present inhabitants of Jerusalem will flee
   - <u>punishment and future restoration</u> of Judah
  b´ **oracle about Judah's neighbor, Tyre (23:1–18)**
   - themes: <u>wailing</u> (*yll*), <u>weeping</u>, <u>cessation of rejoicing</u>, <u>singing</u>, playing the <u>harp</u> (*kinnôr*), <u>water and sea</u>
   - ends: <u>seventy years</u> relating to coming punishment
a´ **fall of "the lofty city" (Babylon) and Judah's restoration (24:1–27:13)**
   - <u>darkening of sun and moon</u>; shaking, trembling of earth
   - permanent desolation of "the lofty city"; it <u>struck</u> (*nkh*) others, it will be struck; Yahweh will <u>bring it down</u>
   - their agony compared to that of a <u>woman giving birth</u>
   - kings of the earth together in the <u>pit</u> (*bôr*), Sheol
   - Yahweh will not show <u>compassion</u> (*rḥm*) on Judah's enemy
   - ends: <u>Jews will find refuge</u> in Jerusalem

---

ably a single literary unit;[9] it appears to exhibit a seven-part symmetric structure.

The entire unit in chapters 13–27 is possibly arranged in a seven-part symmetry (22.9). The introductory oracle about Babylon (a) is con-

spicuously echoed in the concluding message about the fall of Judah's enemy (Babylon!) and Judah's restoration (a´). Correlation between these two messages includes the following:

1. Babylon's (or the lofty city's) fall is predicted in both messages, along with Judah's restoration.
2. Both messages predict the eternal desolation of the enemy city (13:9, 19–22; 24:10; 25:2; 27:10).
3. Both messages describe the darkening of the sun and moon (13:10; 24:23), the shaking of the earth (14:16; 24:19–20), and suffering like a woman in pain as she gives birth (13:8; 26:17).

9. The message about Egypt and Ethiopia (20:1–6) is certainly connected to the woe upon Ethiopia (18:1–7) and the message about Egypt (19:1–25). Moreover, the woe upon Ethiopia has no introduction but emerges from the message beginning in 17:1 (entitled "oracle for Damascus"). Accordingly, although complex, Isaiah 17–20 forms a single unit with a single theme: the nations around Israel will be defeated, but their remnants will one day join restored Israel in worshiping Yahweh (17:4–7; 18:7; 19:18–25). Supporting this analysis is the unit's being so defined to end, like some of the more easily identifiable units of the collection, with a note about the number of years involved in the coming punishment upon the nation (in this case, as with Moab [16:13], three years).

4. Both messages feature scenes of the kings of nations in Sheol ("pit," *bôr*) (14:9–19; 24:21–22).

5. Assyria is mentioned in both messages and nowhere else in these chapters (14:25; 27:13).

6. In both messages, the enemy has "struck" (*nkh*) others but will now itself be "struck" (14:5–6, 29; 27:7) and "brought down" to the earth by Yahweh (14:11–12, 15; 25:11, 12; 26:5–6).

7. Both messages end with a prediction of the remnant's finding refuge in Jerusalem (14:32; 27:12–13).

8. Mention of "Euphrates" in 27:12–13 provides a link with the Babylon oracle.

Likewise, the second and next-to-last units may be intended as matches: both oracles deal with Israel's immediate neighbors: Moab (b) and Tyre (b′); they both contain themes of "wailing" (*yll*) (15:2, 3; 16:7; 23:1, 6), weeping (cf. 15:4, 5, 7, 8, 9, 11; 23:14), the cessation of rejoicing (16:9, 10; 23:2, 4, 12), singing (16:10; 23:16), playing the "harp" (*kinnôr*) (16:11; 23:16), and water and sea (15:6, 9; 16:8; 23:3, 4, 11); and both oracles end with a prediction of the number of years the nations' punishment will last.[10]

The third and third-to-last units of the collection, the oracle involving Egypt and Ethiopia (c) and the oracle about Jerusalem (c′), at first seem unrelated. There may, however, be a possible connection. A large portion of the oracle in chapter 22 (vv. 15–25) focuses on the condemnation of Shebna, who may have been an Egyptian agent serving in Jerusalem.[11] Also, both units focus on the coming punishment and restoration of Yahweh's own people: Israel (cf. 17:3–9) and Judah. Jerusalem, the central focus of chapter 22, is also a focal point in chapters 17–20. It will be the place to which foreigners come to worship Yahweh (18:3–7). Admittedly, all this is tenuous.

The central unit (d) of the collection is "the oracle concerning the 'Wilderness by the Sea' "— presumably Babylon (cf. 21:9)! If so, the entire collection not only opens and closes with units about Babylon, but also has an oracle about Babylon at its center—highlighting the author's focus in this collection.[12]

These oracles establish the author's case that Yahweh alone is worthy of Judah's trust, for it is he and he alone who determines the fate of nations and peoples. He will one day restore Judah and punish their enemies, including mighty Bablyon.

Collection of Woe-Messages (Isaiah 28–35)

Between the oracles against the nations in chapters 13–27 and the historical narratives in chapters 36–39 is a collection of woe-oracles—messages of condemnation, most beginning with the word "woe" (*hôy*; 28:1; 29:1, 15; 30:1; 31:1; 33:1). S. R. Driver analyzes this section as comprising seven units (five of which begin with *hôy*):[13]

---

a coming fall of proud Samaria (and condemnation of Judah) (28:1–29)

b coming siege of Jerusalem (29:1–24)

c failure of the Egyptian negotiations (30:1–33)

d disappointment to be expected from Egypt (31:1–32:8)

e condemnation of the indifference of Judah's women (32:9–20)

f coming failure of the Assyrians to take Jerusalem (33:1–24)

g contrasted future of Edom and of Israel (34:1–35:10)

Driver's identification of the first three units is convincing.[14] The message beginning in 30:1,

---

10. It is noteworthy that, of the central five units, four end with a brief concluding pericope involving the number of years regarding the upcoming judgment upon that people (16:13–14; 20:1–4; 21:16–17; 23:15–18). In fact, two of these are similar: "But now Yahweh says, 'In three years, like the years of a hireling (*śākîr*), the glory of Moab will be brought into contempt . . . and those who survive will be very few' " (Isa. 16:13–14); "For Yahweh said to me, 'Within a year, according to the years of a hireling (*śākîr*), all the glory of Kedar will come to an end; and the remainder of the . . . sons of Kedar will be few' " (Isa. 21:16–17). These four endings, together with the brief declarations of hope marking the conclusions of the first and last units, appear to have been employed by the author/editor to mark the ends of six of his seven units. The oracle about Jerusalem has no such end marker, unless the addendum regarding Shebna was itself considered an obvious end marker.

11. See Otto Kaiser, *Isaiah 13–39*, trans. R. A. Wilson (Old Testament Library; Philadelphia: Westminster, 1974), 150–51.

12. The final seven verses of Isaiah 21, including the two enigmatic verses addressed poetically to Edom and the five to Arabia (both of whom were participants with Babylon in Judah's fall), are probably intended as the completion of this central unit. The concluding reference (21:16–17) to the time left before the fall of punishment marks this unit's end.

13. Driver, *Introduction to the Literature of the Old Testament*, 223–26. Similarly, Duhm (see Eissfeldt, *Old Testament: An Introduction*, 306), sees Isaiah 28–33 as containing seven sayings beginning either with "woe" (28:1; 29:1, 15; 30:1; 31:1; 33:1) or "see" (*hēn*) (32:1), with Isaiah 34–35 functioning as the conclusion to Isaiah 1–33.

14. The message of Isaiah 28 is bracketed by the introductory "woes" (28:1; 29:1) and concluded by a closing note of hope. The beginning of the next message, in Isaiah 29, is also conspicuous because of the shift to a new focus (Jerusalem's fall). The message of Isaiah 30 begins with another introductory "woe" and a shift to a new topic (warning against depending on Egypt). The occurrence of another "woe" in 29:15 appears to mark the beginning of a secondary unit within the larger oracle of Isaiah 29. The topics of 29:1–14, such as seeing and not seeing (29:10), not being able to read the words of a book (29:11–12), and learning/teaching (29:13–14), continue to the end of the chapter (29:15–18, 24)—indicating the unity of the message in Isaiah 29.

22.10 The future king (Isaiah 32–33)

a **future rule of the righteous king** and the transformation of society (32:1–8)
  - topics: king, streams of water, eyes that see, musing <u>hearts</u> (*lēbāb*) of the rash and fools, secure dwelling places, safety from storms, "the tongue of the stammerers" that will speak so that people can understand

b **coming judgment upon the land and the <u>women</u>** (32:9–14)
  - begins: <u>rise up</u>! (from *qûm*); exhortations to <u>hear</u> and <u>tremble</u>
  - failure of <u>food supplies</u> for haughty women

c **future blessings upon the land** (32:15–20)
  - <u>transformation</u> of the <u>wilderness</u> into <u>fertile fields</u>
  - resultant <u>peace</u> (*šālôm*); people living in trust

d **CENTER: a prayer:** Yahweh, be our salvation! (33:1–6)

c′ **present languishing of the land** (33:7–9)
  - <u>transformation</u> of the <u>fertile fields</u> into a <u>wilderness</u>
  - weeping envoys of <u>peace</u> (*šālôm*); people living in mistrust

b′ **coming judgment upon the land;** people addressed as if <u>women</u> ("you conceive . . . give birth to . . .") (33:10–16)
  - begins: now I will <u>rise up</u>! (from *qûm*); exhortation to <u>hear</u>; <u>trembling</u> seizes them
  - security of <u>food supplies</u> for the righteous

a′ **future rule of Yahweh as king** and the transformation of society (33:17–24)
  - topics: the king, rivers and streams, eyes that will see, musing <u>hearts</u> (*lēb*) of the wise, "an immovable tent whose stakes will never be plucked up," and "the strange tongue" that cannot be understood

---

22.11 Collection of woe-messages (Isaiah 28–35)

a **Yahweh's coming overthrow of Judah's enemy to the north, Samarïa** (28:1–29)
  - promise and warning to Judah

b **coming (Assyrian) siege of Jerusalem and promise of Yahweh's rescue** (29:1–24)
  - exhortation to people of Judah; eyes that see/do not see; lips; <u>mind</u> (*lēb*)

c **warning to Judah: do not rely on Egypt!** (30:1–14)

d **CENTER: trust in Yahweh!** (30:15–33)

c′ **warning to Judah: do not rely on Egypt!** (31:1–9)

b′ **coming (Assyrian) attack of Jerusalem, and promise of Yahweh's rescue**, restoration, and rule over the city (32:1–33:24)
  - exhortation to people of Judah; eyes that see/do not see; lips; <u>mind</u> (*lēbāb*)

a′ **Yahweh's coming overthrow of Judah's enemy to the south, Edom** (34:1–35:10)
  - Judah's glorious future return to Zion

---

however, probably ends in 30:14, with 30:15 introducing a new message (its beginning marked by the expression *kî* + "thus says the Lord Yahweh, the Holy One of Israel"), with a new theme that encompasses 30:15–33. Similarly, the message introduced in 31:1, warning against trusting in Egypt, extends only to the end of chapter 31; a new message with a new focus begins in chapter 32, introduced by the common beginning marker *hēn* ("behold").[15] The message beginning in 32:1 most likely extends through chapter 33, since a number of themes and topics in chapter 32 continue throughout chapter 33 (king, establishment of righteousness, streams of water, stammering tongues, etc.). Moreover, the seemingly disparate parts in chapters 32–33 form a symmetry that indicates their unity (22.10).

Chapters 34–35, the final unit in the collection of woe-messages, functions as a majestic conclusion to the entire section, drawing together the themes developed throughout chapters 28–33 (transformation of the wilderness into fertile land, eyes of the blind, ears of the deaf, rivers, highways, Yahweh's victory over Judah's enemies, etc.). Like the book's first two units, this one ends with a celebrative grand finale.

The unity of chapters 28–35 is created in part by the singularity of its theme, which could be summarized as follows: place your trust in Yahweh, not Egypt, because it is only by Yahweh's decree that Judah's present enemies—such as Samaria and Edom—will fall; and it is only Yahweh who can save Jerusalem from the even greater threat of the coming (Assyrian) attack against Jerusalem. The arrangement of this section reinforces its cohesion. Its seven constituent messages appear to form a symmetry, with the call to trust in Yahweh positioned, notably, as the highlighted center (22.11).

The stage is now set for the narrative that follows, which recounts the story of the Assyrian invasion and Yahweh's deliverance, a story that vindicates the call to trust in Yahweh alone!

---

15. As Duhm argues; see Eissfeldt, *Old Testament: An Introduction*, 306.

22.12 Historical narratives (Isaiah 36–39)

a **arrival of the hostile Assyrian emissary** (36:1–22)
   - Assyrian king sends envoy to Hezekiah with threatening message and an army
   - Hezekiah does not even receive them into the city or give them a reply.
b **Hezekiah's distress and his appeal to Yahweh for help** (37:1–7)
   - begins: Hezekiah hears the bad news of the Assyrian message
   - Hezekiah appeals to Isaiah to pray to Yahweh for help
   - Isaiah's message of reassurance: Yahweh will deliver you from the Assyrian king!
   c **Sennacherib's blasphemous message to Hezekiah**: "don't be deceived by your god!" Yahweh cannot deliver you! (37:8–13)
      d **CENTER: Hezekiah's prayer to Yahweh**: "save us . . . that all may know that you alone, Yahweh, are God!" (37:14–20)
   c′ **Yahweh's response to Sennacherib's blasphemous message and Hezekiah's prayer**: because of Sennacherib's mockery of Yahweh, and in response to Hezekiah's prayer, Yahweh will deliver Hezekiah and punish Sennacherib. Yahweh delivers Jerusalem! Sennacherib is assassinated (37:21–38)
b′ **Hezekiah's sickness and his appeal to Yahweh for help** (38:1–22)
   - begins: Hezekiah hears the bad news about his approaching death
   - Hezekiah appeals to Yahweh directly for help
   - Isaiah's message of reassurance: Yahweh will deliver you from the Assyrian king and will add fifteen years to your life! Hezekiah's praise
a′ **arrival of the friendly Babylonian emissaries** (irony!) (39:1–8)
   - Babylonian king sends envoys to Hezekiah with peaceful message and a gift
   - Hezekiah welcomes them into the city and shows them all his treasures

Collection of Historical Narratives (Isaiah 36–39)

The fourth—and central—unit in Isaiah is the collection of historical narratives in chapters 36–39. This unit functions as the book's pivot, providing the transition from the Assyrian threat that dominates the first half of the book, to the Babylonian captivity that will be the focus of the book's second half. Isaiah 36–37 recounts the Assyrian invasion and Yahweh's deliverance of Jerusalem, bringing to a grand conclusion all that was feared and promised in the first half of Isaiah. Isaiah 38–39 relates the visit of the Babylonian envoys, with Isaiah's prediction that (ironically) it will be Babylon (not Assyria) that will one day conquer and exile Jerusalem. The audience is thus prepared for the major shift in focus in the second half of the book.

The narratives in Isaiah 36–39 comprise seven episodes, chiastically arranged (22.12). The symmetric scheme has been achieved, however, at the expense of chronological order, for the events of chapters 38–39 occurred before the events in chapters 36–37.

This central unit in the Book of Isaiah functions to demonstrate that Yahweh alone is God (cf. 37:20); that he alone can stop mighty armies (no pagan "gods" could do this; cf. 37:11–12); and that he knows what will happen in the future (chap. 39). The audience is now prepared for the thrust of the next unit, which will expand upon these two themes—that Yahweh is superior to the pagan gods and that he alone knows the future.

Yahweh's Supremacy over the Worthless Idols of the Nations (Isaiah 40–48)

It is generally agreed that chapters 40–48 form a self-contained unit focusing on the theme of Yahweh's superiority over useless idols (40:19–20; 41:6–7, 28–29; 42:17; 44:9–20; 45:20; 46:1–7; 48:5), particularly demonstrated in his ability to determine and know what will happen in the distant future. This intensively developed theme runs throughout chapters 40–48 and then abruptly ends when chapter 49 introduces a new set of themes. Other themes that tie Isaiah 40–48 together include the following:

1. Yahweh's plans to raise up a future king from the east, named Cyrus, to carry out Yahweh's will
2. Yahweh's plans to bring the Jewish exiles back from their Babylonian captivity
3. Yahweh's care over the poor, blind, and weak among the returning exiles

Though there is a general consensus regarding the parameters of this section, a conspicuous lack of agreement remains over the identification of its constituent units. J. L. McKenzie complains about the apparent chaos encountered here and throughout Second Isaiah:

Critics distinguish separate utterances; but there is no general agreement on their number nor on the points of division. There are, it is true, repetitions of themes and returns to points already made. . . . But the arrangement makes it more difficult to isolate separate sayings than it is in Amos, Hosea, or [First] Isaiah. Most critics now count about fifty to seventy

22.13 Yahweh's supremacy over the idols (Isaiah 45:20–46:13)

  a **Yahweh is the only one who can** <u>save</u> (*yšʿ*); invitation to nations who pray to wooden idols that cannot <u>save</u> (*yšʿ*), to <u>draw near</u> (45:20–21a)

    b **Yahweh is incomparable,** declaring the future; turn to him! (45:21b–25)

      c **idols are helpless:** they must be <u>carried</u> (*nśʾ*) (46:1–2)

        d **CENTER:** in contrast to the idols, **Yahweh has** <u>made</u> (*ʿśh*) **and** <u>carried</u> (*nśʾ, sbl*) **Israel** from the beginning (46:3–5)

      c′ **idols are** <u>made</u> (*ʿśh*) by humans and must be <u>carried</u> (*nśʾ, sbl*) (46:6–7)

    b′ **Yahweh is incomparable,** declaring the future; consider this! (46:8–11)

  a′ **Yahweh brings near his** <u>salvation</u> (*yšʿ*) for those who are far; his <u>salvation</u> (*yšʿ*) is given to Zion; it is not <u>far off</u> (46:12–13)

---

separate sayings in Second Isaiah. . . . In the first major part [chaps. 40–48] we have arranged the sayings in twenty-two poems of varying lengths.[16]

One conspicuous boundary marker in this section is the periodic occurrence of summary promises that Yahweh will help, guide, strengthen, protect, and (in some cases) provide water for the returning exiles on their arduous journey home. These often occur at points that seem by their content to function as conclusions of units: 40:29–31; 41:17–20; 42:16–17; 43:2–7; 45:13–14; 48:17–22. And in four instances these conclusions are followed by abrupt shifts in mood, with Yahweh challenging the nations to assemble in court for a case involving them and him (41:1; 41:21–22; 43:8–9; 45:20–21).

By themselves these markers delineate six units: 40:1–31; 41:1–20; 41:21–42:17; 42:18–43:7; 43:8–45:19; 45:20–48:22. Of these, the last two are exceptionally long. Closer examination suggests that the fifth unit is probably self-contained[17] and that the final unit is comprised of two subunits: 45:20–46:13 and 47:1–48:22. The symmetric layout of 45:20–46:13 suggests its unity (22.13).

At the same time, chapters 47–48 appear to form a single unit about Yahweh's rescuing his people from Babylon by decreeing the city's fall and by bringing his exiled people back home.[18]

If all this is more or less correct, chapters 40–48 could be analyzed as comprising seven main literary units arranged in a symmetry (22.14).

Messages about the Suffering Servant and Mother Israel's Restoration (Isaiah 49–54)

Isaiah 49 introduces the book's next section with an abrupt shift to the first-person discourse of an unidentified servant of Yahweh: "Listen to me . . . you distant lands. Before I was born Yahweh called me" (49:1). The focus of the new section is this enigmatic suffering servant, together with the restoration of Israel—depicted as a barren/bereaved mother who will be given many new children. The extent and internal organization of this section is disputed.[19] Careful analysis suggests that the collection extends neither to chapter 57 (Delitzsch) nor chapter 55 (others) but to chapter 54. The themes introduced in chapter 49 continue only through chapter 54; and chapter 55 introduces a new set of themes (exhortations to repentance, condemnations, etc.) that will continue throughout the next section.

The constituent units of Isaiah 49–54 include 49:1–26 and 50:1–11 (both arranged in seven-part chiasmuses); 51:1–16 (united by the theme of Yahweh's mighty salvation, past and future); 51:17–23 (focusing on the fall of Jerusalem's oppressors); 52:1–12 (united by the theme of Jerusalem's restoration and purification); 52:13–53:12 (the suffering servant); 54:1–17.

The main function of this section seems to be to persuade the future exiles in Babylonian exile that they—like Hezekiah of old—should place their faith and hope in almighty Yahweh alone; for he has wonderful plans for them, including their salvation through his humble servant and

---

16. J. L. McKenzie, *Second Isaiah* (Anchor Bible 20; Garden City: Doubleday, 1968), 15–100. Delitzsch (*Isaiah*, 2.128) analyzes Isaiah 40–48 as a unit comprised of nine addresses: 40:1–31; 41:1–29; 42:1–43:13; 43:14–44:5; 44:6–23; 44:24–45:25; 46:1–13; 47:1–15; 48:1–22.

17. Isaiah 43:8–44:8 begins with the assertion that Yahweh alone is God; and Israel will be witnesses to that because he is declaring ahead of time his plans to bring them back from captivity in Babylon, restoring and forgiving them. The center (44:9–20) presents the vivid contrast of the folly of idolatry. This is followed by Yahweh's assertion that he alone is God and creator, as shown by his declaring ahead of time his plans to raise up Cyrus to bring his people back from captivity (44:21–45:19). The a-b-a′ structure suggests unity.

18. As several of the other units began with a calling of the nations to come and assemble in court, this final unit begins similarly by calling Babylon to come down and sit (but not on a throne) and to hear Yahweh's case and verdict against it. Others are then called to "assemble," to "draw near" (48:14, 16), and hear Yahweh's final words.

19. Delitzsch (*Isaiah*, 2.256–383) proposes that the collection extends through chap. 57, its end being marked by the refrain "there is no peace, says my God, for the wicked" (57:21)—which echoes the closing of the previous collection (48:22). He identifies nine units in this section: 49:1–26; 50:1–11; 51:1–23; 52:1–12; 52:13–53:12; 54:1–17; 55:1–13; 56:1–8; 56:9–57:21. More typical of modern scholars, McKenzie, *Second Isaiah*, 103–45, extends the unit only through chap. 55 and divides the material into eight parts: 49:1–6; 49:7–13; 49:14–50:3; 50:4–11; 51:1–52:12; 52:13–53:12; 54:1–17; 55:1–13.

22.14 Yahweh's supremacy over the idols, and Jerusalem's future restoration (Isaiah 40–48)

a **good news for Jerusalem!** (40:1–31)
  - Yahweh has forgiven Jerusalem: its punishment is completed; it will now be blessed and he will bring his people home!
  - Yahweh is the one who created the heavens and stars (40:12, 22, 26)
  - Jerusalem's punishment is declared adequate

b **Yahweh, superior to all the idols, is raising up one from the east (*mimmizrāḥ*)** (41:1–20)
  - the idol makers make and secure with nails their idols; meanwhile, Yahweh has established and made Israel secure
  - begins: exhortation to approach (*ngš*) and come together (*yaḥdāw*)
  - manufacturing of idols; work of the goldsmith (*ṣōrēp*) (41:7)
  - securing of the idol so that it cannot be moved

c **Yahweh's challenge to idols: can they tell the future as he can?** (41:21–42:17)
  - declaration: in the future he will raise up one from the north and east who will conquer rulers; his other servant
  - theme: helping the blind

d **CENTER: call to sinful Israel to respond to Yahweh** and his punishment; promise of Israel's restoration (42:18–43:7)

c′ **Yahweh's challenge to idols: can they tell the future as he can?** (43:8–45:19)
  - declaration: in the future he will raise up a king named Cyrus, who will send exiled Israel home from their captivity
  - theme: helping the blind

b′ **Yahweh, superior to all the idols, is calling a bird of prey from the east (*mimmizrāḥ*)** (45:20–46:13)
  - idol makers make and secure with nails their idols; in contrast, Yahweh has established and made Israel secure
  - begins: exhortation to approach (*ngš*) and come together (*yaḥdāw*)
  - manufacturing of idols; work of the goldsmith (*ṣōrēp*) (46:6)
  - securing of the idol so that it cannot be moved from its place

a′ **bad news for Babylon!** (47:1–48:22)
  - Babylon's period of prosperity is completed: it will now be punished and Yahweh will bring his people home
  - Babylon seeks help in vain from the heavens and stars
  - Israel's punishment is explained (48:8–11)

the marvelous restoration of Jerusalem and their ruined land.

There are some indications that the unit's seven constituent parts are arranged with a symmetric touch, reinforcing its unity (22.15).

Final Messages of Condemnation, Pleading, and Future Restoration (Isaiah 55–66)

Isaiah 55 introduces the book's final collection of messages. These final messages—like those in the book's first unit—are a combination of present-oriented and future-oriented oracles: the prophet condemns and warns his contemporaries, pleading with them to return to Yahweh; but he also speaks of future hope and restoration. There is wide difference of opinion regarding the internal structure of this collection.[20]

The collection's first unit, despite current opinion, is probably the entirety of chapters 55–56, which features an invitation to come (back) to Yahweh, with the promise of future blessing. The unit's arrangement follows the typical seven-part symmetric scheme (22.16).

The second message of the collection, in chapter 57, centers on the condemnation of Israel's idolatrous practices. The unit, likewise arranged in a seven-part symmetry (the units are verses 1–2, 3–6, 7–10, 11–13, 14–15, 16–18, 19–21), begins and ends with a focus on the "peace" (*šālôm*) that the righteous will experience and that the wicked will not experience (57:1–2; 19–20).

Isaiah 58–59 forms a third literary unit[21] dealing with the hypocrisy of Israel's religious activity and simultaneous social injustice. Oppression and justice are prominent themes. The structure, a seven-part chiasmus, ties the material together (22.17).

Isaiah 60 forms the fourth and central literary unit of this section. Its structure is also symmetric (22.18).

The fifth unit, Isaiah 61:1–62:9, proclaims good news for Jerusalem: it is to be rebuilt and restored. This is followed by a sixth unit, 62:10–64:12 [62:10–64:11], which presents a message of promise for the righteous and a threat for Yahweh's enemies. This unit is introduced by the sweeping series of imperatives in 62:10–11 and is closed by the prophet's prayer in 63:7–64:12 [63:7–64:11].

The seventh and final unit is chapters 65–66. It represents Yahweh's response to the prayer of

---

20. Delitzsch (*Isaiah*, 2.128) analyzes Isaiah 55–66 as containing twelve messages: 55:1–13; 56:1–8; 56:9–57:21; 58:1–14; 59:1–21; 60:1–22; 61:1–11; 62:1–12; 63:1–6; 63:7–64:12 [63:7–64:11]; 65:1–25; 66:1–24. Smith (*Isaiah*, 2.397–445) detects four parts in Isaiah 54–66: 54:1–56:8; 56:9–59:21; 60:1–63:7; 63:8–66:24. Driver (*Introduction to the Literature of the Old Testament*, 245–46) analyzes Isaiah 56–66 as containing seven units: 56:1–8; 56:9–57:13a; 58:1–59:21; 60:1–62:12; 63:7–64:12; 65:1–66:24 (presumably).

21. See Driver, *Introduction to the Literature of the Old Testament*, 245–46.

22.15 The suffering servant (Isaiah 49–54)

a **restoration of Mother Jerusalem and her children through the servant** (49:1–26)
- Zion, a barren/bereaved mother, will unexpectedly have many new children
- her numerous new children will require expanding her living quarters (49:20)
- Yahweh's love is more enduring than the love of a mother for her suckling child
- Yahweh's compassion (*rḥm*) for his afflicted (*ʿănî*) people (49:13)
- Yahweh's forsaking (*ʿzb*) and forgetting (*škḥ*) Israel (49:14–15)
- sing for joy (*ronnû*), break forth (*pṣḥ*) in singing (*rinnâ*) (49:13)
- themes: covenant (*bĕrît*), mountains (*hārîm*), nations (*gôyim*), etc.

b **the suffering servant and Israel's sins** (50:1–11)
- the servant is beaten (*nkh*) and humiliated (50:6–7)
- he did not "hide (*str*) his face (*pānîm*) from shame" (50:6)
- Israel punished for its iniquities (*ʿăwōnōt*) and transgressions (*pĕšaʿîm*)
- Yahweh will help and vindicate the servant (50:7–9)
- ends: behold (*hēn*) and who? (*mî*) (50:8–11)

c **almighty Yahweh will rescue his people** (51:1–16)
- awake, awake, put on strength (*ʿûrî ʿûrî libšî-ʿōz*)
- themes: singing, joy, return from exile

d **CENTER: Mother Jerusalem, bereaved of her children, will be restored!** (51:17–23)

c′ **almighty Yahweh will rescue his people** (52:1–12)
- awake, awake, put on your strength (*ʿûrî ʿûrî libšî ʿuzzēk*)
- themes: singing, joy, return from exile

b′ **the suffering servant and the forgiveness of Israel's sins** (52:13–53:12)
- the servant is beaten (*nkh*) and humiliated (53:3–8)
- he is "as one from whom people hide (*str*) their faces (*pānîm*)" (53:3)
- "he was wounded for our transgressions (*pĕšaʿîm*) and bruised for our iniquities (*ʿăwōnōt*)" (53:5)
- Yahweh will help and vindicate the servant (52:13; 53:10–12)
- begins: behold (*hinnēh*) and who? (*mî*)

a′ **restoration of Mother Jerusalem and her children** (54:1–17)
- Israel, once a barren mother, will unexpectedly have many new children (54:1)
- her numerous new children will require expanding her living quarters (54:2)
- Yahweh's love is more enduring than the permanent mountains and hills (54:10)
- Yahweh's compassion (*rḥm*) for the afflicted one (*ʿănî*) (54:8–11)
- Yahweh's forsaking (*ʿzb*) and forgetting (*škḥ*) Israel (54:4–8)
- sing for joy (*ronnî*), break forth (*pṣḥ*) in singing (*rinnâ*) (54:1)
- themes: covenant (*bĕrît*), mountains (*hārîm*), nations (*gôyim*), etc.

22.16 Invitation to return to Yahweh (Isaiah 55–56)

a **invitation to people to come and eat** (a happy invitation!) (55:1–3a)
- begins: vocative introduced by all, every (*kol*)
- themes: eating (*ʾākal*), wine (*yayin*)

b **promise to people: Yahweh will make a covenant with them** (55:3b–5)
- Yahweh's covenant (*bĕrît*), which is eternal (*ʿôlām*) and will include foreign nations

c **call to righteousness** (55:6–9)

d **CENTER: promise of future blessing** (55:10–13)

c′ **call to righteousness** (56:1–2)

b′ **promise to foreigners and eunuchs who keep Yahweh's covenant** (56:3–8)
- those who keep Yahweh's covenant (*bĕrît*) will be given an eternal (*ʿôlām*) name; inclusion of foreigners

a′ **invitation to animals to come and eat** (a foreboding warning!) (56:9–12)
- begins: vocative introduced by all, every (*kol*)
- themes: eating (*ʾākal*), wine (*yayin*)

22.17 Hypocrisy of Israel's religious activity (Isaiah 58–59)

a **Yahweh does not see (*rāʾâ*)** or respond to their fasting because of their transgressions (*pešaʿ*) and lack of righteousness (*ṣĕdāqâ*) (58:1–3a)

b **social injustice and violence** is the cause of Yahweh's unresponsiveness (58:3b–5)

c **true fast** (not "pursuing your own business") (58:6–7)

d **CENTER: blessings of obedience** (58:8–12)

c′ **true Sabbath** (not "pursuing your own business") (58:13–14)

b′ **social injustice and violence** is the cause of Yahweh's unresponsiveness (59:1–15a)

a′ **Yahweh does see (*rāʾâ*)** their injustice; he will respond to those who turn from transgression (*pešaʿ*); he clothes himself in righteousness (*ṣĕdāqâ*) (59:15b–21)

22.18 The light of Yahweh (Isaiah 60)

a   **the light of Yahweh will dawn on you** (60:1–3)
   • themes: <u>brightness</u> (*nōgah*), <u>glory</u>, <u>light</u> (*ʾôr*)
  b   **nations will bring you gifts** (gold, etc.) (60:4–7)
   c   **foreigners will bring your children to you** (60:8–9)
    d   **CENTER: Yahweh will restore the glory of Jerusalem** and his temple; foreign nations will serve Israel (60:10–13)
   cʹ   **children of your (foreign) oppressors will come to you** (60:14–16)
  bʹ   **nations will bring you gifts** (gold, etc.) (60:17–18)
aʹ   **Yahweh will be your light**: no more need for sun and moon (60:19–22)
   • themes: <u>brightness</u> (*nōgah*), <u>glory</u>, <u>light</u> (*ʾôr*)

22.19 Final invitation to return to Yahweh (Isaiah 55–66)

a   **invitation to wicked and promise of future restoration** (55:1–56:12)
   • themes: <u>Sabbath</u> observance (56:2, 4, 6), <u>inclusion of Gentiles</u> in worship at Jerusalem (56:3–8), <u>regathering of exiles</u> (55:12–13; 56:8)
   • "<u>seek</u> Yahweh while he may be found" (55:6)
   • <u>transformation of nature</u>: plants (55:12–13)
   • references to <u>heaven</u> and <u>earth</u>
  b   **condemnation of God's wicked people**, with a note of hope (57:1–21)
   • "<u>build up, build up, prepare the way, remove every obstruction</u> from my people's way" (57:14)
   c   **call to restoration of true righteousness** (58:1–59:21)
    • theme: justice—"will you <u>proclaim</u> (*qārāʾ*) this . . . a day <u>acceptable to Yahweh</u> (*rāṣôn layhwh*)?" (58:5)
    • "to loose the bonds of wickedness, to undo the thongs of the yoke, to let the oppressed go free" (58:6)
    • <u>rebuilding the ancient ruins</u>, raising up the broken foundations, repairing the breaches (58:12)
    • "he put on righteousness as a breastplate, and a helmet of <u>salvation</u> . . . garments of vengeance for clothing" (59:17)
    d   **CENTER: glorious future restoration of Israel** (60:1–22)
   cʹ   **future restoration of true righteousness** (61:1–62:9)
    • theme: justice—"to <u>proclaim</u> (*qārāʾ*) the year <u>acceptable to Yahweh</u> (*rāṣôn layhwh*)" (61:2)
    • "to bind up the brokenhearted, to proclaim liberty to the captives, to open the prison to those who are bound" (61:1)
    • <u>rebuilding the ancient ruins</u>, raising up the broken foundations, repairing the breaches (61:4)
    • "he has clothed me with the garments of <u>salvation</u>, he has covered me with the robe of righteousness" (61:10)
  bʹ   **condemnation and coming punishment of God's wicked people**, with a prayer for forgiveness and restoration (62:10–64:12 [62:10–64:11])
   • "prepare the way for the people; <u>build up, build up the highway, clear it of stones</u>" (62:10)
aʹ   **invitation to wicked and promise of future restoration** (65:1–66:24)
   • themes: <u>Sabbath</u> (66:23), <u>inclusion of Gentiles</u> in Jerusalem's restoration (66:18–21), <u>regathering of exiles</u> and others (66:18–21)
   • "I was ready to be found by those who did not <u>seek</u> me" (65:1)
   • <u>transformation of nature</u>: animals and humans (65:20, 25)
   • references to <u>heaven</u> and <u>earth</u> (65:17; 66:1, 22)

---

the previous unit (cf. 64:12 [64:11]; 65:6). The unit is tied together by references, near the beginning and end, to "eating swine's flesh," cultic impurities "in the gardens," and other "abominations" (65:3–4; 66:17), Yahweh's creation of "new heavens and a new earth" (65:17; 66:22) and by the theme of rejoicing and being glad in/with Jerusalem (65:18–19; 66:10); etc.

The seven units in chapters 55–66 are arranged symmetrically, with chapter 60, the message about the glorious restoration of Jerusalem and the inclusion of the Gentiles, serving as the centerpiece (22.19). This central unit is flanked by two messages dealing with the restoration of true righteousness and justice (c and cʹ). These are flanked in turn by two messages of condemnation and promise (b and bʹ). And framing the entire collection are two messages of future restoration and hope (a and aʹ). These two messages mirror one another and serve as literary clamps holding together the material of chapters 55–66. Shared features include (among others) the Sabbath, the emphasis on God's house and his holy mountain, the involvement of foreigners in the offerings at the temple, and God's renewed responsiveness to prayer.

Overall Layout of the Book of Isaiah

In summary, the Book of Isaiah in its final form comprises seven larger literary units. The fourth section, the narrative interlude in chapters 36–39, functions remarkably well as the book's thematic centerpiece (the vindication of trust in Yahweh, who is superior to all nations and pagan gods) and its turning point (from the present threat of Assyria [chaps. 36–37] to the future conquest by Babylon [chaps. 38–39]). The function of chapters 36–39 as the book's center and turning point presents the intriguing possibility that the entire book may be designed to form an overall symmetry.

Correspondence of First and Last Collections (Isaiah 1–12; 55–66)

Norman Gottwald's observation that "there are striking links in vocabulary and motifs between chaps. 1 and 65–66, strongly pointing to a redactional inclusio for the finished book"[22] can be expanded to include the entirety of chapters 1–12 and chapters 55–66. Both collections, for example, comprise a series of messages to idolatrous and rebellious Jerusalem that contain condemnations, warnings, calls to repentance, and predictions of a glorious future restoration of Jerusalem. In both collections, Judah's empty religious practices and simultaneous lack of justice and righteousness are condemned (1:10–15; 58:1–14). Both collections begin with messages containing calls to repentance (1:16–18; 55:1–56:1—and no other such calls to repentance occur in the book). Both collections contain promises of a future transformation of nature and human life. Numerous literary ties also link the two units, ties that appear to be deliberate:

1. similar wording of condemnations
   a. The book's opening verse ("they have rebelled against me" [$p\bar{a}\check{s}\check{u}$ $b\hat{i}$]; 1:2) is echoed by its final verse ("those who have rebelled against me" [$p\bar{o}\check{s}\check{e}\hat{i}m$ $b\hat{i}$]; 66:24).
   b. Both collections speak of unacceptable and acceptable sacrifices (1:11–13; 56:7; 65:3–7; 66:3, 20) and condemn drunkenness (5:11–12, 22; 56:12) and lying (5:18–20; 59:3–4, 13).
   c. Both collections declare that Yahweh has hidden his face and will not hear their prayers because their hands—lifted in prayer—are full of blood (1:15; cf. 8:17; 59:1–3; cf. 57:17; 64:7 [64:6]; 65:16).
   d. Both collections speak of Israel's desecration of the new moon and Sabbath—a theme found nowhere else in the book (1:13; 56:2, 4, 6; 58:13; cf. 66:23).
2. similar depictions of Judah's punishment
   e. Both units depict the devastation of Judah and Jerusalem as "desolate" ($\check{s}\check{e}$-$m\bar{a}m\hat{a}$) and "burned with fire" ($\acute{s}rp$ $\grave{e}\check{s}$) (1:7; 64:10–11 [64:9–10]). Both frequently warn that the wicked will be punished by fire (e.g., 1:7, 31; 5:24; 9:18, 19 [9:17, 18]; 10:16–17; 64:1–2 [63:19b–64:1]; 64:11 [64:10]; 66:15–16, 24); and

for "rebels" ($p\bar{o}\check{s}\check{e}\hat{i}m$) against Yahweh, this fire will not be "extinguished" (kbh) (1:31; 66:24).
   f. Both units depict Yahweh's punishment in terms of "quaking" (rgz) mountains (5:25; 64:1–3 [63:19b–64:2]), ravaging by wild animals (5:29; 56:9), and the "growing" ($\bar{a}l\hat{a}$) of thorns and briers (5:6; 55:13).
3. similar calls to repentance and promises of restoration
   g. Both sections call for social justice and helping the weak (1:16–17; 56:1; 58:6–7).
   h. Both sections invite sinners to return, introduced by "come" ($l\check{e}k\hat{u}$) (1:18; 55:1) and with the promise of forgiveness of their sins (1:18; 55:7).
   i. Both sections contain promises that Yahweh will gather the "outcasts of Israel" ($nidh\hat{e}$ $yi\acute{s}r\bar{a}\grave{e}l$, an expression that occurs in 11:12 and 56:8 and nowhere else in Isaiah).
   j. Both sections list specific nations from which Yahweh will gather his people, each list ending with the "coastlands" (11:11; 66:19).
   k. Both sections promise that in the future Yahweh will provide Zion with glorious light by night and by day (4:5; 60:19–20) and that the darkness that once covered the land will be transformed into brilliant light (9:2 [9:1]; 60:1–3).
   l. Both sections promise in almost identical wording the future transformation of animals (and both these passages mention changes in the lives of infants; 11:6–8; 65:20, 23):

> The wolf shall dwell with the lamb . . .
> the cow and the bear shall feed together; . . .
> and the lion shall eat straw like the ox. . . .
> They shall not hurt or destroy
> in all my holy mountain.
> —Isaiah 11:6–9
> The wolf and the lamb shall feed together,
> the lion shall eat straw like the ox. . . .
> They shall not hurt or destroy
> in all my holy mountain.
> —Isaiah 65:25

   m. Both sections predict that Yahweh's spirit will be upon the Messiah (11:1–2; 61:1), followed by a description of the Messiah's role, which includes helping the unfortunate (11:3–4; 61:1–3).
   n. Both sections speak of the moral qualities (e.g., "righteousness") that clothe

---

22. Gottwald, *Hebrew Bible*, 384.

Yahweh or his Messiah (11:5; 59:16–17; 61:10).[23]

With chapters 55–66, then, the Book of Isaiah comes full circle, ending with some of the same themes with which it began.

Correspondence of Second and Next-to-Last Collections (Isaiah 13–27; 49–54)

At first glance, the connection between the book's second and next-to-last units is not so apparent. There seems to be little in common between the collection of oracles to the nations in chapters 13–27 and the servant messages in chapters 49–54. There are, to be sure, several general features shared by these two units, such as their almost exclusively future orientation and their focus on Yahweh's plans for the nations. They also exhibit similar arrangements: both units feature a prominent theme (Babylon's fall in the first unit, Mother Jerusalem's rise in the second) at the unit's beginning, middle, and end. And of course the recurring theme of Babylon's fall in chapters 13–27 stands in matching contrast to the recurring theme of Mother Jerusalem's restoration in chapters 49–54 (this ironic contrasting of the humiliation of the proud and the simultaneous exaltation of the humble is highlighted throughout the book).[24] But none of these (except perhaps the

last one) are striking enough to connect the two units.

There is, however, one prominent connection between these two units: two conspicuously contrasted key figures—the haughty king of Babylon (chaps. 13–14) and the humble servant of Yahweh (49:1–26; 50:5–7; 52:13–53:12). There are a surprising number of contrastive correspondences in the descriptions of these two key figures (22.20).

This conspicuous contrasting of the two most prominent figures in these two collections apparently reflects an intentional link between the two collections. This link is reinforced by the similarly contrastive fates of the two most prominent cities in these collections: Babylon and Jerusalem. As suggested earlier, proud Babylon's future fall is featured in the first, middle, and last positions of the first collection; and humbled Jerusalem's future restoration is featured in the first, middle, and last positions of the second collection. Other correspondences abound. Additional links between these two sections include the following:

1. Throughout the oracles to the nations there is weeping, mourning, and the cessation of joy and singing because Yahweh is overthrowing the nations (e.g., chaps. 15–16); throughout Isaiah 49–54 there is rejoicing and singing, because Yahweh is restoring Israel and the nations (49:13; 51:3, 11; 52:7–10; 54:1).
2. Both sections contain exhortations to those who are dead, asleep, or in hopelessness, to arise, awake, and sing (26:19; 51:9, 11; 52:1, 9; 54:1).
3. Both sections contain references to Sheol, the "pit" (bôr, šaḥat) (14:15, 19; 24:22; 51:14).
4. In both sections, nature rejoices at the end of the Babylonian oppression (14:7–8; 49:12–13).
5. The cutting off of Babylon's descendants (14:20–22) stands in contrast to the restoration of Israel's children (49:19–23; 54:1–17).
6. In 14:17, the king of Babylon "did not let his prisoners (ʾăsîrîm) go"; in 49:9, Yahweh says to the prisoners (ʾăsûrîm), "Come forth."

---

23. Both also contain the figure of the changing of apparel representing the change of fortune. The warning in 3:24–26: "Instead of perfume there will be rottenness; and instead of a girdle, a rope . . . instead of a rich robe, a girding of sackcloth; instead of beauty, shame" (and a reference to mourning) is reversed in 61:3: "To grant to those who mourn in Zion—to give them a garland instead of ashes, the oil of gladness instead of mourning, the mantle of praise instead of a faint spirit."

24. These two sections are notably future oriented. Unlike the lengthy condemnations and the pleading for repentance in the first and last units, these two units simply describe Yahweh's future plans for the nations and Israel. Both collections also speak of Yahweh's plans to restore Israel through the suffering of a third party. In the second unit, Israel's restoration will be achieved through Yahweh's punishment of the nations (cf. 14:1–6, 32; 16:4–5; 18:7; 19:16–25; 23:17–18; 24:21–23; 25:1–26:21). In the next-to-last unit, Israel's restoration will be secured through the suffering of the servant (50:5–7; 52:13–53:12). Moreover, the theme of the fate of the nations in Isaiah 13–27 is echoed in Isaiah 49–54, in which the effects of the servant's ministry on the foreign nations is a major focus. The first message of the unit is addressed to the foreign nations: "Listen to me, O coastlands, and hearken, you peoples from afar" (49:1). In this message the servant is told by Yahweh (49:6): "It is too light a thing that you should be my servant to raise up the tribes of Jacob. . . . I will give you as a light to the nations, that my salvation may reach to the end of the earth." Foreign nations, with their rulers, kings, queens, and princes, are mentioned in this message (49:7, 12, 22–26), and the theme continues throughout the unit: "My justice [will go forth] for a light to the peoples. . . . My arms will rule the peoples; the coastlands wait for me,

and for my arm they hope" (51:4–5); Egypt and Assyria are mentioned (52:4); the servant "shall startle many nations; kings shall shut their mouths because of him" (52:15); and it is promised that restored Israel "will possess the nations" (54:3). Another noteworthy echo: the central unit of the oracles to the nations (21:1–17) and the central unit of the servant messages (51:17–23) share a number of common themes, including drinking, staggering, and falling.

22.20 The king of Babylon and the suffering servant

King of Babylon	Suffering Servant
contrasting lives	
• "smote (*nkh*) peoples with unceasing blows (*nkh*)" (14:6)	• is himself "smitten" (*nkh*), stricken, wounded, bruised, beaten (53:4–5, 10)
• "slew" and "oppressed" (*ngś*) peoples (14:2, 4, 20)	• is himself "oppressed" (*ngś*) and slain to secure forgiveness for his people (53:7–8)
• "shook the earth" (14:16) and boasted: "I will ascend to heaven; above the stars of God I will set my throne on high!" (14:13–14)	• is humble and quiet: "like a lamb . . . he opened not his mouth" (53:7)
• is "wicked" (14:5), filled with pomp, splendor (14:11), and feared by all nations (14:16)	• is "righteous" (53:11), has "no form or comeliness that we should look at him, and no beauty that we should desire him" (53:2); deemed unimportant; and "despised" and "not esteemed" (53:3)
contrasting reversals of fortunes	
• exalts himself, boasting that he is the "Day Star," "son of Dawn," and plots to set his throne on high, "above the stars of God" (14:12–14); will be brought down to (dark) Sheol (14:15)	• has humbly remained hidden in Yahweh's (dark) quiver; will be exalted, honored, and made "the light to the nations" (49:2–6)
• began with such greatness and aspired to such heights ("I will ascend to heaven; I will set my throne on high. . . . I will ascend above the heights of the clouds"; 14:13–14); in the end is "laid low," "cut down," "brought down to Sheol," and reduced to complete humiliation (14:8, 10–12, 15)	• beginning is humble ("like a root out of dry ground," 53:2); in the end "shall be highly exalted and lifted up, and shall be very high" (52:13)
contrasting deaths	
• dies and his life is over (14:18–20)	• dies, but "he shall prolong his days" and a life of great reward will follow his death (53:10–12)
• offspring and "seed" (*zera*) will be "cut off" (*krt*) and will "nevermore be named" (14:20–22)	• though "cut off" (*gzr*) from the land of the living, will "see his seed (*zera*)" (53:8–10)
• not buried in his own "tomb" (*qibrĕkā*) or in dignity with the other kings; is "cast out . . . like a dead body trodden under foot" (14:18–20)	• not buried in his own tomb, but is given a "tomb" (*qibrô*) with the wicked; buried "with the rich(?)" (a burial of dignity after all?) (53:9)
contrasting responses from kings	
• the kings of the earth, in Sheol, are startled when they "see" (*rāʾâ*) the pompous king of Babylon arrive in humiliation (14:9–11, 16)	• when the kings "see" (*rāʾâ*) the servant, they are likewise startled—but for the opposite reason: this humbled person has been highly exalted! (52:14–15)
• when the deceased kings of earth see the king of Babylon arriving in Sheol, they "arise" (*qûm*) (instead of bowing!), speak out, and contemptuously taunt him (14:9–20)	• when the kings of the earth see the servant, they "shut their mouths because of him" (52:15), "arise" (*qûm*), and prostrate themselves" before him (49:7)

7. The fate of Moab (chaps. 15–16) stands in contrast to what will happen to Israel (chap. 54): overthrow versus restoration; pride reduced to humiliation versus humiliation changed into glory; weeping versus rejoicing; etc.

8. Tyre's fate in the earlier collection is contrasted with Israel's fate in the latter: for example, Tyre is exhorted: "Wail . . . be still . . . be ashamed . . . : 'I have neither travailed nor given birth, I have neither reared young men nor brought up virgins' " (23:4); Israel, on the other hand, is told, "Sing, O barren one, who did not bear; break forth into singing and cry aloud, you who have not been in travail! For the children of the desolate one will be more than the children of her that is married . . . you will forget the shame of your youth" (54:1, 4).

9. Both sections conclude with the fate of Jerusalem: in 27:10–11, Zion is "solitary, a habitation deserted and forsaken . . . ; he who made them will not have compassion on them"; in chap. 54, Zion, who was "forsaken," "desolate," whom Yahweh had forsaken, will be shown compassion (54:7, 8, 10) and will be become a populous, inhabited city once again (54:1–2).

10. The expiation of Israel's sins is spoken of in both sections (27:9; 53:1–12).

11. The enlargement of Israel's borders occurs in both sections (26:15; 54:1–3).

12. The motif of the people/earth staggering in drunkenness (having drunk from the cup of God's wrath) occurs in both sections (24:20; 51:21–22).

13. The first message of the earlier collection and the last message of the servant section declare that Israel will one day take possession of other nations (14:1–2; 54:3).

Correspondence of Third and Third-to-Last Collections (Isaiah 28–35; 40–48) and the Pivotal Function of Isaiah 36–39

The Book of Isaiah's third and third-to-last units likewise match. A major connection between the two is their warnings against misplaced trust. Isaiah 28–35 warns against trusting in other earthly powers, particularly Egypt, rather than in Yahweh alone (30:1–18; 31:1–5). For example, 31:1–3 declares:

> Woe to those who go down to Egypt for help
> and rely on horses, . . .
> but do not look to the Holy One of Israel
> or consult with Yahweh. . . .
> The Egyptians are human and not God;
> and their horses are flesh and not spirit. . . .
> The helper will stumble, and he who is helped will fall,
> and they will all perish together.

Isaiah 40–48 warns against trusting in worthless idols instead of Yahweh alone. These two varieties of Israel's misplaced trust are denounced by other prophets, and Israel's history is full of examples of both (as seen, for example, in the Book of Kings). These two sins are treated in Isaiah as two sides of the same coin, as shown in chapters 36–39, the narrative between chapters 28–35 and chapters 40–48. The key point of this narrative is the vindication of Hezekiah's trust in Yahweh. The Assyrian commander mocks Judah's trust in powers human or divine, declaring that neither power can save it:

> On what do you rest this confidence of yours? . . . On whom do you now rely? . . . Are you relying on Egypt, that broken reed of a staff, which will pierce the hand of anyone who leans on it? Such is pharaoh king of Egypt to all who rely on him. But if you say to me, "We rely on Yahweh our God" . . . Do not let Hezekiah convince you to rely on Yahweh by saying, "Yahweh will surely deliver us." . . . Has any of the gods of the nations delivered his land out of the hand of the king of Assyria? Where are the gods of Hamath and Arpad? . . . Who among all the gods of these countries have delivered their countries out of my hand, that Yahweh should deliver Jerusalem out of my hand?
>
> —Isaiah 36:4–20

When the Egyptian army arrives in a vain attempt to help Judah, Sennacherib sends a similar message to Hezekiah (37:9–13): "Do not let your God on whom you rely deceive you. . . . Have the gods of the nations delivered them?" And Hezekiah's subsequent prayer centers on this same issue (37:15–20). In this prayer, Hezekiah expresses his trust in Yahweh alone:

> O Yahweh, . . . you are God, you alone, of all the kingdoms of the earth; you have made heaven and earth. . . . Surely, O Yahweh, the kings of Assyria have laid waste all the nations and their lands, and have cast their gods into the fire; for they were not gods, but the work of men's hands, wood and stone. . . . So now, O Yahweh our God, save us from his hand, that all the kingdoms of the earth may know that you alone are God.

Hezekiah's trust in God is vindicated: Yahweh delivers Jerusalem from Sennacherib.

The author seeks to establish two key points by the narrative in chapters 36–39: (1) Yahweh is superior to all human powers, including the two great powers at the time, Egypt and Assyria, and (2) Yahweh is superior to all other gods; no god but Yahweh was able to protect his people from mighty Assyria. Thus the narrative in the middle of the book links chapters 28–35 (with its warnings against trusting Egypt and other nations rather than Yahweh) with chapters 40–48 (with its warning against trusting other gods rather than Yahweh).

Similar vocabulary reinforces the link between these related themes in the two units:

1. The term *ʿzr* ("help") is used in both units to establish Yahweh's superiority over Egypt and idols. The worthless help of Egypt is mentioned six times in the first unit (30:5, 7; 31:1, 2, 3 [twice]). The word is used once in the second unit of the idol makers who must "help" one another in making their idols and four times of Yahweh, who, in contrast to the idols, is Israel's true "help" (41:10, 13, 14; 44:2). *ʿzr* occurs only six times elsewhere in Isaiah.
2. The verb *hôʿîl* ("to profit") is also used in both units to develop these same themes. In 30:5–6 the word is used three times in declarations that helpless Egypt will not "profit." In chapters 40–48 the term occurs four times to declare that there is no profit in the idols (44:9–10) or in idolatrous sorcery (47:12), but only in Yahweh (48:17). *Hôʿîl* occurs only once elsewhere in Isaiah.
3. The word *bōšet* ("shame") also appears in both units: twice of the shame resulting in trusting Egypt (30:3, 5) and once of the shame resulting in trusting in idols (42:17). Similarly, the verb *bôš* ("to be ashamed") is used of the shame that will come upon the one who trusts in Egypt (30:5) and of the shame of those who trust in idols (42:17; 44:9, 11; 45:16)—in contrast to the one who

trusts in Yahweh who "will not be put to shame" (45:17; cf. 45:24).

4. The contrasting terms *ʾādām* ("human") and *ʾĕlōhîm* ("God") create a similar echo. The Egyptians are declared to be simply human, not God (31:3), and the heathen idols are repeatedly declared not to be God; Yahweh alone is God, and idol makers are merely human (44:6, 8–11).[25]

5. Although different terms are used, the "emptiness" (*hebel*) of Egypt's help (30:7) is echoed in the "emptiness"/"nothingness" (*ʾepes*, *ʾayin*, etc.) of the lifeless idols (41:11, 12, 24, 29; 44:9).

Various other thematic and verbal links connect the two units. For example, both units speak of the ridiculous idea of a clay pot giving advice to its maker:

Shall the potter be regarded as the clay;
that the thing made shall say of its maker,
"He did not make me";
or the thing formed say of him who formed it (*yôṣĕrô*),
"He has no understanding"?
—Isaiah 29:16

Woe to the one who strives with the one who formed him (*yōṣĕrô*),
an earthen vessel with the potter!
Does the clay say to him who fashions it, "What are you making?"
or, "Your work has no handles"?
—Isaiah 45:9

One particularly conspicuous link between the two collections is the correspondence between chapters 35 and 40 (the final unit of the first collection and the opening unit of the second). These two units have a striking number of connections:

1. "wilderness" (*midbār*) and "desert" (*ʿărābâ*) (35:1; 40:3)
2. the way through the wilderness is made easier to traverse (35:6–7; 40:3–4)
3. flowers (35:1–2; 40:6–7)
4. Lebanon (35:2; 40:16)
5. "our God" (*ʾĕlōhênû*) (35:2; 40:3, 8)
6. "the glory of Yahweh" (*kābôd yhwh*) that is "seen" (*rāʾâ*) (35:2; 40:5)

7. "behold" (*hinnēh*), God "is coming" (*yābôʾ*), bringing his reward and recompense with him (35:4; 40:10)
8. a newly constructed "highway" (*maslûl, mĕsillâ*) and "road" (*derek*) in the "wilderness" (*midbār*) or "desert" (*ʿărābâ*) (35:6–8; 40:3)
9. new strength for the weak and renewed mobility for those who have "stumbled" (*kšl*) (35:3; 40:29–31)

Other thematic links include the following:

10. Both units contain sharp repudiations of idols (throughout Isa. 40–48; and sporadically in Isa. 28–35); for example: "In that day everyone shall cast away your idols of silver and your idols of gold, which your hands have sinfully made" (31:7; cf. 30:22).
11. Both units contain similar predictions of future blessings: new rivers in Israel's mountains (30:25; 41:18), streams in the desert (32:2; 35:7; 44:3), the sight of the blind will be restored (32:3; 35:5; 42:7; cf. 42:16), and relief for the "weary" (*ʿāyēp/yāʿēp*) (28:12; 40:30–31).
12. Both units speak of the relationship between trust in Yahweh and the ability to travel swiftly. In the first unit the people who trust in the speed of horses instead of Yahweh will be overtaken and captured by swifter pursuers (30:15–17); in the second unit, those who trust in Yahweh will have renewed strength, so that they will be enabled to run, even "mount up with wings like eagles" (40:29–31).
13. The first unit speaks of mourning over the "highways" (*mĕsillôt*) that lie waste (33:7–8); the second unit announces the rejoicing involved in the creation of a new "highway" (*mĕsillâ*) for Yahweh's coming (40:3).

The entire Book of Isaiah thus appears to exhibit a grand seven-part symmetry (22.21).

Conclusion

The foregoing structural analysis helps explain why many of the larger and smaller units appear where they do in the Book of Isaiah. For instance, Isaiah's call appears, not at the very beginning of the book, but in chapter 6, because there it stands at the highlighted center of the book's symmetrically arranged opening unit. The story of the amiable visit of the Babylonian envoys in chapter 39 is out of chronological order, in part, for a structural reason: in its present, dischronologized position it symmetri-

---

25. For another echo, the first unit states that the Egyptians will stumble, and those they help will fall, so that the two will perish together (*yaḥdāw*) (31:3); the second unit states that the idol makers will be confounded and go in confusion together (*yaḥdāw*) (45:16).

22.21 The Book of Isaiah

a **introductory messages of condemnation, pleading, and future restoration** (1:1–12:6)
- begins: message calling for <u>repentance</u> (1:1–31)
- condemnation of <u>empty religious practices</u> (1:12–15), <u>social injustice</u>, wickedness
- Yahweh's eyes <u>hidden</u>; he <u>won't hear their prayers</u>: their <u>hands are full of blood</u> (1:15)
- themes: <u>devouring beasts</u>, <u>Sabbath observance</u>, <u>briers and thorns</u>, unacceptable sacrifices, drunkenness, punishment by burning, darkness transformed to light
- "<u>the wolf shall dwell with the lamb</u> . . . the cow and the bear shall feed together . . . and <u>the lion shall eat straw like the ox</u> . . . they shall not hurt or destroy in all my holy mountain" (11:6–9)

b **oracles to nations: humiliation of proud king of Babylon** (13:1–27:13)
- <u>fall of proud Babylon</u> (first, middle, and last units)
- <u>lofty beginning</u> of unit's key figure, king of Babylon: <u>proud</u>, <u>boastful</u>, <u>respected and feared</u>, <u>wicked</u>, <u>smites</u> (*nkh*), <u>oppresses</u> (*ngś*), <u>slays peoples</u>, <u>exalts himself</u> above stars, <u>bright morning star</u> (14:1–20)
- <u>humbling of king of Babylon</u>: humiliated, brought low; <u>kings shocked to see him</u>, <u>rise up</u> (*qûm*) and <u>taunt</u> him; he has <u>no offspring</u>

c **collection of woes: don't trust in earthly powers!** (28:1–35:10)
- Egypt's <u>help</u> is empty; it will not <u>profit</u>; <u>shame</u> will be the result of <u>trusting</u> Egypt; they are <u>people</u>, not <u>gods</u>; <u>trust Yahweh!</u>
- folly of idols (30:22; 31:7) and of <u>vessel advising potter</u> (29:16)
- <u>highway in desert</u>; <u>flowers</u>, <u>glory of Yahweh</u> being <u>seen</u>; <u>coming</u> with reward; strengthening the weak (35:1–10)

d **CENTER: historical narratives** showing <u>Yahweh's supremacy</u> over all earthly and divine powers (36:1–39:8)

c′ **Yahweh's supremacy over idols: don't trust in idols!** (40:1–48:22)
- idols are <u>worthless</u> and <u>empty</u>; Yahweh is Israel's true <u>help</u>; idols will not <u>profit</u>; <u>shame</u> from <u>trusting</u> idols; <u>trust Yahweh!</u>
- repudiation of idols; folly of <u>vessel advising potter</u> (45:9)
- <u>highway in desert</u>; <u>flowers</u>, <u>glory of Yahweh</u> being <u>seen</u>; <u>coming</u> with reward; strengthening the weak (40:1–31)

b′ **servant messages: exaltation of the humble servant** (49:1–54:17)
- <u>restoration of humbled Jerusalem</u> (first, middle, and last units)
- <u>humble beginning</u> of unit's key figure, Yahweh's servant: <u>humble</u>, <u>quiet</u>, <u>not esteemed</u>, <u>righteous</u>, <u>smitten</u> (*nkh*), <u>oppressed</u> (*ngś*), <u>slain</u> for his people, <u>remains lowly</u>, hidden in <u>dark obscurity</u>
- <u>exaltation of servant</u>: exalted, raised up; <u>kings shocked to see him</u>, shut mouths, <u>rise up</u> (*qûm*) and <u>bow before him</u>; his <u>offspring</u>

a′ **concluding messages of condemnation, pleading, and future restoration** (55:1–66:24)
- begins: message calling for <u>repentance</u> (55:1–56:1)
- condemnation of <u>empty religious practices</u> (58:1–14; 66:3), <u>social injustice</u>, wickedness
- Yahweh's face <u>hidden</u>; he <u>won't hear their prayers</u>: their <u>hands are bloody</u> (59:1–3)
- themes: <u>devouring beasts</u>, <u>Sabbath observance</u>, <u>briers and thorns</u>, unacceptable sacrifices, drunkenness, punishment by burning, darkness transformed to light
- "<u>the wolf and the lamb shall feed together</u>, <u>the lion shall eat straw like the ox</u> . . . they shall not hurt or destroy in all my holy mountain" (65:25)

cally matches the story of the hostile visit of the Assyrian envoy (the Rabshakeh); and in that matchup it highlights the irony that, contrary to appearances, it would be the Babylonians, not the Assyrians, who would eventually destroy Jerusalem. Similar observations could be made about the locations of dozens of units, such as the two similar and chiastically matched messages condemning reliance on Egypt (30:1–14; 31:1–9); the matched units denouncing the pride of Jerusalem's men (2:6–22) and women (3:16–4:1); and the two visions about the Messiah (chaps. 9, 11).

The analysis helps clarify the function of many of the book's units. For example, the historical narrative in chapters 36–39 may be positioned at the highlighted center of the book's overall symmetric arrangement to underscore the book's central message: trust Yahweh alone rather than earthly powers or other gods. The unit may also function as the book's pivot. It provides the transition from the Assyrian threat that dominates the first part of the book, to the future Babylonian captivity that will dominate much of the book's second half. The apparent matching of chapters 28–35 and 40–48 may suggest that their respective themes—the warning against trusting earthly powers such as Egypt and the warning against trusting worthless idols—represent two sides of the same coin in the book's message.

The internal structure of the oracles against the nations in chapters 13–27 suggests that the enigmatic enemy in chapters 21 and 24–27 is Babylon. That the unit may feature Babylon's fall at the beginning, middle, and end (chaps. 13–14; 21; 24–27) suggests the central importance of this theme in the unit. And this may help clarify a similarly recurring theme in the matching chapters 49–54, where three messages predict the future restoration of Mother Jerusalem (these messages are likewise positioned at the beginning, middle, and end of the unit). The matchup of chapters 13–27 and chapters 49–54 seems to draw attention to the ironically contrasting fates of these two cities: the exalted city of Babylon will fall, and the humbled city of Jerusalem will be exalted. The correspondence between these two units also draws attention to the ironically contrasting personalities and fates of these two units' main characters: the haughty king of Babylon (chap. 14) who "smote" the nations and exalted himself, and Yahweh's humble servant (chaps. 50–53) who was "smitten" for his people and remained quietly submissive as he was humiliated. In the end Yahweh will bring the mighty king of Babylon down in humiliation, and he will raise up and highly honor his suffering servant. (Such reversals of fortunes are thematically developed throughout the Book of Isaiah.)

The book utilizes structured repetition throughout to reinforce its central concerns. These include the pervasiveness of Judah's sinfulness, idolatry, injustice, and religious hypocrisy; the worthlessness of empty religious activity; the warning of coming punishment if Judah continues its spiritual revolt; the call to repentance; the reassurance that Yahweh is worthy of Judah's trust; the folly of idolatry and the supremacy of Yahweh over idols; the ability of Yahweh to determine and know the future; the future reign of the Messiah; the future return from exile; the future restoration of Jerusalem; the key role of the suffering servant in Israel's redemption; and the glorious future role of Israel on earth.

The book's overall structure may also provide some new insights on the issue of its composition. At the very least, the foregoing analysis suggests that someone, whether a single author or a final editor, thoroughly organized the material of Isaiah from one end to the other, arranging it into a masterfully structured presentation according to its well-developed central theme: trust in Yahweh!

23

Jeremiah

Prophet to a Hostile Nation

Jeremiah was God's final prophet to preexilic Judah. His message to the nation was almost entirely negative: if Judah does not repent from its suicidal course of rebellion against Yahweh, it will be destroyed by the Babylonians. The leaders and people of Judah rejected Jeremiah's message—foolishly, as history would prove. The beleaguered prophet was persecuted, beaten, imprisoned, and eventually left to die (to be saved, ironically, by a foreigner).

The Book of Jeremiah is the longest book in the Old Testament. It is also one of the most fascinating, with its lively accounts of Jeremiah's troubled experiences and his heated exchanges with both God and humans. The internal arrangement of the Book of Jeremiah is notoriously complex. As John Bright complains:

What makes these books [i.e., Jeremiah and some other prophetic books] particularly, and one might say needlessly, difficult is the very manner of their arrangement—or to be more accurate, their apparent lack of arrangement. The reader who meets them for the first time is likely to be quite at a loss. All seems confusion. There is no narrative for him to follow, nor can he trace any logical progression running through them and binding their parts together into a coherent whole. No sooner has he grasped a line of thought, and prided himself that he is following it tolerably well, than it breaks off and something quite different is being discussed. The impression he gains is one of extreme disarray; and one can scarcely blame him for concluding that he is reading a hopeless hodgepodge thrown together without any discernible principle of arrangement at all.[1]

J. A. Thompson agrees:

When we come to inquire whether any principle of arrangement can be observed in the Book of Jeremiah, we have to admit that any consistent principles escapes us. . . . The one thing that does become

clear is that the Book of Jeremiah as we have it today was the result of a long and complex process. The very complexity of the process accounts for the seeming disarray of the book to our modern logic-oriented thinking.[2]

R. K. Harrison, following H. T. Kuist, suggests that the book's disorder reflects the strife, uncertainty, and turmoil of the period.[3]

Clearly the book is not arranged chronologically. For example, the successive messages in chapters 21–37 date from the reigns of various kings:

21–24	Zedekiah
25	Jehoiakim
26	Jehoiakim
27	Zedekiah
28–29	Zedekiah
30–31	(undated)
32	Zedekiah
33	Zedekiah
34	Zedekiah
35	Jehoiakim
36	Jehoiakim
37	Zedekiah

Nor is a strictly topical order followed, although, as Bright points out, if any principle could be observed, it might be a topical one, since there do seem to be larger blocks of topically arranged material in the book. For example, Jeremiah's various oracles against foreign nations are grouped together in chapters 46–51, his messages of future hope in chapters 30–33, narratives about his troubled ministry in chap-

---

1. John Bright, *Jeremiah: Introduction, Translation, and Notes* (Anchor Bible 21; Garden City: Doubleday, 1965), lvi.

2. J. A. Thompson, *The Book of Jeremiah* (New International Commentary of the Old Testament; Grand Rapids: Eerdmans, 1980), 82.

3. R. K. Harrison, *Jeremiah* (Downers Grove, Ill.: Inter-Varsity, 1973), 32; H. T. Kuist, *Jeremiah* (London: SCM, 1961), 12.

ters 36–44, and messages of condemnation and warning in chapters 1–25.[4] But, as Bright admits, beyond these broad generalities, the topical scheme frequently breaks down. The material in chapters 34–37, for example, includes a message of hope for Zedekiah (34:1–7), a scathing condemnation of Zedekiah for his treatment of the slaves (34:8–22), a story about the faithful Rechabites (35:1–19), a narrative about Jehoiakim burning Jeremiah's scroll (36:1–32), and the story of Jeremiah's imprisonment during the reign of Zedekiah (37:1–21).[5]

A study of the book's layout suggests, however, that there are seven fairly well-defined larger units that make up the book, each with its own artful internal organization:

a introductory oracles against Judah (1:1–12:17)
b collection of messages about Judah's exile and suffering (13:1–20:18)

---

4. Bright, *Jeremiah*, lix.

5. The controversial theory of the composition of Jeremiah posited by Bernhard Duhm (1901) and popularized by Sigmund Mowinckel (1914) (see standard introductions) likewise fails to account for the present arrangement of the book. As Bright (*Jeremiah*, lx) observes: "[This analysis does not] furnish any key to [the book's] arrangement, but rather add[s] to its chaotic appearance, for the book is certainly not arranged according to its literary types. On the contrary, these are found commingled through its various parts in what can only be called a grand disarray." Several attempts have been made to account for the book's order by proposing various stages of growth and development. Kuist identifies chaps. 1–20 as the earliest edition of the Book of Jeremiah, representing, apart from numerous intrusions, the scroll dictated to Baruch by Jeremiah after his first scroll was burned (Jer. 36:32). The bulk of Jeremiah 21–52 comprises Baruch's own memoirs of Jeremiah's life and messages. Later on, Deuteronomic editors (Kuist followed Mowinckel's view) combined the two earlier works, interspersing their own material throughout. This and similar views are highly speculative. Few scholars, for example, grant that Jeremiah 1–20 should be identified with Baruch's scroll. Moreover, even if it were true, the present lack of order within the various parts of the book must still be accounted for. William Holladay makes a valiant pioneering effort to solve the mystery of the book's order in his monograph *The Architecture of Jeremiah 1–20* (London: Associated, 1976). In a detailed analysis of Jeremiah 1–10, Holladay discovers significant repetitions of keywords within particular blocks of material. He concludes that a number of Jeremiah's sermons have been carefully crafted and joined into "cycles" or "complexes" of sermons, each of which repeats a particular keyword, or set of keywords. There is, for example, a "harlotry cycle" in Jeremiah 2–3 and a "foe cycle" in Jeremiah 4–6 and 8. Holladay only briefly examines Jeremiah 11–20 and concludes that this latter section is far more difficult to analyze than Jeremiah 1–10; it appears to have been compiled in several stages, with later compilers often inserting new material as seemed best at the time. Holladay's analysis is intriguing and full of exegetical insights, but it is not entirely convincing. Some of the intricate parallels, connections, foreshadowings, and echoes that he finds could hardly have been intended by the author/editor. Moreover, what Holladay identifies as a cycle or complex might simply be a single message, unified by one or more keywords (e.g., chaps. 2–3; 4–6).

c dated messages of judgment (21:1–29:32)
d messages of future hope (30:1–33:26)
e dated messages of judgment (34:1–35:19)
f narratives about Jeremiah's suffering (36:1–45:5)
g oracles against the nations (46:1–51:64)
   appendix: fall of Jerusalem (52:1–34)

Jeremiah's Call and Messages of Condemnation and Coming Disaster (Jeremiah 1–12)

Jeremiah opens his book with a unit that condemns Israel's unfaithfulness, pleads with it to return, and warns of the frightening consequence of its continued revolt—namely, "disaster from the north." The cohesion of this first unit is well developed. It is framed by opening and closing dialogues. The first is a dialogue between Jeremiah and Yahweh featuring Jeremiah's call; and the second is a dialogue between the prophet and God, which deals with some of the same topics covered in the first. These dialogues enclose a group of seven messages. Unlike most of the later messages in the book, none of these messages is dated to the regnal year of a specific king, addressed to specific kings or individuals, or accompanied by details or narratives about its delivery (with the minor exception in 7:2a).

Two themes recur throughout these messages: (1) Judah's idolatrous unfaithfulness to Yahweh and (2) the disaster Yahweh is preparing to bring upon Judah from the north. Each of the seven messages is clearly introduced,[6] and they are arranged in a symmetry that places emphasis on the central message, the temple message and its call to repentance (23.1).

Yahweh's Plans for Judah's Fall and Exile and Jeremiah's Complaints (Jeremiah 13–20)

Like the first collection, the book's second collection of messages also has seven messages arranged chiastically (23.2). In contrast to the first group of messages, in this collection Jeremiah's own involvement in the delivery of the messages is given more prominence. Most are accompanied by his symbolic actions (a, b', a') or nonactions ("don't pray" [b]; "don't go" [c]). The recurrence of Jeremiah's complaints throughout this unit serves to tie the unit together and set it apart from the others (the first of these com-

---

6. The introductions are 1:4; 2:1–2; 3:6; 4:3; 7:1–3a; 8:4 (with its instructions to deliver the message, addressees, and introductory message formula); 10:1–2a; 11:1. Only the final unit, 11:18–12:17, has no formal introduction. It is set off instead by the abrupt shift to dialogue between Jeremiah and God.

23.1 Jeremiah's call and introductory messages of condemnation (Jeremiah 1–12)

introduction: Jeremiah's call: <u>dialogue between God and Jeremiah</u> (1:1–19)
- mention of Jeremiah's <u>family</u> and priests of <u>Anathoth</u> (1:1)
- commission to <u>prophesy</u> (*nbʾ*) (1:5–10); God <u>knew</u> (*yādaʿ*) Jeremiah before birth (1:5)
- prediction of enemy opposition and promise of divine protection (1:17–19)
- task of <u>uprooting</u> (*nātaš*), <u>destroying</u> (*ʾbd*), <u>planting</u> (*nātaʿ*), and <u>building</u> (*bānâ*) <u>nations</u> (*gôy*); promise of enemy opposition and divine protection

a   **condemnation of Judah**: (marital) unfaithfulness to Yahweh (2:1–3:5)
- begins: review of <u>exodus</u> and gift of <u>good land</u> (2:2–7)
- revolt of <u>ancestors</u> (2:5–6); in trouble, people <u>cry out to Yahweh</u> (2:27)
- <u>you have as many gods as you have towns, O Judah!</u> (2:28)
- Judah's gods cannot save in a <u>time of trouble</u> (*ʿēt rāʿâ*) (2:28)

b   **condemnation of <u>Israel</u> for idolatry** and invitation to abandon idolatry and return to Yahweh (3:6–4:2)
- shamefulness of idolatry; promise that if Israelites abandon idolatry, <u>nations</u> will be blessed

c   **disaster from the north!** (4:3–6:30)
- terrifying scenes of enemy invasion <u>from the north</u>
- <u>gather together! let us flee into the fortified cities!</u> (4:5)
- alarm in <u>Dan</u>; <u>horses</u>; exhortations to weep, mourn
- <u>"peace, peace," they say, when there is no peace</u> (6:12–15)
- 6:12–15 repeated verbatim in 8:10–12

d   **CENTER: temple message: call to repentance** (7:1–8:3)

c′   **disaster from the north!** (8:4–9:26 [8:4–9:25])
- terrifying scenes of enemy invasion <u>from the north</u>
- <u>gather together! let us flee into the fortified cities!</u> (8:14)
- alarm in <u>Dan</u>; <u>horses</u>; exhortations to weep, mourn
- <u>"peace, peace," they say, when there is no peace</u> (8:10–12)
- 8:10–12 a verbatim repetition of 6:12–15

b′   **condemnation of <u>house of Israel</u> for idolatry** and exhortation to Israel and nations to abandon idolatry (10:1–25)
- foolishness of idols and <u>nations</u> who taught Israel senseless idolatry

a′   **condemnation to Judah**: covenantal unfaithfulness to Yahweh (11:1–17)
- begins: review of <u>exodus</u> and gift of the <u>good land</u> (11:4–7)
- revolt of <u>ancestors</u> (11:7–8); in trouble, people <u>cry out to Yahweh</u>
- <u>you have as many gods as you have towns, O Judah!</u> (11:13)
- Judah's gods cannot save in a <u>time of trouble</u> (*ʿēt rāʿâ*) (11:12)

conclusion: Jeremiah's complaint: <u>dialogue between God and Jeremiah</u> (11:18–12:17)
- mention of Jeremiah's <u>family</u> and people of <u>Anathoth</u> (11:21)
- Jeremiah's <u>prophesying</u> (*nbʾ*) challenged; God <u>knows</u> (*yādaʿ*) Jeremiah
- enemies oppose Jeremiah and plot to kill him; divine help
- themes: <u>uprooting</u> (*nātaš*), <u>destroying</u> (*ʾbd*), <u>planting</u> (*nātaʿ*), and <u>building</u> (*bānâ*) <u>nations</u> (*gôy*) (12:2, 14–17)

---

plaints appeared at the end of the previous unit). These complaints, placed strategically throughout the unit, are Jeremiah's prayers to Yahweh in response to the suffering he is experiencing as Yahweh's prophet. They contain appeals to Yahweh for help.

The messages of this collection are more specific in details of delivery than those of the first unit, but are still less specific than the messages of the next collection, where the messages will be dated to the reigns of specific Judean kings and will contain frequent references to specific kings (none of which we find here).[7] As in the first unit, this unit's conclusion is also marked by a prayer (20:7–18) hearkening back to Jeremiah's call in chapter 1. This prayer echoes both the concluding prayer of

the previous unit (11:18–12:17) and the call account in chapter 1.[8]

Collection of Dated Messages about Specific Kings, Prophets, and Groups (Jeremiah 21–29)

The book's third unit features a collection of messages, each of which is introduced by information providing the message's historical setting. Some are accompanied by accounts of the audience's reaction (the first account of audience

---

7. See David A. Dorsey, "Broken Potsherds at the Potter's House: An Investigation of the Arrangement of the Book of Jeremiah," *Evangelical Journal* 1 (1983) 3–16.

8. Echoes with the call narrative include the following: (1) Jeremiah's "prevailing" (*yākōl*) in his conflicts with his enemies (1:19; 20:7, 9, 10, 11); (2) Jeremiah's commission to "speak" (*dibbēr*) for God (1:6–9; 20:8–9); (3) God's word internalized in Jeremiah (1:9; 20:9); (4) God's promise of being "with" Jeremiah as he faces his enemies (1:19; 20:11); (5) promise that God will "rescue" (*hiṣṣîl*) him (1:19; 20:13); (6) references to Jeremiah's birth (1:5; 20:14–17); and (7) references to Jeremiah's time in his mother's "womb" (1:5; 20:17–18). It should also be noted that there are a number of literary ties between this complaint and the one in 11:18–12:17 (e.g., 11:20 is repeated almost verbatim in 20:12).

23.2 Yahweh's negative plans against Judah, and Jeremiah's complaints (Jeremiah 13–20)

  a **symbolic-action message: ruining the purchased linen sash (13:1–27)**
  - instructions to <u>go and buy</u> a linen sash (which is whole), then ruin it by burying it, as a symbol of the coming destruction of the people of Israel
  - <u>breaking a wine bottle</u> used as <u>metaphor</u> of God's <u>breaking of Judah</u> (13:12–14)
  - theme: coming <u>exile to Babylon</u>

  b **message occasioned by drought**: God won't relent; so don't pray for these people! (14:1–15:21)
    - <u>God will not relent</u>: judgment is inevitable
    - topics: <u>famine</u> and <u>sword</u> (14:13, 15, 18, etc.)
    - ends: <u>Jeremiah's prayer regarding his enemies</u> (15:10–21)

    c **don't marry or go into houses of mourning or feasting! (16:1–17:4)**
      - <u>failure of ancestors</u> and present generation to keep God's <u>law</u>
      - <u>future blessings</u> when people are restored
      - ends: <u>threat of fire</u> (ʾēš) that will burn forever (17:4)

      d **CENTER: message of individualized judgment (17:5–18)**
        - ends: <u>Jeremiah's prayer regarding his enemies</u>

    c′ **Sabbath message: don't bring loads out of your houses on Sabbath days! (17:19–27)**
      - <u>failure of ancestors</u> and present generation to keep <u>Sabbath</u>
      - <u>future blessings</u> if people will change
      - ends: <u>threat</u> of unquenchable <u>fire</u> (ʾēš) (17:27)

  b′ **message occasioned by potter's house experience**: God will relent if Judah repents (18:1–23)
    - <u>God will relent</u> if people repent: judgment is not inevitable
    - topics: <u>famine</u> and <u>sword</u> (18:21)
    - ends: <u>Jeremiah's prayer regarding his enemies</u> (18:18–23)

  a′ **symbolic-action message: breaking the purchased clay jar (19:1–15)**
  - instructions to <u>go and buy</u> a clay pot (which is whole), then destroy it by smashing it, as a symbol of the coming destruction of the people of Israel
  - <u>breaking the bottle</u> used as <u>metaphor</u> of God's <u>breaking of Judah</u>
  - theme: coming defeat and <u>exile to Babylon</u> (cf. 20:4–6)

  conclusion: Jeremiah's persecution and final complaint (20:1–18)

---

reaction is found at the conclusion of the previous unit). For the first time in the book we hear about specific Judean kings, Jeremiah's messages to them, and their reactions (along with the reactions of other leaders) to his messages. Specific false prophets and other groups (particularly the exiles in Babylon) are also addressed.

This unit contains seven messages, each introduced by a statement providing the message's historical setting, always in terms of a particular Judean king's reign (21:1–2; 24:1; 25:1; 26:1; 27:1; 28:1; 29:1). These messages focus on the inevitability of Judah's fall and the upcoming seventy-year period of exile. The doom of Jerusalem's present occupants (particularly its leadership) is contrasted with the relative fortune of those already exiled to Babylon. The exiles are encouraged to settle down, build houses, plant gardens, etc., because God has good plans for them and will bring them home in seventy years. Every message speaks about Judah's leadership. Most condemn the false prophets, who are giving the exiles and inhabitants of Judah false hope.

The entire collection of messages exhibits a conspicuous seven-part symmetric layout that centers on the story about Judah's religious leaders spurning Jeremiah's message (23.3). The seven messages are balanced both in date

(roughly) and in content. The first message is the longest of the group, its parameters marked by the introductory formulas in 21:1 and 24:1. That chapters 21–23 form a single literary unit, despite its length, is indicated by its internal, self-contained structure (23.4).

Messages of Hope (Jeremiah 30–33)

The fourth and central unit in the Book of Jeremiah is his collection of messages of hope. It has long been recognized that chapters 30–33 form a unit of positive messages. The beginning of the unit is well marked: it commences with Yahweh's instructions to "write in a book all the words I have spoken to you; for the days are coming" (30:2). Shifts in topic and mood also mark the new beginning. The positive tone continues only through chapter 33; chapter 34 introduces the next unit, another collection of condemnatory messages.

The entire collection of messages in chapters 30–33 is tied together by many recurring themes and verbal connections:

1. the promise of a future return from captivity and a restoration of Israel in her land
2. the reestablishment of the Davidic dynasty
3. Yahweh's covenant with Israel

23.3 Collection of dated messages (Jeremiah 21–29)

a **message against Judah's kings and false prophets (21:1–23:40)**
  - date: Zedekiah's reign
  - message to Zedekiah: Jerusalem *will* fall; so surrender to Babylonians and live!
  - fate of <u>Jehoiachin</u> and <u>Queen Mother</u> (22:24–30)
  - major theme: do not listen to the <u>false prophets</u>!

 b **two baskets of figs: promise to bring exiles home (24:1–10)**
   - date: early in Zedekiah's reign
   - employment of <u>visual symbol</u>, on the <u>temple mount</u>
   - message: doom of present inhabitants of Judah; blessings upon exiles
   - "<u>Jehoiachin son of King Jehoiakim of Judah</u> and the officials and craftsmen . . . of Judah were carried into exile to Babylon" (24:1)

  c **cup message: seventy years of Babylonian rule (25:1–38)**
    - date: fourth year of Jehoiakim's reign
    - <u>all the nations will be conquered by Babylon</u>, including "Edom, Moab, Ammon, . . . Tyre, and Sidon" (25:21–22)
    - Yahweh will make the nations drink from cup of Babylon
    - <u>symbolic action</u>: Jeremiah gives Babylon's cup to nations

   d **CENTER: religious leaders spurn Jeremiah's message** and seek his death (26:1–24)
     - date: early in Jehoiakim's reign

  c′ **yoke message: three generations of Babylonian rule (27:1–22)**
    - date: early in Zedekiah's reign
    - <u>all the nations will be conquered by Babylon</u>, including "Edom, Moab, Ammon, . . . Tyre, and Sidon" (27:3)
    - Yahweh will make the nations bear the yoke of Babylon
    - <u>symbolic action</u>: Jeremiah bears Babylon's yoke for nations

 b′ **prophet Hananiah's prediction that Yahweh will bring exiles home in two years; Jeremiah's response (28:1–17)**
   - date: early in Zedekiah's reign
   - employment of <u>visual symbol</u>, on the <u>temple mount</u>
   - message: exiles *will not* return soon; doom of Hananiah
   - "I will bring back <u>Jehoiachin son of King Jehoiakim of Judah</u> and the other exiles from Judah who went to Babylon" (28:4)

a′ **message to exiles (including exiled king) and opposition by false prophet (29:1–32)**
  - date: Zedekiah's reign
  - message to exiles: Jerusalem *will* fall; so settle in Babylon and prosper!
  - topics: <u>Jehoiachin</u> and <u>Queen Mother</u> (29:2)
  - major theme: do not listen to <u>false prophets</u>! false prophet Shemaiah (29:24–32)

23.4 Messages against Judah's kings and false prophets (Jeremiah 21–23)

a **message to Zedekiah and Jerusalem** <u>when they ask Jeremiah for an oracle</u> (21:1–10)
 b **message to Judah's nobility**: <u>I am against you</u> (21:11–14)
  c **exhortation to house of David** to be righteous and just, with promise of <u>future kings of David's line</u> who will reign (22:1–9)
   d **message concerning specific kings of Judah** (22:10–30)
     (1) **Shallum**: <u>he will never return</u> (22:10–12)
     (2) **Jehoiakim** (22:13–23)
     (1′) **Jehoiachin**: <u>he will never return</u> (22:24–30)
  c′ **failure of Davidic kings** to be righteous and just; resulting judgment; and promise of <u>future righteous branch from David's line</u> (23:1–8)
 b′ **message to Judah's prophets**: <u>I am against you</u> (23:9–32)
a′ **message for priests, prophets, or people** <u>when they ask for an oracle</u> (23:33–40)

---

4. the statement "they will be my people, and I will be their God" or the like (30:22; 31:1, 33; 32:38)
5. the promise "I will restore their fortunes" (*ʾāšîb ʾet-šĕbûtām*) or the like (30:3, 18; 31:23; 32:44; 33:7, 11, 26)
6. the frequent phrase "in that day" or the like
7. references to rejoicing and celebration (30:19; 31:7–14; 33:11)

Although an argument could be made for a more complex arrangement scheme, the design apparently intended by the author is a simple threefold symmetry (23.5).

Collection of Dated Messages to Specific Kings and Groups (Jeremiah 34–35)

Next comes a group of several messages given by Jeremiah during the reigns of Jehoiakim and Zedekiah. The beginning of the collection is marked by a shift in theme—from the future restoration of Israel to the fate of particular kings and groups.

23.5 Messages of hope (Jeremiah 30–33)

a **restoration of exiled Israel and the new covenant** (30:1–31:40)
  - date: not given
b **symbolic-action message: purchased field** (32:1–44)
  - date: tenth year of Zedekiah
a′ **restoration of exiled Israel and the eternal covenant** (33:1–26)
  - date: while Jeremiah was still confined in the courtyard of the guard

---

23.6 Messages to Zedekiah and the Rechabites (Jeremiah 34–35)

a **message of hope to Zedekiah** (34:2–7)
b **condemnation of Zedekiah** and the Jerusalemites for breaking their promise (34:8–22)
a′ **message of hope for Rechabites**, who have kept their promise (35:1–19)
  - (date: Jehoiakim's reign)

The end of the unit is less certain. The beginning of the next unit, a collection of biographical narratives about Jeremiah, could arguably be placed at 36:1, 37:1, or 37:11. There are three indications that 36:1 should be viewed as the beginning of the new unit. First, the instructions to Jeremiah to take a scroll and "write on it all the words I have spoken to you . . . from the time I began speaking to you in the reign of Josiah till now" seem to suggest a new beginning, as the similar instructions did in 30:1–2. Second, the narrative about Jehoiakim's rejection of the scroll of Jeremiah and Baruch in chapter 36 fits into the organizational scheme of the collection of narratives that follows. The narrative in chapter 36 would then be the first in a series of chronologically ordered stories about Jeremiah's negative experiences in his prophetic ministry to Israel. Lastly, the story of the burning of Baruch's scroll in chapter 36 is matched by the message to Baruch ("in the fourth year of Jehoiakim . . . after Baruch had written on a scroll the words of Jeremiah"; 45:1) at the conclusion of these narratives, which additionally suggests that chapters 36 and 45 form an inclusion bracketing these narratives.

If this is correct, the book's fifth unit is a relatively brief collection of three messages (like the fourth unit), which feature words of doom for Zedekiah and the Judeans, as well as promises of merciful treatment for Zedekiah himself and the Rechabites. Based on each message's final verdict, the order of the three appears to be symmetric (23.6).[9]

---

9. On the other hand, based on their dates, perhaps these messages are arranged in an a-a′-b order. And on the basis of theme, it could be argued that they are laid out in an a-b-b′ scheme—with the last two messages dealing with the topic of keeping a promise.

Narratives about Jeremiah's Suffering as Yahweh's Prophet (Jeremiah 36–45)

The collection of narratives about Jeremiah's suffering spans the period from before to after the fall of Jerusalem. The narratives have been carefully selected to establish the point that Judah's leaders and people rejected and mistreated God's prophet Jeremiah and therefore deserved the divine punishment they received. The narratives form a series of relentlessly condemnatory stories about the people of Judah. The exceptions prove the rule; the two men who treated Jeremiah kindly and freed him from prison were foreigners: Ebed-melech the Cushite and Nebuzaradan the Babylonian!

The unit has been shaped into a seven-part presentation that is primarily linear, following a chronological order (with the exception of the conclusion, chap. 45). In addition, the passage also has a conspicuous symmetric touch, with units involving Baruch framing the narrative and the account of the fall of Jerusalem positioned, significantly, at its highlighted center (23.7).

Oracles against the Nations (Jeremiah 46–51)

The concluding unit in Jeremiah (apart from the appendix) is the group of oracles about the nations. The arrangement of the nine nations addressed is intriguing. The two major powers of the biblical world, Egypt and Babylon, are addressed first and last, with Babylon, the most powerful, in the climactic final position. Sandwiched between these two major powers are seven smaller nations. The arrangement of the seven oracles against these nations is apparently geographical, from nearest to farthest:

---

a neighboring countries: Philistia, Moab, Ammon, Edom
b more distant country: Aram
c most distant countries: Kedar, Elam

23.7 Jeremiah's suffering as Yahweh's prophet (Jeremiah 36–45)

introduction: Baruch's scroll burned by Jehoiakim (36:1–32)
- date: fourth year of Jehoiakim

a **Jeremiah's warning**: the Egyptians will not save Judah from Nebuchadnezzar; Jeremiah beaten and imprisoned (37:1–21)
- ends: Jeremiah remained in the courtyard of the guard (37:21)

b **wicked Judean leaders throw Jeremiah into a cistern to die** because of his message (38:1–13)
- Jeremiah's message: surrender to the Babylonians and live
- rescued by Ebed-melech
- ends: Jeremiah remained in the courtyard of the guard (38:21)

c **Jeremiah's conversations with faithless Zedekiah** (38:14–28)
- Zedekiah returns Jeremiah to prison
- ends: Jeremiah remained in the courtyard of the guard until Jerusalem's capture (38:28)

d **CENTER: fall of Jerusalem** (39:1–14)
- ends: Babylonians released Jeremiah from the courtyard of the guards" (39:14)

c′ **Jeremiah's conversation with kind Nebuzaradan** (39:15–40:6)
- Nebuzaradan releases Jeremiah from prison
- ends: and he remained with [Gedaliah] (40:6)

b′ **wicked Judeans assassinate Gedaliah and throw victims they kill into a cistern** (40:7–43:7)
- Jeremiah's message to remnant: stay in the land and live in submission to the Babylonians
- ends: disobedient Judeans take Jeremiah with them to Egypt

a′ **Jeremiah's warning**: Egypt will not protect you from Nebuchadnezzar! (43:8–44:30)

conclusion: message to Baruch "after he had written the scroll" (45:1–5)
- date: fourth year of Jehoiakim

There is also a general south–north order in the arrangement of the nine nations:[10]

a south: Egypt, Philistia
b east: Moab, Ammon, Edom, Aram, Kedar
c north: Elam, Babylon

The two great powers form a literary inclusio bracketing the entire unit. The seven intervening countries are arranged in a linear, not symmetric, order:[11]

a world power: Egypt (to south; with a message to Judah) (46:1–28)
  (1) Philistia (near neighbor to south) (47:1–7)
  (2) Moab (near neighbor to east) (48:1–47)
  (3) Ammon (near neighbor to east) (49:1–6)
  (4) Edom (near neighbor to east) (49:7–22)
  (5) Damascus (more distant nation to east) (49:23–27)
  (6) Kedar (even more distant nation to east) (49:28–33)
  (7) Elam (most distant nation to north) (49:34–39)
b world power: Babylon (to north; with a message to Judah) (50:1–51:64)

Appendix (Jeremiah 52)

The book closes with an appendix, the account of the fall of Jerusalem. Much discussion has

been devoted to why this chapter was placed here. Part of its function is probably to answer with subtle finality the accusation that Jeremiah was a false prophet. He had proclaimed throughout his ministry that God would destroy Jerusalem if it did not repent. He had been maligned, rejected, and imprisoned because the people refused to believe that such a message could be from God. Jeremiah 52 stands as a quiet but powerful vindication of Jeremiah's ministry. It is highlighted by its final position. The account forms a rhetorically powerful conclusion to the book.

Overall Layout of the Book of Jeremiah

The seven main units in the Book of Jeremiah are designed to form an overall symmetry with the oracles of hope (chaps. 30–33) serving as the center.[12]

Correspondence of First and Last Units (Jeremiah 1–12; 46–51)

The intentionality of this overall symmetric layout can be seen, for example, in the correspondence between the book's opening and closing units. Most obvious are the similar descrip-

---

10. Also, the first and last sets of messages are introduced in some detail (Egypt and Philistia, Elam and Babylon), while the central messages are simply introduced: "Concerning x" (Kedar, Moab, Ammon, Edom, Aram).

11. This arrangement, incidentally, is far more likely to be original than the puzzling arrangement found in the Septuagint: Elam, Egypt, Babylon, Philistia, Edom, Ammon, Kedar, Damascus, Moab.

12. The symmetric layout of the entire Book of Jeremiah is sensed by Joel Rosenberg, "Jeremiah and Ezekiel," in *The Literary Guide to the Bible*, ed. Robert Alter and Frank Kermode (Cambridge: Harvard University Press, 1987), 184–206. Rosenberg's analysis (pp. 190–91) differs considerably from the one offered here; but he similarly places the messages of hope at the center of book's symmetry and matches chaps. 1–10 with chaps. 46–51.

tions of the military disasters portrayed in the first and last units. The theme of Judah's coming devastation in chapters 1–12 is echoed by the theme of the nations' coming disaster in chapters 46–51. The same kinds of military disasters and suffering that Judah will experience according to the book's opening unit are to be experienced by the other nations according to the closing unit. Particularly notable is Babylon's and the other nations' destruction by an enemy "from the north" (46:20, 24; 47:2; 50:3, 9, 41; 51:48) just as Judah was (1:13, 14, 15; 4:6; 6:1, 22; 10:22). The descriptions of the invasion of Judah as if by an eyewitness in the first unit (4:5–6:26; 8:14–10:22) are echoed by the eyewitnesslike descriptions of the invasions of the other nations in the book's final unit, in language conspicuously echoing the descriptions of Judah's invasion.

Whole passages from the first unit are repeated verbatim, or nearly verbatim, in the last. For example, the terrifying vision of the invasion of Judah by an enemy from the north (namely, Babylon) is repeated in the oracle against Babylon—with the words adapted to apply to Babylon:

> Look, an army is coming from the land of the
>   north! . . .
> They sound like the roaring sea
> as they ride on their horses;
> They come like warriors in battle formation
> to attack you, O daughter <u>Zion</u>.
> <u>We</u> have heard reports about them,
> and <u>our</u> hands hang limp.
> Anguish has gripped <u>us</u>,
> pain like that of a woman in labor.
>   —Jeremiah 6:22–24

> Look, an army is coming from the land of the
>   north! . . .
> They sound like the roaring sea
> as they ride on their horses;
> They come like warriors in battle formation
> to attack you, O daughter <u>Babylon</u>.
> <u>The king of Babylon</u> has heard reports about them,
> and <u>his</u> hands hang limp.
> Anguish has gripped <u>him</u>,
> pain like that of a woman in labor.
>   —Jeremiah 50:41–43

Likewise, "I will make <u>Jerusalem</u> a heap of ruins, a haunt of jackals" (9:11a [9:10a]) becomes "<u>Babylon</u> will be a heap of ruins, a haunt of jackals" in the oracle against Babylon (51:37); and "I will lay waste to <u>the towns of Judah</u> so that no one can live there" (9:11b [9:10b]) is adapted to "Yahweh . . . will lay waste to <u>the land of Babylon</u> so that no one can live there" (51:29).

These echoes reinforce the theme that Babylon will be repaid for its invasion of Judah. What it did to Judah will be done to it!

The book opens with Jeremiah's being appointed "over the nations and kingdoms, to uproot and tear down, to destroy and overthrow" (1:10); and it concludes with his fulfillment of this mission, with his messages against the nations. The book's opening unit features a one-verse message in Aramaic to the nations (10:11), followed by a declaration about the folly of idolatry and the greatness of Israel's God, Yahweh (10:12–16). In the book's final unit, the collection of messages against the nations, the declaration of 10:12–16 is repeated almost verbatim (51:15–19).

Other conspicuous links connect the two units:

1. shared themes of military invasion, sounds and scenes of battle, war horses, trumpet alarms, swords, bows, casualties, destruction and desolation of cities, fugitives, and exiles
2. exhortations to weep and wail over a nation's fall (4:8; 6:26; 9:20 [9:19]; 48:17, 20; 49:3; 51:8)
3. messages to the nations (9:25–26 [9:24–25]; 10:11, 25; 12:14–17; 46:1–51:64)
4. the declaration in the first unit, "the days are coming, says Yahweh, when I will punish . . . Egypt, Judah, Edom, Ammon, Moab, and all who live in the desert" (9:25–26 [9:24–25]), foreshadows the oracles against Egypt, Edom, Ammon, Moab, and Kedar in chapters 46–51
5. references to "balm" in Gilead and healing (8:22; 46:11; cf. 51:8)

Correspondence of Second and Next-to-Last Units (Jeremiah 13–20; 36–45)

The connection between the book's second unit and next-to-last unit is likewise strong. The second unit features messages predicting the coming fall and exile of Judah, interspersed with Jeremiah's complaints about his persecution and rejection; it closes with the first recorded incident of Jeremiah's mistreatment, when he is beaten and put in stocks (20:1–2). This unit is echoed by the book's next-to-last unit, which narrates the fall and exile of Judah, and Jeremiah's persecution and rejection (37:15–21; 38:4–13; 38:28). In the earlier unit Jeremiah was beaten and put in stocks at the Benjamin Gate by a priest named Pashhur (chap. 20); in the latter unit Jeremiah is arrested at the Upper Benjamin Gate and beaten and im-

23.8 The Book of Jeremiah

a **oracles against Judah: coming invasion and disaster <u>from the north</u>** (1:1–12:17)
- Jeremiah appointed <u>over the nations</u> to declare God's judgments against them (1:10);
- messages to nations (10:11, 25; 12:14–17); including <u>Egypt</u>, <u>Edom</u>, etc. (9:25–26 [9:24–25])
- eyewitnesslike depictions of Judah's invasion, including <u>battle scenes</u>, <u>horses</u>, <u>trumpet alarms</u>, <u>swords and bows</u>, <u>casualties</u>, <u>destruction of towns</u>, <u>exiles</u>, etc.
- exhortations to <u>weep and wail</u> over Judah's fall (4:8; 6:26; 9:20 [9:19])
- theme: disaster coming <u>from the north</u> (1:13–15; 4:6; 6:1, 22; 10:22)
- nearly verbatim repetitions: 6:22–24 || 50:41–43 and 10:12–16 || 51:15–19

b **Judah's exile and suffering predicted** (13:1–20:18)
- Jeremiah's complaints of his <u>persecution</u>
- Jeremiah <u>beaten and imprisoned</u> at Upper Benjamin Gate by <u>Pashhur</u> (20:1–18)
- Jeremiah's complaints about his <u>persecution</u>; God will save him from enemies
- Jeremiah's prayer that he be <u>vindicated and avenged</u>
- themes: <u>sword</u>, <u>famine</u>, <u>plague</u> (or variations)

c **dated messages of judgment** about specific kings and groups (21:1–29:32)
- begins: message to Zedekiah <u>during siege</u>: city will <u>fall</u> to Babylonians and be <u>burned</u>; Zedekiah will be <u>captured</u> (21:1–7)
- <u>failure of Davidic kings</u> to be <u>just</u> and to <u>rescue oppressed</u> (21:12; 22:3–5)
- symbolic-action message: <u>cup of wine</u> to nations (25:1–38)

d **CENTER: messages of future hope** (30:1–33:26)

c′ **dated messages of judgment** about specific kings and groups (34:1–35:19)
- begins: message to Zedekiah <u>during siege</u>: city will <u>fall</u> to Babylonians and be <u>burned</u>; Zedekiah will be <u>captured</u> (34:1–3)
- <u>failure of Davidic kings</u> to be <u>just</u> and to <u>rescue oppressed</u> (21:12; 22:3–5)
- symbolic-action message: <u>cups of wine</u> to Rechabites (35:1–19)

b′ **Judah's fall and exile** (36:1–45:5)
- stories of Jeremiah's <u>persecution</u>
- Jeremiah arrested at Benjamin Gate; <u>beaten and imprisoned</u> by <u>Pashhur</u> and others
- Jeremiah's <u>persecution</u> documented; Jeremiah is saved from enemies repeatedly
- Jeremiah is <u>vindicated</u> (predictions come true) <u>and avenged</u> (Judah fails)
- themes: <u>sword</u>, <u>famine</u>, <u>plague</u> (or variations)

a′ **oracles against the nations: coming invasions and disasters <u>from the north</u>** (46:1–51:64)
- Jeremiah declares God's judgments <u>against the nations</u>, including <u>Egypt</u>, <u>Edom</u>, etc.
- eyewitnesslike depictions of nations' invasion, including <u>battle scenes</u>, <u>horses</u>, <u>trumpet alarms</u>, <u>swords and bows</u>, <u>casualties</u>, <u>destruction of towns</u>, <u>exiles</u>, etc.
- exhortations to <u>weep and wail</u> over various nations' fall (48:17, 20; 49:3; 51:8)
- theme: disaster coming <u>from the north</u> (46:20, 24; 47:2; 50:3, 9, 41; 51:48)
- nearly verbatim repetitions: 6:22–24 || 50:41–43 and 10:12–16 || 51:15–19

appendix: fall of Jerusalem (52:1–34)

---

prisoned by a group of officials including Pashhur and Gedaliah son of Pashhur (chaps. 37–38). The latter unit provides a narrative account of Jeremiah's suffering as described in his complaints in the earlier unit. For example, Jeremiah bemoans that "the whole land strives and contends" with him; "I have neither lent nor borrowed, yet everyone curses me!" (15:10). Jeremiah 36–45 provides a series of stories documenting the validity of these complaints. God's promise to Jeremiah, "I will make your enemies plead with you in times of disaster and times of distress" (15:11), finds its fulfillment in chapters 37–44, where Jeremiah's enemies, including Zedekiah and the people of Judah, keep coming to him for a word from God or to request that he plead with God on their behalf. God's frequent promises to protect and save Jeremiah from his persecutors (15:11, 20–21; 17:14–17; etc.) are fulfilled in chapters 36–45. Jeremiah's prayers that God will punish his persecutors (15:15;

17:18; 18:21–23; 20:11–13) are fulfilled in the accounts of Judah's fall and exile in chapters 36–45. The prediction of "sword, famine, and plague" (or variations) is a theme in both chapters 13–20 (14:12, 13, 15a, 15b, 16; 15:2; 16:4; 18:21) and chapters 36–45 (42:17, 22; 44:12, 13, 18, 27).

Correspondence of Third and Third-to-Last Units (Jeremiah 21–29; 34–35)

The book's third and third-to-last units also match. Both units begin with messages to Zedekiah during the Babylonian siege of Jerusalem (21:1–2; 34:1–2). Both messages declare the same bad news: (1) Jerusalem will fall to the Babylonians, (2) Zedekiah will be captured, and (3) the city will be burned down. Also, these units comprise the book's only two collections of messages against Judah dated to the regnal years of specific kings. Another connection is the echoed condemnation of the house of David for injustice and for failure to rescue the oppressed from their oppressors (21:12; 22:3–5; 34:8–22). Both messages of condemnation were delivered in Jerusalem's final moments, during the Babylonian siege.

There may be a contrastive correspondence between chapters 25 and 35, both of which feature Jeremiah's symbolic action of serving cups of wine to people and asking them to drink. In chapter 25, God instructs Jeremiah, "Take . . . this cup filled with the wine of my wrath and have the nations . . . drink it." Jeremiah then reports, "So I took the cup . . . and had all the nations . . . drink it" (25:15–17). God warns, "If they refuse to take the cup from your hand and drink, tell them, 'This is what Yahweh Almighty says: you must drink it!'" (25:28). The result of drinking the wine is destruction. This is apparently echoed in the message involving the Rechabites in chapter 35, where God instructs Jeremiah, "Go to the Rechabites . . . and give them wine to drink." Jeremiah reports, "So I set before them bowls full of wine and some cups before the Rechabites . . . and said to them, 'Drink from the wine!'" The Rechabites, being abstainers, naturally refuse; unlike the nations, though, they are not only allowed to refuse but are even praised for it and promised that when God punishes the land, he will spare them.

The entire Book of Jeremiah, therefore, forms a grand symmetry with the messages of hope standing, significantly, at the center (23.8).

Conclusion

Several observations can be made regarding the interplay of structure and meaning in the Book of Jeremiah. The placement of the messages of future hope at the center, in the position of greatest emphasis, suggests that the author considered this hope to be of central importance to his audience. Unlike many prophetic books, the central slot here does not feature a climactic call to repentance. This undoubtedly reflects the historical situation. The book was written after the fall of Jerusalem, when it was too late for the people of Judah to avoid judgment by repenting. Judgment had already fallen. The author chooses, therefore, to structurally highlight the message of hope by placing it at the center. The exiles should wait patiently for God's restora-

tion; he has promised that he will bring them back home in the future.

The book's layout also reflects an interest in establishing the validity of Jeremiah's ministry and message. Closing the book with the appendix is probably intended to underscore the point that Jeremiah's message of Jerusalem's coming fall (for which he was persecuted, beaten, and imprisoned) turned out to be true. The balancing of his predictions of Judah's fall and exile (the second unit) with the accounts of Judah's fall and exile (the next-to-last unit) likewise serves to underscore this point.

The repetition of the theme of Jeremiah's persecution in the second and next-to-last units draws attention to this theme. In chapters 13–20 the audience hears Jeremiah's prayers decrying his rejection and persecution by the people of Judah; then chapters 36–45 provide actual accounts of the prophet's persecution and rejection. The reason for the emphasis should be obvious. By documenting Judah's mistreatment of God's final prophet to the nation, the author reinforces God's case against his people. Theodicy is an underlying concern here. This point is strengthened in the internal design of chapters 36–45, where instances of Jeremiah's persecution by the people of Judah are juxtaposed with stories of how he was treated kindly by foreigners, including Ebed-melech the Cushite and the Babylonians Nebuchadnezzar and Nebuzaradan. Judah's wickedness is made to appear all the more heinous against the backdrop of the kindness of foreigners.

Opening and closing the book with units announcing the divinely decreed fall of nations (Judah in the first unit, other nations in the last) emphasizes to the exilic audience that their disaster was not the result of Yahweh's failure, but their own. Yahweh did not fail to protect Judah; to the contrary, both Judah and various other nations fell because Yahweh decreed that they should fall because of their wickedness (cf. the similar theme in the Book of Kings). Yahweh is above all nations and all gods. He alone determines the destinies of the nations. He alone caused Judah to fall. And he alone can be trusted to take care of the exiles in their captivity and to bring them home again as he has promised.

24

Lamentations

His Mercies Are New Every Morning

The Book of Lamentations is an excellent example of how structure can reinforce or enhance a composition's meaning.[1] The book is written in the form of a eulogy mourning the tragic fall of Jerusalem in 586 B.C. To understand the significance of its structure, we must first understand the unique verse structure of Hebrew eulogies. Verse structure in standard Hebrew poetry generally features couplets (or verses) made up of two matching lines. The two matching lines normally balance one another in both thought and length and generally have three stress accents each. Psalm 19:1–2 [19:2–3] demonstrates well this a-b-c ‖ a′-b′-c′ pattern:

a	the heavens
b	declare
c	God's glory
a′	the skies
b′	proclaim
c′	his craftsmanship

a	day by day
b	they express
c	words
a′	night by night
b′	they utter
c′	knowledge

An exception to this standardized pattern is the special verse form found in eulogies (or "laments"), called the qinah pattern (qînâ is the Hebrew term for "lament"). In a lament, the second line of the couplet is normally shorter than the first, usually following a 3+2 pattern (a-b-c ‖ a′-b′ or variations). It is speculated that the shortening of the second line gives the sense that the line is "cut off" before its anticipated completion, which represents in literary form the tragic "cutting off" of the mourned person's life before its natural completion. The pattern is sometimes referred to as the "dying out" or "dying away" pattern. English translations often obscure the 3+2 pattern in biblical eulogies; but the following examples from Lamentations 3:4 and 3:9 illustrate the pattern a-b-c ‖ a′-b′:

a	he withers
b	my skin
c	and my flesh
a′	he breaks
b′	my bones

a	he walls up
b	my ways
c	with cut stones
a′	he twists
b′	my paths

An ancient author pondering how to organize an extensive eulogy might well have considered using some kind of 3+2 pattern for the eulogy's overall arrangement. Such a design would convey the same sense of "dying out" on the larger level of the eulogy as would already occur on the verse level. The mournful beat of the lament would then be felt on both the verse level and the level of the eulogy's larger structure.

This is precisely what the author of Lamentations did. The book is made up of five poems (corresponding to its five chapters in our Bibles). The first three poems are matched: all are relatively long, and all are precisely the same length. Each is an acrostic poem, arranged alphabetically according to the twenty-two letters of the Hebrew alphabet. Each poem has twenty-two stanzas, with three poetic verses (or couplets) in each stanza—giving a total of sixty-six poetic verses in each poem. In the first two poems, only the first verse in each stanza begins with the appropriate letter of the Hebrew alphabet; in the third poem all three verses in each stanza begin with the appropriate letter (creating the sense of a quickening pace).

1. See David A. Dorsey, "Lamentations: Communicating Meaning through Structure," *Evangelical Journal* 6 (1988) 83–90.

These three long poems are followed by two shorter poems. The fourth poem is alphabetically arranged like the first three, but it is shorter. Each of its twenty-two stanzas has only two verses (only forty-four lines in all), which immediately conveys the impression that the eulogy itself is "dying out." This impression is reinforced by the final poem. Like the others, this poem has twenty-two stanzas (if one can call them such). But the sense of disintegration is completed by two new features: each stanza now has only one verse (for a total of only twenty-two verses) and the orderly alphabetical arrangement is now abandoned. The chapter has the correct number of verses for an acrostic poem (twenty-two), but the verses are in alphabetical disorder. This scheme conveys a sense of disintegration, of "dying away."[2] Overall, the book's 3+2 layout may be viewed as follows:

---

a three long poems
Lamentations 1: long acrostic poem: 66 lines
Lamentations 2: long acrostic poem: 66 lines
Lamentations 3: long acrostic poem: 66 lines
b two shorter poems
Lamentations 4: shorter acrostic poem: 44 lines
Lamentations 5: even shorter poem, not acrostic: 22 lines

There may be yet another structural scheme functioning simultaneously in the book. Bo Johnson argues that Lamentations is chiastically arranged, with 3:21–42 as the climax.[3] He notes that the first third of chapter 3 (3:1–20) has at least some connections with the last third (3:43–66). Furthermore, chapter 1, which is composed of what he terms a "fact half" (1:1–11) and an "interpretation half" (1:12–22), and chapter 2, which also comprises two similar halves (2:1–11; 2:12–22), are echoed in chapter 4, which also consists of a "fact half" (4:1–11) and an "interpretation half" (4:12–22). He is not sure of the function of chapter 5, except that in content it is similar to chapters 1 and 2. Johnson's analysis therefore tentatively suggests a seven-part chiasmus, or modified chiasmus:

---

a Lamentations 1: fact half, interpretation half
　b Lamentations 2: fact half, interpretation half
　　c Lamentations 3:1–20
　　　d Lamentations 3:21–42
　　e Lamentations 3:43–66: connections with 3:1–20

---

f Lamentations 4: fact half, interpretation half
g Lamentations 5: some connections with chaps. 1–2

Johnson's analysis has much to commend it. That 3:21–42 is intended as the climax or counterpoint of the book is quite appealing: these verses form a beautiful, serene paean of hope and faith in the midst of a maelstrom of despair. Careful analysis of Lamentations, however, suggests that though Johnson's sense of the presence of a symmetry is correct, the book's symmetric scheme is more highly developed than he realized.

Throughout the eulogy one cannot help but notice the periodic shift in person, for example, from third-person ("she . . . she . . . her") in 1:1–11 to first-person ("I . . . I . . . my") in 1:12–22. These shifts in person have the effect of creating a series of units. Based primarily on these periodic shifts in person, the eulogy may be divided (quite apart from the five-part scheme created by the acrostic poems) into thirteen units, with the seventh or central unit being, not surprisingly, 3:21–32. Further, the final six units chiastically match the first six, with correspondences that are obvious and significant.

Unit 1: Lamentations 1:1–11

The Book of Lamentations begins with Zion's depiction as a woman weeping over her desolation. Some sixty grammatical instances of the third-person feminine singular govern the entirety of the unit: her virgins have been humbled, her people are hungry, she suffers bitterly, there is none to comfort her.

Unit 2: Lamentations 1:12–22

In 1:12 the eulogy's perspective shifts to the first-person singular. Now we hear Zion itself speaking, decrying its destitution and suffering: "Is there any sorrow like my sorrow that was brought upon me? . . . For these things I weep; my eyes flow with tears." The shift to first-person singular is rhetorically powerful (nearly fifty occurrences of this grammatical feature dominate the unit), drawing the audience into the tragedy of the eulogy by having them hear Zion's story from its own mouth.

Unit 3: Lamentations 2:1–8

The next unit is set off by another shift in person, as fifty grammatical instances of third-person masculine singular conspicuously dominate these verses. The focus of this section is Yahweh: it is he who has destroyed Jerusalem;

---

2. See further William H. Shea, "The *Qinah* Structure of the Book of Lamentations," *Biblica* 60 (1979) 103–7, who also sees this pattern. His study of the book's 3+2 structure is very helpful.

3. Bo Johnson, "Form and Message in Lamentations," *Zeitschrift für die alttestamentliche Wissenschaft* 97 (1985) 58–73.

"Yahweh has covered daughter Zion with the cloud of his anger; he has hurled down Israel's splendor . . . he has not remembered his footstool in the day of his anger."

Unit 4: Lamentations 2:9–12

Next comes a brief section dominated by the third-person plural (some thirteen occurrences), in which the people of Jerusalem are the focus. Their suffering is depicted: "The elders of daughter Zion sit on the ground in silence; they have cast dust on their heads; they put on sackcloth."

Unit 5: Lamentations 2:13–22

The fifth unit is marked by a shift to the second-person feminine singular: about thirty occurrences of this grammatical feature are used to address daughter Zion. Here, in another rhetorically effective stroke, the poet addresses Zion directly, speaking with her about her tragic suffering and desolate state: "O daughter Zion, to what can I compare your suffering? How can I comfort you? Your wound is as deep as the sea." Having established the tragedy of Jerusalem's disaster and its divine cause in the first four units, the poet now begins to subtly move his audience toward the desired response. His admonition is cleverly couched in the guise of words of encouragement to the grieving daughter Zion: "Cry aloud (feminine singular) to Yahweh. . . . Let your tears flow like a river. . . . Pour out your heart like water before Yahweh. Lift up your hands to him in prayer. Plead for your children as they faint . . . in the streets (2:18–19)." This exhortation is climaxed by a suggested prayer that Zion might pray to Yahweh (2:20–22).

Unit 6: Lamentations 3:1–20

The eulogy now turns poignantly personal.[4] It shifts to the first-person singular (about forty occurrences), as in the second unit, but here the speaker is not daughter Zion but the poet himself (the speaker is a man, not a woman; cf. 3:1). The poet, who is an integral part of the population of Judah, speaks here of the terrible suffering he himself has experienced as Yahweh has executed his angry judgment against him as part

of the people of Judah. The poet knows first-hand the suffering of which he speaks.

Along with the predominant first-person singular comes the almost equally dominant third-person masculine singular, with nearly thirty references to Yahweh. Virtually every statement in this section combines the two persons, juxtaposing the poet and Yahweh (3:1–8):

> I myself have seen the affliction
> that comes from the rod of his wrath.
> He has driven me away;
> he has made me walk in darkness. . . .
> He has turned his hand against me
> so I cannot escape. . . .
> He has broken my bones. . . .
> He has weighed me down. . . .
> Even when I cry out . . .
> he closes out my prayer.

Unit 7: Lamentations 3:21–32 (central unit)

The audience is ready for words of hope. These come in the seventh unit, whose inspiring lines form the high point and center of the book. This unit stands apart from its context simply by virtue of its positive content. Its lines express the poet's own resolution of the problem caused by the experience of Yahweh's judgment. The words indirectly serve as advice to his hearers: "Yahweh's kindness never ends; his love never ceases; it is renewed every morning; great is your faithfulness! . . . Therefore I will wait for him. Yahweh is good to those whose hope is in him, to the one who seeks him. . . . Yahweh will not cast off forever. Though he brings grief, he will show love, according to the greatness of his kindness!"

It is not at all clear where this unit ends; and, to make matters worse, the boundaries of the next unit are also difficult to determine (perhaps due to textual and interpretive uncertainties). This central unit of hope probably closes with 3:32, concluding the unit as it opened (3:22)—with a proclamation of Yahweh's "love" (rḥm) and "kindness" (ḥesed).

Unit 8: Lamentations 3:33–39 (sixth-to-last unit)

After the inspiring central unit, the poet returns to his lament, which will continue through the remainder of the book. The final six units chiastically match, in some significant ways, the opening six units. In contrast to the first half of the eulogy, the second half is pervaded with a sense of cautious hope. Each unit offers considerations that mitigate the despair expressed in its counterpart in the first half.

The boundaries of the eighth unit are difficult to determine. I propose that the unit begins at

---

4. The end of this unit is not certain. The third-person masculine singular occurrences end in 3:16. But 3:17–21 continues the domination of the first-person singular as well as the rehearsal of the poet's suffering. The shift to the central unit of hope begins in 3:22; it could be argued that 3:21 might begin this central unit—although in that case a new unit would begin, oddly, two-thirds of the way through a stanza (3:21 is the third verse in the *zayin* stanza).

3:33 and ends with 3:39. These verses are exceedingly difficult to interpret; and any conclusions here must be tentative. The unit apparently offers some positive considerations about divine punishment. Yes, Yahweh is the one who punished his people; everything that happens, bad as well as good, is from God (3:34–38). But Yahweh never enjoys bringing affliction or grief upon human beings (3:33). When people suffer because of their sin, they should not complain (3:39).

This section seems to correspond to the sixth unit, at least weakly.[5] The prominence of the third-person masculine singular in 3:33–39 (about seven times) seems to echo its prominence in 3:1–20 (in both, "he" refers to Yahweh). Also, the opening and closing of these units chiastically match. The sixth unit opens with a complaint that the poet is the "man" (*geber*) who has suffered "affliction" (*ʿānî*) and closes with a vow to remember his "affliction" (*ʿānî*); the eighth unit opens with the statement that Yahweh does not enjoy "afflicting" (*ʿnh*) people (3:33) and closes by mentioning that "a man (*geber*) should not complain when it is for his sins (*ḥăṭāʾîm*; cf. BHS) that he is suffering" (3:39).

Unit 9: Lamentations 3:40–66 (fifth-to-last unit)

The ninth unit addresses Yahweh in the second-person. Second-person elements (about twenty-five times) dominate, which seems to correspond to the fifth unit, the only other unit in the eulogy where second-person predominates. The fifth unit mainly features second-person feminine singular (referring to daughter Zion), with second-person masculine singular becoming predominant only toward the end (2:20–22). On the other hand, the ninth unit exclusively features the second-person masculine singular.

These two units correspond in obvious ways. Both feature prayers to Yahweh (2:20–22; 3:42–47, 55–66), introduced by exhortations to "lift up" (*nśʾ*) the "hands" and to lift up/pour out the "heart" "to Yahweh" (2:19; 3:41). Parallels abound. For example:

You (Yahweh) have slain (*hrg*) . . . without pity (*ḥml*).

—Lamentations 2:21

You (Yahweh) have slain (*hrg*) without pity (*ḥml*).

—Lamentations 3:43

All your enemies
have opened their mouths wide (*pāṣû pîhem*)
    against you.

—Lamentations 2:16

All our enemies
have opened their mouths wide (*pāṣû pîhem*)
    against us.

—Lamentations 3:46

Let your tears descend (*yrd*) like a river,
day and night;
don't cease (*pûgat*);
don't give rest (*ʾal-tiddōm*) to your eyes (*ʿênayim*).

—Lamentations 2:18

Streams of water descend (*yrd*) from my eyes
    (*ʿênayim*); . . .
my eyes (*ʿênayim*) flow and don't rest (*tidmeh*)
or cease (*pûgôt*).

—Lamentations 3:48–49

While the fifth unit is entirely negative, the ninth unit is more positive. According to the fifth unit, the people cried out to Yahweh but received no answer (2:19–22); whereas in the ninth unit the poet cries out to Yahweh and is heard: "You have heard my plea! . . . You came near when I called you, and you said, 'Do not fear!' O Yahweh, you have taken my case; you have redeemed my life! You have seen the wrong done to me" (3:55–59). Furthermore, whereas the fifth unit merely mourns the wrongs Judah has suffered at the hands of its enemies, the ninth unit calls for Yahweh to right the wrongs and pay back their enemies for what they have done (3:59–66).

Unit 10: Lamentations 4:1–10 (fourth-to-last unit)

The tenth unit, like the fourth, features the predominance of the third-person plural. As in the fourth unit, the suffering survivors of Jerusalem are now the focus. In both units, the same categories are mentioned: "nurslings" (*yôneq*), "little children" (*ʿôlēl*), princes, young women, and mothers. In both units, the starvation of the survivors in Jerusalem is the main theme. In both, the fainting and starving of the children is said to be taking place, not in their homes, but out in the streets/town squares (2:11–12; 4:3–4). In both units, the thirst of the nurslings is described (2:11c–12a; 4:4). In both units, the scenes of suffering are in the streets or squares of the city (2:11–12; 4:1, 5, 8). The statement in 2:12b that the starving people "collapse like casualties (*ḥālāl*)" is echoed in 4:9a: "The casualties (*ḥālāl*) of the sword were better off than these casualties (*ḥālāl*) of famine." The fourth

---

5. There also seem to be some echoes of the sixth unit in 3:24–31: "therefore I will hope" (*ʿal-kēn ʿôḥîl*; 3:21, 24), "being sated" (*śbʿ*; 3:15, 30), "man" (*geber*; 3:1, 27), "dust" (3:16, 29), and "abandon" (*znḥ*; 3:17, 31).

unit begins with a line about Zion's "destruction" (*šeber*); its matching unit concludes with the phrase "the destruction (*šeber*) of my people" (4:10b). Conversely, while the fourth unit closes with the question "where?" (*ʾayyēh*), asking about those whose lives "are poured out (*hištappēk*) in the town plazas" (2:12); its matching unit opens with the question "where?" (*ʾēkâ*), asking about the stones that "are poured out (*hištappēk*) at the head of every street" (4:1).

In contrast to the hopelessness of the fourth unit, however, this unit offers a mitigating consideration to help make sense of this tragedy: "The iniquity of my people was greater than the sinfulness of Sodom!" (4:6a).

Unit 11: Lamentations 4:11–16 (third-to-last unit)

Echoing the third unit, the third-to-last unit returns to the predominate use of the third-person masculine singular. The correspondence between these two units is reinforced by the repetition of the theme of Yahweh's "anger" (*ʾappô*; 2:1a, 1b, 3, 6; 4:11) and "wrath" (*ḥămātô*; 2:4c; 4:11a), which Yahweh has "poured out" (*šāpak*; 2:4c; 4:11a) and which has "devoured" (*ʾkl*) Zion's structures like "fire" (*ʾēš*; 2:3–4; 4:11). Both units open with a declaration about God's "anger" (*ʾappô*) against his people (2:1; 4:11). Both units also mention religious leaders, particularly "priests" (*kōhēn*; 2:6; 4:13).

Again, however, the entirely despairing tone of the earlier unit is tempered in the later unit by mitigating considerations. In the third unit we hear only of Yahweh's fierce anger against Zion, whereas in the third-to-last unit we hear the reason for his destructive anger against Zion: "It was because of the sins of its prophets and the iniquities of its priests, who shed within it the blood of the righteous" (4:13). This mitigating note is like the one in the previous unit (4:6): they both occur near the center of their respective units, and they offer the same reason for Zion's suffering: the people's "iniquities" (*ʾăwōn*) and "sins" (*ḥaṭṭāʾt*).

Unit 12: Lamentations 4:17–22 (next-to-last unit)

The next-to-last unit, like the second, uses the first-person; but now it is the first-person plural ("we"), rather than singular ("I"). The poet speaks in the first-person of the nation's suffering. This next-to-last unit corresponds to the second unit in various conspicuous ways. The central theme of both units is the failure of Judah's former allies and neighbors to support it in its

time of distress. They failed to send military help (1:17, 19; 4:17) and offered Judah neither comfort nor assistance (2:16–19, 21; 4:17; cf. 4:21–22). Both units relate that Judah appealed to fickle allies in vain for help (1:17, 19a; 4:17). Both close with a cry of vengeance against Judah's enemies, and both express the wish or prayer that what happened to Judah will now happen to its enemies (1:21–22; 4:21–22). Both also mention that Judah's enemies or neighbors heard about its fall and "rejoiced" (*śûś*; 1:21; 4:21).

In contrast to the second unit, which is entirely hopeless and in which Zion can only cry out to Yahweh to repay its enemies and "deal with them as you have dealt with me" (1:21–22), the next-to-last unit provides a promise that Yahweh will right the wrongs Judah has experienced: "To you [Edom] will the cup also be passed; you will be drunk and stripped naked; O daughter Zion, your punishment will end; he will not prolong your exile. But, O daughter Edom, he will punish your sin and expose your iniquity" (4:21–22). It is worth noting that for the fifth time the mitigating consideration in the later unit involves Yahweh's justice, the fourth time that the justice issue has involved "sins" (*ḥaṭṭāʾt*), and the third time it has involved both "sins" (*ḥaṭṭāʾt*) and "iniquity" (*ʾăwōn*).

Unit 13: Lamentations 5:1–22 (last unit)

The eulogy's closing unit is, fittingly, a prayer. It is the eulogy's own prayer as representative of all the people. The poet prays that Yahweh will "remember" what has happened to the people of Judah, that he will look upon their disgrace (5:1), and that he will "restore" (*hēšîb*) them so they can "return" (*šûb*) and be renewed (5:21). This final unit is governed by about forty occurrences of the first-person plural. By this shift, the poet identifies himself with the people and speaks to Yahweh on behalf of all the survivors: "Remember, O Yahweh, what has happened to us; look and see our disgrace. . . . Restore us" (5:1, 21). The prayer climaxes in 5:19–22, which serves as the book's hope-filled grand conclusion: "You, O Yahweh, reign forever . . . restore us to yourself, Yahweh, that we may return; renew our days as of old."

This unit matches the eulogy's first unit. Both units detail the terrible reversal of Judah's fortunes, from prosperity to horrible suffering. Both mention the prosperous "days of old" (*yĕmê qedem*; 1:7; 5:21). Both depict the awful fate of Judah's princes (1:6; 5:12). The desolation of Jerusalem, once bustling with people, is depicted in both units—at the beginning of the

24.1 The Book of Lamentations

a **she—Zion—is desolate and devastated** (1:1–11)
- terrible reversal of Judah's fortunes
- prosperous days of old (*yĕmê qedem*) are over
- gates are desolate
- fate of princes
- desperation to acquire bread
- pursuers allow no rest; reason: she has sinned

  b **I—Zion—was betrayed and defeated: there is none to help or comfort me** (1:12–22)
  - they rejoice over my fall
  - vain hope for help from allies
  - cry for vengeance

    c **he—Yahweh—has caused this in his anger** (2:1–8)
    - Yahweh has poured out his anger and wrath, which has devoured Zion like fire

      d **they—princes, maidens, nurslings, children, mothers—suffer** (2:9–12)
      - children starve and perish in the town squares

        e **you—Zion—should cry out to God** (2:13–22)
        - let tears stream down like a river without ceasing or rest
        - enemies open mouths against you
        - Yahweh has slain without pity
        - prayer

          f **he—Yahweh—has afflicted (ʿnh) me** (3:1–20)
          - the poet—a man (*geber*)—is afflicted; his complaint

          g **CLIMAX: Yahweh's great love!** (3:21–32)

          f′ **he—Yahweh—afflicts (ʿnh) humans** (3:33–39)
          - mitigating note: Yahweh does not enjoy afflicting humans
          - a man (*geber*) shouldn't complain if he suffers for sins

        e′ **you—Yahweh—to you I cry out** (3:40–66)
        - mitigating note: prayer for Yahweh's justice
        - my tears stream down like a river without ceasing or rest
        - enemies open mouths against me
        - Yahweh has slain without pity
        - prayer

      d′ **they—princes, maidens, nurslings, children, mothers—suffer** (4:1–10)
      - mitigating note: Yahweh is just; his punishment was because Judah's sins and iniquities were worse than Sodom's
      - children starve and perish in the town squares

    c′ **he—Yahweh—caused this in his anger** (4:11–16)
    - mitigating note: Yahweh is just; his punishment was for Judah's sins and iniquities
    - Yahweh has poured out his anger and wrath, which has devoured Zion like fire

  b′ **we—the people of Zion—were betrayed and defeated** (4:17–22)
  - mitigating note: Yahweh is just; he will restore Judah and punish Edom for her sins and iniquities
  - our allies failed to help
  - Edom rejoices

a′ **we—the people of Zion—are desolate and devastated** (5:1–22)
- mitigating note: poet's prayer, "Restore us, so that we may return!"
- terrible reversal of Judah's fortunes
- prosperous days of old (*yĕmê qedem*) are over
- gates are desolate
- fate of princes
- desperation to acquire bread
- pursuers allow no rest; reason: we have sinned

---

first unit and at the end of the last (not counting the final four-verse concluding prayer) (1:1; 5:18; cf. 1:4, 6). The eulogy opens with "how deserted lies the city, once so full of people" (1:1) and ends with "Mount Zion lies desolate; jackals prowl over it" (5:18). In both units, the once busy gates are said to be empty (1:4; 5:14). Both units speak of how foreigners have taken over the land (1:5, 10; 5:2, 8). Both mention the "pur- suers" (*rdp*) (1:3, 6; 5:5) who allow the fugitives no "rest" (*nwḥ*). Both mention the captivity and enslavement of the children/young people (1:5; 5:13; cf. 5:3). Both speak of the people's desperation to acquire "bread" (*leḥem*) (1:11; 5:6, 9). Both charge that Judah suffered because it sinned (1:5, 8; 5:16). Both contain a prayer to God to "look upon" (*rāʾâ*) their affliction/disgrace (1:9; 5:1).

 252

The Book of Lamentations, then, exhibits a thirteen-part symmetry centering on the inspiring passage of hope in 3:21–32 (24.1).

Conclusion

The foregoing analysis offers several helpful insights regarding the form and message of the Book of Lamentations. First, it suggests that chapter 5 is part of the original eulogy, since this chapter plays an integral role in both the book's *qinah* layout and its symmetric scheme. The effect achieved by the overall 3+2 layout is a sense of grief, which is the dominant mood of the book. The author conveys by this structure, as well as by the book's contents, a profound sense of sadness over the tragic fall of the city of Jerusalem.

Also, since the last six units are designed to offer mitigating considerations to soften the despair of the earlier six units, it seems safe to say that the poet intended his eulogy to offer hope and encouragement to the survivors of Jerusalem's fall. That virtually all these hope-inspiring notes seek to justify Yahweh's actions against Judah indicates that the poet wishes to help the audience deal with the problem of theodicy—Yahweh's justice in his treatment of his people.

The placement of the prayer for restoration in the highlighted final position (5:19–22) suggests that the author views Yahweh's gracious restoration of Judah as vital to its future. The placement of the climactic declaration of Yahweh's love at the center of the eulogy, in the position of greatest emphasis, suggests, moreover, that Yahweh's love and compassion is central and key to Judah's restoration. Through these divine qualities the Judean survivors will be able to find restoration and peace with the God who has destroyed them.

25

Ezekiel

Visions of the Glory of God

The Book of Ezekiel is a compilation of messages delivered by the prophet Ezekiel to the Jewish community in Babylonia before and after the fall of Jerusalem in 586 B.C. When Ezekiel began his ministry the exiled community was undoubtedly troubled by events transpiring in their homeland of Judah. Their thoughts and prayers would have been with their relatives and friends there and with their beloved temple. Ezekiel's message to them was not encouraging regarding the fate of Judah and the temple. Yet in other respects his words were very encouraging and served to inspire the exiled community long after the fall of Jerusalem.

Several studies have examined the internal structure of the Book of Ezekiel.[1] Since all the dated messages in the book (1:1–2; 8:1; 20:1; 24:1; 26:1; 29:1, 17; 30:20; 31:1; 32:1, 17; 33:21; 40:1) are in chronological order with the single exception of 29:17,[2] the book's messages appear to be arranged in roughly chronological order.

But we can also observe examples of groupings by topic, for example, the collection of oracles against the nations in chapters 25–32 and the grouping of messages of hope and restoration at the end of the book. Another prominent organizational technique used in the book—and one that has mostly gone unnoticed—is a sevenfold structuring scheme. Study of Ezekiel's structure reveals that the entire book comprises seven main sections, each composed of seven smaller units (25.1).

The book opens with a lengthy group of messages that spans the entire first half of the book. This almost unbroken series of messages finally concludes in chapter 24 with the beginning in chapters 25–32 of the self-contained collection of Ezekiel's oracles against the nations. Although chapters 1–24 might appear to form a single, rather unwieldy series of messages, closer examination reveals several seams in the collection. The author used a simple formula to mark the beginning of each group. At regular intervals, about equally spaced throughout the first twenty-four chapters, occur four similar introductions: 1:1–3; 8:1; 14:1–2; 20:1–2. Each of these introductions, except the third, includes a date. In fact, except for the date in 24:1 (where the date is the central point of the message), these three introductions contain the only dates in the entire twenty-four chapters. Moreover, each except the first includes a statement about the "elders of Judah/Israel" coming to Ezekiel and "sitting" before him, followed by a formulaic introduction to a revelation from God. These four introductions are as follows:

> In the thirtieth year, in the fourth month, on the fifth day of the month, as I was among the exiles . . . the heavens were opened and I saw visions of God. On the fifth day of the month (it was the fifth year of the exile of King Jehoiachin), the word of the Lord came to Ezekiel.
>
> —Ezekiel 1:1–3

---

1. For bibliography, see H. Van Dyke Parunak, *Structural Studies in Ezekiel* (Ph.D. diss., Harvard University, 1978), 573–81. In his extensive work, devoted primarily to microstructural investigations, Parunak proposes that the book comprises three major sections or panels: (1) the material focusing on Ezekiel's call (1:1–3:15), (2) the complex of messages of judgment (3:16–33:33), and (3) the complex of messages of future restoration (34:1–48:35). Within the latter two panels he identifies "blocks" of messages. The second panel contains four such blocks: (a) 3:16–7:27; (b) 8:1–11:25, a complex chiastic adaptation of the *rîb* pattern centered about the vision in chap. 10 of the departure of the glory of the Lord; (c) 12:1–23:49, comprising two subunits: 12:1–15:8 and 16:1–23:49 (the latter subunit bracketed by the inclusio formed by chaps. 16 and 23); and (d) 24:1–33:33, which includes the oracles to the nations (this last section is bracketed by the inclusio created by 24:25–27, in which Ezekiel is told that a messenger will come and tell him that the temple is destroyed, and 33:21–22, in which the messenger arrives with the message). The third panel comprises three blocks: (a) miscellaneous oracles of restoration (34:1–37:28), (b) Gog and Magog (38:1–39:29), and (c) the vision of the restored temple (40:1–48:35).

2. One of the seven messages about Egypt, this message has been logically placed together with the other six despite the violation of the overall chronological scheme.

25.1 Seven major sections of the Book of Ezekiel

a **Ezekiel's call and first collection of messages about coming judgment** (1:1–7:27)

b **second collection of messages about coming judgment** (8:1–13:23)

c **third collection of messages about coming judgment** (14:1–19:14)

d **fourth collection of messages about coming judgment** (20:1–24:27)

e **oracles against the nations** (25:1–32:32)

f **messages about Israel's punishment and future restoration** (33:1–39:29)

g **vision of the new temple and the new land** (40:1–48:35)

25.2 Ezekiel's call and first collection of messages about coming judgment (Ezekiel 1–7)

a **vision 1: Ezekiel's call and commissioning near the Chebar River** (1:1–3:11)
- the hand of Yahweh was upon him (1:3)
- vision of the glory of Yahweh
- vision followed by Ezekiel's falling facedown, then receiving Yahweh's message about his prophetic task

b **vision 2: Ezekiel receives further instructions about his task** (3:12–21)
- the hand of Yahweh was upon me (3:14)
- vision of the glory of Yahweh (3:12–13)
- vision followed by Ezekiel's being overwhelmed, then receiving Yahweh's message about his prophetic task

c **vision 3: more instructions about Ezekiel's task** (3:22–27)
- the hand of Yahweh was upon me (3:22)
- vision of the glory of Yahweh (3:23)
- vision followed by Ezekiel's falling facedown, then receiving Yahweh's message about his prophetic task

d **symbolic action: siege of Jerusalem and the clay tablet** (4:1–17)
- begins: and you, son of man, take for yourself

e **symbolic action: exile and judgment and Ezekiel's hair** (5:1–17)
- begins: and you, son of man, take for yourself

f **message against the mountains of Israel** (6:1–14)
- begins: the word of Yahweh came to me: "Son of man"
- ends: then they will know that I am Yahweh

g **message about the coming disaster upon Israel** (7:1–27)
- begins: the word of Yahweh came to me: "Son of man"
- ends: then they will know that I am Yahweh

In the sixth year, in the sixth month, on the fifth day of the month, as I sat in my house, with the elders of Judah sitting before me, the hand of the Lord God fell there upon me. Then I beheld, and lo. . . .

—Ezekiel 8:1–2

Then came certain of the elders of Israel to me, and sat before me. And the word of the Lord came to me.

—Ezekiel 14:1–2

In the seventh year, in the fifth month, on the tenth day of the month, certain of the elders of Israel came to inquire of the Lord, and sat before me. And the word of the Lord came to me.

—Ezekiel 20:1–2

Ezekiel's Call and First Collection of Messages about Coming Judgment (Ezekiel 1–7)

Ezekiel's first group of messages dates from the fifth year of the exile. This introductory collection of messages begins, appropriately, with Ezekiel's divine call, featuring three inaugural experiences in which Ezekiel sees visions of Yahweh's glory, in each instance accompanied by Yahweh's instructions to Ezekiel about his prophetic task. These three units are followed by a collection of four clearly delineated messages about Jerusalem's coming devastation. They are arranged in pairs: the first two are symbolic-action messages and the last two are paired by their identical beginnings and endings (25.2).

Ezekiel's Second Collection of Messages about Coming Judgment (Ezekiel 8–13)

Ezekiel 8:1 dates the next collection of messages to the sixth year of the exile. As with the first collection, this one opens with a series of visions of the same divine glory that Ezekiel saw in the beginning: "In the sixth year . . . the hand of the Lord God fell upon me. Then I beheld, and, lo, a form that had the appearance of a human being. . . . It brought me in visions of God to Jerusalem . . . and behold, the glory of the God of Israel was there, like the vision that I saw in the plain." Like the first collection, this one also has seven parts and begins with a series of visions, which is followed in turn by mes-

25.3 Second collection of messages about coming judgment (Ezekiel 8–13)

a   **vision, part 1: idolatry in the temple** (8:1–18)
   • stage 1: glory of God <u>is in the temple</u>
b   **vision, part 2: slaying of Jerusalem's wicked citizens** (9:1–11)
   • stage 2: glory of God <u>moves from Holy of Holies to temple threshold</u>
c   **vision, part 3: burning of Jerusalem** (10:1–22)
   • stage 3: glory of God <u>ascends into the air from temple threshold</u>
d   **vision, part 4: corrupt rulers of Jerusalem and their punishment** (11:1–25)
   • stage 4: glory of God <u>departs from the city and stands above the mountain east of the city</u> (four-part vision concluded in 11:24–25)
e   **symbolic action: exile and Ezekiel's luggage** (12:1–16)
   • ends: <u>then they will know that I am Yahweh</u>
f   **symbolic action: coming devastation and Ezekiel's eating** (12:17–20)
   • ends: <u>then you will know that I am Yahweh</u>
g   **message about false visions and divinations** (12:21–13:23)*
   • ends: <u>then you will know that I am Yahweh</u>

*The material in unit g is tied together by the common themes of visions, false visions, and divinations. H. Van Dyke Parunak, *Structural Studies in Ezekiel* (Ph.D. dissertation, Harvard University, 1978), 219, analyzes this section as a single message.

25.4 Third collection of messages about coming judgment (Ezekiel 14–19)

a   **message against idolatry** (14:1–11)
b   **message about coming judgment and God's justice** (14:12–23)
c   **allegory of the useless vine** (15:1–8)
d   **allegory of the adulterous wife** (16:1–63)
e   **allegory of the two eagles and the vine** (17:1–24)
   f   **message about individual responsibility for sin and God's justice** (18:1–32)
      g   **lament over the kings in exile** (19:1–14)

sages of judgment, the first two involving symbolic actions (25.3).

Ezekiel's Third Collection of Messages about Coming Judgment (Ezekiel 14–19)

Ezekiel's third collection of messages, presumably dating from the sixth or seventh year of Israel's exile, features seven clearly delineated and self-contained messages.[3] Each of the first six messages is introduced by a formula that occurs nowhere else in these chapters: "the word of Yahweh came to me: 'Son of man' " (14:1–3, 12–13; 15:1–2; 16:1–2; 17:1–2; 18:1 [following the reading in the Septuagint and the Syriac]). And each message ends with the expression "declares the Lord Yahweh," except for the fifth message, which closes with the declaration "I, Yahweh, have spoken, and I will do it" (17:24). The collection covers a variety of topics and concludes with a lament (25.4).[4]

Ezekiel's Fourth Collection of Messages about Coming Judgment (Ezekiel 20–24)

Ezekiel's fourth collection of messages dates from the seventh to the ninth year of the exile (20:1; 24:1). Like the preceding collections, this one focuses on Judah's guilt and approaching judgment. Each of the seven messages begins with the formula "the word of Yahweh came to me: 'Son of man' "[5] and ends with a concluding line such as "declares the Lord Yahweh" or "then you will know that I am Yahweh" (or variations). These seven messages cover several topics (25.5).

Oracles against the Nations (Ezekiel 25–32)

The most easily identified major unit in the book is the collection of oracles against the nations found in chapters 25–32. The author gathered Ezekiel's oracles about specific nations, dating from various periods in Ezekiel's ministry, and grouped them together to form a homogeneous unit. Seven nations are addressed: Ammon, Moab, Edom, Philistia, Tyre, Sidon, and Egypt. The seventh nation, Egypt, has not one but seven messages addressed to it, six dated

---

3. See Parunak, *Structural Studies in Ezekiel*, 230–85; W. Eichrodt, *Ezekiel: A Commentary*, trans. Cosslett Quin (Old Testament Library; Philadelphia: Westminster, 1970), 185–258.
4. It is tempting to propose that a symmetric scheme has been used in this collection. The issue of God's justice is treated in the second and next-to-last messages; and the figure of the vine is prominent in the third and third-to-last messages. But there seems to be no correspondence between the first and last message.

5. This introduction also occurs in 12:8 and 12:18–19 (but the material introduced here continues the themes of 12:1–7).

25.5 Fourth collection of messages about coming judgment (Ezekiel 20–24)

- a **message about Israel's rebellion** (20:1–44)
- b **message against the south** (20:45–49 [21:1–5])
- c **message about Yahweh's sword of judgment** (21:1–32 [21:6–37])
- d **message of indictment of Jerusalem** (22:1–31)
  - e **allegory of Oholah (Samaria) and Oholibah (Judah)** (23:1–49)
  - f **allegory of the boiling pot** (24:1–14)
    - g **message involving death of Ezekiel's wife**: Judah's judgment is impending (24:15–27)

25.6 Impending judgment and future restoration (Ezekiel 33–39)

- a **message about individual responsibility and Yahweh's justice** (33:1–20)
- b **message on the eve of Jerusalem's fall** (33:21–33)
  - c good news: **shepherds and sheep** (34:1–31)
  - d good news: **Edom's fall and Israel's restoration** (35:1–36:38)
  - e good news: **valley of dry bones** (37:1–14)
  - f good news: **one future nation under one king** (37:15–28)
  - g good news: **Gog and Magog** (38:1–39:29)

25.7 The new temple (Ezekiel 40–48)

- a **measurements of the temple** (40:1–42:20)
- b **arrival of the glory of God to the temple from the east** (43:1–12)
  - • Ezekiel is brought to <u>the gate that faces east</u> to witness the glory of God coming to the temple from the <u>east</u>; "the sound of his coming was like the sound of many waters"
  - c **temple regulations** (43:13–44:31)
    - d **CENTER: measurements of the holy sector** (45:1–12)
  - c′ **temple regulations** (45:13–46:24)
- b′ **departure of river from the temple, toward the east** (47:1–12)
  - • Ezekiel is brought to <u>the gate that faces east</u> to witness the river (comprising much water) coming from the <u>east</u> side of the temple and flowing eastward, the direction from which the glory of God had come
- a′ **measurements of land of Israel**, culminating in the measurements and description of Jerusalem, "with the sanctuary of the temple in its midst" (47:13–48:35)

and one undated.[6] A geographical order controls the arrangement of the oracles within the unit: the six Levantine nations surrounding Judah are addressed in a clockwise order, and then the more distant Egypt is highlighted by its final position. The seven messages about Egypt are arranged in roughly chronological order.

Collection of Messages about Impending Judgment and Future Restoration (Ezekiel 33–39)

Sandwiched between the oracles against the nations and the vision of the new temple is a collection of seven, mostly future-oriented, messages. Each of the seven messages begins with the identical formula: "The word of Yahweh came to me: 'Son of man' " (in the second message this formula is preceded by a brief, stage-setting his-

torical note). The messages are arranged into two groups: two condemnatory messages followed by five messages about Israel's future restoration. These seven messages are arranged in a negative-to-positive progression, moving from condemnation to punishment to the rescue of a remnant to Israel's future restoration (25.6).[7]

Vision of the New Temple and the New Land (Ezekiel 40–48)

Ezekiel's vision of the new temple is a well-defined and self-contained unit. In this unit, dated to the twenty-fifth year of the exile, Ezekiel is taken by vision to Jerusalem, where an angel leads him about and instructs him regarding the new temple. The unit has seven parts, delineated by shifts in genre/topic. The opening, central, and closing parts feature Ezekiel's measuring the restored land; and these parts are in an order from smaller to larger: temple, sacred land around the temple, entire land of Israel. The seven units exhibit a symmetric design (25.7).

6. Walther Zimmerli, *Ezekiel*, trans. Ronald E. Clements (Hermeneia; Philadelphia: Fortress, 1979, 1983), 1.3–4, argues that the number seven is intentional and has played a determining role in the editorial shaping of the unit. He compares the heptadic structuring here to the heptad of nations addressed by Jeremiah in the year of the battle of Carchemish (Jer. 46:1–49:33) and to the message against the seven foreign nations featured in the first two chapters of Amos.

7. Parunak (*Structural Studies in Ezekiel*, 454–79) argues from structural considerations that chapters 35–36 form one message and one literary unit.

25.8 The Book of Ezekiel

a **Ezekiel's call and first collection of messages about coming judgment** (1:1–7:27)
   (1) vision: Ezekiel's commissioning near the Chebar River (1:1–3:11)
   (2) vision: Ezekiel's second message of commissioning (3:12–21)
   (3) vision: Ezekiel's third message of commissioning (3:22–27)
      (4) symbolic act: siege of Jerusalem and the clay tablet (4:1–17)
      (5) symbolic act: exile and judgment and Ezekiel's hair (5:1–17)
         (6) message against the mountains of Israel (6:1–14)
         (7) message about the coming disaster upon Israel (7:1–27)

b **second collection of messages about coming judgment** (8:1–13:23)
   (1) vision, part 1: idolatry in the temple (8:1–18)
   (2) vision, part 2: slaying of Jerusalem's wicked citizens (9:1–11)
   (3) vision, part 3: burning of Jerusalem (10:1–22)
   (4) vision, part 4: corrupt rulers of Jerusalem (11:1–25)
      (5) symbolic act: exile and Ezekiel's luggage (12:1–16)
      (6) symbolic act: coming disaster and Ezekiel's eating (12:17–20)
         (7) message about false visions and divinations (12:21–13:23)

c **third collection of messages about coming judgment** (14:1–19:14)
   (1) message against idolatry (14:1–11)
   (2) message about coming judgment and God's justice (14:12–23)
      (3) allegory of the useless vine (15:1–8)
      (4) allegory of the adulterous wife (16:1–63)
      (5) allegory of the two eagles and the vine (17:1–24)
         (6) message about individual responsibility and God's justice (18:1–32)
            (7) lament over the kings in exile (19:1–14)

d **fourth collection of messages about coming judgment** (20:1–24:27)
   (1) message about Israel's rebellion and the impending judgment (20:1–44)
   (2) message against the south (20:45–49 [21:1–5])
   (3) message about Yahweh's sword of judgment (21:1–32 [21:6–37])
   (4) message of indictment against Jerusalem (22:1–31)
      (5) allegory of Oholah and Oholibah (23:1–49)
      (6) allegory of the boiling pot (24:1–14)
         (7) message involving death of Ezekiel's wife (24:15–27)

e **oracles against the nations** (25:1–32:32)
   (1) Ammon (25:1–7)
   (2) Moab (25:8–11)
   (3) Edom (25:12–14)
   (4) Philistia (25:15–17)
   (5) Tyre (26:1–28:19)
   (6) Sidon (28:20–26)
   (7) Egypt (29:1–32:32)

f **messages about Israel's punishment and future restoration** (33:1–39:29)
   (1) message about individual responsibility and Yahweh's judgment (33:1–20)
   (2) message on the eve of Jerusalem's fall (33:21–33)
      (3) good news: shepherds and sheep (34:1–31)
      (4) good news: Edom's fall and Israel's restoration (35:1–36:38)
      (5) good news: valley of dry bones (37:1–14)
      (6) good news: one future nation under one king (37:15–28)
      (7) good news: Gog and Magog (38:1–39:29)

g **vision of the new temple and the new land** (40:1–48:35)
   (1) measurements of the temple (40:1–42:20)
      (2) arrival of the glory of God from the east (43:1–12)
         (3) temple regulations (43:13–44:31)
            (4) measurements of land's sacred sector (45:1–12)
         (3') temple regulations (45:13–46:24)
      (2') departure of river to the east (47:1–12)
   (1') measurements of the land of Israel (47:13–48:35)

Conclusion

It appears that the Book of Ezekiel has been rigorously designed in a grand sevenfold structuring scheme. The book's four introductory units plus the three concluding units create seven major units, and each of these contains seven smaller units (25.8).

The book is not arranged in an overall symmetry; but there is a significant symmetric touch involving the opening and closing of the book. The book opens with the vision of the glory of God arriving in Babylonia. This conveys one of the book's major themes: Yahweh is abandoning his temple in Jerusalem (cf. chap. 8) and his presence will now be among the exiles. The book closes with the reversal of this: God's glory arrives back at the temple in Jerusalem—after God's judgment upon the city, initiating a new and glorious era. This final vision emphasizes another main theme in Ezekiel: Yahweh has a wonderful future for his people, and it involves a new temple back in Jerusalem. Opening the book with the vision of God's glory in Babylonia encouraged the exilic audience that God's presence is among them. Closing the book with the vision of God's return to his new temple encouraged them to remain faithful, because God has wonderful future plans for them. This design suggests that the book is written to encourage and uplift the exiles, who had every reason to think God had punished them by banishing them (rather than their fellow Judeans, who remained back home). The intent to encourage is also suggested by the placement of the messages of hope and future restoration (chaps. 25–48) at the end of the book. This layout leaves the audience with uplifting visions and messages that point them toward better days to come. The book is arranged and composed to inspire the exiled audience to sever their emotional ties with the doomed temple in Jerusalem and to place their trust in Yahweh, whose glorious presence is now among them and whose glorious presence will one day return with them to their homeland.

26
Daniel
God's Supremacy over All Earthly Powers

The Book of Daniel is written to demonstrate Yahweh's supremacy and control over all earthly powers and to establish that in his omnipotence he is able to protect his people wherever they may be.[1] The book is made up of three sections: a Hebrew introduction, an Aramaic section, and another Hebrew section. Within these language-determined divisions are a total of ten literary units, most introduced by dates and other stage-setting details (26.1).

Based on content, these ten literary units fall into two groups that do not correspond to the language-based divisions. The first group (chaps. 1–6) is made up of six inspiring stories in which Daniel and/or his three friends—godly Jews in pagan courts—succeed in various difficult circumstances because of the protection and knowledge of their powerful God. The stories are full of drama and suspense. Nearly every story ends with Daniel and/or his three friends being honored or promoted by a pagan king. The second group (chaps. 7–12) comprises the book's final four units. Unlike those in the first group, the stories in these units are not filled with high drama and suspense. They are simply accounts of visions, dreams, or prayers of Daniel, followed by interpretations or explanations by an angelic being.

There is also another conspicuous structural pattern in the book. Both the Aramaic and longer Hebrew sections are arranged with a touch of symmetry (26.2).

Although none of the visions in chapters 7–12 appears to be chiastically arranged or contain

seven parts, each of the six stories in chapters 1–6 exhibits a seven-part chiasmus. In each of these, the central, fourth part serves as the story's climax or turning point (26.3).

It is interesting to note that an almost identical structural design is used in the two martyr stories in chapters 3 and 6:

1. introduction
2. plot by enemies to kill martyrs by attacking martyrs' loyalty to God
3. martyrs remain faithful; are thrown to their probable deaths; king's distress
4. the miracle: they are unharmed!
5. martyrs come unhurt out of structure into which they were thrown; king's delight
6. revenge on enemies: they are killed in the very way they plotted to kill martyrs
7. conclusion: martyrs are honored and promoted

Several observations can be made about the relationship of structure and meaning in the Book of Daniel. The structuring effect of the alternation of language is striking. These language shifts may serve to reinforce the book's successive shifts in focus. Opening the book with Hebrew immediately identifies the book's audience as Hebrew-speaking Jews. Other peoples of the empire spoke Aramaic; but no other people spoke Hebrew. The author begins where his audience is (a good rhetorical technique), with their own native tongue. Moreover, the opening story is about four Jewish young men who had just arrived in Babylon from Judah, presumably still speaking Hebrew, their native tongue.

The shift in chapters 2–7 to Aramaic, the international language at the time, coincides with the shift in these chapters to a focus on the international events of world history. Also, the Jewish participants in chapters 2–7 are now fully assimilated members of the court in Babylon and certainly speak Aramaic. The milieu of this section

---

1. The structure of the Book of Daniel has been studied by various scholars: A. Lenglet, "La Structure Littéraire de Daniel 2–7," *Biblica* 53 (1972) 169–90; D. W. Gooding, "The Literary Structure of the Book of Daniel and Its Implications," *Tyndale Bulletin* 32 (1981) 43–79; William H. Shea, "Further Literary Structures in Daniel 2–7: An Analysis of Daniel 4," *Andrews University Seminary Studies* 23 (1985) 193–202; L. F. Hartman and A. A. Di Lella, *The Book of Daniel* (Anchor Bible 23; Garden City: Doubleday, 1978), 9–11; J. E. Goldingay, *Daniel* (Word Biblical Commentary 30; Dallas: Word, 1989), 324–26.

26.1 Language divisions in the Book of Daniel

Hebrew introduction
  a **Daniel and his three friends in Nebuchadnezzar's court** (1)
Aramaic section
  b **Nebuchadnezzar's dream** and Daniel's interpretation (2)
  c **Daniel's three friends** are kept safe in the fiery furnace (3)
  d **Nebuchadnezzar's insanity**: his dream of the tree and Daniel's interpretation (4)
  e **Belshazzar's feast**: the handwriting on the wall and Daniel's interpretation (5)
  f **Daniel kept safe in the lions' den** (6)
  g **vision of four beasts**; explanation by angel (7)
Hebrew section
  h **vision of the ram and goat**; explanation by angel (8)
  i **Daniel's prayer and the seventy weeks**; explanation by angel (9)
  j **vision of two kingdoms**; explanation by angel (10–12)

26.2 Symmetry in the Book of Daniel

Hebrew introduction: Daniel and his three friends in king's training (1)
Aramaic section (2–7)
  a **vision of the <u>four kingdoms</u>** (in human image) (2)
    b **<u>martyr story</u>**: God saves Daniel's three friends in the fiery furnace (3)
      c **Nebuchadnezzar's <u>pride</u>** and <u>Yahweh's sovereignty</u> (4)
      c′ **Belshazzar's <u>pride</u>** and <u>Yahweh's sovereignty</u> (5)
    b′ **<u>martyr story</u>**: God saves Daniel in the lion's den (6)
  a′ **vision of the <u>four kingdoms</u>** (in images of beasts) (7)
Hebrew section (8–12)
  a **vision of <u>two kingdoms</u>** (Persia and Greece; metaphor of beasts) (8)
    b **vision of the seventy "sevens"** (9)
  a′ **vision of <u>two kingdoms</u>** (Persia and Greece; metaphor of man) (10–12)

is the Aramaic-speaking capital of the empire in Babylon. The use of the international language in these chapters underscores the theme (particularly emphasized in this section) that Israel's God has knowledge of and jurisdiction over not only his Hebrew-speaking people, but all the nations of the earth.

The shift back to Hebrew in the final section of the book may help reinforce the simultaneous shift in focus, back to Israel's future, and how the two present world powers, Persia and Greece, will affect the Hebrew-speaking people of Israel in their restored, native homeland.

The three sections marked off by these language shifts address the concerns of Jews in three successive historical situations: the early exilic community, the later exilic community, and the postexilic communities. Furthermore, each section employs the language appropriate for the people whose particular concerns are being addressed in the three sections. Daniel 1, in Hebrew, addresses concerns encountered by Hebrew-speaking exiles—like Daniel and his three friends—who arrive in a foreign land. These Hebrew-speaking Jews needed to know that their God was still with them in exile, that he expected them to remain faithful to him, and that he would bless them for following his laws.

Daniel 2–7, in Aramaic, addresses the concerns of Aramaic-speaking Jews who, like Daniel, had become acclimated to life in exile and who from time to time faced tensions and opposition because of their faith. Was their God powerful enough to protect them in the face of opposition or persecution in foreign lands? Perhaps their God was just a minor deity after all, and it really did not matter whether his exiled people were faithful to him. The Aramaic portion of Daniel seeks to show that the God of Israel is almighty, that he is powerful enough to protect his people against all earthly powers (even mighty Nebuchadnezzar's fiery furnace or King Darius's lions' den!), and that they should continue to trust and obey him, because it is he alone who ultimately controls all earthly powers and the events of world history (as shown by the visions of the great image and the four beasts). Even the greatest world monarchs are helpless before him, as demonstrated in the stories of Nebuchadnezzar's madness and Belshazzar's fateful banquet.

Daniel 8–12, in Hebrew, addresses issues that will be faced by the Hebrew-speaking people back in Israel following the exile. What will happen to them now? Will God still be with them? The visions of this section seek to demonstrate that God knows in detail all that will happen to

26.3 Godly Jews in pagan courts (Daniel 1–6)

story 1: Daniel and his three friends in Nebuchadnezzar's court (1:1–21)
- a introduction: Judah conquered by Nebuchadnezzar (in first year of Babylon's king) (1:1–2)
  - b Daniel and three friends chosen for three years' training for king's service (1:3–7)
    - c ritually "pure" diet proposed on trial basis; God's favor (1:8–14)
      - d CLIMAX: success! they become healthier than the rest! (1:15)
    - c' ritually "pure" diet continued on permanent basis; God's favor (1:16–17)
  - b' Daniel and three friends chosen at end of three years; enter king's service (1:18–20)
- a' conclusion: Daniel continues in service until first year of Persia's king (1:21)

story 2: Nebuchadnezzar's dream and Daniel's interpretation (2:1–49)
- a introduction: Nebuchadnezzar has disturbing dream (2:1)
  - b magicians fail to recount and explain king's dream (2:2–13)
    - c Daniel and Arioch: Daniel goes to king with proposal (2:14–16)
      - d CLIMAX: God reveals and explains dream to Daniel! (2:17–23)
    - c' Daniel and Arioch: Daniel goes to king with answer (2:24–25)
  - b' Daniel succeeds; he recounts and explains king's dream (2:26–45)
- a' conclusion: Nebuchadnezzar glorifies God and promotes Daniel (2:46–49)

story 3: Daniel's three friends in the fiery furnace (3:1–30)
- a introduction: golden image to be worshiped (3:1–7)
  - b enemies speak against Daniel's friends (3:8–12)
    - c friends are thrown into fiery furnace because of faithfulness to God (3:13–23)
      - d CLIMAX: they are unharmed! (3:24–25)
    - c' friends emerge from fiery furnace (3:26–27)
  - b' king praises Daniel's friends and their God: no one is to speak against their God (3:28–29)
- a' conclusion: promotion of three Jews (3:30)*

story 4: Nebuchadnezzar's madness (4:1–37 [3:31–4:34])
- a introduction: king offers opening praise of God's eternal kingdom and dominion (4:1–3 [3:31–33])
  - b king, prospering in his palace, has dream; seeks magicians to interpret dream (4:4–7 [4:1–4])
    - c Daniel interprets dream: seven years of insanity; entreats king to repent (4:8–27 [4:5–24])
      - d CLIMAX: God's message comes true; king becomes insane (4:28–33 [4:25–30])
    - c' king repents after seven years of insanity; his sanity is restored (4:34–35 [4:31–32])
  - b' king returns to palace in even greater prosperity; is sought out by advisers (4:36 [4:33])
- a' conclusion: king offers closing praise of God, "King of heaven" (4:37 [4:34])

story 5: Belshazzar's feast (5:1–31 [5:1–6:1])
- a introduction: Belshazzar in prosperity; his feast and mockery of Yahweh's vessels (5:1–4)
  - b handwriting on the wall (5:5–6)
    - c magicians are summoned; failure of magicians to interpret the writing (5:7–9)
      - d TURNING POINT: Daniel is remembered (5:10–12)
    - c' Daniel is summoned; failure of magicians recounted (5:13–16)
  - b' handwriting on the wall interpreted by Daniel (5:17–28)
- a' conclusion: Daniel is honored and Belshazzar's kingdom is overthrown (5:29–31 [5:29–6:1])

story 6: Daniel in the lion's den (6:1–28 [6:2–29])
- a introduction: Daniel's exaltation in the government (6:1–3 [6:2–4])
  - b Daniel's enemies plot his death (6:4–9 [6:5–10])
    - c Daniel is thrown into lions' den because of his faith; king distraught (6:10–18 [6:11–19])
      - d CLIMAX: Daniel is unharmed! (6:19–22 [6:20–23])
    - c' Daniel is brought out of lions' den; Daniel's faith; king delighted (6:23 [6:24])
  - b' Daniel's enemies are put to death in his place (6:24 [6:25])
- a' conclusion: further exaltation of Daniel and his God (6:25–28 [6:26–29])

*Daniel 3:30 is not a clear match of 3:1–7.

their country in the future and that everything at that time will still be under his control. He will continue to protect the righteous in the land, even when it appears that wicked earthly forces wield ultimate control over them. He is worthy of their trust and obedience. And they are reassured—in their native tongue—of his continued protection and control.

Other observations about the interplay of structure and meaning in Daniel can be made. The theme of the importance of following God's laws even in foreign lands is emphasized by its prominent coverage in the book's structurally highlighted opening story, where Daniel and his three friends are blessed and rewarded for their adherence to God's dietary laws. The author's

Major Prophets

placement of this story here underscores his concern over this issue.

Structured repetition is used throughout Daniel to emphasize the book's two main themes: Yahweh's supremacy over all earthly powers and the importance for Jews to remain loyal to their God, even in exile. For example, the matching stories of how God protected Daniel and his friends when they remained loyal to him, despite the threat of death (chaps. 3, 6), underscores these themes. The theme of Yahweh's supremacy over all earthly kingdoms and powers is highlighted by the matching visions of Yahweh's knowledge of and ultimate triumph over the four great earthly powers (chaps. 2, 7) and by the two analogous matching visions of the two great earthly powers (chaps. 8, 10–12). The same theme is emphasized by the matching stories about Yahweh's supremacy over the two powerful and proud Babylonian monarchs: Nebuchadnezzar and Belshazzar (chaps. 4, 5).

The message of the Book of Daniel is clear. Mighty earthly kingdoms will arise, these kingdoms will wield great power, and they may even persecute God's people. But God's people should remain loyal to their God and his laws, even in the midst of fiery persecution, because Yahweh, God of Israel, is more powerful than all earthly forces. He knows all about human kingdoms—past, present, and future—and he controls their destinies. He has demonstrated his sovereignty over the proud and mighty monarchs of the past. And he will ultimately establish his supremacy over all earthly powers and set up his own magnificent kingdom, in which all those who have been loyal to him will be rewarded. The God of Israel is Lord of heaven and earth, and he is worthy of the trust and obedience of his people.

Unit 6
Minor Prophets

27

Hosea

Come Home, Unfaithful Israel

The Book of Hosea presents Yahweh's message to the rebellious and idolatrous northern kingdom of Israel in the eighth century B.C., during the reign of Jeroboam II. The book offers a remarkable picture of God, the divine husband, attempting to win back his faithless wife, Israel. The book's structure is notoriously difficult to analyze. Granted, chapters 1–3 form a well-defined and tightly structured unit tied together by the topic of Hosea's marriage to Gomer. But the rest of the book seems to ramble on in an unstructured succession of repetitive discourses and sayings. Part of the difficulty, as Francis I. Andersen and David N. Freedman observe, is the lack of clear unit boundary markers:

Is Hosea 4–14 made up of unrelated oracles, or does it consist of paragraphs joined together in continuous discourse? Except for the familiar "Oracle of Yahweh" (11:11), it lacks the rubrics which are often used to mark the onset of a new unit. Nor are there many grammatical clues which show the beginning or the ending of a self-contained composition.[1]

Andersen and Freedman suggest that a rough outline of chapters 4–14 might include three divisions: the state of the nation (chaps. 4–7), the spiritual history of Israel (chaps. 8–11), and retrospect and prospect (chaps. 12–14).[2] They admit, however, that even this analysis breaks down:

The themes in each of these divisions are so numerous and so diverse that it is misleading to give a title to any of them. When attention is paid to the numerous topics and the abrupt transitions from one to the next, it is easy to conclude that the whole is a congeries of brief oracles, assembled without any recognizable principles of order. Probably a majority of scholars hold such an opinion.[3]

The seeming lack of unit markers in chapters 4–14 might suggest that this material simply forms one large unit, comprising an exceedingly long series of many smaller paragraphs and sentences. But writers generally eschew such lengthy stretches of unorganized, rambling discourses; and it would be more likely that there is an internal structure here. Careful attention to beginning markers, end markers, and other structuring techniques suggests that the entire Book of Hosea, including chapters 4–14, is well organized. The book appears to comprise seven larger units arranged in an overall symmetry,[4] with each of these units, in turn, exhibiting its own artful internal organization (27.1).

Hosea's Marriage to Gomer: Sign of Yahweh's Experience with Israel (Hosea 1–3)

All agree that the book's first major unit is chapters 1–3. The unit is bracketed by narrative accounts of Hosea's troubled experiences with his wife, Gomer. Hosea 1 recounts (in third-person) Hosea's marriage to Gomer, and chapter 3 tells (in first-person) the story of his remarriage to her. These two narratives frame Yahweh's message about his own troubled marriage to his wife Israel. The message in chapter 2 moves from topic to topic, creating a series of smaller constituent units. The first literary unit of Hosea is, then, tripartite, opening and closing with episodes about Hosea's marriage and remarriage to faithless Gomer, with a seven-part, symmetrically arranged message about God's marriage and remarriage to faithless Israel at the center (27.2).

In the first of these subunits (a), God addresses Israel's "children," exhorting them to

---

1. Francis I. Andersen and David N. Freedman, *Hosea: A New Translation with Introduction and Commentary* (Anchor Bible 24; Garden City: Doubleday, 1980), 314.

2. Ibid., 314.

3. Ibid.

4. On 4:11–14 and 8:9–13, see J. R. Lundblom, "Poetic Structure and Prophetic Rhetoric in Hosea," *Vetus Testamentum* 29 (1979) 300–308. See also M. DeRoche, "Structure, Rhetoric, and Meaning in Hosea iv 4–10," *Vetus Testamentum* 33 (1983) 185–98.

27.1 The Book of Hosea

a Israel is God's wayward wife: he will cause her to return home (1:1–3:5)

  b condemnation of Israel's spiritual prostitution and idolatry (4:1–5:7)

    c condemnation for political faithlessness and corruption and empty sacrifices; Yahweh's efforts to bring Israel back (5:8–6:11a)

      d CENTER: Israel has not returned to Yahweh, though he has called it to return (6:11b–7:16)

    c′ condemnation for political faithlessness and corruption and empty sacrifices; Yahweh's efforts to bring Israel back (8:1–9:7b)

  b′ condemnation of Israel's spiritual prostitution and idolatry (9:7c–10:15)

a′ Israel is God's wayward son: God invites him to return (11:1–14:9 [11:1–14:10])

27.2 Hosea's marriage to Gomer (Hosea 1–3)

opening narrative: sign of Hosea's unfaithful wife and their three children (1:1–11 [1:1–2:2])

a Yahweh's first punishment: Yahweh will no longer love the children of wayward Israel, and he will remove her land's fertility (2:1–5a [2:3–7a])

    • he will make her a desert, slaying her with thirst

    • begins: say (ʾāmar); My People (ʿammî) and Loved (ruḥāmâ)

  b Yahweh's second punishment: Yahweh will stop Israel from going after her lovers, until she returns to him in desperation (2:5b–7 [2:7b–9])

    • nature is made to oppose Israel

    c Yahweh's third punishment: Yahweh will take back all the gifts he gave Israel because they continue to worship Baal and attribute the gifts to him (2:8–13 [2:10–15])

      • topic: Baal and Baals

      d TURNING POINT: Yahweh will woo Israel back (2:14–15 [2:16–17])

    c′ Yahweh's positive action in response to the third punishment: he will take the names of the Baals from Israel's lips (2:16–17 [2:18–19])

      • topic: Baal and Baals

  b′ Yahweh's positive action in response to second punishment: he will remarry returning Israel (2:18–20 [2:20–22])

    • nature is made to cooperate in Israel's restoration

a′ Yahweh's positive action in response to first punishment: Yahweh will restore the land's fertility, and he will love Israel's people (children) again (2:21–23 [2:23–25])

    • he will restore her fertility; rains and wine

    • ends: "I will love Not Loved (lōʾ ruḥāmâ) and will say (ʾāmar) to Not My People (lōʾ ʿammî), you are My People (ʿammî)"

closing narrative: sign of Hosea's unfaithful wife and his taking her back (3:1–5)

---

confront their adulterous mother, or he will withhold his love from both her and her children and will turn her land into a desert. The subunit is tied together by references to "pity" (ruḥāmâ; 2:1, 4 [2:3, 6]) and "mother" (ʾēm; 2:2, 5a [2:4, 7a]) and the focus on Israel's children (2:1, 2, 4, 5 [2:3, 4, 6, 7]).

The second subunit (b) speaks of Israel's fickleness. First, she decides to go after "other lovers"; but when Yahweh prevents her from doing this, she decides to come back to him. The subunit opens and closes with Israel's two decisions, introduced identically: "She said, 'I will go' (ʾāmĕrâ ʾēlĕkâ)" (2:5, 7 [2:7, 9]).

The third subunit (c) relates Yahweh's plans to take away the gifts he has given her. The expression "says Yahweh" (nĕʾum-yhwh) marks the unit's conclusion and prepares the audience for what will be a major shift—from judgment to promise of restoration in the subsequent units. The fourth subunit (d), introduced by the common beginning marker "therefore" (lākēn), represents the turning point of the message: God

still loves Israel and resolves to win her back: "Behold, I will allure her and bring her into the wilderness and speak tenderly to her." This turning point is bracketed by the expression "says Yahweh" (nĕʾum-yhwh; 2:13, 16 [2:15, 18]).

Each of the final three units is introduced by the expression "in that day" (bayyôm hahûʾ). These three units describe the successive steps that Yahweh will take to restore Israel as his wife; and they match, in reverse order, the first three units.

In the fifth subunit (c′) Yahweh declares that he will no longer allow Israel to speak of her former lovers, the Baals. Even when she speaks of Yahweh she will use only the term ʾîš ("husband") for husband and not baʿal ("husband" or "lord"). The prominence of the name Baal here, occurring in both the singular and plural, links this subunit with the third subunit (c), where the name likewise occurs, again in both the singular and plural (Baal is mentioned nowhere else in chap. 2).

The sixth subunit (b′) corresponds to the second (b). In the second subunit Yahweh blocked

Israel's path to her lovers so that she finally had to return to Yahweh. In the sixth subunit Yahweh declares that he will take her back and remarry her! In the former subunit he utilized nature (thorns) to block her way to her lovers; now he will harness nature to provide for her prosperity.

The final subunit (a') represents the reversal of the punishments described in the first subunit (a). There God withheld Israel's material blessings; now he commands that these be restored (2:21–22 [2:23–24]). In place of a parched land and Israel's thirst, now the skies are called upon to "respond" to the earth (i.e., provide rain), and the earth will "respond" with new wine. In place of his threat to "make her a desert," Yahweh now promises to "plant her for myself in the land" (2:23 [2:25]). The first subunit opened with the statement "say (*ʾāmar*) of your brothers, 'My People' (*ʿammî*), and of your sisters, 'Loved' (*ruḥāmâ*)" (2:1 [2:3]). The final subunit closes with the statement "I will love (*rḥm*) 'Not Loved' (*lōʾ ruḥāmâ*), and I will say (*ʾāmar*) to 'Not My People' (*lōʾ ʿammî*), you are 'My People' (*ʿammî*)" (2:23 [2:25]).

Opening his book with such a unit is rhetorically astute. The tragic story of Hosea's marriage instantly engages the audience. It functions as a "hook"—an illustration that everyone understands. The unit also presents, in capsulized form, Hosea's entire message: Yahweh loves Israel as a husband loves his wife; but she has betrayed him as a faithless wife betrays her husband; he plans to punish her, but after that he will attempt to woo her back. The remainder of the book fills in the details.

Condemnation of Israel's Adultery and Prostitution (Hosea 4:1–5:7)

Andersen and Freedman identify Hosea's second unit as 4:1–5:7, pointing out that this segment is "integrated by rhetorical devices similar to those already observed" in chapters 1–3.[5] This new unit is introduced by the standard introductory formula "hear the word of the Lord, O Israelites" (4:1); and it is tied together by its central theme: God's "case" (*rîb*; cf. 4:1b) against his adulterous wife Israel. Emphasis on Israel's shameful adultery and prostitution (both spiritual and literal) is achieved by the intensive twelvefold repetition of *znh* in keywords such as *zĕnûnîm* ("prostitution"), *zānâ* ("serve as a prostitute"), and *zōnâ* ("a prostitute"). Other terms, such as "commit adultery" (*nāʾap*; occurring

three times), are also used. The unit is also tied together by themes such as Israel's failure to "know" (*yādaʿ*) Yahweh (4:1, 6a, 6b; 5:4), the involvement of the priests in Israel's unfaithfulness (4:4, 6, 7, 9; 5:1), and the picturing of Israel's sin as "stumbling" (*kāšal*; 4:5a, 5b; 5:5b, 5c). The primary target of this extended accusation is the northern kingdom, called alternately Israel and Ephraim (Judah is mentioned only once or twice). The four specific place-names mentioned in these verses are from the northern kingdom (4:15; 5:1–2).

The end of this unit is not entirely obvious. The introduction in 5:1, "hear this (*šimʿû-zōʾt*), you priests," might be taken as the beginning of a new unit. But the following verses continue the themes of chapter 4, including the focus on the northern kingdom (5:1b, 3, 5a–b), Israel's prostitution (5:3–4; cf. especially the expression *rûaḥ zĕnûnîm* ["spirit of prostitution"] in 5:4 and 4:12), "stumbling" (5:5b–c), the culpability of the priests (5:1), and Israel's failure to "know" Yahweh (5:4). The unit more likely extends to 5:7, with 5:8 heralding a new beginning, introduced by the abrupt call to sound a trumpet alarm: "Blow the horn in Gibeah, the trumpet in Ramah . . . lead forth (into battle), O Benjamin!"—which are all Judean places. The addressees of the following verses will now be Ephraim and Judah (cf. 5:9–10, 11–12, 14; 6:4, 10–11).

The internal structure of 4:1–5:7 is difficult to analyze, perhaps due in part to the difficulty of the Hebrew text (27.3). The possibility of an a-b-c-d-c'-a'-b' modified chiasmus is intriguing; but is not certain. Certainly units a and a' correspond with their formulaic introductory "hear" + vocative of addressees and with the condemnation of Israel's failure to "know" Yahweh (4:1; 5:4). Moreover, the themes of "stumbling" (*kāšal*) and "children" in units b and b' seem to connect these two sections. Themes of prostitution, drunkenness, cultic sins, and "disgrace" (*qālôn*; 4:7, 18) link units c and c', which leaves unit d (the condemnation for involvement in prostitution) as the center.

Condemnation of Israel for Political Faithlessness, Corruption, and Empty Sacrifices (Hosea 5:8–6:11a)

A shift in geographical focus ties together the book's third unit. Now both Israel and Judah are addressed. The alternation of references to Ephraim and Judah occurs throughout these verses (5:(8–)9, 10–11, 12, 13, 14; 6:4, 10–11). As the text stands, this unit has no clear end

---

5. Andersen and Freedman, *Hosea*, 317.

27.3 Israel's adultery and prostitution (Hosea 4:1–5:7)

- a **indictment of Israel**: enumeration of their evil deeds (4:1–3)
  - begins: "<u>hear</u> (*šimʿû*) the word of Yahweh, O people of Israel"
  - "there is . . . <u>no knowledge of God</u> in the land" (4:1)
  - <u>beasts</u>, <u>birds</u>, and <u>fish</u> are to be taken away (4:3)
  - b **coming judgment** (4:4–6)
    - "you shall <u>stumble</u> (*kāšal*) . . . and the prophet shall <u>stumble</u> (*kāšal*) <u>with</u> (*ʿim*) you" (4:5)
    - their <u>children</u> (*bānîm*) will be forgotten by God (4:6)
    - c **condemnation and warning** (4:7–11)
      - <u>ignominy</u> (*qālôn*) (4:7)
      - drunkenness and prostitution (4:10–11)
      - d **CENTER: guilt of Israel's prostitution (4:12–14)**
    - c′ **condemnation and warning** (4:15–19)
      - <u>ignominy</u> (*qālôn*) (4:18)
      - "a band of drunkards . . . give themselves to prostitution" (4:18)
  - a′ **indictment of Israel**: "their deeds do not permit them to return to their God" (5:1–4)
    - begins: "<u>hear</u> (*šimʿû*) this, O priests; give heed, O house of Israel"
    - "they <u>do not know Yahweh</u>" (5:4)
    - devices for capturing <u>animals</u>, <u>birds</u>, and <u>fish</u>(?) mentioned (5:1–2)
  - b′ **coming judgment** (5:5–7)
    - "Ephraim shall <u>stumble</u> (*kāšal*) . . . and Judah will <u>stumble</u> (*kāšal*) <u>with</u> (*ʿim*) them" (5:5)
    - they have borne illegitimate <u>children</u> (*bānîm*) (5:7)

27.4 Condemnation of Israel for corruption and injustice (Hosea 5:8–6:11a)

- a **raising the alarm in Benjamin**, including Gibeah and Beth-aven (i.e., <u>Bethel</u>) (towns involved in the horrible Benjaminite crimes during the period of the judges); Ephraim will be ruined (as Benjamin was?) (5:8–9)
  - b **social injustice** and crime in Judah and Ephraim (5:10–12)
    - c **God will tear Judah and Israel to pieces** like a lion (5:13–15)
      - Israel turned to Assyria, instead of Yahweh, for healing
      - d **CENTER: call to repentance (6:1–3)**
    - c′ **God has cut Judah and Israel to pieces** by his prophets (6:4–6)
      - Israel has offered sacrifices, instead of loving and knowing Yahweh, for restoration
  - b′ **social injustice** and crime in Ephraim (6:7–9)
- a′ **the horrible thing that has occurred in <u>Bethel</u>** [Masoretic Text]; Israel has been "defiled" (as the concubine was in Benjamin during the time of the judges?); Judah will also be judged (6:10–11a)

---

marker nor does the introduction of the next unit exhibit a clear beginning marker. A clue here might be the relatively rhythmic alternation of references to Ephraim and Judah, which ends in 6:11a; the following discourse contains no further mention of Judah.[6] The internal symmetric structure of 5:8–6:11a seems to support this conclusion (27.4).

The placement of the call to repentance in the highlighted central position underscores this plea. By bracketing the call to repentance with matching units that describe Yahweh's power to destroy Israel, the author emphasizes the urgency of the invitation. Yahweh is not to be trifled with. Like a ferocious lion, he has the power to kill them. The terrifying vision of an invading enemy in the introduction of this unit serves as an effective attention-getter. The matched units denouncing Israel's moral corruption in the sec-

ond and next-to-last positions reinforces the theme of Yahweh's disapproval of Israel's sins.

Indictment of Israel and Its Leaders; Israel's Failure to Return (Hosea 6:11b–7:16)

The book's fourth unit probably should be identified as 6:11b–7:16. This unit focuses on the indictment of the northern kingdom and its leaders. Judah is nowhere mentioned. The unit's beginning is apparently marked by the shift in addressees from Israel and Judah to only Israel. The end of the unit is marked by the dramatic new beginning of the next unit in 8:1: "Set the trumpet to your lips"—an introduction parallel to the one opening the third unit (5:8). This indictment of Israel appears to comprise seven smaller units arranged with a symmetric touch (27.5).

The placement of the complaint about Israel's failure to return at the beginning, at the center, and at the end certainly serves to highlight this point. Israel has refused to return to Yahweh,

---

6. One could also argue that 6:11b–7:3 belongs to the previous unit, particularly with the references to "return" (*šûb*) and "heal" (*rāpāʾ*) in 6:11b–7:1.

27.5 Israel's failure to return to Yahweh (Hosea 6:11b–7:16)

  a **God's failed efforts to cause Israel to <u>return</u> (šûb) (6:11b–7:2)**
- his efforts are spoiled by Israel's <u>wickedness</u> (rāʿôt)

  b **debauchery and drunkenness (7:3–7)**
- people become inflamed with wine and heated up like bread baking in an oven
- "none of them <u>cry out to me</u> (qōrēʾ ʾēlay)" (7:7)
- condemnatory reference to sleeping throughout the night

    c **condemnation for mixing with nations (7:8–9)**
- "Ephraim is like a half-baked cake"

      d **CENTER: Israel has not <u>returned</u> (šûb) to Yahweh;** after all this, they have not sought him (7:10)

    c′ **condemnation for appealing to nations for help (7:11–12)**
- "Ephraim is like a dove . . . calling to Egypt, going to Assyria"

  b′ **debauchery and drunkenness (7:13–14)**
- people will not cease from their debauchery; new wine and grain (echoing references to drinking wine and baking bread in 7:3–7?)
- "they do not <u>cry out to me</u> (zāʿăqû ʾēlay)" (7:14)
- condemnatory reference to activity(?) in their beds at night(?) (7:14)

  a′ **God's failed efforts to cause Israel to <u>return</u> (šûb) (7:15–16)**
- he disciplines them, but his efforts are in vain
- they devise <u>evil</u> (raʿ) and <u>return</u> (šûb) to Baal

---

despite all his efforts. The material between these highlighted positions fills in the details of Israel's unfaithfulness and guilt. It is an exceedingly negative unit; and its structure reinforces its negative tone.

Condemnation for Political Faithlessness and Corruption and Empty Sacrifices (Hosea 8:1–9:7b)

A fifth unit begins, much as the third, with a call to sound the trumpet alarm (8:1; cf. 5:8). The focus now shifts from the debauchery of Israel's leaders and their failure to return to Yahweh to Israel's cultic failure, from sociopolitical corruption to religious transgression. The Israelites will be punished because of their wickedness, particularly their sins involving the worship of the calf-idols (at Dan and Bethel? cf. 8:4b–6) and their empty sacrifices and religious activities devoted to Yahweh (8:11–13; 9:4–5).

It is difficult to determine the end of this unit. Andersen and Freedman suggest that it extends to 8:14, as indicated by the "clear ending at 8:14 (which may be an editorial gloss), and the new beginning with 9:1."[7] But this is not likely. The themes of returning to Egypt, eating unacceptable sacrificial food, and sacrifices that do not please the Lord in 9:3–4 are the same themes found in 8:13–14. The unit more likely extends to either 9:7b (ending with "let Israel know this") or 9:9. Of these, the former appears more likely.

This unit is tied together by the themes of unacceptable sacrifices (8:11–13; 9:4), returning to

Egypt (8:13; 9:3), going to Assyria (8:9; 9:3), selling themselves as prostitutes (8:9–10; 9:1), and silver (8:4; 9:6). Unfortunately, the internal organization of this unit is exceedingly difficult to ascertain. The analysis in 27.6, suggesting a seven-part chiastic scheme, is very tentative.

If correctly analyzed, this unit's structure, like the structures of the previous units, reinforces the theme of Israel's guilt by repetition in matching paragraphs. The theme of coming punishment is particularly highlighted by its occurrence in all three positions of prominence: beginning, middle, and end.

Condemnation of Israel's Spiritual Prostitution and Idolatry (Hosea 9:7c–10:15)

The beginning of the sixth unit is uncertain (9:7c and 9:10 are two possible introductions of the new unit). The shift from third-person to second-person in 9:7c offers at least partial support for identifying it as the new beginning. The unit's focus on Israel's past and present sins against Yahweh, including their sins at specific towns such as Gibeah (9:9; 10:9–10), Baal-peor (9:10–11), Gilgal (9:15), Beth-aven (10:5–8), and Bethel (9:8b [probably]; 10:15), and its repeated declaration that Israel will be punished for these sins, supports this section's unity. The theme of Israel's "children" (9:11–16; 10:14–15) may also tie the section together. These themes continue through chapter 10, suggesting that 9:7c–10:15 forms the book's sixth unit.

The unit's internal structure is created by the successive references to specific towns where Israel sinned. The references to Gibeah in 9:9 and 10:9–10 suggest the presence of a symmetric

---

7. Andersen and Freedman, *Hosea*, 482.

27.6 Condemnation for political faithlessness and corruption (Hosea 8:1–9:7b)

a **announcement of coming judgment** (8:1–3)
- Israel claims to <u>know</u> (*yd*ʿ) Yahweh

b **condemnation for making kings and making idols** of <u>silver</u> and gold, actions that were not of God (8:4–6)
- Israel has <u>made</u> (ʿā*śâ*) idols; the calf-idol was <u>made</u> (ʿā*śâ*) by an artisan

c **condemnation for alliances with other nations** (8:7–13)
- "they have gone up to <u>Assyria</u>" but will <u>return</u> (*šûb*) to <u>Egypt</u>
- <u>crop failures</u>, especially grain crops
- Ephraim has <u>hired</u> lovers; they have <u>hired</u> allies
- Yahweh is not pleased with their <u>sacrifices</u>

d **CENTER: Israel has forgotten Yahweh**; coming punishment of Judah and Israel (8:14)

c′ **condemnation for alliances with other nations** (9:1–4)
- "they will eat unclean food in <u>Assyria</u>" and <u>return</u> (*šûb*) to <u>Egypt</u>
- <u>crop failures</u>, especially grain crops and vineyards
- Ephraim has loved a harlot's <u>hire</u>
- Yahweh is not pleased with their <u>sacrifices</u>

b′ **punishment for cultic sins; loss of <u>silver</u> treasures** (used for idols?) (9:5–6)
- "what will you <u>make</u> (ʿā*śâ*) for the religious festival?"

a′ **announcement of coming judgment** (9:7a–b?)
- "let Israel <u>know</u> (*yd*ʿ) this!"

27.7 Israel's spiritual prostitution (Hosea 9:7c–10:15)

a **sins at Bethel** (9:7c–8)

b **sins at Gibeah** (9:9)
- topics: <u>their sin</u> (*ḥaṭṭōʾwtām*), God's coming <u>punishment</u>, the expression <u>as in the days of Gibeah</u> (*kîmê haggibʿâ*)

c **sins at Baal-peor** (9:10–14)
- involved fertility cult: thus Yahweh will destroy Israel's fertility ("no birth, no pregnancy, no conception"; "wombs that miscarry and breasts that are dry")

d **sins at Gilgal** (9:15–10:4)

c′ **sins at Beth-aven** (10:5–8)
- involved idolatry at cultic high places; thus Yahweh will take away their idol and destroy their cultic high places

b′ **sins at Gibeah** (10:9–10)
- topics: <u>you sinned</u> (*ḥāṭāʾtā*), God's coming <u>punishment</u>, the expression <u>from the days of Gibeah</u> (*mîmê haggibʿâ*)

a′ **sins at Bethel** (10:11–15)

---

structure. If 9:8 reads *bêt ʾel* ("Bethel") instead of *bêt ʾĕlōhāyw* ("house of his god"),[8] symmetry appears (27.7).

The historical-geographical structuring here helps convey the point that Israel's rebellion has a long history, going back to the time of Moses and to the period of the judges, and that it is widespread, involving Israel's most sacred and historically important places: Bethel, Beth-aven, Gibeah, and Gilgal.

Israel—Yahweh's Wayward Son; Invitation to Return (Hosea 11:1–14:9 [11:1–14:10])

Hosea 11–14 is probably intended to form the book's final literary unit. Indeed, these closing chapters appear to echo the book's opening unit. Hosea 1–3 portrayed Israel as God's wayward wife whom God would one day take back. Hosea 11–14 portrays Israel as God's wayward son whom God will one day take back.

The theme of Yahweh's relations (past, present, and future) with his son Israel ties these final chapters into a single unit. "When Israel was a young boy (*naʿar*), I loved him, and out of Egypt I called my son (*bēn*)" (11:1). God states, "It was I who taught Ephraim to walk" (11:3). God asks, "How can I give you (masculine singular) up, O Ephraim?" (11:8). God speaks of the birth of the boy and how he later wrestled with God (12:3–4 [12:4–5]; cf. also 12:12–13 [12:13–14]). God is going to "give up" his son Israel because of his waywardness (cf. 11:5–8; 13:8–9, 15–16 [13:15–14:1]); but the orphaned son, Israel, is exhorted to "return, O Israel, to the Lord. . . . Take with you these words: 'Take away our iniquity. . . . In you let the orphan (masculine singular) find mercy!'" (14:1–3 [14:2–4]). And God promises to restore "him" in a series of promises in 14:5–8 [14:6–9]—all referring to Israel in the masculine singular.

The layout of chapters 11–14 supports its identification as a self-contained unit. The sec-

---

8. The text may originally have read "were in Bethel" (*běbêt-ʾel hāyû*).

27.8 Yahweh's wayward son (Hosea 11–14)

a **Yahweh's son, Israel, has refused to <u>return</u> (*šûb*) to Yahweh** (11:1–11)
  - God brought his son Israel out of Egypt; but he will <u>bring him back</u> (*šûb*) to Egypt because of Israel's <u>waywardness</u> (*měšûbâ*, related to *šûb*); he will give him up (make him an orphan)
  - yet in the future God will <u>bring Israel back</u> (*šûb*) home
  - keyword: <u>return</u> (*šûb*) occurs four times

b **the deceitful son** (11:12–12:8 [12:1–9])
  - from the womb Israel has been deceitful (a reference to Jacob's birth); looks to other nations for political help

c **Yahweh is the one who led Israel up from Egypt** (12:9–14 [12:10–15])
  - Israel has spurned Yahweh; punishment is coming
  - begins: <u>I am Yahweh your God, from the land of Egypt</u>

d **CENTER: summary of Yahweh's case against Israel** (13:1–3)

c′ **Yahweh is the one who led Israel up from Egypt** (13:4–9)
  - Israel has forgotten Yahweh; punishment is coming
  - begins: <u>I am Yahweh your God, from the land of Egypt</u>

b′ **the foolish son** (13:10–16 [13:10–14:1])
  - like a foolish child who would not come to the opening of the womb (contra Jacob at his birth, who was aggressive in his coming out of the womb!), Israel refuses to turn to Yahweh for help; looks to nation's kings and princes for help

a′ **Yahweh's invitation to his orphaned son Israel: "<u>return</u> (*šûb*) to Yahweh!"** (14:1–8 [14:2–9])*
  - despite Israel's <u>waywardness</u> (*měšûbâ*, related to *šûb*), God offers to <u>take him back</u> and love him again
  - Yahweh will <u>turn away</u> (*šûb*) his anger
  - keyword: <u>return</u> (*šûb*) occurs four times

*Hosea 14:9 [14:10] should be considered a closing addendum.

27.9 The Book of Hosea

a **Israel is God's wayward wife; but he will cause her to return home** (1:1–3:5)
  - <u>God has loved Israel like a wife</u>; his past care for her
  - Israel has been <u>unfaithful</u> to God; she has loved the Baals
  - theme: <u>exodus</u>
  - message of hope: God will receive back his divorced wife, Israel, and forgive her
  - keyword: <u>return</u> (*šûb*)

b **condemnation of Israel's spiritual prostitution and idolatry** (4:1–5:7)
  - warnings mentioning <u>Beth-aven</u> and <u>Gilgal</u>
  - Israel's <u>spiritual prostitution</u> (and idolatry)
  - theme: <u>shame</u> (*bōš*) and <u>glory</u> (*kābôd*) (cf. 4:7, 19)
  - condemnation of the <u>altars</u> (*mizběḥôt*)

c **condemnation for political faithlessness and corruption and empty sacrifices**; Yahweh's efforts to bring Israel back (5:8–6:11a)
  - begins: "sound the <u>trumpet</u> (*šôpār*)"
  - addressed to both Israel and <u>Judah</u>
  - Yahweh is <u>not pleased</u> with Israel's <u>sacrifices</u> to him
  - Israel has <u>turned to Assyria</u>, rather than Yahweh

d **CENTER: Israel has not <u>returned</u> (*šûb*) to Yahweh**, though he has called her to <u>return</u> (*šûb*); corruption of Israel's rulers (6:11b–7:16)

c′ **condemnation for political faithlessness and corruption and empty sacrifices**; Yahweh's efforts to bring Israel back (8:1–9:7b)
  - begins: "[sound] the <u>trumpet</u> (*šôpār*)"
  - addressed to both Israel and <u>Judah</u> (cf. "Yahweh's temple"; 8:1; 9:4)
  - Yahweh is <u>not pleased</u> with Israel's <u>sacrifices</u> to him
  - Israel has <u>turned to Assyria</u>, rather than Yahweh; exile to Assyria

b′ **condemnation of Israel's spiritual prostitution and idolatry** (9:7c–10:15)
  - warnings mentioning <u>Beth-aven</u> and <u>Gilgal</u>
  - Israel's <u>spiritual prostitution</u> (and idolatry) at various cities (9:10)
  - theme: <u>shame</u> (*bōš*) and <u>glory</u> (*kābôd*) (cf. 9:11; 10:6)
  - condemnation of the <u>altars</u> (*mizběḥôt*)

a′ **Israel is God's wayward son; God invites him to return** (11:1–14:9 [11:1–14:10])
  - <u>God has loved Israel like a son</u>; his past care for his son
  - Israel has been <u>unfaithful</u> to God; his idolatry
  - theme: <u>exodus</u>
  - message of hope: God will receive back his orphaned son, Israel, and forgive him
  - keyword: <u>return</u> (*šûb*)

tion appears to exhibit a standard sevenfold, symmetric design (27.8).

Overall Layout of the Book of Hosea

Identification of the larger units making up the Book of Hosea is exceedingly difficult. The preceding analysis should be considered preliminary and tentative. If it is correct, the book consists of seven larger units, most of which comprise seven smaller parts. There are some indications that the book's seven units are arranged in a symmetry, with the highlighted central unit declaring that—despite Yahweh's efforts—Israel has not returned to him (27.9).

This symmetric configuration, then, underscores the book's negative thrust: Israel continues in her waywardness. She has refused to return to Yahweh, her divine husband.

On the other hand, the linear organization of the book's seven units serves to move the audience toward repentance. The condemnatory opening unit (chaps. 1–3) presents Yahweh's case against his faithless wife Israel, immediately capturing the audience's attention with the gripping metaphor of Hosea's own experience. Yet the audience is given a reason to hope (and to keep listening!), because this unit also declares Yahweh's intentions to win back his wayward people.

Having begun with the larger picture—including both the bad news and the good news—Hosea proceeds in the next five units to focus on the bad news. Each of the next five units exposes and condemns Israel's faithlessness, speaks of Yahweh's disappointment, and describes Yahweh's plans to punish Israel. These central units are almost entirely negative. They comprise an intense, sustained series of repeated condemnations and warnings. The audience hears the same message of condemnation, five times over, from five different vantages. The negative emphasis cannot be missed.

After this intensely negative series, the tone of the book softens, and the closing unit returns to the bad news/good news pattern featured in the opening unit. The audience is once again given hope by being reminded that Yahweh intends to win his wayward people back. In the concluding section of this closing unit, the audience finally hears—and they are certainly ready for it now!—the long-awaited invitation to return to Yahweh (14:1–3 [14:2–4]),[9] followed, encouragingly, by the promise that their repentance will be rewarded by Yahweh's forgiveness and wonderful blessing (14:4–9 [14:5–10]). Closing the book on this note suggests that the book's central purpose is to encourage the audience to repent. Although Israel has been utterly unfaithful to the Lord, he still invites them to return to him and be forgiven.

---

9. It is possible that 6:1–3 and 10:12 also represent invitations to repent, although both of these could be otherwise interpreted.

28
Joel
Yahweh Thunders at the Head of His Army

The Book of Joel predicts a great locust plague that will devastate the land of Judah, a plague that will be a harbinger of an even more dreadful day of Yahweh that Judah will face if it does not repent. The book's overall arrangement, comprising a seven-part modified chiasmus (28.1), is similar to that of several other prophetic books: (1) it has seven parts, (2) the fourth, central position contains the call to repentance, and (3) the reversal of judgment and messages of hope and restoration in the final three units balances the messages of judgment featured in the first three units.[1]

The Locust Plague (Joel 1:2–2:11)

The book's first three units depict, in progressively worse terms, Judah's devastation from a great locust plague. The first unit (1:2–14) is introduced by the common beginning marker "hear!" (šim'û) + vocative of addressees ("you elders"). The unit serves as an effective attention-getter: using a rhetorically effective structure, it announces the disastrous locust plague about to occur in Judah. The unit alternates between tight clusters of imperatives calling for action ("listen!" "wail!" "grieve!" etc.; all in the masculine plural) and more lengthy segments depicting the coming devastation. This alternating pattern ceases with 1:15, and a new pattern begins. The unit exhibits a seven-part layout (28.2), which is configured symmetrically (28.3).

The second unit in Joel (1:15–20) introduces an even more frightening revelation: the approaching locust plague is not happenstance; it is part of the day of Yahweh. This unit focuses on the aftermath of the locust plague, particularly the despair experienced by both people and beasts. The exclamatory "alas!" ('ăhāh) marks the unit's beginning; and the double occurrence of the line "for fire has devoured the open pastures" (1:19, 20) marks its conclusion.

The third unit (2:1–11) provides an even more ominous revelation: the locust plague is an invincible army commanded by Yahweh himself: "Yahweh thunders at the head of his army!" (2:11).[2] This unit dashes any hope that Yahweh might save his people from the coming devastation. The abrupt call to sound the trumpet alarm ("sound the trumpet in Zion!" 2:1) marks the unit's beginning. The unit is tied together by the military imagery, framed by references to "the day of Yahweh" (2:1, 11). Its layout is symmetric (28.4).[3]

---

1. The unity of the Book of Joel has been a matter of dispute among scholars since the latter half of the nineteenth century, mainly because the portrayal of the locust plague in 1:2–2:27 seems to be from a different pen than the eschatological material of 2:28–3:21 [3:1–4:21]; see Hans W. Wolff, *Joel and Amos: A Commentary on the Books of the Prophets Joel and Amos*, trans. Waldemar Janzen, S. Dean McBride Jr., and Charles A. Muenchow (Hermeneia; Philadelphia: Fortress, 1977), 6; and James L. Crenshaw, *Joel: A New Translation with Introduction and Commentary* (Anchor Bible 24c; Garden City: Doubleday, 1995), 29–34 (Crenshaw's survey of the various views is particularly helpful). But even among those who take the book as a unity, little is offered in the way of a detailed structural analysis. Wolff (*Joel and Amos*, 7), for example, alludes to the following units in the book: (a) lament over the current scarcity of provisions (1:4–20); (b) announcement of the eschatological catastrophe imminent for Jerusalem (2:1–11); (c) call to return to Yahweh (2:12–17); (d) promise that the calamity of the crop failure will be reversed (2:18–27); (e) pouring out of the spirit and deliverance of Zion (2:28–32 [3:1–5]); (f) promise that Jerusalem's fortunes will be reversed (3:1–21 [4:1–21]). The book's unity, Wolff argues, is demonstrated by its symmetry: the turning point is the junction between 2:17 and 2:18, which marks the transition from the preceding cries of lament to the following oracles where divine response to the pleas is assured. The lament over the crop failure is then balanced by the promise of the reversal of that failure; the eschatological catastrophe imminent for Jerusalem is balanced by the promise that Jerusalem's fortunes will be reversed; and the call to return to Yahweh is balanced the pouring out of the spirit and the deliverance of Zion. This yields an a-b-c-a'-c'-b' pattern for the overall structure of the book.

2. The third unit is correctly identified as 2:1–11 by Wolff, *Joel and Amos*, 39–40.

3. C. Van Leeuwen, "Tekst, Structuur en Betekenis van Joel 2:1–11," *Nederlands Theologisch Tijdschrift* 42 (1988) 89–98, sees the same basic layout of this passage, with 2:6 at the center.

28.1 The Book of Joel

a **devastating locust invasion** (1:2–14)
  b **suffering of all creatures from the locust plague** (1:15–20)
    c **Yahweh himself brings the locust army against Judah** (2:1–11)
      d **CENTER: call to repentance** (2:12–17)
a′ **promise that devastation of locust invasion will be reversed** (2:18–27)
  b′ **Judah will experience Yahweh's spiritual blessings** (2:28–32 [3:1–5])
    c′ **Yahweh will bring the nations against Judah, but he will destroy them and restore Judah** (3:1–21 [4:1–21])

28.2 Introduction to the locust plague (Joel 1:2–14)

a imperatives: **hear! listen!** (1:2a)
  • details of coming disaster (1:2b)
b imperatives: **tell!** (1:3)
  • details of coming disaster (1:4)
c imperatives: **wake up! wail! wail!** (1:5a–c)
  • details of coming disaster (1:5d–7)
d imperatives: **mourn!** (1:8)
  • details of coming disaster (1:9–10)
e imperatives: **despair! wail! grieve!** (1:11a–c)
  • details of coming disaster (1:11d–12)
f imperatives: **put on! mourn! wail! come! stay!** (1:13a–c)
  • details of coming disaster (1:13d)
g imperatives: **prepare! call! gather! cry out!** (1:14)
  • no details of coming disaster (breaking the pattern to mark the end of series)

28.3 Symmetry in the opening portrayal of the locust plague (Joel 1:2–14)

a **exhortation** to the <u>elders</u> and <u>all the inhabitants of the land</u> to listen (1:2)
  b **instructions to tell future generations** about this disaster (1:3–4)
    c **call to <u>wail</u>** (*hêlîlû*); devastation of <u>vines</u> (*gepen*) and <u>figs</u> (*tĕʾēnâ*) (1:5–7)
      d **mourn!** the disaster has reached temple! (1:8–10)
    c′ **call to <u>wail</u>** (*hêlîlû*); devastation of <u>vines</u> (*gepen*) and <u>figs</u> (*tĕʾēnâ*) (1:11–12)
  b′ **instructions for immediate actions** to deal with this disaster (1:13)*
a′ **exhortation** to the <u>elders</u> and <u>all the inhabitants of the land</u> to cry out, call (1:14)
*Unit b′ is not a clear match of unit b.

28.4 Yahweh thunders at the head of his army (Joel 2:1–11)

a **day of Yahweh approaches**: <u>large</u> (*rab*) and <u>mighty</u> (*ʿāṣûm*) army comes (2:1–2)
  b **effects of locust invasion**: <u>before them</u> (*lĕpānāyw*) (2:3)
    c **military likeness** of locust march: <u>they are like . . .</u> (2:4–5)
      d **CENTER: reaction of terror in land** (2:6)
    c′ **military likeness** of locust march: <u>they are like . . .</u> (2:7–9)
  b′ **effects of locust invasion**: <u>before them</u> (*lĕpānāyw*) (2:10)
a′ **day of Yahweh will be great**: Yahweh's army is <u>large</u> (*rab*) and <u>mighty</u> (*ʿāṣûm*) (2:11)

Call to Repentance (Joel 2:12–17)

With all hope of avoiding the disaster dispelled, the audience is now ready to hear what they need to do, which the fourth, central unit provides.[4] Judah must "return" (*šûb*) to Yahweh with the hope that God may "turn" (*šûb*) and bless Judah. The beginning of the unit is marked by an expression that often introduces new units: "and so now" (*wĕ . . . ʿattâ*), followed by "says Yahweh" (*nĕʾum-yhwh*), a divine speech formula occurring nowhere else in Joel (thus highlighting this unit).

Tied together by the repetition of masculine plural imperatives calling for repentance (return, rend, return, blow, consecrate, call, assemble, consecrate, gather, assemble), this unit alternates between exhortations to repent (2:12–13; 2:15–17c)[5] and rhetorical questions providing the rationale for repentance ("who knows? he may relent" [2:14]; "why should they say . . . ?" [2:17d]). The unit offers no hope of avoiding the locust plague; rather, it promises that if Judah repents and appeals to Yahweh, he

---

4. See Wolff, *Joel and Amos*, 40; the other possibility here is that this central unit extends only to 2:14.

5. The second section (2:15–16a) of exhortations to repentance opens with a series of seven imperatives in the masculine plural: sound! sanctify! call! gather! sanctify! assemble! gather!

28.5 The Book of Joel

a **devastating locust invasion** (1:2–14)
  - four locust species <u>devouring</u> (*ʾākal*) the land: *gāzām*, *ʾarbeh*, *yeleq*, *ḥāsîl* (1:4)
  - devastation of <u>grain</u> (*dāgān*), <u>new wine</u> (*tîrôš*), and <u>oil</u> (*yiṣhār*) (1:10)
  - withering of <u>trees</u> (*ʿēṣîm*), <u>vine</u> (*gepen*), and <u>fig tree</u> (*tĕʾēnâ*) (1:12)
  - themes: dried up, withered, destroyed, empty, wailing, mourning

b **suffering of all creatures from the locust plague** (1:15–20)
  - short unit
  - topic: <u>coming</u> (*bwʾ*) of the <u>day of Yahweh</u>
  - "I will <u>call</u> (*qāraʾ*) on you, O Yahweh"
  - all creatures, including all the animals, suffer from the devastation

c **Yahweh himself brings the locust army against Judah** (2:1–11)
  - day of Yahweh is <u>near</u> (*qārôb*); destruction of agriculture
  - locusts as <u>warriors</u> (*gibbôrîm*) and <u>soldiers</u> (*ʾanšê milḥāmâ*)
  - earth (*ʾereṣ*) <u>quakes</u>, <u>heavens</u> (*šāmayim*) <u>shake</u> (*rāʿāšû*)
  - <u>sun and moon are darkened</u> (*šemeš wĕyārēaḥ qādārû*), <u>stars no longer shine</u> (*wĕkôkābîm ʾāsĕpû nāgĕhām*), <u>Yahweh thunders</u> (*nātan qôlô*) at the head of his army (2:10–11)
  - Judah becomes a <u>desert waste</u> (*midbar šĕmāmâ*)

d **CENTER: call to repentance** (2:12–17)

a' **promise that devastation of locust invasion will be reversed** (2:18–27)
  - reversal of devastation of four species of locusts that <u>devoured</u> (*ʾākal*) the land: *gāzām*, *ʾarbeh*, *yeleq*, *ḥāsîl* (2:25)
  - restoration of <u>grain</u> (*dāgān*), <u>new wine</u> (*tîrôš*), and <u>oil</u> (*yiṣhār*) (2:19, 24)
  - rejuvenation of <u>trees</u> (*ʿēṣîm*), <u>vine</u> (*gepen*), and <u>fig tree</u> (*tĕʾēnâ*) (2:22)
  - themes: rains and watering, renewal, replenishing, filling, rejoicing, gladness

b' **in the future all the inhabitants of Judah will experience Yahweh's spiritual blessings** (2:28–32 [3:1–5])
  - short unit
  - topic: <u>coming</u> (*bwʾ*) of the <u>day of Yahweh</u>
  - "everyone who <u>calls</u> (*qāraʾ*) on the name of Yahweh will be saved"
  - all people will experience Yahweh's spiritual blessings

c' **in future, Yahweh will bring the nations' armies against Judah, but he will destroy them and restore Judah** (3:1–21 [4:1–21])
  - day of Yahweh is <u>near</u> (*qārôb*); restoration of agriculture
  - <u>warriors</u> (*gibbôrîm*) and <u>soldiers</u> (*ʾanšê milḥāmâ*)
  - <u>heavens</u> (*šāmayim*) and <u>earth</u> (*ʾereṣ*) <u>shake</u> (*rāʿāšû*)
  - <u>sun and moon are darkened</u> (*šemeš wĕyārēaḥ qādārû*), <u>stars no longer shine</u> (*wĕkôkābîm ʾāsĕpû nāgĕhām*), <u>Yahweh thunders</u> (*nātan qôlô*) from Jerusalem
  - Edom will become a <u>desert waste</u> (*midbar šĕmāmâ*)

may be merciful and help them in the plague's aftermath.

Promise of Future Restoration (Joel 2:18–3:21 [2:18–4:21])

Following this call to repentance, Joel closes his book with three units of hope and promise. The book's fifth unit (2:18–27) offers the promise that Yahweh will reverse the devastation of the locust plague.[6] He will drive the invading locusts out of the country and will restore the land and its crops "so that you may know that I am Yahweh your God."

The sixth unit (2:28–32 [3:1–5]) goes further. Introduced by the temporal clause "and it shall be that after this" (*wĕhāyâ ʾaḥărê-kēn*), this unit announces that after Yahweh has reversed the effects of the locust plague, he will bestow spiritual gifts and abilities upon the entire Judean

population, male and female, young and old (2:28–29 [3:1–2]), and that all who call upon him will be saved (2:30–32 [3:3–5]).

The seventh unit (3:1–21 [4:1–21]) goes even further. This final unit is introduced by two phrases indicating yet another time frame: "Indeed (*kî*), behold, in those days and at that time, when I return the exiles of Judah and Jerusalem, I will . . ." (3:1 [4:1]). This unit promises that Yahweh will one day punish the nations for what they have done to Judah, in a great battle orchestrated by Yahweh himself. He will wondrously restore Judah, so that it will never again experience an invasion by a foreign army (locust or human!) and its land will know fertility and plenty as never before.

Overall Layout of the Book of Joel

The Book of Joel appears to be arranged in a seven-part modified symmetry (a-b-c ‖ d ‖ a'-b'-c'), which centers on the important call to repen-

---

6. It is possible that 2:18 closes the fourth unit and should be translated, "Yahweh may. . . ."

tance (28.5).[7] Certainly the first unit is echoed by the fifth unit (a'), which depicts (using many of the same terms) how Yahweh will reverse the effects of the locust plague described in unit a. For example, the first unit lists the four species of locusts that will "devour"(*ʾākal*) Judah: *gāzām*, *ʾarbeh*, *yeleq*, *ḥāsîl* (1:4); the fifth unit lists these same four species (which are listed nowhere else in the book) in Yahweh's promise to repay Judah for what the four species have "devoured" (*ʾākal*) (2:25). The first unit lists the agricultural products that will be devastated: "grain" (*dāgān*), "new wine" (*tîrôš*), and "oil" (*yiṣhār*) (1:10); the fifth unit lists the same three products in the same order when Yahweh twice promises to restore to his people these products (2:19, 24). The prediction (1:12) that the land's "trees" (*ʿēṣîm*) will wither is echoed in the promise that Yahweh will cause the trees to once again bear fruit (2:22). The withering and drying up of the "vine" (*gepen*) and "fig tree" (*tĕʾēnâ*) (1:12) is echoed by the promise that these plants will yield their riches (2:22). Moreover, the themes of being dried up, withered, destroyed, and empty in unit a are contrasted to the themes of rains and watering, renewal, replenishing, and filling in unit a'; in the same way, the themes of wailing, crying, mourning, etc., find their contrastive echoes in the themes of rejoicing and gladness.

The matching of the second and sixth units is not as certain. These two units correspond in that they are both short (in contrast to the book's other units). They also appear to correspond in two other respects: they both feature the "coming" (*bwʾ*) of the day of Yahweh (1:15; 2:31 [3:4]); and each speaks of "calling" (*qārāʾ*) on Yahweh (1:19; 2:32 [3:5]). Moreover, while unit b describes the day of Yahweh's judgment upon Judah, unit b' speaks of the time when Yahweh will pour out his spiritual blessings on Judah. Admittedly, these are weak connections, and it is not certain that the two units are intended to match.

The third and seventh units have a bit more in common. Both depict Yahweh's bringing an army against his people Judah, in the first instance a locust horde, in the second, the armies of all the nations. Yahweh's purposes echo one another in contrastive matching: in the third unit, he intends to devastate Judah with the locust invasion, destroying the land's agricultural prosperity; in the seventh, he brings the armies of the nations against Judah to destroy these armies, while saving Judah and restoring the agricultural prosperity to its land once again. There are also verbal

correspondences. In unit c the locusts attacking Judah are likened to "warriors" (*gibbôrîm*) and "soldiers" (*ʾanšê milḥāmâ*) (2:7); in unit c' Yahweh summons the nations' warriors and soldiers to come against Judah (3:9 [4:9]). In unit c we read of the great signs accompanying the locust invasion, and in unit c' we hear the echo in the great signs accompanying Yahweh's judgment upon the nations that have invaded Judah:

Before them the earth (*ʾereṣ*) quakes,
the heavens (*šāmayim*) shake (*rāʿāšû*);
the sun and moon are darkened (*šemeš wĕyārēaḥ qādārû*),
and the stars no longer shine (*wĕkôkābîm ʾāsĕpû nāgĕhām*).
Yahweh thunders (*wayhwh nātan qôlô*)
at the head of his army.

—Joel 2:10–11

The sun and moon are darkened (*šemeš wĕyārēaḥ qādārû*),
and the stars no longer shine (*wĕkôkābîm ʾāsĕpû nāgĕhām*).
Yahweh . . . thunders (*wayhwh . . . yittēn qôlô*) . . . . . . from Jerusalem.
The heavens (*šāmayim*) and the earth (*ʾereṣ*) shake (*rāʿāšû*).

—Joel 3:15–16 [4:15–16]

In the third unit (2:3), Judah becomes a "desert waste" (*midbar šĕmāmâ*); whereas in the last unit, Judah will be restored, Egypt will be turned into a "waste" (*šĕmāmâ*), and Edom will become a desert waste (3:19 [4:19]). In the third unit the day of Yahweh is "near" (*qārôb*), so the trumpet should be sounded "in Zion . . . my holy hill (*har qodšî*)" (2:1); the last unit also stresses that the day of Yahweh is near (3:14 [4:14]) and on that day the people of Judah will know that Yahweh is "in Zion . . . my holy hill" (3:17 [4:17]).

Conclusion

Several tentative conclusions may be drawn regarding the interplay of the structure and message in the Book of Joel. The highlighted central position of the call for repentance underscores the central importance of repentance in the author's thinking. Repentance is crucial for the reversal of Judah's fortunes. The negative-positive layout of the book, beginning with words of warning and judgment and ending with words of hope and future restoration, indicates that the book is intended to uplift and motivate the audience to a positive response by leading them from despair to hope. The placement of the promise of restoration after the call to repentance emphasizes the point that Judah's repentance must precede restoration.

---

7. For a different analysis, see Lena Lee, "The Structure of the Book of Joel," *Kerux* 7.3 (1993) 4–24, who analyzes Joel as a five-part symmetric configuration, with 2:10–32 at the center.

29

Amos

The Lion Has Roared

The Book of Amos, like the Book of Hosea, represents God's message of warning to the northern kingdom of Israel during the latter part of the eighth century B.C. Under Jeroboam II's reign, Israel had grown powerful and wealthy; but it had also become corrupt. The rich trampled the poor, social injustice was rife, and God's final judgment was swiftly approaching. God sent Amos to call the nation back from its suicidal course of rebellion.

The book is a masterpiece of rhetorical skill; and it is carefully and effectively structured.[1] One of the book's most striking structural features is the prolific use of sevenfold structuring.[2] James Limburg notes eleven sevenfold groupings in Amos,[3] to which I have added twelve more (nos. 12–23). There are . . .

1. seven oracles against Israel's seven neighbors (1:3–2:5)
2. seven clauses describing Israel's sins (2:6–8): sell, trample, push, go, desecrate, spread out, drink
3. seven clauses depicting the inescapability of punishment (2:14–16): perish, not retain, not escape, not stand, not escape, not escape, flee[4]
4. seven rhetorical questions (3:3–6)[5]
5. seven imperatives in the sarcastic exhortation (4:4–5): come, transgress, multiply, bring, offer, call, proclaim
6. seven first-person perfect verbs depicting Yahweh's punishment (4:6–13): gave, withheld, sent rain, smote, laid waste, sent, overthrew[6]
7. seven verbs of Yahweh's mighty acts in the hymnic piece (5:8–9): make, turn, darken, call, pour, make flash, come (or "bring"; cf. BHS)
8. seven empty ritual activities by Israel (5:21–23): feasts, assemblies, burnt offerings, grain offerings, peace offerings of fatted beasts, noise of songs, melody of harps
9. seven verbs depicting the sins of the wealthy (6:4–6): lie, stretch out, eat, sing, invent, drink, anoint
10. seven things the wealthy do (8:4–8): sell, offer to sell, make small, make great, deal deceitfully, buy, sell

1. Important previous studies of the literary structure of Amos include R. Gordis, "The Composition and Structure of Amos," *Harvard Theological Review* 33 (1940) 239–51; S. W. Eubanks, *Amos: Artist in Literary Composition* (Ph.D. diss., Southern Baptist Theological Seminary, 1943); Z. Weisman, "Stylistic Parallels in Amos and Jeremiah: Their Implications for the Composition of Amos," *Shnaton* 1 (1975) 129–49; K. Koch, *Amos: Untersucht mit den Methoden einer strukturalen Formgeschichte* (3 vols.; Alter Orient und Altes Testament 30; Kevelaer: Butzon & Bercker, 1976); J. De Waard, "The Chiastic Structure of Amos v 1–17," *Vetus Testamentum* 27 (1977) 170–77; W. A. Smalley, "Recursion Patterns and the Sectioning of Amos," *Bible Translator* 30 (1979) 118–27; Yehoshua Gitay, "A Study of Amos's Art of Speech: A Rhetorical Analysis of Amos 3:1–15," *Catholic Biblical Quarterly* 42 (1980) 293–309; Hartmut Gese, "Komposition bei Amos," in *Congress Volume: Vienna 1980*, ed. J. A. Emerton (Vetus Testamentum Supplement 32; Leiden: Brill, 1981), 74–95; A. Van Der Wal, "The Structure of Amos," *Journal for the Study of the Old Testament* 26 (1983) 107–13; N. J. Tromp, "Amos v 1–17: Towards a Stylistic and Rhetorical Analysis," *Oudtestamentische Studiën* 23 (1984) 65–85. See also David A. Dorsey, "Literary Architecture and Aural Structuring Techniques in Amos," *Biblica* 73 (1992) 305–30; and the insightful study of Victor M. Wilson, *Divine Symmetries: The Art of Biblical Rhetoric* (New York: University Press of America, 1997), 157–80.

2. See the provocative article by James Limburg, "Sevenfold Structures in the Book of Amos," *Journal of Biblical Literature* 106 (1987) 217–22.

3. Ibid., 219–21.

4. The five central clauses are negative, whereas the first and last are positive. This heptad is also noted by Francis I. Andersen and David N. Freedman, *Amos: A New Translation with Introduction and Commentary* (Anchor Bible 24a; Garden City: Doubleday, 1989), 339.

5. The first five questions are introduced by interrogative *hē*, the last two by *ʾim*; see Andersen and Freedman, ibid., 386, 393, for additional heptadic schemes in 3:3–6.

6. This heptad could be fortuitous since two imperfects with past meanings are also used in this series. Andersen and Freedman (ibid., 413) suggest that the number seven here "may be of some significance."

29.1 The Book of Amos

a **coming judgment upon Israel and its neighbors** (1:1–2:16)

  b **the prophet's compulsion:** destruction of Israel and Bethel's cult center (3:1–15)

    c **condemnation of wealthy Israelite women:** empty religious activity and Yahweh's judgment (4:1–13)

      d **CENTER: call to repentance and lament** (5:1–17)

    c′ **condemnation of wealthy Israelite men:** empty religious activity and coming judgment (5:18–6:14)

  b′ **the prophet's compulsion:** destruction of Bethel's cult center (7:1–8:3)

a′ **coming judgment upon Israel** (scattering among the nations) and future restoration among the nations (8:4–9:15)

11. seven first-person singular verbs (or syntactic equivalents) depicting Yahweh's punishing acts (9:1–4): slay, take, bring down, search out and take them, command, command, set[7]

12. seven classes of soldiers who will not escape (2:14–16): swift, strong, warrior, archer, infantry, chariotry, mighty[8]

13. seven verbal clauses depicting Yahweh's coming punishment (3:14–15): punish, punish, be cut off, fall, smite, perish, come to an end[9]

14. seven poetic verses comprising the sarcastic exhortation (4:4–5)

15. seven plagues (4:6–11): famine, drought, blight, locusts, pestilence, sword, "overthrow" (or earthquake or fire)[10]

16. seven verbs of exhortation in the call to repentance (5:4–6a): seek, live, do not seek, do not come, do not go, seek, live

17. seven poetic verses expressing Israel's guilt (5:10–13)

18. seven verbs of exhortation or promise (5:14–15): seek, you will live, it will be, hate, love, establish, he will be gracious

19. seven participles in the woe-oracle (6:1–6)[11]

20. seven occurrences of the name "Israel" (7:9–17)[12]

21. seven lines comprising the *ʾim . . . miššām* series (9:2a–4a)[13]

22. seven first-person singular verbs depicting the good things Yahweh will do for Israel in the future (9:11–15): raise up, repair, raise up, build, restore, plant, give

23. seven third-person plural verbs depicting things Israel will do or not do in the last days (9:14–15): build, dwell, plant, drink, make, eat, not be plucked up

Careful analysis suggests that the entire book consists of seven symmetrically arranged main units, each fairly well delineated by various literary devices (29.1).[14]

Israel Is as Guilty as Its Neighbors (Amos 1–2)

A series of oracles against seven foreign nations and Israel constitutes the book's first major unit. The series exhibits a cadenced repetition that binds chapters 1–2 into a self-contained unit. Each oracle contains the same elements, in the same order, making it easy for the audience to follow Amos's successive points:

1. standardized introduction: "Thus says Yahweh, 'For three transgressions of *x*, even for four, I will not revoke the punishment.'"

2. statement of nation's sin, introduced by "because they/he . . ."

3. standardized pronouncement of coming punishment by fire (except eighth stanza): "So I will send fire upon *x*, and it shall devour the strongholds of *y*."

4. specific details of Yahweh's upcoming judgment upon that nation

The eighth oracle, against Israel, stands apart from the first seven by its greater length. Both its accusation section and its punishment section are several times longer than those of the preceding oracles, serving to highlight this oracle. The importance of this oracle is also underscored by its final position in the unit's linear arrangement, serving as the climax of the series. The structuring design suggests that the first seven messages simply build toward and set the stage for the unit's primary objective—the condemnation of Israel, Amos's own audience.

---

7. The five middle lines are introduced by *ʾim* or *wĕʾim*, whereas the first and last assertions lack the introductory *ʾim* protasis.

8. Andersen and Freedman, *Amos*, 340.

9. Ibid., 410.

10. Ibid., 440, 447.

11. Ibid., 545–49.

12. Ibid., 637.

13. Ibid., 681.

14. Limburg ("Sevenfold Structures in the Book of Amos," 218, 222) likewise argues that Amos is composed of seven parts. His analysis, based mainly on the distribution of divine speech formulas, differs from the one presented here in two respects: (1) he identifies 1:1–2 as the book's first unit, and (2) he joins 5:1–17 and 5:18–6:14 into a single unit. Neither of these conclusions are convincing.

Further, the 7+1 structuring scheme creates a rhetorical surprise.[15] An Israelite audience would have every reason to think that Amos's seventh point, the oracle against Judah, is the sermon's finale. But just as they applaud approvingly (so to speak) at what they think is the final point of this fine seven-part sermon, to their surprise Amos unleashes an eighth point, which turns out to be the sermon's main point: their own indictment. It is a clever rhetorical technique.

Some scholars doubt the genuineness of the oracles against Tyre, Edom, and Judah, primarily because of their marked differences from the other oracles. But variety does not necessarily indicate nongenuineness.[16] In fact there is notable variety even among the other four oracles (Aram, Philistia, Ammon, Moab). For example, the repeated line in the first pair of oracles (Aram and Philistia), "I will cut off the inhabitants of *x* and him who holds the scepter from *y*," is entirely missing in the third pair (Ammon and Moab). Conversely, references to "shouting" (*bitrûʿâ*) and the shared fate of the nation's ruler "and his princes" (*wĕśārāyw*; cf. BHS) in 1:14–15 and 2:2–3 are entirely absent in the first pair.

The matching of the Aram and Philistia oracles and the matching of the Ammon and Moab oracles leads one to expect a comparable matching of the intervening Tyre and Edom oracles; and this is precisely the case. This pair, like the other two pairs, displays features that simultaneously link them together and set them apart from the others, particularly their shared references to the treatment of "brothers" (*ʾaḥîm*) and the abbreviated length of their punishment sections.

Of the seven oracles to foreign nations, only Judah's, with its lengthened accusation and abbreviated threat, is unmatched. The result is an a-a'-b-b'-c-c'-d scheme, with the final unit, Judah, carrying the supposed emphasis. The sevenfold structure sets the audience up for the unit's 7+1 surprise. The layout of this introductory message helps Amos effectively convey three points:

1. Yahweh is almighty and not be trifled with; he has the power to destroy not only Israel but all the nations.

2. Yahweh holds all nations accountable for their behavior and will punish wickedness.

3. Israel, once Yahweh's special, holy people, has become like the pagan nations, included in the same list with other wicked nations that are to be punished.

The Lord God Has Spoken; Who Can But Prophesy? (Amos 3)

At least four indicators mark 3:1 as the beginning of a new major unit:[17]

1. The series of identically structured oracles in chapters 1–2 ends with the Israel oracle (3:1 does not introduce a ninth nation nor does it continue the judgment section of the eighth).

2. The phrase *nĕʾum-yhwh* ("oracle of Yahweh") in 2:16 suggests the closure of that unit (this phrase is frequently used in prophetic discourses to signal the end of a message).[18]

3. The exhortation in 3:1 is a typical introduction to a new prophetic message: *šimʿû ʾet-haddābār hazzeh ʾăšer dibber yhwh ʿălêkem bĕnê yiśrāʾēl* ("hear this message that Yahweh has for you, O sons of Israel"), containing three elements: "hear!" + "this word" + vocative.[19]

---

15. See S. M. Paul, *Commentary on the Book of Amos* (Hermeneia; Minneapolis: Fortress, 1991), 22–24, for an excellent discussion of the 7+1 (or seven-eight) pattern in ancient Near Eastern literature, in the Bible, and in the present text.

16. See S. M. Paul, "Amos 1:3–2:3: A Concatenous Literary Pattern," *Journal of Biblical Literature* 90 (1971) 397–403; idem, *Book of Amos*, 16–26.

17. That 3:1 marks the beginning of the book's second major unit is commonly agreed; see W. Rudolph, *Joel–Amos–Obadja–Jona* (Kommentar zum Alten Testament 13/2; Gütersloh: Mohn, 1971), 150; Hans W. Wolff, *Joel and Amos: A Commentary on the Books of the Prophets Joel and Amos*, trans. Waldemar Janzen, S. Dean McBride Jr., and Charles A. Muenchow (Hermeneia; Philadelphia: Fortress, 1977), 175; V. Maag, *Text, Wortschatz und Begriffswelt des Buches Amos* (Leiden: Brill, 1951), 12–13, following Karl Budde, "Zu Text und Auslegung des Buches Amos," *Journal of Biblical Literature* 43 (1924) 75–76, who argues, unconvincingly, that 3:1–2 forms the conclusion of the message of 1:2–2:16.

18. The expression frequently marks the conclusion of a prophetic discourse or saying: Isa. 3:15; 54:17; Jer. 1:19; 12:17; 15:9; 29:23; 32:44; 39:18; 49:6; 49:39; Ezek. 12:28; 14:11, 23; 15:8; 16:63; 24:14; 32:32; 39:29; Hos. 11:11; Obad. 4; Hag. 2:9; Zech. 3:10; cf. H. Eising, "נְאֻם, *nĕʾum*," in *Theological Dictionary of the Old Testament*, ed. G. Johannes Botterweck, Helmer Ringgren, and Heinz-Josef Fabry; trans. David E. Green (Grand Rapids: Eerdmans, 1998) 9:109–13. It can also occur in the midst of a discourse, functioning simply to remind the audience of the identity of the (divine) speaker: Isa. 1:24; 14:22; 17:3; 19:4; 30:1; 55:8; Jer. 2:9; 17:24; 31:33; Ezek. 11:8; Joel 2:12; Obad. 8; Mic. 4:6; Zeph. 1:10. In Amos 1–2 the expression occurs only twice: in 2:11 it stands in the middle of a saying (presumably to remind the audience of the speaker); and in 2:16 it concludes the final clause of the final pericope of chap. 2 and communicates the impression of closure to the hearer.

19. This introduction is a variation of the standard formula used throughout the prophets to introduce new messages and major literary units. This standard introduction normally contains three elements, virtually always in the same order: (1) the verb *šimʿû* ("hear!") in the (usually plural)

29.2 Yahweh will punish (Amos 3)

a **Yahweh will <u>punish</u> (*pqd ʿl*) Israel for its <u>sins</u> (3:1–2)**
  • begins: <u>hear</u> (*šimʿû*)
  b **coming disaster declared by the prophets (3:3–8)**
    • theme: <u>lion and its prey</u>
    c **foreign <u>fortresses</u> (*ʾarměnôt*) called to assemble against the mountains of Samaria (3:9)**
      d **CENTER: Israel does not know how to do right (3:10)**
    c′ **Israel's <u>fortresses</u> (*ʾarměnôt*) and strongholds will be destroyed (3:11)**
  b′ **coming of near-total disaster (3:12)**
    • theme: <u>lion and its prey</u>
a′ **Yahweh will <u>punish</u> (*pqd ʿl*) Israel for its <u>sins</u> (3:13–15)**
  • begins: <u>hear</u> (*šimʿû*)

4. The shift in focus in 3:1 (from Israel's guilt to its impending judgment) is followed by a new format—a succession of rhetorical questions (3:3–8).

The new unit, which extends to 3:15,[20] is tied together by several keywords and themes: "the land of Egypt" (*ʾereṣ miṣrayim*; 3:1, 9), "visit"/ "punish" (*pqd ʿl*; 3:2, 14a, 14b), "know" (*ydʿ*; 3:2, 10), the "lion" (*ʾaryēh* and *ʾărî*) and its prey (3:4, 8, 12), and Israel's coming punishment and destruction.

The unit appears to be laid out in a seven-part symmetry, with each of the constituent paragraphs containing a divine speech formula (the last contains two). The first, middle, and last paragraphs call attention to Israel's guilt, while the other paragraphs offer warnings of the coming punishment. This structure underscores the close connection between Israel's guilt and its coming judgment (29.2).

---

imperative, (2) the direct object of *šimʿû*, generally *děbar yhwh* ("the word of the Lord") but also *haddābār hazzeh* ("this word") or *zōʾt* ("this"), and (3) vocative of the addressees (e.g., "O house of Israel"). The formula is used in Hosea 4:1, for example, to introduce the second part of that book. This same formula or a variation introduces the first messages of three prophetic books: Isaiah (1:2), Joel (1:2), and Micah (1:2); and it signals the beginnings of new messages and major literary units throughout the prophets: Isa. 7:13; 36:13; 49:1; 51:1; Jer. 7:1–2; 10:1; 11:1; 17:19–20; 19:1–3; 21:11; 22:1–2; Ezek. 13:1–2; 25:3; Hos. 5:1; Mic. 3:1; 6:1; cf. Deut. 4:1; 5:1; 9:1; 1 Sam. 15:1; 1 Kings 22:19; 2 Kings 7:1; 18:28; 20:16. A number of scholars understand this formula as functioning to introduce the major units or messages of Amos, including S. R. Driver, *An Introduction to the Literature of the Old Testament* (9th ed.; Edinburgh: Clark, 1913), 315; Otto Eissfeldt, *The Old Testament: An Introduction*, trans. Peter R. Ackroyd (New York: Harper & Row, 1965), 398; Brevard S. Childs, *Introduction to the Old Testament as Scripture* (Philadelphia: Fortress, 1979), 403; see Dorsey, "Literary Architecture and Aural Structuring Techniques in Amos," 309 n. 10.
20. Cf. Limburg, "Sevenfold Structures in the Book of Amos," 217–18; Ernst R. Wendland, "The 'Word of the Lord' and the Organization of Amos," *Occasional Papers in Translation and Textlinguistics* 2.4 (1988) 11–12; Eissfeldt, *Old Testament: An Introduction*, 398; Childs, *Introduction to the Old Testament as Scripture*, 403; Gitay, "Study of Amos's Art of Speech."

Israel's Guilt Despite Yahweh's Efforts (Amos 4)

Amos 4:1 introduces the next major unit. The transition is marked in several ways:

1. The expression *něʾum-yhwh* in 3:15 marks closure; it last occurred at the conclusion of the previous unit in 2:16.
2. The introductory "hear this word" (*šimʿû haddābār hazzeh*) + the vocative in 4:1 is the same basic formula that introduced the previous message in 3:1 (following the pattern "hear!" + "this word" + vocative).
3. The addressees abruptly shift in 4:1 from Israelites in general to the Israelite women who live in Samaria ("you cows of Bashan").
4. The focus shifts from impending judgment to an exposé of Israel's guilt and a survey of Yahweh's past efforts to bring Israel to repentance.

The new message features a 5+1 (or 7+1) series. In 4:6–11 Amos reviews, in five successive stanzas (units c–g), the successive disasters that Yahweh brought upon Israel to induce it to return. Each stanza ends identically: *wělōʾ-šabtem ʿāday něʾum-yhwh* ("'yet you did not return to me,' declares Yahweh"). The expression *něʾum-yhwh*, which closed the book's first two major units, functions here to close each individual stanza within the unit. Like the two 7+1 series featured in the book's first two units, this series builds toward its climactic conclusion: "Therefore . . . prepare to meet your God!" (4:12). The five stanzas plus the dramatic conclusion create a 5+1 scheme. This five-part series is preceded by two stanzas (units a and b), each likewise ending with *něʾum-yhwh* and each approximately the same length as each stanza of the five-part series. The result, apparently intentional, is a unit made up of seven stanzas or sayings ending with *něʾum-yhwh* plus a conclusion (29.3).

The linear arrangement of this unit emphasizes the climactic final position. This climax de-

---

29.3 Prepare to meet God (Amos 4)

a **condemnation:** wickedness of Israel's wealthy women (4:1–3)

b **condemnation:** Israel's hypocritical religious activity (4:4–5)

  c **Yahweh's first failed effort** to get Israel to return to him: lack of bread (4:6)

  d **Yahweh's second failed effort** to get Israel to return to him: lack of water (4:7–8)

  e **Yahweh's third failed effort** to get Israel to return to him: crop failure (4:9)

  f **Yahweh's fourth failed effort** to get Israel to return to him: plagues and war (4:10)

  g **Yahweh's fifth failed effort** to get Israel to return to him: natural disasters (4:11)

    conclusion: "therefore . . . prepare to meet your God!" (4:12–13)

29.4 Call to repentance (Amos 5:1–17)

a **lamentation over fallen Israel** (5:1–3)

  b **call to repentance:** "<u>seek</u> (dirŝû) me and <u>live</u> (wiḥyû)" (5:4–6a)

    • seven verbs of exhortation

    c **condemnation of Israel's injustice:** "you who turn <u>justice</u> into wormwood and cast down <u>righteousness</u> to the earth" (5:6b–7)

      d **CENTER: hymn of Yahweh's power;** seven verbs (5:8–9)

    c′ **condemnation of Israel's injustice:** "you who afflict the <u>righteous</u> and deprive the poor of <u>justice</u>" (5:10–13)

  b′ **call to repentance:** "<u>seek</u> (dirŝû) good, not evil, that you may <u>live</u> (tiḥyû)" (5:14–15)

    • seven verbs of exhortation or promise

a′ **coming lamentation** (5:16–17)

---

clares that since Yahweh's preliminary efforts have failed, he is now coming against Israel himself! With *něʾum-yhwh* closing each of the unit's seven stanzas, the author utilizes a majestic hymnic exclamation (4:13) to close the entire unit.

Seek Good That You May Live (Amos 5:1–17)

Immediately following this hymnic piece is the introductory formula *šimʿû ʾet-haddābār hazzeh . . . bêt yiśrāʾēl* ("hear this word, . . . O house of Israel"; 5:1), again featuring the pattern "hear!" + "this word" + vocative. The new beginning in 5:1 is further marked by the abrupt shift in genre, from prophetic discourse to lament (5:1–3).[21]

This new unit extends to 5:17, with the intervening material tied together by the themes of lamentation and seeking Yahweh. The unit's cohesion is strengthened by the symmetric arrangement of the seven constituent parts. The lament in unit a is echoed by the lamenting in unit a′. The repeated exhortation in unit b to "seek" (dirŝû) Yahweh and "live" (wiḥyû) mirrors the exhortation in unit b′ to "seek" (dirŝû) Yahweh so that you may "live" (tiḥyû). The warning and accusation of lack of justice and righteousness in unit c′ echoes the warning and accusation of lack of justice and righteousness in unit c. And standing strategically at the center of this seven-part symmetry is the book's second hymnic piece (d).

The symmetry of this unit has been seen and discussed independently by J. De Waard and others.[22] The layout should most likely be analyzed as a seven-part chiasmus (29.4).

The arrangement of this unit is rhetorically effective. The attention-getting lament over fallen Israel opens the unit; the two calls for repentance are placed between the words of sure judgment (the laments) and the words of condemnation. At the center stands the exclamation of Yahweh's awesome power: he is almighty, and he is not to be ignored! The message is clear. Yahweh is planning to destroy Israel; but if the people repent he will spare them. The matched repetition of the call to repentance underscores its importance.

Woe to You Who Desire the Day of the Lord! (Amos 5:18–6:14)

Several considerations suggest that 5:18 introduces the next unit.[23] The concluding *ʾāmar yhwh* ("says Yahweh") in 5:17b communicates

---

21. Most scholars see 5:1 introducing a new major literary unit: Wolff, *Joel and Amos*, 231; Eissfeldt, *Old Testament: An Introduction*, 398; Limburg, "Sevenfold Structures in the Book of Amos," 217–18; Wendland, "Organization of Amos," 14; Andersen and Freedman, *Amos*, 461; Paul, *Amos*, 158.

22. De Waard, "Chiastic Structure of Amos v 1–17"; see also Tromp, "Amos v 1–17"; Wendland, "Organization of Amos," 14; Gary V. Smith, *Amos: A Commentary* (Grand Rapids: Eerdmans, 1989), 155–60; idem, "Amos 5:13—The Deadly Silence of the Prosperous," *Journal of Biblical Literature* 107 (1988) 289–91. The only significant difference between the analysis proposed here and that of De Waard's is that he identifies unit d as 5:8a–c, unit e as 5:8d, and unit d′ as 5:9—whereas the analysis here takes 5:8–9 as a single unit.

23. That 5:18 begins a new major unit is supported by Wendland, "Organization of Amos," 14–16; De Waard, "Chiastic Structure of Amos v 1–17"; Douglas Stuart, *Hosea–Jonah* (Word Biblical Commentary 31; Waco: Word, 1987), 344; Smith, *Amos*, 149–60; cf. Wolff, *Joel and Amos*, 254.

29.5 Coming judgment (Amos 5:18–6:14)

a **coming disaster** (5:18–20)
- woe to those who look forward to the day of Yahweh
- disaster depicted by unlikely events involving wild animals
- <u>poisonous</u> snake

b **what Yahweh <u>hates</u> (śānēʾ) and despises**: self-righteous religious activity, with all the noise and worship of Yahweh; he prefers that it cease (5:21–24)

c **threat of <u>exile</u> (glh)** (5:25–27)

d **CENTER: sevenfold woe** (6:1–6)

c′ **threat of <u>exile</u> (glh)** (6:7)

b′ **what Yahweh <u>hates</u> (śānēʾ) and detests**: the pride of Jacob and his strongholds; Yahweh will cause these evil people to be quiet and to fear even mentioning Yahweh's name (6:8–10)

a′ **coming disaster** (6:11–14)
- coming punishment upon those who proudly recall past victories
- disaster depicted in terms of absurd actions of domesticated animals
- reference to <u>poison</u>

---

closure. Neither *něʾum-yhwh* nor a concluding *ʾāmar yhwh* occurs anywhere else in 5:1–17, so that its occurrence here conveys completion. In addition, the chiasmus begun in 5:1 is completed in 5:17. Also, 5:18 begins with *hôy* ("woe"), an interjection employed throughout the prophets to mark the beginning of a woe-oracle.[24] Lastly, the abrupt shift in genre, from lament and calling for repentance to a condemnatory woe-oracle, signals a new unit.

The new unit extends to 6:14 and is tied together by the woe-oracle motif. Woe-oracles generally feature two elements: (1) a pejorative description of the subjects against whom the oracle is directed, usually depicted by a series of participles governed by the definite article (functioning as a relative); and (2) a series of reasons why these (often apparently prosperous) subjects are to be pitied or considered unfortunate—normally because Yahweh is going to bring judgment upon them. In addition, woe-oracles often exhibit a third formal feature: one or more repetitions of the exclamatory *hôy*.[25] All three of these features have been utilized to shape the material of 5:18–6:14: (1) the word *hôy* is repeated in 6:1, (2) the subjects of the oracle are described in condemnatory language, with defined participles generously employed (5:18, 21–23; 6:1–6, 12–13), and (3) Yahweh's coming judgments upon the (presently prosperous) subjects are announced (5:18–20, 26–27; 6:7–11, 14).

Francis Anderson and David Freedman analyze the sayings of this section as comprising eight units:[26]

a day of Yahweh (5:18–20)
b justice (5:21–24)
c threat of exile (5:25–27)
d seven woes (6:1–6)
e the exiles (6:7)
f the oath (6:8–10)
g last woes (6:11–13)
h final threat (6:14)

Of these delineations, at least the last is suspect: 6:11 and 6:14, both beginning with *kî* + *hinnēh* followed by a judgment decree, seem to form an inclusio bracketing 6:11–14. If Anderson and Freedman are correct (with this one caveat), the unit might bear a symmetric touch (29.5).[27]

The arrangement of this unit is characterized by the alternation of words of condemnation and words of warning, underscoring the close connection between Israel's corruption and its coming punishment. The unit is tied together not only by the woe language and motifs, but also by the recurring line *ʾāmar/něʾum-yhwh ʾĕlōhê [haṣ]ṣěbāʾôt* ("says Yahweh, God of hosts"; 5:27; 6:8, 14). In 6:14 this expression marks the unit's conclusion.[28]

I Am Neither a Prophet nor the Son of a Prophet (Amos 7:1–8:3)

Amos 7:1 introduces Amos's collection of narratives. The abrupt shift to an entirely new genre (from woe-oracle to narrative) signals the be-

---

24. For example, Isa. 5:8; 10:1; 18:1; 28:1; 29:1; 30:1; 31:1; 33:1; 55:1; Jer. 23:1; 48:1; Ezek. 34:2; Mic. 2:1; Nah. 3:1; Hab. 2:6; Zeph. 3:1.

25. Cf. Isa. 5:8; 10:5; 45:9; Ezek. 13:3; Hab. 2:6.

26. Andersen and Freedman, *Amos*, 519–608.

27. This analysis is tentative. One wonders, for example, whether 6:7 could be intended as a saying separate from 6:1–6 (although *lākēn* and *ʿattâ*, the verse's first two words, do normally introduce a new phase of an accusation; i.e., the announcement of sentencing) or whether 6:8–10 and 6:11–14 indeed echo 5:18–20 and 5:21–24.

28. See Dorsey, "Literary Architecture and Aural Structuring Techniques in Amos," 317 and n. 23.

ginning of the new unit.[29] Other signals include (1) the new series of vision reports beginning in 7:1, (2) the abrupt transition from poetry to prose, and (3) the shift from Yahweh as main speaker (throughout chaps. 1–6) to Amos as main speaker.

The four vision reports in this unit (7:1–3, 4–6, 7–9; 8:1–3) follow a similar pattern in their first portions: each is introduced by *kōh hir'anî 'ădōnāy yhwh wěhinnēh* ("thus the Lord Yahweh showed me, and behold"; see BHS on 7:7), followed by a report of what the prophet saw. As Anderson and Freedman observe, the four visions exhibit a progression in the length of their descriptions: the first report contains eighteen words; the second, thirteen; the third, eight; and the fourth, three.[30]

Another progression is also discernible. The conclusions of visions 1 and 2 follow one pattern, and the conclusions of visions 3 and 4 follow another. In the first two, the prophet sees the vision and intercedes: "O Lord Yahweh, forgive/cease, I beseech you! How can Jacob stand? He is so small!" (7:2, 5); and in both cases Yahweh relents: "Yahweh repented of this. 'It [also] shall not happen,' [the Lord] Yahweh said" (7:3, 6). In visions 3 and 4, on the other hand, the prophet's vision report is followed by Yahweh's question, Amos's response, and Yahweh's explanation of the vision: "And Yahweh/he said, 'Amos, what do you see?' And I said, 'an *x*.' Then Yahweh said . . ." (7:8; 8:2). Moreover, unlike visions 1 and 2, the last two visions have no intercession by Amos and no relenting by Yahweh. Therefore the visions proceed from less ominous to more ominous—from potential judgment to certain judgment. This technique of pairing hearkens back to the pairing seen in chapters 1–2. The gradual building toward greater severity is also typical of other units (e.g., 4:6–12); and it is designed to create a desired rhetorical effect.

The highly structured series of vision reports in 7:1–8:3 ties this unit together, despite the eight-verse narrative interlude in 7:10–17.[31] Of course,

one must ask: Why is the narrative episode of Amos's confrontation at Bethel (7:10–17) inserted into this series of visions? The episode is presumably placed in this particular unit because it shares with the vision reports a common narrative genre (unlike the rest of the book) and, again like the vision reports, features the book's only dialogue between Amos and another party.

But why not place the episode at the beginning, middle, or end? Why insert it between the third and fourth visions? The reason for this is probably that the narrative naturally follows the concluding line of the third vision (7:9): "The high places of Isaac shall be made desolate, the sanctuaries of Israel will be laid waste, and I will rise against the house of Jeroboam with the sword." The narrative recounts Israel's official reaction to this scandalous declaration. Moreover, the narrative involves two topics unique to the third vision: the high places and sanctuaries of Israel (Bethel) and Jeroboam.[32] In addition, as Andersen and Freedman note, the episode is rhetorically tied to the third vision.[33] The visionary declarations of doom in 7:9b ("I will rise against the house of Jeroboam with the sword") and 7:17b ("and Israel will surely go into exile away from its land") together with the two utterances quoted by Amaziah in his report to Jeroboam in 7:11 ("Amos has said, 'Jeroboam shall die by the sword, and Israel will go into exile away from its land' ") form a rhetorical envelope around the narrative.[34]

Similar to that of the previous unit (6:14), the end of this unit is marked by a concluding *nĕ'um 'ădōnāy yhwh* ("declares the Lord Yahweh"; 8:3), which like the former occurs in the middle of the concluding verse. The absence of any other *nĕ'um* formulas between 6:14 and 8:3 reinforces the listener's sense of closure here.[35]

---

29. That 7:1 begins a new major unit is generally held: cf. Wolff, *Joel and Amos*, 294; Eissfeldt, *Old Testament: An Introduction*, 398; Childs, *Introduction to the Old Testament as Scripture*, 404; Limburg, "Sevenfold Structures in the Book of Amos," 218; Wendland, "Organization of Amos," 19–21; Smith, *Amos*, 215; Van Der Wal, "Structure of Amos," 107–8.

30. Andersen and Freeman, *Amos*, 619.

31. On the other hand, the brief vision of 9:1a is not adequately linked with the visions of 7:1–8:3; it has an entirely different form and structure, is much briefer, and is too distant from the collection to have been connected to these in the minds of the listeners; see Andersen and Freedman, *Amos*, 679.

32. Moreover, since this third vision contains Amos's first proclamation against a specific Israelite king, the listener might well ask how such an inflammatory utterance was received by the powers that be. The reaction narrated in 7:10–17 apprises us that Jeroboam, when informed, did not even give Amos's warning the dignity of a response, but merely instructed his official at Bethel to send the troublesome prophet home. Yahweh's anger at Israel and the two visions of certain judgment bracketing this episode are justified.

33. Andersen and Freedman, *Amos*, 760–61.

34. The unit appears to contain a total of five parts: four vision reports plus the narrative. The narrative, however, is composed of three reported speeches: (1) Amaziah's report to Jeroboam (7:10–11), (2) Amaziah's address to Amos (7:12–13), and (3) Amos's prophecy against Amaziah and Israel (7:14–17). The three speech reports plus the four vision reports make a total of seven parts of approximately equal length, although this might be fortuitous.

35. Also, *hās* ("silence!"), the final word of the line (if textually sound), might function as an additional (and rhetorically dramatic) concluding word.

In That Day I Will Raise up the Fallen Booth of David (Amos 8:4–9:15)

Amos 8:4 heralds the beginning of another major unit by the conventional signal: *šimʿû* ("hear!") + "this" + vocative (8:4–6). The new beginning is also marked by the abrupt shift in genre from narrative back to prophetic discourse.[36]

In all probability 8:4–9:15 is intended as a self-contained major unit, despite the variety of its constituent parts and despite source-critical questions about the prehistory of some of these parts.[37] The cohesion of the material is achieved in part by the recurring phrases *bayyôm hahûʾ* ("in that day") and *hinnēh yāmîm bāʾîm* ("behold, days are coming"; 8:9, 11, 13; 9:11, 13). The latter expression occurs nowhere else in the book, and *bayyôm hahûʾ* occurs only twice elsewhere (2:16 and 8:3, where it may function as anticipatory to the book's final unit). As in the third unit, the measured, periodic repetition of *nĕʾum [ʾădōnāy] yhwh* also rhetorically ties the unit together (8:9, 11; 9:7, 8, 12, 13).

The material is thematically united by its completely future-oriented perspective (the appellatives of 8:4–6 and the hymnic piece in 9:5–6/7 do not disrupt this perspective). This orientation is formally communicated not only through the periodic repetition of the expressions "in that day" and "the days are coming," but also by the almost unbroken succession of first-person declarations of divine future actions. Within these twenty-six verses Yahweh states twenty-four times, "I will. . . ."

The internal structure of this final unit is obscure, in part due to textual and exegetical uncertainties. The various sayings of the unit may possibly be intended to form a sevenfold symmetry with the hymn at its center (29.6).[38]

As in the third unit, the author/editor uses the *nĕʾum-yhwh* formula to punctuate this unit's various sayings (8:9, 11; 9:7, 8, 12, 13). To mark the end of the unit he uses a variation of the formula (as he did to close the fourth unit): *ʾāmar yhwh ʾĕlōhêkā* ("says Yahweh your God"; 9:15).[39]

Overall Layout of the Book of Amos

Although the seven main units in the Book of Amos are arranged in a logical linear progression,[40] their order also features a symmetric touch (29.7).[41] A variety of correspondences between matching units creates the symmetry. For example, the book's first and last units correspond in a number of respects:

1. Yahweh's dealings with Syria, Philistia, and Edom are treated in both units (and nowhere else in the book).
2. Both units list seven sins of the wealthy (2:6–8; 8:4–6).
3. The statement that "they sell the righteous for silver, and the needy for a pair of shoes (*ʾebyôn baʿăbûr naʿălāyim*)" (2:6) corresponds to the similar "they buy the poor for silver, and the needy for a pair of shoes (*ʾebyôn baʿăbûr naʿălāyim*)" (8:6).
4. In the first unit, the wealthy are "those who trample (*haššōʾăpîm*) the head of the poor" (2:7), and in the last they are "those who trample (*haššōʾăpîm*) the needy" (8:4—this verb occurs nowhere else in Amos).
5. Both units feature a series portraying the inescapability of the coming judgment (2:14–16; 9:1–4).
6. The first unit states three times that particular groups of warriors "will not escape" (*lōʾ-yimallēṭ*; 2:14–15), and the last unit states that the fugitive "will not escape" (*lōʾ-yĕmmālēṭ*; 9:1—this verb occurs nowhere else in Amos).
7. The root *nûs* ("fleeing") occurs twice in each unit (2:14–16; 9:1).
8. Yahweh's assertion that "I brought you up out of Egypt" (2:10) is repeated almost verbatim: "Did I not bring you up out of Egypt?" (9:7).
9. Yahweh's threat that "the people of Aram will go into exile to Kir" (1:5) has its reflex in "I brought Aram from Kir" (9:7).

---

36. The shift from addressing Israel in third-person to second-person further signals the beginning of a new unit for the audience.

37. Most see 8:4–9:15 as composed of at least three separate units (many taking 9:11–15 as a secondary addition): Wolff, *Joel and Amos*, 321–55; Smith, *Amos*, 252–80; Stuart, *Hosea–Jonah*, 382–400; cf. Wendland, "Organization of Amos," 22–26. Limburg ("Sevenfold Structures in the Book of Amos," 218), on the somewhat tenuous basis of formula patterns in divine speech, considers 8:4–9:15 a single major unit.

38. This analysis is appealing but open to further scrutiny. Amos 8:9–10 could be intended as a subunit separate from 8:11–14; 9:11–12 might form an integral part of 9:11–15; and the correspondences between 8:4–8 and 9:13–15 and between 8:9–14 and 9:11–12 are weak.

39. This makes a total of seven divine-saying formulas in the unit, as there were in the third unit.

40. See Dorsey, "Literary Architecture and Aural Structuring Techniques in Amos."

41. A chiastic structure of the entire book also suggested by J. De Waard and W. A. Smalley, *A Translator's Handbook on the Book of Amos* (Stuttgart: United Bible Societies, 1979) 194–95; cf. Smalley, "Recursion Patterns and the Sectioning of Amos." The main differences between their analysis and the one proposed here primarily involve unit boundaries and the number of units (twenty, in their analysis).

29.6 The fallen booth of David (Amos 8:4–9:15)

a **land's coming destruction**: Yahweh will overthrow the land because of the sins of the rich inhabitants (8:4–8)
  - theme: sins involving the land's <u>agricultural products</u>

  b **Yahweh will punish Israel** (8:9–14)
  - begins: <u>in that day</u> (*bayyôm hahû³*)
  - ends: "they will <u>fall</u> (*nāpal*) and not <u>rise</u> (*qûm*) again"

    c **Yahweh's judgment: no escape** (9:1–4)
  - killing <u>by the sword</u>
  - <u>I will command</u> (*ṣiwwâ*)
  - wherever they flee, Yahweh will find and kill them
  - ends: "I will set my <u>eyes</u> against them"

      d **CENTER: hymnic exclamation**: seven poetic lines (9:5–7)

    c′ **Yahweh's judgment: righteous remnant will be spared** ("no pebble of grain will fall to the ground") (9:8–10)
  - dying <u>by the sword</u>
  - <u>I will command</u> (*ṣiwwâ*)
  - Yahweh will scatter Israel throughout the nations, and all the sinners will die
  - begins: "the <u>eyes</u> of Yahweh are against . . ."

  b′ **Yahweh will restore devastated Israel** (9:11–12)
  - begins: <u>in that day</u> (*bayyôm hahû³*)
  - begins: "I will cause to <u>rise</u> (*qûm*) the booth of David that has <u>fallen</u> (*nāpal*)"

a′ **land's future restoration**: Yahweh will restore Israel and the land's fertility (9:13–15)
  - restoration of land's <u>agricultural products</u>

29.7 The Book of Amos

a **coming judgment upon Israel and its neighbors** (1:1–2:16)
  - sevenfold condemnation of wealthy: "<u>they sell the righteous for silver</u>, the <u>needy</u> for a <u>pair of shoes</u> (*³ebyôn baʿăbûr naʿălāyim*)" and "<u>trample</u> (*haššōʾăpîm*) the poor"
  - inescapability of judgment: they <u>not escape</u> (*lōʾ-yĕmallēṭ*); <u>fleeing</u> (*nûs*)
  - themes: <u>exodus</u> from Egypt, <u>Philistines</u>, <u>Edom</u>, Yahweh's exiling <u>Aram to Kir</u>
  - topics: <u>top of Carmel</u> (*rōʾš hakkarmel*), drinking wine, planting, uprooting, etc.

  b **the prophet's compulsion: announcement of coming destruction of Israel and Bethel's cult center** (3:1–15)
  - when Yahweh speaks, his prophets must prophesy
  - royal <u>houses</u> and Bethel's altars will be demolished

    c **condemnation of wealthy Israelite women: empty religious activity and Yahweh's judgment** (4:1–13)
  - to "the cows of Bashan who are <u>in the mountain of Samaria</u>"
  - condemnation of <u>wealthy women who idly drink</u>
  - prediction: these women will <u>go into exile</u> toward Harmon (Hermon?)
  - <u>empty religious activities</u> depicted, including sacrifices and offerings
  - Israel <u>loves</u> these activities
  - Yahweh is coming; he turns morning <u>into darkness</u>

      d **CENTER: call to repentance, and lament** (5:1–17)

    c′ **condemnation of wealthy Israelite men: empty religious activity and coming judgment** (5:18–6:14)
  - to "those who feel secure <u>in the mountain of Samaria</u>"
  - condemnation of <u>wealthy men who drink wine</u> (6:6)
  - prediction: these men will be first <u>into exile</u> "beyond Damascus"
  - <u>empty religious activities</u> depicted, including sacrifices and offerings
  - Yahweh <u>hates</u> and "despises" these activities (5:21)
  - the day of Yahweh will be <u>darkness</u>, not light (5:18, 20)

  b′ **the prophet's compulsion: visions of coming judgment; Amos announces coming destruction at the Bethel cult center** (7:1–8:3)
  - Yahweh has spoken, therefore Amos prophesies
  - prophecy at Bethel: Yahweh will destroy Israel's sanctuaries and rise against Jeroboam's <u>house</u>

a′ **coming judgment upon Israel (scattering among the nations) and future restoration among the nations** (8:4–9:15)
  - sevenfold condemnation of wealthy: "<u>they buy the poor for silver</u>, the <u>needy</u> for a <u>pair of shoes</u> (*³ebyôn baʿăbûr naʿălāyim*)" and "<u>trample</u> (*haššōʾăpîm*) the needy"
  - inescapability of judgment: they will <u>not escape</u> (*lōʾ-yimmālēṭ*); <u>fleeing</u> (*nûs*)
  - themes: <u>exodus</u> from Egypt, <u>Philistines</u>, <u>Edom</u>, Yahweh brought <u>Aram from Kir</u>
  - topics: <u>top of Carmel</u> (*rōʾš hakkarmel*), drinking wine, planting, uprooting, etc.

10. The reference in 1:2 to "the top of Carmel" (*rōʾš hakkarmel*) is echoed exactly in 9:3 (Carmel is not mentioned anywhere else in the book).[42]

The second and next-to-last units also correspond, although the linkage is not as extensively developed as that between units a and a'. Both units share the topic of the prophet and his responsibility to prophesy. In addition, both units involve the cultic sanctuary at Bethel and specifically speak against the royal house of Israel (3:13–15; 7:9–12).

The third and third-to-last units are more rigorously linked:

1. The third unit is addressed to "the cows of Bashan who are in the mountain of Samaria" (4:1)—that is, the wealthy women of Samaria—and the third-to-last unit is addressed to "those who feel secure in the mountain of Samaria" (6:1)—that is, the wealthy men of Samaria.
2. Both units condemn the wealthy aristocrats who idly drink (4:1; 6:6).
3. The third unit declares that the wealthy women will all go into captivity (4:3), and the third-to-last declares that the wealthy men will go into captivity (6:7).
4. In both units the exile is said to be in the direction of Damascus (4:3; 5:27—if Harmon refers to Mount Hermon).[43]
5. Both units graphically depict the same empty religious activities of the Israelites: sacrifices and offerings rejected by Yahweh (4:4–5; 5:21–23). In the former, these activities are what Israel "loves" to do (4:5), whereas in the latter, they are "hated" and "despised" by Yahweh (5:21).
6. In the third unit, Yahweh turns the morning into darkness (4:13); in the third-to-last unit, the day of Yahweh will be a day of darkness, not light (5:18, 20).

7. The dramatic declaration *nišbaʿ ʾădōnāy yhwh bĕqādĕšô/bĕnapšô* ("the Lord Yahweh has sworn by his holiness/soul") occurs in both units (4:2; 6:8).

At the center of the book's seven-part symmetry stands, appropriately, the book's centerpiece: the call to repentance.

Conclusion

A great deal of deliberate and well-conceived structural designing characterizes the final formation of the Book of Amos. The use of sevenfold and 7+1 patterns is particularly noteworthy. Most important, some of the seeming structural anomalies in Amos (e.g., the hymnic pieces, the three "secondary" strophes in the oracles against the nations, the interruptive Bethel narrative, the abrupt genre shifts, and the disjunction of thematically related sayings) function crucially in the book's surface structure.

Several observations can be made regarding the interplay of structure and meaning in the book. The repetition of matched units (c and c') focusing on condemnation serves to highlight the theme of Israel's social and ethical corruption, a corruption extending to both sexes and involving, in particular, the abuse of the poor. The reiteration of the theme of Israel's approaching judgment in matching units (a and a') also underscores this warning. The double occurrence of Amos's claims of divine compulsion for his prophesying (b and b') emphasizes the point that these are not Amos's, but Yahweh's words. Amos is delivering this message only because Yahweh compelled him. The implication: if Israel rejects Amos's message, they are rejecting Yahweh's message.

Most obvious is the highlighting of Amos's call to repentance. By placing the call to repentance in the central unit (and by duplicating it there for emphasis) Amos underscores its importance in his message. Yahweh is preparing to destroy the land; but it is still not too late. If Israel will only seek Yahweh, it will be spared.

---

42. Other correspondences include references to drinking wine (2:8, 12; 9:13, 14); planting/uprooting (2:9; 9:14–15); and the sword (1:11; 9:4, 10).

43. So argues Wolff, *Joel and Amos*, 204, 207.

30
Obadiah
Edom's Fall and Judah's Rise

The Book of Obadiah, like Habakkuk, addresses the issue of divine justice. At issue is Edom's mistreatment of helpless Judeans at the time of Judah's fall (probably during the Babylonian destruction of Jerusalem). After Judah's fall, the land lay devastated and depopulated, while proud Edom continued to prosper. Where was God's justice in all this?

Obadiah is the shortest book in the Old Testament—only twenty-one verses in length—but even short compositions have structure. In fact, Obadiah's brief message has clear signs of internal organization, such as the tightly arranged series of seven wrongs committed by Edom (12–14) and the vision of Judah's future expansion (19–21). The structure of the Book of Obadiah has received a great deal of scholarly attention.[1] Most commentators suggest that Obadiah has five units, as does, for example, A. Condamin:[2]

a 1–4 (begins and ends with "Yahweh")
b 5–7
c 8–10
d 11–14 (tied together by the repetition of "day" and by the refrain "in the day of distress" in 12 and 14)
e 15–21 (begins and ends, like the first strophe, with "Yahweh")

and Carl Keller:[3]

a 1b: prophetic vision
b 2–9: divine oracle comprising two strophes (2–4, 5–7) and an envoi (message) (8–9)
c 10–15: prophetic accusation consisting of three strophes (10–11, 12–13aα, 13aβ–14) and a concluding couplet serving as an envoi (15)

d 16–18: divine declaration to Israel comprising two strophes (16–17a, 17b–18)
e 19–21: final series of prose comments

Of all analyses, the most convincing is that by Georg Fohrer, who uses a combination of form criticism and strophic analysis to identify six units in the book:[4]

a 1b–4: ends "oracle of Yahweh"
b 5–7: warning; its end indicated by the new beginning in 8
c 8–11: begins "oracle of Yahweh"; ends with a concluding line
d 12–14, 15b: series of eight warnings, which may be concluded by the misplaced 15b
e 15a, 16–18: threat framing a promise; ends "for Yahweh has spoken"
f 19–21: promise with a final short line

It is more likely, however, that the Book of Obadiah has seven units, as will be presented on the following pages.

Constituent Units

Obadiah's first unit announces that, despite Edom's sense of security, Yahweh will bring it down in defeat. The unit's beginning is marked by the introductory "thus says Yahweh God concerning Edom," and its end is signaled by the concluding nĕʾum-yhwh ("says Yahweh").

The second unit is bracketed by two occurrences of nĕʾum-yhwh, one closing unit a, the other opening unit c. The beginning of unit b is marked by the abrupt appearance of a series of rhetorical questions that assert that Edom will be thoroughly devastated and plundered by the very nations Edom once trusted. The new unit is also marked by a shift in topic (from Edom's defeat to its plundering) and a new perspective regarding the agent of the disaster (from Yahweh

---

1. See the surveys by Ernst Sellin and Georg Fohrer, *Introduction to the Old Testament* (Nashville: Abingdon, 1968); and Leslie C. Allen, *The Books of Joel, Obadiah, Jonah, and Micah* (New International Commentary of the Old Testament; Grand Rapids: Eerdmans, 1976).

2. A. Condamin, "L'Unité d'Abdias," *Revue Biblique* 9 (1900) 261–68.

3. Carl A. Keller, *Osée, Joël, Amos, Abdias, Jonas* (Commentaire de l'Ancien Testament 11a; Neuchâtel: Delachaux & Niestlé, 1965), 251–62.

4. Georg Fohrer, "Die Sprüche Obadjas," in *Studia Biblica et Semitica: Theodoro Christiano Vriezen . . . Dedicata* (Wageningen: Veenman & Zonen, 1966), 81–93.

30.1 Linear sequence in the Book of Obadiah
a **Edom will be defeated**, despite its present strength and security (1–4)
• Edom's fortune: bad
b **Edom will be utterly plundered** (5–7)
• Edom's fortune: worse
c **Edom's population will be annihilated** (8–11)
• Edom's fortune: worst
d **reason**: Edom's sins against Israel (12–14)
e **the nations, who exulted over Israel's fall, will themselves fall** (15–16)
• Israel's fortune: good
f **the remnant of Israel will retake their own land** and plunder Edom (17–18)
• Israel's fortune: better
g **restored Israel will conquer and rule** over all the surrounding nations (19–21)
• Israel's fortune: best

himself in to Edom's former allies). The "I will" in unit a is replaced by "they will" in unit b.

The third unit, like the second, is introduced by a rhetorical question. The beginning of this unit is marked by shifts in topic (from Edom's plundering to the slaughtering of its population), the agent of disaster (back to Yahweh), and time (expressed by "in that day" + the structural marker *něʾum-yhwh* ["says Yahweh"]). The unit is tied together by the terms "day" (*yôm*; 8, 11) and "cut off" (*krt*; 9–10) and by its singular point that Edom's population will be annihilated because of what it did to Israel. And now, for the first time, the audience hears the reason for Edom's upcoming punishment.

The fourth unit is introduced by the shift to a new, tightly structured series of seven parallel rebukes, each introduced by the negative particle *ʾal* or *wěʾal* with a second-person verb ("you should not have . . .") and each concluded with a clause introduced by *běyôm* ("in the day of . . ."), followed by a noun referring to Judah's fall. For example, "You should not have (*wěʾal*) plundered his goods in the day of (*běyôm*) his calamity" (13c). The seventh rebuke is longer than the first six, containing one *běyôm* conclusion and two *wěʾal* clauses, representing a sort of grand finale to the series. This unit serves to detail the specific wrongs that Edom committed against Israel.

The fifth unit opens with a common beginning marker, *kî* ("surely"), followed by a new topic: the day of Yahweh. This new unit appears to extend through 16, and it makes a single point: on Yahweh's day of judgment, Edom and the nations will be punished in retaliation for what they did to Jerusalem: "They shall be as though they had not been" (= annihilated?).[5]

This is the third unit in succession to address the reason for Edom's coming punishment.

The book closes with two units of good news regarding Israel's own future. The sixth unit announces the restoration of Israel. Its beginning is marked by the shift to a new focus: Israel and its own future. The unit is tied together by the fivefold repetition of *bêt* ("house of") and by the singularity of its message: the survivors of Israel will repossess their possessions and will be like a devouring fire, consuming Edom. The unit's end is marked by the concluding clause: *kî yhwh dibber* ("for Yahweh has spoken").

It is generally agreed that 19–21 forms the book's final unit (although some argue that it is a later addition). Bracketed by references to "Yahweh" at the end of 18 and at the end of 21, the unit is tied together by the series of six or seven (the text is difficult here) declarations of how future Israelites from various regions of Israel will take possession of neighboring lands. The series opens and closes (not surprisingly) with predictions of their conquest of "Mount Esau" (19a, 21a).

Arrangement of Units

The linear sequence of Obadiah's seven parts is interesting (30.1). The book opens with a series of three units announcing in succession what appear to be ever-worsening disasters that will befall Edom, concluded with a fourth unit detailing Edom's guilt. The final three units announce the reversal of Israel's tragic history in

---

5. The weak point of Fohrer's analysis ("Die Sprüche Obadjas") is his treatment of 15–16, where he chooses to rearrange 15a–b in order to provide what he feels would be a proper closing for 12–14 and a proper beginning for 16–18. A simpler solution is to take 15–16 as a separate unit altogether, functioning as a self-contained unit and providing a transi-

tion between 12–14 and 17–18, in some respects concluding the previous unit and providing the introduction to the next one. The parallelism in 15b and 16a suggests that these two lines belong to the same strophe. Moreover, 17a does seem to begin a new unit by its sudden shift in tenor, from threat to promise. It is at least possible, therefore, that 15–16 and 17–18 form two separate units, the first dealing with the coming judgment upon Edom and the nations, the second describing the future success of Israel at Edom's expense. This reconstruction obviates the need to rearrange the text of 15.

30.2 Symmetry in the Book of Obadiah

a **proud Edom will be defeated** by the nations (1–4)
  - Yahweh will <u>bring Edom down</u> (*yrd*), despite its sense of security in its lofty position
  - the nations are exhorted to <u>rise up</u> against Edom
  - Edom will be made small among <u>the nations</u>

  b **Edom will be completely plundered** by its former allies and nothing will be left (no "gleanings") (5–7)

    c **Edom's population will be slaughtered** (8–11)
  - topic: future <u>day</u> (*yôm*) of judgment
  - reason: because of the violence <u>they did against Israel</u>

      d **CENTER: indictment of Edom** (12–14)

    c′ **Edom and the nations will be judged (annihilated[?])**, becoming "as if they never were" (15–16)
  - topic: future <u>day</u> (*yôm*) of Yahweh's judgment
  - reason: because of what <u>they did against Israel</u>

  b′ **Israel will regain what it has lost and will plunder** ("devour") Edom (17–18)

a′ **humbled Israel will be victorious** over the surrounding nations (19–21)
  - "saviors"(?) will one day <u>go up</u> (cf. the Septuagint) from Jerusalem <u>to rule Edom</u>
  - restored Israel will defeat and rule over <u>the nations</u>

"the day of Yahweh," with each successive unit featuring Israel's increasingly favorable good fortunes. There also appears to be a symmetric touch in the book's overall layout (30.2).

On the smaller level, each of the book's seven constituent units may be composed of seven smaller parts, in each case arranged in linear rather than symmetric patterns.[6] It is also worth

noting that six of the book's seven units (the central one being the exception) close with a terse concluding clause, which is apparently the author's way of further marking the ends of units.[7]

Conclusion

The structure of the Book of Obadiah serves to reinforce its message. The balancing of the portrayal of proud Edom's future fall (units a and b) with the declaration of fallen Israel's future rise and ascendancy over Edom (units b′ and a′) highlights the theme that Yahweh will right the wrongs that Edom has committed against Israel by reversing the fortunes of the two nations. Placing the unit detailing Edom's sins at the center of the book, in the position of prominence, emphasizes Yahweh's justice as the driving force behind Edom's punishment. The placement of the good news for Judah at the end of the book, concluding the book on a "good note," indicates that the author's purpose is to encourage and console a Judean audience who may still be reeling from an atrocity that called Yahweh's justice into question. In this sense, the Book of Obadiah may be categorized as a theodicy (a study of God's justice), since it, like Habakkuk, Nahum, and Job, seeks to defend the ultimate rightness of Yahweh's actions. Obadiah's message is this: it may appear for the moment that evil has triumphed; but be assured, in the end Yahweh will right all wrongs. Yahweh is still in control; and he is worthy of Israel's trust.

---

6. An examination of the internal structure of these seven units reveals a preference for a septenary scheme. Fohrer ("Die Sprüche Obadjas," 85) analyzes the book's first unit as comprising seven lines: 1b, 1c, 2, 3a, 3b, 4a, 4b. Except for an inconsequential question regarding the break between the fourth and fifth units, Fohrer's analysis seems acceptable. The second unit is emended (rearranged) somewhat by Fohrer, and in his resulting text he finds five lines. There appear to be seven, however, as correctly presented in BHS: 5a, 5b, 5c, 6 (an appropriate center for the piece), 7a, 7b, 7c, with a short, detached, concluding phrase (unless this is a gloss; cf. BHS) analogous to the *nĕʾum-yhwh* phrase that ending the first unit. The third unit is again analyzed by Fohrer as comprising seven lines: 8a, 8b, 9 (except the last word, which goes with 10), 10 (an appropriate center of the unit, representing the turning point), 11a, 11b, 11c (a short, detached comment marking the end of this unit). The central unit (12–14) comprises a series of eight parallel lines (see above), each beginning with *ʾal* + second-person jussive verb and concluding with a temporal phrase introduced by *bĕyôm*. The single exception is the seventh line (14a), which breaks the pattern in its second half. Seven lines, therefore, follow precisely the same pattern and an eighth represents a variation. This exception seems to suggest a textual corruption; but there is no textual support for emendation. (Notice the 3+2+3 pattern in the introductory *waw*s, creating a chiasmus of sorts.) The fifth unit consists of six sentences: 15a, 15b, 15c, 16a–b, 16c, 16d. Splitting the relatively long (for this section) sentence in 16a–b into its two constituent clauses creates a total of seven clauses of approximately equal length in this unit, and it seems quite possible that the author intended this unit to be so taken. The final two clauses (16c, 16d) are exceptionally short, apparently conforming to the author's tendency to mark the ends of his units with short lines, except here he does so with two consecutive short lines. The sixth unit likewise comprises seven sentences (omitting, with Fohrer [p. 91] the two words at the end of 17a) plus a concluding "for Yahweh has spoken" at the end of 18: 17a, 17b, 18a, 18b, 18c, 18d, 18e. The seventh unit comprises seven sentences

(19a, 19b, 19c, 19d, 20a, 20b, 21a) plus a short concluding line "and the kingdom will be Yahweh's" (21b).

7. This pattern, incidentally, supports the textual authenticity of the brief line closing 7.

31

Jonah

A Lesson on Mercy

The story of Jonah is one of the best known narratives in the Bible. It is about an eighth-century B.C. Israelite prophet who reluctantly took God's message of warning to the city of Nineveh.

An analysis of the literary structure of Jonah elucidates several aspects of the book's message. In particular, it may clarify the significance of Jonah's prayer in chapter 2 and Yahweh's lesson in 4:5–11. It may also help identify the author's purpose in writing the book.[1]

Overall Layout of the Book of Jonah

Most people reading the Book of Jonah recognize that the book is composed of a series of episodes. There appear to be seven, each marked off for the audience by shifts in setting, genre, and characters (31.1).[2]

These seven episodes are arranged in chronological order. But a secondary parallel arrangement scheme is also relatively conspicuous. The first three episodes (Jonah's first commission, his first experience with the pagans, and his first prayer) are matched by the second three episodes (his second commission, his second experience with the pagans, and his second prayer) in an a-b-c ‖ a'-b'-c' configuration. Following these six episodes is Yahweh's lesson for Jonah, which concludes the book. The seven episodes

of the book thus exhibit a parallel arrangement: a-b-c ‖ a'-b'-c' ‖ d. This parallel scheme invites further examination.

Correspondence of the Two Commissioning Accounts (Jonah 1:1–3; 3:1–3a)

The two episodes of Jonah's call echo one another through the verbatim repetition of Yahweh's commissioning. This repetition highlights the only significant difference between the two episodes, namely, Jonah's drastically different responses:

> The word of Yahweh came to Jonah son of Amittai: "Arise, go to Nineveh, the great city, and proclaim against it. . . ." And Jonah arose and <u>fled to Tarshish</u> from the presence of Yahweh.
>
> —Jonah 1:1–3

> The word of Yahweh came to Jonah a second time: "Arise, go to Nineveh, the great city, and proclaim against it. . . ." And Jonah arose and <u>went to Nineveh</u> according to the word of Yahweh.
>
> —Jonah 3:1–3a

The repetition also serves to underscore Yahweh's determination to reach the Ninevites with his message of warning. It suggests his resolve, even in the face of his own prophet's disobedience, to extend to sinners an opportunity to repent. Israel's God obviously cares about the fate of sinners, even pagan sinners.

Correspondence of the Two Episodes Involving Jonah and the Pagans (Jonah 1:4–16; 3:3b–10)

The two commissioning episodes are followed by two matching stories about Jonah and the pagans—sailors and Ninevites. These two episodes are designed to echo one another, for in both . . .

1. Jonah finds himself among idolatrous pagans with whom he interacts.
2. The action is recounted in lively detail.

---

1. For two similar structural analyses of Jonah, with similar conclusions regarding the meaning of the book, see David A. Dorsey, "Literary Architecture and Meaning in the Book of Jonah," in *To Understand the Scriptures* (William H. Shea Festschrift), ed. David Merling (Berrien Springs, Mich.: Andrews University, 1997), 57–69; and Victor M. Wilson, *Divine Symmetries: The Art of Biblical Rhetoric* (New York: University Press of America, 1997), 146–56.

2. See James Limburg, *Jonah: A Commentary* (Old Testament Library; Louisville: Westminster/John Knox, 1993), 28, who likewise analyzes the book as composed of these same seven units. The only difference between my analysis and his regards 4:4, which probably belongs with 4:1–3. He places it with 4:5–11. Phyllis Trible, *Rhetorical Criticism: Context, Method, and the Book of Jonah* (Minneapolis: Augsburg Fortress, 1994), 207–25, likewise sees 4:5/6–11 as the book's final, separate unit.

31.1 The Book of Jonah

	setting	genre	characters
Jonah's commissioning and flight (1:1–3)	Israel	succinct narrative	Yahweh and Jonah
Jonah and the pagan sailors (1:4–16)	at sea	detailed narrative and dialogue	Jonah and sailors
Jonah's prayer (1:17–2:10 [2:1–11])	fish's belly	prayer	Jonah (addressing Yahweh)
Jonah's recommissioning and obedience (3:1–3a)	somewhere on dry land (on seashore?)	succinct narrative	Yahweh and Jonah
Jonah and the pagan Ninevites (3:3b–10)	Nineveh	detailed narrative and dialogue	Jonah and Ninevites
Jonah's prayer (4:1–4)	(not given; presumably somewhere in Nineveh)	prayer	Jonah (addressing Yahweh)
Yahweh's lesson for Jonah (4:5–11)	outside Nineveh	narrative and dialogue	Yahweh and Jonah

3. Jonah's arrival brings with it the ominous judgment of his God Yahweh.

4. The pagans respond immediately, vigorously, and with great conviction.

5. The pagans cry out (*qārā*ʾ) to Jonah's God for mercy.

6. Their leader (the captain, the king) participates.

7. The leader expresses the hope that God may show mercy and relent.

8. Yahweh spares the pagans.

9. Yahweh spares the guilty parties—Jonah and the Ninevites.

10. Jonah seems remarkably detached; he is a reluctant participant.

Through these repetitions the author highlights three points: (1) Yahweh's power extends throughout the earth, and all people are accountable to him; (2) sinners, when confronted with Yahweh's impending judgment, should respond in repentance (the only sane response!); and (3) Yahweh may relent from his planned judgment if the guilty parties repent.

Correspondence of Jonah's Two Prayers (Jonah 1:17–2:10 [2:1–11]; 4:1–4)

The two stories about the pagans are followed by Jonah's two prayers to Yahweh. The correspondence of these two prayers is fairly obvious:[3] both are in response to Yahweh's sparing a guilty party (Jonah, the Ninevites); both are introduced with "and Jonah prayed (*wayyitpallēl*) to Yahweh" (2:1–2 [2:2–3]; 4:1–2); and both contain three of the same keywords: "love" (*ḥesed*), "my life" (*ḥayyay*), and "my soul" (*napší*).

What is striking, however, is their differences. The first, Jonah's prayer of thanksgiving to Yahweh for sparing him, is beautiful, almost serene. It is steeped in piety and rich theology. In contrast, the second prayer, in which Jonah reacts angrily to Yahweh's sparing pagan Nineveh, is the opposite: it is not beautiful, serene, pious, or theologically rich. Rather, it is an indignant outburst, petty, small, mean-spirited. In the first prayer Jonah celebrates Yahweh's "kindness" (*ḥesed*), which pagans forfeit (2:8 [2:9]); in the second Jonah complains that Yahweh's *ḥesed* has been extended to the pagans—as Jonah feared it would (4:2). In the first prayer Jonah is grateful that his "life" (*ḥayyay*) and "soul" (*napší*) have been saved (2:5–7 [2:6–8]); in the second he angrily entreats Yahweh to take his "life" (*ḥayyay*) and "soul" (*napší*). In the first prayer, Jonah praises Yahweh for sparing him—one person—from the punishment he deserved (although he apparently has not repented of his disobedience!); whereas in the second prayer Jonah is angry that Yahweh has spared many thousands of *innocent* children, as well as people who *have* sincerely repented.

That the pious prayer of chapter 2 is matched by the mean-spirited prayer of chapter 4 helps the reader, in retrospect, to see the first prayer as the author intended: self-righteous, hypocritical, and selfish.[4]

Yahweh's Object Lesson (Jonah 4:5–11) and the Overall Layout of the Book of Jonah

Two structural considerations suggest that the author intended 4:5–11 to serve as the climax to the Book of Jonah. First, this is the book's only unmatched unit, which gives it a natural emphasis. Second, it stands in the sev-

---

3. That the author of Jonah intends his readers to compare and contrast these two prayers is suggested by George M. Landes, "The Kerygma of the Book of Jonah," *Interpretation* 21 (1967) 3–31; Leslie C. Allen, *The Books of Joel, Obadiah, Jonah, and Micah* (New International Commentary of the Old Testament; Grand Rapids: Eerdmans, 1976), 198–99; Trible, *Rhetorical Criticism*, 202.

4. The hypocrisy of this prayer and its function as an integral part of the book is admirably explored by John C. Holbert, " 'Deliverance Belongs to Yahweh!': Satire in the Book of Jonah," *Journal for the Study of the Old Testament* 21 (1981) 59–81.

31.2 The Book of Jonah

a **Jonah commissioned to go to Nineveh**; his disobedience (1:1–3)
  - "arise, go to Nineveh, the great city . . . and Jonah arose to flee"

b **Jonah and the pagan sailors (1:4–16)**
  - begins: Yahweh threatens judgment the pagan ship
  - sailors <u>respond immediately</u> and vigorously with conviction
  - sailors <u>cry out</u> (qārāʾ) to Jonah's God for mercy
  - their <u>leader</u>, the captain, participates in the effort, expressing hope that <u>God may show mercy and relent</u>
  - ends: Yahweh <u>spares the contrite pagans</u> of the ship

c **Jonah's grateful, beautiful prayer (1:17–2:10 [2:1–11])**
  - "and Jonah <u>prayed</u> (wayyitpallēl) to Yahweh"
  - boasts about Yahweh's <u>love</u> (ḥesed) that pagans forfeit
  - Jonah is grateful that his <u>life</u> (ḥayyay) and <u>soul</u> (napšî) have been saved (although he has not repented)

a′ **Jonah recommissioned to go to Nineveh**; his obedience (3:1–3a)
  - "arise, go to Nineveh, the great city . . . and Jonah arose and went"

b′ **Jonah and the pagan Ninevites (3:3b–10)**
  - begins: Yahweh announces judgment against the pagan city
  - Ninevites <u>respond immediately</u> and vigorously with conviction
  - Ninevites <u>cry out</u> (qārāʾ) to Jonah's God for mercy
  - their <u>leader</u>, the king, participates in the effort, expressing hope that <u>God may show mercy and relent</u>
  - ends: Yahweh <u>spares the contrite pagans</u> of the city

c′ **Jonah's resentful, mean-spirited prayer (4:1–4)**
  - "and Jonah <u>prayed</u> (wayyitpallēl) to Yahweh"
  - complains about Yahweh's <u>love</u> (ḥesed) that the pagans have received
  - Jonah resents that the pagans have been spared; wishes that his <u>life</u> (ḥayyay) and <u>soul</u> (napšî) would be taken

d **CLIMAX: Yahweh's lesson for Jonah (4:5–11)**

---

enth and final position, the standard place for the climax in seven-part parallel arrangements (e.g., the creation story). The book's parallel layout (a-b-c ‖ a′-b′-c′ ‖ d), therefore, highlights Yahweh's lesson for Jonah at the end (31.2).

Internal Structuring within the Constituent Units

The internal structures of some of the individual episodes are instructive. Whereas the two brief commissioning units are constructed in a simple a-b pattern (divine commission, prophet's response),[5] the internal arrangements of the other units are more complex and invite closer scrutiny.

Jonah and the Pagan Sailors (Jonah 1:4–16)

Though the episode of Jonah and the pagan sailors is primarily linear in arrangement—following a chronologically sequential order—the episode exhibits a decidedly symmetric touch. Its structuring as an extended chiasmus is noted by a number of scholars—although analyses differ in details.[6] Rudolf Pesch, for ex-

ample, sees the story as comprising fifteen chiastically arranged units.[7] In all probability, however, the story is intended to comprise thirteen parts, with the central, seventh unit being Jonah's great confession (1:9; see 31.3).[8]

The opening two events of the episode are obviously matched by the two closing events, dramatically capturing the transformation that occurred with respect to the pagan sailors and Yahweh:

---

a Yahweh <u>hurls</u> (hēṭîl) a great wind <u>upon the sea</u> (ʾel-hayyām) (1:4)

b sailors <u>cry out</u>—in vain—to their gods (1:5a)

---

5. Norbert Lohfink, "Jona ging zur Stadt hinaus (Jon 4,5)," *Biblische Zeitschrift* 5 (1961) 200–201, analyzes Jonah's actions in 1:3 as forming a seven-part chiasmus, an analysis with which Trible (*Rhetorical Criticism*, 127–31) agrees.

6. See the various arrangements proposed by Lohfink, "Jona ging zur Stadt hinaus" (five parts); Carl A. Keller, "Jonas: Le Portrait d'un Prophète," *Theologische Zeitschrift* 21 (1965) 329–40; Landes, "Kerygma of the Book of Jonah"; Jonathan Magonet, *Form and Meaning: Studies in Literary Techniques in the Book of Jonah* (Bern/Frankfurt: Lang, 1976),

56–57; G. H. Cohn, *Das Buch Jona im Lichte der biblischen Erzählkunst* (Studia Semitica Neerlandica 12; Assen: Van Gorcum, 1969), 51; Limburg, *Jonah*, 47–48.

7. Rudolf Pesch, "Zur konzentrischen Struktur von Jona 1," *Biblica* 47 (1966) 577–81: (a/a′) narrative and response of fear (4–5a, 15–16a); (b/b′) sailors' prayer (5b, 14); (c/c′) narrative (5c–6a, 13); (d/d′) captain's speech (6b, 12); (e/e′) sailors' speech (7a, 11); (f/f′) narrative (7b, 10c); (g/g′) sailors' speech (8, 10b); center: Jonah's statement and the response of fear (9–10a). Apart from several minor (and inconsequential) points in Pesch's analysis, two items need comment: (1) the splitting of 1:7 into two units seems artificial: the verse makes a single statement: the sailors decided to cast lots and Jonah was found to be the culprit; (2) extracting 1:10c from the rest of 1:10 and granting it the status of a separate unit ("Erzählung") seems unlikely; verse 10c is simply an explanatory remark completing the thought of 1:10, of which it is an integral part.

8. The precise delineations of the units in this analysis are tentative. One could easily argue that the author did not intend so many units. Also, the correspondences of unit d with d′ and unit e with e′ seem somewhat weak.

31.3 Jonah and the pagan sailors (Jonah 1:4–16)

  a **Yahweh** <u>hurls</u> (*hēṭîl*) **a great wind** <u>upon the sea</u> (*ʾel-hayyām*) (1:4)

    b **sailors** <u>cry out</u> (in vain) <u>to their gods</u> (1:5a)

      c **sailors' frantic and futile efforts** to save ship by throwing cargo overboard (1:5b–c)

        d **Jonah does nothing to save the ship:** he remains down in the hold, uninvolved; captain pleads with him to help save the ship (1:6)

          e **sailors' efforts to ascertain what to do:** inquiry by lots—Jonah is guilty (1:7)

            f **sailors demand an explanation** from Jonah: <u>tell</u> (*haggîdâ*) us (1:8)

              g **CLIMAX: Jonah's testimony** (1:9)

            f′ **sailors demand an explanation** from Jonah because of what he had <u>told</u> (*higgîd*) (1:10)

          e′ **sailors' efforts to ascertain what they must do:** inquiry of Jonah—the guilty party (1:11)

        d′ **Jonah finally acts to save the ship:** he proposes that he be thrown overboard (1:12)

      c′ **sailors' frantic and futile efforts** to save ship by rowing harder (1:13)

    b′ **sailors** <u>cry out</u> to Yahweh (1:14)

  a′ **sailors** <u>hurl</u> (*hēṭîl*) **Jonah** <u>into the sea</u> (*ʾel-hayyām*), and the sea becomes still (1:15)

  conclusion: sailors greatly feared Yahweh and made sacrifices and vows to him (1:16)

31.4 Jonah's first prayer (Jonah 1:17–2:10 [2:1–11])

  a **narrative introduction:** great fish swallows Jonah (1:17 [2:1])

    b **prayer** (2:1–9 [2:2–10])

      (1) **report of Yahweh's deliverance** (2:1–2 [2:2–3])

        (2) **description of distress** (2:3–6b [2:4–7b])

      (1′) **report of Yahweh's deliverance** (2:6c–7 [2:7c–8])

        (3) **concluding promise of future service:** Jonah piously contrasts himself with pagans and promises to offer praise and <u>sacrifice</u> and to pay <u>vows</u> to Yahweh in future (2:8–9 [2:9–10])

  a **narrative conclusion:** great fish vomits Jonah out (2:10 [2:11])

---

    b′ sailors (having heard Jonah's testimony and instructions) <u>cry out</u> to the true God, Yahweh—and not in vain (1:14)

  a′ obeying Yahweh's prophet, sailors hurl (*hēṭîl*) Jonah <u>into the sea</u> (*ʾel-hayyām*), and the winds that Yahweh had caused cease (1:15)

This layout underscores the contrast between the futility of the sailors' appealing to their own pagan gods and the remarkable results when they call upon Yahweh and obey his prophet. Jonah's God is truly the God "who made the sea and dry land" (1:9).

The intervening episodes of the story move the audience inexorably toward the identification of Jonah as the culprit and to the story's natural center and turning point, Jonah's grand confession (1:9). Then, in reverse order, the story moves outward to its resolution (31.3). And by repeating the scenes of the sailors' heroic efforts to save themselves through their own desperate efforts and through their appeals for divine mercy (units b–c and c′ b′), the author highlights these commendable responses.

The episode concludes with a statement standing outside the tightly constructed chiasmus, giving it prominence. The statement recounts three things the sailors did as a result of their experience: "Then the men greatly feared Yahweh; they sacrificed a sacrifice to Yahweh, and they made vows" (1:16). This response by the pagan sailors, underscored by its position, will become significant as the audience hears Jonah's prayer that follows.

Jonah's First Prayer (Jonah 1:17–2:10 [2:1–11])

Jonah's psalm of thanksgiving comprises four parts,[9] framed by a narrative inclusio. His prayer is arranged symmetrically, except that its final part stands outside the symmetry and serves as an unmatched (and thus highlighted) conclusion (31.4).

Like the preceding episode about Jonah and the sailors, this prayer features a highlighted

---

9. John T. Walsh, "Jonah 2,3–10: A Rhetorical Critical Study," *Biblica* 63 (1982) 219–29, divides the prayer into four parts (using Hebrew verse numbers here and throughout this note): 2:3, 4–5, 6–8, 9–10. This is accepted by Trible, *Rhetorical Criticism*, 163–65, who sees these four stanzas as forming an a-b-b′-a′ chiasmus. Frank M. Cross, "Studies in the Structure of Hebrew Verse: The Prosody of the Psalm of Jonah," in *The Quest for the Kingdom of God: Studies in Honor of George E. Mendenhall*, ed. H. B. Huffmon, F. A. Spina, and A. R. W. Green (Winona Lake, Ind.: Eisenbrauns, 1983), 159–67, also analyzes it with four parts, but with differences: 2:3–4, 5, 6–7, 8–10. Duane L. Christensen, "The Song of Jonah: A Metrical Analysis," *Journal of Biblical Literature* 104 (1985) 217–31, sees five parts: 2:3, 4–5, 6–7a, 7b–8, 9–10. Jack Sasson, *Jonah: A New Translation with Introduction, Commentary, and Interpretation* (Anchor Bible 24b; New York: Doubleday, 1990), 166, has three parts: 2:3–4, 5–9, 10. In an excellent study, M. L. Barré, "Jonah 2,9 and the Structure of Jonah's Prayer," *Biblica* 72 (1991) 237–48, proposes seven units, in three parts: (1) proem (2:3), (2) part I (2:4; 2:5; 2:6–7b), (3) part II (2:7c–8b; 2:8c–9; 2:10). The only improvement on Barré's analysis is that his part II be subdivided.

31.5 Jonah and the Ninevites (Jonah 3:3b–10)

a **Yahweh's judgment announced** (3:3b–4)
  b **people repent** with <u>fasting and wearing sackcloth</u> (3:5)
    (c **word reaches the <u>king</u>** [3:6a])
      d **CENTER: king repents** (3:6b)
    (c′ **word goes out from the <u>king</u>** to people [3:7a])
  b′ **people commanded to repent** with <u>fasting and wearing sackcloth</u> (3:7b–9)
a′ **Yahweh's judgment canceled**; he relents and spares the city (3:10)

31.6 Jonah's angry prayer (Jonah 4:1–4)

a **introduction**: Jonah's <u>anger</u> (*ḥrh*) (4:1)
  b **prayer** (4:2–3)
    (1) **complaint about Yahweh's mercy**: I said this would happen! (4:2a)
      (2) **excuse** for disobedience: this is why I fled (4:2b)
    (1′) **complaint about Yahweh's mercy**: I knew this would happen, that you would act mercifully! (4:2c)
      (3) **concluding request**: take my life! (4:3)
a′ **conclusion**: Jonah's <u>anger</u> (*ḥrh*) questioned by Yahweh (4:4)

final unit that also speaks of vows and sacrificing to Yahweh (2:9 [2:10])—which of course invites the audience to compare the two passages. The ironic contrast between the two is unmistakable. In the latter, Jonah's boasts: "Those who serve empty idols forfeit (your) kindness; but I, on the other hand, will offer you sacrifice with thanksgiving; I will pay my vows!" (2:8–9 [2:9–10]). Ironically, while the rebellious prophet is making these self-righteous boasts and promises from the fish's belly, the praiseworthy pagan sailors are up above, happy recipients of Yahweh's kindness, doing precisely what Jonah can mostly only promise to do (and what he assumes nobody except faithful Israelites like himself do): they are sacrificing to Yahweh and making vows to him (1:16)! By this structuring strategy the author helps the audience understand how Jonah's pious prayer is to be heard—as hypocritical!

Jonah and the Pagan Ninevites (Jonah 3:3b–10)

As in the episode involving Jonah and the sailors, the episode about Jonah and the Ninevites exhibits a secondary symmetric touch, in this case comprising either five or seven parts (31.5).

In an artistic touch, this symmetry moves upward (socially) as it moves toward its center (from people to king), then downward again as it proceeds from the center to the end (from king back to people). The impression created is that the entire city repents, from top to bottom (or more accurately: from bottom to top to bottom again), with the king, appropriately, taking the lead. Placing the king's own repentance at the center highlights the king's pivotal spiritual role in Nineveh's repentance (with the implied message: the same kind of leadership is needed

among Israelite kings). The king's response in 3:6b, at the center of this chiasmus, is itself symmetric:[10]

a he arose from his throne
  b he took off his robe
  b′ he put on sackcloth
a′ he sat in the dust

Also, the matched repetition of the people's earnest repentance (b and b′) underscores this commendable response (as did the similar repetition in the story of the sailors).

Jonah's Angry Prayer When Yahweh Spares Nineveh (Jonah 4:1–4)

Jonah's terse, angry prayer appears to have precisely the same arrangement as that of his earlier prayer. As there, the prayer here is framed by a narrative (4:1, 4).[11] The prayer itself, like its earlier counterpart, is composed of four parts, the first three forming an a-b-a′ pattern and the fourth standing outside the symmetry and functioning as the prayer's (highlighted) conclusion (31.6).

The similarity of the design of these two prayers draws attention to their differences. The symmetric portion of the first prayer was introduced and concluded by Jonah's praises of Yahweh's kindness to him; here Jonah's complaints about Yahweh's kindness to the Ninevites ironically occupy the same two slots. Like-

---

10. Noted by Trible, *Rhetorical Criticism*, 183.
11. Trible (*Rhetorical Criticism*, 196–205) also notices the parallel between 4:1 and 4:4, and she includes 4:4 in this opening unit of chap. 4. She is ambivalent about 4:5, but eventually decides to place it at the end of the present unit (4:1–5) rather than at the beginning of the next. In all probability, however, 4:5 is intended as the introduction to the book's final unit.

31.7 Yahweh's object lesson (Jonah 4:5–11)

setting (4:5)

a **Yahweh prepares a plant for Jonah** (4:6a)

  b **Jonah's response:** he rejoices (4:6b)

a′ **Yahweh destroys the plant** and causes hot wind to blow on Jonah (4:7–8a)

  b′ **Jonah's response:** he is upset (4:8b)

a″ **Yahweh asks:** should you feel so badly about this plant, Jonah? (4:9a)

  b″ **Jonah's response:** yes! I should feel badly enough to die! (4:9b)

    c **CLIMAX: Yahweh's lesson** (4:10–11)

---

wise, the conclusions of both prayers stand in striking contrast: in his first prayer, after Yahweh had spared him, Jonah concluded with a joyous vow to serve Yahweh; in contrast, Jonah's second prayer, following Yahweh's sparing of the Ninevites, concludes with an ignoble wish to die—which serves to underscore the prophet's hypocrisy.

Yahweh's Object Lesson (Jonah 4:5–11)

The book's final unit is arranged in a seven-part a-b ‖ a′-b′ ‖ a″-b″ ‖ c scheme, with the final, unmatched seventh unit standing in the position of prominence. The narrative (following the stage-setting introduction in 4:5) alternates between Yahweh and Jonah as subjects as it builds toward the grand finale (31.7).

The alternating organization of this unit helps convey the image of Yahweh's patiently walking Jonah through this object lesson. Yahweh causes a chain of events that leaves Jonah feeling badly about a little plant that died. Now Yahweh asks Jonah to see why Yahweh feels so badly about the impending destruction of an entire city full of many thousands of people, including thousands of innocent children and animals.

Conclusion

Does the structure of the Book of Jonah hold any clues as to the author's purpose in writing it? Several observations can be made. The foregoing analysis reveals that the author highlighted at least four themes by the technique of structured, matching repetition:

1. the accountability of all people to Yahweh's authority
2. Yahweh's earnest concern over the fate of sinners
3. the importance of repentance when confronted by Yahweh's threatened judgment
4. the likelihood that Yahweh will be merciful if sinners repent

By his structuring strategy the author also underscored a fifth theme: the hypocrisy of rejoicing at one's own salvation while resenting the salvation of others. He emphasizes this theme in two ways: (1) by the intentional contrasting of the two prayers and (2) by the highlighted position at the climactic conclusion of the book of Yahweh's lesson about this kind of hypocrisy. In light of these observations, it seems that the author has written with two main purposes in mind: (1) to encourage sinners under Yahweh's threatened judgment to repent and (2) to warn against hypocritically resenting the mercy Yahweh shows to sinners outside one's own group.

What circumstances might have occasioned these concerns? The encouragement to repent would fit almost any time in Israel's history, particularly during the ministries of any of the prophets. This theme is central, for example, in Jeremiah 18. On the other hand, it is difficult to identify any known circumstances that might have called for the warning against resenting Yahweh's mercy on others. One might speculate that such resentment may have surfaced in Judah when Yahweh spared the sinful northern kingdom during the reign of Jeroboam II (2 Kings 14:25–27), during Jonah's own lifetime. Or perhaps pious Judeans resented God's sparing wicked Manasseh following his repentance (2 Chron. 33:12–13) or sinful Judah during the reign of Josiah (2 Kings 22–23).

In conclusion, one could compare the message of Jonah to Jesus' parable of the prodigal son. That parable develops the same two themes found in Jonah: hope for the repentant sinner and a plea for understanding on the part of the (self-)righteous faithful—who like rebellious Jonah also need to repent.[12]

---

12. Several of the insights offered here, both structural and theological, are also found in the excellent article by James S. Ackerman, "Jonah," in *The Literary Guide to the Bible*, ed. Robert Alter and Frank Kermode (Cambridge: Harvard University Press, 1987), 234–43.

32
Micah
Walk Humbly with Your God

Micah was a contemporary of Amos, Hosea, and Isaiah. His message to the southern kingdom of Judah complemented the messages of Amos and Hosea to the northern kingdom. Samaria was going to fall, Micah predicted, and unless the people of Judah turned from their own social and moral corruption, they too would be punished. The structure of the Book of Micah is difficult to analyze. In his commentary on Micah, Leslie Allen quotes Martin Luther's complaint about the lack of internal order in the prophetic books: "They have a queer way of talking, like people who, instead of proceeding in an orderly manner, ramble off from one thing to the next, so that you cannot make head or tail of them or see what they are getting at."[1] After himself complaining that "the book of Micah is a blatant example of this seeming jumble, so that a search for literary structure is at first sight an impossible task," Allen then suggests, as have others, that the book is in fact well organized.[2]

---

1. Leslie C. Allen, *The Books of Joel, Obadiah, Jonah, and Micah* (New International Commentary of the Old Testament; Grand Rapids: Eerdmans, 1976), 257.

2. According to Allen (*Joel, Obadiah, Jonah, and Micah,* 257–60), Micah 1 is parallel with Micah 6: both begin with the summons "hear" (1:2; 6:1), both oracles are the first in a series of warnings, and both are followed by short oracles of promise (2:12–13; 7:8–20). With Micah 1–2 and 6–7, therefore, forming the first and last divisions of the book, Micah 3 (also introduced by "hear") begins the central division of the book. This central portion of Micah (chaps. 3–5) was previously analyzed in detail by three other scholars: Eduard Nielsen, *Oral Tradition: A Modern Problem in the Old Testament Introduction* (Studies in Biblical Theology 11; London: SCM, 1954), 79–93; Bernard Renaud, *Structure et Attaches Littéraires de Michée iv–v* (Paris: Gabalda, 1964); and J. T. Willis, *The Structure, Setting and Interrelationships of the Pericopes in the Book of Micah* (Ph.D. diss., Vanderbilt Divinity School, 1966). Nielsen discovers a five-part chiasmus in Micah 4–5: (a) promises of purified worship and peace (4:1–4); (b) promises to the remnant (4:6–8); (c) nucleus (4:9–5:6); (b') promises to the remnant (5:7–9); (a') removal of armaments and objects of Canaanite worship (5:10–15). Nielsen further divides the nucleus into two portions: a negative subunit dealing with the distress of Jerusalem (4:9–5:1) and a positive subunit dealing with the birth of a Davidic king and deliverance from Assyria (5:2–6). Renaud suggests a scheme

Careful analysis of the book's layout reveals a seven-part symmetric arrangement (32.1) that is artful and at the same time highlights Micah's central themes, particularly (1) Israel's social sins, (2) the moral failure of its leadership, and (3) the ultimate establishment of Yahweh's own benevolent kingship over the land.

First Three Units (Micah 1–3)

The book opens with a frightening message about the approaching destruction of both Israel and Judah (chap. 1). This introductory message is an excellent attention-getter, designed with a clever and effective layout. It opens with an alarming vision of Yahweh's terrifying approach, followed by a review of the cities that will experience Yahweh's punishment, moving (as does Amos in his introductory unit) from the audience's more distant neighbor (Samaria) to a closer neighbor (Jerusalem) to the audience's own territory (the towns of the southern Shephelah). The message appears to comprise seven units (32.2).

Micah 2:1 introduces a new unit, whose beginning is marked by the common beginning marker *hôy* ("woe"), as in Isaiah, Ezekiel, and other prophetic books. The focus now shifts. Whereas chapter 1 announced the approaching

---

that corresponds almost exactly to that of Nielsen's; his only significant modifications are slight adjustments to Nielsen's verse groupings (4:8–5:1; 5:7–8) and breaking Nielsen's nucleus into two separate units, thereby creating a six-part chiasmus. Willis, on the other hand, analyzes 3:9–5:15 as a group of seven units that are neither sequential nor chiastic but parallel to one another. Each consists of two parts: a depiction of the present hopeless situation and a promise of deliverance or vindication (3:9–4:5; 4:6–8; 4:9–10; 4:11–13; 5:1–6; 5:7–9; 5:10–15). With minor modifications, Allen follows Willis's analysis. He sees Willis's seven units as forming a modified chiasmus, with the three central units (4:9–10; 4:11–13; 5:1–6 [4:14–5:5]) in a parallel rather than chiastic relationship. The entire Book of Micah, therefore, falls into three parts according to Allen and forms an a-b-a' chiasmus, with the central unit itself comprising seven parts arranged in a modified chiasmus: 1:1–2:13; 3:1–5:15 [3:1–5:14]; 6:1–7:20.

32.1 The Book of Micah

a **coming defeat and destruction** (1:1–16)

   b **corruption of the people** (2:1–13)

      c **corruption of leaders** (3:1–12)

         d **CENTER: glorious future restoration** under Yahweh's own strong and righteous rule (4:1–5:15 [4:1–5:14])

      c′ **corruption of leaders**; Yahweh's provision of good leaders in past and Yahweh's requirements as Israel's divine ruler (6:1–16)

   b′ **corruption of the people**; don't trust anyone except Yahweh (7:1–7)

a′ **future reversal of defeat and destruction** (7:8–20)

32.2 Coming defeat and destruction (Micah 1)

part 1: introduction (1:2–5)

   a **Yahweh's terrifying and destructive approach** (1:2–4)

   b **reason for Yahweh's coming action**: Israel's sin (1:5)

part 2: cities that will experience disaster (1:6–15)

   c **coming disaster in Samaria** (1:6–7)

      • distant neighbor

   d **coming disaster in Jerusalem** (1:8–9)

      • close neighbor

   e **coming disaster in six towns in Micah's own region** (1:10–12)

      • closer neighbor

   f **coming disaster in five other towns in Micah's own region**—including Micah's own town! (1:13–15)

      • closest neighbor

part 3: conclusion (1:16)

   g **call to mourning** (1:16)

32.3 Corruption of the leaders (Micah 3)

group 1: civil leaders (3:1–4)

   a **condemnation** of the <u>heads of Jacob</u> and <u>rulers of the house of Israel</u> (3:1–3)

      • seven verbs depicting their sins

      • begins: <u>hear now</u> (*šimʿû-nāʾ*) + vocatives

   b **coming punishment** of these rulers (3:4)

group 2: prophets (3:5–8)

      c **condemnation of false prophets** (3:5)

         d **CENTER: coming punishment of false prophets**: seven punishments (3:6–7)

      c′ **in contrast to false prophets**, Micah is a true prophet (3:8)

group 3: civil leaders (3:9–12)

   a′ **condemnation** of the <u>heads of the house of Jacob</u> and the <u>rulers of the house of Israel</u> (3:9–11)

      • seven verbs depicting their sins

      • begins: <u>hear now</u> (*šimʿû-nāʾ*) + vocatives

   b′ **coming punishment** because of these rulers (3:12)

---

destruction, chapter 2 primarily deals with the reason for the destruction—the people's sins. The first chapter was a warning; the second chapter is an indictment. Several interpretive and textual uncertainties make structural analysis of the internal organization of this unit difficult.[3]

Micah 3:1 introduces the next major unit with "then I said, 'Listen, you leaders of Jacob.' " Introductory *šimʿû* ("hear") + vocative commonly marks new messages throughout the prophets. The focus now shifts from the corruption of the people to the corruption of the leadership. The internal arrangement of chapter 3 follows a symmetric scheme: it begins with seven verbs

---

3. For example, is 2:12–13 a message of warning or hope? The former is more likely.

---

condemning the sins of "the heads/rulers of the house of Jacob/Israel," which is followed by a short prediction of coming punishment, and ends with seven more verbs again condemning the sins of "the heads/rulers of the house of Jacob/Israel," which is again followed by a short prediction of coming punishment. In the middle are three paragraphs focusing on the prophets, the central one of these listing seven punishments to be experienced by the false prophets. The entire unit, therefore, comprises either a three or a seven-part symmetry (32.3).

Central Unit (Micah 4–5)

The central unit in the Book of Micah introduces a new topic: God's future good plans for

32.4 Message of hope (Micah 4–5)

a **establishment of Yahweh's reign over all the <u>nations</u> (gôyim)** (4:1–5)
  - all <u>war machinery</u> will be converted to peacetime instruments
  - nations will come to Jerusalem to learn the ways of Yahweh
  - begins: <u>and it shall be</u> (wĕhāyâ) + <u>in the latter days</u>

  b **good news for the exiles, the <u>remnant</u> (šĕʾērît)** (4:6–7)
    - Yahweh will make them into a strong <u>nation</u> (gôy) over which he himself will rule

    c **<u>rulership</u> (memšālâ) <u>from an earlier time will come to Migdal-eder (by Bethlehem)</u>** (4:8–10)
      - the region's present suffering is likened to that of a <u>woman in labor</u> (yôlēdâ)
      - begins: <u>and you</u> (wĕʾattâ) + vocative of place-name

      d **TURNING POINT: Israel's present hopeless situation will be reversed by Yahweh** (4:11–5:1 [4:11–14])
        - begins: <u>and now</u> (wĕʾattâ)

    c' **a <u>ruler</u> (mōšēl) <u>from an earlier time will come to Bethlehem</u>** (5:2–5a [5:1–4a])
      - the region's present suffering is likened to that of <u>woman in labor</u> (yôlēdâ)
      - begins: <u>and you</u> (wĕʾattâ) + vocative of place-name

  b' **good news for the <u>remnant</u> (šĕʾērît)** (5:5b–9 [5:4b–8])
    - Yahweh will enable them to be victorious over all the <u>nations</u> (gôyim) in which they now live

a' **establishment of Yahweh's transforming control over the <u>nations</u> (gôyim)** (5:10–15 [5:9–14])
  - <u>war machinery</u> will be destroyed
  - false religion and idolatry will end
  - begins: <u>and it shall be</u> (wĕhāyâ) + <u>in the latter days</u>

32.5 God's case against Israel (Micah 6)

a **introduction** of Yahweh's case against Israel (6:1–2)
  b **Yahweh's past acts of kindness** to Israel (6:3–5)
    c **Israel's (or an Israelite's) questions** about how to secure Yahweh's <u>forgiveness</u> for sins (6:6–7)
      d **CENTER: Yahweh's central requirements** (6:8)
    c' **Yahweh's questions** about whether he can <u>forgive</u> Israel's sins (6:9–11)
  b' **Yahweh's future acts of judgment** against Israel (6:12–15)
a' **conclusion:** summary of accusation and punishment (6:16)

Israel under the leadership of Yahweh and his own rulers.[4] The message of this unit is tied together not only by the common theme of hope and future restoration but also by its internal structure, comprising seven symmetrically arranged stanzas (32.4).

The message begins and ends with a majestic prediction that Yahweh will establish his rule over all the "nations" (gôyim) (4:2; 5:15 [5:14]). This will involve the conversion/destruction of all war machinery and the end of idolatry and false religion. Both predictions are introduced by "and it shall be" (wĕhāyâ) + "in the latter days/that day" (4:1; 5:10 [5:9]).

The unit's second stanza (b), introduced by "in that day," shifts to good news for the "remnant" (šĕʾērît), whom Yahweh will make into a strong "nation" (gôy). This is echoed in the next-to-last stanza (b'), which likewise declares good news for the "remnant" (šĕʾērît), whom Yahweh will

enable to be victorious over all the "nations" (gôyim) in which they now find themselves.

The third stanza (c) is introduced by the vocative "and you (wĕʾattâ), Migdal-eder [a town near Bethlehem; cf. Gen. 35:21]." The prophet predicts that "rulership" (memšālâ) from earlier times will come to Migdal-eder. This prophecy is matched by the third-to-last stanza (c'), which likewise begins with a vocative ("and you [wĕʾattâ], Bethlehem") and in which the prophet predicts that "one who will rule" (mōšēl), "whose goings forth are from earlier times," will come from Bethlehem. In both stanzas, Israel's present suffering is likened to a woman in "labor" (yôlēdâ).

The central stanza (d), introduced by "and now" (wĕʾattâ), announces that Yahweh is going to reverse the present hopeless situation.

Final Three Units (Micah 6–7)

The fifth unit of Micah is introduced by "hear now" (šimʿû-nāʾ; 6:1), the same expression that introduced the third unit (3:1). The theme of this new unit is God's "case" (rîb) against Israel. The end of the unit is probably 6:16, since 7:1 appears

---

4. The only possible interruption of the good news of this section is the prediction of coming destruction upon military installations and idolatry in 5:10–15 [5:9–14]; and this most likely should be understood as directed to the nations (matching the first unit in 4:1–5), not Israel, and therefore represents yet more good news.

32.6 Message of hope (Micah 7:8–20)

a **I will bear God's anger,** for I have <u>sinned</u> against him; but he will restore me (7:8–9)

  b **my enemies will <u>see</u> (*rā'â*),** and <u>shame</u> (*bûšâ*) will cover them (7:10)

    c **promise of restoration:** boundaries to Egypt and Assyria; "they will come to you from <u>Egypt</u>" (7:11–13)

      d **CENTER: prayer to Yahweh** to shepherd his people as in the days of old! (7:14)

    c' **promise of restoration:** God will do great things, "as in the days when you came out of the land of <u>Egypt</u>" (7:15)

  b' **the nations shall <u>see</u> (*rā'â*)** and be <u>ashamed</u> (*bôš*) (7:16–17)

a' **God does not stay angry forever;** he will forgive our <u>sins</u> (7:18–20)

32.7 The Book of Micah

a **coming defeat and destruction** (1:1–16)

  • theme: <u>sin</u> (*peša'* and *ḥaṭṭā't*), of which Israel is guilty

  • the people are <u>going into exile</u>

  • God will destroy the <u>walls</u> of Samaria, down to the foundations

b **corruption of the people** (2:1–13)

  • begins: <u>woe</u> (*hôy*)

  • <u>social evils</u> and greed

c **corruption of leaders** (3:1–12)

  • begins: <u>hear now</u> (*šim'û-nā'*)

  • corruption of <u>rulers</u>, prophets, and priests

  • condemnation of <u>dishonesty</u> and <u>social injustice</u>

  • prophets prophesying for pay (3:5, 11)

  • they abhor <u>justice</u> (*mišpaṭ*) and <u>love</u> (*'āhab*) evil (3:1–2, 8–9)

  • topics: <u>eating</u> (*'ākal*) and <u>mouth</u> (*peh*)

    d **CENTER: glorious future restoration** under Yahweh's own strong and righteous rule (4:1–5:15 [4:1–5:14])

c' **corruption of leaders;** Yahweh's provision of good leaders in past and Yahweh's requirements as Israel's divine ruler (6:1–16)

  • begins: <u>hear now</u> (*šim'û-nā'*)

  • topics: past good <u>rulers</u> and priest (Moses, Aaron, Miriam) Yahweh gave Israel, and corruption of present leaders

  • condemnation of <u>dishonesty</u> and <u>social injustice</u>

  • prophet Balaam (hired to prophesy for pay)

  • do <u>justice</u> (*mišpaṭ*); <u>love</u> (*'āhab*) kindness

  • topics: <u>eating</u> (*'ākal*) and <u>mouth</u> (*peh*)

b' **corruption of the people;** don't trust anyone except Yahweh (7:1–7)

  • begins: <u>woe</u> (*'alĕlay*)

  • <u>social evils</u> and greed

a' **future reversal of defeat and destruction** (7:8–20)

  • theme: <u>sin</u> (*peša'* and *ḥaṭṭā't*), which God will forgive

  • the people will <u>return from exile</u>

  • future rebuilding of <u>walls</u>

to initiate a new unit, marked by the sudden shift to the lament genre: "woe is me!" (cf. the beginning of the book's second unit in 2:1). This unit has seven parts, arranged with a symmetric touch. Its highlighted center declares Yahweh's foremost requirements of his people (32.5).

The sixth unit, its beginning marked by the introductory exclamation, "woe!" (7:1), decries the pervasiveness of evil that filled the land of Israel. The unit is bracketed by the first-person statements in 7:1 and 7:7.

The final unit of Micah is the message of hope in 7:8–20. Its beginning is heralded by the shift in mood from condemnation to joyous anticipation of future restoration. The entire unit is upbeat, and it comprises seven symmetrically arranged parts, with the center, fittingly, being a prayer to Yahweh for leadership and restoration (32.6).

Overall Layout of the Book of Micah

The seven major literary units in the Book of Micah exhibit a symmetric arrangement (32.7). The introductory message of destruction and punishment is balanced by the concluding message of rebuilding and forgiveness. The indictment of people in the second unit is echoed by the similar indictment of the people in the next-to-last unit. The condemnation of the leaders, priests, and prophets for their deceit and social injustice in the third unit is matched by the condemnation of the leaders and the rich for their deceit and social injustice in the third-to-last unit. The central unit of Micah's seven-part symmetry is his majestic message of hope.

Conclusion

What can we learn from structural analysis of the Book of Micah? First, the matching repetition of the units decrying Israel's corrupt leadership and the corruption of Israelite society indicates the importance of these two themes to the author. The placement of the messages of future restoration in the book's two positions of prominence, the central and final slots, suggests that Micah saw these messages as important motivational keys for his audience. That the book concludes with a message of wonderful hope indicates that the book is designed to encourage, not dishearten.

The last three parts of Micah not only correspond to the first three, but also offer practical help in view of the dilemmas posed by the first three units. For example, the book's first unit depicts the upcoming devastation of the country because of Israel's sins, and the last unit offers prayers to Yahweh to forgive Israel's sins and to restore it (7:19–20 is a prayer rather than a prediction). Likewise, the second unit decries the corruption of society, and the next-to-last unit advises the reader not to trust anyone in society, but rather trust Yahweh. The third unit exposes the corruption of the leadership; in response, the third-to-last unit invites the people to reconsider Yahweh's leadership. Unlike Israel's greedy and corrupt human leaders, Yahweh has selflessly served them throughout their history, in love and justice. He has not exploited them. And his requirements are not demanding. He asks only three things of his people:

To act justly, to love kindness,
and to walk humbly with your God.

—Micah 6:8

33

Nahum

Where Now Is the Lion's Den?

The Book of Nahum addresses the issue of divine justice. How could Yahweh permit the Assyrians, that cruel and wicked people, to crush the peoples around them, including Israel, and then go on prospering, unpunished? Scholars generally agree that the Book of Nahum comprises six to eight separate literary units.[1] The book appears to be a sevenfold, chiastically arranged work (33.1).

Individual Units in the Book of Nahum

The Book of Nahum's first literary unit is an attention-getting acrostic poem arranged according to the first half of the Hebrew alphabet,

from *ʾālep* (א) to *kap* (כ), and describing the terrifying power and anger of Yahweh. The poem's introduction (a) and conclusion (a′) speak of Yahweh's "vengeance" (*nqm*; cf. BHS) upon "his enemies" (*ʾōyĕbāyw*) and "his adversaries" (*ṣārāyw*; cf. BHS). The second and next-to-last subunits counterbalance this terrifying image with positive statements about Yahweh's patience (b) and goodness (b′) to those who trust him. The three central subunits (c, d, c′) return to the frightening image of Yahweh's vengeance, creating an overall symmetry (33.2).

The book's second unit is a message of reassurance to Judah, whom Yahweh will rescue from Assyria. The shift to second-person feminine singular (1:11, 12, 13, 15 [2:1]; 1:14 is exceptional here) marks the beginning of the new unit here. The unit deals with the coming reversal of the fates of Israel and Assyria. Any analysis of the unit's internal configuration, however, must remain tentative due to its difficult textual and interpretive problems. It possibly unfolds as a typical seven-part symmetry (33.3).

Nahum's third major unit (2:1–10 [2:2–11]) opens with an abrupt shift in mood, from a measured prediction of Yahweh's reversal of the fates of Judah and Assyria to a series of frantic imperatives calling for the defense of Assyria. It begins with exhortations to strengthen(?) "faces" (*pānayim*) and "loins" (*mātĕnayim*); using the same terminology, it closes with references to the paling of faces and the trembling of loins. The unit features a vivid description of the fall of Nineveh. The prophet describes, in the literary form of an eyewitness account, scenes of the enemy's breaking into the city, the desperate, futile attempts to defend the city, and plundering. The style is lively. Its staccato bursts and rapid-fire shifts in scene serve to convey the sense of the terrifying rapidity of events as Nineveh falls.

The central unit of the book functions as a quiet interlude. The frantic pace of the previ-

---

1. Otto Eissfeldt (*The Old Testament: An Introduction*, trans. Peter R. Ackroyd [New York: Harper & Row, 1965], 414), for example, analyzes the Book of Nahum in six literary units: (a) alphabetic psalm, a hymn on the epiphany of Yahweh, which can be traced as far as 1:9 (1:2–9); (b) promise to Judah and threat against the enemy (alternating themes in an apparently disordered section) (1:10–2:2 [1:10–2:3]); (c) threat against Nineveh (2:3–13 [2:4–14]); (d) vivid description of the capture of Nineveh, introduced by "woe" (3:1–7); (e) fate of Thebes, cruelly destroyed by the Assyrians, will be repeated at Nineveh (3:8–17); (f) final dirge over Nineveh—following the Septuagint and taking the last word from 3:17, "woe" (3:18–19). Ernst Sellin and Georg Fohrer's analysis (*Introduction to the Old Testament* [Nashville: Abingdon, 1968], 449–50) is identical. Brevard Childs (*Introduction to the Old Testament as Scripture* [Philadelphia: Fortress, 1979], 441–45) also follows this analysis, his only minor adjustment being to stop the first unit at 1:8. Robert H. Pfeiffer (*Introduction to the Old Testament* [New York: Harper, 1948], 594–96), on the other hand, traces the first unit through 1:10 and subdivides 2:1–3:19 [2:2–3:19] somewhat differently: 2:1–5 [2:2–6]; 2:6–10 [2:7–11]; 2:11–13 [2:12–14]; 3:1–3; 3:4–6; 3:8–17. Most recently, R. L. Smith (*Micah–Malachi* [Word Biblical Commentary 32; Waco: Word, 1984], 68–69.) offers an analysis following Eissfeldt, with two modifications: (1) the taunt song against Nineveh in 2:11–13 [2:12–14] should be identified as a separate unit (as does Pfeiffer); and (2) Eissfeldt's unit 3:8–17 actually comprises two units: 3:8–13 (the analogy of Thebes) and 3:14–17 (satirical warnings for Nineveh). This gives Smith a total of eight units, counting the brief final dirge in 3:18–19. Careful attention to the wording of Nahum suggests that the analyses by Eissfeldt, Sellin and Fohrer, and Smith are essentially correct. Smith's two modifications are necessary, plus one more: the brief dirge in 3:18–19 should be included as part of the final unit: 3:13–19.

33.1 The Book of Nahum

  a **Yahweh, like a terrible force of nature, avenges his enemies** but is good to those who trust him (1:2–10)
    b **Yahweh will destroy Nineveh** but restore Judah (1:11–15 [1:11–2:1])
      c **vivid description of the attack upon Nineveh** (2:1–10 [2:2–11])
        d **CENTER: lament over fall of Nineveh,** the lions' den (2:11–13 [2:12–14])
      c′ **vivid description of the looting of Nineveh** (3:1–7)
    b′ **Nineveh will be destroyed:** it is vulnerable, like Thebes (3:8–13)
  a′ **Nineveh, likened to a destructive force of nature, will be destroyed** (3:14–19)

33.2 Yahweh's vengeance (Nahum 1:2–10)

  a **Yahweh's <u>vengeance</u> (*nqm*)** upon his <u>enemies</u> (*ʾōyĕbāyw*) and <u>adversaries</u> (*ṣārāyw*) (1:2)
    b **tempering quality:** Yahweh's patience (1:3a)
      c **scorching effects of Yahweh's arrival:** waterways dry up and vegetation withers (1:3b–4)
        d **CENTER: whole earth quakes at Yahweh's arrival** (1:5)
      c′ **scorching effects of Yahweh's arrival:** "like fire" (1:6)
    b′ **tempering quality:** Yahweh's goodness to those who trust him (1:7–8a)
  a′ **Yahweh's <u>vengeance</u> (*nqm*,** cf. BHS) upon his <u>enemies</u> (*ʾōyĕbāyw*) and <u>adversaries</u> (*ṣārāyw*, cf. BHS) (1:8b–10)

33.3 Reversal of fates (Nahum 1:11–15 [1:11–2:1])

  a <u>**wicked**</u> **(*bĕlîyyāʿal*) Assyria plots evil** against Yahweh (1:11)
    b **Assyria will perish,** despite its <u>allies</u>(?) (*šlm*; 1:12a)
      c **Judah will <u>no longer</u> (*lōʾ . . . ʿôd*) be afflicted** by Yahweh (1:12b)
        d **CENTER: Yahweh will free Judah from Assyria** (1:13)
      c′ **Assyria will <u>no longer</u> (*lōʾ . . . ʿôd*) prosper;** its end (1:14)
    b′ **Judah will be restored;** once again it will <u>pay</u> (*šlm*) vows (1:15a–b [2:1a–b])
  a′ <u>**wicked**</u> **(*bĕlîyyaʿal*) Assyria will invade Judah no more** (1:15c [2:1c])

33.4 The lions' den (Nahum 2:11–13 [2:12–14])

  part 1: description of the lions' den (2:11–12 [2:12–13])
    a **where is the lions' den?** (2:11a [2:12a])
    b **there the lion brought its prey** for its cubs (2:11b [2:12b])
    c **the lion captured and killed prey** for his cubs and lionesses (2:12a [2:13a])
    d **he filled his den with prey** (2:12b [2:13b])
  part 2: judgment upon the lions' den (2:13 [2:14])
    e **"behold, I am against you,"** declares Yahweh of hosts (2:13a [2:14a])
    f **your lair(?) and young lions will be destroyed** (2:13b [2:14b])
    g **your prey will be cut off;** the sound of your goings forth(?) will no longer be heard (2:13c [2:14c])

ous unit now gives way to a relaxed, almost wistful tone. The unit is introduced by *ʾayyēh* ("where?"), a word often used to introduce a lament. This unit is a dirge over the fall of Nineveh. The city is likened to a lion's den, and the motif of a lion and its young persists throughout these verses, tying them together into a literary unit. The unit comprises seven poetic lines (cf. BHS), the first four maintaining the metaphor of the lions' den. Whereas the last three shift to more literal terms, the metaphor of the lion is still retained ("your young lions," "your prey"), but now there are references to the literal realities: "your chariots" and "your messengers."[2] The last three lines, introduced by *hinnēh* ("behold"), also represent a shift

from description to verdict and judgment and create a 4+3 structure reminiscent of the Hebrew *qinah* (dirge) pattern (33.4).

Nahum's fifth unit is identified by most commentators as a separate literary unit. It is introduced by the common beginning marker, *hôy* ("woe"). In this unit the prophet returns to his vivid ("eyewitness") description of the fall of Nineveh, echoing the similarly graphic depiction of the city's fall in the book's third unit. There is, however, now a slightly different perspective: the city has fallen, and while the enemy chariots still rush about in the city's streets, there is no resistance, no fighting. The depiction of the slain and the corpses of Ninevites indicates that the battle is over and that the rushing about is now for booty.

The internal structure of the fifth unit is similar to that of the previous one: seven parts, ar-

---

2. On the other hand, these latter two words are textually uncertain, and readings continuing the lion metaphor ("your lair," "your young lions/goings forth," etc.) are quite possible.

33.5 Fall of Nineveh (Nahum 3:1–7)

part 1: the fallen city of Nineveh (3:1–4)
  a **woe to the city** once full of bloodshed and victims; four phrases (3:1)
  b **inside the fallen city**: enemies and chariots everywhere! seven phrases (3:2–3c)
  c **the city is full of casualties and corpses**; four phrases (3:3d–g)
  d **reason for fall**: Nineveh's spiritual harlotry (3:4)
part 2: Yahweh's judgment against Nineveh (3:5–7)
  e **Yahweh is against Nineveh**; he will shame it before the nations (3:5)
  f **he will humiliate her** and make it a spectacle (3:6)
  g **Nineveh will be in ruins**, with no one to mourn for it (3:7)

33.6 Nineveh's vulnerability (Nahum 3:8–13)

part 1: Thebes, though strong, fell (3:8–10)
  a **Thebes's fortifications also included a river** (3:8)
  b **Thebes also had strong allies** (3:9)
  c **yet Thebes fell and went into exile** (3:10a)
  d **the people of Thebes were killed** or became slaves (3:10b–c)
part 2: Nineveh, like Thebes, will fall (3:11–13)
  e **Nineveh also will go into exile** (3:11)
  f **Nineveh's fortresses will fall** (3:12)
  g **Nineveh's cities will be broken into** (3:13)

33.7 The fall of Nineveh (Nahum 3:14–19)

part 1: end of Nineveh (feminine): the locust plague of the earth (3:14–17)
  a **introduction**: desperate siege preparations preceding Nineveh's fall (3:14)
  b **your city will be devoured** by fire and the sword, like locusts (3:15)
  c **your merchants have multiplied**; but they will disappear, like locusts (3:16)
  d **your princes(?) and marshals(?) have multiplied like locusts**; but they will disappear, like locusts (3:17)
part 2: end of Nineveh (masculine) (3:18–19)
  e **your people are scattered**, with no one to gather them (3:18)
  f **your wound is fatal**, with no one to heal it (3:19a)
  g **no one will mourn over you** when people hear of your fall (3:19b–c)

ranged in a 4+3 pattern (again, suggesting a dirge), with the fifth part marking the shift in the unit (33.5). In fact, this fifth part is introduced in precisely the same words as the fifth part of the previous unit: "Behold (*hinnēh*) I am against you, declares Yahweh of hosts" (3:5). The unit is bracketed by references to lamenting over the fallen city (3:1 begins with "woe," and 3:7 asks "who will mourn her?").

The sixth unit of the book should be identified as 3:8–13. Nahum 3:14, with its sudden, staccato imperatives calling for the defense of Nineveh, must be taken as the beginning of the seventh unit. Moreover, the resultant two units, 3:8–13 and 3:14–19, are not only balanced in length, but each also exhibits its own internal unity. The theme of the sixth unit is Nineveh's vulnerability. Nineveh is likened to Thebes, a seemingly invincible fortified city by a body of water, which fell to the Assyrians. Now it is Nineveh's turn: Nineveh is like a ripe fig ready to be shaken from the tree to be eaten; its troops and fortifications are weak and vulnerable.

Like the previous two units, the sixth unit comprises seven parts (each comprising two po-

etic verses) structured in a 4+3 scheme—again, reminiscent of the Hebrew dirge rhythm. The first four parts recall the fall of Thebes and the last three parts assert that Nineveh's fate will be like that of Thebes (33.6).

The final unit describes the fall of Nineveh. Its beginning is marked by the shift in 3:14 to a rapid-fire series of frantic orders given (in vivid prophetic imaging) as the city of Nineveh is about to fall: "Draw water for the siege, strengthen your forts, go into the clay, tread the mortar."

The unit comprises seven parts and, like the previous three units of Nahum, is structured in a 4+3 pattern that reflects the rhythm of a Hebrew eulogy (33.7). The first four parts address Nineveh in the second-person feminine singular: her fall is likened to the devastation of a locust plague; then she herself is likened to a locust plague, which disappears with the coming of winter. In 3:18–19 a shift in the gender to the second-person masculine singular signals that the city (or its king) is now addressed. The locust plague metaphor is dropped, but the theme of Nineveh's demise continues.

33.8 The Book of Nahum

a **Yahweh, like a terrible force of nature, avenges his enemies** but is good to those who trust him (1:2–10)
  - his anger is poured out like <u>fire</u> (*ʾēš*) (1:6)
  - <u>mountains</u> (*hārîm*) quake before him (1:5)
  - he pursues his enemies into(?) darkness (1:8)
  - he makes an end of his enemies' <u>place</u> (*māqôm*) (1:9)

b **Yahweh will destroy Nineveh** but restore Judah (1:11–15 [1:11–2:1])
  - <u>Assyrians will become drunk</u> (1:10)
  - they will be <u>consumed</u> (*ʾākal*) like dry chaff (1:10)
  - Yahweh will <u>break Assyria's bonds</u> that bind Judah (1:13)

c **vivid description of the attack upon Nineveh** (2:1–10 [2:2–11])
  - staccato, as if a live <u>eyewitness account</u>
  - wounded, <u>dying soldiers</u> (2:3a [2:4a])
  - <u>chariots</u> rushing back and forth (2:3b–4 [2:4b–5])
  - they are like <u>lightning</u> (*bārāq*) (2:4 [2:5])
  - the city's defenders <u>stumble</u> (*kāšal*) as they race to the walls (2:5 [2:6])

d **CENTER: lament over fall of Nineveh**, the lions' den (2:11–13 [2:12–14])

c′ **vivid description of the looting of Nineveh** (3:1–7)
  - staccato, as if a live <u>eyewitness account</u>
  - <u>dead soldiers</u>, corpses, everywhere (3:3)
  - <u>chariots</u> rushing about (3:2–3)
  - spears flashing like <u>lightning</u> (*bārāq*) (3:3)
  - enemies <u>stumble</u> (*kāšal*) over corpses (3:3)

b′ **Nineveh will be destroyed**: it is vulnerable, like Thebes (3:8–13)
  - <u>Assyrians will become drunk</u> (3:11)
  - their fortresses are ready to be <u>eaten</u> (*ʾākal*) (3:12); fire has <u>consumed</u> (*ʾākal*) the bars of their gates (3:13)
  - Assyria's dignitaries will be <u>bound</u> in chains (3:10)

a′ **Nineveh, likened to a destructive force of nature, will be destroyed** (3:14–19)
  - they will be consumed with <u>fire</u> (*ʾēš*) (3:15; cf. 3:13)
  - Assyria's people will be scattered upon the <u>mountains</u> (*hārîm*) (3:18)
  - Assyria's <u>place</u> (*māqôm*) will not even be known (3:17)
  - the locust plague is dispersed by the rising of the sun (3:17)

Overall Structure

It is striking that the 4+3 pattern is used in each of the final four units of the Book of Nahum. Its employment in these units may serve to reflect on a larger level the rhythm of the Hebrew dirge (*qinah*) pattern. Certainly each of the four units featuring this 4+3 pattern depicts the fall of Nineveh and the demise of the Assyrian empire. It is true that the first three units also touch upon Nineveh's fall; but the tone in these earlier units is aggressive and bold, expressing prophetic anger rather than mourning. The tone of the final units, on the other hand, is somber, almost wistful, creating a mood representative of a dirge.

The book's seven units may possibly exhibit a symmetric touch. The center of the book, the lament over the lions' den, functions appropriately as the midpoint of a symmetric arrangement and serves as a somber interlude. Immediately before and after this central dirge are units characterized by vivid, graphic, rapid-fire depictions of Nineveh's fall, as if coming "live" (to borrow a modern communications term) from an eyewitness. These two units clearly correspond to one another.

The remaining four units (a and a′, b and b′), while not strongly linked, do exhibit some minor correspondences. In light of the clearly symmetric arrangement of the central three units, it is possible that the author intended the entire book to form a symmetry (33.8).

Conclusion

The foregoing analysis reveals several interesting insights about the Book of Nahum. The use of a 4+3 pattern (echoing the cadence a Hebrew dirge) in the book's final four units reinforces the sense of a eulogy over Nineveh's demise in these final units. The shift to this pattern in the second half of the book may reflect the subtle shift in perspective at this point, from viewing Nineveh as if it will surely fall (in the first three units) to viewing it as already fallen. This progression underscores the certainty of Nineveh's fall: Yahweh's prophet not only believes that it will happen; he composes dirges as though it has already happened. The placement of the eulogy over the "lions' den" in the book's highlighted central position reinforces this sense of certainty.

The two matching units featuring eyewitness-like accounts of the frantic final moments of

Nineveh's fall also convey the certainty of its fall. The prophet is not just idly speculating that the city may fall. He provides the audience with vivid descriptions of the actual fall, as he has already seen it through prophetic vision. Moreover, these vivid descriptions are rhetorically powerful, functioning to hold the audience spellbound by their intensity.

Introducing the book with the awesome vision of Yahweh's avenging arrival is equally riveting. This opening vision is an effective attention-getting device, and it also introduces the issue of the cause of Nineveh's fall, to which Nahum will subsequently return. Nineveh is going to fall because Israel's God, Yahweh, has declared it to be guilty, and he has arrived in his terrifying might to carry out its punishment. Yahweh controls the destinies of all nations; he holds all nations accountable for their actions; and he will ultimately right all wrongs. The people of Israel, who had been crushed by the mighty forces of wicked Assyria, needed to know these truths.

34
Habakkuk

The Just Shall Live by Faith

The Book of Habakkuk is another book that deals with the issue of God's justice. The prophet Habakkuk was probably a contemporary of Jeremiah; and the focus of his book is his own struggle to understand God's justice in dealing with Judah and the Babylonians in his day. The structure of the book is instructive. Habakkuk has taken quite varied material—including a dialogue with God, a woe-oracle, and a psalm—and has organized it into an artistic and effective presentation.[1] The book is generally analyzed as comprising six units:[2]

---

a Habakkuk's first complaint about Yahweh's justice (1:2–4)
b Yahweh's response to Habakkuk's first complaint (1:5–11)
c Habakkuk's second complaint about Yahweh's justice (1:12–17)
d Yahweh's response to Habakkuk's second complaint (2:1–5)
e five woes (2:6–20)
f Habakkuk's psalm (3:1–19)

The possibility of an overall symmetric configuration is enhanced by the position of Habakkuk 2:1–5 (which seems to function as the

1. For an early study on the structure of Habakkuk, see H. H. Walker and N. W. Lund, "The Literary Structure of the Book of Habakkuk," *Journal of Biblical Literature* 54 (1934) 355–70.

2. Robert H. Pfeiffer, *Introduction to the Old Testament* (New York: Harper, 1948), 597–98; Ernst Sellin and Georg Fohrer, *Introduction to the Old Testament* (Nashville: Abingdon, 1968), 453; R. L. Smith, *Micah–Malachi* (Word Biblical Commentary 32; Waco: Word, 1984), 97; cf. Brevard S. Childs, *Introduction to the Old Testament as Scripture* (Philadelphia: Fortress, 1979), 448–54. S. R. Driver, *An Introduction to the Literature of the Old Testament* (9th ed.; Edinburgh: Clark, 1913), 337–38, on the other hand, suggests that the five woes (2:6–20) are part of the unit that begins in 2:1 and comprises Yahweh's response, giving the book only five units. It is also possible to see the book as comprising five parts (with chap. 2 forming a single unit—Yahweh's response to Habakkuk's second complaint), creating a logically progressing linear pattern: (1) the four-part dialogue between Habakkuk and Yahweh, in which Yahweh satisfactorily answers Habakkuk's series of questions about divine justice, and (2) Habakkuk's joyful concluding psalm, expressing the resolution of his concerns. With differing genre, 2:1–5 appears to form a separate unit from the woe-oracles in 2:6–20.

book's climax) at about the midpoint of the book.[3] The problem is that three well-defined units precede 2:1–5 but only two clearly defined units follow it (the section of woe-oracles in 2:6–20 and the psalm of chap. 3).

Could it be that Habakkuk's psalm is intended to form two of the book's parts instead of just one? The psalm does fall into two parts: the theophany (3:3–15) and Habakkuk's concluding response of faith (3:16–19). Certainly the entire psalm forms a single larger unit, since the title (3:1) and the concluding liturgical notation (3:19c) bracket the whole psalm and mark it off as a self-contained unit. On the other hand, listeners would certainly perceive the psalm's personal conclusion in 3:16–19—Habakkuk's autobiographical response and resolution of faith—as separate from the grand vision of Yahweh's arrival for battle in 3:3–15. Moreover, some of the book's other constituent units are themselves also parts of even larger units. For example, the three separate, unintroduced speeches in chapter 1 are parts of the larger dialogue of chapter 1. The collection of woe-oracles in chapter 2 is an unintroduced second part of Yahweh's larger response to Habakkuk in chapter 2 (with the only introduction to the material of this chapter being 2:2). So 3:16–19 might serve two distinct structural roles; namely, the conclusion of Habakkuk's psalm and the seventh part of the entire book.

What makes this possibility particularly appealing is that the seven resulting parts of Habakkuk would form a fairly conspicuous symmetry.

Correspondence of Habakkuk's Opening Complaint (Habakkuk 1:2–4) and His Final Resolution (Habakkuk 3:16–19)

Habakkuk's opening complaint in 1:2–4 is ech-

3. Habakkuk 2:5 is so textually difficult (as is 2:6) that any decision as to its function in the book's structure must remain tentative.

oed in several ways by his personal resolution of faith at the conclusion of the book. Both units (and otherwise only the central unit) feature extended first-person discourses ("I . . . I . . . me" etc.)—so that Habakkuk's more personal expressions are featured at the book's beginning, middle, and end. The final unit represents the resolution of the opening unit. In Habakkuk's opening complaint he asks God, "How long . . . shall I cry out to you, but you do not save (ys̆ʿ)?" The closing unit provides Habakkuk's resolution to this question: "I will wait patiently . . . though the fig tree does not bud, and there are no grapes on the vines . . . yet I will rejoice in God my Savior (ys̆ʿ)."[4] The root ys̆ʿ ("save") also links these two units. The two verbs by which Habakkuk expresses his distress to God, "I *call out* for help" and "I *cry out* to you," which occur in his opening complaint (1:2), are balanced in the closing unit by two opposite verbs expressing his joy toward God: "I *will be joyful* in Yahweh, I *will rejoice* in God my Savior" (3:18). Lastly, the verb "to hear" (s̆mʿ) appears in the introductory line of both units, playing significantly different roles. In the opening unit Habakkuk complains that Yahweh does not hear his cries for help (1:2)—and Habakkuk is very disturbed by this. In the closing unit we have the other side of the coin: Habakkuk hears the thunderous, mighty sound of Yahweh arriving to save his people, and as a result his inner struggle is resolved.

Correspondence of Yahweh's First Response (Habakkuk 1:5–11) and the Theophany (Habakkuk 3:1–15)

Yahweh's answer to Habakkuk's first complaint constitutes a rather terrifying vision:

> Look . . . I am raising up the Babylonians,
> that ruthless . . .
> people who sweep across the whole earth
> to seize dwelling places not their own. . . .
> Their horses are swifter than leopards,
> fiercer than wolves . . .
> their cavalry gallops headlong . . .
> they fly like vultures to devour . . .
> they gather prisoners like sand . . .
> they deride kings . . .
> they capture fortified cities . . .
> they sweep on like the wind.
> —Habakkuk 1:6–11

This frightening depiction of the advance of this unstoppable military force has its conspicuous counterpart in the majestic theophany. Yahweh's militaristic arrival to rescue his people (from the Babylonians) is depicted in similar but even more awe-inspiring language:

> God comes from Teman . . .
> his splendor covers the heavens . . .
> rays flash from his hand . . .
> plague goes before him and pestilence follows close behind . . .
> he stops and shakes the earth . . .
> he makes the nations tremble . . .
> the mountains crumble . . .
> the hills collapse . . .
> you [Yahweh] ride your horses . . .
> you uncover your bow . . .
> you split the earth . . .
> the mountains writhe . . .
> your flying arrows . . .
> your flashing spear . . .
> in anger you thresh the nations . . .
> you crush the leader of the wicked land . . .
> you strip him from head to foot . . .
> with his own spear you pierce his head . . .
> you trample the sea with your horses.
> —Habakkuk 3:3–15

These two depictions have a great deal in common. Both are highly militaristic in their descriptions. Both use some of the same verbs to describe the advance of the human/divine army, including "come" (bôʾ), "proceed" (hālak), and "go forth" (yāṣāʾ) (1:6–9; 3:3, 5, 11, 13). Both refer to the Babylonians' intentions "to devour" (leʾĕkōl) their enemies (1:8; 3:14). Both refer to the "horses" (sûsîm) accompanying the human/divine force (1:8; 3:8, 15). Both begin with a statement about Yahweh's "work" (pʿl). In both, the geographical origin of the invading army is specified: "they [the Babylonians] come from (yābōʾû min) a distant place" (1:8); "he [Yahweh] comes from (yābôʾ min) Teman . . . and from Mount Paran" (3:3).

The two descriptions also stand in intentional and instructive contrast, with the forces of Yahweh purposely depicted as more powerful. The Babylonian force is described first, and it seems formidable; it overwhelms dwellings, kings, and fortified cities. But Yahweh's power is portrayed as vastly superior. Yahweh overwhelms the heavens, earth, mountains, hills, sea, nations— and the forces of Babylon! This contrast is partially accomplished by designing the description of Yahweh's terrifying approach to be twice as long as the description of the approaching Babylonian army.

---

4. The Hebrew root ys̆ʿ occurs elsewhere in the book only in 3:13 (twice) and possibly 3:8 (the reading here is textually uncertain).

34.1 The Book of Habakkuk

a **Habakkuk's first complaint**: <u>how long must I wait</u> for your justice? (1:2–4)
- begins: God does not <u>hear</u> (*šmʿ*) Habakkuk's cries for help
- extended <u>first-person</u> speech
- how long Habakkuk must wait for God's <u>salvation</u> (*yšʿ*)?
- Habakkuk's frustrated cry to God, <u>who is not saving him</u> (1:2)

b **Yahweh's first answer**: <u>coming of the powerful army of Babylon</u> (1:5–11)
- begins: statement about Yahweh's <u>work</u> (*pʿl*)
- highly militaristic portrayal of an <u>unstoppable powerful army</u>
- they <u>come</u> (*bôʾ*), <u>proceed</u> (*hālak*), and <u>go forth</u> (*yāṣāʾ*)
- their <u>horses</u> (*sûsîm*); intentions to <u>devour</u> (*leʾĕkōl*) their enemies
- origin of army: "they <u>come from</u> (*bôʾ min*) a distant place" (north)

c **Habakkuk's second complaint**: how can you allow the wicked to destroy nations more righteous than themselves (1:12–17)
- begins: rhetorical question <u>is it not?</u> (*hălôʾ*) (1:12)
- focus on wickedness of Babylonians in their conquests
- the Babylonians' foolish, human-originated idolatry (1:15–16)
- Yahweh's justice with Babylonians questioned

d **CENTER: wait, for in the end the wicked will be punished**, but <u>the righteous will live by faith</u> (2:1–5)

c′ **Yahweh's answer to second complaint**: "woes" upon wicked: they will be punished; all wrongs will be righted (2:6–20)
- begins: rhetorical question <u>is it not?</u> (*hălôʾ*) (2:6)
- focus on wickedness of Babylonians in their conquests
- the Babylonians' foolish, human-originated idolatry (2:18–19)
- Yahweh's justice with Babylonians answered

b′ **Yahweh's final answer**: <u>coming of the even more powerful army of Yahweh</u>, who will vanquish Babylon and rescue Israel (3:1–15)
- begins: statement about Yahweh's <u>work</u> (*pʿl*)
- highly militaristic portrayal of Yahweh's <u>unstoppable powerful army</u>
- his advance: <u>comes</u> (*bôʾ*), <u>proceeds</u> (*hālak*), and <u>goes forth</u> (*yāṣāʾ*)
- his <u>horses</u> (*sûsîm*); Babylon's intentions to <u>devour</u> (*leʾĕkōl*) peoples
- origin of Yahweh's army: "he <u>comes from</u> (*bôʾ min*) Teman" (south)

a′ **Habakkuk's final resolution of his first complaint**: <u>I will wait</u> for God's help as long as it takes, no matter what; he is my source of joy (3:16–19)
- begins: Habakkuk <u>hears</u> (*šmʿ*) Yahweh's arrival to help and is silenced(?)
- extended <u>first-person</u> speech
- Habakkuk will wait, no matter what, for God is his <u>salvation</u> (*yšʿ*).
- Habakkuk's joyful cry to the <u>God who saves</u> (3:18)

Correspondence of Habakkuk's Second Complaint (Habakkuk 1:12–17) and the Woe-Oracles (Habakkuk 2:6–20)

Habakkuk's second complaint forms the book's third unit, and in it he questions God's justice in allowing the wicked (Babylonians) to "swallow up those more righteous than themselves" (1:13), particularly since these wicked people, after destroying other nations, revel in their own self-centered idolatry (1:16–17). Habakkuk's problem centers on God's justice in allowing the wicked to continue destroying nations more righteous than themselves:

Yahweh . . . your eyes are too pure to look on evil;
you cannot look tolerantly on wrong.
Why then will you look tolerantly on these treacherous people?
Why are you silent while the wicked swallow up those more righteous than themselves,

while [the wicked one] . . .
catches [people of other nations] in his nets. . . .
Shall he keep on emptying his net,
destroying nations without mercy?

— Habakkuk 1:12–17

The series of woe-oracles in 2:6–20 is Yahweh's answer to Habakkuk's second complaint. His answer is this: for the moment it may seem unjust that the Babylonians go on destroying and plundering many nations, but in the end they themselves will be punished for all the wrongs they have done. The atrocities they have committed against other nations will be done to them. Yes, they have made other nations drink from the "cup" of disgrace; but in the end Yahweh will punish them, making them drink from this same cup.

The two units correspond in several ways. Both units begin with a rhetorical question introduced by *hălô* ("is it not . . . ?"; 1:12; 2:6; cf. 2:7, 13). Both units focus on the wickedness of the Babylonians in their cruelty and mistreatment of conquered nations and peoples. Both units address the issue of the Babylonians' foolish idolatry (1:15–16; 2:18–19). Finally, both units deal with the issue of Yahweh's justice in allowing the Babylonians to destroy other nations, including Judah. Habakkuk's complaint raises the issue, and Yahweh's response addresses it.

Overall Layout of the Book of Habakkuk

The layout of the Book of Habakkuk, therefore, follows a seven-part symmetric scheme centering on the key message of 2:1–5 (34.1).

Conclusion

The linear layout of the Book of Habakkuk, beginning with the negative and closing with the positive, suggests that the purpose of the book is to take the audience from confusion and despair to clarification and hope. The composition poses some serious questions about divine justice in the opening units (questions that godly Israelites might well have had); and it answers those questions in the three closing units. This organization leaves the audience on a note of hope. It in-

dicates that the author designed the book to clarify and encourage rather than dishearten.

The theme of waiting is highlighted by its occurrence at the beginning, middle, and end of the book. These structurally prominent units (particularly the central and final units) declare that God will ultimately right all wrongs, but his people must wait with patience for this to happen. The arrangement suggests that this theme is central to Habakkuk's message. Also, the matched repetition of units dealing with Yahweh's justice regarding the wicked Babylonians (b and b′) highlights the importance of this theme.

The matching of the two vivid descriptions of the approaching forces of Babylon and Yahweh invites the audience to compare the two. The similarities are striking; but the contrast between the two forces is even more striking: Yahweh is vastly superior to Babylon; and he will destroy it. The point is clear. There are powerful human forces out there, and Yahweh may use some of these forces to do his destructive work of punishment. But do not fear them. Rather, place your trust in Yahweh, whose power is vastly superior to any human force. Faith in almighty Yahweh is well-placed faith.

35
Zephaniah

The Day of Yahweh Is Near

Zephaniah was a seventh-century prophet related to the royal family of Judah. His brief message condemns Judah's leadership (including his own relatives?) and calls the people of Judah to repent before the arrival of Yahweh's day of judgment. The book is generally analyzed as comprising seven or eight parts. S. R. Driver, for example, identifies eight constituent units (1:2–6, 8–13, 14–18; 2:1–3, 4–15; 3:1–7, 8–13, 9–20).[1] R. L. Smith divides the book into seven units, following Otto Eissfeldt's analysis fairly closely:[2]

a	announcement of universal judgment (1:2–6)
b	announcement of the day of Yahweh (1:7–2:3)
c	oracles against the nations (2:4–15)
d	judgment on Jerusalem (3:1–5)
e	judgment on the nations (3:6–8)
f	a great change coming (3:9–13)
g	a new song (3:14–20)

Adele Berlin prefers to work with six units (1:1–9; 1:10–18; 2:1–4; 2:5–15; 3:1–13; 3:14–20) plus the superscription, although she does not suggest that these represent compositional units.[3] I analyze the book as forming a seven-part symmetry (35.1), which supports Driver's analysis, except that his seventh and eighth units should probably be seen as a single unit (3:8–20).

1. S. R. Driver, *An Introduction to the Literature of the Old Testament* (9th ed.; Edinburgh: Clark, 1913), 341. Robert H. Pfeiffer, *Introduction to the Old Testament* (New York: Harper, 1948), 600, analyzes the book in a similar fashion, with only minor differences in his treatment of the first chapter. Otto Eissfeldt, *The Old Testament: An Introduction*, trans. Peter R. Ackroyd (New York: Harper & Row, 1965), 423–24, follows the same basic scheme, with several modifications: he sees 1:2–6 + 1:8–13 as a single unit and divides chap. 3 into four units: 3:1–4, 5–7, 8–13, 14–20.
2. R. L. Smith, *Micah–Malachi* (Word Biblical Commentary 32; Waco: Word, 1984), 124.
3. Adele Berlin, *Zephaniah* (Anchor Bible 25a; New York: Doubleday, 1994), 17–20.

Announcement of Coming Judgment upon Judah (Zephaniah 1:2–6)

The tightly knit first unit announces the details of Yahweh's planned overthrow of Judah (35.2). The unit is made up of seven poetic lines arranged in an a-a'-a" ǁ b ǁ c-c'-c" pattern. The first three lines announce Yahweh's plans to destroy every living creature from the face of the "earth" (*ădāmâ*)—a term ambiguous enough to leave the audience in temporary suspense, wondering whether the land of Judah or the entire earth is intended. The first and third lines are closed by the same phrase, "from the face of the earth, declares Yahweh," which serves to tie the first three lines together, as does the fourfold repetition of the verb "sweep away" (*ʾsp*) and the fourfold repetition of "humankind"/"earth" (*ʾādām*/*ădāmâ*).

Next comes the startling statement that it is Judah and Jerusalem that are the targets of Yahweh's punishment. This declaration, in turn, is followed by three poetic verses listing the categories of people Yahweh is planning to destroy. The verb *hikrît* ("cut off"), used in the final line of the first grouping (1:3b), is employed again to introduce this new grouping. Now the ambiguity of the first three lines is completely removed: it is the idolatrous inhabitants of Judah and Jerusalem that God is going to punish! Each of the final three verses begins by identifying one category of people that Yahweh will cut off, followed by two additional groups that will also be cut off.

Yahweh's Plans to Punish the Wicked Leaders and the Rich of Jerusalem (Zephaniah 1:7–13)

Zephaniah's second unit is introduced by a foreboding imperative: "Be silent! For the day of Yahweh is approaching!" (1:7). Now the focus shifts to the day when Yahweh will "punish" (*pāqad*) the wicked leaders and rich of Jerusalem. As in the first unit, this unit contains seven smaller units or stanzas. Each of the first four

35.1 The Book of Zephaniah

- a **coming judgment upon the wicked of Jerusalem** (1:2–6)
  - b **coming judgment of corrupt <u>leaders</u> (*śārîm*) and rich of Jerusalem** (1:7–13)
    - c **Yahweh's judgment of all nations:** great and terrible day of Yahweh (1:14–18)
      - d **CENTER: call to repentance** (2:1–3)
    - c′ **Yahweh's judgment of all nations:** oracles against the nations (2:4–15)
  - b′ **coming judgment of corrupt political <u>leaders</u>** (including *śārîm*) and religious leaders of Jerusalem (3:1–7)
- a′ **coming restoration of Jerusalem and its fortunes** (3:8–20)

35.2 Judgment upon Judah (Zephaniah 1:2–6)

- a **I will destroy** everything <u>from the face of the earth</u>, says Yahweh (1:2)
- a′ **I will destroy** humans and beast, birds and fish (1:3a)
- a″ **I will cut off** humans <u>from the face of the earth</u>, says Yahweh (1:3b)
  - b **CENTER: Judah and Jerusalem are the targets of this destruction!** (1:4a)
    - c **I will cut off** from this place the remnant of Baal (1:4b)
    - c′ **(I will cut off)** those who worship the hosts of heaven (1:5)
    - c″ **(I will cut off)** those who do not seek Yahweh (1:6)

35.3 Coming judgment of corrupt leaders (Zephaniah 1:7–13)

- a **be silent!** <u>because</u> (*kî*) the day of Yahweh is at hand (1:7)
  - b **<u>and it shall be</u> (*wĕhāyâ*), I will punish (*ûpāqadtî ʿal*)** + plural noun; <u>coming punishment</u> of officials and princes who wear exotic attire (1:8)
    - c **punishment** of those who fill their lordly <u>houses</u> (*bayit*) by means of misconduct and deceit (1:9)
      - d **CENTER: distress throughout Jerusalem** in that day (1:10)
- a′ **wail!** <u>because</u> (*kî*) the time of prosperity is over (1:11)
  - b′ **<u>and it shall be</u> (*wĕhāyâ*), I will punish (*ûpāqadtî ʿal*)** + plural noun; <u>coming punishment</u> of those who live in luxury and complacency (1:12)
    - c′ **plundering** of goods and <u>houses</u> (*bātîm*); they will build <u>houses</u> (*bātîm*), but they will not dwell in them (1:13)

35.4 The coming day of Yahweh (Zephaniah 1:14–18)

- a **the day of Yahweh** is near; it is quickly approaching! (1:14a)
- a′ **the day of Yahweh** will be characterized by sounds of bitterness, etc. (1:14b)
- a″ **that day will be a day of wrath**, darkness, etc. ("day" repeated seven times) (1:15–16)
  - b **CENTER: reason for punishment:** "for they have sinned against Yahweh" (1:17a)
    - c **their blood** shall be poured out like dust (1:17b)
    - c′ **their wealth** will not be able to deliver them (1:18a)
    - c″ **all the land**, all its inhabitants, will be consumed by his wrath (1:18b)

stanzas refer to the "day" (*yôm*) of Yahweh's approaching judgment. The fifth is a call to wail; and the last two are declarations of who is to be punished and how they will be punished.

The arrangement follows a parallel structure: a-b-c ‖ d ‖ a′-b′-c′ (35.3). The first and fifth stanzas begin with abrupt—and opposite—imperatives relating to speech: "be silent!" (1:7) and "wail!" (1:11); and in each case the exhortation is followed by a clause giving a reason, introduced by *kî* ("because"). The second and sixth stanzas begin with *wĕhāyâ* ("and it shall be") and are followed by the announcement "I will punish" (*ûpāqadtî ʿal*), which governs a plural noun designating the recipients of the punishment. The third and seventh stanzas are tied together by the theme of "houses" (*bātîm*), which have been filled with valuables by misconduct and deceit. The central stanza, highlighted not only by its position but by the appearance of the

only divine-speech formula in the entire unit (*nĕʾum-yhwh*, "says Yahweh"), speaks of the sounds of pain and destruction(?) that will arise throughout Jerusalem "on that day." The technique of "pearling" (each successive stanza repeating a keyword from the previous stanza) is used in the first five stanzas.

The Coming Day of Yahweh When "All the Earth" Will Be Judged (Zephaniah 1:14–18)

The third unit of the book begins with the same terrifying alarm that began the second: "The day of Yahweh is near!" This unit also appears to have seven smaller units that, as in the book's first unit, are arranged in an a-a′-a″ ‖ b ‖ c-c′-c″ pattern (35.4). In the first three, "day" (*yôm*) occurs nine times, announcing in apocalyptic terms the approaching day of Yahweh. The fourth unit gives the reason for the coming pun-

35.5 Call to repent (Zephaniah 2:1–3)

part 1: call to assemble (2:1–2)

  a **come together** and assemble, O shameless(?) nation (2:1)

  b <u>before</u> (*bĕṭerem*) you are driven away like the drifting chaff (2:2a)

  c <u>before</u> (*bĕṭerem*) the anger of Yahweh comes upon you (2:2b)

  d <u>before</u> (*bĕṭerem*) the day of Yahweh's anger comes upon you (2:2c)

part 2: call to seek (2:3)

  e <u>seek</u> (*baqqĕšû*) **Yahweh**, you humble of the land, who do his commands (2:3a)

  f <u>seek</u> (*baqqĕšû*) **righteousness** and humility (2:3b)

  g **perhaps you will be hidden** on the day of Yahweh's anger (2:3c)

35.6 Oracle against Philistia (Zephaniah 2:4–7)

  a **Gaza and Ashkelon will become deserted** (2:4a)

    b **Ashdod will be driven out at noon; Ekron will be uprooted** (2:4b)

      c **woe to the people of the <u>seacoast</u>** (*ḥebel hayyām*) (2:5a)

        d **SUMMARY: Yahweh will destroy Philistia** (2:5b)

      c′ **the <u>seacoast</u>** (*ḥebel hayyām*) **shall become pastures for shepherds** (2:6)

    b′ **Judean survivors will pasture** among the houses of Ashkelon at evening (2:7a)

  a′ **exiled Judeans will be restored to their land** (2:7b)

35.7 Woe upon the Leaders (Zephaniah 3:1–7)

  a **woe to the oppressing <u>city</u>** (*ʿîr*) **who is rebellious** (3:1)

    b **Judah does not <u>take correction</u>** (*lāqĕḥâ mûsār*); it does not trust in Yahweh or listen or draw near to him (3:2)

      c **Judah's corrupt human leaders;** its officials and <u>judges</u> (*špṭ*) <u>in its midst</u> (*bĕqirbāh*) are like wolves that leave nothing <u>in the morning</u> (*labbōqer*) (3:3)

        d **CENTER: its prophets and priests are corrupt** (3:4)

      c′ **Judah's righteous divine leader;** Yahweh <u>in its midst</u> (*bĕqirbāh*) does no wrong; his <u>justice</u> (*špṭ*) shows forth <u>every morning</u> (*babbōqer babbōqer*) (3:5)

  a′ **Yahweh has destroyed other(?) <u>cities</u>** (*ʿîr*) **and nations** (3:6)

    b′ **Judah does not <u>take correction</u>** (*tiqḥî mûsār*); it will not fear Yahweh; but even more eagerly corrupts its deeds (3:7)

---

ishment: "For they have sinned against Yahweh." The final three units return to the description of the terrifying approaching judgment (here, however, "day" is mentioned only once).

Exhortation to Repent (Zephaniah 2:1–3)

Zephaniah's fourth unit is a call to repentance. The unit falls into two parts, with four lines in the first and three lines in the second, making a total of seven lines (35.5). Each part is similarly organized: (1) exhortation to repent and (2) reason or motive for repenting. Each part ends with the words "the day of Yahweh's anger." Interestingly, the five central lines begin with the letter *bêt* (ב), whereas the first and last lines begin with a guttural letter.

Oracles against the Nations (Zephaniah 2:4–15)

The fifth unit of Zephaniah is a group of brief messages against foreign nations. This unit falls into three parts:

  a oracle against Philistia (2:4–7)

  b oracle against Moab and Edom (2:8–11)

  c oracle against Ethiopia(?) and Assyria (2:12–15)

The lines of these oracles follow almost without exception the 3+2 rhythm of the *qinah* (dirge) pattern, conveying the feeling of a eulogy here. The first two oracles appear to have seven lines apiece, and the message against Philistia seems to exhibit a symmetric touch (35.6). The final oracle is difficult to analyze (a textual problem relates to the seemingly intrusive mention of Ethiopia in 2:12); but as it stands, the lines dealing with Assyria are nine in number, virtually all in the 3+2 pattern.

Pronouncement of Woe upon Israel's Political and Religious Leaders (Zephaniah 3:1–7)

After completing the messages against the nations, a new unit is introduced by the common beginning marker *hôy* ("woe"). This unit is a condemnation of the rulers and religious leaders of Jerusalem. It is a highly negative unit, with its main points highlighted by their repeated treatment in matched verses. The internal structure of this unit appears to be a sevenfold modified symmetry, which places structural emphasis on the condemnation of Judah's religious leaders (35.7).

35.8 Future restoration of Judah (Zephaniah 3:8–20)

a **Yahweh will <u>gather</u> (ʾāsap) the peoples (3:8)**
- he will <u>gather</u> (qibbēṣ; cf. BHS) the kingdoms to punish them
- <u>all the earth</u> (kol-hāʾāreṣ) will be consumed
- begins: <u>says Yahweh</u> (nĕʾum-yhwh) (seven phrases/clauses)

b **Yahweh's renewed relationship with his people**: his purification of their speech; they will call on him again; the renewal of their worship of him (3:9–10)
- ends: <u>in that day</u> (cf. BHS)

c **Yahweh will <u>remove</u> (hēsîr) the proud <u>out of your midst</u> (miqqirbēk) (3:11)**
- topic: <u>rejoicing</u> (ʿlz)
- ends with prediction: lōʾ + imperfect verb + ʿôd: "<u>you will no longer</u> be haughty"

d **CENTER: restoration of righteous remnant (seven clauses) (3:12–13)**

c′ **Yahweh will <u>remove</u> (hēsîr) his judgments against Judah; Yahweh will once again be <u>in your midst</u> (bĕqirbēk) (3:14–15)**
- topic: <u>rejoicing</u> (ʿlz)
- ends with prediction: lōʾ + imperfect verb + ʿôd: "<u>you will no longer</u> fear evil" (seven clauses)

b′ **Yahweh's renewed relationship with Jerusalem**: he will give victory, rejoice over his people, he will renew them in love (3:16–18a; cf. BHS)
- begins: <u>in that day</u> (seven clauses)

a′ **Yahweh will <u>gather</u> (qibbēṣ) Judah's outcasts (3:18b–20)**
- he will <u>gather</u> (qibbēṣ and ʾāsap) the Judeans
- he will make them renown in <u>all the earth</u> (kol-hāʾāreṣ), restoring their fortunes
- ends: <u>says Yahweh</u> (ʾāmar yhwh)

35.9 The Book of Zephaniah

a **coming judgment upon the wicked of Jerusalem (1:2–6)**
- they are <u>idolatrous</u>, follow Baal, swear by Molech, and <u>do not seek Yahweh or inquire of him</u>

b **coming judgment of corrupt <u>leaders</u> (śārîm) and rich of Jerusalem (1:7–13)**
- their greed, <u>violence</u> (ḥāmās), and corruption
- the view held by these people: <u>Yahweh will do no good, nor will he do ill</u>

c **Yahweh's judgment of all the nations**: great and terrible day of Yahweh (1:14–18)
- against <u>all the earth</u> and <u>all the inhabitants</u> (yōšĕbîm) <u>of the earth</u>

d **CENTER: call to repentance (2:1–3)**

c′ **Yahweh's judgment of all the nations**: oracles against the nations (2:4–15)
- Yahweh will be against <u>all the gods of the earth</u> and against the <u>inhabitants</u> (yōšĕbîm) of the seacoast, etc.

b′ **coming judgment of corrupt political <u>leaders</u> (including śārîm) and religious leaders of Jerusalem (3:1–7)**
- their greed, <u>violence</u> (ḥāmās) against the law, and corruption
- but <u>Yahweh is righteous; he does no wrong</u>

a′ **coming restoration of Jerusalem and its fortunes (3:8–20)**
- they <u>seek refuge in Yahweh and call upon his name</u>, serve him (<u>not idols</u>) with one accord
- Yahweh will purify the (<u>idolatrous</u>) speech of his people

---

Announcement of the Future Restoration of Judah (Zephaniah 3:8–20)

The book closes with a message of hope announcing the reversal of the disasters portrayed in the book's opening units. This unit is introduced by lākēn ("therefore"), a word commonly used to introduce a concluding unit. Most commentators divide 3:8–20 into two units: 3:8–13 and 3:14–20. And indeed, 3:14 does seem to herald a new unit with its imperatives: "sing!" "shout!" "rejoice!" But careful analysis of the internal structure of this section suggests that a single unit extends from 3:8 through 3:20. The unit comprises seven smaller units arranged with a symmetric touch (35.8).[4]

---

4. Moreover, most of its constituent units comprise seven lines/clauses/phrases (the second and third units are exceptions, containing three lines apiece).

Overall Layout of the Book of Zephaniah

The seven major units in the Book of Zephaniah exhibit a symmetric configuration. The announcement of coming judgment in the first unit is balanced by the announcement of coming restoration in the final unit. The condemnation of Jerusalem's princes and wealthy people in the second unit is balanced by the condemnation of the wicked princes and leaders of Jerusalem in the next-to-last unit. The description of the terrible day of Yahweh in the third unit is balanced by the depiction of Yahweh's judgment against the nations in the third-to-last unit. The book's fourth, central unit, is Zephaniah's call to repentance (35.9).

Conclusion

The linear arrangement of the Book of Zephaniah is rhetorically effective. Zephaniah begins with an attention-getting announcement of the coming destruction of Judah's idolatrous population (unit a), followed by a more specific prediction of the coming punishment of Judah's corrupt leadership (unit b) and, proceeding up the ladder of power, a prediction of the coming punishment of all the nations (unit c). Next is the call to repentance (unit d). The final three units provide motivation for returning to Yahweh: Yahweh can defeat Judah's enemies and in fact plans to do so (unit c'); unlike Judah's leaders, Yahweh is not corrupt or unjust or evil—and is thus worthy of Judah's loyalty (unit b'); and Yahweh has wonderful plans for Judah in the future—an added incentive to return to him (unit a').

In the book's symmetric layout, the repeated mention of Judah's corrupt princes and leaders in matching units highlights this theme, which suggests that the point was important to Zephaniah, himself of noble blood. (That Judah's leaders were perhaps Zephaniah's own relatives might explain why he was particularly ashamed of their corruption.) The placement of the call to repentance at the center of the symmetry underscores its key role for the reversal of Judah's fortunes. And closing the book with encouraging, uplifting units of promise and hope indicates the positive motivational purpose of the book. Zephaniah calls the people of Judah, including its leaders, to turn back to their gracious and forgiving God.

36

Haggai

Rebuild the Temple!

The Book of Haggai is a collection of messages delivered by the prophet Haggai to encourage the postexilic community to rebuild the temple. The internal structure of the Book of Haggai is relatively simple. The book consists of four dated messages and one narrative episode accompanied by a fifth dated message, all arranged in chronological order (36.1).

The book's five parts form a significant linear progression: Haggai's message of rebuke and exhortation is followed by the people's positive response, which is followed in turn by three messages of divine encouragement and promise (36.2). This layout highlights the book's main theme: Israel's obedience, particularly in regard to the temple, will result in God's favor and blessing.[1]

On the smaller level, several of the book's units exhibit carefully designed internal structures. Both of the following examples feature symmetric structures with a highlighted center exhorting the people to rebuild the temple (underscoring Haggai's central message).

Message of Rebuke and Exhortation to Begin Rebuilding the Temple (Haggai 1:2–11)

The book's first message appears to be arranged in a seven-part symmetry (36.3). Each of the

first six subunits of this message is introduced or marked off by "thus says Yahweh" (or some variation), whereas the final subunit is introduced by ʿal-kēn ("therefore"), an expression often used to introduce a concluding section.

Promised Glory of the New Temple (Haggai 2:1–9)

The second message in the book deals with the disappointment experienced by the older people when they saw how modest the new temple would be in contrast to the splendid temple of Solomon. Haggai's message is one of encouragement and promise of future glory. The message appears to have a seven-part symmetric design, although textual difficulties make this analysis tentative (36.4).

Conclusion

The central importance of rebuilding the temple is reinforced in the Book of Haggai by the symmetric arrangements of the two messages examined here (1:2–11; 2:1–9). Each of these features Haggai's call to rebuild the temple at the center of the message, in the position of emphasis. Other themes highlighted in the structured repetitions of these two messages include the following:

1. the importance of obeying Yahweh with regard to the temple, since failure here will bring judgment, and obedience will bring blessing
2. the promise of Yahweh's presence among the people in response to their obedience
3. the promise that in the future, God will bless the temple that the people have built, humble though it may be at present

The linear arrangement of the Book of Haggai—moving from Haggai's initial exhortation to a report of the people's obedience to three final messages of encouragement and promise—

---

1. Brevard S. Childs, *Introduction to the Old Testament as Scripture* (Philadelphia: Fortress, 1979), 469–70, sees an a-b-a´-b´ pattern that alternates messages tying the present poverty of the people to the disregard of God's temple (the first and third oracles: 1:2–15; 2:10–19) with those reiterating Israel's eschatological hope (the second and fourth oracles: 2:1–9; 2:20–23). Childs argues that this canonical reshaping of the book was carried out intentionally to communicate that God's future blessing was intricately tied to Israel's obedience. P. Verhoef (*The Books of Haggai and Malachi* [New International Commentary of the Old Testament; Grand Rapids: Eerdmans, 1987], 20–25) prefers to see the book as comprising two parts: (1) message of rebuke and exhortation (1:2–11), with the people's favorable response (1:12–15a), and (2) messages of hope and promise (1:15b–2:23). The second half is itself composed of three subunits: (a) the promised glory of the new temple (1:15b–2:9), (b) blessings for a defiled people (2:10–19), and (c) Zerubbabel, the Lord's chosen signet ring (2:20–23).

36.1 The Book of Haggai

a **message of rebuke** and exhortation to rebuild the temple (1:2–11)
- date: sixth month, first day

b **report of people's response** and new message; temple begun (1:12–15)
- date: sixth month, twenty-fourth day

c **message of encouragement** about temple now being built (2:1–9)
- date: seventh month, twenty-first day

d **message of promise:** Yahweh will now bless the people (2:10–19)
- date: ninth month, twenty-fourth day

e **message about Zerubbabel's significance** (2:20–23)
- date: ninth month, twenty-fourth day

36.2 Linear progression in the Book of Haggai

a **message of rebuke** and exhortation to rebuild the temple (1:2–11)

b **report of people's obedient response;** temple begun (1:12–15)

c **messages of encouragement and promise** (2:1–23)
- (1) **message of reassurance** and encouragement in the work (2:1–9)
- (2) **message of promise:** Yahweh will now bless them (2:10–19)
- (3) **message about Zerubbabel's significance** (2:20–23)

36.3 Message of rebuke (Haggai 1:2–11)

a **introduction:** these people say, "The time has not yet come for Yahweh's house to be built" (1:2)

b **question:** is it a time for you to live in your paneled <u>houses</u> (*bayit*) while this <u>house</u> (*bayit*) remains a <u>ruin</u> (*ḥārēb*)? (1:3–4)

c **you planted <u>much</u> (*harbēh*) but it <u>brought little</u> (*hābēʾ mĕʿāṭ*);** you eat, drink, put on clothes, etc., but still lack (1:5–6)

d **CENTER: therefore, build my house!** (1:7–8)

c′ **you expected <u>much</u> (*harbēh*) but got <u>little</u> (*mĕʿāṭ*);** what you <u>brought</u> (*hăbēʾtem*) home, I blew away (1:9a–b)

b′ **question:** why? because my <u>house</u> (*bayit*) remains a <u>ruin</u> (*ḥārēb*) while you are busy in your own <u>houses</u> (*bayit*) (1:9c–d)

a′ **conclusion:** this is why there is scarcity and crop failure (1:10–11)*

*Unit a′ has little correspondence with unit a.

36.4 Message of encouragement (Haggai 2:1–9)

a <u>splendor</u> (*kābôd*) of the <u>former temple</u> (*hārīʾšôn*) was greater than this small <u>present temple</u> (*habbayit hazzeh*) being built (2:3)

b **encouragement** to take courage (2:4a–c)

c **reassurance** of Yahweh's presence (2:4d)

d **CENTRAL POINT: carry out(?) the terms of the covenant** that Yahweh commanded when he brought his people out of Egypt (particularly: "build him a dwelling!") (2:5a)*

c′ **reassurance** of Yahweh's presence (2:5b)

b′ **encouragement:** soon Yahweh will shake the nations and bring their wealth and fill this temple with it (2:6–8)†

a′ <u>splendor</u> (*kābôd*) of this <u>present temple</u> (*habbayit hazzeh*) will surpass that of the <u>former temple</u> (*hārīʾšôn*) (2:9)

*Reading a command here depends on a possible textual emendation: moving the word *waʿăśû* ("do!") from 2:4d to 2:5a.
†Unit b′ does not correspond tightly with unit b.

underscores the pattern that Israel's obedience in regard to the temple results in Yahweh's favor and blessing. Before the people began to build the temple they were experiencing poverty; but after they began to obey Yahweh's prophet and build the temple, their fortunes turned. In addition, Yahweh sent them new messages of hope, with promises of even greater prosperity in the future. The decision to conclude the book with such positive messages suggests that the purpose of the book is to encourage the postexilic community, particularly its leaders. They should be reassured that God is pleased with their obedience; and they should be encouraged to continue in their obedience, because God has wonderful plans for them and their newly built temple.

37
Zechariah

Yahweh Will Again Live among His People

Zechariah was a contemporary of Haggai; and his message to the postexilic Jewish community in Jerusalem was similar to that of Haggai: "Build the temple!" Many scholars believe that the Book of Zechariah is the work of two different authors: chapters 1–8 by Zechariah son of Berechiah (1:1), and chapters 9–14 by an unknown author. The two parts of the book differ significantly in both subject matter and style, and a theory of dual authorship is one way to account for this difference. The following structural analysis, however, will explore the book in its present form, setting aside the question of its original composition.

In one respect, the book's internal organization is relatively easy to analyze because its messages are so clearly delineated. Three messages are introduced by a date (the only dates in the book) followed by the standard introduction to a prophetic message:

In the eighth month of the second year of Darius, the word of Yahweh came to the prophet Zechariah son of Berechiah son of Iddo.

—Zechariah 1:1

In . . . the eleventh month of the second year of Darius, the word of Yahweh came to the prophet Zechariah son of Berechiah son of Iddo.

—Zechariah 1:7

In the fourth year of King Darius, in the ninth month, . . . the word of Yahweh came to me.

—Zechariah 7:1–4

Two other messages are introduced by a title, the same in both instances: "an oracle" followed by the introductory "the word of Yahweh" (9:1; 12:1). And the remaining two messages (6:9–15; 11:4–17) are self-contained symbolic-action messages, each introduced by Yahweh's instructing the prophet to do a particular act, followed by a prophetic message based on the action. This yields a total of seven

messages in the present form of the Book of Zechariah (37.1).[1]

The most obvious pattern in the book's arrangement is the chronological scheme followed in the first half of the book. Conceivably a chronological arrangement pattern governed the layout of the entire book (as in Ezekiel and Haggai); but this is speculative, since no dates occur in the book's second half. No overall structural scheme (such as symmetry) clearly ties the two parts of Zechariah together. Though both halves of the book share various elements (horses, cleansing from sin, Judah's leaders, cessation of lying in Yahweh's name, restoration of Jerusalem, punishment of Judah's enemies, etc.), and though the central (fourth) message of the book func-

---

1. Otto Eissfeldt (*The Old Testament: An Introduction*, trans. Peter R. Ackroyd [New York: Harper & Row, 1965], 429–40) sees six parts in the book: (a) introductory oracle calling for repentance (1:2–6); (b) eight (or seven) night visions of the prophet (1:7–6:8); (c) crown of silver and gold for the ruler of Judah (6:9–15); (d) complex of messages introduced by the question about fasting, including the seven promises in 8:1–17 (7:1–8:23); (e) complex of messages introduced by "oracle, the word of Yahweh," including subunits 9:1–17; 10:1–2; 10:3–12; 11:1–3; 11:4–17 (the latter is the symbolic tending of Yahweh's flock, involving the two staffs, "Grace" and "Union" (9:1–11:17); (f) a second complex of messages introduced by "oracle, the word of Yahweh against Israel," including subunits 12:1–13:6; 13:7–9; 14:1–21 (12:1–14:21). Eissfeldt (p. 440) is uncertain about 11:4–17, admitting that "there is in fact little relationship between the prophecies of ix,1–xi,3 and the parable of xi,4–17." R. L. Smith, *Micah–Malachi* (Word Biblical Commentary 32; Waco: Word, 1984), 181, and others analyze the book in a similar fashion. J. Alberto Soggin, *Introduction to the Old Testament: From Its Origins to the Closing of the Alexandrian Canon*, trans. John Bowden (3d ed.; Louisville: Westminster/John Knox, 1989), 330–33, 350, also subdivides chaps. 9–11 into 9:1–11:3 and 11:4–17, the latter representing "two important symbolic actions . . . described in rhythmic prose which is almost poetry." That 11:4–17 is to be understood as a separate unit seems clear since it is introduced by the common beginning marker "thus said Yahweh to me." It represents a complete break from the message before it, and it does not naturally lead into the following message. Moreover, the genre shift, from oracle to prophetic symbolic action and back to oracle indicates to the reader a separate unit. There seems no question that the casual reader would assume that 11:4–17 was intended as a separate unit.

37.1 The Book of Zechariah

a **call to repentance** (1:1–6)
  - begins: date (second year, eighth month) plus introductory message formula

b **Zechariah's nighttime vision** (1:7–6:8)
  - begins: date (second year, eleventh month) plus introductory message formula

c **symbolic-action message:** silver and gold crown (6:9–15)
  - begins: introductory message formula

d **message about fasting and call to repentance** (7:1–8:23)
  - begins: date (fourth year, ninth month) plus introductory message formula

e **Israel's future restoration** (9:1–11:3)
  - begins: title ("an oracle") plus introductory message formula

f **symbolic-action message:** shepherd and two staffs (11:4–17)
  - begins: introductory message formula

g **Israel's future restoration** (12:1–14:21)
  - begins: title ("an oracle") plus introductory message formula

37.2 Prophetic visions (Zechariah 1:7–6:8)

a **four horsemen,** four horns, and four smiths (horses of four different colors) who <u>patrol the earth</u> (*hithallēk bāʾāreṣ*): Israel and the nations (1:7–21 [1:7–2:4])

  b **man and the measuring line:** Yahweh is coming to dwell in Jerusalem; the exiles should <u>leave Babylon and return to Jerusalem</u>, which will be restored (2:1–13 [2:5–17])

    c **Yahweh's house (temple) purified**; high priest's iniquity is removed; <u>sin</u> of the land will be removed (3:1–10)

      d **CENTER: the temple will be completed!** lampstand and olive trees; <u>prophet awakes</u> (4:1–14)

    c′ **every sinner's house is cursed:** the scroll (same dimensions as tabernacle) with the curses goes out over the land to bring a curse on any <u>sinner</u> (5:1–4)

  b′ **women and the measuring basket** (ephah): Israel's iniquity is carried <u>back to Babylon</u>, where a house will be built for it to dwell in (5:5–11)

a′ **four chariots** (with horses of four different colors) who <u>patrol the earth</u> (*hithallēk bāʾāreṣ*): Israel and the nations (6:1–8)

---

tions nicely as the book's centerpiece, with its call to repentance and its exhortation to rebuild the temple (7:9–10; 8:9, 13, 16–17), there does not seem to be an overall symmetric scheme.[2]

The book falls into two parts based on topic. Chapters 1–8 focus on rebuilding the temple, with exhortations to the postexilic community to build the temple and to repent of their former sinful ways. Chapters 9–14 shift to the topic of Israel's future restoration. Zechariah, then, exhibits the same overall negative-to-positive arrangement as Haggai, Ezekiel, and other prophetic books.

The arrangement of the eight visions in 1:7–6:8 has long puzzled scholars. Several suggest that one of the visions (the fourth) is spurious,[3]

and others attempt to rearrange the visions by subject matter.[4] Although tentative, another possibility would be to see the brief second vision as part of the first. This combined first vision would then match the final vision, and all seven visions would unfold in a symmetry (37.2).[5]

---

2. On the other hand, symmetry may have played a small part in the overall design. The first three messages form an a-b-a′ pattern (page count from BHS): (a) message 1 (one-half page); (b) message 2: visions (six pages); (a′) message 3 (one-half page). The final three messages also form a similar symmetry, which may, however, simply be fortuitous: (a) message 5: message of hope (three pages); (b) message 6: condemnatory symbolic action message (one page); (a′) message 7: message of hope (three pages).

3. A number of scholars (C. Jeremias, Karl Elliger, Alfred Jepsen, Theophane Chary; see Smith, *Micah–Malachi*, 186) argue that the fourth vision does not belong to the collection, which originally had only seven. The fourth vision, it is held, is so different from the others in form that it probably has been added.

4. See Smith, *Micah–Malachi*, 185. H. G. Mitchell, *A Critical and Exegetical Commentary on Haggai, Zechariah, Malachi, and Jonah* (International Critical Commentary; Edinburgh: Clark, 1912), 115, argues that the visions are already arranged topically: the first three deal with the return from captivity; the fourth and fifth, the anointed of Yahweh; and the last three, the removal of sin. Joyce Baldwin, *Haggai, Zechariah, Malachi: An Introduction and Commentary* (Tyndale Bible Commentary; London: InterVarsity, 1972), 85, arranges the eight visions in a chiastic pattern: a-b-b-c-c-b-b-a. The first and last speak of horses and chariots patrolling the earth and the earth is at rest. The central visions come in pairs: the second and third deal with the threat of the nations against Judah and God's defense of his people; the fourth and fifth deal with Judah's anointed leaders; and the sixth and seventh describe the cleansing of the land. What makes this analysis seem forced is that the only link Baldwin sees between the second/third and the sixth/seventh visions is that the nations meet retribution in the second and evil meets retribution in the sixth.

5. The obvious problem with this proposal is that the vision of the four horns and four smiths in 1:18–21 [2:1–4] appears to comprise a separate unit. It is introduced by the same formula ("I lifted up my eyes and saw") that introduces the vision of the man with the measuring line (2:1 [2:5]) and two other visions (5:1; 6:1—these latter two also contain *šûb*, "again"). Moreover, the four horns and four smiths seen in this vision do not seem to be directly related to the previous

37.3 Message about fasting (Zechariah 7–8)

a **people from Bethel** <u>come to Jerusalem to entreat Yahweh</u> (7:1–3a)

  b **fasting**: condemnation for fasting selfishly (7:3b–6)

    c **past call to righteousness and justice** by prophets was rejected; thus ancestors exiled and land made desolate (7:7–14)*

      d **CENTER: rebuild the temple!** Yahweh will return the exiles and restore Jerusalem; so "let your hands be strong!" (8:1–13)

    c′ **present call to righteousness and justice**: obey and Yahweh will do good to the people and land (8:14–17)

  b′ **fasting**: fasts will be turned to feasts of joy (8:18–19)

a′ **people from many cities** will <u>come to Jerusalem to entreat Yahweh</u> in the future (8:20–23)

*Verse 8 should perhaps be omitted.

37.4 Israel's future restoration (Zechariah 9:1–11:3)

a **coming judgment upon Lebanon and other nations**: Tyre will be <u>devoured by fire</u> (*ʾēš tēʾākēl*) (9:1–7)

  b **Yahweh will return to his temple** and reign <u>over all the earth</u>, "from <u>sea to sea</u>, and from the Euphrates to the <u>ends of the earth</u>" (9:8–10)

    c **Yahweh will <u>save</u>** (*hôšîaʿ*) **and restore Israel**, "for they are his <u>sheep</u> (*ṣōʾn*)" (9:11–17)

      d **CENTER: appeal to Yahweh, not idols!** (10:1–2b)

    c′ **Yahweh will <u>save</u>** (*hôšîaʿ*) **Israel**; they wander like <u>sheep</u> (*ṣōʾn*); but Yahweh "cares for <u>his flock</u>" (10:2c–7)

  b′ **Yahweh will cause the exiles to return** from <u>all over the earth</u>, "from the land of Egypt and . . . from Assyria . . . and they shall pass through the <u>sea</u>" (10:8–12)

a′ **coming judgment upon Lebanon and other regions**: "<u>fire</u> (*ʾēš*) will <u>devour</u> (*tōʾkal*) your [Lebanon's] cedars" (11:1–3)

37.5 Shepherd and two staffs (Zechariah 11:4–17)

a **bad shepherds are replaced**: Israel's bad shepherds sold the flock; prophet told to take over flock (11:4–6)

  b **the equipment of a good shepherd**: two good staffs, Grace and Union; becomes a good shepherd over flock, protecting oppressed (11:7–8a)

    c **good shepherd breaks the staff "Grace"** when sheep spurn him; <u>breaks</u> (*prr*) covenant with the nation (11:8b–10)

      d **CENTER: good shepherd is humiliated**: the shameful wages of thirty shekels of silver (11:11–13)

    c′ **good shepherd breaks the staff "Union"**; <u>breaks</u> (*prr*) relationship between Judah and Israel (11:14)

  b′ **the equipment of a bad shepherd**: flock will not be cared for; oppressed will not be protected (11:15–16)

a′ **bad shepherd is back**: Israel ends up where it started—with a worthless shepherd who deserts the flock (11:17)

Regarding the structure of the book's other units, most (if not all) of them are designed with a symmetric touch; and most appear to have seven parts, with the fourth, central part functioning as the position of emphasis. For example, the final four units all have similar structures (37.3, 37.4, 37.5, 37.6).

vision. On the other hand, the introductory formula used in 1:18 [2:1] does not always introduce a new vision in this section: it occurs in the middle of the vision of the ephah of iniquity (5:9), functioning there as an internal division marker. Furthermore, the very short vision of 1:18–21 [2:1–4] (just six lines in BHS) could be seen as the conclusion of the first vision: pagan lands, according to the patrols, are at rest; the angel cries out, "How long?"; the Lord says, "I am very angry with the nations" (who brought disaster upon Judah); and the sight of the four horns and four smiths brings with it the fitting conclusion to the first vision: "These have come to destroy them, to cast down the horns of the nations who lifted up their horns against the land of Judah." This entire first vision is perfectly balanced by the last vision, in which the patrols "who go toward the north country have set my spirit at rest in the north country" (6:8)—that is, the nations (Assyria, Babylon) that brought disaster upon Judah, to whom the smiths were sent in the first vision, have been dealt with; all is taken care of now—a fitting inclusio for the visions of 1:7–6:8. The five central visions (2:1–5:11) then focus on Judah and Jerusalem.

* * *

Unfortunately, the foregoing structural analysis of the Book of Zechariah does not resolve the debate over the book's unity. No overarching symmetric or parallel design seems to connect the book's two halves. On the other hand, the case for its unity gains some support from the book's containing seven parts and from its overall two-part arrangement, beginning with messages of condemnation and exhortation followed by messages of future restoration, which is the same organizational pattern found in other prophetic books (e.g., Ezekiel and Haggai).

Throughout the book, various themes are highlighted by the structure. The importance of righteousness and justice is emphasized by its double coverage in matching units at the book's center (7:7–14 and 8:14–17). The key role of repentance is underscored by the placement of this theme in the prominent first position (1:1–6).

Another dominant theme is Yahweh's wonderful plans for Israel. The promise of Israel's future prosperity under Yahweh's rule is high-

37.6 Israel's future restoration (Zechariah 12–14)

a **all the nations of the earth will gather (ʾsp)** against Jerusalem, but <u>Yahweh will defeat them</u> (12:1–4)

  b **Judah's leaders will be strengthened**; they will be "like a <u>blazing</u> (ʾēš) pot in the midst of wood, like a <u>flaming</u> (ʾēš) torch among sheaves" (12:5–9)

    c **repentance of house of David** and the people (12:10–14)

      d **CENTER: cleansing from sin and uncleanness** (13:1–2)

    cʹ **repentance of prophets** (13:3–6)

  bʹ **Judah's leader will be struck and the sheep scattered**; one-third will remain; "and I will put this third into the <u>fire</u> (ʾēš)" (13:7–9)

aʹ **all the nations will gather (ʾsp)** against Jerusalem; but <u>Yahweh will defeat them</u> and become their king; he will have them assemble every year in Jerusalem to worship him (14:1–21)

lighted by its repetition in matching subunits in the lengthy section of prophetic visions that open the book (1:7–6:8) and elsewhere throughout the book (e.g., 7:1–3a ǁ 8:20–23; 7:3b–6 ǁ 8:18–19; 9:8–10 ǁ 10:8–12; 9:11–17 ǁ 10:2c–7).

The most prominent theme of the book, however, is the call to rebuild the temple. The collection of visions in 1:7–6:8 is arranged to underscore this message, particularly with the vision about the future completion of the temple (chap. 4) standing at the highlighted center of the collection. Similarly, the book's central message in chapters 7–8 has at its center the exhortation to complete the temple: "Let your hands be strong so that the temple may be built!" (8:9). Yahweh has great plans for restored Israel; and these plans center around the temple, where he will once again graciously dwell among his people. As the book now stands, the placement of the messages about Israel's future restoration (chaps. 9–14) after the central exhortation to rebuild the temple conveys the point that Israel's glorious restoration must be preceded by obedience with regard to God's temple: So rebuild the temple!

38

Malachi

How Have We Robbed God?

Malachi lived many years after the temple had been rebuilt by the postexilic Jewish community. Judah had obeyed God in rebuilding his temple (inspired by such prophets as Haggai and Zechariah); but now a new problem had arisen. The priests and people were lapsing into practices that dishonored God, particularly bringing him inferior offerings as if it really did not matter. And why not? Did it really matter? Was Yahweh really paying attention to his people, rewarding the righteous and punishing wrongdoers?

The Book of Malachi is arranged in a way that effectively addresses this new situation. The arrangement helps highlight the book's main points: (1) condemnation of the negligence at the temple, (2) the key leadership role of the priests and Levites in restoring rightful worship of Yahweh, and (3) the truth that Yahweh does indeed reward those who serve him and punishes the wicked.

At first it might seem daunting to analyze the internal organization of the book, since—unlike Haggai and Zechariah—there are no introductory date formulas to help mark the beginnings of its constituent units. Despite this, the book's units are relatively easy to identify. Most scholars analyze the book as composed of six units plus an appendix:[1]

a Yahweh has "loved" Judah and "hated" Edom (1:2–5)
b condemnation of priests for bringing Yahweh inferior offerings (1:6–2:9)
c condemnation of the people for being faithless (2:10–16)
d future refining of the Levites (2:17–3:6)
e condemnation of people for inferior offerings (3:7–12)
f future punishment of wicked and reward of righteous (3:13–4:3 [3:13–21])
   appendix (4:4–6 [3:22–24])

These unit identifications seem to be correct, or nearly so. All except the third begin the same way: a new topic is introduced by the literary device of a verbal exchange between Yahweh and the people. These introductory exchanges follow a short pattern (1:2–3; 2:17; 3:13–15):

a Yahweh's introductory statement
b people's objection
a′ Yahweh's second statement

or a longer pattern (1:6–8; 3:7–8):

a Yahweh's introductory statement
b people's objection
a′ Yahweh's second statement
b′ people's objection to second statement
a″ Yahweh's third statement

Furthermore, all but one of these units (the first) are closed by the concluding formula "says Yahweh of hosts" (ʾāmar yhwh ṣĕbāʾôt; 1:14; 2:8, 16; 3:5, 12; 4:3 [3:21]).[2]

The only significant problem has to do with the exceedingly lengthy second unit. Evidence suggests that this section comprises not one, but two units: 1:6–14 and 2:1–9.[3] Admittedly, several

---

1. See S. R. Driver, *An Introduction to the Literature of the Old Testament* (9th ed.; Edinburgh: Clark, 1913), 355–56 (with one reservation); Robert H. Pfeiffer, *Introduction to the Old Testament* (New York: Harper, 1948), 612; Otto Eissfeldt, *The Old Testament: An Introduction*, trans. Peter R. Ackroyd (New York: Harper & Row, 1965), 441–42; Ernst Sellin and Georg Fohrer, *Introduction to the Old Testament* (Nashville: Abingdon, 1968), 469–70; Brevard S. Childs, *Introduction to the Old Testament as Scripture* (Philadelphia: Fortress, 1979), 489; J. Alberto Soggin, *Introduction to the Old Testament: From Its Origins to the Closing of the Alexandrian Canon*, trans. John Bowden (3d ed.; Louisville: Westminster/John Knox, 1989), 343–44; R. L. Smith, *Micah–Malachi* (Word Biblical Commentary 32; Waco: Word, 1984), 299; Norman K. Gottwald, *The Hebrew Bible: A Socio-Literary Introduction* (Philadelphia: Fortress, 1985), 509–10. See also the provocative study of Ernst R. Wendland, "Linear and Concentric Patterns in Malachi," *Bible Translator* 36 (1985) 108–21.

2. This expression is also sometimes used to close smaller units within these larger messages.

3. Joyce Baldwin, *Haggai, Zechariah, Malachi: An Introduction and Commentary* (Tyndale Bible Commentary; London: InterVarsity, 1972), 219, and Walter C. Kaiser, *Malachi: God's Unchanging Love* (Grand Rapids: Baker, 1984), 17, treat the passage as comprising two separate units, although they

38.1 Priests and people have cheated Yahweh (Malachi 1:6–14)

a **as Israel's father and <u>lord</u> (*ʾădônîm*)**, Yahweh <u>is not honored or feared</u> (*yrʾ*) (1:6a)
  - ends: <u>says Yahweh of hosts</u>
  b **priests have offered Yahweh <u>polluted</u> (*mĕgōʾāl*) food**, and Yahweh's <u>table</u> (*šulḥan*) is <u>despised</u> (*nibzeh*) (1:6b–8)
    - ends: <u>says Yahweh of hosts</u>
    c **Yahweh will not accept offerings** <u>from your hands</u> (*miyyedkem*) (1:9)
      - ends: <u>says Yahweh of hosts</u>
      d **CENTER: close the temple!** (1:10a)
        - ends: <u>says Yahweh of hosts</u>
    c′ **Yahweh will not accept offerings** <u>from your hands</u> (*miyyedkem*); but his name will be great among the nations (1:10b–11)
      - ends: <u>says Yahweh of hosts</u>
  b′ **priests have offered Yahweh unacceptable sacrifices**, so that Yahweh's <u>table</u> (*šulḥan*) is <u>polluted</u> (*mĕgōʾāl*) and his food <u>despised</u> (*nibzeh*) (1:12–13a)
    - ends: <u>says Yahweh of hosts</u>
a′ **as Israel's king and <u>lord</u> (*ʾădônîm*)**, Yahweh has been <u>dishonored by Israel's sacrifices</u>; but his name will be <u>feared</u> (*yrʾ*) among the nations (1:13b–14)
  - ends: <u>says Yahweh of hosts</u>

---

considerations favor the unity of the entire section;[4] but even more compelling reasons favor two distinct units here.[5] Perhaps the most compelling of these is the self-contained structure of 1:6–14. This section is made up of seven parts, each concluded by the identical formula: "says Yahweh of hosts" (*ʾāmar yhwh ṣĕbāʾôt*; 1:6, 8, 9, 10, 11, 13, 14). Moreover, these seven parts form an unmistakable symmetry that ties the material together in a distinct literary package (38.1).

If 1:6–14 and 2:1–9 are indeed separate units, then Malachi contains, not six, but seven main units plus an appendix.[6] Further, these seven units appear to exhibit a symmetric arrangement (38.2).

The symmetric touch is particularly obvious in the second and next-to-last units. Both units feature an accusation against the priests/people for bringing unacceptable offerings to Yahweh (a theme not explicitly treated elsewhere in the book). In unit b, the priests have cheated Yahweh of his due by "offering polluted food on my altar" (1:7) and by offering defective animals (1:8, 13–14); whereas in unit b′ the people have "robbed" God by failing to bring acceptable tithes and offerings to him (1:8–9). In both units, a curse is upon those who rob or cheat God in this matter (1:14; 3:9). In the second unit, God wishes someone would "shut the doors" of his sanctuary so that no more offerings could be brought in (1:10); whereas in the next-to-last unit, he exhorts the people to bring offerings for his temple, and he will "open the windows" of heaven (3:10). Both units, unlike all the others in the book, begin with a five-part series of questions and responses (1:6–8; 3:7–9). Lastly, in both units the five-part introduction is followed by an exhortation that, if

---

concede that the two units perhaps function as subunits of the larger unit 1:6–2:9. Kaiser feels justified in handling these as two separate units not only because of the exceptional length of 1:6–2:9 but also because of the "suitable climax in 1:14." Smith (*Micah–Malachi*, 310–11), who notes that this lengthy unit accounts for twenty-three of the book's fifty-five verses, calls 2:1–9 "the second part" of 1:6–2:9.

4. These considerations include the following: (1) the focus of both 1:6–14 and 2:1–9 is the priests, and 2:1–9, while comprising a new phase of the argument, continues Yahweh's case against the priests; (2) the verb *bāzâ* ("to despise") seems to tie the entire section together: the section begins with the accusation that the priests have "despised" Yahweh's name (1:6) and ends with the threat that Yahweh will make the priests "despised" (2:9); and (3) the statement-question-statement interchange that generally introduces new units throughout the book is missing in 2:1–17.

5. There are at least four reasons to see distinct units here: (1) the section 1:6–2:9 would be a surprisingly long unit—forty-two lines in BHS—in a book where all the other units are much shorter (the remaining units comprise seven, sixteen, sixteen, thirteen, and eighteen lines respectively): seen as two units, however, their lengths correspond to those in the rest of the book: twenty-four lines (nineteen if the pairs of short lines are combined) in 1:6–14 and eighteen lines in 2:1–9; (2) the introductory *wĕʿattâ* + vocative in 2:1 is often used in the Hebrew Bible to introduce new literary units; (3) that 2:1–17 does not begin with the standard interchange (i.e., statement-question-statement) does not necessarily mean this is not a new unit: the unit in 2:10–16 also has no such beginning; and (4) that both parts deal with a common topic does not necessarily mean that they are part of the same literary unit: both 2:17–3:6 and the final unit also deal with identical topics but are clearly separate units.

6. Virtually all agree that 4:4–6 [3:22–24] forms an appendix or epilogue to the book (whether added by the author himself or by another hand) and is not part of the final unit. Driver (*Introduction to the Literature of the Old Testament*, 356), on the other hand, seems to consider 3:13–4:6 [3:13–24] the book's final unit. Careful reading of the entire section, however, suggests that these final three verses are not functioning as the end of the previous unit; they broach new topics, and they read like a sweeping epilogue or conclusion to the entire book (cf. Eccles. 12:9–14) rather than the completion of the preceding section.

38.2 The Book of Malachi

a **Yahweh is just: he "loves" (the faithful remnant of) Israel but will utterly destroy wicked Edom** (1:2–5)
- judgment upon the <u>wicked</u> (*rišʿâ*) country: Yahweh has destroyed Edom, and "though they rebuild, I will tear down"

b **priests and people have cheated Yahweh in their offerings** (1:6–14)
- <u>unacceptable and inferior offerings</u> have been brought
- <u>curse</u> upon those who have cheated Yahweh in their offerings
- Yahweh wishes someone would <u>shut the doors</u> of his temple so that no more unacceptable offerings could be brought in (1:10)
- <u>five-part introduction</u>, followed by exhortation and promise

c **in the past Levi served in righteousness**, but <u>Levites have turned from Yahweh</u> (2:1–9)
- Levi kept Yahweh's <u>covenant</u> (*běrît*)
- the priest is the <u>messenger</u> (*malʾāk*) of Yahweh
- priests have turned aside from the <u>way</u> (*derek*)
- look back upon a <u>time of Levi's past righteousness</u> (2:5–6)

d **CENTER: stop being faithless!** (2:10–16)

c′ **in the future Yahweh's messenger will come** and <u>Levites will be purified</u> (2:17–3:6)
- he will be the "messenger of the <u>covenant</u>" (*běrît*)
- he will be the <u>messenger</u> (*malʾāk*) of Yahweh
- he will "prepare the <u>way</u> (*derek*) before Yahweh"
- look back upon a <u>time of past righteousness</u> (3:4)

b′ **people have robbed Yahweh in tithes and offerings**; but if they change, God will bless them (3:7–12)
- <u>unacceptable tithes and offerings</u> have been brought
- "you are <u>cursed with a curse</u>, for you are robbing me" (3:9)
- Yahweh exhorts the people to bring acceptable offerings for his temple, with the promise that he will <u>open the windows</u> of heaven (3:10)
- <u>five-part introduction</u>, followed by exhortation and promise

a′ **Yahweh is just: he will reward the righteous but will utterly destroy the wicked** (3:13–4:3 [3:13–21])
- judgment upon the <u>wicked</u> (*rāšāʿ*): Yahweh will bring them to an end, leaving them "neither root nor branch"

conclusion: day of Yahweh (4:4–6 [3:22–24])

---

heeded, will result in God's favor upon the people (1:9; 3:10–12).

The first and last units also seem to match, although their correspondence is weaker. Both units address the criticism that Yahweh treats everyone alike, whether they are his faithful people or evildoers (and so why bother being faithful?). In the first message, Yahweh's "love" for his people Israel is contrasted with his "hatred" for Israel's wicked enemy, Edom. Proof of this is seen in Yahweh's destroying Edom (while Judah has obviously been restored) and continuing to tear down that "wicked land" if they try to rebuild it. The theme of Yahweh's justice is revisited in the last unit, where Yahweh declares that the righteous "shall be mine, my special possession, and I will be tender toward them as parents are tender toward their children" (3:17); but all evildoers will be destroyed (4:1–3 [3:19–21]). In both units, Yahweh's punishment of the wicked is total: "even if they try to rebuild, I will demolish" (1:4); "not a root or branch will be left to them" (4:1 [3:19]). The key terms "wickedness" and "wicked" (*rišʿâ/rāšāʿ*; 1:4; 3:15, 18; 4:1 [3:19]; 4:3 [3:21]) occur nowhere else in the book.

The book's third and third-to-last units share more obvious correspondences. Both units focus on the key role of the Levites in rectifying unacceptable behavior at the temple. Both units focus on Levi or his descendants (2:4, 5, 6, 8; 3:3)—and Levi is mentioned nowhere else in the book. In unit c, the present wayward priests are contrasted with their faithful forefather Levi (2:6); whereas in unit c′, Yahweh promises that in the future the descendants of Levi will be purified and will once again present right offerings to Yahweh, "as in the days of old" (3:3–4). The third unit looks back to faithful Levi, and the third-to-last unit looks forward to the future faithful sons of Levi—providing the present Levites with encouraging examples from both the past and the future. The term "covenant" (*běrît*) occurs only in these two units and in the central one (2:4, 5, 8, 10, 14; 3:1). Also, the topic of Yahweh's "messenger" (*malʾāk*) is featured in these two units (2:7; 3:1) and nowhere else in the book. In unit c the levitical priests were supposed to be Yahweh's messengers to the people, but were "turning the people from the way (*derek*)"; in unit c′ Yahweh will send his own messenger, who will prepare the "way" (*derek*) before him. In unit c Yahweh has "sent" (*šālaḥ*) a curse upon the priests (2:2, 4); whereas in unit c′ he will graciously "send" (*šālaḥ*) his messenger to them (3:1); this verb occurs elsewhere only in the appendix.

The book's central unit features the book's call to repentance. Here Malachi appeals to the people to stop being faithless. The theme of this unit is the faithlessness of the people—in their social relations, their spiritual obligations, and their marital relations. The term *bāgad* ("be faithless") ties this unit together; it occurs throughout the unit (2:10, 11, 14, 15, 16) and nowhere else in the book.

Three themes find particular emphasis by their parallel coverage in the Book of Malachi's symmetric layout. The first and last units in the symmetry (positions of prominence) underscore the point that Yahweh rewards faithfulness and punishes wickedness (a truth that the author apparently thinks the people need to hear). The twofold condemnation of the priests and people for cheating and robbing Yahweh with their inferior offerings, in the second and next-to-last units, draws attention to this theme. And the double coverage of the key role of the Levites in renewal, in the third and third-to-last units, highlights their importance in Israel's religious life. In addition, the placement of the call to repentance at the center of the book's symmetric arrangement emphasizes the key role

that repentance must play if the people are to receive God's forgiveness and blessing.

The book's linear layout reflects a negative-to-positive scheme. The first four units are primarily condemnatory, while the final three units (plus the appendix) offer words of hope and promise. This layout, culminating in an uplifting, inspiring message of hope, suggests that the book is designed primarily to encourage.

The appendix, because it both concludes the book and stands outside the symmetric arrangement, is doubly highlighted. It serves as the book's grand finale, capsulizing Malachi's message: Yahweh has wonderful plans for his people. He is going to send his representative to his people to take charge and to right all wrongs—someone like the prophet Elijah. He will bring Israel back to Yahweh. So take heart! And most important: "Remember the law of my servant Moses, the decrees and laws I gave him at Horeb for all Israel" (4:4 [3:22]).

With this closing injunction, we have come full circle in the Old Testament, which began, it will be recalled, with the Book of the Law of Moses. Malachi calls Israel to return to that law, to return to its original treaty with God.

Unit 7
Conclusion

39
Some Final Thoughts

I have attempted in this study to be comprehensive in scope, investigating the literary architecture of every book in the Hebrew Bible. Such a broad inquiry naturally leaves many questions unanswered—or even unasked. For example, I have focused primarily on the larger units of the Hebrew Bible, leaving the structures of the smaller units, for the most part, unexplored. Much more research remains to be done on the smaller units of books such as the Book of the Law, the historical books, and the major prophets. The literary structure of most of the individual psalms calls for examination.

Many other issues and questions invite further study. For instance, is there any significant overall arrangement scheme in the two collections of Solomonic proverbs in Proverbs 10–22 and 25–29? How are the individual constituent units of the story of Abraham (or Isaac or Jacob) structured, and what do these patterns reveal about those units and their meanings? Do the final units in Daniel exhibit internal structures similar to those in the first part of the book?

There are undoubtedly many other common structuring conventions to be identified in the Hebrew Bible, patterns that I have missed. These other structuring patterns and techniques need to be identified, their functions analyzed, and their usages in specific Old Testament passages investigated.

The interplay of structure and genre remains to be explored. Are different structuring principles at work in poetry than in prose? Do the prophets use arrangement conventions unique to prophetic genres? Moreover, the variation in structuring methods from author to author invites further study. Do certain authors prefer particular structural configurations? (Amos certainly favors nonsymmetric sevenfold groupings.) The identification of an author's unique structuring style (like the identification of unique vocabulary or style of expression) might

be useful in source-critical debates and in determining issues of disputed authorship. Accordingly, it would be of interest to consider whether there are peculiar structuring patterns in the first half of Isaiah that are repeated in the book's second half. And what about the two halves of Zechariah or the various parts of the Pentateuch and Joshua? Do the "Davidic" psalms have structuring conventions that are unique to them?

Questions remain regarding how much of a composition's structure an audience was expected to perceive. Certainly an ancient audience could easily catch and appreciate the pairing pattern in the Joseph story. But could the average listener at the same time have caught the story's overall symmetry? Or the symmetries of the two halves of the story? Was the intricate design intended to be fully appreciated only after several hearings? Were some patterns created primarily to assist the storyteller in remembering the story, or were all structuring schemes intended for the audience's benefit and appreciation? Related to this, the issue of author intentionality needs to be further explored. How much structuring in the Old Testament is unintentional and unplanned, the result of authors unconsciously following natural or highly common arrangement patterns?

The relationship of structure and meaning also requires further study. I have considered some of the uses of parallel and symmetric patterns in conveying meaning, particularly the technique of highlighting material through utilization of matched repetition and through positions of prominence. But how else were these patterns used to convey meaning? And in what ways did biblical authors exploit linear configurations to help communicate their messages?

Certainly it is time for surface-structural analysis to take its place among the important disciplines within biblical studies. Old Testament authors communicated their message through the *arrangement* of their compositions as well as through *verbal content*. Modern commentators devote much effort to clarifying the verbal content of passages of scripture but give relatively little attention to the arrangement of this content. If we are to understand more fully the books of the Hebrew Bible, we must pay greater attention to their structures and to what those structures reveal about their meaning. The purpose of the present work is to encourage renewed interest in this promising and important aspect of interpretation.

Bibliography

Alter, Robert. *The Art of Biblical Narrative*. New York: Basic Books, 1985.

———. *The World of Biblical Literature*. New York: Basic Books, 1992.

Alter, Robert, and Frank Kermode (eds.). *The Literary Guide to the Bible*. Cambridge: Harvard University Press, 1987.

Bar-Efrat, S. *Narrative Art in the Bible*. Translated by Dorothea Shefer-Vanson. Journal for the Study of the Old Testament Supplement 70. Atlanta: Almond, 1989.

———. "Some Observations on the Analysis of Structure in the Biblical Narrative." *Vetus Testamentum* 30 (1980) 154–73.

Beekman, John, John Callow, and Michael Kopesec. *The Semantic Structure of Written Communication*. Dallas: Summer Institute of Linguistics, 1981.

Berlin, Adele. *Poetics and Interpretation of Biblical Narrative*. Sheffield: Almond, 1983.

Boys, Thomas. *Key to the Book of Psalms*. London: Seeley, 1825. Revised by E. W. Bullinger. London, 1890.

Bullinger, E. W. *The Companion Bible*. London: Oxford University Press, n.d.

Callow, Kathleen. *Discourse Considerations in Translating the Word of God*. Grand Rapids: Zondervan, 1974.

Cassuto, Umberto. "The Sequence and Arrangement of the Biblical Sections." Vol. 1 / pp. 165–69 in *World Congress of Jewish Studies 1947*. Jerusalem: Magnes, 1952. Reprinted in *Biblical and Oriental Studies*, vol. 1, pp. 1–6. Jerusalem: Magnes, 1973.

Di Marco, Angelico. *Der Chiasmus in der Bibel*. Bonn: Linguistica Biblica Bonn, 1975.

Dorsey, David A. "Can These Bones Live? Investigating Literary Structure in the Bible." *Evangelical Journal* 9 (1991) 11–25.

———. "Literary Architecture and Aural Structuring Techniques in Amos." *Biblica* 73 (1992) 305–30.

———. "Literary Architecture and Meaning in the Book of Jonah." Pp. 57–69 in *To Understand the Scriptures* (Festschrift for William H. Shea). Edited by David Merling. Berrien Springs, Mich.: Andrews University Press, 1997.

———. "Literary Structuring in the Song of Songs." *Journal for the Study of the Old Testament* 46 (1990) 81–96.

Fishbane, Michael. "Recent Work on Biblical Narrative." *Prooftexts* 1 (1981) 99–104.

———. *Text and Texture: Close Readings of Selected Biblical Texts*. New York: Schocken, 1979.

Fokkelman, Jan P. *Narrative Art and Poetry in the Books of Samuel: A Full Interpretation Based on Stylistic and Structural Analysis*. 4 vols. Studia Semitica Neerlandica. Assen: Van Gorcum, 1981–93.

Forbes, John. *The Symmetrical Structure of Scripture*. Edinburgh: Clark, 1854.

Gooding, D. W. "The Composition of the Book of Judges." *Eretz-Israel* 16 (1982) 70*–79*.

Grimes, Joseph E. *The Thread of Discourse*. The Hague: Mouton, 1975.

Hollenbach, Barbara. "A Preliminary Semantic Classification of Temporal Concepts." *Notes on Translation* 47 (1973) 2–8.

Jebb, John. *Sacred Literature*. London: Cadell & Davies, 1820.

Licht, Jacob. *Storytelling in the Bible*. Jerusalem: Magnes, 1978.

Limburg, James. "Sevenfold Structures in the Book of Amos." *Journal of Biblical Literature* 106 (1987) 217–22.

Longacre, Robert E. *An Anatomy of Speech Notions*. Lisse: de Ridder, 1976.

——— (ed.). *Discourse Grammar: Studies in Indigenous Languages of Colombia, Panama, and Ecuador*, vol. 1. Dallas: Summer Institute of Linguistics and University of Texas at Arlington, 1976.

———. "The Discourse Structure of the Flood Narrative." *Journal of the American Academy of Religion* 47 supplement (1979) 89–133.

———. *The Grammar of Discourse*. New York: Plenum, 1983.

———. "The Paragraph as a Grammatical Unit." *Syntax and Semantics* 12 (1979) 115–34.

Lowth, Robert. *Lectures on the Sacred Poetry of the Hebrews.* 1753. Reprinted London: Tegg, 1835.

Lund, Nils Wilhelm. *Chiasmus in the New Testament.* Chapel Hill: University of North Carolina Press, 1942.

———. "Chiasmus in the Psalms." *American Journal of Semitic Languages and Literature* 49 (1932–33) 281–312.

———. "The Literary Structure of the Book of Habakkuk." *Journal of Biblical Literature* 53 (1934) 355–70.

Miller, George. "The Magical Number Seven, Plus or Minus Two: Some Limits on Our Capacity for Information Processing." *Psychological Review* 63 (1956) 81–97.

Muilenburg, James. "Form Criticism and Beyond." *Journal of Biblical Literature* 88 (1969) 1–18.

———. "The Linguistic and Rhetorical Usages of the Particle *Kî* in the Old Testament." *Hebrew Union College Annual* 32 (1961) 135–60.

———. "A Study in Hebrew Rhetoric: Repetition and Style." Pp. 97–111 in *Congress Volume: Copenhagen 1953.* Edited by G. W. Anderson et al. Vetus Testamentum Supplement 1. Leiden: Brill, 1953.

Parunak, H. Van Dyke. "Oral Typesetting: Some Uses of Biblical Structure." *Biblica* 62 (1981) 153–68.

———. "Some Axioms for Literary Architecture." Paper delivered at the Midwest Regional Meeting of the American Oriental Society and the Society of Biblical Literature, Ann Arbor, Mich., 23 Feb. 1981.

———. *Structural Studies in Ezekiel.* Ph.D. dissertation, Harvard University, 1978.

Pickering, Wilbur. *A Framework for Discourse Analysis.* Arlington: Summer Institute of Linguistics and University of Texas at Arlington, 1980.

Ryken, Leland, and Tremper Longman III (eds.). *A Complete Literary Guide to the Bible.* Grand Rapids: Zondervan, 1993.

Shea, William H. "The Chiastic Structure of the Song of Songs." *Zeitschrift für die alttestamentliche Wissenschaft* 92 (1980) 379–96.

———. "Further Literary Structures in Daniel 2–7: An Analysis of Daniel 4." *Andrews University Seminary Studies* 23 (1985) 193–202.

———. "The *Qinah* Structure of the Book of Lamentations." *Biblica* 60 (1979) 103–7.

Smalley, W. A. "Recursion Patterns and the Sectioning of Amos." *Bible Translator* 30 (1979) 118–27.

Sternberg, Meir. *The Poetics of Biblical Narrative.* Bloomington: Indiana University Press, 1985.

Trible, Phyllis. *Rhetorical Criticism: Context, Method, and the Book of Jonah.* Minneapolis: Augsburg Fortress, 1994.

Watson, W. G. E. "Chiastic Patterns in Biblical Poetry." Pp. 118–68 in *Chiasmus in Antiquity.* Edited by J. W. Welch. Hildesheim: Gerstenberg, 1981.

Welch, J. W. (ed.). *Chiasmus in Antiquity: Structures, Analyses, Exegesis.* Hildesheim: Gerstenberg, 1981.

Wellek, René, and Austin Warren. *Theory of Literature.* Third edition. Harmondsworth: Penguin, 1963.

Wendland, Ernst R. (ed.). *Discourse Perspectives on Hebrew Poetry in the Scriptures.* New York: United Bible Societies, 1994.

Wilson, Victor M. *Divine Symmetries: The Art of Biblical Rhetoric.* New York: University Press of America, 1977.

Yelland, H. L., S. O. Jones, and K. S. W. Easton. *A Handbook of Literary Terms.* New York: Philosophical Library, 1950.